OXFORD EC LAW LIBRARY

General Editor: F. G. Jacobs
Advocate General, The Court of Justice
of the European Communities

EXTERNAL RELATIONS OF THE EUROPEAN UNION

OXFORD EC LAW LIBRARY

The aim of this series is to publish important and original studies of the various branches of EC Law. Each work provides a clear, concise, and original critical exposition of the law in its social, economic, and political context, at a level which will interest the advanced student, the practitioner, the academic, and government and Community officials.

Other Titles in the Library

External Relations of the European Union

Legal and Constitutional Foundations

PIET EECKHOUT

OXFORD

UNIVERSITY PRESS

OXFORD

UNIVERSITY PRESS

Great Clarendon Street, Oxford OX2 6DP

Oxford University Press is a department of the University of Oxford.
It furthers the University's objective of excellence in research, scholarship,
and education by publishing worldwide in

Oxford New York

Auckland Bangkok Buenos Aires Cape Town Chennai
Dar es Salaam Delhi Hong Kong Istanbul Karachi Kolkata
Kuala Lumpur Madrid Melbourne Mexico City Mumbai Nairobi
São Paulo Shanghai Taipei Tokyo Toronto

Oxford is a registered trade mark of Oxford University Press
in the UK and in certain other countries

Published in the United States
by Oxford University Press Inc., New York

© P. Eeckhout, 2004

The moral rights of the author have been asserted
Database right Oxford University Press (maker)

First published 2004

British Library Cataloguing in Publication Data
Data available

Library of Congress Cataloging in Publication Data
Data available

ISBN 0–19–925165–7

1 3 5 7 9 10 8 6 4 2

Typeset by Newgen Imaging Systems (P) Ltd., Chennai, India
Printed in Great Britain
on acid-free paper by
Biddles Ltd., King's Lynn

General Editor's Foreword

The European Union is a unique construct in which the relations between the Union and its Member States are governed by a system of law. Internally, within the Union, powers are allocated between the Union and its Member States under the constitutional provisions of the Treaties.

The external dimension of the European Union (embracing the European Community) is in some respects even more remarkable, especially as the Union takes an increasing role on the world stage, in both economic and political terms. Externally, as internally, powers are allocated between the Union and its Member States in accordance with a system of law. Thus the Community has an express, and exclusive, competence in matters of commercial policy; and it has a wide range of implied external powers. It has a presence alongside its major trading partners in all relevant international forums, not least the World Trade Organization. Moreover, the European Union has a common foreign and security policy; the existence of very profound, and very public, differences between Member States in this arena should not be allowed to obscure the day-to-day, unspectacular achievements of concerted action of a kind never previously witnessed.

This book breaks new ground in explaining and exploring the external relations of the European Union, a subject which, despite its great practical importance and its great intellectual fascination, is still surprisingly neglected.

The author rightly emphasizes the legal and constitutional foundations of the subject. Thus Part One deals with fundamental aspects of the powers or competences of the Union, while Part Two deals with the international foundations—including the different aspects of the relationship between EU law and international law, not least the effects of international agreements within the European legal order.

On the basis of those foundations, Part Three deals with policies: the common commercial policy; the common foreign and security policy; and the interaction of trade and foreign policy, notably economic sanctions and export controls. The final chapter discusses the European Union's human rights policy and includes a typology of human rights clauses contained in the Community's external agreements.

The starting point of the analysis is, necessarily, the Treaty provisions, the European legislation and the case law of the European Courts—the Court of Justice and, increasingly, the Court of First Instance. The remarkable jurisprudence of the Court of Justice on the Community's external competence is fully explored. But these are only starting points: the author examines EU practice and State practice, explores legal scholarship, and—not insignificantly—draws on his own experience at the Court of Justice, where he had the opportunity to work as an official on some of the most interesting issues he addresses here.

In what results, the author's analysis, both vivid and powerful, illuminates the wide-ranging subject area of this book.

November 2003   Francis G. Jacobs

Acknowledgements

Many people have contributed to the effort of writing this book, and I am most grateful to all of them. I should like to single out my various research assistants in the years I was working on this project: Luca Rubini, Ivan Vassilev, and Axelle Lemaire. I have benefited enormously from their support, generously funded by the Centre of European Law. I should like to thank my colleagues at King's College for their support, understanding, and cover, in particular Andrea Biondi and the administrators of the Centre, Christine Copping and Andrea Cordwell-James. The European Commission's Legal Service enabled me to conduct interviews with its staff, and I am very grateful to Dr Pieter-Jan Kuijper, Principal Legal Advisor, for organizing this. I wish to thank those who gave generously of their time, knowledge, and experience, in particular Elisabetta Montaguti, Barbara Eggers, Sybilla Fries, Jörn Sack, Raimund Raith, Eric White, Götz zur Hausen, Thomas Jürgensen, Esa Paasivirta, Frank Hoffmeister, Michael Wilderspin, and Bernd Martenczuk. The people at OUP have been marvellous in their guidance, support, and efficiency; I wish to thank in particular John Louth, Kate Elliott, Fiona Barry, and Rebecca Allen. The General Editor of this series deserves much more than an acknowledgement, and I am ever grateful. Last but not least, this book would not have seen the light of day without the domestic encouragement and tolerance, abundantly supplied by 'de jongens' and especially by Hilde, to whom this book is dedicated.

Contents

Table of Cases

European Court of Human Rights

European Court of Justice and Court of First Instance

Alphabetical

Chronological

Germany

International

GATT

World Trade Organization

International Court of Justice

US Court of International Trade

Table of Legislation

European Union

Common Position

Common Strategies

Decisions

Directives

Joint Actions

Regulations

Resolutions

European Treaties

Germany

Other International Instruments

1

Introduction

Constitutional moment

This book was written in a year of great constitutional moment for the European Union's role on the world stage. It was not, however, a moment of universal euphoria over unquestionable progress. At one level the Convention on the Future of Europe was debating the constitutionalization of the EU, charting a course for a proper external projection of the EU phenomenon by constructing the constitutional and institutional foundations for an effective European foreign policy. It proposed abolishing the pillar structure, whose stone-faced mysteries have resisted and confused all conceptual understanding, and have led to much expenditure of ineffective political and institutional energy. It proposed express confirmation of the Union's legal personality, which is in effect an international legal personality. It proposed an assembly of all Treaty provisions on EU external relations, gleaned from the various treaties, renovated, and expanded, in a vital Title of Part III of the new constitution. It proposed a solution for resolving interinstitutional tension between the Commission and the Council, namely the creation of a double-hatted Minister for Foreign Affairs. It proposed, not least, an ambitious, some might say Utopian,[1] formulation of the principles and objectives of the Union's external action. At the outset of this book the projected Article III–193 of the draft Constitution is worth quoting:

1. The Union's action on the international scene shall be guided by, and designed to advance in the wider world, the principles which have inspired its own creation, development and enlargement: democracy, the rule of law, the universality and indivisibility of human rights and fundamental freedoms, respect for human dignity, equality and solidarity, and for international law in accordance with the principles of the United Nations Charter.

   The Union shall seek to develop relations and build partnerships with third countries, and international, regional or global organisations, which share these values. It shall promote multilateral solutions to common problems, in particular in the framework of the United Nations.

2. The Union shall define and pursue common policies and actions, and shall work for a high degree of cooperation in all fields of international relations, in order to:

(a) safeguard the common values, fundamental interests, security, independence and integrity of the Union;

---

[1] R Kagan, *Of Paradise and Power: America and Europe in the New World Order* (Alfred Knopf, 2003).

(b) consolidate and support democracy, the rule of law, human rights and international law;
(c) preserve peace, prevent conflicts and strengthen international security, in conformity with the principles of the United Nations Charter;
(d) foster the sustainable economic, social and environmental development of developing countries, with the primary aim of eradicating poverty;
(e) encourage the integration of all countries into the world economy, including through the progressive abolition of restrictions on international trade;
(f) help develop international measures to preserve and improve the quality of the environment and the sustainable management of global natural resources, in order to ensure sustainable development;
(g) assist populations, countries and regions confronting natural or man-made disasters;
(h) promote an international system based on stronger multilateral cooperation and good global governance.

. . .

If Europe, with all its political, economic, and intellectual resources, could realize only a segment of all this, the world might truly become a better place. The Convention, which clearly appreciated that its work on EU external action was central to its own constitutional moment, might in some measure earn its lofty denomination evoking the best episode of the American dream, and prove that the Age of Enlightenment is not dead.

Yet at the very same time Europe was facing one of its gravest political crises in the form of its inability to speak with one voice about the approach towards the Hussein regime in Iraq. In the corridors of the Convention there were arguments about the futility of the constitution-drafting exercise, in particular as regards EU external action, in the face of such fundamental cleavages between the Member States. The Common Foreign and Security Policy (CFSP), in existence for ten years, but rarely ever noticed by the general public, might as well be abandoned, notwithstanding opinion polls showing strong public support for a united European foreign policy.

Institutions and the law are quite resistant to such radical solutions. The Convention continued its work, attempting to create an adequate constitutional and institutional framework whilst recognizing that it could not itself supply the political will required to make Europe's foreign policy work. All this might suggest to those unfamiliar with the EU that its foreign policy is still in its infancy. Such an assessment would be wholly unjustified. In her book on the intergovernmental pillars of the EU Denza describes the foreign and security relations of a single sovereign State as supported and realized through a range of powerful instruments:[2]

The State by its nature has international legal personality; it may conclude treaties, become a member of international organizations, send and receive diplomatic and consular missions, defend its external interests by domestic legislation and its physical and political integrity by armies and weapons. By exploiting its natural and human resources it has money at its disposal which may be used for internal as well as external purposes.

[2] E Denza, *The Intergovernmental Pillars of the European Union* (OUP, 2002) 85–6.

Denza employs this description to contrast, at least to some extent, the sovereign State with the EU's CFSP. However, it is in fact striking that the EU already possesses and uses most, if not all, of those 'powerful instruments'. Whether the EU, as distinct from the EC, has international legal personality is still a matter of some debate,[3] but Article 281 EC provides that the Community has legal personality, and as early as 1971 the Court of Justice, in the seminal *AETR* ruling, construed this provision as confirming international legal personality.[4] Such personality is not a theoretical construction, as the EC is a party to hundreds of international agreements covering many areas of international lawmaking and establishing links with countries in all corners of the globe. The EC is also a member of a number of other international organizations, a rather unique phenomenon, even if still of limited scope. The EC or EU does not send formal diplomatic and consular missions, but that lacuna is more apparent than real in light of the important role played by European Commission delegations in third countries. The EC has the capacity to enact legislation; indeed in matters of external trade it has exclusive competence, and has wholly replaced the individual Member States. The EU has significant financial resources, an important part of which is spent on external action, often in conjunction with Member States' expenditure (e.g. development co-operation). Finally, the current EU even has a military component, and engages in military operations.[5]

Subject matter and methodology

This book explores the legal and constitutional foundations of the EU's foreign policy, or external relations as is the prevailing denomination. It brings together the various strands of EU external action,[6] focusing on both the EC's (first pillar) and the EU's (second and third pillar) external policies. In doing so it aims to present a unified portrait of the law of the EU's external relations. Indeed, one of the underlying assumptions of the analysis is that the EU is a single organization with a single legal system,[7] notwithstanding differences between the pillars, and differences between EU law and EC law. No attempt is made here to justify that assumption; it is hoped that the book itself may do so.

   The aims of the project which led to this book were the collection, organization, and presentation of the many different aspects and developments of external relations law; to give access to practice, case law, and academic literature linked to external relations; to advance our understanding (or at least this author's understanding) of the role of law in EU external policies; and to offer introduction, survey, analysis, and reflection. The academic approach is largely doctrinal, but with attention to historical development, political and institutional context, and in narrative form. The attempt is to be true

---

[3] See Ch 5.   [4] See Ch 3.   [5] See Ch 11.

[6] The draft Constitution speaks of external action instead of external relations.

[7] A von Bogdandy, 'The Legal Case for Unity: the European Union as a Single Organization with a Single Legal System' (1999) 36 CMLRev 887.

to this series' aim of providing 'a clear, concise, and critical exposition of the law in its social, economic, and political context'. The book may also serve as a basis for further and deeper academic reflection on specific aspects of EU external relations law.

Academic literature on EC or EU law has generally tended to concentrate a lot on the case law of the European Courts, in particular the Court of Justice. There are a number of obvious reasons for this, which need not be explored here. Over the last decade, however, there has been contestation of Court-centred analysis. Academic lawyers have rightly become more critical of the Court, and more attention is devoted to non-judicial actors and developments. Law does not invariably develop through case law, and judicial proclamations may conceal rather than reveal the problems which the polity and society face, and may create legal illusions.

This book none the less devotes a lot of attention to the case law. The rulings by the EU Courts offer a rich record of problems, questions, and issues concerning external relations. Case law has contributed to shaping the constitutional foundations of external action as well as some of the actual policies. It exposes the inter-institutional struggle which explains a lot of basic features, including the pillar structure itself. It is the meeting place for true encounters between EU law and international law, as parties to litigation put the two systems in confrontation. In-depth study of the case law allows one to develop a richer and more nuanced, focused, and calibrated legal discourse on external relations.

The most challenging dimension of the project was to find an overall framework of analysis, which would allow for selection of relevant topics. It was soon realized that the book could not cover all external policies and all international agreements. External EU policies are not confined to 'inherent' domains of external relations such as trade, development co-operation, and foreign and security policy. Most, if not all, of the EU's 'internal' policies have a significant external dimension. Environmental policy is possibly the best example: the Community's environmental policy is perhaps as much constructed through participation in international environmental lawmaking as through internal legislation. Accordingly, a study of all external policies could not be undertaken in this book. The same is true for the treaty-making practice, in particular as regards the variety of agreements, in terms of concepts and subject matter, and as regards the specific features of relations with third countries or groups of third countries. The EC has concluded association, partnership, and co-operation agreements, of some form or other, with so many third countries. Each of those agreements forms the basis for a particular bilateral relationship. Again, a study of those agreements could not be undertaken, and this book does not provide an analysis, as such, of treaty relations between the EC and third countries.

So what does the book cover? As its title suggests, it aims to identify the legal and constitutional foundations of external relations. What are the bases in the founding treaties for the EU's external relations? What powers or competences have been conferred on the EU to act in the international sphere? How does the EU conclude international agreements and become a member of international organizations? What is the role of the various EU institutions in the conduct of external relations?

What is the relationship between EU law and international law? What are the effects of international law, and in particular international agreements, in the EU's legal order? Those are all foundational questions the answers to which this book attempts to unravel. The juxtaposition of 'legal' and 'constitutional' is inspired by a number of considerations. The exclusive use of the term constitutional would require the construction of a conception of constitutionalism which the author would rather refrain from undertaking here. It would give too much specific focus, undermining the attempt at comprehensive treatment, even if that conception were broad as seems to be fashionable. The juxtaposition leaves open whether particular issues are 'constitutional' or simply 'legal'. At the same time, the term constitutional is warranted because the book does indeed aim to explore fundamental questions of government in relation to the EU's external relations.

The book is organized in three parts. The first is called Constitutional Foundations: Powers and Objectives. It is wholly devoted to the Treaty foundations (both EC and EU) for external relations and external policies. It concentrates on the Treaty provisions which confer power to conclude international agreements, which are the core of external action. Ever since the creation of the EEC this has been a big legal battlefield, due to the reluctance, resistance, and inhibitions of the Member States to cede sovereignty to the Community, in particular as regards external relations. Chapter 2 examines the Community's powers in matters of commercial policy, which formed the basis in the original EEC Treaty for external action. From the 1970s onwards the Court of Justice has played a pivotal role in defining the scope and nature of the Community's competence as regards external trade. Chapter 3 complements that analysis by concentrating on the doctrine of implied powers, equally foundational for the Community's external action, and equally contested. Partly on the basis of the analysis in those two chapters, Chapter 4 looks more generally at external competences under the EC Treaty in the main areas of EC policy-making. Chapter 5 concludes Part I by looking at external competences under the TEU, in particular the definition of the scope and remit of the CFSP. In contrast with the previous chapters, there is very little relevant case law on this subject, because the Court of Justice lacks jurisdiction. It is none the less possible to engage in a legal analysis of external powers in this area, including their relationship with the EC's external powers.

The second part of the book is called International Foundations: Treaties and International Law. It contains four chapters on the relationship between international law and treaties, and EU law. Chapter 6 explores the life cycle of international agreements, analysing the EU procedures for negotiation, conclusion, suspension, and termination of treaties and agreements. Such analysis reveals the role of the various EU institutions in the conduct of external relations, and throws up constitutional questions of division of powers, democracy, accountability, and legitimacy. Chapter 7 concentrates on mixed agreements and membership of international organizations. Mixed agreements, i.e. agreements with third countries or international organizations to which both the Community and its individual Member States are parties, are a hallmark of EU external relations, again reflecting the resistance to cession of sovereignty. They give rise to many questions and problems which the chapter aims to analyse. It also focuses on membership of international organizations, for purposes of convenience: even though that is a subject on its own, the issues to which it gives rise are often the same as in the case of mixed agreements, because Community membership is invariably combined with Member States' membership. Furthermore, the concept of an international organization is not easy to define, as many international agreements (often mixed agreements in terms of EC participation) provide for some type of institutional framework. Chapter 8 looks at the role of the European Courts in the interpretation and application of agreements concluded by the Community. It examines the main heads of jurisdiction of those courts, aiming to identify in what way such jurisdiction extends to international agreements. It also offers an analysis of methods of interpretation of such agreements. Chapter 9, lastly, the longest chapter of this book, examines the effects of international agreements and international law in the EU legal order.

There is a third part of the book, even though Parts I and II could be regarded as sufficient for a book on legal and constitutional foundations of EU external relations. This third part concentrates on a few external policies. It is much more selective than Parts I and II, because there are many established and developing external policies which are not analysed. It first focuses on the common commercial policy (Chapter 10), which is historically at the heart of the Community's external relations. Chapter 11 studies the actors and instruments of the CFSP. Chapter 12 explores the links between trade policy and foreign policy in the areas of economic sanctions and export controls. That chapter offers some type of case study of those links. Chapter 13, lastly, provides a survey of the EU's external human rights policy, which cuts across various segments of the EU's external policies. Focus on human rights is also justified from the perspective of constitutionalism.

The purpose of this third part on external policies is to put some flesh on to the bones of constitutional and institutional developments, and to improve the understanding of those developments. Issues of external competence or legal effects of international agreements should not be studied in isolation, because the way in which the law develops is clearly influenced by the substantive policies which are projected and conducted. Analysis of actual policies also further clarifies the role of the various institutions, and throws up additional questions of constitutionalism.

Throughout this book there are also references to and succinct analyses of the relevant provisions of the draft Constitution. The domain of 'external action' is one where that Constitution aims to make significant changes and progress. By incorporating what, at the time of writing, are still only proposals the book is better able to show the direction of external relations law.

Through this book the author hopes to show the importance of this subject, not only in its own right, but for the developing identity of the EU as a whole. The organization of the external relations of the EU and its Member States is crucial for the unique type of federalism which Europe is constructing.[8]

---

[8] Cf JHH Weiler, *The Constitution of Europe* (CUP, 1999) 186–7.

Part I

Constitutional Foundations:
Powers and Objectives

2

Competence in matters of commercial policy

Introduction

The European Union, as it developed out of the European Communities, has some of its legal origins in the GATT. After World War II, the GATT was negotiated with a view to establishing a multilateral legal framework for trade liberalization. It reflected prevailing economic theory on the benefits of free trade, and was centred around the concept of non-discrimination, in reply to the beggar-thy-neighbour policies of the 1930s. Article I GATT spells out the most-favoured-nation principle (MFN), which requires equal treatment of trading partners. If that principle were unqualified, it would not be possible to set up forms of regional economic integration based on preferential terms of trade within the region concerned. The GATT tolerates departures from MFN for integration purposes, provided they take the form of either a customs union or free-trade area and comply with the requirements of Article XXIV GATT. Again this was based on economic theory, which recognizes the potential benefits flowing from closer integration,[1] even though it must be added that the theoretical support is qualified.[2]

When the EEC was set up, it was decided to establish a customs union, the most advanced form of trade integration, since there was the further aim of building a common market, with free movement of factors of production. Accordingly, (current) Article 23(1) EC provides that:

The Community shall be based upon a customs union which shall cover all trade in goods and which shall involve the prohibition between Member States of customs duties on imports and exports and all charges having equivalent effect, and the adoption of a common customs tariff in their relations with third countries.

It may be emphasized that this provision identifies the customs union as the very basis of the Community. The customs union is at the core of the common (or internal) market, and establishing the customs union was among the first major policies which the EEC implemented, in the 1960s, together with the common agricultural policy. The abolition of customs duties in internal trade is now largely of historical (and

---

[1] J Viner, *The Customs Union Issue* (Carnegie Endowment for International Peace, 1950).
[2] See e.g. J Bhagwati, *The World Trading System at Risk* (Harvester Wheatsheaf, 1991) ch 5.

constitutional[3]) interest, and the common customs tariff is discussed in Chapter 10. However, it was clear to the drafters of the EEC Treaty that a common external tariff was only one segment of a common external trade policy, and that indeed such a policy was required if the customs union and the common market were to work well. They therefore wrote a chapter on the common commercial policy which the EEC was to set up and conduct.

The original EEC Treaty chapter on the common commercial policy was short, and it is even shorter at present due to the repeal of some provisions. The chapter opens by identifying the aims of this policy: by establishing a customs union Member States aim to contribute, in the common interest, to the harmonious development of world trade, the progressive abolition of restrictions on international trade, and the lowering of customs barriers (Article 131 EC). Article 132 EC speaks of the progressive harmonization of the systems whereby Member States grant aid for exports to third countries, to the extent necessary to ensure that competition between undertakings of the Community is not distorted. As will be seen below, this notion of undistorted competition is important for understanding some of the functions of the common commercial policy. Then follows the central Article 133 EC, which further describes the measures envisaged to be adopted in the framework of this policy:

The common commercial policy shall be based on uniform principles, particularly in regard to changes in tariff rates, the conclusion of tariff and trade agreements, the achievement of uniformity in measures of liberalization, export policy and measures to protect trade such as those to be taken in case of dumping or subsidies.

The article also sets out the role of the various institutions and the procedure to be followed for the adoption of such measures, and was in this respect substantially amended by the Treaties of Amsterdam and Nice. At this stage, it is important to note that the Commission and the Council are the leading institutions, and that the Council decides by qualified majority. Amsterdam and Nice also amended the Article in terms of broadening the scope of the common commercial policy, as discussed below.

Article 134 EC is a technical and vaguely phrased provision aiming to avoid obstruction—by deflection of trade or in case of economic difficulties—of measures of commercial policy taken by Member States. In practice, it served as a basis for certain restrictions in intra-Community trade which were necessary as long as there was no full uniformity in import conditions.[4]

It may also be noted that the original EEC Treaty chapter on commercial policy contained an additional provision, Article 116 EEC, which was repealed by the TEU for reasons which were not obvious. Indeed, its language was quite strong. It provided that, from the end of the transitional period, Member States were required, in respect of all matters of particular interest to the common market, to proceed

---

[3] It was in this area that the ECJ delivered its foundational ruling in Case 26/62 *Van Gend en Loos v. Nederlandse Administratie der Belastingen* [1963] ECR 1.   [4] See Ch 10.

within the framework of international organizations of an economic character only by common action.[5]

That, then, was the legal basis for the Community's external trade policy, which was to complement the creation of the customs union. In the course of the 1960s the young EEC was successful in removing internal customs duties and adopting the common customs tariff. The latter required common action in the framework of GATT, of which all the Member States were contracting parties. As the Treaty empowered the Commission to conduct trade negotiations, the Commission effectively replaced the Member States in GATT dealings, in a pragmatic arrangement characteristic of the then GATT.[6]

With the advent of the 1970s, however, the EEC lost much of its pristine state, and at the level of trade policy it soon became clear that developing a truly uniform external trade policy, over and above the customs union, was going to be more difficult than had been envisaged. Achieving such uniformity in fact required the abolition of long lists of import restrictions which individual Member States still operated. In a period of economic stagnation and crisis that proved impossible to achieve, and it was only by 1994, twenty-four years after the due date, that complete uniformity of import conditions was reached.[7] In light of such difficulties in establishing what is in effect the core of any external trade policy, it will come as no surprise that there was soon also a legal debate on the exact scope of the common commercial policy. When, as will be seen, the ECJ decided that the EEC's powers to conduct this policy were exclusive of those of the Member States, the legal stakes became even greater. The scene had been set for various turf battles, mostly between the supranational Commission and the intergovernmental Council. This chapter aims to analyse and portray those battles, and the case law and Treaty amendments they gave rise to.[8] It aims to do that from a historical perspective, in the sense of discussing both internal and external events which throw light on how the law on trade policy powers developed. The chapter also aims to show the significant political dimension of these legal battles, so closely interwoven with the classic struggle between supranationalism and intergovernmentalism. In fact, they may be the epitome of this struggle, because of the potent mix of external relations, exclusive powers, and qualified majority—a threesome of political sensitivities.

Opinion 1/75 and the notion of exclusivity

The first case in which the ECJ showed awareness of the significance of the transfer of trade policy powers from the Member States to the EEC was *Hauptzollamt*

---

[5] See Ch 7.
[6] For an account see Joined Cases 21 to 24/72 *International Fruit Company v. Produktschap voor Groenten en Fruit* [1972] ECR 1219.   [7] See Ch 10.
[8] See also C Kaddous, *Le droit des relations extérieures dans la jurisprudence de la Cour de justice des Communautés européennes* (Helbing & Lichtenhahn, 1998) 181–218.

Bremerhaven v. Massey-Ferguson.[9] In issue was the validity of a regulation on valuation of goods for customs purposes. The regulation had been adopted on the basis of (current) Article 308 EC, and it was argued that this legal basis was incorrect. The Court disagreed, but it did point out that the proper functioning of the customs union justified a wide interpretation of the Treaty provisions on the customs union and the common commercial policy, and of the powers which these provisions conferred on the institutions to allow them thoroughly to control external trade by measures taken both independently and by agreement.[10]

That statement was no more than a first indication, but a few years later the Court was to decide its first Opinion on an envisaged international agreement, pursuant to (current) Article 300(6) EC. That provision establishes a procedure enabling the Court to rule on the compatibility of an envisaged agreement with the Treaty, also as regards matters of competence.[11] If it had not existed, there might not have been half as many external competence cases, for it is politically and legally much more difficult to challenge the lawfulness of an international agreement once it has been concluded. The procedure of a request for an Opinion allows the institutions and the Member States to ensure that the envisaged agreement does indeed come within the Community's competence and is adopted under the correct Treaty provision. In practice, however, the procedure has often been used for opposite reasons, particularly by the Commission, namely to disprove Member State competence through the assertion of exclusive Community competence. As will be seen throughout this chapter and the next, those attempts have rarely been wholly successful.[12]

Opinion 1/75 concerned a draft 'Understanding on a Local Cost Standard' which had been drawn up under the auspices of the OECD.[13] This 'Understanding' concerned export credits. The participating governments essentially agreed not to finance or cover credit, in respect of local costs related to export transactions (in effect, payment of the purchase price), for more than 100 per cent of the value of the goods and services exported. The Commission asked whether the Community had the power to conclude the 'Understanding' and, if so, whether that power was exclusive. Thus phrased, the question identified the two vital components in EC external powers claims: the scope of those powers, and whether or not they are exclusive of the powers of Member States.[14] In both respects, *Opinion 1/75* contains important statements.

As regards the scope of the Community's powers,[15] the Court could easily have limited its analysis to (current) Article 132 EC, which specifically addresses aid for exports, and therefore covers the grant of export credits. Instead, it chose to broaden

---

[9] Case 8/73 *Hauptzollamt Bremerhaven v. Massey-Ferguson* [1973] ECR 897.   [10] Ibid, para 4.
[11] See Ch 8.
[12] Cf T Tridimas and P Eeckhout, 'The External Competence of the Community and the Case-Law of the Court of Justice: Principle versus Pragmatism' (1994) 14 YEL 143.
[13] *Opinion 1/75 re Understanding on a Local Cost Standard* [1975] ECR 1355.
[14] A Dashwood and C Hillion, 'Introduction', in A Dashwood and C Hillion (eds), *The General Law of E.C. External Relations* (Sweet & Maxwell, 2000) pp. v–vi.
[15] *Opinion 1/75* (n 13 above), 1362–3.

the discussion by also considering (current) Article 133 EC. The Court pointed out that this provision referred to export policy, and thus necessarily covered systems of aid for exports, particularly export credits. It identified the relevant measures as constituting an important element of commercial policy, and stated that that concept had the same content whether it was applied in the context of the international action of a State or to that of the Community. This rather cryptic statement was to return in later case law, and indicates that international practice in the area of trade policy is one factor for determining the scope of the common commercial policy. The Court also referred to directives concerning credit insurance, which expressly recognized the important role played by export credits in international trade, as a factor of commercial policy. It concluded that the subject matter of the 'Understanding' came within the scope of (current) Articles 132 and 133 EC.

The Court then specifically considered the power to conclude international agreements on commercial policy, as envisaged by the relevant Treaty provisions. It stated that a commercial policy was made up by the combination and interaction of internal and external measures, without priority being taken by one over the others. It further developed that idea, indicating *inter alia* that the common commercial policy was above all the outcome of a progressive development based upon specific measures which could refer without distinction to 'autonomous' and external aspects of that policy, and which did not necessarily presuppose the existence of a large body of rules, but combined gradually to form that body. The Court was thus pointing out that the common commercial policy could be built gradually, through both the adoption of internal legislation and the conclusion of international agreements.

Reading the Opinion up to that point, one might have expected that, in the second part, the Court would have characterized the Community's competence as concurrent with the competence of Member States. That might have seemed more logical in light of the Court's references to the gradual development of this policy. But the Court did not adopt that approach. It described the nature of the Community's powers in the following terms.[16] The common commercial policy was conceived in (current) Article 133 EC in the context of the operation of the common market, for the defence of the common interests of the Community, within which the particular interests of the Member States had to endeavour to adapt to each other. This conception was clearly incompatible with the freedom to which the Member States could lay claim by invoking a concurrent power, so as to ensure that their own interests were separately satisfied, at the risk of compromising the effective defence of the common interests. Any unilateral action on the part of the Member States would lead to disparities in the conditions for the grant of export credits, calculated to distort competition between undertakings of the various Member States in external markets. Such distortion could be eliminated only by means of a strict uniformity. Concurrent powers therefore could not be accepted, and the Treaty provisions on concluding agreements of commercial policy

---

[16] Ibid, 1363–4.

showed clearly that the exercise of concurrent powers was impossible. To accept the contrary would amount to recognizing that, in relations with third countries, Member States could adopt positions which differed from those which the Community intended to adopt, and would thereby distort the institutional framework, call into question the mutual trust within the Community, and prevent the latter from fulfilling its task in the defence of the common interest.

On a further point, no doubt elicited by the fact that the 'Understanding' concerned export credits granted by the Member States from their own resources, the Court considered that it was of little importance that the obligations and financial burdens inherent in the execution of the agreement envisaged were borne directly by the Member States. The 'internal' and 'external' measures adopted by the Community within the framework of the common commercial policy did not necessarily involve a transfer to the institutions of the Community of the obligations and financial burdens which they could involve. Those measures were solely concerned to substitute for the unilateral action of the Member States a common action based upon uniform principles on behalf of the whole Community.

The Court's analysis contained various arguments in support of the exclusive nature of the Community's trade policy powers. They deserve brief comment, particularly as the Court never returned to the subject.

The Court's first argument is that the defence of the Community's common interests requires exclusivity. It is certainly true that trade policies often concern significant economic interests, and that it could be very difficult to map out a meaningful common policy if the Member States were allowed to continue to pursue their own trade policies. Yet it is clear that this is essentially a political argument, which may also be valid for other common policies. One may think of the common transport policy, also prescribed by the EEC Treaty, but in this field the Court never recognized exclusive powers.

A second, but related argument is more persuasive. The Court refers to the distortions of competition between undertakings established in the Community which are likely to arise in the absence of uniform export credit conditions. It is indeed not difficult to see how such distortions could arise: the whole purpose of the OECD 'Understanding' was to limit excessive competition in the grant of export credits. However, the argument is of much broader scope, and connects the common commercial policy as a whole, as regards both imports and exports, with the internal market. Indeed the EU internal market, characterized as it is by strong integration and generalized free movement of products, persons, capital, and companies, could hardly function effectively in the absence of a common external trade policy, which uniformly lays down the external terms of trade. As the common commercial policy took some time actually to be realized in certain sectors, there are numerous examples to illustrate that. Thus, to mention just one, it took until the 1990s before there was a uniform import regime for Japanese cars. Previously, a number of Member States operated restrictions on imports of such cars, evidently to protect their domestic manufacturers. Yet the latter were also in competition with other

European car manufacturers, established and with a large market share in Member States which did not operate such restrictions. The distortion of competition was evident.[17]

As will be seen below, the concept of distortion of competition may be complemented with the notion of deflections of trade. In the absence of a uniform external trade policy, particularly as regards imports, deflections of trade are likely to arise: imports will tend to go to the Member State with the most liberal policy, and will then, by virtue of the internal market, find their way to the less liberal Member States. Such deflections of trade could only be avoided through the erection of barriers to intra-Community trade, but those are anathema to a genuine internal market.[18]

It is worth adding that the notions of competition distortion and trade deflection have their counterparts in the Court's case law on the EC's 'internal' powers to harmonize national laws with a view to establishing the internal market. In the important Tobacco Advertising Directive case, for example, the Court examined whether the directive was aimed at eliminating distortions of competition or obstacles to trade or free movement.[19] The latter notion is the internal counterpart of deflections of trade. Thus it can be seen that essentially the same economic risks justify internal legislative powers and external exclusive competence.

The Court's third argument in *Opinion 1/75* was based on the principle of Member States' loyalty towards the Community and its institutions. That argument may not be very strong: it does not follow from the fact that certain powers are concurrently held by the Community and the Member States that the latter will act contrary to the Community's interests, or will disregard common decisions.

In support of exclusivity, the Court could also have referred to the international legal basis for the customs union. The GATT defines a customs union as the substitution of a single customs territory for two or more customs territories, so that substantially the same duties *and other regulations of commerce* are applied by each of the members of the union to the trade of territories not included in the union.[20] This conjunction of the external tariff and other external trade policies is obvious from an economic perspective and, as the Treaty clearly opted for a single common customs tariff and a uniform common commercial policy, the Court's ruling in favour of exclusive commercial policy powers, which followed the adoption of the common tariff, made eminent sense.

None the less, from a constitutional perspective the Court's decision continues to be remarkable. It may be that it was also in part the child of a particular period in the Court's case law. Waelbroeck has demonstrated that in the early 1970s the case law on competence, not only in the field of commercial policy but also in other fields such as agriculture, wavered between what he called a federalist-conceptualist approach,

---

[17] For further details, also as regards other sectors, see P Eeckhout, *The European Internal Market and International Trade—A Legal Analysis* (OUP, 1994) ch 6.   [18] See further Ch 10.
[19] Case C–376/98 *Germany v. European Parliament and Council* [2000] ECR I–8419.
[20] Art XXIV(8)(a) GATT, emphasis added.

where Community competence is construed as being necessarily exclusive, and a pragmatic approach, where concurrent powers are recognized. Particularly the period 1973–5, when *Opinion 1/75* was delivered, is characterized by Waelbroeck as a period of hesitation between those approaches.[21]

But if that was the case, it must be emphasized that the Court never hesitated to confirm the exclusive nature of the Community's trade policy powers. None the less, as will be seen below as well as in Chapter 10, the Court did not interpret the principle of exclusivity in a strict way, and left considerable scope for a gradual implementation of the common commercial policy and for some measure of recognition of Member States' powers, provided their exercise was regulated by Community law.

The rise of UNCTAD and the broad conception of 'trade'

In light of the principle of exclusivity one might have expected the Court to interpret the scope of the common commercial policy somewhat narrowly. Exclusive competences are exceptional in the EU constitutional order, and politically sensitive, in particular where external relations are involved. The Court did not however adopt such an approach in the 1970s and 1980s. It took a broad view of the notion of trade, against the backdrop of increased worldwide questioning of the free-trade model, especially as regards its effects on developing countries. In 1964 UNCTAD had been established, an organization built on the link between trade and development, and it soon came to be seen as a rival institution of the GATT. Its activities were geared towards establishing preferential terms of trade for developing countries, which implied forms of trade regulation rather than trade liberalization. In 1976 UNCTAD established an 'Integrated Programme for Commodities', designed to improve the conditions for trade in certain commodities which were of particular interest to developing countries. The programme provided that in respect of eighteen such commodities negotiations were to be opened for introducing international arrangements between producer and consumer countries. In that framework a 1978 conference negotiated a draft International Agreement on Natural Rubber. The main feature of the draft agreement was the creation of a buffer stock system designed to stabilize natural rubber prices. The Commission had proposed to the Council that it be given a mandate to conduct the negotiations, since it considered that the draft agreement came within the scope of (current) Article 133 EC. The Council had rejected that view, and had decided that the negotiations were to be conducted by a Community delegation and by delegations from Member States, which were to act on the basis of a common standpoint. The Commission then went to the Court of Justice and requested an Opinion on the scope of the Community's competence.[22]

---

[21] M Waelbroeck, 'The Emergent Doctrine of Community Pre-emption—Consent and Re-delegation', in T Sandalow and E Stein (eds), *Courts and Free Markets* (OUP, 1982) 551 and 556–61.

[22] *Opinion 1/78 re International Agreement on Natural Rubber* [1979] ECR 2871.

This is a classic scenario which, as will be seen, often returns, and which features no real disagreement as to the actual negotiating position to be adopted from the European side, but is more concerned with the respective roles of the Commission, the Council, and delegations from Member States.

Opinion 1/78 is a long and complex judicial text, which analyses and describes the objectives and features of the draft agreement at considerable length. As regards the scope of (current) Article 133 EC, however, the Court discussed the relevant principles in just three paragraphs, which became a classic in EC external relations law.[23]

The Court first referred to the link between the various agreements on commodities: as an increasing number of products which were particularly important from the economic point of view were concerned, it was clear that a coherent commercial policy would no longer be practicable if the Community were not in a position to exercise its powers also in connection with a category of agreements which were becoming, alongside traditional commercial agreements, one of the major factors in the regulation of international trade.

The Court developed this concern in the next paragraph, concentrating on the new type of trade regulation and management which UNCTAD advocated. It would, in the Court's opinion, no longer be possible to carry on any worthwhile common commercial policy if the Community were not in a position to avail itself also of more elaborate means devised with a view to furthering the development of international trade. (Current) Article 133 EC was not to be interpreted so as to restrict the common commercial policy to the use of instruments intended to have an effect only on the traditional aspects of external trade to the exclusion of more highly developed mechanisms. Such a 'commercial policy' would be destined to become nugatory in the course of time. Although it might have been thought that at the time of Treaty drafting liberalization of trade was the dominant idea, the Treaty nevertheless did not form a barrier to the Community's developing a commercial policy aiming at a regulation of the world market for certain products rather than at a mere liberalization of trade.

In the third paragraph the Court confirmed this from the perspective of the text of (current) Article 133. That provision empowered the Community to formulate a commercial 'policy', based on 'uniform principles', thus showing that the question of external trade had to be governed from a wide point of view and not only having regard to the administration of precise systems such as customs and quantitative restrictions. The same conclusion was deduced from the fact that the enumeration in Article 133 of the subjects covered by commercial policy was conceived as a non-exhaustive enumeration which could not close the door to any other process intended to regulate external trade. A restrictive interpretation, the Court concluded, would risk causing disturbances in intra-Community trade by reason of the disparities which would then exist in certain sectors of economic relations with non-member countries.

The concern underlying the Court's reasoning in those paragraphs is obvious and was at the time no doubt justified. Despite the fact that the draft rubber agreement

---

[23] Ibid, paras 43–45.

employed novel conceptions regarding trade relations between developing and developed countries, it was clearly an international agreement on trade in rubber. The decision of principle which the Court thus reached was that the Community had exclusive competence to enter into the agreement. However, at the time of delivering the Opinion it was not yet clear whether the buffer stock, central to the operation of the agreement, was to be financed from the Community budget or by the Member States. The Court considered that this was an important point. It stated that the financing of the buffer stock constituted an essential feature of the whole scheme, and that, if the financing was to be undertaken by the Member States, that would imply their participation in the decision-making machinery or, at least, their agreement with regard to the arrangements for financing envisaged. That in turn would require that the Member States participate in the agreement together with the Community, and '[t]he exclusive competence of the Community could not be envisaged in such a case'.[24]

Opinion 1/78 is thus more mixed than is sometimes thought. On the one hand, the Court took a broad view of the concept of common commercial policy, recognizing extended exclusive Community powers. On the other hand, it allowed for Member State participation, and thus mixed action, through the financing arrangements. That aspect of the ruling has been criticized on the ground that it is inconsistent with *Opinion 1/75*, where the Court decided that the financial side was irrelevant, and on the ground that it put the cart before the horse: instead of allowing finance to determine exclusivity, exclusivity should have determined finance.[25] It is none the less possible to distinguish *Opinions 1/75* and *1/78*. In the former, the 'Understanding' purported to impose a cap on export credit expenditure by the participating States, and in no way required such expenditure. In the latter, the contracting parties had to finance the operation of the agreement, and in effect such financing amounted to development aid, a matter which clearly does not come within the scope of the common commercial policy, even though at the time there were no other express Treaty provisions on such aid.[26] In any event, *Opinion 1/78* will be remembered for its emphasis on a broad interpretation of (current) Article 133 EEC and the commercial policy concept which it embodies.

The bipolar world of *Commission v. Council*

In the course of the proceedings leading up to *Opinion 1/78* the Commission and the Council submitted different views on the scope of the common commercial

---

[24] Opinion 1/78 (n 22 above), para 60. The political outcome was that commodity agreements were concluded as mixed agreements: see Ch 7.

[25] JHH Weiler, 'The External Legal Relations of Non-Unitary Actors: Mixity and the Federal Principle', in D O'Keeffe and HG Schermers (eds), *Mixed Agreements* (Kluwer Law and Taxation Publishers, 1983) 72; idem in *The Constitution of Europe* (CUP, 1999) 174; PJG Kapteyn and P VerLoren van Themaat, *Introduction to the Law of the European Communities* (3rd edn, by LW Gormley, Kluwer Law International, 1998) 1281.   [26] See Ch 4.

policy in attempts to lay down general criteria for the concept of commercial policy. The Commission argued that a measure of commercial policy had to be assessed primarily by reference to its specific character as an instrument regulating international trade (the so-called 'objective/instrumental' approach).[27] The Council, on the other hand, considered that any measure the aim of which was to influence the volume or flow of trade had to be considered as a commercial policy measure (the so-called 'subjective/purposive' approach).[28] Of those contrasting approaches, the former was probably the broader one, whereas the latter left considerable room for manœuvre for the Council, chief legislator in this field, through the definition and description of the aims of the measures which it adopted. At one stage the debate on those theories acquired near scholastic dimensions. It was very much a lawyers' debate, with participation by academics and by lawyers from the legal services of the Commission and the Council,[29] and it may be doubtful whether the institutions themselves and the Member States governments felt well entertained by such discussions. The practice as regards conclusion of international agreements was not in any event greatly affected. The EEC at the time often concluded 'trade and economic co-operation' agreements, and as such agreements contained a non-trade dimension, they were concluded on the basis of (current) Articles 133 and 308 EC.[30]

The Court of Justice never looked at the scope of the common commercial policy in such general terms.[31] Views differed on which thesis was most vindicated in *Opinion 1/78*, but the truth is probably that neither was and that the Court opted for judicial economy, aiming to resolve the problem before it rather than developing an abstract formula for capturing the scope of the common commercial policy.

The Commission and the Council had a re-run of *Opinion 1/78* in 1987, in a case on the correct legal basis for the adoption of generalized tariff preferences (GSP).[32] The Community GSP system was developed in the 1970s, upon recommendation by UNCTAD. It is a unilateral system of tariff reductions for imports from developing countries, and thus again links trade and development.[33] Since 1971, the Council had adopted the relevant EEC regulations without making express reference to the EEC Treaty provisions considered to form the legal basis. It acted by unanimity. The Commission, by contrast, had consistently proposed that the regulations be adopted under (current) Article 133 EC—requiring qualified majority. Before the Court, the Council declared that the regulations were in fact based on (current) Articles 133 and 308 EC, the latter requiring unanimity.

---

[27] *Opinion 1/78* (n 22 above), 2883–4.   [28] Ibid, 2887–8.

[29] See e.g. C-D Ehlermann, 'The Scope of Article 113 of the EEC Treaty', in *Mélanges offerts à Pierre-Henri Teitgen* (Pedone, 1984) 150–1; JHJ Bourgeois, 'The Common Commercial Policy—Scope and Nature of the Powers', in ELM Völker (ed), *Protectionism and the European Community* (2nd edn., Kluwer, 1986) 1–16; J Steenbergen, 'Annotation Case 45/86' (1987) 24 CML Rev 731–7.

[30] E.g. K Lenaerts and E De Smijter, 'The European Community's Treaty-Making Competence' (1996) 16 YEL 23.

[31] K Lenaerts and P van Nuffel, *Constitutional Law of the European Union* (R Bray (ed) and trans, Sweet & Maxwell, 1999) 622.   [32] Case 45/86 *Commission v. Council* [1987] ECR 1493.

[33] See Ch 10.

Commission and Council again presented their theories on the scope of the common commercial policy, but the Court stood firm in its refusal to be drawn into scholastics. Lenz AG finely remarked that in the oral proceedings the parties had conceded that they deployed the different theories according to where their interests lay. Thus, the Commission adopted the 'objective/instrumental' approach so as to support its arguments but a 'subjective/purposive' argument in order to differentiate (current) Articles 133 and 26 EC (on the common customs tariff). Conversely, the Council used a 'subjective/purposive' approach in order to support its view of the interpretation of (current) Article 133 but had to employ the 'objective/instrumental' approach when adopting trade sanctions.[34]

The Court itself, noting the Council's explanation that the use of both (current) Articles 133 and 308 was required because the contested regulations not only had commercial-policy aims, but also major development-policy aims, based its analysis on the principle that in the context of the organization of the powers of the Community the choice of legal basis for a measure could not depend simply on an institution's conviction as to the objective pursued, but had to be based on objective factors which were amenable to judicial review.[35] It thus clearly rejected a purely subjective 'subjective/purposive' approach.[36] The Court then pointed out that (current) Article 308 EC could only be used if there was no other Treaty provision conferring competence.[37] Consequently, the Court examined whether (current) Article 133 alone was a sufficient legal basis. Here it referred to the language of that provision, which refers to 'changes in tariff rates'. It then recalled its statement in *Opinion 1/75* on the concept of commercial policy having the same content whether it was applied in the context of the international action of a State or in that of the Community. The Court considered that the link between trade and development had become progressively stronger in modern international relations, as recognized in the contexts of both UNCTAD and GATT. It was against that background that the model was evolved on which the Community's GSP system was based; that system reflected a new concept of international trade relations in which development aims played a major role. The Court then returned to the text of the Treaty, considering that, in defining the characteristics and the instruments of the common commercial policy, the Treaty took possible changes into account. It pointed in particular to (current) Article 131 EC's reference 'to the harmonious development of world trade' and to the combined provisions of (current) Article 133 EC and (old) Article 116 EEC, encompassing common action also in international organizations which might deal with commercial problems from the point of view of development policy. Lastly, the Court recalled its statements on the broad scope of the common commercial policy in *Opinion 1/78*. It concluded that (current) Article 133 EEC was the correct legal basis, and annulled the regulations.[38]

---

[34] *Commission v. Council* (n 32 above), Opinion Lenz AG, para 59. See below for the case law on economic sanctions, as well as Ch 12.   [35] Ibid, paras 10–11.
[36] There is an analogy with *Germany v. European Parliament and Council* (n 19 above), para 85.
[37] *Commission v. Council* (n 32 above), para 13.   [38] Ibid, paras 14–21.

After *Opinion 1/78*, the judgment in *Commission v. Council* cannot have come as much of a surprise. The Court essentially reiterated its views on a modern commercial policy requiring enclosure of trade measures with development aims.[39] Whilst there may in this context indeed be more emphasis on the instrument used than on the aims pursued, the judgment does not provide unqualified support for the Commission's thesis. The Court does also consider the aims of the measure, but takes the view that development aims are integral to a modern commercial policy. From the perspective of international developments in trade policy since the 1960s, that view is clearly correct.

The internal market and external trade

Opinion 1/75 rightly referred to the link between the unity of the common market (now internal market) and a uniform common commercial policy. The Court considered that this was an argument for exclusive Community competence, but a moment's thought will clarify that it may also serve to delimit the scope of this competence. If indeed potential distortions of competition or deflections of trade in the internal market justify trade policy powers, then those concepts may amount to some form of test for the competence calculus. Where a Member State adopts a measure which bears some relation to external trade, could that measure give rise to distortion of competition or deflection of trade, threatening the unity of the internal market? If so, the measure would in principle have to come within the scope of the Community's exclusive powers.

There are a number of potential measures which are obvious trade measures and clearly fit the bill of the above calculus. An import quota is one of them, but there are also other measures whose covert aim may be to limit trade, particularly imports. For some time France, for example, required all imports of Japanese videorecorders to be cleared through customs in one single small customs office, in Poitiers, in the middle of France.[40] Clearly, deflections of trade and distortions of competition in the European videorecorder market were bound to ensue. However, trade restrictions may just as easily result from measures whose objectives are wholly unrelated to trade. What about a decision to prohibit the marketing of a particular food product, because it is considered harmful for public health? Such a decision, where taken by a Member State, will almost invariably affect domestic products, imports from other Member States, *and* imports from third countries. Is it then, in so far as it affects non-EU imports, a trade policy measure coming within the powers of the Community?

Such questions reveal an important characteristic of modern trade measures: often those measures are taken for achieving non-trade objectives. Those objectives

[39] Cf J Raux, 'Politique de coopération au développement et politique commerciale commune', in M Maresceau (ed), *The European Community's Commercial Policy after 1992: The Legal Dimension* (Martinus Nijhoff, 1993) 157–95.

[40] See GATT, Import Restrictive Measures on Video Tape Recorders, Doc. L/5427.12 December 1982.

may range from protection of the environment, protection of public health, consumer protection, international security, to protection of human rights. Where those objectives are pursued through measures which affect international trade, and, in the EU context, the unity of the internal market, should one simply conclude as to the existence of a trade measure in EC law terms, with the resulting transfer of powers from the Member States to the Community?

In academic literature the link between the internal market and the common commercial policy was further explored in the second half of the 1980s, particularly as regards general market regulation. This investigation coincided with the internal market programme, put on the rails by the 1985 Commission White Paper[41] and the 1986 Single European Act. That programme generally raised the question as to the external dimension of this enormous legislative endeavour, in terms of both substance and legal form. As regards the latter, the question was whether all external policies relating to the establishment and completion of the internal market came within the scope of the Treaty's common commercial policy. That question may sound abstract and legalistic, but in a number of areas it was clearly crucial for the actual direction of future policy. For example, in the field of air transport the reply to the question would determine whether or not the Community acquired sole negotiating authority over air traffic agreements with non-member countries. If external trade in air transport services came within the scope of (current) Article 133 EC, then the Community would have exclusive competence as regards such agreements.[42] This of course presupposed that trade *in services* could be covered by Article 133.

One of the most interesting proposals for the interpretation of (current) Article 133 EC was made by Timmermans.[43] He suggested that the interpretation should dovetail the rule-of-reason approach towards (current) Article 28 EC, set in motion with the *Cassis de Dijon* judgment.[44] Under this rule of reason, Member States are entitled to regulate the market on the basis of 'mandatory requirements', an open-ended list of non-economic concerns of public policy. Timmermans noted that these 'mandatory requirements' in effect recognize Member State competence from an internal market perspective, and that it would make little sense if such non-trade measures, when applied in an external trade context, were to be regarded as coming within the Community's exclusive competence. He therefore proposed to read the rule of reason into the interpretation of (current) Article 133 EC: also in external trade, Member States would continue to be entitled to adopt measures based on 'mandatory requirements' or on the express exceptions in (current) Article 30 EC. Such measures, when proportionate, were not to be considered trade policy measures. From a perspective of internal market unity, Timmermans further argued,

---

[41] *Completing the Internal Market*, COM(85)310 final, June 1985.

[42] Eeckhout (n 17 above), ch 3.

[43] CWA Timmermans, 'La libre circulation des marchandises et la politique commerciale commune', in P Demaret (ed), *Relations extérieures de la Communauté européenne et marché intérieur: aspects juridiques et fonctionnels* (Story, 1986) 91, 96–9.

[44] Case 120/78 *Rewe v. Bundesmonopolverwaltung für Branntwein* [1979] ECR 649.

such a rule of reason was clearly defensible: there was no risk of deflections of trade in the products concerned, as Member States could in any event, also as regards internal trade, erect barriers conforming to the rule of reason.

Timmermans' proposal was welcome and continues to deserve consideration. Where a Member State regulates its market with a view to protecting the environment, its consumers, or public health, and does so in a proportionate manner, without discrimination against imported products, it makes sense (a) not to consider this as an unlawful barrier to trade in so far as imports from other Member States are concerned, and (b) not to consider this as an external trade measure in so far as imports from non-Member States are involved. If the Community considers that such regulation unduly fragments the market, it has competence under e.g. Article 95 EC to harmonize the laws of the Member States.

A weakness of Timmermans' proposal was perhaps that it did not address 'non-trade measures' (in the sense of measures not pursuing commercial or economic aims) which none the less concern only external imports or exports. In 1990 the Court of Justice was confronted with such a measure in the *Chernobyl I* case. Shortly after the nuclear accident in Chernobyl, Ukraine, the Council had adopted a regulation laying down maximum levels of radioactive contamination as regards agricultural products imported from Central and Eastern Europe. Although clearly aimed at protecting public health within the Community, the regulation had been adopted on the basis of (current) Article 133 EC, and the Court accepted that.[45] There is, however, a better opportunity to examine the judgment below in the section on trade and environment. In the recent *BAT* judgment the Court had occasion to delimit Articles 95 (concerning internal market harmonization) and 133 EC.[46] Again the judgment is best examined in the section on trade and environment.

The Uruguay Round and Maastricht

Important as the precise delimitation of the scope of the Community's powers over external trade in goods may be, at the time there were a number of more hotly debated questions. In 1986 the GATT contracting parties initiated a new round of multilateral trade negotiations, the so-called Uruguay Round, which was to be much more innovating than any previous GATT round. The negotiating agenda identified three new topics: trade in services, trade-related aspects of intellectual property rights, and trade-related investment measures. Particularly as regards the first two, services and intellectual property, a debate developed on whether they were covered by the Treaty provisions on the common commercial policy. The answer to those questions

[45] Case C–62/88 *Greece v. Council* [1990] ECR I–1527.
[46] Case C–491/01 *The Queen v. Secretary of State for Health, ex parte British American Tobacco* [2002] ECR I–11453.

was to be of huge political and institutional, if not constitutional, significance, for it would determine whether or not the Community had sole authority to negotiate and conclude the wide-ranging international agreements which were the subject of the Uruguay Round. Yet, interestingly, the debate was again academic in more than one sense. While it was being held, the negotiations went ahead unperturbed, in a pragmatic arrangement with the Commission as European negotiator, closely supervised by the Council and representatives of Member States.[47] Even when the competence issue came to a head, when the agreements had to be signed and concluded, and the Commission went to Court, claiming that the Community had exclusive competence, there remained an awkward gap between legal principle and practice. The Uruguay Round had resulted in the establishment of a new World Trade Organization, and whereas the Commission in its request for an Opinion argued for exclusive competence, it did refer, in its third question, to an 'agreement already reached that [the Member States] will be original Members of the WTO'.[48] The Commission never clarified how exclusive Community competence could be reconciled with such membership.

But before analysing *Opinion 1/94*, it is worth saying a little more about the academic debate and some political developments leading up to the court battle. The debate centred on whether trade in services and trade-related aspects of intellectual property rights were covered by the Treaty provisions on the common commercial policy.

On services there was a range of diverging opinions.[49] Some argued that (current) Article 133 EC had no bearing on services.[50] Others felt that there was some scope for a common commercial policy in this area, but that it had to be confined to services directly related to trade. Again the most interesting analysis came from Timmermans.[51] He considered that, if an international trade organization like the GATT decided to extend its activities to the services sector, the Community had to be able to follow suit, without being hampered by an outdated interpretation of what is commercial policy. He admitted that deflections of trade were unlikely in the case of trade in services, but pointed out that substantial differences in national regimes regarding trade in services could certainly distort competition in the internal market. This did not mean that (current) Article 133 could be applied without more ado to the entire sector of international trade in services. Timmermans proposed a similar approach to the one he defended with respect to goods. The external regime should mirror the internal regime, in the sense that all

---

[47] P van den Bossche, 'The European Community and the Uruguay Round Agreements', in JH Jackson and AO Sykes (eds), *Implementing the Uruguay Round* (OUP, 1997) 25–6.

[48] *Opinion 1/94 re WTO Agreement* [1994] ECR I–5267, 5283.

[49] For a fuller discussion see Eeckhout (n 17 above), 20–34.

[50] E.g. F Perreau de Pinninck, 'Les compétences communautaires dans les négociations sur le commerce des services' (1991) 27 Cahiers de Droit Européen 401–8.

[51] CWA Timmermans, 'Common Commercial Policy (Article 113 EEC) and International Trade in Services', in *Du droit international au droit de l'intégration: Liber Amicorum Pierre Pescatore* (Nomos, 1987) 675–90.

measures directly or indirectly discriminating against external trade in services should fall within the scope of the common commercial policy. In other words, all measures which regulate the 'status' of international services on the national market, ranging from flat prohibitions over special regimes of stricter conditions to granting national treatment whether or not on a basis of reciprocity, should come within exclusive Community competence. What Timmermans in fact argued for was a coherent external dimension to the internal market in services.

As regards intellectual property, the academic debate recognized that exclusive Community trade powers could hardly be considered to cover intellectual property rights as such. However, in light of the clear link between the protection of such rights and international trade Govaere defended a combined application of the Community's internal powers of harmonization (current Article 95 EC) and the Treaty provisions on the common commercial policy.[52]

The debate on the scope of the Community's trade policy powers was not however confined to academe. In the course of 1991, more than halfway through the Uruguay Round, the Treaty on European Union was negotiated. In the context of those negotiations the Commission proposed far-reaching changes to the Community's external powers, no doubt against the backdrop of the ongoing Uruguay Round. It suggested that powers be transferred to the newly established European Union to pursue a 'common external economic policy', which was to include trade, and economic and commercial measures involving services, capital, intellectual property, investment, establishment, and competition. Community powers over all those matters were to be exclusive, but it would be possible to authorize Member States to take some of these measures within certain prescribed limits and conditions. Such authorizations would be granted by the Commission itself.[53]

It is not clear whether the Commission ever really considered that its proposals would form the basis for a serious negotiation between the Member States. The intergovernmental conference brushed aside the Commission's views, and confined the debate on amendments to (current) Article 133 EC to a possible extension to 'services directly related to trade'.[54] But even that modest proposal did not survive the negotiations, and in the end the scope of the common commercial policy was left unmodified. It is an episode which is worth bearing in mind, as it formed the basis for the 'defence' of the Council and some Member State governments in the *Opinion 1/94* battle: the Commission was accused of attempting to get implemented, by means of judicial interpretation, proposals which were rejected at the Maastricht negotiations.[55]

---

[52] I Govaere, 'Intellectual Property Protection and Commercial Policy', in Maresceau (n 39 above), 197–222.

[53] See M Maresceau, 'The Concept "Common Commercial Policy" and the Difficult Road to Maastricht', in Maresceau (n 39 above), 6–10.   [54] Ibid, 10–11.

[55] *Opinion 1/94* (n 48 above), I–5306. There may be an analogy here with *Opinion 2/94 re accession to the ECHR* [1996] ECR I–1759, where the Council may have intended to achieve through judicial interpretation what it could not achieve through internal political negotiation.

The joint competence settlement of *Opinion 1/94*

The Uruguay Round negotiations ended in early 1994. The Agreement establishing the WTO, which brought together nearly all the results of the multilateral negotiations in one single international agreement, was signed at Marrakesh on 15 April 1994. By that time, the legal dispute on competence between the Commission (supported only by the Belgian government) and the Council (supported by most other Member States) was in full swing. The political sensitivity of the issue is perhaps best illustrated by a skirmish at the GATT Ministerial Conference at Marrakesh. As regards the signing of the WTO Agreement, the Commission had suggested that it and the Member State ministers should sign as a group under the collective rubric of the EU. Yet even though the order of signing is a matter of pure protocol, with no effect whatsoever on the legal distribution of powers or on the commitments entered into, the Member State governments refused and insisted that the overall alphabetical order of the list of GATT delegations be followed.[56]

On 6 April 1994 the Commission submitted its request for an Opinion to the Court. Essentially, the Commission asked whether the Community had exclusive competence[57] to conclude the WTO Agreement, on the basis of (current) Article 133 EC on its own, or in combination with implied powers pursuant to (current) Articles 95 and 308 EC. The Court's analysis of implied powers is considered in the next chapter, and the reader is also referred to those pages for a complete view of *Opinion 1/94*. It is perhaps worth adding that the Court was compelled to deliver its Opinion at (judicial) record speed, because the approval and ratification procedures had to be completed by the end of 1994 so as to enable the WTO to start functioning on 1 January 1995. The Court delivered its Opinion on 15 November 1994.[58]

As regards the scope of (current) Article 133 EC, it is somewhat ironic to see that the Commission was effectively compelled to rely on the 'subjective/purposive' approach previously advocated by the Council. The Commission did not expressly refer to that theory, but it is clear that it essentially argued for exclusive Community competence on the basis of (current) Article 133 on grounds of the clear trade policy *objectives* of all the WTO agreements.

Trade in goods

The Court first looked at the multilateral agreements on trade in goods, in Annex 1A of the WTO Agreement. Even though it was generally accepted that the bulk of those

---

[56] *Financial Times*, 14 April 1994.

[57] The Commission's actual questions did not refer to exclusivity, but that was clearly the tenor of its arguments, in the interpretation of the Court: *Opinion 1/94* (n 48 above), paras 13–14.

[58] Other specific analyses include JHJ Bourgeois, 'The EC in the WTO and Advisory Opinion 1/94: An Echternach Procession' (1995) 32 CMLRev 763; M Hilf, 'The ECJ's Opinion 1/94 on the WTO— No Surprise, but Wise?' (1995) 6 EJIL 245; J Dutheil de la Rochère, 'L'ère des compétences partagées'

agreements came within the Community's trade policy powers, questions had arisen over coal and steel products; the Agreement on Agriculture and the Agreement on Sanitary and Phytosanitary Measures (SPS Agreement); and the Agreement on Technical Barriers to Trade (TBT Agreement). The discussion on coal and steel products concerned the interrelationship between the ECSC Treaty and the EC Treaty, and is of only historical interest after the expiry of the former.

As regards the Agriculture and SPS Agreements the Council contended that (current) Article 37 EC, on agriculture, was the appropriate legal basis, rather than (current) Article 133. Its reasoning was that those agreements concerned not just the commercial measures applicable to international trade in agricultural products but also, and above all, the internal rules on the organization of agricultural markets. The United Kingdom government added that the commitments to reduce domestic support and export refunds would affect the common organizations of the markets, and concerned Community products. The Court replied by conceding that it had held that (current) Article 37 EC was the appropriate legal basis for a directive laying down uniform rules on the conditions under which products, including imported ones, could be marketed.[59] However, that directive was intended to achieve one or more of the agricultural policy objectives laid down in (current) Article 33 EC, which was not the case for the Agreement on Agriculture, whose objective was to establish a fair and market-oriented agricultural trading system. The fact that the Agreement required internal measures to be adopted on the basis of (current) Article 37 did not prevent the international commitments themselves from being entered into pursuant to (current) Article 133 alone. The same conclusion was reached for the SPS Agreement, which, according to its preamble, was confined to establishing a multilateral framework for minimizing the negative effects of SPS measures on trade.[60]

As regards the TBT Agreement, the Netherlands government argued that joint participation of the Community and the Member States was justified, since the Member States had their own competence in relation to technical barriers to trade by reason of the optional nature of certain Community directives and because complete harmonization had not been achieved and was not envisaged; an argument more in the nature of implied powers (see Chapter 3) than focused on commercial policy competence. The Court's reply to that argument was that the Agreement was merely designed to ensure that technical regulations and standards, and conformity assessment, did not create unnecessary obstacles to international trade.[61]

The Court concluded that all the WTO agreements on trade in goods came within the Community's commercial policy competence. Even if the Court's analysis was succinct, this is an important dimension of *Opinion 1/94*. With respect to goods, the Court confirmed the broad conception of 'trade', in line with

(1995) 390 RMCUE 461; T Tridimas, 'The WTO and OECD Opinions', in A Dashwood and C Hillion (eds), *The General Law of EC External Relations* (Sweet & Maxwell, 2000) 48–60; A Burnside, 'The Scope of the Common Commercial Policy Post Opinion 1/94: Clouds and Silver Linings', in idem, 152–9.

[59] Case C–131/87 *Commission v. Council* [1989] ECR I–3764, para 27.
[60] *Opinion 1/94* (n 48 above), paras 28–31.   [61] Ibid, paras 32–33.

international developments in trade policy. It is also obvious that here the Court did indeed primarily rely on the trade objectives of the various agreements, and considered that their effect on internal legislation, at Community and Member State level, as well as the need for implementation through internal legislation did not stand in the way of conclusion on the basis of (current) Article 133.

Trade in services

The Court then turned to Annex 1B of the WTO Agreement, the General Agreement on Trade in Services (GATS). Much more was at stake here, as there were diametrically opposing views on whether trade in services was covered by the Treaty provisions on a common commercial policy, and in light of the debate which had taken place in the Maastricht intergovernmental conference. GATS is an agreement which aims to achieve liberalization of international trade in services through the application of basis legal concepts (such as non-discrimination and market access) and liberalization mechanisms (such as schedules of concessions/commitments) borrowed from the GATT. Its logic is that neoliberal economic theory on the benefits of free trade is equally valid for trade in services. GATS also provides for some form of definition of trade in services, a phenomenon much more difficult to capture than trade in goods. In Article I(2) GATS trade in services is defined as comprising four modes of supply: (1) cross-frontier supplies not involving any movement of persons; (2) consumption abroad, which entails the movement of the consumer into the territory of the WTO member country in which the supplier is established; (3) commercial presence, i.e. the presence of a subsidiary or branch in the territory of the WTO member country in which the service is to be rendered; (4) the presence of natural persons from a WTO member country, enabling a supplier from one member country to supply services within the territory of any other member country. That definition is intended to be as comprehensive and inclusive as possible, and the modes of supply are used for structuring the specific commitments entered into by WTO members. Those commitments entail the granting of market access (Article XVI) and national treatment (or non-discrimination, Article XVII) in specific services sectors for the various modes of supply.[62]

The Court tackled the issues straight on. It summarized the Commission's argument in one paragraph, and then proceeded to consider, first, services other than transport. The Court referred to *Opinion 1/75*, where it had decided that the common commercial policy covers credits for the financing of local costs linked to export operations.[63] It pointed out that those local costs concerned expenses incurred for the supply of both goods and services, but that the Court had nevertheless recognized

---

[62] See further MJ Trebilcock and R Howse, *The Regulation of International Trade* (2nd edn., Routledge 1999) 278–91. For a comparison with EC law on services, see P Eeckhout, 'Constitutional Concepts for Free Trade in Services', in G de Búrca and J Scott (eds), *The EU and the WTO—Legal and Constitutional Issues* (Hart, 2001) 211–35.   [63] N 13 above.

exclusive competence, without distinguishing between goods and services. The Court then harked back to its pronouncements in *Opinion 1/78* on the broad interpretation of (current) Article 133. It referred to the Commission's assessment that in certain developed countries the services sector had become the dominant sector of the economy and that the global economy had been undergoing fundamental structural changes: the trend was for basic industry to be transferred to developing countries, whilst the developed economies had tended to become exporters of services and of goods with a high value-added content. This trend, the Court noted, was borne out by the WTO agreements, which were the subject of a single process of negotiation covering both goods and services. The Court's conclusion was that, having regard to this trend in international trade, it followed from the open nature of the common commercial policy that trade in services could not immediately,[64] and as a matter of principle, be excluded from the scope of (current) Article 133.[65]

If the Court had stopped there, the Commission would have won an important victory. But the Court went on, considering that its conclusion had to be made more specific, taking into account the definition of trade in services given in GATS, so as to see whether the overall scheme of the EC Treaty was not such as to limit the extent to which trade in services could be included in (current) Article 133. The Court then described the four modes of supplying services. As regards cross-frontier supplies, it noted that neither the supplier nor the consumer moved, and that this was not unlike trade in goods. There was thus no particular reason why such a supply should not fall within the concept of common commercial policy. However, the same could not be said of the other three modes, namely consumption abroad, commercial presence, and the presence of natural persons. The Court pointed out that, as regards natural persons, it was clear from Article 3 EC, which distinguished between 'a common commercial policy' and 'measures concerning the entry and movement of persons', that the treatment of nationals of non-member countries on crossing the external frontiers of Member States could not be regarded as falling within the common commercial policy. More generally, the Court continued, the existence in the Treaty of specific chapters on the free movement of natural and legal persons showed that those matters did not fall within the common commercial policy.[66]

The Court's reasoning, concise as it may be, is not difficult to understand. The Court was of the Opinion that, in so far as GATS commitments have an effect on cross-border movement of natural and legal persons, they could not come within the notion of commercial policy as encapsulated in the EC Treaty.[67] The reason is not so much that that notion is inherently incapable of extending to movement of persons, but rather that such an approach does not conform to the structure and organization of the EC Treaty, which looks at such movement, both internally and externally, under different chapters. If anything, that perspective was strengthened with the entry into force of the Amsterdam Treaty, inserting into the EC Treaty the new

---

[64] The French version uses the term '*d'emblée*'.   [65] *Opinion 1/94* (n 48 above), paras 36–41.
[66] Ibid, paras 42–46.   [67] Tridimas (n 58 above), 51.

Title IV on visas, asylum, immigration, and other policies related to free movement of persons. It is indeed incontrovertible that the EC Treaty distinguishes between external trade policy and immigration policy.

Notwithstanding the above, the Court's reasoning is not persuasive. As has been noted,[68] GATS is not intended to be an instrument of immigration policy. So much is clear from the GATS Annex on Movement of Natural Persons Supplying Services under the Agreement. In a footnote to that annex, it is stated that 'the sole fact of requiring a visa for natural persons of certain Members and not for those of others shall not be regarded as nullifying or impairing benefits under a specific commitment'. That provision effectively places visa requirements outside the scope of GATS. More generally, the Annex also provides that GATS shall not apply to measures affecting natural persons seeking access to the employment market of a Member, nor shall it apply to measures regarding citizenship, residence or employment on a permanent basis (paragraph 2). It further provides that the GATS shall not prevent a Member from applying measures to regulate the entry of natural persons into, or their temporary stay in, its territory, including those measures necessary to protect the integrity of, and to ensure the orderly movement of natural persons across, its borders, provided that such measures are not applied in such a manner as to nullify or impair the benefits accruing to any Member under the terms of a specific commitment (paragraph 4). It is of course true that GATS commitments may have an effect on immigration. Where a WTO member commits itself to full market access for a particular type of service, provided through commercial presence or the movement of natural persons, it has to allow companies or persons from other WTO members providing such services free access to its territory. Similarly, where market access through consumption abroad is granted, there will have to be free entry by consumers (e.g. tourists). The question however is whether that is sufficient to draw GATS away from the common commercial policy. Provisions on external trade in goods may also have an effect on non-trade policies, as the Court itself recognized in the first part of *Opinion 1/94*. The fact that the Agreement on Agriculture would affect EC common market organizations did not put that agreement outside the scope of (current) Article 133. Nor did the fact that the TBT Agreement affects technical regulations and standards, often embodied in national law rather than Community law, lead the Court to the conclusion that it did not come within the common commercial policy. GATS does indeed affect immigration, but it does that only through the prism of ensuring market access and non-discrimination for internationally traded services.

It is also notable that the Opinion does not refer to the unity of the internal market. The Court does not analyse the risk of deflections of trade or distortions of competition created by non-uniform external trade policies as regards services. Yet such risk is self-evident, in particular as regards distortion of competition.[69] For example, in an integrated and liberalized internal financial services market, different

---

[68] Tridimas and Eeckhout (n 12 above), 161–2.
[69] For an example of deflections of trade in services, see Eeckhout (n 17 above), 25–6.

policies by Member States on access and treatment of foreign financial services companies seeking to operate on that market are just as much likely to distort competition as are different policies on imports of goods. The unity of the internal market in services thus requires a uniform external trade policy.

Perhaps the Court was also influenced by the fact that much of the regulation of services industries continues to be in the province of the Member States rather than that of the EU, and that GATS directly interferes with certain aspects of such regulation, as can be seen when browsing through the GATS commitments of the EC and its Member States. The Court may have been reluctant to effect, through judicial pronouncement rather than political consensus, what it perhaps perceived as a significant transfer of powers from the Member States to the Community, particularly in light of the exclusive nature of the EC's trade policy powers. In any event, the result of the Court's ruling is that the EC's and the Member States' powers to regulate international trade in services are, at least in so far as GATS is concerned, indivisibly linked. The Community's competence over cross-border services is exclusive, and the Member States generally retain competence over the other modes of supplying services.[70] As any meaningful GATS negotiation encompasses all modes of supply, the EC and its Member States are compelled to act in common. Politically, then, the difference between exclusive and shared competence is reduced to the type of decision-making: shared powers require unanimous action by the EC and its Member States, whereas EC trade policy powers are exercised by the Council deciding by qualified majority.

Transport

As the EC Treaty contains a specific chapter on the common transport policy, the Court examined transport services separately. The Commission clearly regarded as important its claim that international agreements of a commercial nature in relation to transport (as opposed to those relating to safety rules) fall within the common commercial policy: if correct, the EC would have gained exclusive competence to negotiate such agreements, e.g. in the air transport sector.[71] By contrast, EC competence under the common transport policy is concurrent;[72] thus there remains more political discretion where a common external policy is to be constructed under such competence. Note also that transport services can be regarded as cross-border services in the meaning of Article I(2) GATS.

The Court was not impressed by the Commission's claim.[73] It referred to its case law on implied powers, in particular the *AETR* judgment, where it had held that competence to conclude international agreements may flow implicitly from

---

[70] But see Ch 3 as regards implied powers.
[71] For an overview of the Commission's proposals in this regard, see Eeckhout (n 17 above), Ch 3. See also Ch 3 below for recent case law regarding air transport.   [72] See Ch 3.
[73] *Opinion 1/94* (n 48 above), paras 48–52.

certain Treaty provisions.[74] That judgment concerned transport policy, and the idea underlying it, the Court pointed out, was that international agreements in transport matters were not covered by (current) Article 133. The distinction which the Commission attempted to draw between agreements on safety rules and those of a commercial nature was rejected, as the *AETR* judgment drew no such distinction and as the later ruling in *Opinion 1/76*, confirming implied external transport powers, concerned an economic agreement.[75]

The Commission had also referred to precedent, in the sense that a number of trade embargoes which the EC had adopted on the basis of (current) Article 133 EC involved the suspension of transport services. The Court regarded those precedents as inconclusive: as the embargoes related primarily to the export and import of products, they could not have been effective without at the same time suspending transport services. Such suspension was therefore a necessary adjunct to the principal measure. In any event, the Court continued, mere practice of the Council could not derogate from the rules laid down in the Treaty and could not, therefore, create a precedent binding on Community institutions with regard to the correct legal basis.

Intellectual property

As regards the TRIPs Agreement the Court started its analysis by stating that the Commission's argument for exclusive Community competence under (current) Article 133 was essentially that the rules concerning intellectual property rights were closely linked to trade in the products and services to which they applied. It then looked at Section 4 of Part III of TRIPs, on enforcement measures to be applied at border crossing points. The Court pointed out that that section of TRIPs had its counterpart in an EC regulation on measures to prohibit the release for free circulation of counterfeit goods,[76] which had been based on (current) Article 133 EC. That was indeed the correct legal basis, the Court reasoned, because the regulation concerned measures to be taken by the customs authorities at the external frontiers of the Community. Since measures of that type could be adopted autonomously by the EC on the basis of (current) Article 133 EC, it was for the Community alone to conclude international agreements on such matters.[77]

However, the above TRIPs provisions form but a small section of the Agreement, and the Court did not accept the Commission's claim for the remainder. It admitted that there was a connection between intellectual property and trade in goods, in that intellectual property rights enabled those holding them to prevent third parties from carrying out certain acts. The power to prohibit the use of a trade mark, the manufacture of a product, the copying of a design, or the reproduction of a book,

---

[74] Case 22/70 *Commission v. Council* [1971] ECR 263, para 16; see Ch 3.

[75] *Opinion 1/76 re Inland Waterways* [1977] ECR 741.

[76] Council Regulation 3842/86 laying down measures to prohibit the release for free circulation of counterfeit goods [1986] OJ L357/1.   [77] *Opinion 1/94* (n 48 above), paras 54–55.

a disc, or video cassette, the Court illustrated, inevitably had effects on trade. Intellectual property rights were moreover specifically designed to produce such effects, but that was not enough to bring them within the scope of (current) Article 133: intellectual property rights did not relate specifically to international trade, but affected internal trade just as much as, if not more than, international trade.[78]

The Court then further examined the TRIPs Agreement and its relationship with intra-Community harmonization of intellectual property law. It pointed out that the primary objective of TRIPs was to harmonize the protection of intellectual property on a worldwide scale. As TRIPs laid down rules in fields in which there were no Community harmonization measures, the conclusion of the agreement would achieve such harmonization and contribute to the establishment and functioning of the common market. If such conclusion were based on (current) Article 133 alone, it would enable the Community institutions to escape the internal constraints in relation to procedures and voting which normally applied in the case of harmonization (the Court referred to current Articles 94, 95, and 308 EC).[79]

As a third element in its analysis the Court did not accept that institutional practice in relation to autonomous measures or external agreements adopted on the basis of (current) Article 133 could alter this conclusion. On the autonomous measures front, the Commission had referred to the so-called new commercial policy instrument, a regulation enabling private parties to complain about third-country trade practices.[80] In a number of cases that regulation had been employed to defend the Community's intellectual property interests, but the Court pointed out that this was unrelated to harmonization of intellectual property protection, and that the actual measures which could be taken under the regulation were clearly trade measures. The Court was likewise not impressed by the Commission's reference to cases of suspension of GSP on grounds of lack of intellectual property protection in the third countries concerned, as again the actual measures were no doubt trade measures. Lastly, the Court did recognize that a number of trade agreements concluded by the Community referred to the protection of intellectual property, but noted that those provisions were extremely limited in scope. The fact that the Community and its institutions were entitled to incorporate in external agreements coming within (current) Article 133 ancillary provisions for the organization of purely consultative procedures or clauses calling on the other party to raise the level of intellectual property protection did not mean that the Community had exclusive competence to conclude an international agreement of the type and scope of TRIPs. Nor was the Court convinced by a precedent as regards protection of

---

[78] Ibid, para 57.   [79] Ibid, paras 58–59.

[80] Council Regulation 2641/84 on the strengthening of the common commercial policy with regard in particular to protection against illicit commercial practices [1984] OJ L252/1. The regulation was replaced by Council Regulation 3286/94 laying down Community procedures in the field of the common commercial policy in order to ensure the exercise of the Community's rights under international trade rules, in particular those established under the auspices of the WTO [1994] OJ L349/71 (the trade barriers instrument: see Ch 10).

description of wines. It therefore concluded that, apart from those of its provisions which concerned the prohibition of the release into free circulation of counterfeit goods, TRIPs did not fall within the scope of the common commercial policy.[81]

The Court's analysis of TRIPs is convincing. Notwithstanding the reference in its name to trade-related aspects, the TRIPs Agreement is indeed primarily concerned with intellectual property protection as such, and not with any specific effects on international trade of such protection. Indeed, it is noteworthy that a particularly significant trade issue resulting from the application and enforcement of intellectual property rights is not addressed by TRIPs: the issue of exhaustion of rights.[82] The question whether rights are exhausted in an international trade context where the intellectual property right holder markets or consents to marketing its own products appears to be left to the discretion of WTO members.[83] TRIPs could thus only be regarded a trade agreement if it were sufficient that its overall objective is to affect trade (but not necessarily promote it), by ensuring general protection of intellectual property. Clearly, in the Court's opinion that overall objective is insufficient to bring the agreement within the Community's exclusive trade policy powers.

The Court's general conclusion in *Opinion 1/94* was that the Community and its Member States were jointly competent to conclude both GATS and TRIPs. There will be opportunity to consider the implied powers dimension of the Opinion in Chapter 3. The discussion of this episode may be concluded by referring to two subsequent rulings, in which the Court confirmed the *Opinion 1/94* approach.

In *Opinion 2/92*, which was in fact requested by the Belgian government one and a half years before the Commission's request for *Opinion 1/94*, and which was before the Court at the same time as *Opinion 1/94*, the Court looked at an OECD decision on national treatment of foreign undertakings. It described this national treatment rule as concerning mainly the conditions for the participation of foreign-controlled undertakings in the internal economic life of the Member States in which they operated. It did recognize that the rule also applied to the conditions of those undertakings' participation in trade between the Member States and non-member countries, conditions which were the subject of the common commercial policy. However, so far as the participation of foreign-controlled undertakings in intra-Community trade was concerned, such trade was governed by the Community's internal market rules and not by the rules of the common commercial policy. It followed that the national treatment rule related only partially to international trade, and that it affected internal trade to the same extent as international trade, if not more so. Therefore, (current) Article 133 did not confer exclusive competence.[84]

---

[81] *Opinion 1/94* (n 48 above), paras 61–71.

[82] Art 6 TRIPs provides that 'for the purposes of dispute settlement . . . nothing in this Agreement shall be used to address the issue of the exhaustion of intellectual property rights'.

[83] On the EC approach in the field of trade marks see e.g. D O'Keeffe and B Keane, 'The Shadow of *Silhouette*' (1999/2000) 19 YEL 139.

[84] *Opinion 2/92 re Third Revised Decision of the OECD on national treatment* [1995] ECR I–521, paras 24–28.

In *Parliament v. Council* the Court entertained a challenge to Council decisions, based on (current) Article 133 EC alone, whose effect was to extend the benefits of EC public procurement rules to US undertakings. As that extension covered services, the Court recalled that in the then state of Community law only cross-border services came within the scope of (current) Article 133. Since the extension also related to supplies made thanks to a commercial presence or the presence of natural persons, the Council decisions should not have been based on (current) Article 133 alone, and were annulled.[85]

Trade and foreign policy

As mentioned above, many different types of measures may affect international trade. Also, trade measures may be taken for the purpose of pursuing policies which are not economic or commercial in nature. One such interface concerns trade and general foreign policy. If one reflects on this a little further, one notices the awkwardness of the European Union's dichotomy between trade policies, devised and implemented under the EC Treaty, and general foreign and security policy, which forms the subject of gradual co-ordination within the framework of the EU's second pillar. From a legal perspective, trade policy appears to dominate. It predates the CFSP, and comes within the exclusive competence of the EC, a competence exercised by supranational institutions capable of adopting legal acts which are directly effective and supreme. Under the CFSP, by contrast, there are no exclusive EU powers, the approach is intergovernmental, and the precise dimensions and effects of legal acts are vague and uncertain.[86] From a political perspective, however, this state of affairs appears to make no sense. How can trade issues be dissociated from general foreign policy? If one looks at the practice of third countries, it is clear that their position and participation in international trade relations form part of a broader foreign policy, and that decisions on trade matters may be guided by such broader policy. If examples are required, one could refer to the approach by the United States towards the accession of China to the WTO. That approach clearly formed part of a general policy aimed at engaging China.

It is similarly clear that the EU's support for China's WTO accession was not only inspired by trade policy considerations, but formed part of a broader policy, pursued by the EU and its Member States. Again this is only an example, and it would be interesting to analyse the EC's trade policy against the broader canvas of international politics. At an aggregate level, this state of affairs poses no particular problems for the EC's exclusive trade policy powers. Those powers are in any event exercised by political institutions, the main one, the Council, representing national governments, and the policy directions there adopted are a matter of political rather than legal concern. When one speaks at a general level of trade relations with third countries

---

[85] Case C–360/93 *Parliament v. Council* [1996] ECR I–1195. [86] See further Chs 5 and 11.

forming part of a broader foreign policy, there appear to be no particular problems for the scope and nature of the EC's common commercial policy. However, matters become more complex when one focuses on certain types of more individualized trade measures which are taken for foreign policy or even external security reasons. It is in such a context that the awkwardness of the dichotomy becomes apparent.

From the 1980s onwards, the EC developed a practice of adopting various types of economic sanctions, particularly in the trade field.[87] Trade restrictions and embargoes are indeed a preferred instrument for exercising political and economic pressure on countries and regimes, and they may be decreed by the UN Security Council. Even though the reasons behind such measures may be wholly discon-nected from commercial policy as such, it is difficult to see them as anything but trade measures, given their marked effects on trade. However, the authority to adopt trade sanctions would then appear to come within the EC's exclusive powers. Somewhat surprisingly perhaps, the EC's practice confirmed this, and the Council adopted such sanctions by way of regulations based on (current) Article 133 EEC, not, however, without combining this with 'political' decisions taken, at first, under the heading of EPC and subsequently under the successor CFSP. The Treaty on European Union then codified this practice through the introduction of (current) Articles 301 and 60 EC. This acceptance and confirmation of EC involvement were no doubt also inspired by the advantages which regulations offer as a legal instrument: the procedure for their adoption is straightforward (particularly as the European Parliament is not involved), and they apply directly and uniformly in the laws of the Member States.

From a legal perspective, this approach towards economic sanctions raises delicate and difficult issues of interrelationship between the first and second EU pillars. Those issues are discussed in Chapters 5 and 12. But what about the powers of the Member States in those cases where there is no common policy? Are the Member States entitled to restrict trade for foreign policy reasons, or is that not possible in light of the EC's exclusive competence to conduct a common commercial policy?

Those questions came up in two cases which German courts referred to the Court of Justice.[88] Both cases concerned the lawfulness, under Community law, of German legislation which was applied so as to control the export of so-called dual-use goods.[89] In *Werner v. Germany* the German authorities had refused a licence for the export to Libya of a vacuum induction, smelting and cast oven, as well as induc-tion spools for that oven, on the grounds that the products could be used for the production of missiles.[90] In *Leifer and Others* a number of people were criminally prosecuted for having exported to Iraq between 1984 and 1988 plant, parts of plant,

---

[87] See for an overview PJ Kuijper, 'Trade Sanctions, Security and Human Rights and Commercial Policy', in Maresceau (n 39 above), 387. See further Ch 12.

[88] In an earlier judgment, Case C–367/89 *Richardt and 'Les Accessoires Scientifiques'* [1991] ECR I–4621, the Court had analysed the issues purely from an internal market perspective.

[89] I.e. goods which may be used for both civil and military purposes.

[90] Case C–70/94 *Werner v. Germany* [1995] ECR I–3189.

and chemicals without the requisite export licence. The authorities considered that those products were used in Iraq's chemical weapons programme.[91] The German legislation enabled the authorities to curtail contracts and activities in the sphere of foreign trade in order to guarantee Germany's security, prevent a disturbance of peaceful coexistence, or prevent the external relations of Germany from being seriously disrupted. In both cases the German courts asked the Court of Justice whether the export controls and restrictions in issue were compatible with the Community's exclusive competence under (current) Article 133 EC.

The Court's analysis in these judgments was almost identical.[92] The Court started by stating that the question was whether the common commercial policy solely concerned measures which pursued commercial objectives, or whether it also covered commercial measures having foreign policy and security objectives. It recalled the text of (current) Article 133 and referred to the principle of a non-restrictive interpretation of the common commercial policy concept, so as to avoid disturbances in intra-Community trade by reason of the disparities which would then exist in certain sectors of economic relations with non-member countries, a principle established in *Opinion 1/78*.[93] So, the Court continued, measures whose effect was to prevent or restrict the export of certain products could not be treated as falling outside the scope of the common commercial policy on the ground that they had foreign policy and security objectives. The specific subject matter of commercial policy, which concerned trade with non-member countries and, according to (current) Article 133, was based on the concept of a common policy, required that a Member State should not be able to restrict its scope by freely deciding, in the light of its own foreign policy or security requirements, whether a measure was covered by (current) Article 133.

In these cases the Court again displayed a principled approach to the interpretation of (current) Article 133. However, one should not jump to the conclusion that the Court considered *ultra vires* (and thus unlawful) attempts by Member States autonomously to control exports of dual-use goods on foreign or security policy grounds. In both judgments the Court in the end accepted that the German legislation conformed to EC legislation on exports, which enables Member States to adopt restrictions on public security grounds. The legislation thus benefited from a specific Community authorization, which was sufficient to render it compatible with the principle of exclusive Community powers.[94]

The Court returned to the relationship between commercial and foreign policy in *Centro-Com*.[95] That case concerned a trade embargo against the Federal Republic of Yugoslavia (Serbia and Montenegro), decreed by the UN Security Council and implemented through an EC regulation.[96] There was an exception for supplies of

---

[91] Case C–83/94 *Leifer and Others* [1995] ECR I–3231.

[92] *Werner v. Germany* (n 90 above), paras 7–11; *Leifer and Others* (n 91 above), paras 7–11.

[93] *Opinion 1/78* (n 22 above).   [94] See Chs 10 and 12.

[95] Case C–124/95 *The Queen, ex parte Centro-Com v. HM Treasury and Bank of England* [1997] ECR I–81.

[96] Council Regulation 1432/92 prohibiting trade between the European Economic Community and the Republics of Serbia and Montenegro [1992] OJ L151/4.

medical products and foodstuffs, and Centro-Com, an Italian company, had benefited from that exception and exported pharmaceutical goods and blood-testing equipment to Montenegro. When it sought payment through a bank account held by the National Bank of Yugoslavia with Barclays in London, the Bank of England refused release of the funds, in implementation of a new government policy permitting payment only for exports from the United Kingdom. The policy had been adopted so as to combat circumvention of the sanctions. Centro-Com challenged the refusal in the UK courts, and the Court of Appeal referred the case to the Court of Justice. In its first question it asked *inter alia* whether the refusal to release the funds was compatible with the common commercial policy, and with (current) Article 133 EC in particular.

The Court took care to clarify the relationship between measures of foreign and security policy and the common commercial policy.[97] Indeed, one of the UK's arguments was that the measures at issue had been taken by virtue of its national competence in the field of foreign and security policy and that performance of its obligations under the UN Charter and under Security Council resolutions came within that competence. The UK further argued that the validity of those measures could not be affected by the Community's exclusive competence or by the relevant sanctions regulation, which did no more than implement at Community level the exercise of Member States' national competence in the field of foreign and security policy. The Court accepted that the Member States had indeed retained their competence in the field of foreign and security policy. None the less, the powers retained by the Member States had to be exercised in a manner consistent with Community law. Similarly, the Member States could not treat national measures whose effect was to prevent or restrict the export of certain products as falling outside the scope of the common commercial policy on the ground that they had foreign and security objectives. Consequently, while it was for Member States to adopt measures of foreign and security policy in the exercise of their national competence, those measures nevertheless had to respect the provisions adopted by the Community in the field of the common commercial policy provided for by (current) Article 133. It was indeed, the Court continued, in the exercise of their national competence in matters of foreign and security policy that the Member States expressly decided to have recourse to a Community measure, which became the abovementioned sanctions regulation, based on (current) Article 133. As the preamble to the regulation showed, it ensued from a decision of the Community and its Member States which was taken within the framework of political co-operation and which marked their willingness to have recourse to a Community instrument. It followed that, even where measures such as those in issue in the main proceedings had been adopted in the exercise of national competence in matters of foreign and security policy, they had to respect the Community rules adopted under the common commercial policy. The Court then examined whether the UK measure was compatible with the relevant regulations, and found that it was not. That substantive analysis need not concern us here.[98]

---

[97] *Centro-Com* (n 95 above), paras 23–30.   [98] See Ch 12.

The Court's statements on competence are persuasive and consistent with previous rulings, yet at the same time unable to bridge the gap between the exercise of exclusive trade policy powers and foreign and security policy decisions. It is true that the Court points to the link between the political co-operation decision and the regulation, but it does so in a descriptive rather than prescriptive manner. If no political co-operation (or currently CFSP) decision were taken, one should think that the Community would still have full, exclusive powers to adopt trade measures which pursue foreign and security policy objectives. The conclusion to be drawn is that the political subordination of the EC's trade policy is not matched by any legal subordination (except in areas where the EC Treaty expressly provides so, such as pursuant to Article 301 EC). More generally, the above judgments confirm that trade measures are trade measures, whatever the objectives pursued. Import and export measures come within the scope of (current) Article 113 (now Article 133) EC, even if their purpose is wholly unrelated to commercial or economic considerations.

Trade and environment

There are several types of linkages between international trade and environmental protection, and a lot of reflection on those linkages is taking place, at official levels,[99] and in various academic disciplines.[100] One of those connections is that trade measures can be used to pursue certain environmental protection policies. Perhaps a few non-exhaustive examples may be given. A State may regulate production processes or the marketing of certain products or services in a manner which affects international trade. A State may also have concerns over importing products which contribute to environmental degradation when used or consumed. Or it may wish not to export such products, for fear of causing such degradation abroad. A State may further be reluctant to participate in the trade in environmentally valuable goods, such as threatened species. Or it may not wish to trade in products whose production processes cause excessive environmental harm, locally, regionally, or at the level of the global commons. And it also happens that a State uses trade as a means of persuading other States to provide for higher environmental protection, by conditioning its willingness to import upon a certain level of protection. States can do all of that, either through autonomous action or in the framework of international agreements on environmental protection.

In the context of the WTO there is an important debate, fed by case law, on the lawfulness of such measures, and on the link between WTO free trade rules and multilateral environmental agreements.[101] That is a debate on the legal substance of trade and environment policies, but in EU law the debate has a formal, jurisdictional

---

[99] See e.g. the WTO's Committee on Trade and Environment.
[100] For a general treatment see e.g. E-U Petersmann, *International and European Trade and Environmental Law after the Uruguay Round* (Kluwer Law International, 1995); J Wiers, *Trade and Environment in the EC and the WTO—A Legal Analysis* (Europa Law Publishing, 2002).   [101] Ibid.

counterpart. Where does competence lie to take action in the field of trade and environment? Do all environmental measures affecting trade come within the Community's exclusive competence? Or does that depend on the centre of gravity of the measure; whether it is primarily a trade measure or an environmental measure?[102]

Before looking at the Court's case law on such questions, it is useful to point out that, since the SEA, the EC Treaty provides for a Community policy on protection of the environment (see, currently, Articles 174–176 EC). The powers conferred upon the Community in this field extend to external relations, as Article 174(4) provides that, within their respective spheres of competence, the Community and the Member States shall co-operate with third countries and with the competent international organizations. It further provides that the arrangements for Community co-operation may be the subject of agreements between the Community and the third parties concerned. Therefore, the question of the proper competence location of trade-and-environment measures is not so much concerned with whether the Community has any powers at all, but rather with whether the Community's competence is exclusive (under the common commercial policy) or concurrent with those of the Member States (under the Community's environmental policy). It may further be noted that Article 6 EC provides that environmental protection requirements must be integrated into the definition and implementation of all other Community policies (the so-called principle of integration).[103]

In *Chernobyl I*, the Court for the first time looked at trade and environment through the prism of external competence.[104] Following the accident at the Chernobyl (Ukraine) nuclear power station in April 1986 the Member States immediately took action to block imports of contaminated agricultural products from Central and Eastern Europe. Within a couple of weeks the Community got involved and the Council of Ministers adopted a regulation on such imports, based on (current) Article 133 EEC. Greece did not agree with that course of action, and challenged a successor regulation,[105] arguing that in the light of the public health objective of the measure the legal basis was incorrect. Thus, the case did not concern environmental protection in a strict sense, but the EC Treaty provisions on environmental policy were referred to in argument: Greece claimed that the regulation should have been based on Articles 130r and 130s EEC (now, with amendments, Articles 174 and 175 EC), possibly in conjunction with (current) Article 308 EC, or on Article 31 of the EAEC Treaty. The analysis can therefore be fully transposed to pure trade-and-environment measures.

---

[102] For an in-depth, albeit no longer recent, examination, see P Demaret, 'Environmental Policy and Commercial Policy: The Emergence of Trade-Related Environmental Measures (TREMs) in the External Relations of the European Community', in Maresceau (n 39 above), 305–86.

[103] See on that principle D McGillivray and J Holder, 'Locating EC Environmental Law' (2001) 20 YEL 152–6.   [104] *Greece v. Council* (n 45 above).

[105] Council Regulation 3955/87 on the conditions governing imports of agricultural products originating in third countries following the accident at the Chernobyl nuclear power station [1987] OJ L371/4.

The Court's reasoning was as follows.[106] It first referred to the principle it had established in the *GSP* case,[107] i.e. that in the context of the organization of the powers of the Community the choice of legal basis for a measure had to be based on objective factors which were amenable to judicial review. It then analysed the objective of the regulation, as expressed in its preamble, where it was indicated that 'the Community must continue to ensure that agricultural products and processed agricultural products intended for human consumption and likely to be contaminated are introduced into the Community only according to common arrangements', and that those 'common arrangements should safeguard the health of consumers, maintain, without having unduly adverse effects on trade between the Community and third countries, the unified nature of the market and prevent deflections of trade'. The Court further pointed out that the regulation established uniform rules regarding the conditions under which agricultural products likely to be contaminated could be imported into the Community from non-member countries. Having thus examined the objective and content of the regulation, the Court concluded that it was intended to regulate trade between the Community and non-member countries, and that it came within the common commercial policy. The fact that maximum permitted levels of radioactive contamination were fixed in response to a concern to protect public health and that the protection of public health was one of the objectives of Community action in environmental matters could not remove the regulation from the sphere of the common commercial policy. (Current) Articles 174 and 175 EC were intended to confer powers on the Community to undertake specific action on environmental matters, but they left intact the powers held by the Community under other provisions of the Treaty, even if the measures taken under those provisions pursued at the same time any of the objectives of environmental protection. That interpretation was confirmed by the principle of integration, which implied that a Community measure could not be part of Community action on environmental matters merely because it took account of environmental protection requirements.

At the time commentators felt that the Court had accepted too broad an interpretation of (current) Article 133,[108] yet from the perspective of safeguarding the unity of the internal market the judgment made sense. This is well expressed in the Opinion of Darmon AG, where he stated that, in order to avoid any change in patterns of trade and any distortion of competition in dealings with non-member countries, the Community had to be able, under the common commercial policy, to adopt uniform rules regarding the conditions under which products from non-member countries could be imported into its territory. In the Advocate General's conception, those conditions could include in particular compliance with maximum permitted levels of radioactivity without the measure in question thereby being of a different nature or not capable of adoption under (current) Article 133.

---

[106] *Greece v. Council* (n 45 above), paras 13–20.   [107] *Commission v. Council* (n 32 above).
[108] ELM Völker, *Barriers to External and Internal Community Trade* (Kluwer, 1993) 186–8.

The contested regulation seemed to him by its very nature to come within the common commercial policy.[109] One could add that the judgment essentially adopts the same approach as the above cases on trade and foreign policy: trade measures are trade measures, whatever the objectives pursued.

The Court was not again confronted with trade and environment from an external competence perspective until recently, when it had to rule on a request for an Opinion concerning the appropriate legal basis for the Cartagena Protocol on Biosafety.[110] The main difference with *Chernobyl I* is that the Cartagena Protocol is much less clearly concerned with trade, so that the above approach was inappropriate.

The Cartagena Protocol is a protocol to the Convention on Biological Diversity, a mixed agreement to which both the Community and its Member States are parties. The legal basis for conclusion by the Community was (current) Article 175 EC.[111] The Convention aims at 'the conservation of biological diversity, the sustainable use of its components and the fair and equitable sharing of the benefits arising out of the utilization of genetic resources'. Article 19(3) of the Convention provides for the negotiation of a protocol 'in the field of the safe transfer, handling and use of any living modified organism resulting from biotechnology that may have adverse effect on the conservation and sustainable use of biological diversity'. That provision formed the basis for the negotiation of the Cartagena Protocol. It is also worth mentioning that Article 34 of the Convention allows for conclusion of the Convention and any Protocol by States and by regional economic integration organizations. Where such organizations become parties together with their member States, the organization and its member States shall decide on their respective responsibilities for the performance of obligations, and they shall not be allowed to exercise rights concurrently. Further, the relevant organization must declare the extent of its competence.

The Cartagena Protocol was negotiated between 1997 and 2000, and was signed on behalf of the Community and its Member States on 24 May 2000. At that occasion, there was a divergence in the views of the Commission and the Council. The Commission had proposed that the decision authorizing signature be based on Articles 133 and 174(4) EC, but the Council unanimously adopted the decision on the basis of Article 175(1) EC alone. The Commission then requested the Court's Opinion, essentially asking whether its proposal had been correct. It pointed out that there would have to be a declaration regarding the Community's competence, and took the view that the Court's Opinion would ensure a framework of legal certainty for management of the Protocol, in particular when voting rights were exercised. The Commission was thus mainly concerned with the future management of the Protocol, in terms of representation of and decision-making by the Community and its Member States. It accepted that the Protocol would become a mixed agreement, but considered that there was preponderant Community competence under Article 133 EC, which should be reflected in future implementation.

---

[109] *Greece v. Council* (n 45 above), para 32 of the Opinion.
[110] *Opinion 2/00 re Cartagena Protocol on Biosafety* [2001] ECR I–9713.
[111] Council Decision 93/626 [1993] OJ L309/1.

Article 1 of the Cartagena Protocol states that its objective is 'to contribute to ensuring an adequate level of protection in the field of the safe transfer, handling and use of living modified organisms resulting from modern biotechnology that may have adverse effects on the conservation and sustainable use of biological diversity, taking also into account risks to human health, and specifically focusing on transboundary movements'. In accordance with Article 4, and without prejudice to certain specific provisions, the Protocol 'shall apply to the transboundary movement, transit, handling and use of all living modified organisms' that may have the above-mentioned adverse effects. Article 2(2) provides that 'the Parties shall ensure that the development, handling, transport, use, transfer and release of any living modified organisms are undertaken in a manner that prevents or reduces the risks to biological diversity, taking also into account risks to human health'. To that end, the Protocol sets up various control procedures, such as the informed agreement procedure (Articles 7–10 and 12), the procedure for living modified organisms intended for direct use as food or feed, or for processing (Article 11), and a simplified procedure (Article 13). Article 20 creates a Biosafety Clearing-House.

In its Opinion the Court examined whether conclusion of the Protocol should be based on Article 133 EC. It first pointed to settled case law that the choice of legal basis for a measure, including one adopted in order to conclude an international agreement, did not follow from its author's conviction alone, but had to rest on objective factors—in particular the aim and content of the measure—which were amenable to judicial review. The Court then introduced a principle, novel as regards external competence claims, but derived from case law on the legal basis of 'internal' acts. It stated that, if examination of a Community measure revealed that it pursued a twofold purpose or that it had a twofold component and if one was identifiable as the main or predominant purpose or component, whereas the other was merely incidental, the measure had to be founded on a single legal basis, namely that required by the main or predominant purpose or component.[112] By way of exception, the Court emphasized, if it was established that the measure simultaneously pursued several objectives which were inseparably linked without one being secondary and indirect in relation to the other, the measure could be founded on the corresponding legal bases.[113] Since interpretation of an international agreement was in issue, the Court also recalled that under Article 31 VCLT 'a treaty shall be interpreted in good faith in accordance with the ordinary meaning to be given to the terms of the treaty in their context and in the light of its object and purpose'.[114]

Having thus done the groundwork, the Court identified the question in issue as being (a) whether the Protocol, in the light of its context, its aim, and its content,

---

[112] The Court referred to Case C–155/91 *Commission v. Council* [1993] ECR I–939, paras 19 and 21 (*Waste Directive* judgment); Case C–42/97 *Parliament v. Council* [1999] ECR I–869, paras 39–40; and Case C–36/98 *Spain v. Council* [2001] ECR I–779, para 59.

[113] Here the Court referred to Case C–300/89 *Commission v. Council* [1991] ECR I–2867, paras 13 and 17 (the *Titanium Dioxide* judgment), and to *Parliament v. Council* (n 85 above), para 38.

[114] *Opinion 2/00* (n 110 above), paras 22–24.

constituted an agreement principally concerning environmental protection which was liable to have incidental effects on trade in living modified organisms (LMOs), (b) whether, conversely, it was principally an agreement concerning international trade policy which incidentally took account of certain environmental requirements, or (c) whether it was inextricably concerned both with environmental protection and with international trade.[115]

As regards the context of the Protocol, the Court recalled its link with the Convention on Biological Diversity, an instrument indisputably falling within the field of environmental protection. As regards purpose, it was clear beyond doubt that the Protocol pursued an environmental objective, highlighted by its reference to the precautionary principle, a fundamental principle of environmental protection included in Article 174(2) EC. The title of and preamble to the Protocol confirmed this. As regards content, finally, there was a clear reflection of the Protocol's environmental aim in the fundamental obligation to prevent or reduce the risks to biological diversity in the development, handling, transport, use, transfer, and release of any LMO. Article 4 of the Protocol, defining its scope as applying to all LMOs that could have adverse effects on biological diversity, also showed that the Protocol intrinsically concerned environmental protection. Further confirmation was found in the type of control procedures which the Protocol set up. It followed from this examination that the Protocol's main purpose or component was the protection of biological diversity against the harmful effects which could result from activities that involved dealing with LMOs, in particular from their transboundary movement.[116]

The Court did not stop there, but also rebutted the Commission's arguments regarding the common commercial policy. In essence the Commission had relied on a broad interpretation of Article 133 EC, and had pointed out that the Protocol applied to transboundary movements of LMOs, and that the control procedures would specifically relate to such movements, which included trade in LMOs. The Court accepted that, but did not consider that this modified the Protocol's character as an instrument intended essentially to improve biosafety and not to promote, facilitate, or govern trade. First, the Protocol covered any form of movement of LMOs between States, whether or not commercial. Likewise the juxtaposition of the terms 'transfer', 'handling', and 'use' of LMOs indicated the parties' wish to cover any manner in which LMOs were dealt with. Secondly, the Commission's interpretation would effectively render the specific Treaty provisions concerning environmental policy largely nugatory, since, as soon as it was established that Community action was liable to have repercussions on trade, the envisaged agreement would have to be regarded as coming within the common commercial policy. Thirdly, the practical difficulties associated with the implementation of mixed agreements were irrelevant when selecting the legal basis for a Community measure.[117]

The Court thus held that conclusion of the Protocol on behalf of the Community had to be founded on a single legal basis, specific to environmental policy.

---

[115] *Opinion 2/00* (n 110 above), para 25.   [116] Ibid, paras 26–34.   [117] Ibid, paras 35–41.

It also decided that Article 175(1) EC provided such basis, and not Article 174 EC, which only defined the objectives to be pursued in the context of environmental policy.[118]

Does *Opinion 2/00* inaugurate a new, more restrictive reading of Article 133 EC, and, correspondingly, a broader reading of the Community's external competences in matters of environmental policy? Does the Opinion bury the conception that trade measures are trade measures, no matter which objectives they pursue? The reply to those questions need not be affirmative. As was mentioned, the Cartagena Protocol on Biosafety is much less obviously a trade measure than the import restrictions in issue in *Chernobyl I*, or than the export restrictions in *Werner, Leifer*, and *Centro-Com*. At first glance, one may be tempted to identify transborder movement with trade, but the Court was right to look at the Protocol more closely, and to detect that the notion of transborder movement is wider than the notion of international trade; that the Protocol not only regulates such movement, but also other issues; and that there is generally no significant trade or economic dimension to the Protocol. Thus, the fact that the application of the Protocol will no doubt affect trade is insufficient for bringing it within the scope of Article 133 EC. The Court could have added that the Protocol could just as much affect trade between Member States, a matter for the internal market, as it could affect external trade.

The Opinion also reflects the Court's overall approach to trade-and-environment issues. For example, in the case law on the free movement of goods, policies for protection of the environment have been raised almost to the level of an express exception to the prohibition of quantitative restrictions and measures having equivalent effect.[119] In that case law, one also finds indications of the Court's reluctance to protect a principle of free trade in environmentally harmful products, such as waste.[120] Similarly, the case law on the delimitation of the Community's competence to harmonize national laws for the purpose of establishing an internal market and its competence to pursue environmental policies also betrays a reluctance to regard the circulation of environmentally harmful products as an internal market matter.[121] *Opinion 2/00* is in a sense the external competence counterpart of those developments in the case law.

The Commission's request for an Opinion in this case may also have been seen as yet another institutional turf battle, not so much concerned with confirming and defining the external powers of the Community as such, but rather with carving out the respective future roles of the Community institutions (particularly of the Commission, which represents the Community externally) and the Member States. It cannot have helped the Commission's case that all parties recognized that the Protocol would be a mixed agreement in any event, and that it came at least in part within the Community's external environmental competence. As with *Opinion 1/94*,

---

[118] Ibid, paras 42–44. See further Ch 3.
[119] Case C–379/98 *PreussenElektra v. Schleswag* [2001] ECR I–2099.
[120] e.g. Case C–2/90 *Commission v. Belgium* [1992] ECR I–4431.
[121] Case C–155/91 *Commission v. Council* [1993] ECR I–939.

there was again an awkward gap between legal principle and practice. The competence issue was litigated only when the negotiations had taken place, and the
Community and its Member States had managed to take part in those negotiations
on the basis of a common negotiating stance. It cannot be denied that the implementation of mixed agreements may give rise to complex problems of defining the
respective powers of the Community and its Member States, which may threaten the
effective defence of the Community's interests or affect the proper decision-making
procedures. Those problems are further analysed in Chapter 7. However, claiming
exclusive Community competence on the basis of Article 133 EC is perhaps not
a proper strategy for tackling such problems.

That *Opinion 2/00* did not introduce a more restrictive reading of Article 133 EC
is confirmed by the most recent development in the area of trade and environment,
i.e. the Court's judgment in *Commission v. Council*, on the Energy Star Agreement.[122]
In 1992 the United States Environmental Protection Agency set up a voluntary
labelling programme for office equipment, called the Energy Star Programme. The
programme encouraged the vast majority of manufacturers to introduce energy-
saving features and raised consumer awareness of the energy losses of office equipment in stand-by mode. The programme was subsequently extended to cover
other appliances and equipments. The Energy Star logo was introduced for the
labelling of equipment which adhered to certain rules concerning energy consumption. After observing that the Energy Star Programme already established the
standard for office equipment sold on the American market and the Energy Star
requirements were becoming the standard worldwide, including in the Community, the Commission decided that, rather than developing a separate labelling
programme, the better course was to introduce the Energy Star Programme in the
Community. To that effect the Community negotiated and signed the Agreement
between the Government of the United States of America and the European
Community on the co-ordination of energy-efficient labelling programmes for
office equipment.[123]

According to the preamble to the agreement the contracting parties wish 'to
maximize energy savings and environmental benefits by stimulating the supply of
and demand for energy-efficient products'. Article I provides for the use of a common set of energy-efficiency specifications and a common logo, the latter for the
purpose of identifying qualified energy-efficient product types. Under Article V
manufacturers, vendors, or resale agents can enter the Energy Star labelling programme by registering with either the Commission or the US Environmental
Protection Agency, which are designated as management entities responsible for
implementation of the agreement. Articles VI, VII, and VIII deal with co-ordination
of the Energy Star labelling programme between the contracting parties, registration
of the Energy Star marks in the Community, and monitoring by each management
entity of compliance with the provisions on the proper use of the Energy Star marks.

---

[122] Case C–281/01 *Commission v. Council* [2002] ECR I–12049.   [123] See [2001] OJ L172/1.

The Council concluded the agreement on the basis of Article 175(1) EC, in conjunction with the relevant provisions of Article 300 EC.[124] The Commission challenged that decision, arguing that the agreement should have been concluded on the basis of Article 133 EC.

The Court, broadly following the Opinion of Alber AG, agreed with the Commission. It first referred to its statements in *Opinion 2/00* concerning measures pursuing a twofold purpose or having a twofold component. It was not in dispute that the Energy Star Agreement was designed to co-ordinate energy-efficient labelling programmes for office equipment. Such co-ordination necessarily facilitated trade inasmuch as manufacturers needed to refer to just one standard and to comply with just one registration procedure. That co-ordination therefore undoubtedly constituted a commercial policy measure. However, it was also clear that the labelling programme in question was intended to promote energy savings and therefore in itself constituted an environmental policy measure. It followed that the agreement simultaneously pursued a commercial policy objective and an environmental protection objective, and it therefore had to be established whether either objective was the agreement's main or predominant aim, or whether the objectives pursued were inseparable without one being secondary and indirect in relation to the other.[125]

The Court then pointed out that it was clear from the terms in which the agreement was couched that the programme was essentially intended to enable manufacturers to use, in accordance with a procedure for the mutual recognition of registrations, a common logo to identify for consumers certain products complying with a common set of energy-efficiency specifications which they intended to sell on the American and Community markets. An instrument having a direct impact on trade in office equipment was therefore involved. It was true that in the long term, depending on how manufacturers and consumers in fact behaved, the programme should have a positive environmental effect. However, that was merely an indirect and distant effect, in contrast to the effect on trade in office equipment that was direct and immediate. Furthermore, the agreement did not itself contain new energy-efficiency requirements. The commercial policy objective therefore had to be regarded as predominant.[126]

The Court then rejected a number of objections against that conclusion. The non-mandatory nature of the programme did not matter, as the agreement was in any event designed to have a direct impact on trade. In addition, the TBT Agreement (see above, the section on *Opinion 1/94*) clarified that non-binding labelling provisions could constitute an obstacle to international trade. Also, the fact that the Treaty provisions relating to environmental policy had been chosen as the legal basis for the adoption of internal measures regarding eco-labelling was not sufficient to establish that the same basis had to be used when approving an international agreement

---

[124] Council Decision 2001/469, in ibid.   [125] *Commission v. Council* (n 32 above), paras 34–39.
[126] Ibid, paras 40–43.

with similar subject matter: since Article 133 EC related to external trade it could not in any event serve as the legal basis for measures with purely internal effects, or for completion of the internal market. Nor did the fact that certain Member States had adopted their own eco-label stand in the way of recognition of exclusive Community competence under Article 133 EC: those labels did not in fact concern the external trade of the Community.[127] The Court consequently annulled the Council decision in issue.

The Court's judgment is in line with its analysis of the TBT Agreement in *Opinion 1/94*. Technical regulations, standards, and labelling of products, in a context of international trade, appear to have a predominant trade character.[128] If one contrasts the judgment with *Opinion 2/00* the conclusion is clearly that the Court is reluctant to accept a dual legal basis, and prefers to establish the predominant purpose or component of an agreement (or of an autonomous measure).

The judgment in *BAT* also reaffirmed the principles concerning acts having a twofold purpose or component.[129] In issue was the validity of a directive on the approximation of the laws, regulations, and administrative provisions of the Member States concerning the manufacture, presentation, and sale of tobacco products.[130] According to the eleventh recital of the preamble the directive would have consequences for tobacco products exported from the Community. Under Article 3(2) the provisions on maximum yield of cigarettes as regards tar, nicotine, and carbon monoxide also applied to cigarettes manufactured within, but exported from, the Community. In light of this provision the directive had been adopted on the basis of both Articles 95 and 133 EC. BAT challenged this recourse to a dual legal basis. The Court examined whether such recourse was necessary or possible. It first recalled the above principles, and considered that in their light the directive could not simultaneously have Articles 95 and 133 EC for a legal basis. Without there being any need to consider whether, in its provisions affecting tobacco products exported to non-member countries, the directive also pursued an objective linked to the implementation of the common commercial policy under Article 133 EC, that objective was in any event secondary in relation to the aim and content of the directive as a whole, which was primarily designed to improve the conditions for the functioning of the internal market. The Court also accepted that the directive could, on the basis of Article 95, regulate the manufacture of cigarettes for export with a view to avoiding circumvention of its provisions through illicit re-importation.[131]

The Treaties of Amsterdam and Nice

After the delivery of *Opinion 1/94*, where the Court had concluded that there was shared competence for WTO matters, the Community institutions for some time

---

[127] *Commission v. Council* (n 32 above), paras 44–47.   [128] See also Ch 4.
[129] *British American Tobacco* (n 46 above).   [130] Directive 2001/37 [2001] OJ L194/26.
[131] *British American Tobacco* (n 46 above), paras 81–98.

attempted to negotiate what was called a 'code of conduct', which would contain arrangements for the exercise of Community and Member States' competences in the WTO.[132] Those negotiations did not progress much, and got caught up in the IGC which drafted the Treaty of Amsterdam.[133] Despite strenuous attempts by the Commission to have Article 133 modified so as to extend the scope of the common commercial policy to all WTO matters, the IGC could only agree to disagree. It added a fifth paragraph to Article 133, according to which:

The Council, acting unanimously on a proposal from the Commission and after consulting the European Parliament, may extend the application of paragraphs 1 to 4 to international negotiations and agreements on services and intellectual property insofar as they are not covered by these paragraphs.

From a constitutional perspective this provision was awkward. Here the Treaty effectively enabled the Council, an EU institution, to broaden the powers of the Community—exclusive powers, one assumes—so as to include rather ill-defined areas. Indeed, whereas there is no doubt that the amendment was intended to cover WTO negotiations, its language does not refer to the WTO, and many other types of international negotiations could come within its scope. This extension of Community competence could be accomplished without any need for approval by the Member States as such, in accordance with their constitutional principles or provisions. It thus looked as though the Member States, by concluding the Amsterdam Treaty, transferred *Kompetenz-Kompetenz* (the competence to distribute or transfer competence) in this area to the Council of Ministers. Of course Article 133(5) provided for unanimity in the Council of Ministers, but it should be borne in mind that the Council is composed of representatives of the governments of the Member States, and those governments do not generally have power, under domestic constitutional rules, to transfer powers to an international organization.

Dashwood commented upon this amendment by calling it a face-saving device, which would put off any effective amendment of Article 133 until the Greek Kalends.[134] That comment exemplified the risk of making predictions about the constitutional evolution of the EU (more than a misreading of the political currents, as at the time the comment seemed plausible), for at the Nice IGC Article 133 again became the subject of renegotiation and amendment, before the Amsterdam Article 133(5) had ever been applied. The IGC negotiations were characterized by a general willingness to broaden the scope of Article 133 so as to cover WTO matters, but with reservations on the part of some Member States as regards transfer

---

[132] As regards services, such a code of conduct had been agreed before *Opinion 1/94*; for the text see *Opinion 1/94* (n 48 above), at 5365–6. See further Ch 7.

[133] On the IGC debate concerning the common commercial policy see M Cremona, 'External Economic Relations and the Amsterdam Treaty', in D O'Keeffe and P Twomey (eds), *Legal Issues of the Amsterdam Treaty* (Hart Publishing, 1999) 225–47.

[134] A Dashwood, 'External Relations Provisions of the Amsterdam Treaty', in ibid, 205.

of powers and decision-making procedures for certain subjects. The result is a fiendishly complex recast Article 133, introducing three new paragraphs which are best fully quoted for the purpose of analysis.[135]

The new Article 133(5) EC provides:

5. Paragraphs 1 to 4 shall also apply to the negotiation and conclusion of agreements in the fields of trade in services and the commercial aspects of intellectual property, insofar as those agreements are not covered by the said paragraphs and without prejudice to paragraph 6.

By way of derogation from paragraph 4, the Council shall act unanimously when negotiating and concluding an agreement in one of the fields referred to in the first subparagraph, where that agreement includes provisions for which unanimity is required for the adoption of internal rules or where it relates to a field in which the Community has not yet exercised the powers conferred upon it by this Treaty by adopting internal rules.

The Council shall act unanimously with respect to the negotiation and conclusion of a horizontal agreement insofar as it also concerns the preceding subparagraph or the second subparagraph of paragraph 6.

This paragraph shall not affect the right of the Member States to maintain and conclude agreements with third countries or international organizations insofar as such agreements comply with Community law and other relevant international agreements.

There are several comments to be made as regards the meaning and effect of this new provision. First, its scope is more narrowly defined than the Amsterdam Article 133(5), as it refers to *trade* in services and the *commercial* aspects of intellectual property rights. That brings its scope closer to the WTO's current remit. It is none the less clear that the text does not exclude application of this provision to non-WTO negotiations on these subjects.

Secondly, the new paragraph (5) operates a dichotomy between the negotiation and conclusion of international agreements and the adoption of internal Community rules. Article 133, paragraphs (1) to (4), does not operate such a dichotomy, and gives competence to the Community to develop a trade policy through both international and autonomous action. Paragraph (5), by contrast, does not appear to transfer competence for the adoption of internal rules. However, at the same time the new provision does recognize that there may be 'internal' competence as regards trade in services or the commercial aspects of intellectual property, because its second subparagraph provides that the Council shall exercise the new powers by unanimous action where the agreement relates to a field in which the Community has not yet adopted internal rules. That of course presupposes that the new paragraph may also be applied in a field where there are already internal rules. Perhaps the proper reading is that those internal rules relate to services and intellectual property generally, for which there is clearly an internal power of harmonization.[136] If that is so, the question

---

[135] See also HG Krenzler and C Pitschas, 'Progress or Stagnation? The Common Commercial Policy after Nice' (2001) 6 EFARev 291; CW Herrmann, 'Common Commercial Policy after Nice: Sisyphus Would Have Done a Better Job' (2002) 39 CMLRev 7.

[136] See the analysis of *Opinion 1/94* as regards implied powers in Ch 3.

arises whether paragraph (5) enables the Community to adopt autonomous measures with respect to 'trade in services' and 'the commercial aspects of intellectual property', in the absence of an international agreement or more general internal market harmonization. It must be said that the exclusion of such autonomous action would make little sense.

Thirdly, paragraph (5) provides for unanimity in three types of circumstances. The first, referring to an agreement containing provisions for which unanimity is required for the adoption of internal rules, again appears to operate a dichotomy between internal and international action. The presumption is clearly that the internal rules referred to are based on provisions in the Treaty, other than Article 133, and requiring unanimity. The logic is that such unanimity is then extended to international action, thus preventing what might be seen as circumvention of the 'internal' unanimity requirement through external action subject to qualified majority voting. The second type of circumstances is where the Community has not yet exercised its powers by adopting internal rules. In that case unanimity is required for external action, even if the legal basis for internal action may provide for qualified majority. The third type covers horizontal agreements which concern the preceding subparagraph or the second subparagraph of paragraph (6) (see below). One assumes that horizontal here refers to agreements which have broad coverage, and are not confined to the types of circumstances referred to.

This subparagraph of Article 133(5) appears to confuse trade policy powers with implied powers. The circumstances to which it refers are such that under the doctrine of implied powers the EC Treaty provision giving 'internal' powers to the Community would have to be the legal basis for external action. The new paragraph (5) suggests that that is no longer the case, without clarifying its relationship with the doctrine of implied powers.

Fourthly, the last subparagraph appears to characterize the Community's powers under Article 133(5) as concurrent with those of the Member States, since it provides that the new powers do not affect the right of the Member States to maintain and conclude agreements in so far as such agreements comply with Community law and other (one assumes Community) agreements.

A further layer of complexity is added by the provisions of paragraph (6):

6. An agreement may not be concluded by the Council if it includes provisions which would go beyond the Community's internal powers, in particular by leading to harmonization of the laws or regulations of the Member States in an area for which this Treaty rules out such harmonization.

In this regard, by way of derogation from the first subparagraph of paragraph 5, agreements relating to trade in cultural and audiovisual services, educational services, and social and human health services, shall fall within the shared competence of the Community and its Member States. Consequently, in addition to a Community decision taken in accordance with the relevant provisions of Article 300, the negotiation of such agreements shall require the common accord of the Member States. Agreements thus negotiated shall be concluded jointly by the Community and the Member States.

The negotiation and conclusion of international agreements in the field of transport shall continue to be governed by the provisions of Title V and Article 300.

There are again several comments to be made. This paragraph is generally aimed at defining the limits of the Community's competence, flowing from the conferral by paragraph (5). There appears to be some measure of contradiction between the first and the second subparagraphs. Whereas the former rules out Community competence altogether, by providing that the Council may not conclude certain agreements, the latter speaks, 'in this regard', about competences shared with the Member States and about joint conclusion. The two subparagraphs can none the less be reconciled, if one assumes that the agreements on trade in services as defined by the second subparagraph are agreements containing, on the one hand, provisions within the Community's competence, and, on the other, provisions excluded from Community competence by virtue of the first subparagraph.

The first subparagraph again appears to be based on a type of implied powers reasoning. It refers in particular to (but does not seem confined to) harmonization where the Treaty excludes that. Examples of such exclusion are Article 150(4) EC, regarding education, vocational training, and youth; Article 151(5) EC, concerning culture; and Article 152(4) EC, with respect to public health.

As regards the second subparagraph, the central question will be how to define 'trade in cultural and audiovisual services, educational services, and social and human health services'. The desire to exclude Community competence for such services appears to be nourished by anti-globalization sentiments in certain Member States, and the resulting concern to maintain national sovereignty in this area.

The last subparagraph of paragraph (6) confirms the Court's analysis of transport services in *Opinion 1/94*.

Finally, there is paragraph (7) of the new Article 133, which provides:

7. Without prejudice to the first subparagraph of paragraph 6, the Council, acting unanimously on a proposal from the Commission and after consulting the European Parliament, may extend the application of paragraphs 1 to 4 to international negotiations and agreements on intellectual property insofar as they are not covered by paragraph 5.

This provision concerns intellectual property agreements which do not deal with 'the commercial aspects of intellectual property', as referred to in paragraph (5). Again the interpretation exercise is not straightforward, because in *Opinion 1/94* the Court of Justice did not appear convinced that the TRIPs Agreement deals with commercial matters. One therefore wonders whether any future TRIPs negotiation would be covered by paragraph (5) or by paragraph (7). There may thus be debate whether such negotiation requires a unanimous Council decision pursuant to paragraph (7), or whether the Council can act by qualified majority pursuant to paragraph (5) (provided the unanimity requirement of that paragraph does not apply).

On the whole one wonders whether the above complexity implies much modification of the Community's existing competences. Services are in this respect clearly the most important sector, because the current GATS is little more than a framework for liberalization of trade in services, and much work lies ahead. Assuming that GATS continues to be a central legal framework for trade in services, and assuming that the WTO continues to operate through broadly-based negotiation rounds with general coverage, such as the current Doha Round, the effect of the new Article 133 EC will be that the Community and the Member States continue to share competence, and need to act jointly, exactly as the Court held in *Opinion 1/94*.[137] It is also to be feared that, in light of the complexity of the new provisions, it will be impossible to find some form of consensus on their interpretation and application, and that again this will only result in joint action and the conclusion of mixed agreements. In other words, the Treaty drafters could have spared themselves the trouble.

The draft Constitution

The common commercial policy did not appear to be high on the agenda of the Convention on the Future of Europe, but the proposed draft Constitution none the less provides for a very significant expansion of the scope of this policy. Issues concerning the EU's external relations were mainly discussed in the Convention's Working Group on External Action. The final report of this group discussed commercial policy only from the perspective of decision-making. It noted that there was a high degree of support for qualified majority voting 'in all areas of commercial policy, including services and intellectual property, without prejudice to current restrictions on harmonization in internal policy areas'.[138] The final version of the draft Constitution follows that recommendation, and introduces some other provisions which are relevant from the perspective of competence.

Article I–3, which sets out the Union's overall objectives, speaks in paragraph (4) about the relations with the wider world, in which the Union 'shall contribute to . . . free and fair trade'. Those concepts are not further defined, and it is in particular unclear what is meant by fair trade. That notion has traditionally been used as a reference to certain trade-protection instruments such as anti-dumping and anti-subsidy.[139] If that is the intended meaning of fair trade the draft Constitution would be emphasizing a rather protectionist dimension of commercial policy. It is however difficult to see any particular causes for such an, arguably retrograde, step. The reference to fair trade is more naturally read as an instruction to take account of the interests of developing countries in the international trading system, because the reference is juxtaposed to 'the sustainable development of the earth', 'solidarity and mutual respect among peoples', and 'eradication of poverty and protection of human rights and in particular children's rights'. A veiled reference to protectionism seems very much out of kilter with those lofty ideals. No further reference to fair trade is made

---

[137] Krenzler and Pitschas (n 135 above), 311. [138] CONV 459/02, at 7.
[139] On those policies see Ch 10.

in the more specific provisions on external action in Part III of the draft Constitution. Article III–193(2) contains a more detailed list of objectives, which includes under letter (e) 'the integration of all countries into the world economy, including through the progressive abolition of restrictions on international trade'.

The draft Constitution also proposes new language on the nature of the Union's competences. It provides in Article I–11(1) that, where the Constitution confers on the Union exclusive competence in a specific area, only the Union may legislate and adopt legally binding acts, the Member States being able to do so themselves only if so empowered by the Union or for the implementation of acts adopted by the Union. The draft Constitution further confirms that the Union shall have exclusive competence in the area of the common commercial policy (Article I–12(1)). This is a welcome confirmation of the principles resulting from the Court's case law. The most significant innovations are in Article III–217, a reformed version of Article 133 EC. As regards the scope of the common commercial policy the relevant provisions are paragraphs (1), (4), and (5):

1. The common commercial policy shall be based on uniform principles, particularly with regard to changes in tariff rates, the conclusion of tariff and trade agreements relating to trade in goods and services and the commercial aspects of intellectual property, foreign direct investment, the achievement of uniformity in measures of liberalization, export policy and measures to protect trade such as those to be taken in the event of dumping or subsidies. The common commercial policy shall be conducted in the context of the principles and objectives of the Union's external action.

. . .

4. For the negotiation and conclusion of agreements in the fields of trade in services involving the movement of persons and the commercial aspects of intellectual property, the Council of Ministers shall act unanimously where such agreements include provisions for which unanimity is required for the adoption of internal rules.

The Council shall also act unanimously for the negotiation and conclusion of agreements in the field of trade in cultural and audiovisual services, where these risk prejudicing the Union's cultural and linguistic diversity.

The negotiation and conclusion of international agreements in the field of transport shall be subject to the provisions of Section 7 of Chapter III of this Title and Article III–227.

5. The exercise of the competences conferred by this Article in the field of commercial policy shall not affect the delimitation of internal competences between the Union and the Member States, and shall not lead to harmonization of legislative or regulatory provisions of Member States insofar as the Constitution excludes such harmonization.

Compared to the version of Article 133 EC post-Nice, it must be said that the above provision is a model of clarity, thereby offering an excellent illustration of the limits to the intergovernmental method of amending the Treaties and the benefits of the convention approach. The proposed Article III–217 in fact returns to the logic of the pre-Amsterdam version of Article 113 E(E)C, whilst considerably expanding the scope of the Union's exclusive competence. This expansion is clearly intended to reflect the remit of the WTO through the reference to 'trade in goods and services and the commercial aspects of intellectual property'. There can be little doubt that all current WTO matters would come within the scope of the common commercial policy if the Constitution entered into force. In addition, foreign direct investment will also be a Union matter. This extension makes sense, in particular in light of the fact that foreign direct investment by service providers, which is covered by GATS, is already within Community competence subsequent to the entry into force of the Treaty of Nice. It would be rather anomalous not to extend the scope of Community competence to foreign direct investment by all companies, including those manufacturing goods.[140]

It is also to be noted that the extension of the scope of the common commercial policy is, in contrast with the Nice version of Article 133 EC, not confined to the conclusion of international agreements. It is true that Article III–217 speaks of 'the conclusion of tariff and trade agreements relating to trade in goods and services and the commercial aspects of intellectual property', but the list of subjects and measures is not exhaustive ('particularly'),[141] and the underlying conception of the draft is clearly that the notion of trade includes trade in goods and services and commercial aspects of intellectual property.

Paragraph (4) contains an exception to qualified-majority decision-making, continuing the Nice reference to the rules on internal decision-making. As regards trade in services involving the movement of persons and the commercial aspects of intellectual property the institutions will need to investigate whether an agreement contains provisions which, if adopted autonomously by the Union within its internal sphere, would be subject to unanimous decision-making. There is also a voting carve-out for agreements which affect linguistic and cultural diversity, again an exception fed by globalization anxieties.

Paragraph (5) likewise aims to avoid that the new provision is employed so as to circumvent constitutional prohibitions on harmonization of national legislation.

Conclusions

On the basis of the EEC Treaty provisions on a common commercial policy the Court of Justice has been able to construct a firm doctrine of exclusive Community competence, not limited to the internal sphere of adopting 'autonomous' acts but extending to the conclusion of agreements with third countries. The growth of international trade, the expansion of the GATT, in terms of both membership and subject matter, the creation of the WTO with its beyond-trade agenda, and the proliferation of regional trade agreements which was first championed by the Community but is now a general phenomenon have all contributed to making trade

---

[140] Cf Eeckhout (n 62 above).   [141] See also *Opinion 1/78* (n 22 above).

policy the hard core of the EU's external action. The Community's exclusive competence in trade matters thrust the Community on the international scene, as an ineluctable partner for all countries wishing to trade with Europe. The EEC Treaty provisions on a common commercial policy are thus the very constitutional origin of EU external relations, and they were constitutionalized through the Court's interpretation, which interjected the notions of competence, exclusivity, authorization,[142] thereby creating a Community territory in the realm of international relations.

As was pointed out, the Court created such territory with respect for national competence, through an approach which was both principled and pragmatic.[143] It left room for national legislation and measures, and for Member States' membership of the WTO, by using various legal devices, such as deconnecting financing, introducing the concept of authorization, adopting broad interpretations of exceptions contained in EC legislation, and limiting the scope of the Treaty concept of commercial policy in comparison with international developments and conceptions. At the same time, the Court's emphasis on exclusivity required some measure of Community involvement in all trade-related matters, effectively rendering the Community institutions the locus of decision-making on international trade.

The most notable and noted development has been the Court's refusal to allow the notion of commercial policy to expand so as to cover the entire WTO agenda. A majority of commentators takes the view that *Opinion 1/94* was less bold than the Court's previous rulings.[144] This author does not agree. At most, the Court could have gone further as regards services, by adopting the internal-market logic of treating both goods and services as traded products, and by recognizing that both forms of trade require a unified external policy so as to avoid deflections of trade and distortions of competition. To decide, however, that the entire TRIPs agreement came within exclusive Community competence would have signified that any regulatory matter could, simply by using the trade label in an international negotiation, be transferred to Community territory. The halt which the Court called to the coextensive character of the common commercial policy and international trade policy was justified from a constitutional perspective, given the strong (exclusive) traits of Community competence. Managing to attach a trade label to an international negotiation or bringing a subject of economic (or even non-economic) regulation within the sphere of the WTO is not going to be sufficient to decree a transfer of powers from the national to the Community level.

In calling this halt the Court recognized the limits of the concepts contained in the original EEC Treaty, and opened up a space for constitutional development through express amendment. In other matters, too, there are examples of such judicial behaviour.[145] Constitutional amendment has indeed been taking place, and

---

[142] See further Ch 10.   [143] Tridimas and Eeckhout (n 12 above).
[144] E.g. Kaddous (n 8 above).
[145] See, as regards accession to the ECHR, *Opinion 2/94* [1996] ECR I–1759, discussed in Ch 3, and A Arnull, 'Left to Its Own Devices? Opinion 2/94 and the Protection of Fundamental Rights in the European Union', in A Dashwood and C Hillion (eds), *The General Law of EC External Relations* (Sweet &

the draft Constitution actually confirms the way in which institutional practice has moved away from the complex mixity which *Opinion 1/94* seemed to inaugurate.[146] The proposed Article III–217 may seem to introduce a significant expansion of the commercial-policy concept, but in effect it does little more than confirm that, at least as regards WTO matters and negotiations, competence, not in a legal but in a material sense, already lies with the EU institutions. They are the locus of decision-making, and the debate about national competence is really one about modalities of decision-making (unanimity or qualified majority), token sovereignty, and political carve-outs.

In the complex and, at heart, artificial exercise of delineating trade and non-trade policies the Court has managed to develop a convincing and balanced approach, both as regards trade-and-environment and trade-and-foreign-policy. In this area too the Constitution may be able to pacify, by harmonizing both legislative procedure across different legal bases in the Treaty and the procedure for negotiating and concluding international agreements. The distinction between exclusive and shared powers will remain, necessitating knowledge of the scope of the common commercial policy so as to determine what in any event needs to be decided at EU level, but whether, for example, a particular agreement is a trade or an environmental agreement may not matter much once the EU has decided to sign and conclude it. The case law on delimitation of trade and non-trade policies will none the less remain of interest, possibly even for the political debate of reconciling such policies, not from the institutional perspective of competence but from that of content and connection.

If however the case law on the common commercial policy has been of great constitutional significance for the EU's external action, no less great a role was cast for the doctrine of implied powers, to which the next chapter turns.

Maxwell, 2000) 67; as regards standing in an action for annulment by private parties see Case C–50/00 P *UPA v. Council* [2002] ECR I–6677.

[146] On mixity see Ch 7.

3

The doctrine of implied powers

Introduction

In the original EEC Treaty there were not many provisions which expressly referred to external action by the Community. There were the provisions on the common commercial policy, discussed in the previous chapter of this book, which mentioned the conclusion of international agreements on commercial policy. Other references to external relations were confined to the last part of the Treaty, containing 'General and Final Provisions'. There one found Article 228 (now, with amendments, Article 300 EC), on the procedure for concluding international agreements 'where this Treaty provides for' such agreements. Article 229 (now Article 302 EC) instructed the Commission to maintain 'all appropriate relations' with the United Nations, its specialized agencies, the GATT, and other international organizations; Article 230 (now Article 303 EC) provided that the Community was to establish all appropriate forms of co-operation with the Council of Europe; and Article 231 (now Article 304) spoke of establishing close co-operation with the OECD, the details of which were to be determined by common accord.

It is clear that none of those final provisions conferred any substantive powers—in the sense of defining certain policy areas—to act under international law. There was one, last provision which did confer a more broadly-defined external competence: Article 238 (now Article 310 EC) on association agreements, according to which 'the Community may conclude with one or more States or international organizations agreements establishing an association involving reciprocal rights and obligations, common action and special procedures'. That provision was soon and often to be used; its scope and meaning are analysed in Chapter 4.

The question then arose whether the external powers of the EEC were confined to developing a common commercial policy, concluding association agreements, and establishing co-operation with international organizations, or whether the EEC could act externally and conclude international agreements in other areas too. Whether, in other words, the Treaty contained implied external powers. The case law of the Court of Justice on these implied powers is of great constitutional significance,[1] and this chapter is devoted to its analysis. It takes the reader through the entire body

---

[1] JHH Weiler, *The Constitution of Europe* (CUP, 1999) 189; for general analyses see R Kovar, 'Les compétences implicites: jurisprudence de la Cour et pratique communautaire', in P Demaret (ed), *Relations extérieures de la Communauté européenne et marché intérieur: aspects juridiques et fonctionnels* (Story Scientia,

of the case law, offering an extensive account and close scrutiny. In the last section it offers some concluding reflections, and makes the link to the following chapter where this book looks at the main policy areas in the current EC Treaty which are relevant from an external relations perspective.

The *AETR* case: implied v. conferred powers?

The original EEC Treaty did not contain any provisions analogous to Article 101 EAEC Treaty, which was negotiated at the same time.[2] According to that provision, the EAEC could, 'within the limits of its powers and jurisdiction, enter into obligations by concluding agreements or contracts with a third State, an international organization or a national of a third State'. This article established a clear parallelism between internal and external powers. As no comparable provision was inserted into the EEC Treaty, it would not be illogical to assume that the drafters of that Treaty were circumspect about creating general parallelism in the case of the much broader transfer of powers from the Member States to the EEC.

In 1970 the Commission brought the *AETR* case, named after the European Agreement concerning the work of crews of vehicles engaged in international road transport.[3] This agreement was first signed in 1962 under the auspices of the UN Economic Commission for Europe by five of the six EEC Member States and a number of other European States. It did not however enter into force because there was not a sufficient number of ratifications. Negotiations for a revision of the agreement resumed in 1967, and at the same time substantively similar work was undertaken at Community level, resulting in Council Regulation 543/69 on the harmonization of certain social legislation relating to road transport.[4] The Council then discussed the attitude to be taken by the Member States in the AETR negotiations. It decided that those negotiations would continue to be conducted by the Member States, and thus did not agree with the Commission's proposal that the Community should negotiate instead of the Member States. The Council also agreed on a common position in the negotiations. The Commission then brought an action for the annulment of 'the Council proceedings'.

The Court's judgment has a complex structure, in that the examination of the Community's external powers is located in a section on the 'initial question', even

---

1988) 15; I Macleod, ID Hendry, and S Hyett, *The External Relations of the European Communities* (OUP, 1996) 47–55; C Kaddous, *Le droit des relations extérieures dans la jurisprudence de la Cour de justice des Communautés européennes* (Helbing & Lichtenhahn, 1998) 240–55; C Denys, *Impliciete bevoegdheden in de Europese Economische Gemeenschap* (Maklu, 1990); A Dashwood and J Helikoski, 'The Classic Authorities Revisited', in A Dashwood and C Hillion (eds), *The General Law of EC External Relations* (Sweet & Maxwell, 2000) 3–19; D O'Keeffe, 'Exclusive, Concurrent and Shared Competence', in idem, 179–99.

[2] PJG Kapteyn and P VerLoren van Themaat, *Introduction to the Law of the European Communities* (3rd edn, by LW Gormley, Kluwer Law International, 1998) 1257.

[3] Case 22/70 *Commission v. Council* [1971] ECR 263.   [4] [1969] OJ Spec Ed (I) 170.

before the analysis of the admissibility of the action. Indeed, the Council argued that the action for annulment was inadmissible, on the ground that the proceedings in question were not an act subject to review under Article 173 EEC (now Article 230 EC). In order to decide this point, the Court was required to determine which authority was empowered to negotiate and conclude the AETR. The legal effect of the proceedings differed according to whether they were regarded as constituting the exercise of powers conferred on the Community (in which case one could properly speak of a Council act) or as acknowledging a co-ordination by the Member States of the exercise of powers which remained vested in them (in which case there simply was no Council act).[5]

The Commission argued that the Treaty provisions on a common transport policy, and (current) Article 71 EC in particular, applied to external relations just as much as to domestic measures, notwithstanding the absence of an express reference to that effect. The full effect of this provision would be jeopardized if the powers which it conferred, particularly that of laying down 'any appropriate provisions', within the meaning of subparagraph (1)(c) (now (1)(d)) of the Article, did not extend to the conclusion of agreements with third countries. Even if the Community's power did not originally embrace the whole sphere of transport, it would tend to become general and exclusive as and where the common policy in this field came to be implemented. The Council, by contrast, contended that since the Community only had such powers as had been conferred on it, authority to enter into agreements could not be assumed in the absence of an express provision. Article 75 related only to measures internal to the Community and could not be interpreted as authorizing the conclusion of international agreements. And even if it were otherwise, such authority could not be general and exclusive, but at the most concurrent with that of the Member States.[6]

Dutheillet de Lamothe AG essentially agreed with the Council. He was of the opinion that recognizing external powers in the field of transport would involve the Court in a discretionary construction of the law—a judicial interpretation far exceeding the bounds which the Court had so far set regarding its power to interpret the Treaty. He referred to the opening sentence of (current) Article 300 EC, on the procedure for negotiating and concluding international agreements, which spoke of 'where this Treaty provides for the conclusion of agreements'. He did not accept the wide interpretation of that provision advocated by the Commission. In his view, recognition of the Community's authority in this case would concede by implication that the Community authorities exercised, in addition to the powers expressly conferred upon them by the Treaty, those implied powers whereby the US Supreme Court supplemented the powers of the federal bodies in relation to those of the confederated States. The Advocate General, for his part, considered that Community powers should be regarded as 'conferred powers', thereby contrasting that notion with the concept of implied powers.[7]

---

[5] *Commission v. Council* (n 3 above), paras 2–5.   [6] Ibid, paras 6–11.   [7] Ibid, at 289–93.

The constitutional import of the case was thus clearly identified by the time the Court delivered its ruling. The Court's reasoning on the issue of competence consists of two parts. In the first part, the Court examined the question of principle.[8] It started by referring to (current) Article 281 EC which provided that 'the Community shall have legal personality'. This provision, placed at the head of the Treaty's 'General and Final Provisions', meant that in its external relations the Community enjoyed the capacity to establish contractual links with third countries over the whole field of objectives defined in Part One of the Treaty. To determine in a particular case the Community's authority to enter into international agreements, the Court continued, regard had to be had to the whole scheme of the Treaty no less than to its substantive provisions. Such authority arose not only from an express conferment by the Treaty—as was the case with the provisions on tariff and trade agreements and on association agreements—but could equally flow from other provisions of the Treaty and from measures adopted, within the framework of those provisions, by the Community institutions. The Court then specified this: each time the Community, with a view to implementing a common policy envisaged by the Treaty, adopted provisions laying down common rules, whatever form these might take, the Member States no longer had the right, acting individually or collectively, to undertake obligations with third countries which affected those rules. As and when such common rules came into being, the Community alone was in a position to assume and carry out contractual obligations towards third countries affecting the whole sphere of application of the Community legal system. The conclusion was that, with regard to implementation of the provisions of the Treaty, the system of internal Community measures could not be separated from that of external relations.

In the second part of its reasoning the Court applied these principles to the issues at hand.[9] It referred to (current) Article 3(f) EC, which mentions a common policy in the sphere of transport as one of the Community's objectives, and to (current) Article 10 EC, which defines the principle of Member State loyalty. If those provisions were read together, it followed that to the extent to which Community rules were promulgated for the attainment of the objectives of the Treaty, the Member States could not, outside the framework of the Community institutions, assume obligations which might affect those rules or alter their scope. The Court then analysed the Treaty provisions on transport, pointing out that under those provisions the Council could lay down 'any other appropriate provisions'. As regards the scope of the common transport policy, the Court referred to (current) Article 71(1)(a) EC, which speaks of 'international transport to or from the territory of a Member State or passing across the territory of one or more Member States'. This provision was equally concerned with transport from or to third countries, as regards that part of the journey which took place on Community territory. The provision thus assumed that the powers of the Community extended to relationships arising from international

---

[8] Ibid, paras 13–19.   [9] Ibid, paras 20–31.

law, and hence involved the need for agreements with third countries. The Court then looked at Regulation 543/69, whose bringing into force necessarily vested in the Community power to enter into agreements with third countries relating to the subject matter governed by that regulation, as was expressly recognized by Article 3 of the regulation.[10] Since the subject matter of the AETR fell within the scope of the regulation, the Community had been empowered to negotiate and conclude the agreement since the entry into force of the regulation. These Community powers excluded the possibility of concurrent powers on the part of Member States, since any steps taken outside the framework of the Community institutions would be incompatible with the unity of the common market and the uniform application of Community law.

Thus, much like in its first major ruling on the Community's powers under the common commercial policy,[11] the Court not only confirmed external competence but also characterized it as being exclusive. However, and again much as with decisions on the scope of the common commercial policy, the reader must be urged to read the full judgment. The Court, after having thus resolved the 'initial question' with which it was confronted, decided that the Commission's action was admissible, since the Council proceedings constituted an act having legal effects. On the substance, however, the Court rejected the Commission's claim for annulment of the proceedings. Essentially, the Court considered that the AETR negotiations were a mere continuation of the earlier negotiations which in 1962 had resulted in an agreement which could not be ratified. At that time, power to conclude this agreement was still vested in the Member States, because the common transport policy was not yet sufficiently developed and Regulation 543/69 had not yet been adopted. To have suggested to the third countries involved that there was a new distribution of powers might have jeopardized the successful outcome of the negotiations. The Court thus accepted that it was appropriate for the Member States to carry on negotiating, and that the Community's interests were safeguarded through the common position which the Council had adopted and which the Member States would defend in the negotiations.[12]

The Court was thus both principled and pragmatic. On the issues of principle, it is questionable whether the Advocate General's stark contrast between conferred and implied powers was convincing. One of the main themes of this chapter is that it is useful and appropriate to distinguish between the Community's external powers in substantive terms, i.e. in terms of pursuing an external policy in a particular domain, and the Community's power to conclude international agreements in areas where the Treaty does not expressly provide for such agreements. If one makes that distinction, and applies it to an analysis of the *AETR* judgment, it will be seen that the Court was not guilty of effecting through judicial interpretation a significant

---

[10] Art 3 provided: 'The Community shall enter into any negotiations with third countries which may prove necessary for the purpose of implementing this regulation'.

[11] *Opinion 1/75 re Understanding on a Local Cost Standard* [1975] ECR 1355; see Ch 2.

[12] *Commission v. Council* (n 3 above), paras 81–91.

expansion of the Community's powers. In substantive terms, the Court was very careful and no doubt correct to point out that the common transport policy extends to transport from or to third countries, as regards the part of the journey which takes place on Community territory.[13] Also, the actual subject matter of the AETR agreement, working conditions of crews of vehicles engaged in road transport, clearly came within the Community's lawmaking powers, as was confirmed by the adoption of Regulation 543/69. Where the *AETR* judgment was innovative was in its recognition of the power to conclude an international agreement in the absence of an express recognition of such power. Yet here again the analysis was not without foundation in the text of the Treaty. (Current) Article 71 EC does permit the Council to adopt 'any other appropriate provisions', and (current) Article 300 EC does recognize that the Community may conclude international agreements. In fact, if the Court had decided differently, it could only have based itself on a strict interpretation of the principle of conferred powers, and it would have had to disregard both the fact that the subject matter of the AETR agreement came within Community competence and the fact that the Treaty provisions on a common transport policy were imprecise in terms of defining the legal instruments which could be employed. It is doubtful whether such a strict interpretation of the principle of conferred powers would have been justified, also because this principle was nowhere precisely defined in the Treaty. The only reference to it was in (current) Article 7(1) EC which provides that each institution shall act within the limits of the powers conferred upon it by the Treaty. It is not obvious that this provision was ever intended to govern the division of powers between the Community and the Member States. Later on, the TEU inserted what is currently Article 5 EC into the Treaty, whose first sentence provides that 'the Community shall act within the limits of the powers conferred upon it by this Treaty and of the objectives assigned to it therein'. Here the juxtaposition of powers and objectives chimes rather well with the Court's analysis in the *AETR* judgment, where it emphasized the objective of establishing a common transport policy.

As regards the exclusive nature of the Community's competence it is clear from the judgment that this was only a consequence of the adoption of Regulation 543/69, which covered the same subject matter as the AETR agreement. If there had been no such regulation, the Court would no doubt have confirmed concurrent competence. Indeed, that was its ultimate conclusion, based on the fact that the regulation was not yet in force at the time of the adoption of the first version of the AETR agreement.

The crucial language on exclusive competence is that the Member States have no right to enter into international commitments which might affect or alter the scope of 'internal' Community rules. In all likelihood the Court's concern was that, in the absence of exclusive competence, the Member States might, advertently or

---

[13] Dashwood and Helikoski (n 1 above), at 8, refer to the *effet utile* of the Treaty provisions on transport policy.

inadvertently, conclude international agreements whose provisions conflict with
Community law. Member States would then be facing conflicting obligations.
From a strictly legal perspective, the Community law reply to such conflicts could
be to confirm the primacy of Community rules, to which the Member States would
have to give precedence in their internal legal orders, and to leave possible problems
at international level for the Member States themselves to resolve. Apparently, however, the Court was of the opinion that prevention of such conflicts was preferable
to later resolution. Also, from a transfer-of-powers perspective it makes sense to
regard the Community's powers as being exclusive once Community rules in a particular area have been adopted, exclusive in terms of both internal and international
lawmaking. In this respect, the *AETR* judgment has its parallels in the Court's case
law on the effect of Community legislation (through what is often referred to as
occupying the field, or pre-emption) on the powers of the Member States to adopt
internal legislation.[14]

The parallelism approach of *Opinion 1/76*

Some years later the Court handed down a new judgment on implied powers, this
time on a reference from a court in the Netherlands. *Kramer* concerned the North-
East Atlantic Fisheries Convention, an international agreement aimed at ensuring
the conservation of fish stocks in the North-East Atlantic Ocean.[15] All the Member
States except Italy and Luxemburg were parties to that agreement. Pursuant to a
decision which had been taken within the framework of this convention the
Netherlands authorities took measures to restrict catches of sole and plaice. A number of Netherlands fisherman were prosecuted for failing to observe those restrictions, and in their defence they claimed that the Netherlands no longer had the
power to participate in the operation of the convention because that power
belonged exclusively to the Community.

The judgment is comparable to that in the *AETR* case. The Court recalled the
general principles identified in that case, and then examined the Community's competence to act in the field of fish conservation measures. It referred to the Treaty
provisions on the common agricultural policy; to Council Regulations 2141/70
and 2142/70, respectively laying down a common structural policy for the fishing
industry and on the common organization of the market in fishery products;[16] and
to Article 102 of the Act of Accession,[17] which instructed the Council to 'determine conditions for fishing with a view to ensuring protection of the fishing grounds
and conservation of the biological resources of the sea'. The Court considered that

---

[14] See K Lenaerts, 'Les répercussions des compétences de la Communauté européenne sur les compétences externes des Etats membres et la question de "preemption"', in Demaret (n 1 above), 447–72.
[15] Joined Cases 3, 4, and 6/76 *Kramer* [1976] ECR 1279.
[16] [1970] OJ Spec Ed III 703 and 707.
[17] The Act was on the accession of Denmark, Ireland, and the United Kingdom.

it followed from those provisions taken as a whole that the Community had at its disposal, on the internal level, the power to take any measures for the conservation of the biological resources of the sea. It further followed from those provisions, and from the very nature of things, that the rule-making authority of the Community *ratione materiae* also extended—in so far as the Member States had similar authority under public international law—to fishing on the high seas. The only way to ensure the conservation of the biological resources of the sea both effectively and equitably was through a system of rules binding on all the States concerned, including non-member countries. In these circumstances it followed from the very duties and powers which Community law had established and assigned to the institutions of the Community on the internal level that the Community had authority to enter into international commitments for the conservation of the resources of the sea.[18]

Such EC power did not however mean that the Netherlands no longer had the authority to adopt conservation measures. The Court pointed out that at the time of the facts the Community had not yet fully exercised its functions in the matter. The Member States could thus continue to act, provided they did not hinder the Community in carrying out its tasks. They were also under a duty, together with the Community institutions, to use, when the Community decided to start implementing its duties, all political and legal means at their disposal in order to ensure the participation of the Community in the Convention and in other similar agreements.[19]

The Court's judgment needs to be seen in the light of its later case law on the Community's powers as regards fish conservation. Indeed, in the 1981 *Commission v. United Kingdom* case the Court examined the effect of the expiry on 1 January 1979 of the transitional period of Article 102 of the Act of Accession. It held that, since then, the power to adopt, as part of the common fisheries policy, measures relating to the conservation of the resources of the sea had 'belonged fully and definitively to the Community'. Member States were therefore no longer entitled to exercise any power of their own in the matter of conservation measures in the waters under their jurisdiction.[20] In other words, the Community's competence had become exclusive.

The *Kramer* judgment is comparable to the *AETR* case in the sense that the power to conclude international agreements in the field in question was based not only on the relevant Treaty provisions (including the Act of Accession, which has Treaty status) but also on Community legislation. Again one can distinguish between substantive competence and power to conclude agreements. As regards substantive external competence, the Court carefully analysed the relevant provisions of Community law to conclude that such power extended to fishing on the high seas, and was not limited to fishing in the Member States' territorial waters. As regards power to conclude agreements, the Court then rightly indicated that the only way to ensure conservation was through an international system, involving also

---

[18] *Kramer* (n 15 above), paras 21–33.   [19] Ibid, paras 34–45.
[20] Case 804/79 *Commission v. United Kingdom* [1981] ECR 1045, paras 17–18.

non-member countries. Indeed it is difficult to see how fish conservation could ever work in the absence of multilateral treaties and conventions, and in that sense the Community's substantive competence to ensure conservation effectively required that it should also have the power to take part in such international lawmaking.

The further question, whether implied power to conclude agreements is also present in the absence of internal Community legislation covering the same subject matter, was considered by the Court in *Opinion 1/76*.[21] That Opinion concerned a draft Agreement establishing a European laying-up fund for inland waterway vessels. The agreement had been negotiated between the Commission, acting on behalf of the Community, and Switzerland, with the participation of six Member States which were parties to certain conventions on navigation of the Rhine and the Moselle. The objective of the agreement was to introduce a system intended to eliminate the disturbances arising from the surplus transport capacity for goods by inland waterways in the Rhine and Moselle basins and by all the Netherlands and German inland waterways linked to the Rhine basin. The system consisted of formulating an arrangement for the temporary laying-up of capacity in return for financial compensation. A fund was to be responsible for compensation and was to be financed by contributions imposed on all vessels using the inland waterways which were to be subject to the system. The Commission requested the Court's Opinion on the compatibility of the draft Agreement with the Treaty because the sytem envisaged involved for the Community a certain delegation of powers of decision and judicial powers to independent bodies. The Commission also asked for clarification of the Community's competence to conclude the Agreement.

The Court started its analysis by pointing out that the object of the draft Agreement was to rationalize the economic situation of the inland waterway transport industry in a geographical region in which transport by inland waterway was of special importance within the whole network of international transport. Such a system was doubtless an important factor in the common transport policy, the establishment of which was included in the activities of the Community laid down in Article 3 of the Treaty. In order to implement this policy, (current) Article 71 EC instructed the Council to lay down common rules applicable to international transport to or from the territory of one or more Member States. This article also supplied, as regards the Community, the necessary legal basis to establish the system concerned. In the case of the draft Agreement, however, it was impossible fully to attain the objective pursued by means of the establishment of common rules pursuant to Article 71, because of the traditional participation of vessels from a third State, Switzerland, in navigation by the principal waterways in question, which were subject to the system of freedom of navigation established by international agreements of long standing. It had thus been necessary to bring Switzerland into the scheme in question by means of an international agreement with this third State.[22]

---

[21] *Opinion 1/76 re Inland Waterways* [1977] ECR 741.   [22] Ibid, paras 1–2.

The Court then conceded that the power to conclude such an agreement was not expressly laid down in the Treaty. However, it recalled that it had already had occasion to state, most recently in *Kramer*,[23] that authority to enter into international commitments could not only arise from an express attribution by the Treaty, but could equally flow implicitly from its provisions. The Court had concluded *inter alia* that whenever Community law had created for the institutions of the Community powers within its internal system for the purpose of attaining a specific objective, the Community had authority to enter into the international commitments necessary for the attainment of that objective even in the absence of an express provision in that connection. This was particularly so in all cases in which internal power had already been used in order to adopt measures which came within the attainment of common policies. It was, however, not limited to that eventuality. Although the internal Community measures were adopted only when the international agreement was concluded and made enforceable, as was envisaged in the case in question by the proposal for a regulation to be submitted to the Council by the Commission, the power to bind the Community *vis-à-vis* third countries nevertheless flowed by implication from the provisions of the Treaty creating the internal power and in so far as the participation of the Community in the international agreement was, as here, necessary for the attainment of one of the objectives of the Community.[24]

Opinion 1/76 confirmed that there is no requirement of prior internal Community legislation for the exercise of external competence. In later cases and analyses of the Opinion reference has occasionally been made to the Court's statement on internal Community measures only being adopted when the international agreement is concluded and made enforceable. One should see that statement in its context. When the Commission requested the Court's Opinion it had already prepared a proposal for a Council regulation which would, at the same time, conclude the agreement, and implement it through the adoption of internal rules. That is currently no longer the practice of the Community institutions: agreements are concluded by way of Council decision, and any implementing legislation which may be required is adopted by way of a separate act.[25] Whether any implementing legislation is necessary depends on the purport and provisions of the agreement in question, and such legislation is no precondition for the exercise of external competence, which is directly based on the Treaty provisions.

There is a second element in the Court's reasoning which attracted further discussion. The Court twice speaks of the Community's participation in the agreement being 'necessary' for the attainment of the Treaty's objectives. As will be seen, the Commission would rely on this term for the purpose of arguing that the Community had exclusive competence to conclude the WTO Agreement.[26] There will be further scope for discussing the meaning of that term below.

---

[23] *Kramer* (n 15 above).   [24] *Opinion 1/76* (n 21 above), paras 3–4.   [25] See Ch 6.
[26] See the section on *Opinion 1/94*.

A third point of debate on the meaning of the Opinion is whether it established exclusive Community competence to conclude the draft Agreement. Again, this will be further discussed when analysing *Opinion 1/94*, but some comments must none the less be made at this stage. The Court's reasoning as set out above made no reference to exclusive competence. However, the Court did look in the Opinion at what it called 'a special problem' arising because the draft Agreement provided for the participation as contracting parties not only of the Community and Switzerland but also of six Member States (out of nine). Those Member States were parties to two older international conventions, which they undertook to modify in implementation of the draft Agreement. The Court considered that this particular undertaking, given in view of the second paragraph of (current) Article 307 EC,[27] explained and justified the participation of those six States, which had to be considered as being solely for this purpose and not as necessary for the attainment of other features of the system. The Court also pointed out that, except for this special undertaking, the legal effects of the Agreement with regard to the Member States resulted, in accordance with (current) Article 300(7) EC, exclusively from the conclusion by the Community. In those circumstances, the participation of the six Member States was not such as to encroach on the external power of the Community. There was therefore no occasion to conclude that this aspect of the draft Agreement was incompatible with the Treaty.[28]

Clearly, the Court was of the opinion that a particular justification was required for the participation as contracting parties of six Member States. Does that mean that, in principle, the Court regarded the Community's competence to conclude the draft Agreement as exclusive? It cannot be denied that this is a possible reading of the Opinion, but it is not persuasive.[29] First, the Court did not use any language referring to exclusive Community powers. It looked at the issue of participation by Member States as a 'special problem', which it addressed after having established the principle of Community competence. Secondly, in the *AETR* case the Court had clearly established that exclusive implied powers result from internal legislation, which may be affected or whose scope may be altered by the agreement. In the absence of such legislation, the Court had regarded the Community's power to conclude agreements in the sphere of transport as concurrent with the powers of the Member States. If the Court sought to modify that principle in *Opinion 1/76*, one could have expected it to be clearer in that respect. Thirdly, the Court has always regarded the Community's competence to develop a common transport policy as concurrent with the competence of the Member States.[30] It is difficult to see how,

---

[27] Art 307 concerns international agreements concluded by Member States before membership. The second paragraph provides: 'To the extent that such agreements are not compatible with this Treaty, the Member State or States concerned shall take all appropriate steps to eliminate the incompatibilities established. Member States shall, where necessary, assist each other to this end and shall, where appropriate, adopt a common attitude'.   [28] *Opinion 1/76* (n 21 above), paras 6–7.

[29] Cf Dashwood and Helikoski (n 1 above), 13–14; J Helikoski, *Mixed Agreements as a Technique for Organizing the International Relations of the European Community and its Member States* (Kluwer Law International, 2001) 43–4.   [30] Ibid, 13.

if internal legislative competence in transport matters is not exclusive, the Member States could have lost the power to conclude international agreements in this area.

There is an alternative reading of this passage in *Opinion 1/76*. That reading concentrates on the exercise of Community competence rather than on the nature of that competence, exclusive or concurrent, as a matter of principle. What the Court may have observed in *Opinion 1/76* is that, once the decision to exercise Community competence by way of concluding an international agreement is taken, participation by the Member States as contracting parties is permissible only if some parts or provisions of the agreement are not covered by Community competence at all.[31] That does not mean that the Community's competence is exclusive, for if the Community decides not to exercise it, the Member States retain their full powers.

Opinion 1/76 was generally regarded as establishing parallelism between the Community's internal and external powers.[32] That view may be correct, provided one bears in mind the distinction between substantive competence and the power to conclude agreements. Again, the Court did not in the Opinion broaden the competence of the Community in transport matters in substantive terms. The object of the agreement, i.e. rationalizing the inland waterway transport sector as operating in the Rhine and Moselle basins, clearly came within the Community's powers in matters of transport. What the Court recognized was simply the power of the Community to achieve such rationalization through an international agreement rather than through the mere adoption of internal legislation.

The clarity of *Opinion 2/91*

The Court had the opportunity to bring together and further clarify the various principles of external competence in an Opinion on a draft convention which had been negotiated in the ILO. The Community is not a member of the ILO, but has observer status. Apparently that creates a number of problems when conventions are negotiated in the ILO concerning matters covered by Community law. The Community institutions and the Member States have tried to find some *modus vivendi* which should enable the Community's position, where relevant, to be voiced and defended. A dispute arose however over the respective roles of the Community and the Member States in the adoption and implementation of Convention No 170 concerning safety in the use of chemicals at work. Following the adoption of that convention by the ILO Conference, the Commission wrote to the Council stating its view that the Member States were under an obligation to inform the Director-General of the International Labour Office that the competent authorities, within

---

[31] CWA Timmermans, 'Division of External Powers between Community and Member States in the Field of Harmonization of National Law—A Case Study', in CWA Timmermans and ELM Völker (eds), *Division of powers between the European Communities and their Member States in the Field of External Relations* (Kluwer, 1981) 20.

[32] J Groux, 'Le parallèlisme des compétences internes et externes de la Communauté économique européenne' (1978) 14 CDE 1; Dashwood and Helikoski (n 1 above), 12.

the meaning of Article 19(5)(c) of the ILO Constitution,[33] were in this case the Community institutions. Several Member States indicated their refusal to accept that the Community had exclusive competence to conclude the convention. The Commission then sought the Opinion of the Court of Justice, particularly as regards the Community's competence to conclude the convention and the consequences which this would have for the Member States.[34]

This was again a case in which the questions of principle were more important than any specific practical outcome. Indeed, the German and Netherlands governments argued before the Court that the request was inadmissible, because the Community could not itself conclude the agreement, as it was not a member of the ILO; they were referring to the rule that only ILO members can ratify ILO conventions.[35] The Court brushed this objection aside, by stating that the request for an Opinion did not concern the Community's capacity, on the international plane, to enter into an ILO convention, but related to the scope of the competence of the Community and the Member States within the area covered by Convention No 170. It was not for the Court to assess any obstacles which the Community could encounter in the exercise of its competence. In any event, its external competence could, if necessary, be exercised through the medium of the Member States acting jointly in the Community's interest.[36]

The most useful dimension of *Opinion 2/91* is that the Court started its analysis by setting out the principles of external competence.[37] It reasoned as follows. It first pointed out that, as it had stated in *Opinion 1/76*,[38] authority to enter into international commitments could not only arise from an express attribution by the Treaty, but could also flow implicitly from its provisions. There the Court had concluded, in particular, that whenever Community law created for the institutions of the Community powers within its internal system for the purpose of attaining a specific objective, the Community had authority to enter into the international commitments necessary for the attainment of that objective even in the absence of an express provision in that connection. In *Kramer*[39] the Court had already pointed out that such authority could flow by implication from other measures adopted by the Community institutions within the framework of the Treaty provisions or the acts of accession.[40]

Having thus recalled the principles of express and implied powers to 'enter into international commitments', the Court turned to the nature of the Community's external competence, exclusive or concurrent. It stated that the exclusive nature of the Community's competence had been recognized with respect to Article 113

---

[33] Art 19(5)(c) provides: 'Members shall inform the Director-General of the International Labour Office of the measures taken in accordance with this article to bring the Convention before the said competent authority or authorities, with particulars of the authority or authorities regarded as competent, and of the action taken by them'.

[34] *Opinion 2/91 re ILO Convention No 170* [1993] ECR I–1061.

[35] See Art 19(5)(d) ILO Constitution.   [36] *Opinion 2/91* (n 34 above), paras 1–6.

[37] Dashwood and Helikoski (n 1 above), 15.   [38] *Opinion 1/76* (n 21 above).

[39] *Kramer* (n 15 above).   [40] *Opinion 2/91* (n 34 above), para 7.

(*Opinion 1/75*)[41] and to Article 102 of the Act of Accession (*Commission v. United Kingdom*).[42] It followed from that line of authority that the existence of such competence arising from a Treaty provision excluded any competence on the part of Member States which was concurrent with that of the Community, in the Community sphere and in the international sphere.[43] The Court thus recalled that exclusive competence which is based on the Treaty covers both internal lawmaking and the conclusion of international agreements.

The Court then turned to exclusive implied powers. It stated that the exclusive or non-exclusive nature of the Community's competence did not flow solely from the provisions of the Treaty but could also depend on the scope of the measures which had been adopted by the Community institutions for the application of those provisions and which were of such a kind as to deprive the Member States of an area of competence which they were able to exercise previously on a transitional basis. As the Court had stated in the *AETR* case,[44] where Community rules had been promulgated for the attainment of the objectives of the Treaty, the Member States could not, outside the framework of the Community institutions, assume obligations which might affect those rules or alter their scope. Contrary to the contentions of a number of governments, the authority of the decision in that case could not be restricted to instances where the Community had adopted Community rules within the framework of a common policy (the argument by these governments was that the *AETR* principle was limited to what were nominally 'common policies' according to the Treaty, such as the common transport policy). In all the areas corresponding to the objectives of the Treaty, the Court continued, (current) Article 10 EC required Member States to facilitate the achievement of the Community's tasks and to abstain from any measure which could jeopardize the attainment of the objectives of the Treaty. The Community's tasks and the objectives of the Treaty would also be compromised if Member States were able to enter into international commitments containing rules capable of affecting rules already adopted in areas falling outside common policies or of altering their scope.[45]

The Court thus recalled the scope of exclusive implied powers as well as their rationale, which is based on the principle of Member State loyalty. Much of the remainder of the Opinion was devoted to determining whether, and, if so, to what extent, there was Community legislation which could be affected or whose scope could be altered by Convention No 170. It is here too that the Opinion is helpful and clarifies the law. But before engaging in that examination the Court stated a final principle of external competence: an agreement could be concluded in an area where competence was shared between the Community and the Member States. In such a case, negotiation and implementation of the agreement required joint action by the Community and the Member States.[46]

---

[41] *Opinion 1/75* (n 11 above).   [42] *Commission v. United Kingdom* (n 20 above).
[43] *Opinion 2/91* (n 34 above), para 8.   [44] *Commission v. Council* (n 3 above).
[45] *Opinion 2/91* (n 34 above), paras 9–11.   [46] Ibid, para 12.

The Court then applied the above principles. It recalled that Convention No 170 concerned safety in the use of chemicals at work and that its essential objective, according to its preamble, was to prevent or reduce the incidence of chemically induced illnesses and injuries at work by ensuring that all chemicals were evaluated to determine their hazards, by providing employers and workers with the information necessary for their protection, and, finally, by establishing principles for protective programmes. The field covered by Convention No 170 thus fell within the 'social provisions' of the EEC Treaty. Under Article 118a EEC,[47] Member States were required to pay particular attention to encouraging improvements, especially in the working environment, as regards the health and safety of workers, and to set as their objective the harmonization of conditions in this area. In order to help achieve this objective, the Council had the power to adopt minimum requirements by means of directives. It followed from Article 118a(3) that the provisions adopted pursuant to that article were not to prevent any Member State from maintaining or introducing more stringent measures for the protection of working conditions compatible with the Treaty. The Community thus enjoyed an internal legislative competence in the area of social policy. Consequently, Convention No 170, whose subject matter coincided, moreover, with that of several directives adopted under Article 118a, fell within the Community's area of competence.[48]

It may be noted here that the Court again had no difficulty whatsoever in confirming that, in an area where the Community has the power to adopt internal legislation, it also has the power to conclude international agreements. This was so notwithstanding the fact that, at the time, Community competence for health and safety of workers was defined in subsidiary terms. Article 118a EEC referred to the Member States (not the Community) encouraging improvements in health and safety, instructed the Council 'to help achieve the objective' through the adoption of directives, and left intact the power of Member States to adopt more stringent provisions. Yet this subsidiary character of Community competence was not an obstacle for the recognition of treaty-making power.

The Court then examined whether Community competence was exclusive. It pointed out that the provisions of Convention No 170 were not of such a kind as to affect rules adopted pursuant to Article 118a. If, on the one hand, the Community decided to adopt rules which were less stringent than those set out in an ILO convention, Member States could, in accordance with Article 118a(3), adopt more stringent measures or apply for that purpose the relevant ILO convention. If, on the other hand, the Community decided to adopt more stringent measures, there was nothing to prevent the full application of Community law by the Member States under Article 19(8) of the ILO Constitution, which allowed Members to adopt more stringent measures than those provided for in conventions or recommendations adopted by that organization.[49]

---

[47] The provisions of Art 118a EEC are now part, with amendments, of Art 137 EC.
[48] *Opinion 2/91* (n 34 above), paras 14–17.   [49] Ibid, para 18.

The Court was faced here with a rather unique situation, in which, notwithstanding the fact that the international agreement covered the same subject matter as Community legislation, there was no exclusive competence, because both the agreement and the Community legislation allowed for the adoption of more stringent provisions. The tenor of the Court's reasoning is that, in light of that state of affairs, conflicts between the provisions of the convention and those of the Community directives were excluded. One should not however deduce from this reasoning that actual conflicts between Community norms and the provisions of an international agreement are required to vest exclusive competence in the Community.[50] The question of competence in principle arises even before an agreement is negotiated, for one needs to know which authority has power to negotiate. The precise provisions resulting from the negotiation are still unknown at that point, so it will be impossible to establish whether there is conflict or not. The rationale is rather that, where the agreement covers the same subject matter as Community legislation, the Community needs to negotiate so as to avoid conflict, or, alternatively, so as to be persuaded that new rules need to be adopted at international level which may require amendment of existing Community legislation. In the case of Convention No 170, however, no such rationale was present, because of the character of minimum rules of both the Community directives and the provisions of the Convention.

In its submissions in *Opinion 2/91* the Commission had argued that it was sometimes difficult to determine whether a specific measure was more favourable to workers than another, and that Member States might be tempted, in order not to be in breach of an ILO convention, not to adopt provisions better suited to the social and technological conditions specific to the Community. The Court did not accept that argument. It stated that such difficulties, which might arise for the legislative function of the Community, could not constitute the basis for exclusive Community competence.[51]

However, the Court then went on to look at a number of EEC directives, concerning classification, packaging, and labelling of dangerous substances and preparations,[52] which had been adopted pursuant to Articles 100 and 100a EEC (current Articles 94 and 95 EC). The Court compared the provisions of those directives with the provisions of Convention No 170. It concluded that, while there was no contradiction between the provisions of the convention and those of the directives, it nevertheless had to be accepted that Part III of the convention was concerned with an area which was already covered to a large extent by Community rules progressively adopted since 1967 with a view to achieving an ever greater degree of harmonization. In those circumstances, it had to be considered that the commitments arising from Part III of the convention were of such a kind as to affect the Community rules laid down in those directives and that consequently Member

---

[50] See the section below on air transport cases.   [51] *Opinion 2/91* (n 34 above), paras 19–20.
[52] Council Directive 67/548 [1967] OJ Spec Ed 234 and Directive 88/379 [1988] OJ L187/14.

States could not undertake such commitments outside the framework of the Community institutions.[53]

In the penultimate section of the Opinion on the question of competence, the Court looked at the provisions of the convention on implementation. It held that, in so far as it had been established that the substantive provisions of the convention came within the Community's sphere of competence, the Community was also competent to undertake commitments for putting those provisions into effect. It was no obstacle that such implementation required consultation of representative organizations of employers and workers. The Court admitted that co-operation between both sides of industry was a matter falling predominantly within the competence of the Member States, yet it was not entirely withdrawn from the Community's competence: under Article 118b EEC the Commission was required to endeavour to develop the dialogue between management and labour at European level.[54] As regards, further, the implementation of the convention in terms of supervision, again it was no problem that the competent authorities supervising the use of hazardous chemicals were authorities at the level of the Member States: just as, for internal purposes, the Community could provide, in an area covered by Community rules, that national authorities were to be given certain supervisory powers, it could also, for external purposes, undertake commitments designed to ensure compliance with substantive provisions which fell within its competence and implied the attribution of certain supervisory powers to national authorities.[55]

Lastly, the Court accepted that the substantive scope of the convention lay outside the scope of the association scheme for overseas countries and territories (see Articles 182–188 EC), and that consequently it was for the Member States which were responsible for the international relations of those territories and which represented them in that regard to conclude the convention.[56] The Court's overall conclusion was that Convention No 170 came within the joint competence of the Member States and the Community.[57]

The meanderings of *Opinion 1/94*

In Chapter 2 we looked extensively at the GATT Uruguay Round negotiations, resulting in the WTO Agreement, and at *Opinion 1/94* in so far as that Opinion analysed Community competence under Article 113 EC (now Article 133 EC).[58] The reader is referred to those pages for the background to the Opinion. Again the purpose of the Commission's request was to establish exclusive Community competence. The Commission did not confine its arguments to the common commercial

---

[53] *Opinion 2/91* (n 34 above), paras 22–26.
[54] The current provisions of the EC Treaty on such dialogue are much more advanced, see Arts 138 and 139 EC.   [55] *Opinion 2/91* (n 34 above), paras 27–34.
[56] Ibid, para 35.   [57] Ibid, para 39.
[58] *Opinion 1/94 re WTO Agreement* [1994] ECR I–5267.

policy, even if the relevant Treaty provisions offered the most credible basis for the Commission's claim. It also submitted, in a subsidiary argument, that implied powers under other Treaty provisions fully covered the various WTO agreements and that those powers were exclusive of those of the Member States. With respect, that argument had little if any basis in the Court's previous case law, and the Commission's lawyers must have been aware of this. The Court did not go along, and the result, in this author's view, is an Opinion which, in an attempt to defuse arguments which were difficult to understand, does not contribute much to clarifying the law on implied powers.

As the Court accepted that the WTO agreements on trade in goods came within the Community's exclusive competence to develop a common commercial policy, there was no need to consider implied powers in that regard. The Court's analysis concentrated on trade in services (GATS) and intellectual property rights (TRIPs).[59]

GATS

As regards GATS, the Commission's first of three arguments was that there was no area or specific provision in GATS in respect of which the Community did not have corresponding powers to adopt measures at internal level; powers as set out in the Treaty chapters on right of establishment, freedom to provide services, and transport. In the Commission's view exclusive external competence flowed from those internal powers.[60]

In its reply, the Court first referred to transport, and recalled the *AETR* judgment;[61] it accepted that there was external competence but rejected the claim of exclusivity. The Court stated that it was only in so far as common rules had been established at internal level that the external competence of the Community became exclusive. However, not all transport matters were already covered by common rules. The Court also rejected the Commission's argument that the Member States' continuing freedom to conduct an external transport policy would inevitably lead to distortions in the flow of services and would progressively undermine the internal market. It observed that there was nothing in the Treaty which prevented the institutions from arranging concerted action in relation to non-member countries or from prescribing the approach to be taken by the Member States in their external dealings.[62] As a comment, it may be noted that the Commission's argument here was more relevant to the scope of the common commercial policy than to implied powers. The avoidance of distortion of competition in the internal market is a strong justification for a common commercial policy, but the Court did not devote any attention to it in *Opinion 1/94*.[63]

---

[59] See also N Neuwahl, 'The WTO Opinion and Implied External Powers of the Community—A Hidden Agenda?', in A Dashwood and C Hillion (eds), *The General Law of EC External Relations* (Sweet & Maxwell, 2000) 139–51.   [60] *Opinion 1/94* (n 58 above), para 74.

[61] *Commission v. Council* (n 3 above).   [62] *Opinion 1/94* (n 58 above), paras 76–79.

[63] See Ch 2.

The Court then turned to services other than transport. It pointed out that, unlike the chapter on transport, the chapters on the right of establishment and on freedom to provide services did not contain any provision expressly extending the competence of the Community to 'relationships arising from international law'. As had rightly been observed by the Council and most of the Member States which had submitted observations, the sole objective of those chapters was to secure the right of establishment and freedom to provide services for nationals of Member States. They contained no provisions on the problem of the first establishment of nationals of non-member countries and the rules governing their access to self-employed activities. One could not therefore infer from those chapters that the Community had exclusive competence to conclude an agreement with non-member countries to liberalize first establishment and access to service markets, other than those which were the subject of cross-border supplies within the meaning of GATS, which were covered by Article 113 EEC.[64]

This is one of the most significant paragraphs of *Opinion 1/94* and, unfortunately, it contains one turn of phrase which is deceptive. The Court refers to, and puts between quotation marks, 'relationships arising from international law',[65] which may be seen as hinting at the conclusion of international agreements. It is a quotation taken from paragraph 27 of the *AETR* judgment, where this turn of phrase concluded the Court's analysis of the substantive scope of 'external' Community competence: the part where the Court considered that the Treaty rules on the common transport policy extended to international transport to or from third countries, in so far as the transport takes place on Community territory. Similarly, here in *Opinion 1/94* the Court is not so much concerned with the power to conclude international agreements as with the question whether the Treaty chapters on right of establishment and freedom to provide services have a substantive external dimension. Do those chapters extend to first establishment, in the Community, by nationals of non-member countries?[66] Do they cover access by nationals of non-member countries to service markets and to self-employed activities within the EU? For that is the substantive scope of GATS. From the perspective of the Community and the Member States, the GATS deals with access to service markets by and national treatment of service suppliers from non-member countries. As the Court rightly pointed out, however, that is not the scope of the relevant Treaty provisions, which concern the internal market, and extend only to nationals of Member States. It is therefore impossible to base an exclusive external competence on those provisions. Essentially, the Court observes that, as regards services and establishment, the Treaty does not provide for an external dimension (with the exception of cross-border supplies of services), in contrast with goods, where the external dimension comes within the common commercial policy.

[64] *Opinion 1/94* (n 58 above), para 81.
[65] In the French version this is '*des relations relevant du droit international*', which could be translated just as much by relationships coming under international law.
[66] See on that question Y Loussouarn, 'Le droit d'établissement des sociétés' (1990) 26 RTDE 229–39.

The reference to 'relationships arising from international law' is deceptive because the Court is addressing competence in general here, arguably encompassing internal lawmaking just as much as the conclusion of international agreements. Much as the Community cannot claim exclusive competence to conclude agreements on first establishment and access to services markets, it could not claim exclusive competence to regulate those issues by way of Community directives and regulations. The Court does not expressly mention that, perhaps because it was not in issue, but it must be the correct reading to avoid an unworkable dichotomy between the Community's 'internal' and 'external' powers. Does that mean that the Community does not have any competence whatsoever to regulate the external dimension of the internal market in services? As we will see below, that is not the case, since there is some measure of Community competence.

The Commission's second implied powers argument in relation to GATS was based on a particular reading of *Opinion 1/76*.[67] The Commission argued that the Community's exclusive external competence was not confined to cases in which use had already been made of internal powers, but that, whenever Community law had conferred on the institutions internal powers for the purposes of attaining specific objectives, the international competence of the Community implicitly flowed from those provisions. It was enough that the Community's participation in the international agreement was necessary for the attainment of a Community objective. To show such necessity in the case of GATS (and TRIPs) the Commission put forward both internal and external reasons. At internal level, the coherence of the internal market would be impaired without such participation. At external level, the Community could not allow itself to remain inactive on the international stage: the need for the conclusion of the WTO Agreement was not in dispute.[68]

Rightly, the Court did not accept that reasoning, but its reply was not persuasive. It pointed out that the agreement in issue in *Opinion 1/76* was different from GATS, because in the case of the former it was impossible to achieve the objective of rationalization of the inland waterways sector in the Rhine and Moselle basins by the establishment of autonomous common rules, in light of the traditional participation of vessels from Switzerland in navigation on those waterways. It was therefore necessary to bring Switzerland into the scheme. The Court also referred to its case law on conservation of fish resources (see above), in which it had pointed out that restrictions of fishing on the high seas could hardly be effective in the absence of agreements. It was therefore understandable, the Court concluded, that external powers could be exercised, and thus become exclusive, without any internal legislation having first been adopted. That was not the situation in the sphere of services: attainment of freedom of establishment and freedom to provide services for nationals of the Member States was not inextricably linked to the treatment to be afforded in the Community to nationals of non-member countries or in non-member countries to nationals of Member States of the Community.[69]

---

[67] *Opinion 1/76* (n 21 above). [68] *Opinion 1/94* (n 58 above), paras 82–83.
[69] Ibid, paras 85–86.

That reasoning raises various questions. First, it is not clear why the Court felt compelled to examine an argument for exclusive competence when it had not yet established competence as such to begin with. Indeed, in the preceding part of the Opinion the Court stated that the Treaty provisions on right of establishment and freedom to provide services did not cover the subject matter of GATS. Secondly, it is also not clear why the Court referred to its fisheries case law, as there the relevant primary law provisions are interpreted as establishing exclusive Community competence. Thirdly, and most problematic, the Court appears to agree with the Commission's analysis that *Opinion 1/76* was a case of exclusive competence. Above it was argued that such a reading is unconvincing, and the Court does not here clarify the basis for exclusivity. One understands of course that the inland waterways agreement was indispensable if the Community decided to rationalize the transport sector concerned. But that does not make Community competence exclusive. One fails to see on what grounds such rationalization, as an element of transport policy, would be within the Community's exclusive powers when all other transport matters are not. Surely, as a matter of law the Community could have decided not to act in this regard, and to leave the relevant Member States to deal with the issues of excess capacity. It is also not clear what the Court means when it considers that 'it is understandable . . . that external powers may be exercised, and thus become exclusive, without any legislation having first been adopted'. Taken literally, the Court is addressing here the consequences of the exercise of external powers (they thus become exclusive), but that was not in issue. The question was whether, *a priori*, before its exercise either internally or externally, the Community's competence to conclude GATS was exclusive. A couple of paragraphs further down in the Opinion,[70] the Court restates the idea in the following terms: 'Save where internal powers can only be effectively exercised at the same time as external powers . . . , internal competence can give rise to exclusive external competence only if it is exercised'. But how can there be exclusive 'external' competence where the 'internal' competence is not exclusive? In an area where the powers of the Community and the Member States are generally concurrent (let us take environmental protection as an example), what could be the justification for considering that, if the Community's competence can only be exercised usefully through the conclusion of an international agreement, the competence to conclude such an agreement is exclusive? Suppose there is a political desire to protect the tropical rainforests. The Community on its own is clearly unable to provide for such protection through the mere adoption of internal legislation. But on what grounds should that be a justification for exclusive Community competence to conclude an international agreement on the subject? Surely, in the event that the Community does not act the Member States retain the power to conclude such an agreement, as they retain power over environmental protection generally in the absence of Community action. Of course, once the Community has acted in a particular field the Member States to some degree lose power. But, again, that was not in issue in *Opinion 1/94*.

[70] *Opinion 1/94* (n 58 above), para 89.

The Commission's third argument as regards implied powers was that (current) Articles 95 and 308 EC formed the basis for exclusive external competence, an argument if anything more difficult to understand than the two previous ones. The Court's reply to that argument clarified the extent of the Community's external powers in matters covered by GATS, and perhaps this part of the Court's reasoning should have preceded the rebuttal of the Commission's claim. As regards (current) Article 95 EC, the Court pointed out, it was undeniable that, where harmonizing powers had been exercised, the harmonization measures thus adopted could limit, or even remove, the freedom of the Member States to negotiate with non-member countries. However, an internal power which had not been exercised in a specific field could not confer exclusive external competence in that field on the Community. (Current) Article 308 EC, on the other hand, could not in itself vest exclusive competence in the Community at international level. Save where internal powers could only be effectively exercised at the same time as external powers (see comments above), internal competence could give rise to exclusive external competence only if it was exercised, and this applied *a fortiori* to Article 308.[71]

After having thus effectively restated the *AETR* principle, the Court further considered the extent of the Community's powers in matters covered by GATS. Whereas earlier in the Opinion the Court appeared to suggest that the Treaty chapters on services and establishment in no way extended to the treatment of non-nationals, it now qualified that approach. The Court stated that, although the only objective expressly mentioned in those chapters was the attainment of the freedoms in question for nationals of the Member States, it did not follow that the Community institutions were prohibited from using the powers conferred on them in that field in order to specify the treatment which was to be accorded to nationals of non-member countries. It then pointed to and discussed numerous Community acts which contained provisions to that effect, and found that very different objectives could be pursued by the incorporation of external provisions. The Court effectively accepted such practice, and concluded its description thereof by stating that, whenever the Community had included in its internal legislative acts provisions relating to the treatment of nationals of non-member countries or expressly conferred on its institutions powers to negotiate with non-member countries, it acquired exclusive competence in the spheres covered by those acts. The same applied in any event, the Court continued, even in the absence of any express provision authorizing its institutions to negotiate with non-member countries, where the Community had achieved complete harmonization of the rules governing access to a self-employed activity, because the common rules thus adopted could be affected within the meaning of the *AETR* judgment if the Member States retained freedom to negotiate with non-member countries. That was not the case in all services sectors, however, as the Commission had acknowledged. It followed that competence to conclude GATS was shared between the Community and the Member States.[72]

---

[71] Ibid, paras 87–89.   [72] Ibid, paras 90–98.

The Court was surely right in accepting that Community harmonization measures in the areas of establishment and services may have an external dimension. It does not make much sense to harmonize, for example, the legislation of the Member States concerning banking activities in the internal market without at the same time defining, at least to some extent, the treatment of non-Community banks seeking to establish themselves in the Community.[73] The Court therefore acknowledges that the Community's substantive competence as regards establishment and services extends to the treatment of nationals of non-member countries, in so far as this is connected with internal market harmonization.[74] It essentially leaves it to the Community's legislature to decide to what extent provisions to that effect are required. What is noteworthy is that, in this context, the Court also accepts that legislative provisions conferring on the Community external negotiating powers give rise to exclusive external competence. The EC legislature may, in other words, withdraw the competence to conclude international agreements from the Member States either by way of substantive regulation of a particular subject matter, or simply by stating that henceforth it will be for the Community to negotiate internationally.

Similarly, it is logical that once the rules on access to a particular self-employed activity are fully harmonized at Community level, the Member States have lost their freedom to conclude international agreements on access to that activity by nationals of non-member States.

TRIPs

As regards exclusive implied powers to conclude the TRIPs Agreement the Commission relied on the same type of arguments, i.e. the existence of internal legislative acts which could be affected in the meaning of *AETR*; the need to participate in the conclusion in order to achieve one of the objectives of the Treaty; and (current) Articles 95 and 308 of the Treaty. The Court was able to brush those arguments aside in a couple of paragraphs. First, it regarded the reference to *Opinion 1/76* just as disputable here as in the case of GATS, because unification or harmonization of intellectual property rights in the Community did not have to be accompanied by agreements with non-member countries in order to be effective. Secondly, (current) Articles 95 and 308 could not in themselves confer exclusive competence. Thirdly, harmonization within the Community in certain areas covered by TRIPs was only partial, and in other areas there was no harmonization whatsoever. Trade marks were an example of partial harmonization, whereas protection of undisclosed technical information, industrial designs, and patents were subjects

---

[73] For a description of the external dimension of the internal market in financial services at the time of the Opinion, see P Eeckhout, *The European Internal Market and International Trade—A Legal Analysis* (OUP, 1994) ch 2.

[74] A Dashwood, 'The Attribution of External Competence', in Dashwood and Hillion (n 1 above), 130.

where there was no harmonization. The *AETR* principle therefore did not apply to the whole of TRIPs.[75]

The Court could have concluded its analysis there, but it chose to highlight the reverse of the coin as well.[76] Some Member States had argued that the TRIPs provisions on effective protection of intellectual property rights fell within national competence. The Court however pointed out that, if that argument was to be understood as meaning that all those matters were within some sort of domain reserved to the Member States, it could not be accepted. The Community was certainly competent to harmonize national rules on those matters, in so far as, in the words of (current) Article 94 EC, they 'directly affect the establishment or functioning of the internal market'. But the fact remained that the Community institutions had not yet exercised their powers in the field of the 'enforcement of intellectual property rights', with the exception of Regulation 3842/86 laying down measures to prohibit the release for free circulation of counterfeit goods.[77] The Court thus recalled its settled case law that there are no *a priori* areas of exclusive Member State competence. Much as the Court is unwilling to confirm exclusive EC powers other than in certain well-defined areas, it also rejects claims for exclusive national competence.

In the literature *Opinion 1/94* is often characterized as embodying greater reluctance by the Court to confirm EC external competence, compared to earlier case law. It is regarded as signalling a new phase of judicial retrenchment.[78] As regards implied powers, however, it is doubtful whether that perception is justified. The Court left *AETR* and *Opinion 1/76* fully intact. It even accepted the claim, not obvious, that *Opinion 1/76* established exclusive competence. The Court also identified the novel principle that EC legislative acts may bring about exclusive external competence when they speak of the conclusion of international agreements by the Community. It applied the *AETR* principle in much the same way as in its previous case law; the pre-emption argument only extends to the precise and specific subject matter of the internal legislation. In fact, the Commission could have been successful with its implied-powers argument only if the Court had significantly expanded the scope of the relevant principles, or had accepted a new principle, such as a notion of political necessity which would determine exclusive external competence. If the Court had agreed with the Commission, certain external powers would have been exclusive where the corresponding internal competences were not.

As a matter of fact, the next ruling in which the Court addressed implied powers, *Opinion 2/94* on accession to the European Convention on Human Rights (ECHR), displayed far greater judicial restraint to confirm external powers.[79]

---

[75] *Opinion 1/94* (n 58 above), paras 99–103.   [76] Ibid, para 104.   [77] [1986] OJ L357/1.
[78] J de la Rochère, 'L'ère des compétences partagées' (1995) 390 RMCUE 466–8; JHJ Bourgeois, 'The EC in the WTO and Advisory Opinion 1/94: An Echternach Procession' (1995) 32 CMLRev 780–2; M Hilf, 'The ECJ's Opinion 1/94 on the WTO—No Surprise, but Wise?' (1995) 6 EJIL 254 and 258.
[79] The Court essentially repeated the implied powers reasoning of *Opinion 1/94* in *Opinion 2/92 re Third Revised Decision of the OECD on national treatment* [1995] ECR I–521.

The limits of *Opinion 2/94*

The question of the scope and nature of the EU's powers in the area of the protection of human rights is central to European constitutionalism. As the EU grows into an ever more full-blooded polity, with a correspondingly rich legal system, it gets involved in an increasing number of policy areas which may affect basic rights and entitlements of citizens and non-citizens, such as immigration, asylum, non-discrimination, criminal law. Such involvement requires a more intensified human rights discourse (or several competing human rights discourses). However, the constitutional basis for the development of such discourses has long been precarious. The Court of Justice has been compelled to 'discover' the protection of fundamental rights in the EC legal order through the construction of general principles of EC law, which include such rights. Those human rights in the form of general principles of EC law are derived from the constitutional traditions of the Member States, and from international human rights instruments to which the Member States are parties, in particular the ECHR. At the Maastricht intergovernmental conference the Member States, as masters of the Treaties, confirmed the jurisprudence in (current) Article 6(2) TEU.[80] In 2000 a special Convention elaborated a Charter of Fundamental Rights of the European Union, and the recent Convention on the Future of Europe proposed that the Charter be incorporated in the Constitution.

Human rights are not only ever more central to the EU's internal constitutional development; they are at least as vital for the EU's external action. A mere cursory glance at the Treaties confirms the importance of human rights for external policies. According to Article 11 TEU the objectives of the Common Foreign and Security Policy are *inter alia* 'to preserve peace and strengthen international security' and 'to develop and consolidate democracy and the rule of law, and respect for human rights and fundamental freedoms'.[81] If one reflects on the number of trouble-spots in this world from the perspective of democracy and protection of human rights, Article 11 clearly sets a broad and important agenda for the EU's external action. When one turns to the EC Treaty, it is true that the provisions on commercial policy, the EEC's first external policy, do not refer to human rights, but the more recently drafted articles on development co-operation again confirm the central position of human rights. Article 177(2) EC boldly states that 'Community policy in this area shall contribute to the general objective of developing and consolidating democracy and the rule of law, and to that of respecting human rights and fundamental freedoms'.[82] On this constitutional basis the EU is developing a strong external human rights policy. Agreements with non-member countries are now as

---

[80] 'The Union shall respect fundamental rights, as guaranteed by the European Convention for the Protection of Human Rights and Fundamental Freedoms signed in Rome on 4 November 1950 and as they result from the constitutional traditions common to the Member States, as general principles of Community law'.   [81] See Ch 5.

[82] See Ch 4.

a rule predicated on respect for democracy, the rule of law, and human rights, and there are also autonomous external policies which are oriented towards human rights protection, e.g. in the area of trade preferences. Chapter 13 looks more closely at the EU's external human rights policy.

In tandem with the growth of EU human rights policies one sees a strengthening of their constitutional basis. The Charter of Fundamental Rights now constitutes an express catalogue, much as a typical constitution of a nation state contains its enumeration of human and fundamental rights. However, States increasingly define human rights through international lawmaking, in particular the conclusion of human rights treaties. It would seem natural that the EU should also be able to do so, first of all with a view to ensuring that its policies comply with internationally agreed standards, and perhaps also so as to be able to bring its own experience with protection of human rights to an international negotiating table. There are however no provisions in the Treaties which expressly confer competence to conclude human rights treaties. In that context, further issues are posed by the absence of the EU in the system of the ECHR. In practice, the EU institutions need to respect the provisions of the ECHR, because those provisions are general principles of EC law which the Court will uphold, but the lack of formal participation in the ECHR system means that the European Court of Human Rights has no jurisdiction over acts of the EU institutions.[83]

There has been a long and intense debate, in both political and legal terms, about the merits and drawbacks of full EC (or EU) participation in the ECHR system. This is not the place to engage with all aspects of that debate. In the course of 1994, however, the Council of Ministers decided to request the Opinion of the Court of Justice on the compatibility of EC accession to the ECHR with the EC Treaty. Technically, this was a request on an envisaged international agreement, notwithstanding the fact that no negotiations on the subject had taken place or were being conducted in the Council of Europe; there was even no consensus among the Member States on the question of principle whether such negotiations, and a resulting accession, were desirable. The Court none the less admitted the request, or at least one part of it, and took the opportunity to develop a judicial definition of the EC's powers in the field of human rights, including the power to conclude human rights treaties. It is from that angle that we analyse *Opinion 2/94* here.[84]

The Council had requested the Court's Opinion, both as regards (a) competence under the EC Treaty to join the ECHR, and (b) the compatibility of accession with substantive provisions and principles of EC law, in particular the exclusive jurisdiction of the Court of Justice and the autonomy of the Community legal order. The

[83] There are however signs that it is changing its approach: see ECtHR, *Matthews v. United Kingdom*, App. No. 24833/94, judgment of 18 Feb. 1999, (1999) 28 EHRR 361.

[84] *Opinion 2/94 re Accession to the ECHR* [1996] ECR I–1759. See also *inter alia* JHH Weiler and S Fries, 'A Human Rights Policy for the European Community and Union: The Question of Competences', in P Alston (ed), *The EU and Human Rights* (OUP, 1999) 147; A Arnull, 'Left To Its Own Devices? Opinion 2/94 and the Protection of Fundamental Rights in the European Union', in A Dashwood and C Hillion (eds), *The General Law of EC External Relations* (Sweet & Maxwell, 2000) 61–78.

Court admitted only the first part of the request.[85] It considered that it was in the interests of the Community institutions and of the States concerned, including non-member countries, to have the question of competence clarified from the outset of negotiations, and even before the main points of the agreement were negotiated. The only condition was that the purpose of the envisaged agreement be known, and there was no doubt that that was the case as regards accession to the ECHR: the general purpose and subject matter of the ECHR and the institutional signific-ance of accession were perfectly well known.[86] The second part of the request was not however admissible. In order fully to answer the question whether accession would be compatible with the rules of the Treaty, in particular with (current) Articles 220 and 292 EC relating to the jurisdiction of the Court, the Court had to have sufficient information regarding the arrangements by which the Community envisaged submitting to the judicial control machinery established by the ECHR.[87]

The Court's reasoning on competence was as follows. It first referred to (cur-rent) Article 5 EC, which provides that the Community is to act within the limits of the powers conferred upon it by the Treaty and of the objectives assigned to it therein. It followed from that provision that the Community has only those pow-ers which have been conferred upon it. That principle of conferred powers had to be respected in both the internal action and the international action of the Community. The Community acted ordinarily on the basis of specific powers which were not necessarily the express consequence of specific provisions of the Treaty but could also be implied from them. Thus, in the field of international relations it was settled case law that the competence of the Community to enter into international commitments not only flowed from express provisions of the Treaty but could also be implied from those provisions. The Court then referred, more specifically, to the principle that, whenever Community law had created for the institutions of the Community powers within its internal system for the purpose of attaining a speci-fic objective, the Community was empowered to enter into the international com-mitments necessary for attainment of that objective even in the absence of an express provision to that effect.[88]

After having thus identified the issue as one of external implied powers, the Court turned to the subject of human rights. It first pointed out that no Treaty pro-vision conferred on the Community institutions any general power to enact rules on human rights or to conclude international conventions in this field. The Court then stated that, in the absence of express or implied powers, it was necessary to consider whether (current) Article 308 of the Treaty could constitute a legal basis for accession. That provision the Court characterized as designed to fill the gap where no specific provisions of the Treaty conferred on the Community institutions express or implied powers to act, if such powers appeared none the less to be nec-essary to enable the Community to carry out its functions with a view to attaining

---

[85] See also Ch 8.   [86] *Opinion 2/94* (n 84 above), paras 10–12.   [87] Ibid, para 20.
[88] Ibid, paras 23–26.

one of the objectives laid down by the Treaty. However, Article 308 could not serve as a basis for widening the scope of Community powers beyond the general framework created by the provisions of the Treaty as a whole and, in particular, by those that defined the tasks and the activities of the Community. On any view, Article 308 could not be used as a basis for the adoption of provisions whose effect would, in substance, be to amend the Treaty without following the procedure which it provides for that purpose.[89]

In the last part of the Opinion the Court examined accession in the light of the scope of Article 308. It recalled the importance of respect for human rights, as emphasized in various declarations and provisions of the Treaties (see above). It further recalled that it was well settled that fundamental rights formed an integral part of the general principles of law whose observance the Court ensured. Respect for human rights was therefore a condition of the lawfulness of Community acts. However, the Court finally held, accession to the ECHR would entail a substantial change in the Community system for the protection of human rights in that it would entail the entry of the Community into a distinct international institutional system as well as integration of all the provisions of the ECHR into the Community legal order. Such a modification of the system for the protection of human rights in the Community, with equally fundamental institutional implications for the Community and for the Member States, would be of constitutional significance and would therefore be such as to go beyond the scope of Article 308. It could be brought about only by way of Treaty amendment. Therefore, as Community law stood, the Community had no competence to accede to the ECHR.[90]

The Court's reasoning in *Opinion 2/94* is not straightforward, and it is difficult to deduce broader principles from the ruling, in particular as regards general EC competence to conclude human rights treaties. One issue is the relationship between the implied powers doctrine and Article 308 EC. A possible reading is that the Court wrongfoots the student of the Opinion, by first reciting the implied powers principles, and then swiftly turning to Article 308, 'in the absence of express or implied powers'. That seems to suggest that Article 308 is not itself part of the implied powers doctrine, and that the Court needs to analyse it because the Treaty does not elsewhere contain express or implied powers in the human rights field. In itself that approach is unobjectionable, if it were not for the lack of any real analysis of whether other provisions of the Treaty confer implied powers in this field. The Court simply asserts that 'no Treaty provision confers on the Community institutions any general power to enact rules on human rights or to conclude international conventions in this field'. It is true, of course, that there are no specific provisions to that effect. But if respect for human rights is a condition of the lawfulness of Community acts, as the Court confirms further down in the Opinion, can it not then be argued that the institutions have the duty, and therefore the power, in all the areas in which they may exercise conferred competences, to ensure that their acts

---

[89] Ibid, paras 27–30.   [90] Ibid, paras 32–36.

do not violate fundamental rights? One could call this a functional human-rights competence.[91] It is surely arguable that the Community is capable of binding itself, within the limits of the powers conferred upon it, to an international human rights instrument, so as to ensure that its legislation and executive acts comply with internationally agreed human rights standards. In the case of the ECHR, that argument has even more force, because the Court expressly mentions the ECHR in its case-law on protection of fundamental rights. In effect, EC acts need to comply with the ECHR. The Court, however, does not examine any such arguments in the section of its Opinion on implied powers.

Nor does it analyse competence in the sphere of protection of human rights when scrutinizing the scope of Article 308. The article is there to fill the gap where no specific Treaty provisions confer express or implied powers, and such powers none the less appear necessary to enable the Community to carry out its functions with a view to attaining one of the objectives laid down by the Treaty. But the Court does not discuss whether human rights powers come within that category. It jumps to the point that Article 308 cannot be used for the adoption of provisions whose effect would in substance be to amend the Treaty.[92]

That brings us to what is effectively the core of the Court's argument. Accession to the ECHR is in substance Treaty amendment. If one accepts that, it is obvious that no Treaty provision can confer the power to do so by way of conclusion of an international agreement; amendment needs to take place through the proper procedure in the Treaty. In fact the Court could have taken this principle as its starting point, and could have avoided speaking about implied powers and Article 308 altogether.

As regards the constitutional significance of accession to the ECHR, requiring Treaty amendment, the Court points to the 'substantial change in the present Community system for the protection of human rights'. That substantial change includes 'the entry of the Community into a distinct international institutional system' (obviously a reference to the jurisdiction of the European Court of Human Rights) as well as the 'integration of all the provisions of the Convention into the Community legal order'. Such a modification of the system has 'equally fundamental institutional implications for the Community and for the Member States'. The Court, however, does not clarify those implications. At the level of the Community institutions the most fundamental implication is obvious: accession to the ECHR would in effect mean that aggrieved citizens could complain to the ECtHR that their rights were violated by an act of an EC institution. It is not obvious at all, however, what the fundamental implications would be for the Member States. Nor is it obvious that integration of all the Convention provisions into the Community legal order would be of a fundamental character. At the time of the

---

[91] P Eeckhout, 'The EU Charter of Fundamental Rights and the Federal Question' (2002) 39 CMLRev 984–5.

[92] Cf Arnull (n 84 above) 71–2, where he argues that it would be a mistake to conclude that Art 308 is completely devoid of potential in the field of human rights.

Opinion the Court had, for a number of years, already been applying the ECHR in the guise of general principles of EC law, and it is doubtful whether actual incorporation of the ECHR would lead to a stricter application of its provisions. The above dissection therefore reveals one single decisive argument against accession to the ECHR: the implications of external review, mainly by the ECtHR, for the Community institutions, including the Court itself.

The issue of accession to the ECHR is not as such the object of this section. The Convention on the Future of Europe proposes that the EU Constitution contain a provision enabling such accession.[93] But does the EU have broader powers in the human rights field? Is it capable of concluding other international agreements for the protection of human rights? That is an implied powers question, and the answer to that question cannot be derived from *Opinion 2/94*. Whilst that Opinion shows that the Court does not appear favourably disposed towards recognizing broad competence in the field of human rights, its reasoning in the Opinion is too succinct to enable us to draw firm conclusions. One should hope that the opportunity may come for the Court to engage with the argument for a functional human-rights power, as discussed above. That there must be some measure of competence to conclude human rights treaties follows, in the current state, simply from the *AETR* principle. An example are the non-discrimination directives,[94] which are in many respects similar to Protocol 12 of the ECHR, a protocol not yet in force. There is thus exclusive Community competence to conclude that protocol, in so far as it affects those directives.

The air transport cases

The latest development in the implied-powers doctrine consists of a series of parallel judgments concerning EC and national competence to conclude air transport agreements. The Commission has been proposing the development of a common external air transport policy since the start of the 1990s, in parallel with the completion and liberalization of the internal air transport market.[95] The proposal has its merits, because the internal market cannot be genuinely completed and cannot function without distortion of competition as long as individual Member States continue to determine external traffic rights by concluding bilateral aviation agreements with non-member countries. Such agreements typically reserve external traffic rights for domestic carriers, i.e. carriers majority owned or controlled by a Member State's own nationals, whereas competition in the internal market between

[93] Art I–7(2) provides: 'The Union shall seek accession to the [ECHR]. Accession to that Convention shall not affect the Union's competences as defined in this Constitution'.

[94] Directive 2000/43 implementing the principle of equal treatment between persons irrespective of racial or ethnic origin [2000] OJ L180/22 and Directive 2000/78 establishing a general framework for equal treatment in employment and occupation [2000] OJ L303/16.

[95] See Eeckhout (n 73 above), ch 3.

carriers is free. There is in effect a common regime for internal trade in transport services, and a fractured regime involving discrimination on grounds of nationality for external trade.

The Commission's proposals have none the less continued to meet resistance in the Council. At some point the Council agreed that the Commission could start negotiations with *inter alia* the United States on air transport issues, but not negotiations covering exchange of traffic rights.[96] The United States in particular has been using the last decade to conclude so-called 'open skies' agreements with individual Member States. It is generally regarded to have benefited in those negotiations from its stronger negotiating power.

In the proceedings for *Opinion 1/94* the Commission argued that external transport services come within the common commercial policy as defined in (current) Article 133 EC.[97] If the Court had agreed with that argument Community competence to conclude air transport agreements would have been exclusive, and the Member States would have been compelled to relinquish power to the Community. The Court was not impressed, however, and pointed to its case law on implied powers in the transport sector, i.e. *AETR* and *Opinion 1/76*: international agreements in transport matters come within the Treaty provisions on a common transport policy. Implicitly, therefore, but not expressly, the Court confirmed that the power to conclude external transport agreements was concurrent, and not exclusive.

The Commission none the less did not abandon its efforts to bring about an external air transport policy. As its powers of political persuasion proved insufficient, it decided to bring proceedings against a large number of Member States, on the grounds that the 'open skies' agreements with the US violated EC law. The Commission argued that those agreements were in breach of the principle of exclusive external competence, and that the clauses on ownership and control of airlines in those agreements were contrary to (current) Article 43 EC, on right of establishment.[98]

As regards external competence the Commission advanced two arguments. It argued that there was an external competence within the meaning of *Opinion 1/76*, and that such competence was exclusive in nature. It further claimed that there was exclusive competence by virtue of the *AETR* principle: the internal Community legislation on air transport was affected by commitments to exchange traffic rights and to open up access for third-country carriers to the intra-Community market.

[96] Case C–466/98 *Commission v. UK* [2002] ECR I–9427, Opinion of Tizzano AG, para 12.

[97] *Opinion 1/94* (n 58 above), paras 48–52; see Ch 2.

[98] *Commission v. United Kingdom* (n 96 above; in this case the Commission did not make the claim of exclusive competence); Case C–467/98 *Commission v. Denmark* [2002] ECR I–9519; Case C–468/98 *Commission v. Sweden* [2002] ECR I–9575; Case C–469/98 *Commission v. Finland* [2002] ECR I–9627; Case C–471/98 *Commission v. Belgium* [2002] ECR I–9681; Case C–472/98 *Commission v. Luxembourg* [2002] ECR I–9741; Case C–475/98 *Commission v. Austria* [2002] ECR I–9797; and Case C–476/98 *Commission v. Germany* [2002] ECR I–9855.

Opinion 1/76-type competence

The first argument was particularly interesting. The Commission referred to the Court's statements in *Opinion 1/94*, to the effect that *Opinion 1/76* concerned exclusive competence in cases where an international agreement is required for the effective exercise of internal competence; and that external powers may be exercised, and thus become exclusive, without any internal legislation having first been adopted.[99] The Commission claimed that in the field of air transport purely internal measures would hardly be effective, given the international nature of the activities carried on and the impossibility of separating the internal and external markets both economically and legally. The discrimination, the distortions of competition, and the disturbance of the Community market resulting from the bilateral open skies agreements proved that the aims of the common air transport policy could not be attained without the conclusion of an agreement between the Community and the United States.[100]

With this argument the Commission effectively invited the Court to make more sense of its statements in *Opinion 1/94* regarding the meaning of *Opinion 1/76*. Tizzano AG took up the gauntlet and mounted an impressive clarification of the judicial pronouncements in issue.[101] He recalled the Court's statements in *Opinion 1/76*, and compared them to the logic underlying (current) Article 308 EC, which in a sense, he observed, the Court had transposed to the sphere of the Community's external action. He then stressed that the conclusions drawn by the Commission from this case law stemmed from a mistaken belief that in affirming the Community's competence in the situations referred to in *Opinion 1/76*, the Court also held this competence to be automatically exclusive. It was in his view apparent that all the Court had actually affirmed was that the 'necessity' for an agreement could enable the Community to affirm its external competence, but that it would always be the specific recognition of such 'necessity', i.e. the actual exercise of that competence, which would render it exclusive. The subsequent case law (*Opinions 2/91* and *1/94*) corroborated such a reading, but it was above all confirmed by the problems which the Commission's argument raised when one considered how and by whom the assessment should be carried out as to the 'necessity' of an agreement. That could only be done in accordance with the proper Treaty procedures. There could be no recognition of the 'necessity' for an agreement unless there had been a specific assessment by the competent institutions and the procedures prescribed had been followed. It could be debated, possibly even before the Court, whether in a specific case the assessment of the 'necessity' for an agreement was properly carried out (or omitted), but there could certainly be no escaping the fact that the institutions empowered to carry out the assessment and

---

[99] See above.   [100] *Commission v. Germany* (n 98 above), paras 71–74.
[101] *Commission v. United Kingdom* (n 96 above), paras 46–59 of the Opinion (there was one Opinion for all the cases).

the procedures to be followed were those in the Treaty. Otherwise, there was a risk of introducing elements of uncertainty, even arbitrariness, into the division of powers between Community and Member States, and of distorting the procedures and the interinstitutional balances established by the Treaty. Applying those principles to the cases at hand, Tizzano AG pointed out that the Council had consistently rejected the need for an air transport agreement with the United States covering traffic rights. Of course, one could take the view that the Council's assessment was unlawful. But in that case the relevant Council decision should be challenged or an action for failure to act should be brought. In the absence of any steps of that nature, the Council's decisions had to be presumed lawful. In any event, their validity could not be challenged indirectly and by means of inappropriate procedures (such as enforcement proceedings against Member States).

The Advocate General's approach is broadly in line with the reading of *Opinion 1/76* suggested above, in that he recognizes that this ruling did not establish an *a priori* exclusive competence of the kind which exists in matters of commercial policy and conservation of fish resources, or in cases where the Community has previously exercised internal competence by the adoption of internal rules which are liable to be affected by the provisions of an international agreement (*AETR*). It is only the exercise of competence which creates its exclusive character. Again one must repeat that the notion of exclusivity is hardly relevant in such cases, since in the disputes on competence one is invariably dealing with the question whether there is exclusivity prior to exercise. If the Community had already exercised its competences by concluding an air transport agreement with the United States, the cases under consideration could only have been of a radically different character: namely whether any agreements concluded by the Member States complied with the EC agreement with the United States.

The reading of the Advocate General thus effectively emasculates the exclusive nature of the *Opinion 1/76*-type external competence, and rightly so. Here, exclusive competence only becomes nascent at the moment of its exercise. It is then a stillborn concept, for the notion of power, *pouvoir*, or competence, *Kompetenz*, logically precedes its exercise, or the acts adopted under it. Do I have the power to do X? That question disappears once I do X. Do I have the competence to do X? Again the question disappears once I do X. In a legal context, of course, it is possible to challenge the actual exercise of power, competence, on the basis that it was unlawful. But the assessment of lawfulness again takes you back to how the law stood prior to such exercise.

The Court, however, made no effort to clarify its statements linking necessity and exclusivity with the exercise of external competence. Instead, it distinguished the air transport cases from *Opinion 1/76*. The Court first recalled its various statements, reiterating that the hypothesis in *Opinion 1/76* was that internal competence could be effectively exercised only at the same time as the external competence, the conclusion of the international agreement thus being necessary in order to attain objectives of the Treaty that could not be attained by establishing autonomous rules. That was not the case as regards external air transport. The Court pointed out that the institutions could arrange concerted action in relation to the United States or prescribe the approach to be taken by the Member States in their external dealings, so as to mitigate any discrimination or distortions of competition. It had therefore not been established that, by reason of such discrimination or distortions of competition, the aims of the Treaty in the area of transport could not be achieved by establishing autonomous rules. The Court then drew attention to the fact that the Council had considered it unnecessary for the Community to exercise external competence by negotiating an agreement with the United States covering traffic rights.[102] It concluded that its findings could not be called into question by the fact that the measures adopted by the Council in relation to the internal market in air transport contained a number of provisions concerning nationals of non-member countries. Contrary to what the Commission maintained, the relatively limited character of those provisions precluded inferring from them that the realization of the freedom to provide services in the field of air transport in favour of nationals of the Member States was inextricably linked to the treatment to be accorded in the Community to nationals of non-member countries, or in non-member countries to nationals of the Member States. The Community could therefore not validly claim that there was an exclusive external competence, within the meaning of *Opinion 1/76*, to conclude an air transport agreement with the United States.[103]

If the Court did not, in contrast with the Advocate General, clarify *Opinion 1/76*-type exclusive implied powers, it would none the less seem that the scope for such powers is much restricted. One has difficulty imagining cases where internal competence could not be exercised without concluding an international agreement within the strict parameters set by the Court. It is even doubtful whether the agreement in issue in *Opinion 1/76* came within those parameters. In that case the Court stated that limiting inland waterway capacity in the Rhine and Moselle basins required an agreement with Switzerland, because of traditional navigation of Swiss vessels, which were subject to the system of freedom of navigation established by international agreements of long standing.[104] But could not the Council, here too, have arranged for concerted action towards Switzerland in the internal legislation, and could it not have prescribed the approach to be taken by the Member States in their external dealings with Switzerland on this issue?

By way of conclusion on this point, it may be repeated that *Opinion 1/76* is better looked at as a case which did not establish exclusive external competence, but simply confirmed general parallelism between internal and external powers.

---

[102] The Commission did receive a mandate to negotiate with the US, and it is clear from the judgments that it disputed the restricted scope of that mandate. It is also obvious, however, that the Council never agreed to the inclusion of negotiations on traffic rights.
[103] *Commission v. Germany* (n 98 above), paras 80–90.   [104] See above.

AETR-type competence

In the air transport cases the Court also looked at *AETR*-type external competence. Again Tizzano AG offered a comprehensive and persuasive analysis. It is not necessary to describe his entire argument, in particular as the Commission alleged that the agreements concluded by the Member States affected a series of common rules, requiring detailed scrutiny. Instead it may be sufficient to highlight some of the general points which the Advocate General made, and to look at just a couple of applications.

Tizzano first recalled previous judicial statements on the matter. He concluded from them that, in principle, in matters covered by common rules, the Member States could not under any circumstances conclude international agreements, even if these were entirely consistent with the common rules, since any steps taken outside the framework of the Community institutions would be incompatible with the unity of the common market and the uniform application of Community law. Further consequences should however be inferred from the case law. First, Member States could not conclude international agreements, in matters covered by common rules, even if the texts of the agreements reproduced the common rules *verbatim* or incorporated them by reference. The conclusion of such agreements could also prejudice the uniform application of Community law. The 'reception' of common rules into the agreements would be no guarantee that the rules would then in fact be uniformly applied, and that any amendments which might be adopted internally would be fully and promptly transposed into the agreements. Further, any such 'reception' would have the effect of distorting the nature and legal regime of the common rules, and entail a real and serious risk that they would be removed from review by the Court under the Treaty. Secondly, the Member States could not undertake international obligations in matters governed by common rules even in order to eliminate conflicts between those rules and agreements concluded by them before the rules were adopted. Not even the requirement to ensure the full and correct application of Community law could justify unilateral action by Member States; that requirement was in principle to be fulfilled by the Community itself.[105]

The Advocate General also considered that, between the situations of agreements which were in clear conflict with common rules, and agreements which covered the same subject matter as that governed by common rules, there was a considerable area. As an example he mentioned agreements which concerned aspects which were contiguous, so to speak, to those governed by common rules, or agreements which, while they concerned a matter which was to a large extent covered by common rules, related however to aspects not, or not yet, regulated by those rules.[106]

Tizzano further stressed that in order to establish that the common rules were 'affected' it was not enough to cite general effects of an economic nature which the agreements could have on the functioning of the internal market; what was required

---

[105] *Commission v. United Kingdom* (n 96 above), paras 71–74, Opinion of Tizzano AG.
[106] Ibid, para 75.

instead was to specify in detail the aspects of the Community legislation which could be prejudiced by the agreements.[107]

The Advocate General then proceeded to apply those principles, and the manner in which he did so perfectly illustrates the *AETR* doctrine. One example is the Commission's claim that the agreements with the United States affected Regulation 2407/92 on licensing of air carriers[108] and Regulation 2408/92 on access for Community air carriers to intra-Community air routes.[109] According to the Commission, those regulations laid down exhaustively the conditions for access to intra-Community routes, with regard to all air carriers, and the disputed agreements effectively permitted US carriers not satisfying the requirements of Regulation 2407/92 also to operate on intra-Community routes. Tizzano replied, however, that the Commission had misread the regulations. They only secured access to intra-Community routes for Community air carriers, and did not concern third-country carriers. The disputed agreements and the regulations therefore applied to different situations.[110]

A second, contrasting, example concerns Regulation 2409/92 on fares and rates for air services.[111] That regulation explicitly restricts to Community carriers the right to introduce lower fares than the ones existing for identical products within the Community. The Advocate General considered that it thereby indirectly but unequivocally excluded that right for non-Community carriers, who were thus prohibited from introducing such fares. He then established that the disputed agreements did amend the pricing rules contained in earlier bilateral agreements, and therefore infringed exclusive Community competence. It was irrelevant that some of the disputed agreements effected only minor amendments, and that some of the amendments were in fact intended to preserve the application of the regulation. The Member States should have allowed the Community to negotiate on these matters, and, if that proved impossible, they should have acted within the framework of the Community institutions by seeking authorization to negotiate the necessary amendments, in concert and in close co-operation with those institutions.[112]

The Court essentially followed the approach of its Advocate General. It first examined whether the *AETR* reasoning actually applied to air transport, in light of the wording of (current) Article 80(2) EC, which merely enabled the Council to 'decide whether, to what extent and by what procedure appropriate provisions may be laid down for . . . air transport'. The Court none the less considered that, if the Member States were free to enter into international commitments affecting the common rules adopted on the basis of Article 80(2), that would jeopardize the attainment of the objective pursued by those rules and would thus prevent the Community from fulfilling its task in the defence of the common interest. The *AETR* findings thus applied.[113]

The Court then recalled all its previous pronouncements on *AETR*-type exclusive competence. Those paragraphs in the judgments usefully collate the various ways

---

[107] Ibid, para 77.   [108] [1992] OJ L240/1.   [109] [1992] OJ L240/8.
[110] *Commission v. United Kingdom* (n 96 above), paras 81–84, Opinion of Tizzano AG.
[111] [1992] OJ L240/15.   [112] *Commission v. United Kingdom* (n 96 above), paras 89–97.
[113] *Commission v. Germany* (n 98 above), paras 104–106.

in which international agreements may affect common rules, thereby giving rise to exclusive Community competence. In other words, what follows is the most up-to-date, authoritative formulation of the relevant principles.

Exclusive competence arose, the Court stated, where the international commitments fell within the scope of the common rules, or in any event within an area which was already largely covered by such rules. In the latter case, the Member States could not enter into international commitments outside the framework of the Community institutions, even if there was no contradiction between those commitments and the common rules. Thus it was that, whenever the Community had included in its internal legislative acts provisions relating to the treatment of nationals of non-member countries or expressly conferred on its institutions powers to negotiate with non-member countries, it acquired an exclusive external competence in the spheres covered by those acts. The same applied, even in the absence of any express provision authorizing its institutions to negotiate with non-member countries, where the Community had achieved complete harmonization in a given area, because the common rules thus adopted could be affected within the meaning of the *AETR* judgment if the Member States retained freedom to negotiate with non-member countries. On the other hand, any distortions in the flow of services in the internal market which might arise from bilateral 'open skies' agreements concluded by Member States with non-member countries did not in themselves affect the common rules adopted in that area and were thus not capable of establishing an external competence of the Community. There was nothing in the Treaty to prevent the institutions arranging, in the common rules laid down by them, concerted action in relation to non-member countries or to prevent them prescribing the approach to be taken by the Member States in their external dealings.[114]

The Court's application of those principles to the cases at hand dovetailed Tizzano AG's Opinion. The Court established that there were was exclusive Community competence as regards the setting of fares and rates by non-Community carriers (Regulation 2409/92),[115] as regards computerized reservation systems (CRS) used by such carriers in the Community (Regulation 2299/89 on a code of conduct for computerized reservation systems),[116] and as regards the allocation of slots at Community airports (Regulation 95/93).[117] To the extent that Member States had included provisions on these matters in the disputed agreements they had violated the *AETR* principle. The Court characterized those violations as a breach of the combined provisions of Article 10 EC, embodying the principle of loyalty, and the regulations in issue.

Conclusions

It may be useful at this stage of this book's analysis to offer some further reflections on the doctrine of implied powers, as elaborated in the above case law. It is in

---

[114] *Commission v. Germany* (n 98 above), paras 108–112.   [115] N 111 above.
[116] [1989] OJ L220/1.   [117] [1993] OJ L14/1.

particular important to identify with precision the rules and principles which the Court established.[118]

As suggested there is a basic distinction between two different dimensions of the external power question, which gives us a key for a better understanding of the case law. That distinction is between (a) the material scope, the reach in terms of subject matter, of powers conferred upon the Community in specific policy fields, *both* as regards internal lawmaking *and* the conclusion of international agreements; and (b) what, in so far as external relations are concerned, may be called the core implied-powers question, i.e. does the EC have capacity to conclude international agreements in areas within its competence where the Treaty does not mention such capacity?

The latter, core question was clearly the most vital one for the Court to answer. The EEC Treaty had conferred broad internal legislative powers in matters pertaining to the common market, transport, agriculture, competition. It had however been much meaner with express powers to conclude international agreements, limiting those essentially to commercial policy and association agreements. Article 228 EEC (current Article 300 EC) appeared to confirm that the Community's treaty-making powers were limited to those instances by laying down provisions on procedure which were to apply 'where this Treaty provides for the conclusion of agreements'. None the less, the Court replied to this core implied-powers question with a resounding yes. It set the tone in *AETR* by emphasizing the Community's legal personality, which it construed as including *international* legal personality, and which it saw as overriding the absence of express Treaty language, in specific areas, on the conclusion of international agreements. In matters of transport it was sufficient that the Treaty authorized the Council to adopt 'appropriate provisions'. *Opinion 1/76* was also concerned with transport, but the language in both *AETR* and that Opinion was general, and suggested that the Community could act by way of entering into international commitments in all its areas of activity. *Post* the first substantial amendment of the EEC Treaty through the Single European Act, involving a first expansion of the Community's competences, the Court even accepted treaty-making capacity in an area, health and safety of workers, where the powers conferred upon the Community were rather weak. Article 118a EEC instructed the *Member States* to pay particular attention to encouraging improvements as regards the health and safety of workers, and to set as their objective the harmonization of conditions in this area. The Council's task was only to help achieve that objective by adopting, by means of directives, *minimum* requirements for *gradual* implementation, which could not prevent any Member State from maintaining or introducing more stringent measures. None the less, the Court confirmed in *Opinion 2/91* that in this area, too, there was treaty-making power.

Obviously, there must be some limit to the Community's implied treaty-making capacity. In certain areas, such as culture and public health, the Treaty excludes harmonization of laws,[119] and it seems incontrovertible that this exclusion cannot be

---

[118] Compare with Dashwood and Helikoski (n 1 above), 18–19.
[119] See Arts 151(5) and 152(4)(c) EC.

circumvented by concluding an international agreement which would in effect amount to such harmonization. But even in such areas the conclusion of international agreements on matters which do come within the Community's competence, e.g. cultural subsidies, should be possible in light of the case law.

What is the broader meaning and import of this core implied power? The Court of Justice appears to have realized and valued the growing significance of international lawmaking.[120] By affirming general treaty-making power it asserted the Community's international capacity and laid the foundations for an effective international legal personality. It may be noted, in that regard, that such legal personality ultimately depends on the willingness of other international actors to contract, and cannot be unilaterally decreed.[121] Yet, obviously, no such willingness could have been forthcoming if the Court had erected a constitutional barrier to the conclusion of treaties. The Court's broad affirmation no doubt assisted in the actual development of the Community's involvement and formal participation in international lawmaking, and contributed to the gradual acceptance of the Community as an international actor. Today one may forget all too easily that such acceptance did not come automatically, witness the refusal of Soviet-dominated communist countries to recognize the Community.[122] And even today, there continues to be a particular form of international action which poses a lot of problems, namely membership of international organizations.[123]

When one compares the Community with other organizations between States, the implied-powers case law confirmed the general political character of the Community, its function to establish a European polity which transcends the format of traditional international organizations. Indeed, this case law, and the international action which it set in motion and enabled, is one of the hallmarks of such transcendence. Which other international organizations have capacity to conclude international agreements, in diverse policy areas, which bind not only their institutions but also their Member States? From that perspective, the implied-powers doctrine is rightly regarded as a core component of European constitutionalism.

Beyond this core of the implied-powers doctrine, there is a second, and different, dimension to the above case law. The Court may have unreservedly supported the claim to treaty-making power, but that support should not be identified with judicial laxness concerning the material scope of EC powers. In *AETR* Dutheillet de Lamothe AG contrasted implied powers with conferred powers. The latter principle, of conferred and limited powers, is at the very heart of EU constitutional law.[124] But the case law on implied powers does not in any way abandon it. In all of the above rulings the Court takes great care to define and circumscribe the material

---

[120] Cf M Cremona, 'External Relations and External Competence: The Emergence of an Integrated Policy', in P Craig and G de Búrca, *The Evolution of EU Law* (OUP, 1999) 147–8.

[121] See further Ch 5.

[122] See J Maslen, 'European Community–CMEA: institutional relations', in M Maresceau (ed), *The Political and Legal Framework of Trade Relations between the European Community and Eastern Europe* (Martinus Nijhoff, 1989) 85–92.   [123] See Ch 7.

[124] A Dashwood, 'The Limits of European Community Powers' (1996) 21 ELR 113.

scope of EC powers, the subject area in which the EC may act, with reserve and precision.[125] It does not accept broad expansion of EC powers in material terms. *AETR* and *Opinion 1/76* concerned agreements regulating matters clearly within Community competence, i.e. social legislation relating to road transport and inland waterway capacity on the Rhine and Moselle basins. The ILO Convention in issue in *Opinion 2/91* clearly concerned health and safety of workers; indeed internal EC legislation had already been adopted as regards the use of chemicals. In *Opinion 1/94* the Court rejected the Commission's expansionist claim that the Treaty chapters on right of establishment and freedom to provide services were a basis for regulating external trade in services. It did not exclude that internal market harmonization could extend to the treatment of non-nationals, but refused a sweeping extension of Community competence from the internal market in services to external trade. In *Opinion 2/94* the Court denied the Community general powers in the human rights field, notwithstanding the requirement of respect for human rights as general principles of EC law.

This dimension of the implied-powers case law is in line with jurisprudence on 'internal' competence. There, too, the Court is careful, or at least has become careful, to uphold the limits to powers conferred upon the Community.[126] At the same time, the implied-powers case law also displays a degree of respect for the division of powers (or institutional balance) between the various political institutions, as well as between the legislature and the judiciary. Even if powers are limited, there is some latitude for the institutions vested with the authority to exercise such powers. Thus, in *Opinion 1/94* the Court accepted that there is exclusive treaty-making power where internal legislative acts confer powers to negotiate. In the air transport cases the Court also regarded it as vital that the Council had not decided that an agreement on traffic rights with the United States was necessary. Within the boundaries set by the Treaty, the Community legislature may to some extent determine the scope of external competence. In particular the recognition that the legislature may legislate on external competence is remarkable from a constitutional perspective. *Kompetenz-Kompetenz* does not seem to be limited to the Member States as *Herren der Verträge* (Masters of the Treaties). In fact, the masters of the Treaties themselves established such *Kompetenz-Kompetenz* for the Council in the Amsterdam and Nice amendments to Article 133 EC.[127] There is obviously some tension between the idea of limited powers and respect for the political discretion of the legislature, yet there need not be contradiction. Where the Treaties confer powers on the Community to act, it is natural that the institutions which have been given authority to exercise those powers are the first interpreters of the scope of such powers. There must of course be judicial review, but some degree of deference to the legislature seems appropriate. As regards *Kompetenz-Kompetenz* it is also worth

---

[125] Cf A Dashwood, 'The Attribution of External Relations Competence', in Dashwood and Hillion (n 1 above) 128.

[126] See in particular Case C–376/98 *Germany v. European Parliament and Council* [2000] ECR I–8419 (the *Tobacco Advertising Directive* case). [127] See Ch 2.

piercing the institutional veil. Where the Court recognizes that the Council may, for example, confer exclusive negotiating authority by providing for negotiations in Community legislation, it is doubtless aware of the Council's function of representing the Member States, masters of the Treaties.

A third dimension of the implied-powers case law is the notion of exclusive competence. As can be seen, enormous institutional battles have been fought over the reach of exclusivity. Instead of simply concentrating on whether the Community has competence to conclude an agreement, the case law's real focus has been on exclusive competence. The cause is the antagonism between the Commission and the Council which, in the domain of international negotiations and the conclusion of international agreements, epitomizes the struggle between supranationalism and intergovernmentalism; perhaps more so than in any other domain of Community action. The Commission has consistently, over three or four decades, perceived the Council as the bodyguard of national competence, greatly reluctant to recognize and exercise external competence. The Council, i.e. the Member State governments, see the Commission as purely intent on increasing its own, supranational powers, for it is the Commission which negotiates international agreements, and the negotiator holds many cards.[128] If proof there need be of this antagonism, it is to be found in the EU Treaty's provisions on CFSP, which do not provide for any significant Commission role. The Convention on the Future of Europe also struggled with this dimension of foreign policy.

It is understandable that the Court was drawn into the battle, for it has ultimate authority to interpret the scope and meaning of the Treaties. One none the less wonders whether all the judicial energy spent on defining exclusive implied powers has had much effect on actual practice. As is discussed in Chapter 7, that practice is founded on the notion of mixity. Whenever there is doubt as to the scope of Community powers international agreements are concluded as mixed agreements, requiring signature and conclusion by the Community and by each Member State. If the case law on exclusive implied powers has led to any actual expansion of the Community's involvement with the negotiation and conclusion of international agreements, it is barely visible.

A proper understanding of the case law is none the less indispensable. It may be helpful to look at the doctrine of exclusive implied powers (or *AETR*) as located somewhere in between pure conflict pre-emption and *a priori* Treaty-based exclusive competence, such as in matters of commercial policy and conservation of fish resources. As emphasized by Tizzano AG in the air transport cases, and recognized by the Court, there need not be conflict between the provisions of an international agreement and internal Community legislation for the *AETR* principle to operate. There are many more positions, including where provisions of the agreement copy EC provisions; where they are contiguous to common rules; where an area is largely regulated by the Community, and the provisions of the agreement affect that area;

---

[128] See Ch 6.

where there is complete harmonization; where Community legislation provides for international negotiations on a particular subject. The draft Constitution codifies those principles in Article I–12(2) in the following terms:

The Union shall have exclusive competence for the conclusion of an international agreement when its conclusion is provided for in a legislative act of the Union, is necessary to enable the Union to exercise its competence internally, or affects an internal Union act.

The rationales for exclusive implied powers can perhaps be reformulated as follows. Particularly in the domain of action under international law one cannot leave possible conflicts or frictions between provisions of EC law and, effectively, provisions of national law (albeit in the form of an international agreement concluded by a Member State) to resolution once the respective provisions have been enacted. The resolution itself would be straightforward: EC law prevails over national law, under any circumstances. But Member States may find themselves faced with conflicting commitments. Further, one should not separate the internal, in the sense of Community legislation, from the external, conclusion of international agreements. Where the Community legislates, the Member States effectively lose autonomous powers, including as regards treaty-making. A separation of the internal and the external would risk undermining the uniform interpretation of Community law. It would also affect the proper role and function of the Community institutions which have legislated on a particular matter. It would affect review by the Court of Justice. Lastly, it would undermine the autonomy of the Community legal order.

The case law is generally convincing, except for the characterization of *Opinion 1/76* as a case involving exclusive competence. One may refer here to the comments above. *Opinion 1/76* is simply better understood as establishing general parallelism, by emphasizing that implied external powers are Treaty-based and therefore not confined to areas where the Community has already legislated.[129] The notion that, in certain cases, exclusivity arises out of the necessity of concluding an international agreement so as to achieve the Treaty's objectives disregards the general distinction between exclusive and concurrent powers. It is only in areas where powers are concurrent that the question of exclusive implied external powers arises, for where Community powers are *a priori* exclusive there can be no debate. In such areas of concurrent competence, one fails to see on what basis treaty-making should, in contrast with the power to make legislation, be exclusive on grounds of necessity. Exclusive implied powers are best confined to the *AETR* doctrine.

The Court has rejected general effects on the internal market as a criterion for exclusive implied powers. The risk of distortion of competition, for example in the air transport market, even if central to the idea of an internal market,[130] is no basis for exclusive treaty-making power. Here the Court does not adopt its well-known teleological and contextual methods of interpretation of the Treaty. The internal

---

[129] Cf D McGoldrick, *International Relations Law of the European Union* (Longman, 1997) 61.

[130] *Tobacco Advertising Directive* case (n 126 above).

market, vital as it has been for the development of the Community and of Community law, is not such a strong imperative as to establish exclusive external competence, other than through the common commercial policy. Instead of a broad economically-oriented, teleological, and contextual approach to implied powers, the Court has preferred a more doctrinal, constitutional, and institutional approach, which focuses on the autonomy and protection of the EC legal order. Again, this confirms the central function of implied powers in European constitutionalism.

To sum up, the ultimate conclusion from the analysis and the above reflections is that the Court did establish genuine parallelism between 'internal' and 'external' powers. It established such parallelism by giving the Community the authority to conclude international agreements in all areas where powers have been conferred on it. It confirmed such parallelism by adopting a consistent approach towards the material scope of EC powers, whether exercised through the adoption of legislation or the conclusion of an international agreement. Even exclusive implied powers are nothing more than an extension, to the field of treaty-making, of the doctrine of legislative pre-emption.

On this basis, it is now possible to discuss in the next chapter the main domains in which the Community may act on the international scene.

4

Express and implied powers
under the EC Treaty

Introduction

The case law of the Court of Justice on the scope and nature of the common commercial policy and on the implied powers doctrine, discussed and analysed in the preceding chapters, offers a solid foundation for understanding the EC's external powers. However, the Treaty has much evolved from its original approach where references to the conclusion of international agreements were limited to commercial policy and association. The aim of this chapter is to take a further look at external competence, in the main areas of EC policy-making where there is substantial external action. Before we look at specific areas, it is worth setting out the evolution of the E(E)C Treaty itself, in a short overview.

The Single European Act inserted a title on Research and Technological Development into the Treaty. The Community's policies in that area were to have an external dimension, as (current) Article 170 EC provides that the Community may make provision for co-operation with third countries or international organizations, and that the detailed arrangements for such co-operation may be the subject of agreements between the Community and the third parties concerned, to be negotiated and concluded in accordance with Article 300 EC. Similar provision for international co-operation was made in the new title on environmental policy, also inserted by the Single European Act. (Current) Article 174(4) EC states that, within their respective spheres of competence, the Community and the Member States shall co-operate with third countries and international organizations, and may conclude agreements to that effect. Due to the pace and dimensions of international environmental law making, this proved to be an important expansion of external Community competence.

The Treaty on European Union also inserted provisions in the EC Treaty concerning international action and the conclusion of international agreements. One of the main objectives of the TEU was to set in motion the development of Economic and Monetary Union. In the sphere of monetary policy, (current) Article 111 EC enables the Council to conclude international agreements on an exchange-rate system for the ECU (now euro) in relation to non-Community currencies.

With respect to education (Article 149(3) EC), vocational training (Article 150(3) EC), culture (Article 151(3) EC), and public health (Article 152(3) EC), where the TEU also created an express Treaty basis for Community policies, the EC Treaty merely provides that the Community and the Member States shall foster co-operation with third countries and the competent international organizations. It does not expressly mention the conclusion of international agreements, but in light of the implied powers doctrine there is no doubt that there is competence to conclude agreements for the purpose of such co-operation. The same is true as regards trans-European networks, where Article 155(3) EC states that the Community may decide to co-operate with third countries.

The Treaty on European Union also inserted a new Title on development co-operation, which is of course a purely external policy. In practice, development co-operation is one of the main pillars of EU external action, and before the EC Treaty was amended the Community had already been involved in such co-operation. In this domain Article 181 EC speaks, evidently, of co-operation with third countries and with the competent international organizations, and provides for the conclusion of international agreements to that effect.

The Amsterdam Treaty did not make further express provision for EC international action. It did however insert a new title, taken from the Third Pillar, on visas, asylum, immigration, and other policies related to the free movement of persons, which is currently the Community side of the Area of Freedom, Security, and Justice. The external dimension of those Community policies is obvious, and it is remarkable that no mention is made of the conclusion of international agreements. Again, though, the implied-powers doctrine no doubt fills the gap. The same comment applies to the expansion of EC social policy which the Amsterdam Treaty enabled by the effective inclusion of the Agreement on Social Policy (current Articles 136–145 EC), to which the United Kingdom had been unwilling to sign up at Maastricht.

The Treaty of Nice, lastly, inserted a title on economic, financial, and technical co-operation with third countries, effectively codifying a longstanding practice of including co-operation provisions in general agreements with non-member countries. Article 181a EC provides, rather obviously, for the conclusion of international agreements, and for co-operation with third countries and the competent international organizations.

This short *aperçu* sets the scene for a more intense examination of external competence in the main areas of EC policy-making. We have already looked at commercial policy, and will hereafter consider association agreements, development co-operation, the internal market, environmental protection, social policy, EMU, and the Community side of the Area of Freedom, Security, and Justice. In a number of those areas there is Court case law on external competence; in others there are no specific judicial statements as yet, but the principles of external competence none the less enable us to make some observations. It must be stressed that the object of this chapter is not to provide a comprehensive overview of actual external practice.[1] That is beyond the scope of this book, and references to practice are by way of illustration rather than anything else. The emphasis is on the relevant principles.

Association agreements

Article 310 EC provides:

The Community may conclude with one or more States or international organisations agreements establishing an association involving reciprocal rights and obligations, common action and special procedures.

The text is not a model of clear drafting. As noted by Stein, it highlights the structural components but resonates in silence on the substance.[2] Virtually any international agreement would involve reciprocal rights and obligations, and many agreements involve common action and special procedures. The concept of association itself is not defined. One possible reading is that, as the drafters of the EEC Treaty only mentioned the conclusion of agreements in matters of commercial policy and association, they envisaged that the EEC's international action was limited to trade agreements and general agreements with countries wishing to 'associate' themselves to the newborn organization. They seem to have been looking to provide a Treaty basis for agreements creating closer links with certain countries, and indeed international organizations, but the provision has never been used for agreements with the latter.

Article 310 EEC was immediately used to conclude association agreements with Greece, which was later to become a Member State,[3] and Turkey, which continues to aspire to membership.[4] Both those agreements made explicit reference to the prospect of future membership, and that became a feature of many association agreements. There are however other agreements concluded on the basis of Article 310 which never embodied prospective membership, expressly or by implication.[5] The provision was, for example, also used to manage the EEC's approach to relations with colonies of the Member States gaining independence, relations which developed into the broad partnership with ACP countries under the Lomé and, currently, Cotonou conventions.[6] It may further be noted that nearly all association agreements were concluded as mixed agreements, even if the Treaty provided for unanimity

[1] For recent surveys of types of agreements concluded by the Community see S Peers, 'EC Frameworks of International Relations: Co-operation, Partnership and Association', in A Dashwood and C Hillion (eds), *The General Law of EC External Relations* (Sweet & Maxwell, 2000) 160–76 and K Lenaerts and E De Smijter, 'The European Community's Treaty-Making Competence' (1996) 16 YEL 20–5; for an earlier attempt at classification see C Flaesch-Mougin, *Les accords externes de la Communauté économique européenne—Essai d'une typologie* (Editions de l'ULB, 1979).

[2] E Stein, 'External Relations of the European Community: Structure and Process', in *Collected Courses of the Academy of European Law (1990)—Community Law*, Vol I, Book 1 (Martinus Nijhoff, 1991) 151.

[3] [1974] OJ Spec Ed 2nd Series, PEI, 4.   [4] [1964] JO 217.

[5] E.g. with Southern Mediterranean States: see Peers, n 1 above, at 162.

[6] For the Cotonou Agreement see [2000] OJ L317/3.

within the Council thereby enabling all Member States to have a decisive voice and right of veto. Much as in other areas, the Commission argued for pure Community agreements, but was unable to persuade the Council.[7]

The Court of Justice did not before 1987 clarify the scope of EC competence to conclude association agreements. *Demirel v. Stadt Schwäbisch Gmünd*[8] concerned Mrs Demirel, a Turkish national, who in 1984 came to Germany under a tourist visa, so as to join her husband who lived there. She remained in the country after the expiry of her visa, and was threatened with expulsion. Before the *Verwaltungsgericht* (Administrative Court) Stuttgart she sought to rely on provisions of the association agreement with Turkey, a mixed agreement. The court referred questions on the interpretation and effect of those provisions to the Court of Justice for a preliminary ruling. In those proceedings the German and United Kingdom governments argued that the Court had no jurisdiction to reply to the questions, because the provisions in issue, on free movement of workers, had to be regarded as coming within the competence of the Member States, and not that of the Community.

Darmon AG emphasized the fact that the agreement aimed to 'establish ever closer bonds between the Turkish people and the peoples brought together in the European Economic Community', and created the prospect of accession. Those factors alone were in his opinion enough to classify the agreement as an act in the meaning of (current) Article 234 EC on preliminary rulings. When such a convention looked towards a further accession, he argued, the Community had of necessity to hold the most extensive powers to conclude agreements with non-member countries in order to cover all the fields of activity contemplated by the Treaty. There was no need to have recourse to the implied powers doctrine, as there was the express basis in Article 238 EEC (now 310 EC), and the power which it conferred had to be exercised in keeping with the goal pursued and the interests of the Community, and was not to be contrued restrictively. He none the less confined that analysis to agreements concluded with a view to accession, pointing out that there were agreements which had been based on Article 238 EEC which had aroused discussion as to their true nature. However, since one of the aims of an agreement concluded with a view to accession was the approximation of the economic and legal systems—and indeed political ones—in order to achieve 'full acceptance' by the associate country of the obligations arising out of the Treaty, it was necessary that all the subjects which were *a priori* to be covered by such acceptance be set out by the agreement in a Community perspective and that it be possible to interpret them with a view to their uniform application. That of course included the fundamental freedoms required for the establishment of the common market.[9]

The Court was much shorter. It followed the Advocate General's approach, but did not mention the dimension of prospective accession, and ruled on the scope of

---

[7] Stein (n 2 above), 151.
[8] Case 12/86 *Demirel v. Stadt Schwäbisch Gmünd* [1987] ECR 3719.
[9] Ibid, Opinion of Darmon AG, para 14.

(current) Article 310 EC in general terms. The Court held that, since the agreement in question was an association agreement creating special, privileged links with a non-member country which was required, at least to a certain extent, to take part in the Community system, (current) Article 310 EC necessarily empowered the Community to guarantee commitments towards non-member countries in all the fields covered by the Treaty. Since freedom of movement for workers was one of the fields covered by that Treaty, it followed that commitments regarding free movement fell within the powers conferred by Article 310. Thus the question whether the Court had jurisdiction to rule on the interpretation of a provision in a mixed agreement containing a commitment which only the Member States could enter into in the sphere of their own powers did not arise.[10]

The Court's analysis offers limited clarification of the concept of an association, by (a) referring to the creation of special, privileged links, and (b) requiring the associated country, at least to a certain extent, to take part in the Community system. The first dimension is self-explanatory, but the second is more ambiguous. Surely, the Court did not have in mind genuine participation by the associated country in the work of the Community and its institutions. No association agreement provides therefor.[11] The reference to participation in the Community system is in all likelihood to be interpreted in material terms. The system of the Treaty must in some policy areas, e.g. the internal market, or competition policy, be in some measure extended to the associated country.[12] Whether all agreements effectively adopted on the basis of (current) Article 310 EC comply with those criteria is not entirely free from doubt, but the tone of the *Demirel* ruling does not suggest strict scrutiny by the Court.

The most remarkable aspect of the judgment is that, particularly at the time of the case, it established broader external competence than under any other Treaty provisions. One should not be deceived by the Court's reference to free movement of workers, and its extension to Turkey. The Court's ruling effectively established that, in an association agreement, the Community could contract on matters of immigration. Turkey was, and is, a third country, and therefore provisions on the treatment of Turkish workers in the Community are effectively provisions on immigration and employment of third-country nationals. There was clearly at the time no basis in the Treaty for an EC immigration policy, but the Court none the less accepted that in the context of an association the Community could regulate immigration. It is therefore only in the context of association that one sees the full and complete external dimension of Community policies. For associations which prepare for accession, such broad EC competence is appropriate, but whether that is also the case for other associations may be more doubtful. However, with the gradual expansion of EU external powers such questions are increasingly irrelevant;

---

[10] Ibid, para 9.
[11] The EEA Agreement goes furthest because of its ambitious objective of extending the internal market, and even that agreement only establishes pre-legislative consultation: see Arts 97–104 ([1994] OJ L1/3).   [12] Lenaerts and De Smijter (n 1 above), 17.

immigration, for example, is currently expressly within Community competence (see below).

If the Court's judgment was among the most expansive in terms of Community competence, it did not much change the practice of concluding association agreements in mixed form. Often the official justification for mixity is that the agreement also establishes a political dialogue, which is outside Community competence.[13]

Association agreements continue to be a preferred instrument for preparing non-member countries for accession.[14] They are also used for establishing privileged links, across a broad spectrum of EU policies.[15]

Development co-operation and other co-operation policies

Development co-operation prior to the TEU

The European Union is a major global actor in the sphere of development co-operation. It works *in tandem* with the Member States, and together they make up the largest international donor.[16] The development of policies in this domain came naturally, in the first stages as a by-product of the EEC's other external policies, i.e. commercial policy and association. The association formula was quickly used for creating a framework for relations with the ACP countries, in the Yaoundé and subsequently Lomé Conventions (see above). Those relations are predicated on the notion of development. The commercial policy sphere witnessed a shift of emphasis in the 1970s, away from a strict non-discrimination approach (MFN), and towards the idea that preferential terms of trade are necessary for developing countries.

The use of the association formula for EEC–ACP relations was never challenged, particularly as the Conventions were concluded as mixed agreements. However, as we have seen in Chapter 2, there has been a strong debate on whether EEC competence in matters of commercial policy extended to trade agreements or trade measures with a strong development component. In *Opinion 1/78* the Court confirmed that such competence covered commodities agreements which regulated rather than liberalized trade agreements drafted in the framework of UNCTAD and thus specifically geared towards aiding the development of producer countries. It none the less allowed the financing of such agreements and the buffer-stock systems which they

---

[13] Cf Lenaerts and De Smijter, 24.

[14] e.g. the Europe Agreements: see M Maresceau and E Montaguti, 'The Relations between the European Union and Central and Eastern Europe: A Legal Appraisal' (1995) 32 CMLRev 1327–67.

[15] Cotonou Agreement (n 6 above) and agreements with Mediterranean countries: see C Flaesch-Mougin, 'Differentiation and Association within the Pan-Euro-Mediterranean Area', in M Maresceau and E Lannon (eds), *The EU's Enlargement and Mediterranean Strategies—A Comparative Analysis* (Palgrave, 2001) 63–96.

[16] According to the Commission the EU and its Member States provide about 55% of all international official development assistance, see <http://europa.eu.int/pol/ext/overview_en.htm>.

set up to be supplied by the Member States rather than the Community, in which case mixity was required.[17] What from a constitutional perspective seemed like making small allowance for pragmatism by recognizing Member States' involvement[18] became, as will be shown, an important factor in the Community's development co-operation policies, where financing is obviously crucial. After *Opinion 1/78* the Court confirmed the broad approach towards the notion of commercial policy in the *GSP* case.[19] Unilateral trade preferences for developing countries also come within the scope of the common commercial policy.

If association agreements and trade policy offered vehicles for a Community development co-operation policy, their limitations were obvious. It is impossible to conclude association agreements with all developing countries, and the notion of development is much broader than the notion of trade, however generously defined. Community efforts turned for example towards humanitarian aid, where only (current) Article 308 EC could be used as a legal basis, and even then under a broad reading of doubtful constitutionality.[20] The same Treaty provision had to be employed for concluding co-operation agreements with non-member countries outside the Yaoundé and Lomé framework.[21]

The precarious constitutional foundations of the Community's development co-operation policy prior to the TEU are evident for the close reader of two ECJ judgments dating from 1993 and 1994.[22] In *Parliament v. Council and Commission* (the *Bangladesh* case) the Parliament challenged decisions on emergency aid for Bangladesh, claiming that they infringed its prerogatives in budgetary matters.[23] The decision of principle had been taken by the 'Member States meeting in the Council'. The Court pointed out that such decisions, which were not acts of a Community institution, could not be challenged under (current) Article 230 EC. It none the less examined whether, having regard to its content and all the circumstances in which it was adopted, the act in question was not in reality a decision of the Council. If that had been the case, the Court would have had jurisdiction. However, one of the factors which led the Court to the conclusion that *in casu* there was no Council act was that the Community did not have exclusive competence in the field of humanitarian aid, and that consequently the Member States were not precluded from exercising their competence in that regard collectively in the Council or outside it.[24] The Court followed the Opinion of Jacobs AG according to whom 'it [was] common ground that in the field of humanitarian aid the competence of the Community is not exclusive but concurrent with that of the Member

---

[17] *Opinion 1/78 re International Agreement on Natural Rubber* [1979] ECR 2871.

[18] T Tridimas and P Eeckhout, 'The External Competence of the Community and the Case-Law of the Court of Justice: Principle versus Pragmatism' (1994) 14 YEL 143.

[19] Case 45/86 *Commission v. Council* [1987] ECR 1493.

[20] Cf JHH Weiler, *The Constitution of Europe* (CUP, 1999) 54, n 117.   [21] Peers (n 1 above), 163.

[22] For analysis see A Ward, 'Community Development Aid and the Evolution of the Inter-institutional Law of the European Union', in Dashwood and Hillion (eds), n 1 above, 42–7.

[23] Joined Cases C–181/91 and C–248/91 *Parliament v. Council and Commission* [1993] ECR I–3685.

[24] Ibid, paras 14–16.

States'.[25] Neither the Advocate General nor the Court, however, identified the legal basis in the Treaty for a Community humanitarian aid policy, and might have found themselves in some difficulty if they had opted to do so. In the end, the Court had no problems with allowing the Member States collectively to finance emergency aid, taking decisions when meeting in the Council, but not as Council, and entrusting co-ordination to the Commission, and yet acting outside the framework of the Treaty and of the budget.

In *Parliament v. Council* (the *Lomé IV* case) the Parliament again challenged its lack of involvement with the financial side of development co-operation policies.[26] The financial provisions of the Yaoundé and Lomé Conventions are traditionally implemented by means of a European Development Fund (EDF), set up for each convention by an internal agreement of the Member States. The EDF never formed part of the Community budget, despite pressure by the Parliament, the Commission, and the Court of Auditors.[27] Indeed, at the time of writing the EDF continues to be separate from that budget.[28] In the *Lomé IV* case the Parliament argued that the Financial Regulation of Lomé IV was adopted on the wrong legal basis, because the expenditure concerning the development aid provided for by the Convention was Community expenditure. The procedure of (current) Article 279 EC should have been used.

Much of the argument in the case focused on external competence. Jacobs AG indicated that, with regard to development aid to the ACP States, there was nothing in the Treaty, or in provisions adopted by the Community institutions pursuant to the Treaty, which pointed to the conclusion that the Community's competence was exclusive. In the absence of any indication to the contrary, it could be accepted that the Community and the Member States shared competence in this field. It followed that not only the Community but also the Member States, acting individually or collectively, could enter into international agreements to provide development aid to the ACP States. The Advocate General did not accept the Parliament's argument that, once the Community undertook an obligation by entering into an international agreement, the Member States were necessarily excluded from undertaking that obligation jointly with the Community. As a general rule, he pointed out, in an area where the Community and the Member States enjoyed concurrent competence, they could exercise their competences concurrently by undertaking joint action and joint obligations *vis-à-vis* third parties. He concluded that it was possible for the Community and the Member States to undertake jointly the obligation to provide development aid to the ACP States, and that, since the Community and the Member States enjoyed concurrent competence in that field, it was possible for them to agree that the funds necessary to finance the development aid were to be provided directly by the Member States outside the Community budget.[29]

---

[25] Joined Cases C–181/91 and C–248/91, Opinion of Jacobs AG, para 25.
[26] Case C–316/91 *Parliament v. Council* [1994] ECR I–625.
[27] Ibid, Opinion of Jacobs AG, paras 13–14.
[28] See Financial Regulation applicable to the 9th European Development Fund [2003] OJ L83/1.
[29] *Parliament v. Council* (n 26 above), Opinion of Jacobs AG, in particular paras 40, 50, and 53.

The Court followed that approach. It held that the Community's competence in the field of development co-operation was not exclusive, and that the Member States were accordingly entitled to enter into commitments themselves *vis-à-vis* non-member States, either collectively or individually, or even jointly with the Community. The Court then interpreted the Convention in order to identify the parties which had entered into commitments. It established that, in accordance with the essentially bilateral character of the co-operation, the obligation to grant 'the Community's financial assistance' fell on the Community and its Member States, considered together. As for the question whether it was for the Community or for its Member States to perform that obligation, the Court again noted the non-exclusive nature of Community competence, so that the Member States were entitled collectively to exercise their competence in that field with a view to bearing the financial assistance to be granted to the ACP States. It followed that the competence to implement the Community's financial assistance was shared by the Community and its Member States and that it was for them to choose the source and methods of financing. The choice had been for the expenditure to be assumed directly by the Member States and distributed by a Fund which they had set up by mutual agreement, with the administration of which the Community institutions were associated. Consequently, the expenditure was not Community expenditure and the action failed.[30]

The Court's statements on the non-exclusive character of Community competence in the area of development co-operation could hardly be criticized. However, the conclusions it drew from those statements for the system of financing of EC–ACP development co-operation are less straightforward. Apparently, in budgetary matters one does not need to draw a clear line between the Member States and the Community. Once it had established that competences were shared, the Court accepted that the system of financing could be of a hybrid character, for that is what the EDF amounts to. It is financed from the budgets of the Member States, but operates under a Financial Regulation adopted by the Council, and involving the Commission, the European Investment Bank, the European Parliament, and the Court of Auditors.[31] Yet it remains outside the Community budget. In this case, as in *Opinion 1/78* and the *Bangladesh* case, the Court left great discretion to the Member States and the Community institutions as regards the systems of financing.

The EC Treaty provisions on development co-operation

In the *Lomé IV* case both the Advocate General and the Court referred to the new EC Treaty provisions on development co-operation, inserted by the TEU. Indeed, the case was decided after the entry into force of the TEU, but the facts predated it. Those provisions confirmed the non-exclusive nature of EC competence. In fact,

---

[30] Ibid, paras 24–39.		[31] Financial Regulation (n 28 above).

the terms used in (current) Article 177(1) EC refer to the 'complementary' character of Community powers, rather than to the notion of concurrent competence: 'Community policy . . . shall be complementary to the policies pursued by the Member States'.[32] As is discussed below, the Convention on the Future of Europe distinguishes between concurrent and shared competences.

Let us take a brief look at the Treaty provisions on development co-operation. Article 177(1) provides, next to confirming the complementary character of EC competence, that policy in this sphere shall foster:

—the sustainable economic and social development of the developing countries, and more particularly the most disadvantaged among them;
—the smooth and gradual integration of the developing countries into the world economy;
—the campaign against poverty in the developing countries.

As Martenczuk notes, this provision highlights that development co-operation is not limited to questions of economic or social development, but aims to address all the causes of poverty and under-development.[33]

Article 177(2) provides that 'Community policy in this area shall contribute to the general objective of developing and consolidating democracy and the rule of law, and to that of respecting human rights and fundamental freedoms'. It puts development co-operation squarely in the context of human rights, broadly defined. Article 177(3) requires that the Community and the Member States comply with the commitments and take account of the objectives they have approved in the context of the United Nations and other competent international organizations.

Article 178 refers to the principle of integration: the Community shall take account of the above objectives in the policies which are likely to affect developing countries.[34]

Article 179 offers a legal basis for measures adopted by the Council under Article 251 EC (co-decision procedure), and provides that such measures may take the form of multi-annual programmes (paragraph 1). The European Investment bank shall contribute to the implementation of those measures (paragraph 2). The provision does not however affect co-operation with the ACP countries (paragraph 3). One may understand the latter provision as confirmation of the special, association-based framework of EC–ACP relations.[35]

Article 180(1) instructs the Community and the Member States to co-ordinate their policies and to consult each other on their aid programmes, including in international organizations and during international conferences. They may undertake

---

[32] A declaration attached to the TEU on the EDF confirmed the intention that the Fund would continue to be financed by national contributions.

[33] B Martenczuk, 'Cooperation with Developing and Other Third Countries: Elements of a Community Foreign Policy', in S Griller and B Weidel (eds), *External Economic Relations and Foreign Policy in the European Union* (Springer, 2002) 385–417.

[34] On the notion 'developing country' see ibid, 389–90.

[35] I Macleod, ID Hendry, and S Hyett, *The External Relations of the European* Communities (OUP, 1996) 341; Martenczuk (n 33 above), 397.

joint action, and Member States shall contribute if necessary to the implementation of Community aid programmes. That Treaty language appears to confirm the Court's approach in the *Bangladesh* and *Lomé IV* cases on the broad discretion for organizing co-operation between the Member States and the Community.

Article 181 contains the classic provision on co-operation with third countries and with international organizations. Such co-operation is to take place within the respective spheres of competence of the Community and of the Member States, and the arrangements for Community co-operation may be the subject of agreements negotiated and concluded in accordance with Article 300 EC. This competence is 'without prejudice to Member States' competence to negotiate in international bodies and to conclude international agreements'. A declaration attached to the TEU states that the latter provision, as well as (current) Article 111 on monetary policy and (current) Article 174 on environmental policy, 'do not affect the principles resulting from the judgment handed down by the Court of Justice in the AETR case'. It is however unclear whether such a declaration has any particular legal status.

Portugal v. Council

Questions as to the scope and nature of Community competence under the above provisions have only once come before the Court of Justice, in a Portuguese action against the conclusion of a Co-operation Agreement between the EC and India (a pure Community agreement).[36] The agreement was based on (current) Articles 133 and 181 EC. Portugal's challenge was broad. It considered that those Treaty provisions did not confer on the Community the necessary powers to conclude the Agreement as regards, first, the provision therein relating to human rights and, secondly, the provisions relating to various specific fields of co-operation (energy, tourism, and culture; drug abuse control; intellectual property; and commercial policy). Portugal further considered that recourse should also have been had to (current) Article 308 EC and to participation of all the Member States in the conclusion of the Agreement.

La Pergola AG started his analysis by looking at the origins of the newly established Treaty provisions on development co-operation. He identified three types of development co-operation agreements since the first Yaoundé Convention. In the first-generation agreements the main focus was on Community aid; the second-generation agreements were basically geared to economic co-operation; and the third-generation agreements take into account the social structure of the developing countries as well as commercial relations.[37] The Advocate General then turned to

---

[36] Case C–268/94 *Portugal v. Council* [1996] ECR I–6177. For the agreement see Council Decision concerning the conclusion of the Co-operation Agreement between the European Community and the Republic of India on Partnership and Development [1994] OJ L223/23. For academic comment see S Peers, 'Fragmentation or Evasion in the Community's Development Policy? The Impact of Portugal v. Council', in Dashwood and Hillion (n 1 above), 100–12.

[37] Ibid, Opinion of La Pergola AG, para 9.

the new provisions, regarding it as clear from (current) Article 177(1) EC that the objectives of Community development co-operation reflected a complex vision of development, the product of interaction between its economic, social, and political aspects.[38] He described Community competence as equal and complementary to that of the Member States. He did not however agree with the claim that Community competence was subordinate to that of the Member States. The Treaty provisions on co-ordination and consultation referred to both national and Community policy, and (current) Article 179 EC, on the adoption of measures by the Council, implied that the Community was empowered to conduct its own development co-operation policy.[39] There was no room for applying (current) Article 308 EC, because the Treaty specifically provided for a development co-operation policy.[40]

Those observations were useful, particularly as the Court itself did not engage in such general analysis. The Advocate General then turned to the human rights clause in Article 1(1) of the EC–India Agreement, which provided:

Respect for human rights and democratic principles is the basis for the co-operation between the Contracting Parties and for the provisions of this Agreement, and it constitutes an essential element of the Agreement.

He first pointed out that the case law of the Court, as embodied in (current) Article 6(2) TEU, made respect for human rights an objective that must inform Union action as a whole. The Treaty interdependence of human rights and development co-operation (see Article 177(2) EC) did not mark a new departure in Community action: La Pergola AG traced and described various political resolutions and statements linking the two. He considered that the inclusion of the human-rights clause in issue was specifically intended to adjust co-operation policy in line with respect for human rights. It was also designed to allow the Community to exercise the right to terminate the Agreement, in accordance with Article 60 of the Vienna Convention on the Law of Treaties (VCLT), where the non-member State failed to respect human rights within its own legal system.[41] The Advocate General went even further. The whole of Community action in this area illustrated the importance attaching to respect for human rights in development aid policy. If that was properly taken into account, the democracy clause had to be deemed necessary if development co-operation policy was to be lawfully pursued, and it would be fail-ure to adopt a clause of that type that would compromise the legality of Community action.[42]

The Court's approach was similar. It pointed out that (current) Article 177(2) EC required the Community to take account of the objective of respect for human rights when it adopted measures in the field of development co-operation. The mere fact that Article 1(1) of the Agreement provided that such respect 'constitutes an essential element' of the Agreement did not justify the conclusion that that provision

---

[38] *Portugal v. Council* (n 36 above), para 13.   [39] Ibid, paras 14–17.   [40] Ibid, para 20.
[41] See Chs 6 and 13.   [42] *Portugal v. Council* (n 36 above), paras 25–29.

went beyond the objective of Article 177(2). The very wording of that article demonstrated the importance to be attached to respect for human rights and democratic principles, so that, amongst other things, development co-operation policy had to be adapted to the requirements of respect for those rights and principles. With regard to the argument that the characterization of respect for human rights as an essential element of co-operation presupposed specific means of action, it first had to be stated that to adapt co-operation policy to respect for human rights necessarily entailed establishing a certain connection between those matters whereby one of them was made subordinate to the other. In that regard, it had to be borne in mind that a provision such as Article 1(1) could be an important factor for the exercise of the right to have a development co-operation agreement suspended or terminated where the non-member country violated human rights. Furthermore, the heading of Article 1 ('Basis and objectives') and the wording of the first paragraph provided confirmation that the question of respect for human rights and democratic principles was not a specific field of co-operation provided for by the Agreement.[43]

The Portuguese claims were not confined to human rights. The applicant also contested provisions of the Agreement concerning specific co-operation matters, as going beyond the combined Treaty provisions on commercial policy and development co-operation. Here the Court started its analysis at a general level. The Portuguese arguments, the Court stated, raised the question of the extent to which an agreement concluded on the basis of (current) Article 181 EC could lay down provisions on specific matters without there being any need to have recourse to other legal bases, or indeed to participation of the Member States in the conclusion of the agreement. The Court described the Community's competence in matters covered by the Treaty title on development co-operation as not exclusive but complementary to that of the Member States. In order to qualify as a development co-operation agreement, the agreement had to pursue the objectives in Article 177 EC. Article 177(1) in particular made it clear that those were broad objectives in the sense that it had to be possible for the measures required for their pursuit to concern a variety of specific matters. That was so in particular in the case of an agreement establishing the framework of such co-operation. That being so, to require a development co-operation agreement to be based on another provision as well as on Article 181 and, possibly, also to be concluded by the Member States whenever it touched on a specific matter would in practice amount to rendering devoid of substance the competence and procedure described in Article 181. It therefore had to be held that the fact that a development co-operation agreement contained clauses concerning various specific matters could not alter the characterization of the agreement, which had to be determined having regard to its essential object and not in terms of individual clauses, provided that those clauses did not impose such extensive obligations concerning the specific matters referred to that those

---

[43] Ibid, paras 23–28.

obligations in fact constituted objectives distinct from those of development co-operation.[44]

The Court then tested the EC–India Agreement against those requirements, first in general, and then in specific areas identified by Portugal (see above). At a general level the Court was satisfied that the provisions of the Agreement on specific matters established the framework of co-operation, and were limited to determining the areas for co-operation and to specifying certain of its aspects and various actions to which special importance was attached. By contrast, those provisions contained nothing that prescribed in concrete terms the manner in which co-operation in each specific area envisaged was to be implemented.[45] The Court also made it clear that the mere inclusion of provisions for co-operation in a specific field did not necessarily imply a general power such as to lay down the basis of a competence to undertake any kind of co-operation action in that field. It did not, therefore, predetermine the allocation of spheres of competence between the Community and the Member States or the legal basis of Community acts for implementing co-operation in such a field.[46]

At the level of specific areas of co-operation, Portugal took objection to *inter alia* the provisions on drug abuse control, under which the Contracting Parties affirmed their resolve to increase the efficiency of policies and measures to counter the supply and distribution of narcotic and psychotropic substances as well as preventing and reducing drug abuse. The co-operation in this field comprised training, education, health promotion, and rehabilitation of addicts; measures to encourage alternative economic opportunities; assistance in the monitoring of precursors' trade, prevention, treatment, and reduction of drug abuse; and exchange of all relevant information, including that relating to money laundering.[47] The Portuguese government argued that those matters came within the TEU provisions on Justice and Home Affairs (the Third Pillar, as then in force).

The Court first held that drug abuse control could not, as such, be excluded from the measures necessary for the pursuit of the objectives referred to in Article 177, since production of narcotics, drug abuse, and related activities could constitute serious impediments to economic and social development. It then had to be considered whether Article 19 of the Agreement remained within limits which did not necessitate recourse to a competence and to a legal basis specific to the sphere of drug-abuse control. The Court noted that the text of Article 19(1) contained nothing more than a declaration of intent to co-operate in drug-abuse control. In addition, it stated that the contracting parties were to act in conformity with their respective competences. The substance of the co-operation, defined in Article 19(2), constituted measures falling within the sphere of the development co-operation objectives. Here the Court specifically focused on exchange of information: it was in fact only in so far as that exchange made a contribution that was intimately linked to the other measures provided for by Article 19 that it could be included amongst

---

[44] *Portugal v. Council* (n 36 above), paras 35–39.   [45] Ibid, para 45.   [46] Ibid, para 47.
[47] Art 19 of the Agreement (n 36 above).

the actions falling within the field of development co-operation, and a restrictive interpretation was called for.[48]

As regards the agreement's provisions on energy, tourism, and culture, the Court simply considered that they only established the framework of co-operation, and laid down obligations to take action which did not constitute objectives distinct from those of development co-operation.[49]

On intellectual property the Court observed, first, that the improvement in protection of intellectual property rights sought by Article 10 of the Agreement contributed to the objective in Article 177(1) EC of smoothly and gradually integrating the developing countries in the world economy, and, secondly, that Article 10 merely provided that the contracting parties undertook to ensure as far as their laws, regulations, and policies allowed that suitable and effective protection was provided for intellectual property rights, reinforcing this protection where necessary. The further obligation to facilitate access to the databases of intellectual property organizations had only a very limited scope and was ancillary in nature, even in relation to the substance of intellectual property protection. Again, therefore, the obligations in this field constituted objectives distinct from those of development co-operation.[50]

Two dimensions of the Court's ruling in *Portugal v. Council* are of general significance. First, there is the location and precise meaning of the objective to develop and consolidate democracy and the rule of law, and to respect human rights. Peers notes that the Court transformed respect for human rights as an objective of development policy into an obligation to make such policy subject to the protection of human rights.[51] La Pergola AG indeed ventured to state that respect for human rights could constitute a condition for the legality of Community measures, but the Court did not confirm this in so many words. It did hold that 'development co-operation policy must be adapted to the requirement of respect for those rights and principles'.[52] It is therefore in any event clear that respect for human rights must permeate the whole sphere of development co-operation, and must be fully integrated into the Community's policy. There is however debate on whether human rights protection constitutes an objective in its own right, or whether it is only a general condition for the Community's policy.[53] The debate is linked to the contested scope for Community action in the domain of human rights generally.[54] On the basis of the text of the Treaty, however, one does not see what would preclude the Community from adopting measures or concluding agreements relating specifically to respect for human rights, where such respect is a development issue. It is true that the Treaty in Article 177 distinguishes between the objectives of development

---

[48] *Portugal v. Council* (n 36 above), paras 60–66.   [49] Ibid, para 54.

[50] Ibid, paras 73–76. The Court also recalled at para 77 its statements in *Opinion 1/94* on, from a perspective of commercial policy, the ancillary character of provisions for the organization of purely consultative procedures or clauses calling on the other party to raise the level of protection of intellectual property; see Ch 2.   [51] Peers (n 36 above), 103.

[52] *Portugal v. Council* (n 36 above), Opinion of La Pergola AG, para 24.

[53] E.g. E Fierro, *The EU's Approach to Human Rights Conditionality in Practice* (Martinus Nijhoff, 2003) 263–6.   [54] See Chs 3 and 13.

co-operation policy, described in paragraph 1, and the requirement that Community policy contribute to human rights protection etc., set out in paragraph 2. The basis for the distinction is not difficult to see, though. In paragraph 2 respect for human rights etc. is rightly characterized as a 'general objective', to which development co-operation policy must contribute. Indeed it is self-evident that human rights protection is not only a development issue. The European Union itself is founded on the principles of liberty, democracy, respect for human rights and fundamental freedoms (Article 6(1) TEU). Human rights protection is a much broader objective, going beyond the domain of development co-operation. Seen from that angle, there appears to be every scope for specific development co-operation measures or agreements to concentrate on democracy, the rule of law, and human rights—again, in so far as those are development issues. One does not see on what ground the Treaty could be seen to preclude specific measures oriented towards a specific dimension of development co-operation policy.

The Court also drew attention to the function of the human rights clause in the EC–India Agreement of permitting suspension or termination of the agreement in the case of non-respect of that provision. Indeed, the clause did not appear to have much other function, and the Agreement did not envisage specific measures for the promotion of human rights. As with much of the EU's involvement with human rights, the respect-and-control function was preferred over the active promotion of human rights.[55] In Chapter 13 we will further look at EU experience with suspension and termination of agreements.

The conclusion that the EU may well adopt specific measures of human rights protection in the context of its development co-operation policy brings us to the second dimension of *Portugal v. Council*. The Court visibly struggled with the tension between the ever broader and inclusive notion of development and the principle of limited Community powers. The Agreement's provisions on drug abuse control are a good example. Drug abuse is clearly a major development issue in a number of developing countries, yet the Community has virtually no general powers under the Treaty to develop an effective drugs policy. In so far as crime policy is concerned, the Third Pillar may be relevant, but not the First. The Court appears to fear that, through development co-operation policies, the limits of Community powers may be circumvented.[56] Theoretically, indeed, this is conceivable. The Community might, for example, conclude an agreement on drug abuse control with a developing country which is so detailed and specific that it necessitates the development of an internal Community policy on drugs. Imagine that such an agreement contains provisions on specific criminal penalties for narcotics trade and drug abuse in the contracting parties. Clearly, it would not be within the Community's competence

---

[55] P Alston and JHH Weiler, 'An "Ever Closer Union" in Need of a Human Rights Policy: The European Union and Human Rights', in P Alston (ed), *The EU and Human Rights* (OUP, 1999) 1, in particular 9–14.

[56] Cf M Cremona, 'External Relations and External Competence: The Emergence of an Integrated Policy', in P Craig and G de Búrca, *The Evolution of EU Law* (OUP, 1999) 161.

to conduct a development co-operation policy which would have the effect of binding the Community and the Member States as regards such criminal penalties. Furthermore, such an agreement would not only aim at development co-operation as one may assume that the EU is developed.

Whether there is a genuine threat of such abuse of the Treaty provisions on development co-operation is doubtful, but the Court is none the less correct in drawing attention to the limits of Community powers.[57] The right balance is difficult to strike, though. One may read the judgment as proclaiming that development co-operation agreements may only, in specific areas, provide for a general framework for co-operation. Yet effective development co-operation cannot be achieved through the mere establishment of such a general framework. All kinds of specific measures and actions may be required. Even if the Court did not accept Portugal's claims, it may have been too restrictive in its analysis, putting up high constitutional hurdles for an effective Community development co-operation policy.

The Treaty of Nice and the Convention on the Future of Europe

The Court's rather restrictive approach in *Portugal v. Council* may be one of the causes of the insertion into the EC Treaty of a further title on 'Economic, Financial and Technical Cooperation with Third Countries'.[58] The Treaty of Nice created this title, which is limited to one single provision, Article 181a EC. It provides:

1. Without prejudice to the other provisions of this Treaty, and in particular those of Title XX, the Community shall carry out, within its spheres of competence, economic, financial and technical co-operation measures with third countries. Such measures shall be complementary to those carried out by the Member States and consistent with the development policy of the Community.

Community policy in this area shall contribute to the general objective of developing and consolidating democracy and the rule of law, and to the objective of respecting human rights and fundamental freedoms.

2. The Council, acting by a qualified majority on a proposal from the Commission and after consulting the European Parliament, shall adopt the measures necessary for the implementation of paragraph 1. The Council shall act unanimously for the association agreements referred to in Article 310 and for the agreements to be concluded with the States which are candidates for accession to the Union.

3. Within their respective spheres of competence, the Community and the Member States shall co-operate with third countries and the competent international organisations. The arrangements for Community co-operation may be the subject of agreements between the Community and the third parties concerned, which shall be negotiated and concluded in accordance with Article 300.

---

[57] See also Ch 3.   [58] See also Martenczuk (n 33 above), 399–410.

The first subparagraph shall be without prejudice to the Member States' competence to negotiate in international bodies and to conclude international agreements.

This article clearly complements the provisions on development co-operation in several ways. First, it provides a legal basis for concluding co-operation agreements with all non-member States, not only developing countries. There is a well-established practice in this field, as the Community sought to broaden bilateral trade agreements by adding on provisions on economic co-operation. In the absence of an express Treaty provision Article 308 EC had to be relied upon for concluding such agreements.[59]

Secondly, the provision confirms the 'general objective' of development and consolidation of democracy and the rule of law, and of respect for human rights. It supports the conception that human rights are a transversal objective, and underlie the whole sphere of the EU's external action; indeed they should underlie the whole sphere of all EU action.

Thirdly, Article 181a EC appears to take care of the problem of the limits, identified in *Portugal v. Council*, of Community competence in matters of development co-operation. It addresses economic, financial, and technical co-operation 'within [the Community's] spheres of competence'. The subject matter of such co-operation is therefore defined in the broadest terms, and the provision offers a specific legal basis for such co-operation, obviating the need for recourse to different Treaty provisions depending on the subject of co-operation. For example, an agreement providing for technical co-operation in matters of transport, environmental protection, and agriculture does not need to be based on the express or implied external powers in those areas.

The concepts of economic, technical, and financial co-operation are not defined in the Treaty, but should not present major difficulties of interpretation, in particular in the light of established practice. They can be contrasted with the law making function of international agreements, where a particular policy is pursued through the establishment of binding rules destined to be integrated into domestic legal systems. A co-operation agreement in matters of intellectual property, for example, could not involve harmonization of intellectual property law.

The draft Constitution confirms that development co-operation is a matter of shared competence, and adds that the exercise of EU competence may not result in Member States being prevented from exercising theirs (Article I–13(4)). Chapter IV of Part III concerns 'Co-operation with Third Countries and Humanitarian Aid'. Article III–218 provides that EU development co-operation policy shall have as its primary objective the reduction and, in the long term, the eradication of poverty. Article III–222 deals with urgent financial aid which the situation in a third country may require. The draft Constitution also introduces a provision on humanitarian aid (Article III–223). It concerns 'operations . . . intended to provide ad hoc assistance, relief and protection for people in third countries and victims of natural

---

[59] Peers (n 5 above); Martenczuk (n 33 above), 399–400.

or man-made disasters, in order to meet the humanitarian needs resulting from different situations'. In the three areas of development co-operation, economic, financial, and technical co-operation, and humanitarian aid, the EU may conclude agreements with third countries.[60]

Environment

The Community has a longstanding involvement with environmental protection policies. It is of course in the nature of many environmental problems that they cross borders between States, and increasingly such problems are of a global character. Therefore, much as Community involvement is logical, Community policy cannot stop at the external border. Policies are increasingly developed in international concert, leading to multilateral environmental agreements. Community competence in matters of environmental protection would be severely limited if there was no capacity to participate in the negotiation and conclusion of such agreements.[61]

As was mentioned, the SEA inserted environmental protection policy into the EEC Treaty, and from the start provided for external action. (Current) Article 174(4) EC provides:

Within their respective spheres of competence, the Community and the Member States shall co-operate with third countries and with the competent international organizations. The arrangements for Community co-operation may be the subject of agreements between the Community and the third parties concerned, which shall be negotiated and concluded in accordance with Article 300.

The previous subparagraph shall be without prejudice to Member States' competence to negotiate in international bodies and to conclude agreements.

In Chapter 2 we looked at the relationship between trade policy and environmental policy from an external competence perspective. In *Greece v. Council* the Court accepted that a regulation laying down the maximum level of radioactive contamination for imported agricultural products came within the common commercial policy.[62] In *Opinion 2/00*, by contrast, the Court established that the Cartagena Protocol is essentially concerned with environmental protection, and not with trade.[63] In the *Energy Star Agreement* case the conclusion was that an agreement with the United States on the labelling of products as regards their energy-efficiency is predominantly concerned with trade.[64] The reader is referred to those pages for further analysis of the delimitation of commercial policy and environmental policy, which may well continue to pose problems, particularly in light of

---

[60] Arts III–219(2), III–221(3), and III–223(4).
[61] For a more in-depth analysis of external competence see JH Jans, *European Environmental Law* (2nd edn., Europa Law Publishing, 2000) ch 2.
[62] Case C–62/88 *Greece v. Council* [1990] ECR I–1527.
[63] *Opinion 2/00 re Cartagena Protocol on Biosafety* [2001] ECR I–9713.
[64] Case C–281/01 *Commission v. Council* [2002] ECR I–12049.

the exclusive nature of Community competence in matters of trade and the concurrent character of powers in the field of environmental protection.

There can be no attempt here to define Community competence in matters of environmental protection in material terms. The Treaty sets a number of objectives for Community policy and refers to a number of principles which must guide Community action (the precautionary principle, the principle of preventive action, and the polluter-pays principle).[65] It provides for different methods of decision-making.[66] The co-decision procedure is the rule, but in certain areas the Council decides unanimously. In many areas environmental policy is developed through general action programmes.[67] The Treaty also specifies that Community measures shall not prevent any Member States from maintaining or introducing more stringent provisions.[68] It is clear from those provisions, and from the practice, that Community competence in environmental matters is wide and inclusive, yet shared with the Member States.

There is one further, particular issue which needs to be looked at. The text of the Treaty provisions may suggest that all external action in matters of environmental protection must be based on the express provision of Article 174(4) (see above). That is however not the case. In *Opinion 2/00*[69] the Court of Justice held that Article 174 defines the objectives to be pursued in the context of environmental policy, while Article 175 constitutes the legal basis for the adoption of environmental measures. The latter provision contains alternative modes of EC decision-making, depending on the subject matter of the measures, but it does not expressly refer to the conclusion of international agreements. The Court appeared to confine the use of Article 174(4) to 'arrangements for Community co-operation' with third parties, and pointed out that the Protocol did not merely establish such arrangements but laid down precise rules on the environmental issues which it covered. Accordingly, Article 175(1) EC was the appropriate legal basis for the conclusion of the Protocol, and not, as the Commission had argued, Article 174(4).[70] It is not wholly clear from the Opinion why the Commission took this view. It may have been concerned about the possible application of Article 176 EC, according to which 'the protective measures adopted pursuant to Article 175 shall not prevent any Member State from maintaining or introducing more stringent protective measures', something the Commission might seek to avoid in relation to the Cartagena Protocol. If that was indeed the Commission's concern, it would in any event seem questionable whether Article 176 EC constitutes sufficient authority for the Member States to adopt protective measures more stringent than those provided for by the Protocol. According to Article 300(7) EC agreements concluded by the Community are

---

[65] See Art 174 EC.   [66] Art 175 EC.

[67] E.g. Decision 1600/2002 of the European Parliament and of the Council laying down the Sixth Community Environment Action Programme [2002] OJ L242/1.   [68] Art 176 EC.

[69] N 63 above.

[70] See also, as regards the respective scope of paras 1 and 2 of Art 175, Case C–36/98 *Spain v. Council* [2001] ECR I–779.

binding on the Community institutions and on the Member States, and it is submitted that the question whether more stringent measures are allowed is to be resolved on the basis of the proper construction of the Cartagena Protocol.

Be that as it may, the Opinion does clarify that the Community's external environmental powers are not confined to the arrangements referred to in Article 174(4), but extend to all areas of Community environmental law making.[71] The Opinion thus recognizes implied external powers, and its approach may be relevant for other policy areas where the Treaty contains similar provisions on international co-operation.

It may further be recalled that the Opinion established, for external competence, the principle that when an agreement has a twofold purpose or component, one should aim to determine the predominant purpose or component. Only if the agreement simultaneously pursues several objectives which are inseparably linked without one being secondary and indirect in relation to the other may the agreement be founded on the corresponding legal bases.[72] This principle will no doubt become increasingly important, as agreements pursue multiple aims, and as the founding treaties have become more express on matters of competence.

The internal market

Community policies to establish and complete a well-functioning internal market, which operates like a single national market, are central and foundational for much of the Community and EU construct, even if the current EU clearly transcends the core economic functions of the original EEC. Internal market policy is of course primarily an 'internal' policy, and it may at first glance seem curious to consider opportunities for external action and for the conclusion of international agreements in this sphere. The issue none the less needs to be considered, because there are important questions of scope of Community powers in internal market-related matters.

The first point to note is that the common commercial policy complements the internal market; indeed it is a component of the internal market. In the conception of the Treaty a common policy on external trade is vital for internal free movement, since the internal market covers all products, those originating in the Community and those which are imported.[73] The scope and nature of Community competence in external trade matters are extensively analysed in Chapter 2.

That does not however mean that all Community measures which affect imported products come within the scope of the common commercial policy. One classic mechanism for having a well-functioning internal market is harmonization of national product regulations, based on Article 95 EC. Such measures of harmonization, usually in the form of directives, govern all products on the internal market, including imported products. For example, the directive on toys lays down certain

---

[71] Cf A Dashwood, Annotation Opinion 2/00 (2002) 39 CMLRev 368.
[72] *Opinion 2/00* (n 63 above), paras 22–24.   [73] Arts 23 and 24 EC; see also Ch 10.

essential requirements for the safety etc. of toys,[74] with which all toys traded on the internal market need to comply, be they produced in the EU or, for that matter, China. A directive on toys comes within the scope of internal market competence, even if it also applies to Chinese toys, whereas a regulation limiting imports of toys from China[75] falls within the common commercial policy. At the level of internal (domestic) legislation the distinction between general harmonization and import or export measures may be rather straightforward, but when it comes to concluding international agreements on product regulations (or technical regulations and standards, as is the current term of art) the issue of competence is less obvious.[76] What is the legal basis in the Treaty for the adoption of such agreements?

In *Opinion 1/94* the Court briefly looked at the WTO Agreement on Technical Barriers to Trade (TBT) and the Agreement on Sanitary and Phytosanitary Measures (SPS). As regards the former, the Netherlands government argued that the joint participation of the Community and the Member States was justified, since the Member States had their own competence in relation to technical barriers to trade by reason of the optional nature of certain Community directives in that area, and because complete harmonization had not been achieved and was not envisaged. The Court most succinctly replied by stating that the provisions of the TBT Agreement were designed merely to ensure that technical regulations and standards and procedures for assessment of conformity with technical regulations and standards did not create unnecessary obstacles to trade (see the preamble and Articles 2.2 and 5.1.2. TBT). It thus followed that the agreement came within the ambit of the common commercial policy. As regards the SPS Agreement the Court similarly referred to the preamble, according to which the agreement was confined to 'the establishment of a multilateral framework of rules and disciplines to guide the development, adoption and enforcement of sanitary and phytosanitary measures in order to minimise their negative effects on trade'. Such an agreement could be concluded on the basis of (then) Article 113 EC alone (now, with amendments, Article 133).[77]

The Court's approach was logical for agreements which are predominantly oriented towards avoiding the negative effects on trade of technical regulations and standards, and of sanitary and phytosanitary measures, and which do not themselves provide for harmonization of such regulations and measures. However, in the *Energy Star Agreement* case the Court appeared to go a little further.[78] There the Court considered that the predominant purpose of an agreement effectively extending the US Energy Star programme to the Community was of a commercial–policy rather than environmental–policy nature, even if the programme itself ultimately aimed at greater environmental protection. The Court concentrated on the immediate and direct

---

[74] Directive 88/378 on the approximation of the laws of the Member States concerning the safety of toys [1988] OJ L187/1.
[75] Regulation 519/94 on common rules for imports from certain third countries and repealing Regulations 1765/82, 1766/82, and 3420/83 [1994] OJ L67/89.
[76] See for further analysis ELM Völker, *Barriers to External and Internal Community Trade* (Kluwer, 1993) ch 5.   [77] *Opinion 1/94 re WTO Agreement* [1994] ECR I–5267, paras 28–33.
[78] *Commission v. Council* (n 64 above).

impact on trade of common labelling rules, rather than on the longer-term and indirect objective of environmental protection. The judgment goes further than *Opinion 1/94* because there was an element of material harmonization in the agreement. It would however be wrong to conclude that all international agreements laying down technical regulations, standards, or common labelling rules come within the scope of the common commercial policy. In some cases, no doubt, effective harmonization will be more predominant than international trade concerns. Such agreements will have to be concluded on the basis of the Treaty provision enabling such harmonization, the most general one being Article 95 EC.[79]

The above observations apply to the production of and trade in goods. As regards services, the second type of products traded in the internal market, the position is different. Before the entry into force of the Treaty of Nice, external trade in services was only covered by the common commercial policy in so far as it took place under the cross-border mode.[80] Currently, the complex provisions of Article 133(5) and (6) EC apply.[81] Those provisions should cover many international negotiations on services, at least those in the WTO, which are definitely concerned with 'trade' in services. However, where an international negotiation does not concern the trade dimension of services, there may none the less be scope for EC involvement, on the basis of the internal market provisions in the Treaty. For example, an international agreement establishing certain accounting standards for the protection of investors may well be insufficiently trade-related to come within the scope of the amended Article 133 EC. It should be possible to conclude such an agreement on the basis of the Community's implied external powers in the sphere of the internal market, if the provisions in the agreement contribute to removing obstacles in the internal market or distortion of competition.[82] Furthermore, it follows from *Opinion 1/94* that the Community has exclusive competence for agreements concerning services where (a) provisions in EC legislation provide for international negotiations, or (b) there is complete harmonization of a particular self-employed activity.[83]

In the sphere of establishment the above principles also apply, with the proviso that establishment by non-EU nationals or legal persons comes within the concept of trade in services where the economic activity involved consists of the provision of services. Indeed, the notion of 'services' under WTO law is broader than under the EC Treaty. GATS applies to commercial presence, which covers permanent establishment by non-domestic service providers.[84] Where establishment is not related to an economic activity in the services sector, external competence needs to be linked to the internal market.

---

[79] It is noteworthy that in the *Energy Star Agreement* case the Court hinted at the fact that EC directives on eco-labelling should have been based on Art 95 EC rather than Art 175 EC: ibid, para 46.

[80] *Opinion 1/94* (n 77 above); see Ch 2.   [81] See again Ch 2.

[82] Cf Case C–376/98 *Germany v. European Parliament and Council* [2000] ECR I–8419 (*Tobacco Advertising Directive* case).   [83] *Opinion 1/94* (n 77 above); see Ch 3.

[84] For further reflections see P Eeckhout, 'Constitutional Concepts for Free Trade in Services', in G de Búrca and J Scott, *The EU and the WTO—Legal and Constitutional Issues* (Hart, 2001) 221–3.

As regards workers it is not clear whether prior to the Treaty of Amsterdam the Treaty's internal market provisions offered any firm basis for external action, particularly in so far as non-EU citizens were involved. As analysed above, the Court in *Demirel* had no difficulty in accepting that an association agreement could cover provisions on non-EU workers,[85] but outside the context of associations the scope of Community competence was uncertain. One could argue that the Community had competence as regards non-EU workers legally resident and employed in a Member State, on the ground that the treatment of such workers could affect the internal labour market, but as regards access by non-EU citizens to the labour market and the connected subject of immigration there was no basis in the Treaty for Community competence.[86] The Treaty of Amsterdam changed that by projecting in the new Title IV a Community migration policy as part of the Area of Freedom Security and Justice (see below). It also provided, in (current) Article 137 EC (social policy), for measures regarding 'conditions of employment for third-country nationals legally residing in Community territory'.

In the domain of capital and payments, by contrast, there is clear-cut external competence. The Treaty not only prohibits restrictions on movement of capital and payments between Member States, but also between Member States and third countries, subject to those restrictions which existed on 31 December 1993 under either national law or Community law, which involve direct investment, establishment, the provision of financial services or the admission of securities to capital markets (Articles 56 and 57(1) EC). It is therefore clear that, after that date, the Member States are no longer entitled to introduce additional restrictions; only the Council may do so under either Article 57(2) EC (again as regard direct investment, establishment, provision of financial services, or admission of securities to capital markets), Article 59 EC (safeguard measures), or Article 60 EC (economic sanctions).[87] Those combined provisions in effect establish exclusive Community competence, subject to the identified exceptions. Such exclusive competence extends to the conclusion of international agreements on capital or payment restrictions.

In the specific sectors of agriculture, fisheries, and transport the case law analysed in Chapters 2 and 3 identifies the basis for and scope of Community competence. In *Opinion 1/94* the Court clarified that agreements on trade in agricultural products come within the scope of the common commercial policy, even if they affect the Common Agricultural Policy (CAP) as strongly as does the WTO Agreement on Agriculture.[88] An agreement not concerned with trade, by contrast, would come within the scope of the Community's implied external powers provided by the Treaty provisions on agriculture, if it can be linked to the objectives

---

[85] N 8 above.

[86] Cf Joined Cases 281, 283 to 285, and 287/85 *Germany and Others v. Commission* [1987] ECR 3203, para 30.

[87] In the latter case, a Member State may none the less, for serious political reasons and on grounds of urgency, take unilateral measures; see further Ch 12.

[88] *Opinion 1/94* (n 77 above), paras 28–31.

of the CAP. Those provisions do not confer exclusive competence, but there is so much Community legislation that the *AETR* principle would often apply. In the sphere of conservation of fish resources, there is exclusive Community competence, flowing from the relevant provisions of primary law.[89] As regards transport, *Opinion 1/94* and the implied-powers case law supply the relevant principles, and the reader may be referred to the analysis in the previous chapters. The Community's competition policy is a further dimension of the internal market. In this area, too, the Community no doubt has competence to conclude international agreements, for example regarding co-operation with non-EU competition authorities.[90]

Social policy

The development of an EU social policy is a difficult process, largely owing to political differences regarding the aims and reach of EU involvement in this area. The original EEC Treaty envisaged little more than close co-operation between the Member States (Article 118 EEC), and did not confer legislative competence. The Single European Act changed that, but only as regards health and safety of workers (Article 118a EEC). At the Maastricht negotiations there was strong pressure to create a much more meaningful social policy, but the United Kingdom resisted such pressure, leading to the Agreement on Social Policy between eleven Member States. At Amsterdam the Member States agreed on making that agreement part of the Treaty, leading to the current chapter on 'Social Provisions', Articles 136–145 EC.

In Chapter 3 we analysed *Opinion 2/91*,[91] where the Court examined competence to conclude an ILO Convention concerning safety in the use of chemicals at work. It had no difficulty in confirming that Article 118a EEC conferred competence to conclude international agreements, even if the Community's internal legislative competence in the field of health and safety of workers was defined in rather subsidiary terms.[92]

On the basis of that ruling and the other implied powers case law, there can be no doubt that the Community may conclude agreements in the sphere of social policy. Article 137 EC defines the areas in which the Community shall support and complement the activities of the Member States, which it may do by adopting, by means of directives, minimum requirements for gradual implementation. Those areas include health and safety of workers; working conditions; information and consultation of workers; integration of persons excluded from the labour market; equality between men and women. Here the co-decision procedure applies. In other areas the Council acts unanimously; they include social security and social protection of workers;

---

[89] See Ch 3; for further analysis see Macleod, Hendry, and Hyett (n 35 above), ch 10.

[90] See e.g. Decision 98/386 concerning the conclusion of the Agreement between the European Communities and the Government of the United States of America on the application of positive comity principles in the enforcement of their competition laws [1998] OJ L173/26, based on (current) Art 83 EC.

[91] *Opinion 2/91 re ILO Convention No 170* [1993] ECR I–1061.   [92] See Ch 3.

protection of workers where their employment contract is terminated; representation and collective defence of the interests of workers and employers; conditions of employment for third-country nationals legally residing in Community territory; and financial contributions for promotion of employment and job creation. In all those areas the Community may act under international law. The same no doubt goes for the competence conferred by Article 141(3) EC to adopt measures to ensure the application of the principle of equal opportunities and equal treatment of men and women in matters of employment and occupation, including the principle of equal pay for equal work of equal value. It may be added that such external competence is exclusive where there is Community legislation which could be affected by the provisions of an international agreement. However, as the Court found in *Opinion 2/91*, that principle does not operate where both the Community legislation and the international agreement only provide for minimum rules.

Whereas there is thus extensive external competence in the field of social policy, a major obstacle to the exercise of such competence is that the Community is not a member of the ILO, and cannot as such participate in the conclusion of ILO Conventions.[93] The ILO Constitution admits only States as members (Article 1(2)) and does not provide for ratification of ILO Conventions by non-members. In the ILO, therefore, the Community needs to be represented by its Member States.[94]

Economic and Monetary Union

The Treaty on European Union laid down provisions for the establishment of an Economic and Monetary Union (EMU), which is at present in full operation (the so-called third phase), with a single currency, even if a number of Member States do not yet participate in that final phase. The distinguishing feature of EMU, as compared with other Community policies, is that there is a specific institutional framework, the European System of Central Banks (ESCB), which comprises the European Central Bank (ECB) and the national central banks.

The Treaty distinguishes between economic and monetary policy. The chapter on economic policy does not confer strong law making powers on the Community. It mostly contains instructions for the Member States and the Community institutions, including prohibitions on overdraft facilities (Article 101 EC), on privileged access to financial institutions (Article 102 EC), on bail-outs (Article 103 EC), and on excessive government deficits (Article 104 EC). Co-ordination of economic policies is to take place within the Council, which may issue recommendations setting out broad guidelines following conclusions reached by the European Council (Article 99(1) and (2) EC). The Council and the Commission have general monitoring and supervisory powers (see Articles 99(3)–(5) and 104 EC).

---

[93] See *Opinion 2/91* (n 91 above) and Ch 7.
[94] So much follows from the duty of co-operation: see Ch 7.

The Treaty chapter on economic policy does not provide for express external powers, nor is there much scope for the application of the implied-powers doctrine. The kind of powers conferred on the Community do not lend themselves to the conclusion of formal international agreements,[95] and there are no examples of agreements concluded on the basis of any of the relevant Treaty provisions. There is however clearly scope for Community involvement in informal international co-ordination of economic policies, such as takes place in various international fora (e.g. the G8).

The EU's monetary policy is carried out through the ESCB, whose primary objective is to maintain price stability, and which shall support the general economic policies in the Community (Article 105(1) and (2) EC). The basic tasks of monetary policy are: [96]

—to define and implement the monetary policy of the Community;
—to conduct foreign exchange operations consistent with the provisions of Article 111;
—to hold and manage the official foreign reserves of the Member States;
—to promote the smooth operation of payment systems.

The ESCB shall moreover contribute to the smooth conduct of policies pursued by the competent authorities relating to the prudential supervision of credit institutions and the stability of the financial system (Article 105(5) EC), and the Council may confer upon the ECB specific tasks concerning policies relating to the prudential supervision of credit institutions and other financial institutions with the exception of insurance undertakings (Article 105(6) EC). The ECB has the exclusive right to authorize the issue of banknotes (Article 106(1) EC). Further provisions on the powers of the ECB are laid down in the Statute of the ESCB, and the ECB may exercise those powers by adopting its own regulations, decisions, and recommendations and opinions (Article 110 EC).

It is obvious that the running of a single currency and of monetary union may require action under international law, including the conclusion of international agreements. The EC Treaty recognizes that in Article 111, which contains the relevant provisions. The first two paragraphs concern the exchange rate of the euro in relation to non-Community currencies:

1. By way of derogation from Article 300, the Council may, acting unanimously on a recommendation from the ECB or from the Commission, and after consulting the ECB in an endeavour to reach a consensus consistent with the objective of price stability, after consulting the European Parliament, in accordance with the procedure in paragraph 3 for determining the arrangements, conclude formal agreements on an exchange-rate system for the ECU [euro] in relation to non-Community currencies. The Council may, acting by a qualified majority on a recommendation from the ECB or from the Commission, and after consulting the ECB in an endeavour to reach a consensus consistent with the objective of price stability, adopt, adjust or abandon the central rates of the ECU within the exchange-rate system.

---

[95] C Zilioli and M Selmayr, 'The External Relations of the Euro Area: Legal Aspects' (1999) 36 CMLRev 289.   [96] Art 105(2) EC.

The President of the Council shall inform the European Parliament of the adoption, adjustment or abandonment of the ECU central rates.

2. In the absence of an exchange-rate system in relation to one or more non-Community currencies as referred to in paragraph 1, the Council, acting by a qualified majority either on a recommendation from the Commission and after consulting the ECB or on a recommendation from the ECB, may formulate general orientations for exchange-rate policy in relation to these currencies. These general orientations shall be without prejudice to the primary objective of the ESCB to maintain price stability.

The Treaty thus permits Community participation in a formal exchange-rate system, such as that of Bretton Woods or as existed in the Community prior to EMU. Short of the establishment of such a system, the Council may also formulate general orientations for exchange-rate policy.

   Article 111(3) EC confers general power to conclude agreements concerning monetary or foreign-exchange regime matters, and lays down the procedure to be followed for the negotiation and conclusion of such agreements:

3. By way of derogation from Article 300, where agreements concerning monetary or foreign-exchange regime matters need to be negotiated by the Community with one or more States or international organisations, the Council, acting by a qualified majority on a recommendation from the Commission and after consulting the ECB, shall decide the arrangements for the negotiation and for the conclusion of such agreements. These arrangements shall ensure that the Community expresses a single position. The Commission shall be fully associated with the negotiations.

   Agreements concluded in accordance with this paragraph shall be binding on the institutions of the Community, on the ECB and on Member States.

Paragraphs (4) and (5) of Article 111 concern, respectively, international representation and the scope for agreements concluded and negotiated by the Member States:

4. Subject to paragraph 1, the Council, acting by a qualified majority on a proposal from the Commission and after consulting the ECB, shall decide on the position of the Community at international level as regards issues of particular relevance to economic and monetary union and on its representation, in compliance with the allocation of powers laid down in Articles 99 and 105.

5. Without prejudice to Community competence and Community agreements as regards economic and monetary union, Member States may negotiate in international bodies and conclude international agreements.

As can be seen, those Treaty provisions lay down a complete system for the conduct of external relations in monetary matters. The core provision is Article 111(3) EC, which generally allows for the conclusion of international agreements on 'monetary or foreign-exchange regime matters'. As with other external competences of the Community, one needs to determine both the scope and the nature of those competences.

This section cannot offer an extensive analysis of the concept of monetary policy and of the internal and external powers conferred upon the Community in this field. There is, in any event, little or no practice as yet, and there is no case law on Article 111 EC. It may none the less be noted that the concept of 'monetary or foreign-exchange regime matters' appears broad, and can be read as encompassing all aspects of Community monetary policy. Through the broad reference in Article 111(3) EC the Treaty thus appears to establish full parallelism between the Community's internal and external powers. In the literature it has none the less been suggested that the scope of Article 111(3) EC is more limited, and extends only to 'monetary regime' and 'foreign-exchange regime' matters. The former notion is said to be confined to situations in which the monetary regime of the euro is extended to a third country.[97] It is indeed true that the different language versions of Article 111(3) EC are inconclusive as to the precise meaning of the phrase 'monetary or foreign-exchange regime matters', some of them indicating that all 'monetary questions' are covered, others providing that external competence concerns 'monetary regime' matters. However, the correct conclusion rather seems to be that little independent meaning is to be attributed to the use of the notion of 'regime'. There is in any event no indication in the Treaty that the term 'monetary regime' has the precise and limited meaning referred to above.

As regards the nature of Community competence in the sphere of monetary policy, it is submitted that it is exclusive, in so far as the euro and the Member States participating in the final phase of EMU are involved.[98] Indeed it is in the nature of a single currency that there is a single monetary and exchange-rate policy (see Article 4(2) EC), and the draft Constitution expressly recognizes exclusive EU competence.[99] Thus, the Community's external powers under Article 111 EC are also of an exclusive character, notwithstanding the reference in Article 111(5) EC to national competence, which in any event is 'without prejudice to Community competence'.[100] This has important consequences for Community representation in certain international organizations, in particular the IMF. At present the Community as such cannot become a member of the IMF because the latter admits only States, but as in the case of the ILO the Member States are required to act in common, representing the Community, in all matters of exclusive Community competence.[101]

There is a further point to examine. Zilioli and Selmayr have mounted an impressive and elaborate argument, to the effect that the ECB has international legal personality, separate from that of the Community. In their conception, there are two

---

[97] Zilioli and Selmayr (n 95 above), 299–301; see also J Dutheil de la Rochère, 'EMU: Constitutional Aspects and External Representation' (1999–2000) 19 YEL 441.

[98] Zilioli and Selmayr (n 95 above), 277; CW Herrmann, 'Monetary Sovereignty over the Euro and External Relations of the Euro Area: Competences, Procedures and Practice' (2002) 7 EFA Rev 18.

[99] Art I–12, referring to 'monetary policy, for the Member States which have adopted the euro'.

[100] *Contra* Zilioli and Selmayr (n 95 above), 297; Dutheil de la Rochère (n 97 above), 441–3.

[101] Ibid, 444–5; J Lebullenger, 'La projection externe de la zone euro' (1998) 34 RTDE 468–78.

supranational entities capable of entering into international commitments concerning monetary matters, i.e. the Community and the ECB. They argue that this follows from the Treaty's confirmation of the ECB's legal personality (Article 107(2) EC) and of the ECB's independence (Article 108 EC). They take the view that the ECB is not a Community institution like those enumerated in Article 7 EC, but is an independent international legal person created by the EC Treaty. The ECB is said to be the natural bearer of external competences in the field of monetary policy, and the competences of the Community are said to be limited to those expressly provided for in Article 111 EC. Zilioli and Selmayr claim that the ECB may exercise implied external competences, including the conclusion of agreements on an exchange rate system for the euro in relation to Community currencies, agreements on payment systems, administrative agreements, and agreements on banking supervision.[102]

The thesis of Zilioli and Selmayr has attracted strong criticism in the literature,[103] and is not widely shared. The assumption that the ECB is not a Community institution and is to be distinguished from the Community as such is contradicted by recent case law. In *Commission v. ECB* the Court entertained an action for annulment which the Commission had brought against an ECB decision on fraud prevention.[104] That decision purported to establish a separate ECB anti-fraud regime,[105] parallel to that operated by the European Anti-Fraud Office (OLAF), notwithstanding a Parliament and Council regulation concerning OLAF investigations, providing for such investigations in 'the institutions, bodies, offices and agencies established by, or on the basis of, the Treaties'.[106] The Commission argued that the ECB decision violated that regulation. Part of the ECB's defence was to argue that the regulation undermined its independence, as established by the Treaty. The Court recognized that the Treaty draftsmen clearly intended to ensure that the ECB should be in a position to carry out independently the tasks conferred upon it by the Treaty. However, other Community institutions such as, notably, the Parliament, the Commission, or the Court itself, also enjoyed independence and guarantees comparable in a number of respects to those afforded to the ECB. As was clear from the wording of Article 108 EC, the outside influences from which that provision sought to shield the ECB and its decision-making bodies were those likely to interfere with the performance of the tasks which the Treaty and the ESCB Statute assigned to the ECB. Article 108 EC sought, in essence, to shield the ECB from all political pressure in order to enable it effectively to pursue the objectives attributed to its tasks, through the independent exercise of the specific powers conferred on it for that purpose by the EC Treaty and the ESCB Statute. By contrast, recognition that the ECB had such independence did

---

[102] Zilioli and Selmayr (n 95 above), *passim*.

[103] R Torrent, 'Whom Is the European Central Bank the Central Bank of? Reaction to Zilioli and Selmayr' (1999) 36 CMLRev 1229–41; Herrmann (n 98 above), 1–24.

[104] Case C–11/00 *Commission v. ECB*, judgment of 10 July 2003, not yet reported.

[105] Decision 1999/726 of the ECB on fraud prevention [1999] OJ L291/36.

[106] Regulation 1073/1999 concerning investigations conducted by the European Anti-Fraud Office (OLAF) [1999] OJ L136/1; see Art 1(3).

not have the consequence of separating it entirely from the European Community and exempting it from every rule of Community law. The ECB was to contribute to the achievement of the Community's objectives, it was subject to various kinds of Community controls, and it was not the intention of the Treaty draftsmen to shield the ECB from any kind of legislative action taken by the Community legislature. There were thus no grounds which *prima facie* precluded the Community legislature from adopting, by virtue of the powers conferred on it by the EC Treaty and under the conditions laid down therein, legislative measures capable of applying to the ECB.[107] The Court annulled the *ECB* decision.

The Court thus clearly regards the ECB as a Community institution, and so does the draft Constitution.[108] The thesis that the ECB is a supranational institution of its own, with international legal personality in parallel with the Community, is therefore untenable. The ECB is not the natural bearer of external competences in the monetary field. The better view is that, even if there may be some measure of international legal personality for the ECB, founded on Article 107(2) EC, it is of limited scope. As Herrmann points out, it is only in the small world of banking operations that the ECB is recognized as an international legal person with certain powers, stemming from the merely operational tasks it is entrusted with.[109]

The conclusion must be that Article 111 EC is the core provision concerning the conduct of external relations in the sphere of monetary policy. There may be some scope for the implied-powers doctrine, in so far as certain aspects of monetary policy are considered not to be covered by Article 111 EC. It is however more natural to read the Treaty as establishing full parallelism between internal and external powers, through a broad interpretation of the concept of 'monetary or foreign-exchange regime matters' in Article 111(3) EC.

Area of freedom, security, and justice

Introduction

The Treaty on European Union created the so-called Second and Third Pillars of EU action, respectively in the areas of foreign and security policy, and justice and home affairs. The CFSP continues to be located in the TEU, and does not come within the scope of Community law (see Chapter 5). Matters are different, however, as regards justice and home affairs. The Treaty of Amsterdam moved some of the justice and home affairs policies into the EC Treaty, in a separate Title denominated 'Visas, Asylum, Immigration and Other Policies Related to the Free Movement of

---

[107] *Commission v. ECB* (n 104 above), paras 130–136.
[108] The ECB is the first institution described in Chapter II of Part I on 'Other Institutions and Bodies'.
[109] Herrmann (n 98 above), at 9; on the question of the ECB's capacity to conclude international agreements see Ch 6.

Persons' (hereafter Title IV). The denomination is not comprehensive, since there are also provisions on judicial co-operation in civil matters in Title IV. On the other hand, police and judicial co-operation in criminal matters continues to be located in the TEU's Third Pillar, and is thus not subject to Community law, even if the Court of Justice has been given a degree of jurisdiction over Third Pillar matters.[110]

The policies in Title IV and in the Third Pillar share the objective of establishing and maintaining an 'area of freedom, security and justice' (see Article 61 EC). For a number of years this has been one of the main areas of EU activity, leading to the adoption of a series of legislative acts.[111] Unavoidably, such activity also expands to the international level. It is not the purpose of this section to review the external policies which are under development in this area. The section is confined to a succinct analysis of the external powers of the Community under the relevant Treaty provisions, which, as regards treaty-making, are of an implied character, as there are no express provisions on the conclusion of international agreements or action in international organizations. This is somewhat surprising, in light of the nature of some of the policies covered by Title IV, such as visas, asylum, and immigration, which are by definition directed towards non-EU citizens. The section is divided into two parts, reflecting the diverse content of Title IV. External powers in the Third Pillar (Police and Judicial Co-operation in Criminal Matters) are touched upon in the next chapter.

At the outset it may also be noted that not all Member States participate in the policies adopted under Title IV. As regulated in two protocols, the United Kingdom and Ireland do not participate in, and are not bound by, acts adopted under Title IV, unless they opt in,[112] whereas Denmark does not participate at all.[113] This raises specific questions which are beyond the scope of this chapter.[114]

Visas, asylum, and immigration

The Title IV provisions on movement of persons set up a rather complex programme of legislative and administrative action, partly to be implemented within a five-year period after the entry into force of the Treaty of Amsterdam, and subject to different legislative procedures (Article 67 EC). Leaving aside those specific aspects, the

---

[110] See Art 35 TEU.

[111] See e.g. S Peers, *EU Justice and Home Affairs Law* (Longman, 2000); G Papagianni, 'Free Movement of Persons in the Light of the New Title IV TEC: From Intergovernmentalism Towards a Community Policy' (2002) 21 YEL 107.

[112] Treaty of Amsterdam, Protocol on the Position of the United Kingdom and Ireland [1997] OJ C340/99.

[113] Treaty of Amsterdam, Protocol on the Position of Denmark [1997] OJ C340/101.

[114] M Wilderspin and A-M Rouchaud, 'Les conséquences pour la compétence externe de la Communauté européenne de la "communautarisation" du droit international privé', to appear in [2004] Revue Critique de Droit International Privé, No.1.

content of the programme is described in Articles 62 and 63 EC. Under Article 62 the Council shall adopt:

. . .

1. measures with a view to ensuring, in compliance with Article 14, the absence of any controls on persons, be they citizens of the Union or nationals of third countries, when crossing internal borders;
2. measures on the crossing of the external borders of the Member States which shall establish:

(a) standards and procedures to be followed by Member States in carrying out checks on persons at such borders;
(b) rules on visas for intended stays of no more than three months, including:
   (i) the list of third countries whose nationals must be in possession of visas when crossing the external borders and those whose nationals are exempt from that requirement;
   (ii) the procedures and conditions for issuing visas by Member States;
   (iii) a uniform format for visas;
   (iv) rules on a uniform visa;

3. measures setting out the conditions under which nationals of third countries shall have the freedom to travel within the territory of the Member States during a period of no more than three months.

Article 63 EC concerns:

. . .

1. measures on asylum, in accordance with the Geneva Convention of 28 July 1951 and the Protocol of 31 January 1967 relating to the status of refugees and other relevant treaties, within the following areas:

(a) criteria and mechanisms for determining which Member State is responsible for considering an application for asylum submitted by a national of a third country in one of the Member States,
(b) minimum standards on the reception of asylum seekers in Member States,
(c) minimum standards with respect to the qualification of nationals of third countries as refugees,
(d) minimum standards on procedures in Member States for granting or withdrawing refugee status;

2. measures on refugees and displaced persons within the following areas:

(a) minimum standards for giving temporary protection to displaced persons from third countries who cannot return to their country of origin and for persons who otherwise need international protection,
(b) promoting a balance of effort between Member States in receiving and bearing the consequences of receiving refugees and displaced persons;

3. measures on immigration policy within the following areas:

(a) conditions of entry and residence, and standards on procedures for the issue by Member States of long-term visas and residence permits, including those for the purpose of family reunion,
(b) illegal immigration and illegal residence, including repatriation of illegal residents;

4. measures defining the rights and conditions under which nationals of third countries who are legally resident in a Member State may reside in other Member States.

. . .

The measures set out in those provisions are nearly all concerned with non-EU citizens. In that sense, one can say that they form an externally-oriented policy of the EU, even if it mostly consists of the adoption of internal legislation. In the current set-up of the Treaties, these policies are the counterpart of the common commercial policy, as they concern movement of persons into the EU, in contrast to goods. It is obvious however that the Title IV policies are not as comprehensive as the common commercial policy. For a start, there is clearly no exclusive competence as regards visas, asylum, and immigration. Community competence is limited to specific aspects, and in a number of areas only minimum standards are to be adopted. The presumption should therefore be that we are dealing with an area of shared or concurrent competence, which is confirmed by the draft Constitution (see Article I–13(2)).

    The policy area which lends itself most to the conclusion of international agreements is immigration, as defined in Article 63(3) EC, which refers to conditions of entry and residence and to repatriation of illegal residents. Indeed, from its early days the Community has been concluding agreements including provisions on entry and residence of third-country nationals: many association agreements as well as certain co-operation agreements regulate certain forms of immigration from the other contracting parties.[115] However, also in matters of visas and asylum there is clearly scope for international action. As the Treaty generally speaks of the adoption of 'measures', which are nowhere defined, there can be no doubt that there are implied powers to conclude international agreements in the whole sphere of policies concerning visas, asylum, and immigration. The conditions for the exercise of those powers are those resulting from the Court's case law, analysed in Chapter 3. One may note that the *AETR* principle applies, leading to exclusive Community competence for the negotiation and conclusion of international agreements affecting acts adopted under Title IV. For example, once basic harmonization of asylum law is in place, as is the objective of the EU's legislative programme in this area,[116] the development of international asylum law will require Community involvement.

    Hitherto the negotiation of international agreements on the basis of the above provisions of Title IV has been confined to agreements on readmission of illegal immigrants.[117] The EU is also actively exploring the integration of migration issues in its overall relations with third countries.[118]

---

[115] See the section on association agreements above, and case law in Chs 8 and 9.
[116] See the Tampere European Council Conclusions <http://ue.eu.int/en/Info/eurocouncil/index.htm>.
[117] See e.g. Proposal for a Council Decision concerning the signing of the Agreement between the European Community and the Government of the Macao Special Administrative Region of the People's Republic of China on the readmission of persons residing without authorization, COM(2003)151 final.
[118] See COM(2002)703 final, Communication from the Commission to the Council and the European Parliament—Integrating migration issues in the European Union's relations with Third Countries.

Judicial co-operation in civil matters

The second type of policies for which Title IV provides concerns judicial co-operation in civil matters. Article 65 EC describes the scope for such policies in the following terms:

Measures in the field of judicial cooperation in civil matters having cross-border implications, to be taken in accordance with Article 67 and in so far as necessary for the proper functioning of the internal market, shall include:

(a) improving and simplifying:

—the system for cross-border service of judicial and extrajudicial documents,
—cooperation in the taking of evidence,
—the recognition and enforcement of decisions in civil and commercial cases, including decisions in extrajudicial cases;

(b) promoting the compatibility of the rules applicable in the Member States concerning the conflict of laws and of jurisdiction;
(c) eliminating obstacles to the good functioning of civil proceedings, if necessary by promoting the compatibility of the rules on civil procedure applicable in the Member States.

In practice, the most significant acts coming within the scope of this provision concern conflict of laws and of jurisdiction. Again one must presume that Community competence is concurrent, and it is in any event limited to what is necessary for the proper functioning of the internal market. The implied powers doctrine applies, in particular the *AETR*-type exclusive competence. Whenever a Community act is likely to be affected by an international negotiation the Community has exclusive competence. In the area of conflict of laws such exclusive competence will often arise, in light of two centrepieces of Community legislation: Regulation 44/2001 on jurisdiction and the recognition and enforcement of judgments in civil and commercial matters, which is the successor to the first Brussels Convention;[119] and Regulation 1347/2000 on jurisdiction and the recognition and enforcement of judgments in matrimonial matters and in matters of parental responsibility for children of both spouses, the successor to the second Brussels Convention.[120] As many conflict-of-laws conventions touch upon matters of jurisdiction and recognition of judgments, the *AETR* effect will often be triggered. Complex questions are likely to arise as regards the relationship between the relevant Community law provisions and those of international conventions, and there are likely to be many mixed agreements.[121] In the literature it is argued that in this field the various Member States often have diverging approaches, which may create problems for the definition of a common position, and which may give rise to so-called partial mixity (where not all the Member States are parties to a mixed agreement).[122]

---

[119] [2001] OJ L12/1.   [120] [2000] OJ L160/19.
[121] The Council has made a request for an Opinion under Art 300(6) EC as regards competence to conclude the new Lugano Convention on jurisdiction and the recognition and enforcement of judgments in civil and commercial matters (*Opinion 1/03*, see [2003] OJ C101/1).
[122] Wilderspin and Rouchaud (n 114 above).

Conclusions

The analysis in this chapter is of a diverse character, as each Community policy has its own specific characteristics. It none the less demonstrates the wide scope for external action, due to the growing importance of international law making, which affects all significant policy areas. Also, a couple of general observations are worth making.

The analysis confirms the broad parallelism between internal and external powers. The case law examined in this chapter and the previous one generally recognizes that the Community may conclude international agreements in any area of policy-making coming within its competence. Perhaps the strongest confirmation of parallelism comes from *Opinion 2/00*, where the Court decided that the Cartagena Protocol had to be concluded on the basis of Article 175(1) EC, notwithstanding the express reference in Article 174(4) EC to the conclusion of agreements. The Court apparently considered that one should first look at the Treaty provision conferring legislative competence in a particular area for the purpose of finding the correct legal basis for international action.

The draft Constitution confirms such general parallelism. Article III–225(1) provides:

The Union may conclude agreements with one or more third countries or international organizations where the Constitution so provides or where the conclusion of an agreement is necessary in order to achieve, within the framework of the Union's policies, one of the objectives fixed by the Constitution, where there is provision for it in a binding Union legislative act or where it affects one of the Union's internal acts.

This provision links treaty-making power to the Union's policies and objectives. The concept of necessity should not be read as limiting the EU's treaty-making capacity, compared to its 'internal' law making powers. It expresses the principle of conferral (or limited powers, see Article I–9(1)), including the principles of proportionality and subsidiarity. EU competences should not be exercised unduly, indeed only where 'necessary' for achieving one of the EU's objectives, but whether they are exercised through internal legislative action or the participation in international law making does not matter.

If one looks at the current EC Treaty, there is a broad basis for engaging in relations with third countries, covering many different areas, and for participating in multilateral negotiations and agreements. The EC is far beyond the period of external competence in trade matters. Development co-operation policies have gained equal weight; there is now a constitutional basis for co-operation, in all the spheres of Community competence, with any third country; agreements can be concluded on migration and movement of persons just as much as on imports and exports; conflict-of-laws conventions will increasingly require EC participation; there is broad competence in matters of environmental policy, social policy, and monetary policy.

That may raise the question of the appropriate legal basis in the Treaty for certain agreements. The principle that one should identify the predominant purpose or component is no doubt useful, in particular for delineating exclusive competences, such as in matters of commercial policy, and non-exclusive competences. The hope may none the less be expressed that it will be possible to move away from legal conflicts over the scope and nature of external competence, for the benefit of effective international action by the EU and its Member States. The draft Constitution may contribute to that, through its unified procedure for the conclusion of agreements (Article III–227; see Chapter 6) and its confirmation of parallel external powers.

5

External powers under the Treaty on European Union

Introduction

The preceding chapters offer an account of the European Community's powers and objectives as regards external action. The emphasis there was on the first concept, powers or competences, rather than the second, objectives. The original EEC Treaty was sparsely worded as regards the objectives of the Community's external policies, and external action was quickly turned into a legal battleground over the location of the border between the Community's and the Member States' competences, in particular as regards treaty-making. With the amendments made by the Maastricht Treaty came more EC Treaty language on objectives of external action, in particular concerning development co-operation, yet lawyers continue to focus on issues of the nature and delimitation of competences.

The Maastricht Treaty created the European Union, founded, according to Article 1, on the European Communities, but supplementing them by the policies and forms of co-operation established by that Treaty: in the current version, a Common Foreign and Security Policy (CFSP) and Police and Judicial Co-operation in Criminal Matters (PJCCM). The CFSP in particular is a purely external policy, supplementing, to borrow from the TEU again, the external Community policies. Yet its denomination does not suggest a mere supplementary role. Rather, it suggests broad coverage, as nearly any form of external action can be brought within the terms 'foreign and security policy'. This raises difficult questions of interrelationship between EC external policies and the CFSP. Those questions arise against the broader canvas of constitutional confusion over the nature of the European Union, and its three pillars, to use the most used (but increasingly challenged) image.[1] This introduction is hardly the appropriate location in which to engage with the debate concerning the nature of the Union, yet it may be helpful to make some general

---

[1] JHH Weiler, 'Neither Unity Nor Three Pillars—The Trinity Structure of the Treaty on European Union', in J Monar, W Ungerer, and W Wessels (eds), *The Maastricht Treaty on European Union* (European Interuniversity Press, 1993) 49; DM Curtin and I Dekker, 'The EU as a "Layered" International Organization: Institutional Unity in Disguise', in P Craig and G de Búrca (eds), *The Evolution of EU Law* (OUP, 1999) 83; B de Witte, 'The Pillar Structure and the Nature of the European Union: Greek Temple or French Gothic Cathedral?', in T Heukels, N Blokker, and M Brus (eds), *The European Union after Amsterdam* (Kluwer Law International, 1998) 51.

observations. The EC pillar is said to be supranational, with much majority voting, and a strong role for supranational institutions such as the Commission, the European Parliament, and the Court of Justice. Constitutionalism is the hallmark of its legal order, with direct effect and supremacy as the operating systems of such constitutionalism.[2] The EC is governed by Community law, a 'new legal order'.[3] The second and third pillars, by contrast, are said to be intergovernmental in character, with unanimity as a rule and a much smaller role for the supranational institutions. Particularly as regards the CFSP, the Commission and the Parliament stand more or less at the sidelines, and the Court of Justice appears to have no role whatsoever. *Community* law does not apply, and many commentators regard the CFSP as a form of co-operation coming within the sphere of international law instead.[4] The latter view is not uncontested, however. Increasingly the EU is looked at as a single organization, and EU law as a distinct, unified legal discipline, even if not all Community law principles and concepts may as such apply to the second and third pillars.[5] The approach taken by the Convention on the Future of Europe supports that view, as the Convention proposes to demolish the pillars, at least at the level of Treaty structure: all policies, including CFSP and PJCCM, are to be integrated in the Constitution of the European Union.

Such constitutional confusion about the nature of the European Union as a whole, and about the legal nature of the 'policies and forms of co-operation' in the second and third pillars, does not facilitate legal analysis of the nature and scope of the EU's external powers outside the EC framework, in particular under the CFSP. As the Court of Justice has no jurisdiction over Title V TEU (the CFSP title),[6] there is no specific case law on EU external powers. The analysis therefore needs to concentrate on the language and meaning of the TEU itself, and on the practice under that Treaty. As will be seen in the following section, the CFSP provisions in the TEU stand in contrast to the EC Treaty provisions on external relations by their emphasis on broadly worded objectives rather than a more or less precise delimitation of subject matter or a definition of the kind of competences conferred upon the EU. The difficulty of legal analysis is reflected in the dearth of relevant writing. The CFSP forms the subject of a burgeoning political science and international

---

[2] Cf JHH Weiler, *The Constitution of Europe* (CUP, 1999) 221.

[3] Case 26/62 *Van Gend en Loos v. Nederlandse Administratie der Belastingen* [1963] ECR 1.

[4] E Denza, *The Intergovernmental Pillars of the European Union* (OUP, 2002) 19; MR Eaton, 'Common Foreign and Security Policy', in D O'Keeffe and P Twomey, *Legal Issues of the Maastricht Treaty* (Chancery Law, 1994) 222; I McLeod, ID Hendry, and S Hyett, *The External Relations of the European Communities* (OUP, 1996) 412; M Koskenniemi, 'International Law Aspects of the Common Foreign and Security Policy', in M Koskenniemi (ed), *International Law Aspects of the European Union* (Kluwer Law International, 1998) 30.

[5] A von Bogdandy, 'The Legal Case for Unity: the European Union as a Single Organization with a Single Legal System' (1999) 36 CMLRev 887–910; I Pernice, 'Multilevel Constitutionalism and the Treaty of Amsterdam: European Constitution-Making Revisited?' (1999) 36 CMLRev 703–50; CWA Timmermans, 'The Constitutionalization of the European Union' (2002) 21 YEL 1–11.

[6] Art 46 TEU.

relations literature,[7] yet legal science has for a long time shied away from entering such uncertain territory.[8]

In light of the above the reader may wonder whether a chapter on external powers and objectives of the EU under the second and third pillars is justified, and whether it would not be more useful to limit the analysis to the actual policy—which is the subject of Chapter 11. Such an approach would be commendable if the second and third pillars were independent forms of intergovernmental co-operation, completely detached from the EC. That is not however the case. The TEU provisions on the CFSP, in particular, cannot be read in isolation from the EC Treaty provisions on external policies, as the practice exemplifies. Because the Union is 'served by a single institutional framework' (Article 3 TEU) the same institutions take action under the CFSP and under the EC Treaty. In many cases, as will be seen, various forms of external action are complementary. In legal terms the question thus arises how to delimit the CFSP from EC external action. Linked to this question of delimitation, in some sense even in opposition to it, is the issue of overall consistency of the Union's external activities, elevated to official Treaty concern in Article 3 TEU. Those are the kind of issues which this chapter can examine.

Furthermore, there is one particular type of external power which has given rise to much legal debate in the context of the second and third pillars, i.e. the EU's power to conclude international agreements. The uninformed reader of the TEU is no doubt mystified about how that debate could arise. How could it be possible to conduct a 'common foreign and security policy' without concluding international agreements? And since Amsterdam, does not Article 24 TEU expressly provide for such agreements? Again one can understand the question only in light of the constitutional ambiguity of the EU, which in this area has been funnelled into the topos of international legal personality. At the time of Maastricht it seemed that no such personality was created for the Union, thereby preventing the second and third pillars from being anything other than political co-ordination of sovereign national powers. This chapter also addresses the state of the debate on the Union's international legal personality.

The structure of the analysis is as follows. The following section explores the Treaty language concerning the objectives of the CFSP, and the powers conferred upon the EU institutions to pursue those objectives. On that basis, it is possible to analyse the interaction with EC external policies, where we need to examine both the delimitation of competences and the goal of consistency. The chapter then investigates

---

[7] See *inter alia* M Holland (ed), *Common Foreign and Security Policy—The Record and Reforms* (Pinter, 1997); S Keukeleire, *Het buitenlands beleid van de Europese Unie* (Kluwer, 1998); J Peterson and H Sjursen, *A Common Foreign Policy for Europe?* (Routledge, 1998); AW Cafruny and P Peters (eds), *The Union and the World: The Political Economy of a Common European Foreign Policy* (Kluwer, 1998); J Zielonka (ed), *Paradoxes of European Foreign Policy* (Kluwer, 1998); B Soetendorp, *Foreign Policy in the European Union* (Longman, 1999); S Nuttall, *European Foreign Policy* (OUP, 2000).

[8] This is beginning to change, see *inter alia* Denza (n 4 above); R Wessel, *The European Union's Foreign and Security Policy—A Legal Institutional Perspective* (Kluwer Law International, 1999); P Koutrakos, *Trade, Foreign Policy and Defence in EU Constitutional Law* (Hart Publishing, 2001).

the EU's international legal personality and its power to conclude agreements. It also takes a look at the scope of the third pillar (PJCCM), and the opportunities for external action in that sphere of EU policy-making. The last section shortly examines the changes envisaged in the draft Constitution.

CFSP objectives and powers

At the outset it is useful to subject the Treaty language to close scrutiny. In terms of defining the territory of the CFSP, one needs to look at the formulation of the objectives of that policy. Article 2 TEU provides that the Union shall set itself a number of objectives, one of which is:

—to assert its identity on the international scene, in particular through the implementation of a common foreign and security policy including the progressive framing of a common defence policy, which might lead to a common defence, in accordance with the provisions of Article 17.

The objectives of the CFSP are defined in Article 11(1) TEU:

The Union shall define and implement a common foreign and security policy covering all areas of foreign and security policy, the objectives of which shall be:

—to safeguard the common values, fundamental interests, independence and integrity of the Union in conformity with the principles of the United Nations Charter;
—to strengthen the security of the Union in all ways;
—to preserve peace and strengthen international security, in accordance with the principles of the United Nations Charter, as well as the principles of the Helsinki Final Act and the objectives of the Paris Charter, including those on external borders;
—to promote international co-operation;
—to develop and consolidate democracy and the rule of law, and respect for human rights and fundamental freedoms.

This provision does not determine the actual scope of the CFSP, other than through the phrase 'all areas of foreign and security policy'. The 'foreign policy' limb is not further defined. By contrast, Article 17 TEU sheds some further light on the 'security policy' dimension.[9] It provides that the 'common foreign and security policy shall include all questions relating to the security of the Union, including the progressive framing of a common defence policy, which might lead to a common defence, should the European Council so decide'. It further clarifies that the 'progressive framing of a common defence policy will be supported, as Member States consider appropriate, by co-operation between them in the field of armaments'. It also adds: '[q]uestions referred to in this Article shall include humanitarian and rescue tasks, peacekeeping tasks and tasks of combat forces in crisis management, including peacemaking'.

---

[9] Gradually strengthened to form the European Security and Defence Policy (ESDP): see in particular Nice European Council conclusions (<http://ue.eu.int/en/Info/eurocouncil/index.htm>); the draft Constitution speaks of the Common Security and Defence Policy (CSDP).

Those are the objectives and subject matter of the CFSP. In terms of powers to achieve those objectives, the TEU enumerates and defines a number of instruments. They include 'common strategies . . . in areas where the Member States have important interests in common' (Article 13 TEU); 'joint actions' which 'address specific situations where operational action by the Union is deemed to be required' (Article 14 TEU); 'common positions' which 'define the approach of the Union to a particular matter of a geographical or thematic nature' (Article 15 TEU); information and consultation 'on any matter of foreign and security policy of general interest' (Article 16 TEU); and the conclusion of international agreements (Article 24 TEU). The scope and legal effects of those various instruments are examined in Chapter 11, but it will strike the uninformed reader that only the latter two instruments, information and consultation, and international agreements, benefit from instant recognition. Common strategies, joint actions, and common positions are not standard foreign policy instruments. Indeed it is useful to contrast the CFSP instruments with what would normally be regarded as instruments of a full-blown foreign policy. Keukeleire distinguishes diplomatic, military, and economic and financial instruments.[10] Common positions, to some extent joint actions, and CFSP declarations come within the category of diplomatic instruments. The EU's military instruments are limited, even if some joint actions start invading the military terrain.[11] The use of economic and financial instruments for foreign policy purposes, however, appears to be largely an EC matter, as the EC Treaty provides for a common commercial policy, a development co-operation policy, and other co-operation policies, and a common monetary policy for the Eurozone. In terms of *legal* instruments, moreover, it is striking that the CFSP provisions do not appear to envisage legislative action, be it directly, such as in the case of EC regulations, or indirectly, such as in the case of EC directives, which harmonize national laws. The Union can develop a common foreign policy, but it appears unable to legislate in the matter.[12]

It is likewise interesting to contrast the scope of the CFSP, as outlined in the TEU provisions, with the basic constitutional powers which would be required for a European foreign policy 'worthy of its name', in the approach of an eminent international relations scholar.[13] Those powers would need to extend to war and peace; raising armed forces; treaty-making; regulation of commerce (sanctions); external borders (immigration); cession or acquisition of territory. Again it is clear that the CFSP does not come anywhere near covering all that, but that a number of those powers are present within the EC Treaty.

---

[10] Keukeleire (n 7 above), 34–8.

[11] Joint Action 2003/92 on the European Union military operation in the Former Yugoslav Republic of Macedonia [2003] OJ L34/26 and Joint Action 2003/423 on the European Union military operation in the Democratic Republic of Congo [2003] OJ L143/50.   [12] See further Ch 11.

[13] C Hill, 'The Capability-Expectations Gap, or Conceptualizing Europe's International Role' (1993) 31 JCMS 316–17.

As the analysis by Nuttall tracing the political debate leading up to the Maastricht Treaty shows, the grand idea of the CFSP, as expressed in Article 11(1) TEU, was a product of its time, characterized by the momentous changes consisting of the disappearance of the Iron Curtain and the Berlin Wall, and by the success of European integration in the form of the internal market programme. Yet it has disappointed expectations because it has never had a clearly defined objective and purpose, agreed to by consensus.[14]

The actual objectives of the CFSP, as outlined in Article 11(1) TEU, merit some further comment.[15] Keukeleire points out that those objectives are in the nature of underlying policy principles rather than precise operational objectives. This leads him to contrast the 'common' foreign and security policy with common policies under the EC Treaty, which are much more precisely defined. The result is that the CFSP threatens to be squeezed between Community external competences and national competences.[16] The way Denza puts it is that the CFSP is a common, and not a single policy, and that the adoption of legal instruments is not the primary objective of the CFSP.[17] Koskenniemi is critical of the CFSP objectives, arguing that they are meaningless abstract principles, which lay down no substantive priorities for Union foreign policy. He points out that, as always with open-ended standards, power is transferred from the legislators to the executive.[18] It is indeed possible to read the CFSP provisions as the continuation of executive dominance over foreign affairs, as it exists in at least a number of Member States. Such a reading may be more interesting than the traditional approach of contrasting intergovernmentalism and supranationalism, and of explaining the intergovernmental character of CFSP by national sovereignty concerns.

The objectives of the CFSP do have a positive dimension as well. They project and constitutionalize, at least to some degree, certain core values of the European Union. As such they may develop into a strong guiding force for EU external action. From a legal perspective particularly the last objective in Article 11(1) TEU is worth noting: to develop and consolidate democracy and the rule of law, and respect for human rights and fundamental freedoms. As is discussed in Chapter 13, the EU is developing a meaningful and increasingly sophisticated external human rights policy, and one expert commentator takes the view that such a policy is developing into a core component of the CFSP.[19]

Given that the Treaty language is not specific in terms of defining the scope of the CFSP and its objectives, it may be useful to take a look at the actual practice under Title V TEU. Under customary international law principles such practice may guide the interpretation of the Treaty.[20] In this respect the reader is referred to the analysis of joint actions and common positions in Chapter 11.

---

[14] Nuttall (n 7 above), ch 1.   [15] For a detailed analysis see Wessel (n 8 above), 56–70.
[16] Keukeleire (n 7 above), 154.   [17] Denza (n 4 above), 86 and 90.
[18] Koskenniemi (n 4 above), 28.
[19] A Clapham, 'Where is the EU's Human Rights Common Foreign Policy, and How is it Manifested in Multilateral Fora?', in P Alston (ed), *The EU and Human Rights* (OUP, 1999) 627.
[20] Art 31(3)(b) VCLT.

A last point to look at in the overall discussion of the EU's powers under the CFSP concerns the nature of those powers, particularly in relation to the Member States. The CFSP is of course not an exclusive EU competence, in contrast to the EC's common commercial policy. One may use the notion of shared or concurrent competences, but it is not clear that the notion of transfer of competences, as we use it in the EC context, is appropriate for the CFSP.[21] This depends on basic conceptions of the nature of the EU, as identified in the introduction. If one looks at EU law as a single legal system, the discourse of transfer of competences, stemming from *Van Gend en Loos*,[22] may also be appropriate for the second (and third) pillar. If, by contrast, one analyses the TEU provisions on CFSP through the prism of international law, there may be less scope for such a discourse, which is not commonly known in international law. The CFSP is then indeed merely a form of co-operation between sovereign States. But even if one takes the latter approach, the CFSP does not present itself, through the Treaty language, as an *à la carte* form of co-operation, merely *ad hoc* and optional. Article 11(1) TEU does provide that the Union *shall* define and implement a CFSP covering *all* areas of foreign and security policy. Article 11(2) TEU instructs the Member States to support the policy *actively* and *unreservedly* in a spirit of loyalty and mutual solidarity, and to refrain from any action which is contrary to the interests of the Union or likely to impair its effectiveness as a cohesive force in international relations. The Member States are bound by joint actions (Article 14(3) TEU) and common positions (Article 15 TEU). They shall inform and consult one another within the Council on any matter of foreign and security policy of general interest (Article 16 TEU). In international organizations and at international conferences the Member States shall co-ordinate their action, and uphold the common positions. Member States which are members of the UN Security Council will concert and keep the other Member States fully informed, and Member States which are permanent members will, in the execution of their functions, ensure the defence of the provisions and the interests of the Union, without prejudice to their responsibilities under the provisions of the UN Charter (Article 19 TEU).

Those provisions impose strong discipline as regards respect for, implementation of, and participation in, the CFSP by the Member States. As such the Treaty language ought to be sufficient for the construction of a meaningful CFSP. The actual policy, however, is mostly looked at as insufficient, unsatisfactory, and ineffective. Part of the reason may lie in the absence of enforcement mechanisms for the various duties and obligations which the TEU imposes. In contrast to the position under the EC Treaty, no EU institution or Member State can be brought before the Court of Justice for non-compliance. Article 11(2) TEU provides only that the Council shall ensure that the principles in that provision are complied with. As the Council needs to act unanimously (Article 23(1) TEU), one immediately sees the difficulty of actual

---

[21] See below, the section on the draft Constitution.
[22] '[A] new legal order for the benefit of which the States have limited their sovereign rights': *Van Gend en Loos* (n 3 above), 12.

enforcement. In theory, recourse to the International Court of Justice seems possible, but in practice it is hardly conceivable.

Interaction with EC external policies and powers

Treaty language and practice

The above discussion shows that the scope and nature of the EU's powers under the CFSP do not lend themselves to strict legal analysis, because of the open texture of the Treaty provisions and the lack of authoritative interpretation through case law. However, where it comes to the interaction between the CFSP and the EC's external policies and powers we can hardly be satisfied with some general reflections. It matters a lot whether a decision is taken under the first or the second pillar: decision-making procedures are different, parliamentary and judicial scrutiny is different, and the legal effects of the decisions are different.

The paradox of the relationship between EC and CFSP external action—indeed, one could say the original sin of overall EU external action—is that the CFSP *supplements* the first pillar with a less intrusive policy, and yet is intended to cover *all areas* of foreign and security policy. But commercial policy, development co-operation policy, etc., are of course also forms of foreign policy. As Koskenniemi points out, everyone agrees that it is difficult to separate foreign policy from other aspects of policy and that the most credible conception of security is the comprehensive one.[23] This original sin of EU external action produces many effects. Within the supranational Community context it creates concerns about contamination of EC policies by the CFSP. Those concerns have an obvious institutional dimension: as the Council is the central CFSP institution, with only limited roles for the Commission and the Parliament, the latter institutions do not like to see certain types of decisions effectively transferred from the first to the second pillar.[24] Moreover, Community lawyers have been concerned that CFSP decisions, taken unanimously under intergovernmental procedures, could contain instructions for the Community, and could be seen as hierarchically superior.[25] Those concerns were present at the inception of the pillar structure. Accordingly, the TEU contains a number of provisions which are aimed at avoiding undue interference with EC policies. Article 2 TEU provides that one of the Union's objectives is 'to maintain in full the acquis communautaire and build on it with a view to considering to what extent the policies and forms of co-operation introduced by this Treaty may need to be revised with the aim of ensuring the effectiveness of the mechanisms and

---

[23] Koskenniemi (n 4 above), 36.

[24] See e.g. Commission, *Report on the Operation of the Treaty on European Union* (EC Commission, May 1995), as reported by G Edwards, 'Common Foreign and Security Policy' (1994) 14 YEL 545.

[25] CWA Timmermans, 'The Uneasy Relationship between the Communities and the Second Union Pillar: Back to the "Plan Fouchet"?' (1996/1) LIEI 61.

the institutions of the Community'. It thus appears to foreshadow a gradual integration of the pillars.[26] The central provision on the matter is Article 47 TEU:

Subject to the provisions amending the Treaty establishing the European Economic Community with a view to establishing the European Community . . . and to these final provisions, nothing in this Treaty shall affect the Treaties establishing the European Communities or the subsequent Treaties and Acts modifying or supplementing them.

This provision is clearly intended to protect the *acquis communautaire*, and to prevent intergovernmental contamination of supranational decision-making. To vary the pillar image, Article 47 TEU aims to create watertight compartments in the EU vessel between the Community, on the one hand, and CFSP and PJCCM, on the other.

That is not however the entire Treaty picture, because the drafters also realized that, at least at political level, the CFSP needs to be co-ordinated with external Community policies. Article 3, second paragraph, TEU provides that the Union shall ensure the consistency of its external activities as a whole in the context of its external relations, security, economic, and development policies.

In one particular area, that of economic and financial sanctions, the connection between CFSP and EC decisions is clarified in the EC Treaty itself. Article 301 EC provides:[27]

Where it is provided, in a common position or in a joint action adopted according to the provisions of the Treaty on European Union relating to the common foreign and security policy, for an action by the Community to interrupt or reduce, in part or completely, economic relations with one or more third countries, the Council shall take the necessary urgent measures. The Council shall act by a qualified majority on a proposal from the Commission.

That provision illustrates the constitutional and institutional complexity of the intercourse between the pillars. Common positions or joint actions on economic sanctions are adopted by the Council, acting unanimously, and do not require a Commission proposal or initiative. Nevertheless, the Commission then needs to make a proposal for an EC regulation, which the Council will adopt by qualified majority. The Council cannot act without such a proposal. As long as the Council and the Commission co-operate and agree, there are no problems, but there is nothing in the Treaties which regulates disagreement, other than the general provision on the obligation of interinstitutional co-operation in Article 3 TEU.[28]

Economic sanctions are of course not the only example of interaction between the pillars. For the purpose of illustration it may be useful to mention a few other practical instances. Since Amsterdam the TEU provisions on the CFSP have envisaged common strategies as an instrument of foreign policy. Three such strategies have been developed, concerning Russia, the Ukraine, and the Mediterranean region.[29]

---

[26] As indeed takes place under the draft Constitution: see below.   [27] See also Art 60 EC.

[28] On economic sanctions see further Ch 12.

[29] Common Strategy 1999/414 on Russia [1999] OJ L157/1; Common Strategy 1999/877 on Ukraine [1999] OJ L331/1; and Common Strategy 2000/458 on the Mediterranean region [2000] OJ L183/5.

At the same time there are significant EC agreements with the countries concerned, so-called Partnership and Co-operation Agreements with Russia and the Ukraine,[30] and forms of association agreements with Mediterranean countries.[31] The common strategies will obviously affect trade and economic relations with those countries. Strong interaction is also visible in the EU's external human rights policy.[32] EC bilateral agreements with third countries are as a rule predicated on respect for human rights, and where the EU takes action to enforce human rights clauses, such as in a couple of cases involving ACP countries, such action usually follows a political decision in the framework of CFSP.[33] Another example is the Kimberley process, which concerns trade in so-called conflict diamonds.[34] The interaction between the first and second pillar is also strong as regards the fight against terrorism which followed September 11. EU policy is to insist that third countries which enter into agreements with the EC commit themselves to combating terrorism.[35] A last example are the, at the time of writing ongoing, negotiations with Iran on a trade and co-operation agreement, which have a very strong foreign policy dimension, going far beyond pure trade issues.[36] At political level, therefore, the first and second pillars cannot be separated. In legal terms, however, there is a strong need for delimitation of competences.

Delimitation of competences

The Court of Justice does not have jurisdiction over the second pillar, and has only since Amsterdam acquired some measure of jurisdiction over the third pillar (Article 35 TEU). There is none the less one judgment which sheds light on the legal

[30] Agreement on partnership and co-operation establishing a partnership between the European Communities and their Member States, of one part, and the Russian Federation, of the other part [1997] OJ L327/3 and Partnership and co-operation agreement between the European Communities and their Member States, and Ukraine [1998] OJ L49/3. Cf C Hillion, 'Common Strategies and the Interface Between EC External Relations and the CFSP: Lessons of the Partnership Between the EU and Russia', in A Dashwood and C Hillion (eds), *The General Law of EC External Relations* (Sweet & Maxwell, 2000) 287–301.

[31] C Flaesch-Mougin, 'Differentiation and Association within the Pan-Euro-Mediterranean Area', in M Maresceau and E Lannon (eds), *The EU's Enlargement and Mediterranean Strategies—A Comparative Analysis* (Palgrave, 2001) 63–96. [32] Ch 13.

[33] See the example of Zimbabwe as described in Ch 13.

[34] See Common Position 2001/758 on combating the illicit traffic in conflict diamonds, as a contribution to prevention and settlement of conflicts [2001] OJ L286/2 and Council Regulation 2368/2002 implementing the Kimberley Process certification scheme for the international trade in rough diamonds [2002] OJ L358/28.

[35] Annual report from the Council to the European Parliament on the main aspects and basic choices of CFSP, including the financial implications for the general budget of the European Communities (point H, para 40, of the Interinstitutional Agreement of 6 May 1999)—2002 (7083/03), 16 (<http://register.consilium.eu.int/pdf/en/03/st07/st07038en03.pdf>).

[36] See e.g. 'EU to join US in pressing Tehran on nuclear checks', *Financial Times*, 11 June 2003, which reported that 'European diplomats made it clear any trade and co-operation accord would go nowhere if there was no progress on the "political dialogue", including human rights, terrorism and weapons of mass destruction'.

relationship between the pillars. The so-called *Airport Transit Visas* case[37] concerned a Commission challenge to a Council joint action regarding such visas, which had been adopted under the third pillar, on the basis of Article K.3 TEU (pre-Amsterdam version).[38] The objective of that joint action was the harmonization of Member States' policies as regards the requirement of an airport transit visa in order to improve control of the air route which, particularly when applications for entry or *de facto* entry were involved in the course of airport transit, represented a significant way in with a view, in particular, to illegally taking up residence within the territory of the Member States.[39] However, the Commission considered that such an act should have been adopted on the basis of (then) Article 100c EC, concerning the determination of the third countries whose nationals must be in possession of a visa when crossing the external borders of the Member States. The case thus concerned delimitation of competences between the first and third pillars, but there is no reason why the Court's analysis should not also be relevant for demarcating the first from the second pillar.[40]

In light of (then) Article L TEU it was unsurprising that one Member State, the United Kingdom, argued that the Court had no jurisdiction to decide the case. The Commission had brought the action pursuant to (current) Article 230 EC, as an action for annulment of a Council act. Article L TEU excluded ECJ jurisdiction in second and third pillar matters (see current Article 46 TEU). It did however confer jurisdiction over Article M TEU, the current Article 47 TEU, cited above, on respect for the *acquis communautaire*.

Fennelly AG pointed out that the power of judicial review which the Court enjoyed under the jurisdictional clauses of the EC Treaty was extended by Article L in conjunction with Article M, so as to ensure respect for the provisions of that Treaty. The Court therefore had to be able to determine whether anything in the TEU, including acts adopted thereunder, 'affected' the EC Treaty. Indeed, in his view Article M was inserted into the TEU with the very purpose of ensuring that, in exercising their powers under Titles V and VI TEU, the Council and the Member States did not encroach on the powers attributed to the EC. It followed from Article M that, however clear and unambiguous they could be, the provisions of Title VI could not be applied so as to restrict in any way the scope of the provisions of the EC Treaty, interpreted in accordance with the normal canons of construction of Community law. The Advocate General did not accept the argument that the Council had a discretion to resort to Article K.3 TEU even when the conditions for the application of Article 100c EC were met. He conceded that the Court did not have jurisdiction to analyse and interpret Article K.3 as such. However, the Court could interpret acts purporting to be adopted under Title VI TEU, in order to determine whether they dealt with matters which more properly fell within the Community sphere of competence. In so acting, the Court was neither interpreting

---

[37] Case C–170/96 *Commission v. Council* [1998] ECR I–2763.
[38] Joint Action 96/197 [1996] OJ L63/8.   [39] Ibid, preamble.
[40] S Peers, 'Common Foreign and Security Policy 1998' (1998) 18 YEL 661.

provisions of the TEU which were outside its jurisdiction nor deciding whether acts were validly adopted thereunder. It was considering such acts only in their relation to the EC Treaty, where the Court's powers were incontestable. In support, the Advocate General referred *inter alia* to the *AETR*,[41] *Bangladesh*,[42] and *European Development Fund*[43] decisions, in which the Court examined whether certain Council decisions, or decisions of the Member States meeting within the Council, came within the scope of the EC Treaty. To accord acts purporting to be adopted under Title VI immunity from review on the sole basis of their denomination would run contrary to the reasoning adopted by the Court in these cases and deprive Article M of its useful effect. (Current) Article 230 EC clearly intended to confer on the Court jurisdiction only in respect of Council acts adopted within the scope of the EC Treaty. However, in order to exercise that jurisdiction, the Court was not merely empowered but obliged, in accordance with (current) Article 220 EC, to rule on whether a contested Council act was within the scope of the Treaty or not. Fennelly AG therefore considered that the Court had jurisdiction.[44]

The Court followed the Advocate General's Opinion, but was much more concise in its reasoning. It first noted that by its application the Commission sought a declaration that, in light of its objective, the act adopted by the Council fell within the scope of Article 100c EC, so that it should have been based on that provision. Next, Article M TEU made it clear that a provision such as Article K.3 did not affect the provisions of the EC Treaty. In accordance with Article L the provisions of the EC Treaty concerning the powers of the Court of Justice and the exercise of those powers applied to Article M. It was therefore the task of the Court to ensure that acts which, according to the Council, fell within the scope of Article K.3 did not encroach upon the powers conferred by the EC Treaty on the Community. It followed that the Court had jurisdiction to review the content of the act in the light of Article 100c EC in order to ascertain whether the act affected the powers of the Community under that provision and to annul the act if it appeared that it should have been based on Article 100c EC.[45]

On the issue of substance, both the Advocate General and the Court came to the conclusion that the Council act in question did not come within the scope of Article 100c EC, as this provision did not apply to airport transit visas, and the Commission's application was therefore rejected. However, the Commission may none the less have felt that it effectively won the case, as it found the Court prepared to arbitrate the delimitation of competences between the pillars. Indeed the Court clearly adopted an expansive approach of its jurisdiction, and the significance of its ruling could hardly be overestimated, even if the reasoning was succinct.[46] The judgment holds two general and important implications.

---

[41] Case 22/70 *Commission v. Council* [1971] ECR 263; see Ch 3.

[42] Joined Cases C–181/91 and C–248/91 *Parliament v. Council and Commission* [1993] ECR I–3685; see Ch 4.   [43] Case C–316/91 *Parliament v. Council* [1994] ECR I–625; see Ch 4.

[44] *Commission v. Council* (n 41 above), Opinion of Fennelly AG, paras 7–18.

[45] Ibid, paras 13–17 of the judgment.

[46] See further DM Curtin and RH van Ooik, 'Een Hof van Justitie van de Europese Unie?' (1999) 47 SEW 24–38.

The first concerns the nature of the relationship between Community powers under the EC Treaty and Union powers under the TEU. That relationship seems different from that between Community and Member States' powers. The assumption here is that Article 100c EC did not vest in the Community an exclusive, but rather a concurrent or shared competence. The Court did not give any indication to the contrary, and one fails to see the reasons for regarding Community visa competence as exclusive. The current Article 62(2)(b) EC likewise does not appear to vest such exclusive competence in the Community, and the institutions have not acted as if this was in any way the case.[47] If that assumption is correct, non-exclusive EC competences do preclude second or third pillar decisions which come within their scope, whereas they do not preclude national acts, or even acts of the Member State governments meeting in the Council.[48] In other words, no second or third pillar acts may trespass on competences conferred upon the EC, and it does not matter whether such competences are exclusive or not. For example, no second pillar decisions may concern development co-operation in the meaning of Article 177 EC, even if EC competence in this sphere is not exclusive. Thus, in legal terms, the CFSP does not cover 'all areas of foreign and security policy', but only those which do not come within the scope of the EC Treaty. Keukeleire's view, referred to above, that the CFSP risks being squeezed between EC and national competences indeed appears borne out by the *Airport Transit Visas* judgment. The basis for such a restricted approach is (current) Article 47 TEU. The prohibition on second or third pillar acts affecting the EC Treaty precludes that the EU institutions adopt acts under those pillars, if the acts can be adopted under the EC Treaty.

The second implication builds on the first. The above approach makes sense only under a unified conception of EU law. If the TEU were simply a self-standing international agreement between the Member States, truly separate from the EC Treaties, the Court could not have adopted the *Airport Transit Visas* approach. It would have had to follow the *Bangladesh* and *Lomé*-type of reasoning, first by establishing that EC competence was concurrent, and then by accepting that the Member States could act, even in common, as long as the Community did not act. But the TEU is not self-standing. It is organically linked to the EC Treaty; there are too many connections to enumerate, but the most significant one is the single institutional framework. Where the EU institutions act, they can only do so under the relevant provisions of either the EC or EU Treaty, and by virtue of Article 47 TEU competences under the second or third pillar give way to those under the first. The judgment in the *Airport Transit Visa* case lends strong support to the concept of EU law as a distinct, unified legal discipline.

The Court's concern to protect EC competences is also apparent in judgments on export controls and economic sanctions. In *Werner v. Germany* and *Leifer and Others*,[49]

---

[47] Art I–13(2) of the draft Constitution characterizes policies concerning the area of freedom, security, and justice as coming within shared competence.   [48] See the *Bangladesh* case (n 42 above).
[49] Case C–70/94 *Werner v. Germany* [1995] ECR I–3189; Case C–83/94 *Leifer and Others* [1995] ECR I–3231.

cases analysed in Chapter 2, the Court decided that measures whose effect was to prevent or restrict the export of certain products could not be treated as falling outside the scope of the common commercial policy on the ground that they had foreign policy and security objectives.[50] Those judgments affected the EU's practice in the field of export controls: whereas the EU first adopted a regime combining a CFSP joint action with an EC regulation, some years later the Council was persuaded to replace those acts with an EC regulation only, on the basis that export controls come within the common commercial policy.[51]

From the perspective of unity of the EU, it may thus make sense to delimit CFSP and EC external action in the following terms. The CFSP may cover all areas of foreign and security policy, but where the EC Treaty confers upon the Community powers for a specific form of foreign policy, such as commercial policy and development co-operation, those powers take precedence. They are, one could say, *lex specialis*. They should not, however, as *lex specialis* be interpreted narrowly, but rather on their own terms, in no way confined by the TEU provisions on the CFSP. Such a method of interpretation is required by Article 47 TEU.

With the integration of the pillars in the Constitution, as proposed by the Convention on the Future of Europe (see below), the issue of delimitation of competences will not disappear. On the contrary, there are likely to be an increasing number of issues, as the CFSP effectively develops and grows. In the literature it has been suggested that the centre of gravity of a measure should be the criterion for delimiting the various external policies.[52] That suggestion more or less conforms to the Court's latest rulings on external competence in matters of trade and environment, where the determination of the correct legal basis in the Treaty was the issue. Both in *Opinion 2/00* and in the *Energy Star Agreement* case the Court based its analysis on the principle that, if examination of a Community measure reveals that it pursues a twofold purpose or that it has a twofold component and if one is identifiable as the main or predominant purpose or component, whereas the other is merely incidental, the measure must be founded on a single legal basis, namely that required by the main or predominant purpose or component. By way of exception, if it is established that the measure simultaneously pursues several objectives which are inseparably linked without one being secondary and indirect in relation to the other, the measure may be founded on the corresponding legal bases.[53] It remains to be seen whether that principle will also be used for measures concerning external EU action under the new, integrated Constitution. One question is whether dual legal bases will be possible, given the differences in decision-making procedures. This is the problem of so-called cross-pillar mixity. Hitherto there have been no

---

[50] See also Case C–124/95 *The Queen, ex parte Centro-Com v. HM Treasury and Bank of England* [1997] ECR I–81.   [51] See Ch 12 for further details.

[52] RA Wessel, 'The Inside Looking out: Consistency and Delimitation in EU External Relations' (2000) 37 CMLRev 1148–9.

[53] *Opinion 2/00 re Cartagena Protocol on Biosafety* [2001] ECR I–9713; Case C–281/01 *Commission v. Council* [2002] ECR I–12049; see Ch 2 for more details.

EU measures with a dual legal basis, in the EC Treaty and in the EU Treaty, nor have any international agreements been adopted in such a way. The quest for coherence and consistency none the less pleads for allowing such an approach.[54]

Consistency

The strong language in Article 3 TEU, one of the first provisions of that Treaty, shows the drafters' concern that the pillar structure may obstruct coherent and consistent external action. Article 3 provides:

The Union shall be served by a single institutional framework which shall ensure the consistency and the continuity of the activities carried out in order to attain its objectives while respecting and building upon the acquis communautaire.

The Union shall in particular ensure the consistency of its external activities as a whole in the context of its external relations, security, economic and development policies. The Council and the Commission shall be responsible for ensuring such consistency and shall co-operate to this end. They shall ensure the implementation of these policies, each in accordance with its respective powers.

Consistency was also a concern in the Convention's deliberations.[55] At one level the emphasis on consistency is what may be expected in light of the broad scope of EU external action. Globalization leads to an ever-growing importance and sophistication of external policies, thereby inevitably involving a variety of institutional actors, and in individual States too there are mechanisms and procedures for ensuring consistency so as to overcome policy fragmentation and inconsistencies. Nevertheless, within States consistency would rarely be raised to the constitutional level, as is the case in the EU. The fact that consistency is such a high-level concern is no doubt related to the pillar structure itself, and the tension between intergovernmentalism and supranationalism, particularly at institutional level. The CFSP, to recall the main relevant features again, is dominated by the Council acting unanimously. Under the EC Treaty the Commission occupies a much more central role, particularly in external relations, because it is the Community's international negotiator and because in many areas the Council decides by qualified majority, which gives the Commission more room for manœuvre. Unavoidably, the pillar structure created interinstitutional tension in the conduct of EU external relations. From an institutional perspective it matters a lot whether a particular policy is located in the EC Treaty or is pursued as a CFSP matter. As we have seen, it is difficult to delimit competences between the pillars, because the issues are complex and the overall set-up inherently paradoxical, and because the Court has limited jurisdiction. One could say that the constitutional emphasis on consistency is something of a subterfuge, an

---

[54] See further Ch 6.
[55] See Final Report of Working Group VII on External Action, CONV 459/02, 4–5 (<http://european-convention.eu.int/doc_wg.asp?lang=EN>).

attempt to cover up inter-institutional strife, to throw a constitutional blanket on the struggles between the Council and the Commission, not to mention the Parliament.

The inter-institutional dimension of the consistency requirement can be seen in the text of Article 3, second paragraph, TEU, where the Council and the Commission are made responsible for ensuring consistency and an obligation of co-operation is imposed on them. However, the Treaty does not spell out any specific consequences of that obligation. It does not, in particular, resolve the issue of hierarchy between the pillars. As the CFSP covers all areas of foreign and security policy, thus projecting an EU role in general international politics, it is in the nature of things that certain CFSP decisions set policies with ramifications for EC external action. The question therefore arises whether CFSP decisions may contain legally binding instructions for EC action. Nuttall reports that this question crystallized in 1994, on the occasion of deciding upon common positions concerning Rwanda and the Ukraine.[56] The Council had in mind combining action under both the first and second pillars, but the Commission strongly objected to the fact that this combined approach was exclusively defined under the CFSP. The Council legal service took the view that it had not been the intention to exclude matters of EC competence from the CFSP provisions, but admitted that the Commission could not be obliged to act by a decision taken under those provisions, which would impair its autonomy under the EC Treaty. The Commission legal service contested the view that CFSP provisions could apply to EC matters, and denied that the Commission could be reduced to a body for implementing CFSP policy. In its view, common positions were addressed to the Member States and not the Commission. The dilemma was partially resolved when in March 1995 the Council noted an operational guide (*mode d'emploi*) on common positions.[57] This *mode d'emploi* provided that common positions committed the Union as a whole, and respected the consistency of the Union's external activities in accordance with (current) Article 3 TEU; they could thus refer to the Union's external activities as a whole, but had to preserve the powers specific to each institution, including the Commission's power of initiative.[58]

The Commission's position is understandable, and appears correct in so far as CFSP decisions would attempt to interfere with the Commission's right of initiative under the EC Treaty. If, however, consistency is to be meaningful, some degree of political superiority of the CFSP over EC external policies seems unavoidable. It is doubtful whether such superiority risks undermining the supranational character of the first pillar. In the absence of the CFSP, international politics would not disappear, and Member State governments, present in the Council, would also decide on certain external EC policies from a broader political perspective. For example, one can hardly imagine current negotiations on a trade and co-operation agreement with Iran not being affected by high international politics. The benefit of the CFSP is that it makes

---

[56] Nuttall (n 7 above), 263–4.
[57] The *mode d'emploi* is not published. See for a description Wessel (n 52 above), 1154–5.
[58] See also Timmermans (n 25 above), 63–64.

that dimension visible, and subject to a formal process of deliberation. Once such deliberation has taken place, the Member States are bound by its conclusions, including when they act within the EC framework. That may actually be helpful, rather than detrimental, for effective EC decision-making. Of course there is the tension between unanimous CFSP decision-making and EC qualified majority. But it may be something of an illusion to think that, in the absence of a CFSP with the more onerous unanimity requirement, EC decision-making on sensitive external policies would be less fractured and more effective. From that perspective it makes little sense to focus too closely on the question whether the EC is subordinate to the CFSP and whether CFSP decisions can impose legally binding obligations on the Community.[59]

At institutional level it seems clear that the institutions, in particular the Council and the Commission, are in practice in any event required to co-operate.[60] The Commission's role here probably gives it greater effective participation in CFSP decision-making than a bare reading of the TEU may suggest. However, the co-operation obligation is hardly enforceable, largely because of the fundamental credos of the CFSP: its separation from the EC and the lack of Court jurisdiction.

The Treaty of Amsterdam introduced the new instrument of common strategies, which are clearly intended to improve consistency by laying down overall strategies towards certain countries or regions. Whether the attempt has been successful is still unclear. Three common strategies have hitherto been fleshed out.[61] In all three cases the strategy brought together existing policies, mainly within the first pillar, rather than projecting new orientations. Some commentators are therefore critical of the usefulness of the instrument.[62]

International legal personality and power to conclude agreements

The EU and international legal personality

A crucial question concerning the external powers of the EU under the CFSP is whether the EU has the power to conclude international agreements. As mentioned above, the uninformed reader of the TEU will be astonished by the question, in light of the express reference in Article 24 TEU to the negotiation and conclusion of agreements. However, Article 24 was only inserted by the Treaty of Amsterdam, and is itself but one development in a long debate about the EU's international legal

---

[59] A negative reply is given by Wessel (n 52 above), 1156.

[60] Compare with the duty of co-operation between the Community and the Member States: see Ch 7.

[61] Russia, Ukraine, and the Mediterranean region (n 29 above).

[62] e.g. E Decaux, 'Le processus de décision de la PESC: vers une politique étrangère européenne?', in E Cannizzaro (ed), *The European Union as an Actor in International Relations* (Kluwer Law International, 2002) at 37, where he argues that the Union, in spite of the ambition to project an overall vision through common strategies, remains a prisoner of its compartmentalized competences.

personality. In the *AETR* decision on implied powers under the EC Treaty the Court of Justice started its analysis by referring to (current) Article 281 EC, which provides that the Community has legal personality. In the Court's opinion, this provision meant that in its external relations the Community enjoyed the capacity to establish contractual links with third countries over the whole field of objectives of the Treaty.[63] This was the very constitutional starting point of the EC's treaty-making powers. By contrast, when the European Union was set up at Maastricht, no provision on legal personality of the Union was inserted, even if the point had been discussed. Nor were there any provisions on the conclusion of international agreements by the Union, whereas capacity to make treaties is clearly one of the defining features of international legal personality. All this created the opportunity for great legal debate on the topic. Some argued that international legal personality had deliberately been withheld,[64] whereas others viewed the Treaty silence as mere oversight.[65] One could also read the silence as an absence of consensus on the issue.

Be that as it may, since Maastricht the debate on international legal personality has played an awkward role, as it seemed to be directed towards establishing whether there is some type of constitutional/international law barrier to EU action under international law in second and third pillar matters. It is not however obvious that the concept of international legal personality should be ascribed such a normative function.[66] As time goes by, the debate seems ever more irrelevant, in light of Article 24 TEU, the effective use made of that provision, and the draft Constitution which establishes legal personality for the whole Union.[67] The analysis in these sections is thus based on the assumption that the EU's international legal personality is beyond doubt at the time of writing. There is no attempt to present a definitive analysis of the vexed question of international legal personality of international organizations.[68] The account rather aims to reflect how the debate about EU international legal personality got caught in between the fires of international law doctrine, the demands of CFSP practice, and European constitutional politics.

The concept of international legal personality

The decision of the ICJ in the *Reparation for Injuries* case continues to be the most authoritative ruling on international legal personality of international organizations.[69]

[63] *Commission v. Council* (n 41 above); see Ch 3.

[64] Eaton (n 4 above), 225; Wessel (n 8 above), 258.

[65] J Klabbers, 'Presumptive Personality: The European Union in International Law', in M Koskenniemi (ed) (n 4 above), 238–9.   [66] Ibid, 243–4.

[67] Most recent literature accepts that the EU has international legal personality: see A Dashwood, 'External Relations Provisions of the Amsterdam Treaty', in O'Keeffe and Twomey (eds), (n 4 above), 220; A Tizzano, 'The Foreign Relations Law of the EU between Supranationality and Intergovernmental Model', in Cannizzaro (n 62 above), 142–3, and 'La personalità internazionale dell'Unione europea' [1998] Diritto dell'Unione Europea 377; C Tomuschat, 'The International Responsibility of the European Union', in Cannizzaro (above) 181–2; Wessel (n 52 above), 1138.

[68] See Von Bogdandy (n 5 above), 892, for criticism of the scientific relevance of the notion.

[69] *Reparation for Injuries* [1949] ICJ Rep 174.

In issue was the capacity of the United Nations to bring claims under international law. Like the TEU the UN Charter does not expressly provide for legal personality. The Court nonetheless concluded that the UN had such personality. The Organization was intended to exercise and enjoy, and was in fact exercising and enjoying, functions and rights which could only be explained on the basis of the possession of a large measure of international personality and the capacity to operate on the international plane. It could not carry out the intentions of its founders if it was devoid of international personality. It had to be acknowledged that the UN Members, by entrusting certain functions to it, with the attendant duties and responsibilities, had clothed it with the competence required to enable those functions to be effectively discharged.[70]

International law scholars are in no sense unanimous about the meaning and consequences of the decision, and defend different theories on international legal personality.[71] According to the 'will' theory legal personality of an international organization depends first and foremost on the will of its founders, as expressed in the foundational instrument. The will theory also expects recognition of the international organization by the international community. As regards the EU, the will of the founders is difficult to establish, particularly after Amsterdam: no Treaty article expressly confers international legal personality, but there is a provision on the negotiation and conclusion of international agreements, whose scope and meaning are however contested (see below). There is none the less general recognition of the EU by other international actors (States and international organizations).

According to the objective theory the endowment of international legal personality follows quite naturally from the fact that an organization exists. As soon as it meets certain objective standards, it must be deemed to be an international legal person, in much the same way as States, once they meet the criteria of statehood, possess international legal personality. The standards in question relate to whether the organization can act autonomously at international level and whether it is distinct from its members. The will of the founders is relegated to a somewhat subservient status. If one follows the objective theory, there can be little doubt that the EU possesses international legal personality.

Klabbers however proposes a different approach. He argues that international legal personality is not a normative question. In his view the ICJ effectively employed a notion of presumptive personality in the *Reparation for Injuries* case. It did not really establish the UN's personality, particularly in relation to third States, but reasoned on the basis of a presumption of personality which was not rebutted. The Court, Klabbers argues, accepted that the fifty States which set up the UN had the power to create an international legal person, and presumed that they had utilized that power. He draws a parallel with the Court of Justice's ruling in the *AETR*

---

[70] *Reparation for Injuries* (n 69 above), 179.
[71] See in particular Klabbers (n 65 above), on which the following paras are based. See also D McGoldrick, *International Relations Law of the European Union* (Longman, 1997) 26–8.

case, which should be understood as the Court having regarded Article 281 EC as a strong presumption of international legal personality.[72]

According to Paasivirta the implied powers or functional theory is the most widely accepted approach for determining international legal personality. Under that approach personality derives indirectly from the functions of the organization appropriately exercised through its organs, especially when that exercise demonstrates a will separate from its members. In his view, there are three requirements for international legal personality: it must be indispensable to the achievement of the organization's objectives; the organization must have its own organs and special tasks; and it must be distinct from its members.[73]

Further differences of emphasis are laid by Wessel. He argues that when international organizations are distinct from their members they are by definition an international legal person. More important in his view is the determination of the legal capacities of the organization.[74]

It is not easy to find common ground between these different theories and approaches. The EU nevertheless clearly satisfies a number of the criteria which are advanced in literature. It is distinct from its Member States, and possesses its own organs. Perhaps the two most problematic points are the will of the founders, on which there is no agreement, and the international capacities of the organization, particularly as regards the conclusion of international agreements. The following subsection focuses on the evolution of the TEU with regard to those matters, and on the expanding practice.

Treaty evolution and practice

As mentioned above, no provisions on international legal personality or on the conclusion of international agreements were included in the original TEU. At the time this led most commentators to deny that the EU had such personality. Joint actions and common positions were not instruments which appeared to require international capacity, and the EU was seen as a form of intergovernmental co-operation between the Member States, building upon the rather loose European Political Co-operation.[75]

As CFSP practice developed, however, it became increasingly clear that the EU was hampered by its lack of international capacity. This was most apparent when arrangements were made for the Union to administer the city of Mostar, in the context of the conflict in ex-Yugoslavia. The EU could not itself conclude an agreement with the parties involved in the conflict, and a Memorandum of

---

[72] Klabbers (n 65 above), 246–7.
[73] E Paasivirta, 'The European Union: From an Aggregate of States to a Legal Person?' (1997) 2 The Hofstra Law & Policy Symposium 43–4.   [74] Wessel, (n 52 above), 1140.
[75] Cf the *Maastricht* judgment of the *Bundesverfassungsgericht* (German Constitutional Court), BVerfGe 89, 155, [1994] 1 CHLR 57, at 94.

Understanding was signed by the EU and WEU Member States rather than the Union itself.[76]

In the Amsterdam IGC it was considered that, since the creation of the CFSP, the EU had increasingly been acting, and had also been perceived by third States or other international organizations to be acting as an entity distinct from its Member States. It was also felt that, *de facto*, the EU was operating in a manner which implied that it had legal capacity. The IGC considered two basic options. The first was to make express provision for international legal personality, but there was no consensus. The second option was to include a provision on the conclusion of international agreements. That option was accepted, and became Article 24 TEU, not however without ambiguity in the text.[77] In De Witte's assessment, the refusal to make express provision for EU international legal personality had been due to the word-fetishism of the British.[78]

Article 24 TEU provided, in the post-Amsterdam version:

When it is necessary to conclude an agreement with one or more States or international organizations in implementation of this Title, the Council, acting unanimously, may authorize the Presidency, assisted by the Commission as appropriate, to open negotiations to that effect. Such agreements shall be concluded by the Council acting unanimously on a recommendation from the Presidency. No agreement shall be binding on a Member State whose representative in the Council states that it has to comply with the requirements of its own constitutional procedure; the other members of the Council may agree that the agreement shall apply provisionally to them.

The provisions of this Article shall also apply to matters falling under Title VI.

The last sentence of the first paragraph, referring to the position which Member States may take in the Council, could hardly be more enigmatic.[79] It gives rise to the question whether Article 24 agreements are concluded by the EU itself, or whether the Council simply acts on behalf of the Member States. The reply to that question is crucial for the Union's international legal personality and capacity.

The first point to note is that, if the reference to compliance with domestic constitutional procedure for the conclusion of agreements was intended as an expression of the fact that Article 24 agreements are concluded on behalf of the Member States, and not of the Union itself, one would not expect the present optional language.

As Marquardt argues, one needs to interpret Article 24 TEU by applying the rules of treaty interpretation in Article 31 VCLT, focusing on the ordinary meaning of the terms, taking into account their context, and in the light of the agreement's

---

[76] For further details see Special Report 2/96 concerning the accounts of the Administrator and the European Union Administration, Mostar (EUAM) accompanied by the replies of the Commission and the Administrator of Mostar [1996] OJ C287/1; Koskenniemi (n 4 above), 34–5.

[77] S Marquardt, 'The Conclusion of International Agreements under Article 24 of the Treaty on European Union', in V Kronenberger (ed), *The European Union and the International Legal Order: Discord or Harmony?* (TMC Asser Press, 2001) 337; Wessel (n 8 above), 259–60. See also S Peers, 'Common Foreign and Security Policy' (1996) 16 YEL 619–20; N Neuwahl, 'A Partner With a Troubled Personality: EU Treaty-Making in Matters of CFSP and JHA after Amsterdam' (1998) 3 EFARev 181–5.

[78] De Witte (n 1 above), 63.   [79] For further analysis see Ch 6.

object and purpose.[80] Applying that method, the author points out that Article 24 agreements are concluded by the Council, which is an EU institution, and are negotiated by the Presidency, which pursuant to Article 18(1) TEU represents the Union, and not the Member States. He also refers to other TEU provisions, confirming that the EU is distinct from its Member States: Article 11 on the objectives of the CFSP; Article 12 on the Union's own means of action, including common positions and joint actions; Article 23 according to which Member States have a right of abstention but need to 'accept that the decision commits the Union', a provision which also applies to Article 24.[81]

Marquardt's analysis is difficult to rebut.[82] It is shared by Tomuschat, who likewise points out that the words in Article 24 must be read according to their natural meaning. Since Article 24 refers to conclusion by the Council, 'fairly strange intellectual operations would be needed to demonstrate that a treaty concluded under such circumstances has instead created legal bonds between the third party concerned and each one of the Member States of the European Union'.[83] Tomuschat also refers to a further element, beyond Article 24 TEU. He draws attention to the EU's international responsibility, which in no way depends on an express conferral of legal personality. Third States which are adversely affected by the conduct of the EU, for example through European Council statements on political issues outside Europe, may hold it responsible for any injury they may have suffered. Moreover, the EU (including the EC) is an entity with powers going far beyond anything one encounters in the ordinary type of international organizations. Both at quantitative and qualitative level its functions are such that the definitive step towards statehood seems to be crossing no more than a thin red line. The fact that the EU is so close to statehood supports the conclusion that it must be subject to the regime of international responsibility.[84]

Dashwood also takes the view that the EU has international legal personality. He is of the opinion that the text of Article 24 TEU, post-Amsterdam, is ambiguous as regards conclusion of international agreements by the EU, but if, in practice, such agreements are indeed concluded by the Union (there was no practice yet when Dashwood wrote about the subject), then the issue would be beyond doubt.[85]

In the meantime such practice definitively confirms the EU's legal personality. A number of agreements have been concluded on the basis of Article 24 TEU,[86] all of which are agreements between the European Union as such and third States or

---

[80] Marquardt (n 77 above), 338.   [81] Ibid, 340–4.

[82] But see Paasivirta (n 73 above), 58; M Cremona, 'External Relations and External Competence: The Emergence of an Integrated Policy', in Craig and de Búrca (n 1 above) 168; K Lenaerts and P Van Nuffel, *Constitutional Law of the European Union* (R Bray (ed and trans.), Sweet & Maxwell, 1999) 608.

[83] Tomuschat (n 67 above), 181–2.   [84] Ibid, 182–3.

[85] Dashwood (n 67 above), 220. See also Peers (n 77 above), 564 and McGoldrick, (n 71 above), 37.

[86] Council Decision 2001/352 concerning the conclusion of the Agreement between the European Union and the Federal Republic of Yugoslavia (FRY) on the activities of the European Union Monitoring Mission (EUMM) [2001] OJ L125/1; Council Decision 2001/682 concerning the conclusion of the Agreement between the European Union and the Former Yugoslav Republic of Macedonia

an international organization (*in casu* NATO). There is no mention of the EU Member States in the title of any of the agreements, nor is there any reference in the Council decisions of conclusion of any Member State making use of the opportunity in Article 24 to comply with the requirements of its own constitutional procedure. One of the agreements (with FYROM, on the EU-led forces) even concerns an EU military operation. None of the agreements are concluded as mixed agreements, and there is therefore no indication whatsoever that the EU Member States are in some way parties to those agreements. Most of the agreements contain provisions which clearly distinguish the EU from its Member States. For example, the agreements on EU Monitoring Missions in the Republic of Yugoslavia, FYROM, and Albania provide that the head of such missions is appointed by the Council, and other personnel 'shall be seconded by the Member States of the European Union'.[87] The very notion of secondment shows that the EU is distinct from its Member States, and many more indications can be found in the agreements which lead to the conclusion that they are concluded by the EU as a legal person.

The Treaty of Nice has amended and expanded Article 24 TEU, mainly with respect to Council decision-making (by unanimity or qualified majority). However, the new provision also provides, in paragraph 6: 'Agreements concluded under the conditions set out by this Article shall be binding on the institutions of the Union'. The current version of Article 24 thus confirms that the agreements in question are binding both on the Member States (with the exception of Member States which need to comply with the domestic constitutional requirements) and on the EU institutions. It is in this respect in essence indistinguishable from Article 300(7) EC. The reference to the institutions provides further confirmation that Article 24 agreements are concluded by the EU as such.

In light of this EU capacity to conclude international agreements, a capacity which is recognized by third countries, there can no longer be any doubt that the EU as such has international legal personality. The draft Constitution therefore logically confirms such legal personality, in one of its first provisions (Article I–6).

(FYROM) on the activities of the European Union Monitoring Mission (EUMM) in FYROM [2001] OJ L242/1; Council Decision 2002/845 concerning the conclusion of the Agreement between the European Union and Bosnia and Herzegovina (BiH) on the acitivities of the European Union Police Mission (EUPM) in BiH [2002] OJ L293/1; Council Decision 2003/211 concerning the conclusion of the Agreement between the European Union and the North Atlantic Treaty Organization on the Security of Information [1993] OJ L80/35; Council Decision 2003/222 concerning the conclusion of the Agreement between the European Union and the Former Yugoslav Republic of Madedonia on the status of the European Union-led Forces (EUF) in the Former Yugoslav Republic of Macedonia [2003] OJ L82/45; Council Decision 2003/252 concerning the conclusion of the Agreement between the European Union and the Republic of Albania on the activities of the European Union Monitoring Mission (EUMM) in the Republic of Albania [2003] OJ L93/49.

[87] Art III(2) Agreement with the FRY, Art III(2) Agreement with FYROM, and Art 3(2) Agreement with Albania, all n 86 above.

Police and judicial co-operation in criminal matters

The Third Pillar of the EU concerns, in its current version, police and judicial co-operation in criminal matters. Its scope was reduced by the Treaty of Amsterdam, which took out certain aspects of the original Justice and Home Affairs policies, in order to put them in the EC Treaty.[88] According to Article 29 the third pillar policies involve: (a) closer co-operation between police forces, customs authorities, and other competent authorities in the Member States; (b) closer co-operation between judicial and other competent authorities of the Member States; and (c) approximation, where necessary, of rules on criminal matters in the Member States. The instruments at the EU's disposal are common positions, framework decisions for the approximation of the laws and regulations of the Member States, decisions for any other purpose, and conventions concluded between the Member States (Article 34 TEU). As regards external relations Article 38 TEU provides that agreements referred to in Article 24 may cover matters falling under the PJCCM title. In other words, the EU may also conclude international agreements on Third Pillar matters. Also, according to Article 37 TEU the Member States shall defend the PJCCM common positions within international organizations and at international conferences.

The TEU thus permits significant external policies in the area of PJCCM, as is illustrated by the first agreements hitherto negotiated and signed, but not yet concluded. Those agreements are between the EU and the US and concern extradition and mutual legal assistance.[89] The extradition agreement, for example, defines as contracting parties 'the European Union and the United States of America' (Article 2(1)), thereby confirming again that Article 24 agreements are concluded on behalf of the EU, and not on behalf of the Member States. The significance of the agreement is readily apparent: as regards the extradition issues which it covers it purports to override bilateral agreements between the individual Member States and the United States (Article 3).

There is no attempt here to determine with any precision the scope of the EU's powers in the field of PJCCM. It is none the less obvious that issues of demarcation and delimitation are likely to arise, both with EC competences[90] and with the EU's powers under the CFSP. The instant candidates for such issues are policies to combat terrorism. As mentioned above, the EC is currently insisting on the inclusion of anti-terrorism clauses in external agreements.[91] The relevant provisions could be considered to come, either within national competence, or within the scope of CFSP or PJCCM powers, or even within the competences of the EC in so far as EC acts are affected or development co-operation is in issue.

---

[88] See Ch 4.
[89] See Council document 9153/03, available on <www.statewatch.org/news/2003/jun/useu 09153.pdf>.
[90] Cf the provisions on drug abuse control in the co-operation agreement with India (see Ch 4).
[91] N 35 above.

The draft Constitution

As regards the Union's powers to conduct a common foreign and security policy the draft Constitution involves substantial modifications to the existing legal framework. The most significant innovation is the demolition of the pillar structure. The TEU is no longer separate from the EC Treaty. Instead, all the EU's policies are brought together in one single Constitution. As regards external relations, or rather external action, to use the Constitution's terminology, this has enabled the Convention members to bring all constitutional provisions together in a single title (Title V of Part III), called The Union's External Action. Reflecting that creation of unity Article I–6 provides: 'The Union shall have legal personality'. When one reads that provision in combination with the Constitution's unified provision on the negotiation and conclusion of international agreements (Article III–227), which replaces the current Articles 24 TEU and 300 EC, there is no longer any doubt that the Union set up by the Constitution possesses international legal personality.

The CFSP none the less remains a separate policy, and a number of characteristics of the current pillar structure are maintained. It is for example striking that, whereas for the first time an attempt has been made to develop categories of EU competences and to describe the nature of those competences, the CFSP has escaped those attempts. Indeed, Article I–11 distinguishes between exclusive and shared competences, competence to promote and co-ordinate economic and employment policies, competences to support, co-ordinate, or supplement actions of the Member States— and the CFSP. For all other types of competence there is an attempt at defining their character, in particular in their relationship with national policies, but not for the CFSP. Moreover, in Title V of Part III, on The Union's External Action, there is a separate chapter on the CFSP, which is not radically different from the current Title V of the TEU. The CFSP continues to be run through the use of different instruments. Whereas the draft Constitution introduces European 'laws' and 'framework laws', adopted under a legislative procedure involving the Council and the Parliament, Article I–39(7) excludes the use of laws and framework laws for the conduct of the CFSP. Instead, the policy is implemented by way of 'decisions', defined as 'a non-legislative act, binding in its entirety' (Article I–32(1)). Those decisions will concern 'actions' or 'positions' of the Union or their implementation (Article III–195(3)), thereby corresponding to the current joint actions and common positions. The decision-making procedures are not substantially modified, meaning that the Commission and Parliament are much less involved than in other Union policies. Perhaps most important is that the jurisdiction of the Court of Justice continues to be limited. Article III–282 provides that the Court shall not have jurisdiction with respect to Articles I–39 and I–40 (the provisions in Part I on the CFSP and the common security and defence policy, or CSDP) and the provisions of the CFSP chapter in Part III.[92] Further confirmation that the CFSP remains separate territory can be

---

[92] The second para contains an exception for restrictive measures against natural or legal persons: see Ch 11.

found in Article III–209, according to which the implementation of the CFSP shall not affect the EU's other competences, and *vice versa*. That provision reflects current Article 47 TEU, and the Court is expressly given jurisdiction to monitor compliance with it. There will thus continue to be a need to delimit the EU's external competences. In this respect, one may also note that there appears to be some tension between the exclusion of jurisdiction in Article III–282 and the Court's task to protect and safeguard the different competences. If the Court is to protect competences under the CFSP title from incursion through acts adopted under other competences, it will have to interpret the Constitution's provisions on the CFSP.

The exact scope of the CFSP continues to be difficult to determine. Like the TEU the draft Constitution provides that the Union's competence in CFSP matters covers 'all areas of foreign policy and all questions relating to the Union's security, including the progressive framing of a common defence policy, which might lead to a common defence' (Article I–15(1)). In fact, the CSDP, which is an integral part of the CFSP,[93] is better defined than the overal CFSP. According to Article I–40 the CSDP shall provide the Union with an operational capacity drawing on assets civil and military, and the Union may use them on missions outside the Union for peace-keeping, conflict prevention, and strengthening international security; the CSDP shall include the progressive framing of a common Union defence policy.[94] No such precision is available as regards other matters coming within the CFSP.

Furthermore, the CFSP is no longer characterized by a separate set of policy objectives, such as those listed in Article 11(1) TEU, however vague those objectives may be. With a view to creating a more unified approach to the Union's external action, the relevant title in Part III opens with two general provisions, the first of which describes the overall objectives of the Union's external action. Article III–193 provides:

1. The Union's action on the international scene shall be guided by, and designed to advance in the wider world, the principles which have inspired its own creation, development and enlargement: democracy, the rule of law, the universality and indivisibility of human rights and fundamental freedoms, respect for human dignity, equality and solidarity, and for international law in accordance with the principles of the United Nations Charter.

The Union shall seek to develop relations and build partnerships with third countries, and international, regional or global organisations, which share these values. It shall promote multilateral solutions to common problems, in particular in the framework of the United Nations.

2. The Union shall define and pursue common policies and actions, and shall work for a high degree of cooperation in all fields of international relations, in order to:

(a) safeguard the common values, fundamental interests, security, independence and integrity of the Union;

---

[93] Art I–40(1).

[94] See also Art III–209(1), which further defines the relevant tasks as including 'joint disarmament operations, humanitarian and rescue tasks, military advice and assistance tasks, conflict prevention and peace-keeping tasks, tasks of combat forces in crisis management, including peacemaking and post-conflict stabilization'; all those tasks 'may contribute to the fight against terrorism'.

(b) consolidate and support democracy, the rule of law, human rights and international law;
(c) preserve peace, prevent conflicts and strengthen international security, in conformity with the principles of the United Nations Charter;
(d) foster the sustainable economic, social and environmental development of developing countries, with the primary aim of eradicating poverty;
(e) encourage the integration of all countries into the world economy, including through the progressive abolition of restrictions on international trade;
(f) help develop international measures to preserve and improve the quality of the environment and the sustainable management of global natural resources, in order to ensure sustainable development;
(g) assist populations, countries and regions confronting natural or man-made disasters;
(h) promote an international system based on stronger multilateral cooperation and good global governance.

3. The Union shall respect the principles and pursue the objectives listed in paragraphs 1 and 2 in the development and implementation of the different areas of the Union's external action covered by this Title and the external aspects of its other policies.

The Union shall ensure consistency between the different areas of its external action and between these and its other policies. The Council of Ministers and the Commission, assisted by the Union's Minister for Foreign Affairs, shall ensure that consistency and shall cooperate to that effect.

The last subparagraph corresponds to Article 3 TEU, and it appears that there may be as much need for consistency under the new Constitution as before. It must further be noted that the search for more unified external action is also reflected in the second general provision, Article III–194. That provision corresponds to the TEU provisions on common strategies. It states that 'the European Council shall identify the strategic interests and objectives of the Union', and that the relevant decisions 'shall relate to the common foreign and security policy and to other areas of the external action of the Union'. Article III–194 thus confirms the role of general strategies, which should ensure consistent and coherent external policies.

The quest for more unified external action is also reflected at institutional level, through the creation of the Union Minister for Foreign Affairs, the person with the so-called double hat, at once chairing the Council of Ministers as well as taking over the function of the current High Representative for the CFSP, and acting as Vice-President of the Commission (Article I–27).

Conclusions

Several general conclusions can be drawn from this chapter's analysis of the EU's external powers and the objectives of external action under the second and third pillars (in particular the former).

The sphere of action of the CFSP is defined in the broadest terms, as encompassing all areas of foreign and security policy. The objectives of the CFSP, as defined in Article 11(1) TEU, are so general that they do not circumscribe the scope of the CFSP. Indeed, the draft Constitution no longer contains specific CFSP objectives.

A lot of different activities are undertaken within the framework of this policy, but increasingly it appears that its specificity is concentrated in security and defence matters, where the TEU and the draft Constitution clarify the kind of activities which the EU is destined to undertake.

If the CFSP were to exist in isolation, its broad definition, indeed its lack of real definition, would not necessarily raise many issues. However, the CFSP is constitutionally juxtaposed to the EC's external policies, by virtue of Article 47 TEU. Even if the Court has only once applied that provision, it is clear that it is prepared to employ it for policing the boundaries between the second (and third) pillar and the Community's competences. Thus, the CFSP may not trespass on Community external relations territory. As the latter continues to expand, the CFSP may indeed shrink to security and defence policy. Its vocation to cover all areas of foreign and security policy is thus much qualified: there should be a footnote stating that this provision applies only in so far as there is no EC competence. The original fears of a subordination of Community policies to CFSP decision-making, and a resulting infection of the *acquis communautaire* now seem unjustified. Perhaps it is rather the CFSP which is under siege of the Community's expanding external competences.

The way in which the Court policed the borders between the EC Treaty and the TEU also confirms that there is a unified concept of EU law, and that the EU is a single organization, albeit also housing the EC and Euratom. If the EU were truly separate and independent from the EC, the Court could not stop the Member States from using it for co-ordinating national policies in areas where the Member States share competence with the EC. That is however not the Court's conception, and rightly so. The EC Treaty and the TEU are organically linked, and competences therefore have to be allocated. A development co-operation measure, for example, cannot be taken under the CFSP. The draft Constitution wholly confirms this unified concept, by merging the treaties, and by creating the position of Union Minister for Foreign Affairs. One may hope that this will lead to better co-ordination and greater effectiveness of external policies. There will however still be scope for institutional turf battles. The Union Minister may unify the external action administration, but decision-making procedures remain different (e.g. unanimity in CFSP matters) and so does the role of the various institutions.

Recent developments also confirm the EU's international legal personality: the scope for conclusion of agreements under Article 24 TEU, since Nice with some room for qualified majority, the actual agreements concluded by the EU, and the draft Constitution. Already today, before the entry into force of the Constitution, the most convincing thesis is that there is a single international legal personality for the whole of the EU, which includes the EC and Euratom. Third countries contracting with either the EU, under the second or third pillar, or the EC may invoke the responsibility of the EU as a whole.

This chapter concludes the analysis of the legal and constitutional foundations of the EU's external powers and objectives. One must again draw attention to the broad overall scope of such powers. There appear to be virtually no significant areas of international law making in which the EU cannot participate.

Part II

International Foundations: Treaties and International Law

6

The life cycle of international agreements

Introduction

This chapter examines the procedure for the EU's negotiation, conclusion, and termination, of an international agreement.[1] At face value this may seem like a terse and self-referential legal subject. It will be clear however that important constitutional and institutional issues lurk behind the relevant procedural provisions. The scope and depth of the EU's treaty-making practice are such that it has become a central instrument of law making, often of a general normative or legislative character. Policy areas such as trade, development co-operation, fisheries, and environmental protection are obvious examples of areas of EU activity where much law making effectively takes place by way of participation in international negotiations. Examining the role of the various EU institutions (and of the Member States) in the negotiation and conclusion of international agreements therefore implies identifying important constitutional functions.

Those functions can be approached from two perspectives. First, there is the perspective of institutional balance.[2] Each of the EU's political institutions—Commission, Council, and European Parliament—has a particular role to play in the process of entering into international commitments. The definition of that role is an important factor in the overall balance of political power as distributed among those institutions. Secondly, and more fundamentally, there is the perspective of democracy and legitimacy. It is a worn but justified complaint that the EU struggles with questions about the legitimacy and democratic character of its action. In one sense, the EU's participation in international law making is even more remote from the citizen than is the creation of 'internal' legislation. There is a stronger role for the executive, as opposed to representatives of the people, which is a general feature of States' participation in international law making. Indeed, as analysed below, even though the European Parliament needs to give its assent to certain types of international agreements, that does not imply a strong role for the Parliament in the actual negotiation of international commitments. There are thus, in

---

[1] See also I Macleod, ID Hendry, and S Hyett, *The External Relations of the European Communities* (OUP, 1996) 75–105.

[2] See e.g. B De Witte, 'Institutional Principles: A Special Category of General Principles of Law', in U Bernitz and J Nergelius (eds), *General Principles of European Community Law* (Kluwer Law International, 2000) 150–2.

this area, significant issues of legitimacy and democracy which receive remarkably little attention in either public debate or academic literature.

This chapter does not aim to present a definitive analysis of such issues. It aims to describe the law and practice as regards the different phases in the life of an international agreement: negotiation, signature, conclusion, implementation, suspension, and termination. The relevant provisions are contained in Article 300 EC, which was much amended and expanded in the course of time, from two to seven paragraphs, thus reflecting the intense treaty-making activity of the Community and the resulting problems and practices, some of which were addressed through Treaty amendments. Article 300 EC is not however the only provision on the conclusion of agreements. Agreements on an exchange-rate system, or on monetary or foreign exchange regime matters are subject to special procedures described in Article 111(1) and (3) EC. Furthermore, since the Treaty of Amsterdam the EU has also been capable of concluding international agreements concerning the Second or the Third Pillar. Article 24 TEU contains the relevant provisions. Accordingly, each section in this chapter distinguishes between those three procedures.

The draft Constitution aims to integrate the various provisions on negotiation and conclusion, and its proposed provisions are shortly discussed in a separate section. This chapter does not however examine the role of the Court of Justice in the process of negotiation and conclusion. Under Article 300(6) EC the Court can be asked to deliver an Opinion on the compatibility of an envisaged agreement with the Treaty, but that procedure is analysed in Chapter 8.

At the outset a point of legal terminology is also worth noting. Article 300 EC consistently refers to 'agreements', but that term needs to be broadly interpreted as encompassing all forms of international contractual obligations entered into, be they in the form of a treaty, convention, agreement, memorandum of understanding, or any other instrument. So much follows both from the case law of the Court of Justice, which recognizes the Community's general capacity to enter into international commitments and consistently identifies Article 300 EC as the Treaty provision containing the relevant procedural rules,[3] and from established institutional practice.[4] Likewise, the term agreement in Article 111 EC and Article 24 TEU must no doubt be broadly construed.

Negotiations

Article 300 EC

As in most other fields of Community law making the Commission has the prerogative of proposal. Article 300(1) EC provides:

Where this Treaty provides for the conclusion of agreements between the Community and one or more States or international organisations, the Commission shall make recommendations to

---

[3] *Opinion 1/75 re Local Cost Standard* [1975] ECR 1355, 1360.
[4] The VCLT also operates a holistic approach to the concept of a treaty: see Art 2(1)(a).

the Council, which shall authorize the Commission to open the necessary negotiations. The Commission shall conduct these negotiations in consultation with special committees appointed by the Council to assist it in this task and within the framework of such directives as the Council may issue to it.

In exercising the powers conferred upon it by this paragraph, the Council shall act by a qualified majority, except in the cases where the first subparagraph of paragraph 2 provides that the Council shall act unanimously.

In practice, it is fair to say that the initiative to engage in a particular negotiation may come from various corners and that, depending on the type of negotiation, there may be a period of reflection prior to the decision to open negotiations. Often such reflection is accompanied by discussion papers which the Commission produces.[5] The European Council is also actively involved in determining the general direction of policies in the field of external relations. The actual recommendations which the Commission makes to the Council are not published. The Council may then authorize the Commission to proceed; the 'shall' in Article 300(1) EC does not imply an obligation for the Council to agree with the Commission's recommendations.[6] The Council takes that decision by qualified majority or unanimity, depending on the type or content of the agreement, under the same rules as apply to the conclusion of agreements (see below).

The Commission conducts negotiations in accordance with directives which the Council may issue to it. The term 'directives' here does not have the same meaning as in Article 249 EC, which defines the directive as a legislative instrument. In the context of international negotiations, the Council's directives are not addressed to the Member States, but to the Commission.[7] Nor are they published, as this would permit the other party to the negotiations to have knowledge of the Commission's precise brief too easily. The content of the directives is none the less often reported in the press, and the practice appears to be for the directives to be rather general in character. That does not mean that the Commission has a free hand in the negotiations. Through the 'special committees', consisting of national government representatives, the Council machinery keeps a close eye on how the negotiations are evolving. The Commission is therefore often a double negotiator: both with the other party to the negotiations and with Member States' representatives or the Council itself.

Notwithstanding such supervision by the Council, the negotiation of international agreements does amount to a significant Commission prerogative. The Commission is generally in a position to try to find a common denominator of the, often varying, interests of the Member States. Moreover, in some cases the Commission can be quite deft in the use of its authority to negotiate. Two examples, both from the Uruguay Round negotiations leading to the establishment of the WTO, illustrate this.

---

[5] E.g. Communication from the Commission to the European Parliament and the Council—EU relations with the Islamic Republic of Iran, COM(2001)71 final.

[6] Macleod, Hendry, and Hyett (n 1 above), 87.

[7] Ibid, 89. In other language versions the terminology differs.

The first example is the so-called Blair House agreement. Faced with the fact that the Uruguay Round could be successful only if an agreement could be reached with the United States on agriculture, the Commission entered into unofficial negotiations with the United States, resulting, in 1992, in the above outline agreement on the basic principles of the future WTO Agreement on Agriculture, which was the breakthrough which the Round needed. The Commission did this much on its own, and some Member States, with France in the lead, immediately reacted that they could not accept the outcome of the negotiations. However, by the time the Round was concluded (end of 1993) the resistance had melted away, and all Member States accepted the Agreement on Agriculture as part of the overall WTO package.[8]

The second example concerns bananas, and is more technical. Following the adoption of the common market organization on bananas in 1993[9] a number of Latin American countries brought complaints against the Community in the GATT. In reaction the Commission requested the Council's authorization for opening negotiations with the complaining countries on compensation. In March 1994, one month before the final conclusion of the Uruguay Round, the Commission reached a 'framework agreement' with those countries. However, the Commission was aware that the agreement, on its own, would not muster a qualified majority in the Council, and could therefore not as such be concluded by the Community. It then decided to make the agreement part of the Community's tariff commitments in the Uruguay Round, without first seeking the Council's approval, and sent a letter to that effect to the GATT Secretariat. When in April 1994 the WTO Agreement was due to be signed, in Marrakesh, it contained that framework agreement as part of the Community's tariff schedule, and for obvious political reasons none of the Member States was in a position not to sign the WTO Agreement, merely for the sake of trade in bananas. Some Member State delegations fiercely protested against this course of events, and Germany brought two cases against the framework agreement before the Court of Justice. The first was a request for an Opinion under Article 300(6) EC, which Germany made in July 1994, several months before the WTO Agreement entered into force. It argued *inter alia* that the Council had not given the Commission authority to negotiate the framework agreement, or at least that the Commission had gone beyond the Council's instructions. The Court, however, did not examine that claim, as it did not manage to deliver its Opinion before 1 January 1995, when the WTO Agreement, of which the framework agreement formed part, had already entered into force. The request for an Opinion had thus become devoid of purpose, as the Court's Opinion can examine only an envisaged agreement.[10] In its second challenge, an action for the

---

[8] P Van den Bossche, 'The European Community and the Uruguay Round Agreements', in JH Jackson and AO Sykes (eds), *Implementing the Uruguay Round* (OUP, 1997) 62–6.

[9] Council Regulation 404/93 on the common organization of the market in bananas [1993] OJ L47/2; see Ch 10.

[10] *Opinion 3/94 re Framework Agreement on Bananas* [1995] ECR I–4577; see Ch 8.

annulment of the Council's decision to conclude the WTO Agreement in so far as it contained the banana framework agreement, Germany no longer argued that the Commission had failed to respect its negotiating mandate.[11]

It is thus not clear at this stage whether Commission observance of the Council's negotiating directives is subject to judicial review. In principle, any Commission act producing legal effects can be challenged on grounds of violation of the Treaty in an action for annulment. In so far as the Commission adopts such an act in the framework of an international negotiation, it would seem possible to argue a violation of the provisions of Article 300(1) EC. The case is unlikely to arise, however, as the Commission's actions are subject to political review by the Council. If the latter is unhappy with the outcome of a negotiation, it may simply refuse to conclude the agreement. Where it does conclude the agreement, it obviously agrees with the Commission's approach, and a challenge to particular Commission conduct in the course of negotiations would then in any event be unable to affect the outcome, namely conclusion of the agreement, as this is a separate Council act.

The phase of negotiating an international agreement is often concluded by the initialling of the text.[12] This is the act whereby the negotiators authenticate the text resulting from the negotiations. As this forms part of the negotiation, the Commission has authority to undertake such initialling.

It is remarkable that the European Parliament is nowhere mentioned in Article 300(1) EC, and thus has no formal role under the Treaty in either the decision to launch an international negotiation, the directives issued to the Commission, or the supervision of the Commission's conduct of the negotiations. That lack of involvement is even more remarkable given that the Parliament as a rule needs to be consulted before the conclusion of an agreement, and has to give its assent to certain agreements (see below). In practice, the Parliament is not left in the dark as regards the Community's international negotiations. There is an interinstitutional agreement between the Commission and the Parliament which contains provisions on the forwarding of information on international agreements.[13] In that agreement the Commission commits itself to providing early and clear briefing on the preparation phase of agreements, draft negotiating directives, and adopted negotiating directives, in order to be able to take due account of the Parliament's views so far as possible. The Commission shall also keep the Parliament regularly and fully informed of the subsequent conduct and conclusion of international negotiations. Information must be provided in sufficient time for the Parliament to be able to express its views. Also, at the request of the Parliament the Commission shall facilitate the inclusion of Parliament members as observers in Community delegations negotiating multilateral agreements, on the understanding that those members may not take part directly in the negotiating sessions themselves.

---

[11] Case C–122/95 *Germany v. Council* [1996] ECR I–973.
[12] Macleod, Hendry, and Hyett (n 1 above), 90–1.
[13] Framework Agreement on relations between the European Parliament and the Commission [2001] OJ C121/122: see Annex 2.

Article 111 EC

In the monetary field the procedure for the conclusion of international agreements is different, or at least potentially different, since the Treaty leaves it to the Council to decide on the appropriate arrangements. Article 111(3) EC provides *inter alia* that:

the Council, acting by a qualified majority on a recommendation from the Commission and after consulting the ECB, shall decide the arrangements for the negotiation and conclusion of . . . agreements. These arrangements shall ensure that the Community expresses a single position. The Commission shall be fully associated with the negotiations.

The Treaty therefore does not identify the negotiator of agreements based on Article 111(1) or (3) EC, presumably because there may be cases in which the ECB would, in light of its expertise, be the natural negotiator, or at least would need to be involved in the process of negotiation.[14]

Article 24 TEU

Agreements negotiated within the Second or the Third Pillar are also subject to a different procedure. Article 24(1) TEU provides:

When it is necessary to conclude an agreement with one or more States or international organisations in implementation of this title, the Council may authorise the Presidency, assisted by the Commission as appropriate, to open negotiations to that effect. Such agreements shall be concluded by the Council on a recommendation from the Presidency.

As Marquardt points out, the potential role of the Commission is not clearly defined, but the possibility of assistance reflects the general principle that the Commission is 'fully associated' with the work carried out in the CFSP field (Article 27). He also envisages that the Council could, when authorizing the Commission to conduct a negotiation pursuant to Article 300(1) EC, instruct the Commission to include Second or Third Pillar matters if this is deemed more practical.[15] As is discussed below, there are hitherto no agreements which have been concluded on the basis of both the EC and EU Treaties (so-called cross-pillar mixity). Those CFSP agreements which have been concluded were negotiated by the Presidency, and there is no mention of any Commission involvement.[16]

---

[14] See further C Zilioli and M Selmayr, 'The External Relations of the Euro Area: Legal Aspects' (1999) 36 CMLRev 302–3.

[15] S Marquardt, 'The Conclusion of International Agreements Under Article 24 of the Treaty on European Union', in V Kronenberger (ed), *The European Union and the International Legal Order: Discord or Harmony*? (TMC Asser Press, 2001) 340.

[16] Council Decision 2001/352 concerning the conclusion of the Agreement between the European Union and the Federal Republic of Yugoslavia (FRY) on the activities of the European Union Monitoring Mission (EUMM) [2001] OJ L125/1; Council Decision 2001/682 concerning the conclusion of the Agreement between the European Union and the Former Yugoslav Republic of Macedonia (FYROM) on the activities of the European Union Monitoring Mission (EUMM) in FYROM [2001] OJ L242/1; Council Decision 2002/845 concerning the conclusion of the Agreement between the European Union and Bosnia and Herzegovina (BiH) on the activities of the European Union Police

Again there is no formal role whatsoever for the European Parliament, other than the general obligation for the Presidency to consult the Parliament on the main aspects and the basic choices of the CFSP, and to ensure that the views of the Parliament are duly taken into consideration (Article 21 TEU).

Signature and conclusion

Article 300 EC

Concepts

Under international treaty law, as codified in the Vienna Convention on the Law of Treaties, there are various alternative modes of expressing consent to be bound by a treaty.[17] They include signature, exchange of instruments, ratification, acceptance, approval, and accession, the choice between them depending on the treaty in question. Those modalities all concern action on the international plane. It is important to distinguish between such international action and a State's internal legal act enabling that State to engage in such international action.[18] A State's constitution would typically contain a number of rules which have to be followed for undertaking international commitments. Similarly, Article 300(2) EC lays down the Community's internal decision-making procedure for concluding international agreements. It is only by following that procedure that the Community can lawfully—under Community law—express its consent to be bound. The relevant section of Article 300(2) EC provides:

Subject to the powers vested in the Commission in this field, the signing, which may be accompanied by a decision on provisional application before entry into force, and the conclusion of the agreements shall be decided on by the Council, acting by a qualified majority on a proposal from the Commission. The Council shall act unanimously when the agreement covers a field for which unanimity is required for the adoption of internal rules and for the agreements referred to in Article 310.

The provision must be read as applying to all forms of expressing consent on the international plane. Conclusion by the Council is thus a generic term for Council

Mission (EUPM) in BiH [2002] OJ L293/1; Council Decision 2003/211 concerning the conclusion of the Agreement between the European Union and the North Atlantic Treaty Organization on the Security of Information [1993] OJ L80/35; Council Decision 2003/222 concerning the conclusion of the Agreement between the European Union and the Former Yugoslav Republic of Madedonia on the status of the European Union-led Forces (EUF) in the Former Yugoslav Republic of Macedonia [2003] OJ L82/45; Council Decision 2003/252 concerning the conclusion of the Agreement between the European Union and the Republic of Albania on the activities of the European Union Monitoring Mission (EUMM) in the Republic of Albania [2003] OJ L93/49.

[17] See Arts 11–17 VCLT.

[18] JHJ Bourgeois, 'The European Court of Justice and the WTO: Problems and Challenges', in JHH Weiler, *The EU, the WTO and the NAFTA* (OUP, 2000) 77.

decisions on undertaking international commitments. The suggested sequence of signature and conclusion need not always be present. Again this depends on what the agreement itself provides for. The prevailing practice as regards significant treaties or agreements is that, through their signature, the representatives of the contracting parties agree to submit the agreement for domestic approval. In such cases, signature does not express the final consent to be bound, but it does create the obligation not to defeat the object and purpose of the agreement.[19] There are however numerous agreements which are concluded upon signature, in which case the Council has to take a decision on conclusion prior to signature.

Signature may be accompanied by a decision on provisional application before entry into force. This provision was inserted by the Amsterdam Treaty. It reflects Article 25 VCLT, according to which a treaty may provide for such provisional application or the negotiating States may agree to it. The Community regularly makes use of that opportunity in the case of mixed agreements, which require ratification by all Member States, often a time-consuming exercise.[20]

Council decision-making

After some initial hesitation, the Council developed the practice of concluding international agreements by way of decision. Such decisions typically consist of a preamble, identifying *inter alia* the legal basis in the Treaty for the conclusion of the agreement, and a couple of articles expressing conclusion or approval as well as indicating the person (usually the President of the Council) who is instructed to notify the other contracting party or parties of Community conclusion.[21] The decision may of course contain further provisions, for example as regards Community representation in bodies or organs set up by the contracting parties.[22]

It follows from Article 300(2) EC that, as a rule, the Council concludes agreements acting by a qualified majority on a proposal from the Commission. Where however an agreement covers a field for which unanimity is required for the adoption of internal rules the Council shall act unanimously. If, for example, an agreement is concluded on matters of indirect taxation coming within Article 93 EC, the Council is required to act unanimously since that provision provides for unanimous decision-making.

---

[19] Art 18 VCLT. For an application of that obligation see Case T–115/94 *Opel Austria v. Council* [1997] ECR II–39, paras 90–95; see further Ch 9.

[20] A Rosas, 'The European Union and Mixed Agreements', in A Dashwood and C Hillion (eds), *The General Law of EC External Relations* (Sweet & Maxwell, 2000) 208.

[21] See e.g. Council Decision 2002/245 on the conclusion of an agreement on co-operation and customs union between the European Economic Community and the Republic of San Marino and of the Protocol thereto following the enlargement which took effect on 1 January 1995 [2002] OJ L84/41.

[22] See e.g. Decision 2002/309 of the Council, and of the Commission as regards the Agreement on Scientific and Technological Cooperation, on the conclusion of seven Agreements with the Swiss Confederation [2002] OJ L114/1.

Effectively, therefore, Article 300(2) EC confirms the doctrines of implied powers and parallelism between internal and external powers, as it recognizes that Treaty provisions conferring internal legislative competence may form the basis for the conclusion of an international agreement.[23] Unanimity is also required for association agreements referred to in Article 310 EC.

Role of the European Parliament

The Parliament's involvement with the conclusion of agreements is limited. Article 300(3) EC contains the relevant provisions:

The Council shall conclude agreements after consulting the European Parliament, except for the agreements referred to in Article 133(3), including cases where the agreement covers a field for which the procedure referred to in Article 251 or that referred to in Article 252 is required for the adoption of internal rules. The European Parliament shall deliver its opinion within a time limit which the Council may lay down according to the urgency of the matter. In the absence of an opinion within that time limit, the Council may act.

By way of derogation from the previous subparagraph, agreements referred to in Article 310, other agreements establishing a specific institutional framework by organising cooperation procedures, agreements having important budgetary implications for the Community and agreements entailing amendment of an act adopted under the procedure referred to in Article 251 shall be concluded after the assent of the European Parliament has been obtained.

The Council and the European Parliament may, in an urgent situation, agree upon a time limit for the assent.

As a rule, the Parliament is only consulted. In the case of agreements adopted under Article 133 EC (common commercial policy) there is not even any requirement of consultation; there is none the less a practice of informing the Parliament of such agreements, enabling it to take a position.[24] The rule of mere consultation extends to agreements covering a field for which the co-decision or co-operation procedure (respectively Articles 251 and 252 EC) applies for the adoption of internal rules. Thus, Commission and Council may on their own, through the adoption of an international agreement, establish rules which, if adopted internally, would require co-decision or co-operation by the European Parliament. However, Article 300(2) EC also provides that, where an agreement entails amendment of an act adopted under the co-decision procedure, the Parliament's assent is required before the Council may conclude the agreement. There is no compelling logic for limiting the assent requirement to such cases, as one does not see on what grounds the Parliament should be less involved in the conclusion of agreements laying down, for the first time, rules which in the internal decision-making process require co-decision, as opposed to amendment of existing rules. In this context one should also bear in

---

[23] See Ch 3.
[24] Previously under the so-called Luns-Westerterp procedure: see Macleod, Hendry, and Hyett (n 1 above), 98–100; see at present the Framework agreement (n 13 above).

mind that international agreements concluded by the Community may have direct effect (see Chapter 9), and that the provisions of a directly effective agreement may thus have effects similar to those of legislative acts. It is incongruous that the Treaty does not require Parliamentary assent for all acts adopted in a field where the co-decision procedure applies.

Assent must also be obtained for three further types of agreement: association agreements, 'other agreements establishing a specific institutional framework by organising cooperation procedures', and 'agreements having important budgetary implications for the Community'. The first category, association agreements, is easy to define, at least in formal terms: it encompasses all agreements concluded on the basis of Article 310 EC. The second category is more difficult. Its scope is ill-defined, as a great many international agreements contain some type of institutional frame-work,[25] and as it is not clear what is meant by 'organising cooperation procedures'.

The third category, agreements having important budgetary implications, is based on the rationale that the Parliament occupies a central institutional position in budg-etary matters,[26] and that therefore agreements entailing considerable expenditure have to receive the Parliament's assent. Again the terms are open to varying interpretations, and it is very much a matter of judgement as to what constitutes an 'important' effect on the budget. The Parliament has sought further clarification of the provision by chal-lenging a Council decision not to ask for its assent to the conclusion of a fisheries agreement with Mauritania.[27] The agreement was concluded for a period of five years from 1 August 1996, and entailed financial compensation in exchange for fishing rights amounting to ECU 266.8 million (distributed over those five years). The Court made the following analysis. It first rejected the Council's argument that the agree-ment's expenditure should be set against the overall budget of the Community. It pointed out that appropriations allocated to external operations of the Community traditionally accounted for a marginal fraction of the Community budget (barely exceeding 5 per cent in 1996 and 1997). A comparison between the annual financial cost of an agreement and the overall Community budget therefore scarcely appeared significant, and to apply such a criterion might render the relevant Treaty wording wholly ineffective. The Court then examined the three criteria proposed by the Parliament. The first referred to the fact that expenditure is spread over several years, and the Court agreed that relatively modest annual expenditure could, over a num-ber of years, represent a significant budgetary outlay. It did not however accept the criterion of the relative share of the agreement's expenditure in relation to expenditure of the same kind under the budget heading concerned, because budget headings varied considerably in importance so that the relative share could be large even though the expenditure in question was small. Nor did it accept the criterion of the rate of increase

---

[25] J Sack, 'The European Community's Membership of International Organizations' (1995) 32 CMLRev 1238–9; Macleod, Hendry, and Hyett (n 1 above) 102; PJG Kapteyn and P VerLoren van Themaat, *Introduction to the Law of the European Communities* (3rd edn, by LW Gormley, Kluwer Law International, 1998) 1267–8.   [26] See Arts 268–280 EC.
[27] Case C–189/97 *European Parliament v. Council* [1999] ECR I–4741.

in expenditure under the agreement in relation to the financial section of the previous agreement. That rate could be high, whilst the amounts involved could be small. The Court then returned to the criterion of comparison of the expenditure under an agreement with the overall amount of appropriations designed to finance the Community's external operations, which offered an appropriate means of assessing the financial importance which the agreement actually had for the Community. Further, where a sectoral agreement was involved, as in this case, that criterion could in appropriate cases, and without excluding the possibility of taking other factors into account, be complemented by a comparison between the expenditure entailed by the agreement and the whole of the budgetary appropriations for the sector in question, taking the internal and external aspects together. However, since the sectors varied substantially in terms of their budgetary importance, that examination could not result in the financial implications of an agreement being found to be important where they did not represent a significant share of the appropriations designed to finance the Community's external relations. The Court then applied those criteria to the facts of the case. It pointed out that the five-year period of the agreement with Mauritania was not particularly lengthy, and that the financial compensation provided for, whilst exceeding 5 per cent of expenditure on fisheries, represented barely more than 1 per cent of the whole of the payment appropriations allocated for external operations of the Community. This could scarcely be described as important. Lastly, the Court rejected the Parliament's argument that an analogy be drawn with the powers of national parliaments when approving international agreements with financial implications.[28]

The judgment is convincing and useful, and considerably clarifies the term 'important'. None the less, it may not lay to rest differences of opinion between the Council and the Parliament, due to the great imprecision of the Treaty terms, and the Court may have gone about as far as it could in attempting to remedy this. There appear to be two further avenues for greater clarification. The first is to bring a string of further cases before the Court, which is hardly attractive. The second is for the Commission, the Council, and the Parliament to agree on a number of further guiding principles and benchmarks in an interinstitutional agreement.

The Parliament has used its power of assent in a number of cases so as to achieve modifications in agreements, in particular in cases involving human rights.[29]

Commission powers

A last issue concerning the rules on conclusion of international agreements is whether the Commission has autonomous powers to conclude certain agreements.

---

[28] Ibid, paras 26–34.
[29] See for an overview K Lenaerts and P Van Nuffel, *Constitutional Law of the European Union* (R Bray (ed and trans), Sweet & Maxwell, 1999) 659–60.

The question must be raised because of the enigmatic opening phrase of Article 300(2) EC: 'Subject to the powers vested in the Commission in this field, the signing' etc. It is possible to interpret that phrase as recognizing such autonomous powers, but there is no clear indication, in either Article 300 or any other Treaty provision, what those powers may cover or what the limits of those powers may be.

In 1991 the Commission made use of what it regarded as its power to conclude certain types of agreements by signing an agreement with the United States in the field of competition law. The aim of the agreement was to promote co-operation and co-ordination, and to lessen the possibility or impact of differences between the parties in the application of their competition laws. The Commission had consulted the Member States, but had not obtained a mandate from the Council and had refused to take account of objections of principle against its powers to conclude the agreement. Thereupon, France challenged the Commission's decision to conclude the agreement before the Court of Justice.[30] In its defence the Commission argued that the agreement constituted an administrative agreement which it was competent to conclude, and that failure to perform the agreement would not result in an international liability claim but merely in termination. The Court did not agree with that analysis. It pointed out that it was the Community alone, having legal personality, which had the capacity to bind itself by concluding international agreements, and that the agreement in question was no doubt binding on the Community and could give rise to liability at international level. The Court also examined the Commission's claim that it had power to conclude what it called international administrative agreements. To that effect, the Commission had built a complex argument based on the French wording of (current) Article 300(2) EC and on the analogy with Article 101 EAEC Treaty. Essentially, the Commission took the view that it could derive its powers from sources other than the Treaties, such as the practices followed by the institutions, and that under the EC Treaty it had the same powers to conclude agreements as under Article 101 EAEC Treaty.[31] The Court was unimpressed. It referred *inter alia* to (current) Article 7(1) EC, according to which each institution shall act within the limits of the powers conferred upon it by the Treaty. It also pointed out that a mere practice cannot override the Treaty provisions. It regarded the analogy with the EAEC Treaty as inappropriate. Lastly, it rejected the argument that the agreement with the United States could be concluded in light of the Commission's specific powers in the field of competition: that internal power was not such as to alter the allocation of powers between the Community institutions with regard to the conclusion of international agreements. The Court thus upheld the plea of lack of competence, and annulled the act whereby the Commission had concluded the agreement.[32]

From a constitutional perspective the Court's denial of Commission competence to conclude the agreement with the United States is convincing. A vague and

---

[30] Case C–327/91 *France v. Commission* [1994] ECR I–3641.
[31] Under Art 101 EAEC agreements or contracts whose implementation does not require action by the Council and which can be effected within the limits of the relevant budget are negotiated and concluded solely by the Commission.   [32] *France v. Commission* (n 30 above), paras 19–43.

ill-defined provision such as that of the opening sentence of Article 300(2) EC can hardly form the basis for an important law making power, which the conclusion of international agreements constitutes, particularly as the remainder of the provision is clear in its attribution of competence to the Council. The judgment shows that parallelism between external and internal competences is not necessarily reflected in the balance of powers of the institutions.[33] However, the judgment did not resolve the enigma. The Court did not, unfortunately, clarify the meaning of the phrase. The only hint it gave was to refer to the French Government's argument that the Commission powers are limited to agreements to be concluded by the Commission for the recognition of Community *laissez-passer* (Article 7 of the Protocol on the Privileges and Immunities of the European Communities), and to administrative or working agreements, including the establishment of relations with the organs of the United Nations and with other international organizations (see e.g. Article 302 EC).[34] The Court did not however clarify whether it agreed with that submission. The meaning of the opening phrase of Article 300(2) EC thus remains uncertain, and it is not clear whether there are any agreements which the Commission may conclude on its own.[35]

Article 111 EC

Article 111(3) EC, the general provision on the conclusion of agreements concerning monetary or foreign exchange regime matters, simply provides that 'the Council, acting by a qualified majority on a recommendation from the Commission and after consulting the ECB, shall decide the arrangements for the negotiation and for the conclusion of such agreements'. The provision does not mention the European Parliament, but it is no doubt in the Council's power to provide for consultation (or even assent) of the Parliament. The Treaty is more precise as regards formal agreements on an exchange-rate system for the euro in relation to non-Community currencies. Article 111(1) EC provides that 'the Council may, acting unanimously on a recommendation from the ECB or from the Commission, and after consulting the ECB in an endeavour to reach a consensus consistent with the objective of price stability, after consulting the European Parliament' conclude such agreements. The role of the ECB is justified on account of its expertise and function in monetary policy-making. In light of the potential economic importance of international agreements on an exchange-rate system one wonders whether the assent of the Parliament should not be required.

In the literature it has been suggested that the ECB has autonomous powers to conclude international agreements.[36] This argument, which was touched upon in

---

[33] M Cremona, 'External Relations and External Competence: The Emergence of an Integrated Policy', in P Craig and G de Búrca, *The Evolution of EU Law* (OUP, 1999) 150.

[34] *France v. Commission* (n 30 above) para 29.

[35] See for further discussion Macleod, Hendry, and Hyett (n 1 above), 95–6.

[36] Zilioli and Selmayr (n 14 above), 290–335.

Chapter 4, derives from the conception that the ECB is an independent international legal person, distinct from the Community. However, it does not, as was analysed, find support in the case law of the Court of Justice. In light of that case law,[37] which characterizes the ECB as a Community institution, there is no basis for accepting that the ECB has the power to conclude international agreements on monetary matters. It is only in the small world of banking operations that the ECB is recognized as an international legal person with certain powers, stemming from the merely operational tasks it is entrusted with.[38]

Article 24 TEU

The procedure for concluding agreements under the Second and Third Pillars is significantly different from that of Article 300 EC. The most notable feature is that there is a potential, indeterminate role for national authorities in the act of concluding such agreements. It is appropriate to cite the full text of Article 24 TEU, as modified by the Treaty of Nice:

1. When it is necessary to conclude an agreement with one or more States or international organisations in implementation of this title, the Council may authorise the Presidency, assisted by the Commission as appropriate, to open negotiations to that effect. Such agreements shall be concluded by the Council on a recommendation from the Presidency.

2. The Council shall act unanimously when the agreement covers an issue for which unanimity is required for the adoption of internal decisions.

3. When the agreement is envisaged in order to implement a joint action or common position, the Council shall act by a qualified majority in accordance with Article 23(2).

4. The provisions of this Article shall also apply to matters falling under Title VI. When the agreement covers an issue for which a qualified majority is required for the adoption of internal decisions or measures, the Council shall act by a qualified majority in accordance with Article 34(3).

5. No agreement shall be binding on a Member State whose representative in the Council states that it has to comply with the requirements of its own constitutional procedure; the other members of the Council may agree that the agreement shall nevertheless apply provisionally.

6. Agreements concluded under the conditions set out by this Article shall be binding on the institutions of the Union.

The Nice amendments concern paragraphs 2 to 4, introducing qualified-majority voting for the conclusion of certain agreements. Here, too, the Treaty drafters established parallelism between internal and external powers. CFSP acts implementing joint actions and common positions are adopted by qualified-majority voting,

---

[37] Case C–11/00 *Commission v. ECB*, judgment of 10 July 2003, not yet reported.
[38] CW Herrmann, 'Monetary Sovereignty over the Euro and External Relations of the Euro Area: Competences, Procedures and Practice' (2002) 7 EFA Rev 9.

pursuant to Article 23(2) TEU, and that rule extends to international agreements. However, Article 23(2) also provides for majority voting for acts adopted on the basis of a common strategy, and that exception to unanimity does not apply to the conclusion of agreements. As regards PJCCM the parallelism is complete.

There is no role for the European Parliament in the conclusion of EU agreements. From a democracy perspective this is deplorable and unsustainable. The most significant agreements hitherto negotiated on the basis of Article 24 TEU, concerning extradition and mutual legal assistance in EU–US relations are examples of agreements which, because of their potential impact on citizens, should require parliamentary scrutiny and approval.[39] The extradition agreement overrides existing extradition agreements between Member States and the US on a number of points (Article 3). It defines extraditable offences (Article 4), and it lays down extradition procedures. The agreements have been negotiated, on the part of the EU, exclusively by the Presidency, and are concluded by the Council. In other words, only executive organs are formally involved in their negotiation and conclusion.[40] The House of Lords Select Committee on the EU scrutinized the draft agreements, and had great trouble obtaining the text, which was classified as confidential. In its report it noted the 'major constitutional, legal and political issues' arising from the agreements, and considered the 'confidential' classification to be 'contrary to the democratic accountability that ought to inform decisions by the EU institutions regarding access to documents'.[41] It also highlighted possible issues concerning the compatibility of the agreements with the ECHR, and referred with respect to parliamentary involvement to 'the marked contrast to the position in the United States where the Senate advises on and consents to the ratification of Treaties that are not self-executing'.[42]

As argued in Chapter 5, Article 24 agreements are concluded by the Council on behalf of the EU, and not on behalf of the Member States. This follows both from the text of Article 24 TEU, read in its context, and from subsequent practice. Article 24(5) none the less refers to domestic constitutional procedure of the Member States. An agreement is not binding on a Member State whose representative in the Council states that it (the Member State) has to comply with the requirements of its own constitutional procedure. The text further clarifies that the other members of the Council may agree that the agreement shall nevertheless apply provisionally. That indicates that the agreement can enter into force definitively only once the Member State in question has complied with domestic procedure.[43]

This provision is most enigmatic. It appears to presuppose that under the constitutional law of one or more Member States, which are not identified, certain

---

[39] For the text of the agreement, see Council document 9153/03, available on <www.statewatch.org/news/2003/jun/useu09153.pdf>; see also Ch 5.

[40] A number of Member States have however indicated that they wish to make use of the opportunity to comply with their constitutional requirements (see below): see Council Justice and Home Affairs, Outcome of Proceedings, 10409/03, 13 June 2003.

[41] *HL Select Committee on the EU 38th Report, EU/US Agreements on Extradition and Mutual Legal Assistance* (HL Paper (2002–03) no 153), Abstract.   [42] Ibid, para 12.

[43] Marquardt (n 15 above), 345.

procedural requirements may need to be complied with before an agreement, negotiated by the Presidency on behalf of the EU, can be concluded and can thus become binding on that Member State. There is hitherto no relevant practice, as no Council member appears to have made use of the provision. It is beyond the scope of this chapter to engage in an analysis of the constitutional laws of the Member States on the conclusion of international agreements so as to find any specific rules on the matter. Moreover, it is probably unlikely that any of those laws are conclusive as regards such a particular issue as the conclusion by an international organization of an agreement which becomes binding on the members of that organization. The provision of paragraph 5 can none the less be turned to good effect. In most if not all Member States certain types of agreement, where concluded by the Member State itself, require parliamentary involvement or scrutiny of some kind. In light of the absence of any formal role for the European Parliament in the conclusion of Article 24 agreements, a Member State which is concerned about the content of an Article 24 agreement, from the perspective of individual rights for example, could make use of paragraph (5) and require that the agreement be approved by the national parliament.

Cross-pillar mixity

A last point concerns the interaction between Article 24 TEU and Article 300 EC. One can easily envisage negotiations between the EU and a third country involving both Community policies (e.g. trade or development co-operation) and CFSP matters (e.g. political dialogue or arms proliferation). None the less, there are hitherto no examples of agreements which were negotiated and concluded on the basis of Articles 24 TEU and 300 EC (so-called cross-pillar mixity). It is true that the procedural rules are quite different, but there are no objections of principle to a combined application. The different parts of an agreement could be negotiated under different procedures, and the resulting agreement could be concluded by way of two separate Council decisions, one on the basis of the EC Treaty and the other on the basis of the TEU. The agreement would become binding on the Community and Union institutions—which are one and the same anyway—and on the Member States.

Implementation, amendment, and adoption of Community positions

Once concluded, an international agreement needs to be implemented and applied. This raises the question of the effects, in Community law, of an international agreement concluded by the Community. In that respect, Article 300(7) EC merely provides that agreements are binding on the institutions of the Community and on

Member States. Article 111(3) EC likewise provides that the relevant agreements are binding on the institutions of the Community, on the ECB, and on Member States. Article 24(5) TEU also implies that EU agreements are binding on the Member States, and Article 24(6) TEU, inserted by the Treaty of Nice, clarifies that they are binding on the EU institutions. As the question of legal effect of an agreement raises complex issues, it is dealt with separately in Chapter 9.

However, Article 300 EC contains a few further provisions on decision-making related to implementing, applying, and amending an agreement. First, the second subparagraph of paragraph (2) addresses decision-making as regards 'the positions to be adopted on behalf of the Community in a body set up by an agreement, when that body is called upon to adopt decisions having legal effect, with the exception of decisions supplementing or amending the institutional framework of the agreement'. That provision was inserted by the Amsterdam Treaty. Originally, it related only to association agreements, but the Treaty of Nice broadened this to any agreement. Community decision-making on such positions follows the same procedure as that for the conclusion of an agreement. However, the Parliament is not involved by way of consultation or assent; it is merely 'immediately and fully informed on any decision'. The justification for that is said to be the frequency with which such positions may be called for, which would mean that Parliament involvement would impair effective Community participation in these bodies.[44]

Secondly, on the subject of modification of an agreement, Article 300(4) EC provides that the Council may, when concluding an agreement, authorize the Commission to approve modifications on behalf of the Community where the agreement provides for them to be adopted by a simplified procedure or by a body set up by the agreement. The Council may attach specific conditions to such authorization. In the absence of such an authorization one would expect the standard procedure for the conclusion of an agreement to extend to its modification. That follows from the fact that the legal consequences of conclusion and modification are the same: the Community enters into specific international commitments.

As regards 'formal agreements on an exchange-rate system', envisaged in Article 111(1) EC, '[t]he Council may, acting by a qualified majority on a recommendation from the ECB or from the Commission, and after consulting the ECB in an endeavour to reach a consensus consistent with the objective of price stability, adopt, adjust or abandon the central rates of the [euro] within the exchange-rate system. The President of the Council shall inform the European Parliament of the adoption, adjustment or abandonment of the [euro] central rates.'

Article 24 TEU does not contain specific provisions on implementation or amendment.

---

[44] A Dashwood, 'External Relations Provisions of the Amsterdam Treaty' in D O'Keeffe and P Twomey (eds), *Legal Issues of the Amsterdam Treaty* (Hart Publishing, 1999) 207. On the legal effects in Community law of decisions adopted by bodies set up under an agreement, see Ch 9.

Suspension and termination

The original EEC Treaty did not contain provisions on how to suspend or terminate an international agreement. That lacuna is partly filled by the Amsterdam Treaty amendments to Article 300 EC. There is now some Treaty language concerning the suspension of an international agreement, no doubt as the result of a couple of cases of threatened or applied suspension which created problems (see below). There are however no provisions on terminating an agreement: here again one would expect the same procedure to apply as that governing the conclusion of the agreement.

The second and third subparagraphs of Article 300(2) provide that a decision to suspend the application of an agreement follows the procedure for conclusion, only without the Parliament's involvement. As is the case for the determination of the Community position to be adopted in a body set up by an association agreement, the Parliament is only 'immediately and fully informed' of the Council's decision to suspend. The Parliament's lack of real powers here is more noteworthy than with respect to decisions by bodies set up under an agreement. This is an area where the Parliament is often quite vocal, because the (threatened) suspension of an international agreement is a highly political act in external relations. The refusal to involve the Parliament more fully signals a reluctance by the Treaty drafters to enable it to interfere with questions of general foreign policy.[45]

The provisions on suspension must be seen against the backdrop of the Community's policy on suspending international agreements, particularly in the case of human rights violations. After having fared somewhat badly with the suspension of a co-operation agreement with Yugoslavia at the time of the war in and between the various Republics of ex-Yugoslavia, because the agreement did not contain a suspension clause,[46] the institutions developed a considerable practice of including suspension provisions in agreements with third countries. That practice is explored in Chapter 13.[47]

There are no provisions on the termination of agreements in either Article 300 EC, Article 111 EC, or Article 24 TEU. One presumes that the decision to terminate an agreement must be taken under the same procedure as applies to the conclusion of the agreement in question. It must also be noted that suspension and termination raise delicate questions in the case of mixed agreements (see Chapter 7).

The draft Constitution

The draft Constitution removes the distinction between the EC and EU Treaties, and in that sense removes the pillar structure. The provisions on the CFSP none the

---

[45] See also Ch 11.
[46] See Case C–162/96 *Racke v. Hauptzollamt Mainz* [1998] ECR I–3655, analysed in Ch 9.
[47] Art 111 EC contains no provisions on suspension, which means that the procedure of Art 300(2) EC applies; Art 24 TEU also contains no provisions on suspension.

less remain separate from those on other aspects of the EU's external relations, and keep a lot of their defining features, such as a more intergovernmental approach with less involvement of the Commission and the European Parliament.[48] However, the members of the Convention brought together the various provisions on the conclusion of international agreements. In the conception of the draft Constitution, Article III–227 will apply to the negotiation and conclusion of all EU agreements, i.e., previous Community, CFSP, and PJCCM agreements. There are specific provisions, derogating in certain respects from the standard procedure in Article III–227, as regards the common commercial policy (see Article III–217) and as regards monetary matters (Article III–228).

The main innovations are as follows. First, because the standard procedure can be used for both former CFSP and EC agreements, the right to recommend the opening of negotiations may be exercised by either the Commission or the Union Minister for Foreign Affairs, the latter 'where the agreement exclusively or principally relates to the common foreign and security policy' (Article 222(3)). As regards negotiations, the Council nominates the negotiator or leader of the Union's negotiating team, again depending on the subject of the agreement. One presumes that this means that both the Commission and the Union Minister for Foreign Affairs may be involved with a negotiation, where an agreement relates to both CFSP and other matters, which will often be the case.

Secondly, the role of the European Parliament is largely the same (see Article 222(7)), but its consent is required, in addition to the cases provided for in Article 300(3) EC, for Union accession to the ECHR. Consent is also required for 'agreements covering fields to which the legislative procedure applies', thereby broadening the current provision which is limited to agreements amending an act adopted under the co-decision procedure. However, there is no formal role for the Parliament as regards pure CFSP agreements. It is deplorable that not even consultation is required. It must none the less be noted that, because the legislative procedure will apply to PJCCM matters,[49] the Parliament's role in the conclusion of agreements coming within this field is modified from no involvement to consent. This is to be welcomed, given the nature and content of the kind of agreements currently negotiated under the PJCCM heading (see above).

Thirdly, qualified-majority voting continues to be the principle, the exceptions being where the agreement covers a field in which unanimity is required for the adoption of an EU act as well as association agreements and EU accession to the ECHR.

Fourthly, with respect to agreements concerning commercial policy the Commission is under a duty to report regularly to both the special committee appointed by the Council (the equivalent of the current Article 133 Committee) *and* the European Parliament. Moreover, as the legislative procedure applies to the common commercial policy, the Parliament will need to give its consent to trade agreements, whereas currently it has no formal role whatsoever. This constitutes

---

[48] See Chs 5 and 11.   [49] See Arts III–171 to III–178 of the draft Constitution.

important progress from the perspective of democracy and legitimacy, even if one may doubt whether all trade agreements, including minor technical ones, will benefit from parliamentary scrutiny.

Conclusions

The procedure for concluding international agreements has been substantially modified in the course of time, on the whole in the direction of greater involvement of the European Parliament. As such, the modifications correspond to the gradual expansion of the Parliament's role in the internal legislative process. It is of course true that a stronger parliamentary role is no panacea for the issues of democracy and legitimacy afflicting the EU in the conduct of its external relations. Formal democratic processes are no guarantee for effective democracy. Even in the absence of a formal role the Parliament may be able to influence the process of decision-making through the authority of its positions, as has to some extent been the case in the area of trade policy.[50] Such informal input is however no substitute for constitutional guarantees of involvement. Formal parliamentary scrutiny at European level may not be sufficient, but is certainly indispensable for reaching higher levels of legitimacy and accountability. The story of the agreements with the US on extradition and mutual legal assistance shows the defects of negotiations conducted solely by the executive.

One can distinguish three types of argument against greater involvement by the Parliament in the process of negotiating and concluding international agreements. Such involvement may be too cumbersome and time-consuming and thus obstruct effective international decision-making. The open parliamentary process is ill-suited for an international negotiation, which may require a measure of secrecy more conducive to striking deals. And certain agreements are so technical as to resist involvement by non-experts. None of those arguments is convincing. It is clear that parliamentary input is not required for each and every agreement, and the relevant constitutional rules should be aimed at defining those agreements which raise issues necessitating parliamentary scrutiny. The secrecy and effectiveness arguments do not recognize the important law making function of many international agreements. For the negotiation of such agreements, the search for greater effectiveness cannot justify the absence of public debate to which secrecy gives rise.

The current provisions of Article 300 EC go a long way towards recognizing the role of the Parliament. Arguably, they do not go far enough.[51] The lack of any formal role for the Parliament in the conclusion of trade agreements is unjustifiable, and stems from pre-globalization times, when international trade negotiations were more confined to the economic dimension of trade relations. The limitation of the

---

[50] Macleod, Hendry, and Hyett (n 1 above), 98–100.

[51] See M Krajewski, 'Foreign Policy and the European Constitution' (2003) 22 YEL, forthcoming.

assent procedure to agreements amending acts adopted under the co-decision procedure is too narrow. The draft Constitution constitutes substantial progress with respect to both those issues. Further improvements are none the less conceivable.

At present, the Parliament's formal role is limited to the phase of the conclusion of an agreement, where the Parliament is either consulted or needs to give its assent. Conclusion of course takes place when the negotiations are finished, and even if the requirement of parliamentary scrutiny may allow the Parliament to influence the negotiations, in particular where its assent is needed, there is scope for a formal role in the decision to open negotiations and in the negotiations themselves.[52]

The non-participation of the Parliament in decisions to suspend an international agreement and in the establishment of positions to be adopted in a body set up under an agreement (with the exception of institutional-type decisions) is difficult to justify. Decisions on suspension are nearly always highly charged political acts, and the fact that the Parliament may be more vocal in this area does not warrant its exclusion from the decision-making process. As regards decisions by bodies set up under an agreement, often such decisions have a significant law making function,[53] meriting parliamentary involvement as much as the conclusion of agreements in areas where the legislative procedure applies.

The draft Constitution extends the standard legislative procedure to present Third Pillar matters, with the result that the Parliament will need to give its assent to the conclusion of agreements in this field. This constitutes substantial progress. However, the Parliament continues to be excluded from participation in the nego-tiation and conclusion of agreements on CFSP matters. That is clearly untenable. The EU is developing its defence capacity, it is setting up military operations, it is concluding international agreements regarding such operations, and no parliamentary organ is formally involved in the process.

---

[52] Lenaerts and Van Nuffel report that in its Rules of Procedure the Parliament has provided that it may request the Council not to authorize the opening of negotiations until the Parliament has stated its position on the negotiating mandate and that it may adopt recommendations to be taken into account: Lenaerts and Van Nuffel (n 29 above), 653.

[53] E.g. decisions of the EC–Turkey Association Council; see Ch 9 for case law regarding such decisions.

7

Mixed external action and membership of international organizations

Introduction

Previous chapters discussed the Community's external competence and treaty-making powers. The analysis revealed that the EC Treaty enables the Community institutions to engage in external action in many different areas of policy-making, often broadly defined. The EC Treaty provides for an impressive array of legal foundations for external action. The dimensions of the actual practice based on those foundations are equally impressive. However, notwithstanding those firm and broad foundations, that practice is generally characterized by what has come to be denoted as mixity: more often than not, international agreements are concluded by the Community and its Member States acting jointly, rather than the Community simply acting on its own. It is difficult to quantify this phenomenon, as there are so many different types of conventional international lawmaking, but all observers agree that mixity is a hallmark of the Community's external relations.[1] 'Pure' Community agreements are more exceptional than one would expect in light of the legal foundations.

The *prima facie* legal justification for a mixed agreement is that parts of the agreement do not come within the Community's competence, and that conclusion of the agreement therefore requires joint action by the Community and its Member States, the latter complementing, as it were, the otherwise insufficient powers of the Community.

This chapter aims to analyse the law and practice of mixed external action. It does not, however, merely concentrate on the conclusion of international agreements. It also addresses Community membership of international organizations.

---

[1] E.g. I Macleod, ID Hendry, and S Hyett, *The External Relations of the European Communities* (OUP, 1996) 142; D McGoldrick, *International Relations Law of the European Union* (Longman, 1997) 78; C Kaddous, *Le droit des relations extérieures dans la jurisprudence de la Cour de justice des Communautés européennes* (Helbing & Lichtenhahn, 1998) 263; PJG Kapteyn and P VerLoren van Themaat, *Introduction to the Law of the European Communities* (3rd edn, by LW Gormley, Kluwer Law International, 1998) 1263; M Cremona, 'External Relations and External Competence: The Emergence of an Integrated Policy', in P Craig and G de Búrca (eds), *The Evolution of EU Law* (OUP, 1999) 154; K Lenaerts and P Van Nuffel, *Constitutional Law of the European Union* (R Bray (ed and trans), Sweet & Maxwell, 1999) 648; J Helikoski, *Mixed Agreements as a Technique for Organizing the International Relations of the European Community and its Member States* (Kluwer Law International, 2001) 3 and Appendix 1 (list of mixed agreements).

In principle this could be dealt with separately, as such membership presents a number of political and legal problems of its own, and as there is no logical link with mixity: the Community could, in theory, become a member of an international organization without any of its Member States also being a member. In practice, however, there are virtually no examples of sole Community membership. The Community's participation in the work of other international organizations is thus also governed by mixity, and the problems to which the latter gives rise in this context are similar to those created by mixed agreements—as well as often more acute. Further, both the conclusion of mixed agreements and mixed membership of international organizations are governed by the same overarching legal principle identified by the Court of Justice, namely the duty of co-operation between the Member States and the Community institutions.

The structure of this chapter is as follows. It first provides a general and concise overview of the practice and its causes, as regards both mixed agreements and membership of international organizations. It then analyses the case law on the duty of co-operation between the Community and the Member States, and attempts to spell out the foundations and possible impact of that overarching principle. The chapter subsequently turns to a number of the problems and legal issues mixity gives rise to.

Cause and practice of mixed agreements

Competence

The legal justification for mixity is that an agreement cannot be concluded by the Community alone, because its competences do not cover the entire agreement. Several authors have attempted to draw up a classification or typology of mixed agreements, centred around the scope and nature of the Community's competences.[2] However, the practice of mixity does not readily lend itself to such attempts.[3] The interaction between the diverse external powers of the Community and the multitude and variety of international conventions, treaties, and agreements is such that classification may have the effect either of over-simplifying the phenomenon or of rendering it even less accessible. Moreover, such interaction does not take place in a theoretical legal sphere, but rather in the day-to-day politics of the Community. It is therefore preferable to look at the practice on its own merits, and not to base oneself on a pre-conceived typology.

Notwithstanding that approach, it is necessary at the outset to recapitulate and explore a few basic principles of external competence. A first distinction is between

---

[2] See for such a classification A Rosas, 'The European Union and Mixed Agreements', in A Dashwood and C Hillion (eds), *The General Law of EC External Relations* (Sweet & Maxwell, 2000) 203–7.

[3] NA Neuwahl, 'Joint Participation in International Treaties and the Exercise of Power by the EEC and its Member States: Mixed Agreements' (1991) 28 CMLRev 717.

exclusive and non-exclusive powers. The former are limited to commercial policy, conservation of fish resources, monetary policy, and certain implied powers. Whenever the provisions of an international agreement are fully covered by any of those exclusive Community powers only the Community is entitled to conclude the agreement. In practice, such exclusive competence is limited to commercial policy and fisheries, as there are very few examples of international agreements which come wholly within the Community's implied powers. As regards non-exclusive Community powers it is appropriate to distinguish between concurrent and parallel powers.[4] In the case of concurrent powers, the Member States retain power to conclude an agreement for as long as the Community has not made use of its own power, and thus has not 'occupied the field'. Examples of such powers are transport policy and agricultural policy. The term parallel powers can be used where Community and Member States powers are truly parallel, so that they may be exercised independently. Development co-operation is an example.

In the literature on external competence and mixed agreements such non-exclusive treaty-making powers are often termed 'potential' or 'virtual'.[5] It is indicative that this terminology is used only for denoting external powers, and not for the Community's internal legislative competence. The terms are confusing, as the Community's non-exclusive external powers are, in legal terms, every bit as real as (and in many cases co-extensive with) its internal competences. It is in the nature of competences or powers that they enable public action, and the competence question logically precedes its exercise. Potentiality is thus the very hallmark of all competences. However, it is not without reason that non-exclusive external competences have been characterized as potential or virtual. The terminology is in effect a reflection of the fact that, often, a mixed agreement is concluded where it is legally possible for the Community to conclude the agreement on its own, without the participation of the Member States, by making use of these 'potential' or 'virtual' powers. It has been noted that at political level in the Community there is a tendency to consider that, unless an agreement wholly comes within the exclusive competence of the Community, mixity is required.[6]

Practice and case law

The following short survey of the practice is from a historical perspective, and attempts to make reference to the different kinds of mixed agreements as well as to the intervening statements (which are rather limited) by the Court of Justice.

---

[4] A von Bogdandy and J Bast, 'The European Union's Vertical Order of Competences: The Current Law and Proposals for its Reform' (2002) 39 CMLRev 242–8. The draft Constitution speaks of exclusive competence, shared competence, and areas of supporting, co-ordinating, or complementary action: see Arts I–11 to I–16.

[5] CD Ehlermann, 'Mixed Agreements—A List of Problems', in D O'Keeffe and HG Schermers (eds), *Mixed Agreements* (Kluwer, 1983) 6.   [6] Rosas (n 2 above), 206.

The practice of negotiating and concluding mixed agreements has existed since the early days of the Community, and thus predates the case law of the Court of Justice on external competence.[7] Mixity none the less soon came before the Court. Already in the *AETR* case,[8] the Court was confronted with a situation where the Member States were required to engage in further negotiation of the European Road Transport Agreement, on the basis of a common position reached in the Council, constituting the exercise of Community competence in the field of transport. In *Kramer* the Court similarly pointed out that, as long as the Community had not fully exercised its functions in the matter of conservation of fish resources, as was the case at the time, the Member States were under a duty, together with the Community institutions, to use all political and legal means at their disposal in order to ensure participation of the Community in the North-East Atlantic Fisheries Convention.[9] Both judgments were in that respect a first expression and reflection of the need for the Community and its Member States to co-operate in the conduct of external relations.

The Court's first serious attempt to grapple with issues of mixity was *Opinion 1/76*.[10] As discussed in Chapter 3, the Court in this case confirmed and developed the doctrine of implied powers in relation to transport policy. The Court did more than that, however. Chapter 3 discusses the Court's apparent need to find a justification for the participation as contracting parties of the draft agreement by six of the then nine Member States. The analysis there submits that this need is not explained by a finding of exclusive Community competence. The Court did not in the Opinion suggest exclusivity, nor did it at any other time accept that the Community has exclusive competence over transport. Community competence in matters of transport is concurrent with Member State competence. None the less, the Court felt compelled to address the 'special problem' arising from the participation by six Member States. It pointed out that those six States were parties to two earlier conventions, which would need to be amended, as provided for by Article 3 of the draft agreement. The undertaking to carry out such amendment explained and justified the participation by these Member States, which had to be considered 'as being solely for this purpose and not as necessary for the attainment of other features of the system'.[11] The Court moreover considered that, under Article 4 of the agreement, enforceability extended to the territories of all the Member States, and that, except for this special undertaking, the legal effects of the agreement resulted, in accordance with (current) Article 300(7) EC, exclusively from the conclusion by the Community.[12] In those circumstances, the Court decided that the participation

---

[7] See e.g. the association agreements with Greece ([1974] OJ Spec Ed 2nd Series, PE 1, 4) and with Turkey ([1964] JO 217). [8] Case 22/70 *Commission v. Council* [1971] ECR 263; see Ch 3.

[9] Joined Cases 3, 4, and 6/76 *Kramer* [1976] ECR 1279, paras 34–35; see again Ch 3.

[10] *Opinion 1/76 re draft Agreement establishing a European laying-up fund for inland waterway vessels* [1977] ECR 741. [11] Ibid, para 7.

[12] Art 300(7) EC provides that agreements concluded by the Community are binding on the institutions and on the Member States: see Ch 9.

of the six Member States was not such as to encroach on the external power of the Community.[13] By contrast, the Court did consider that the participation of those six States in the negotiations had led to results beyond their objective, as defined above. To summarize the Court's analysis, it pointed out that the part played by the Community institutions in the bodies and organs which the agreement set up was extremely limited, and that the provisions of the agreement called in question the power of the institutions and altered in a manner inconsistent with the Treaty the relationships between Member States within the context of the Community. The agreement constituted both a surrender of the independence of action of the Community in its external relations and a change in the internal constitution of the Community. As a result, the Court's Opinion on the compatibility of these aspects with the Treaty was negative. It expressly mentioned that the possibility that the agreement might constitute the model for future arrangements in other fields had confirmed it in its critical attitude: the repetition of such procedures was in fact likely progressively to undo the work of the Community irreversibly.[14]

Opinion 1/76 thus constituted an attempt by the Court to carry out significant review of a particular manifestation of mixity. Cremona observed that the Court had seen that the danger of mixed agreements (and their attraction for Member States) lay in their tendency to over-emphasize at the expense of the Community the participation of the Member States as traditional international legal persons.[15] In any event, the most convincing reading of this section of *Opinion 1/76* is that, where an agreement comes entirely within the Community's concurrent competences, such as those for developing a common transport policy as was the case here, mixity requires a specific justification and is not simply optional.[16] There is considerable logic in such an approach. As mentioned above, concurrent competences are as real as exclusive ones. The difference between them is only that the Community may decide not to exercise its concurrent competence and leave it to the Member States to act. Thus, in an area of concurrent competence, such as transport or environmental protection, the Community may decide not to participate in an international negotiation or not to conclude a particular agreement. However, where the Community does become a party, and the agreement comes entirely within its competence, one fails to see the justification for mixity. It is as if the Community decides to exercise its competence for only one part of the agreement, and not to exercise it for another. Yet, particularly where all the Member States become parties themselves, as is the standard approach, there is no mistaking that the agreement will establish common rules for the entire Community. In that case, mixity, with all the difficulties associated with it (as discussed below), could be considered to

---

[13] *Opinion 1/76* (n 10 above), para 7.   [14] Ibid, paras 8–14.

[15] M Cremona, 'The Doctrine of Exclusivity and the Position of Mixed Agreements in the External Relations of the European Community' (1982) 12 OJLS 414.

[16] CWA Timmermans, 'Division of External Powers between Community and Member States in the Field of Harmonization of National Law—A Case Study', in CWA Timmermans and ELM Völker (eds), *Division of Powers between the European Communities and their Member States in the Field of External Relations* (Kluwer, 1981) 20.

violate Article 10 EC: by participating in the agreement the Member States may be making it more difficult and cumbersome for the Community to achieve its objectives.

After *Opinion 1/76* the Court did not have, or take, many more opportunities to scrutinize the use of mixity as such. In *Ruling 1/78*, an EAEC Treaty case which is also looked at below, it was undisputed that certain provisions of the convention at issue did not come within the powers of the EAEC, and the Court simply recognized that the convention concerned in part the jurisdiction of the Member States and in part that of the Community.[17] Then came *Opinion 1/78*, on the at the time important question of competence for the conclusion of international commodity agreements in the framework of UNCTAD. The Court's decision in that case, despite affirming the wide scope of the Treaty provisions on a common commercial policy, appeared much more accommodating towards mixity. As discussed in Chapter 2, the Court considered that, if the Member States were to finance the buffer stock which was to be the central element of the International Agreement on Natural Rubber, their participation in the agreement was necessary, and the agreement thus had to be mixed. It also pointed out that, in any event, mixity was required in so far as certain Member States represented 'dependent territories' not belonging to the Community, whilst stressing that the Member States in question could on this basis participate only in their capacity of representatives of these territories.[18] The latter illustrates that mixity may have many different causes.

Opinion 1/78 was criticized for accepting Member State participation too easily, and for not ruling that, as the agreement came within the Community's exclusive trade policy competence, the Community ought to have ensured financing of the buffer stock.[19] The Opinion led to a first major institutional settlement in favour of mixity. In 1981 the Council adopted the so-called 'PROBA 20' arrangement, a compromise 'intended to improve the Community's external image and to strengthen its internal cohesion and solidarity'.[20] It was based on the understanding that all legal and institutional considerations regarding the respective competences of the Community and the Member States were to be set aside, and that instead the Community and the Member States would participate jointly in all the commodities agreements concerned, and that such participation would involve a

---

[17] *Ruling 1/78 re Convention on the Physical Protection of Nuclear Materials, Facilities and Transports* [1978] ECR 2151, para 31.

[18] *Opinion 1/78 re International Agreement on Natural Rubber* [1979] ECR 2871, paras 52–62. As regards overseas countries and territories, see also *Opinion 2/91 re Convention No 170 of the ILO* [1993] ECR I–1061, para 35.

[19] JHH Weiler, 'The External Legal Relations of Non-Unitary Actors: Mixity and the Federal Principle', in O'Keeffe and Schermers (eds) (n 5 above), 72, idem in *The Constitution of Europe* (CUP, 1999) 174; Kapteyn and VerLoren van Themaat (n 1 above), 1281; Cremona (n 15 above), 418–19.

[20] The text was never officially published, but can be found in ELM Völker and J Steenbergen, *Leading Cases and Materials on the External Relations Law of the EC* (Kluwer, 1985) 48. For comments see Ehlermann (n 5 above), 8–9; J Groux, 'Mixed Negotiations', in ibid, 96; KR Simmonds, 'The European Community and the New Law of the Sea' (1989/VI), 218 Hague Recueil 39–40; J Sack, 'The European Community's Membership of International Organizations' (1995) 32 CMLRev 1253–4.

joint delegation expressing the joint position with a single voice.[21] That approach was indeed followed for these types of agreements.[22]

In the 1970s and early 1980s the Community participated, together with the Member States, in negotiations leading to the Convention on the Law of the Sea, one of the most wide-ranging and complex mixed agreements ever to be concluded by the Community.[23] The latter's participation was necessary in light of its exclusive competence in matters of conservation of fish resources. In contrast with most mixed negotiations, the Community and its Member States did not in this case manage to assume an overall common position. Indeed, Simmonds reports a comment according to which the only issue on which the group was united was advocating the right of the Community to become a party to the Convention, and characterizes the comment as harsh, but not unjust.[24] Community signature and participation were not readily accepted by non-member countries, and there was in particular a lack of understanding of, and fear for, the consequences of Community participation if not all the Member States were to become parties. Other delicate problems concerned the consequences for third States of the progressive expansion of the Community's treaty-making powers; membership of Convention institutions and voting rights; responsibility for breach of obligations; and participation in the dispute-settlement procedures.[25] In the end Community signature and participation were permitted, subject however to fairly stringent conditions, laid down in Annex IX of the Convention. The annex enables an international organization to join the Convention, provided a majority of its Member States are joining as well. It also spells out that the organization's participation is limited to matters coming within its competence, and that it does not have rights and obligations beyond those matters. Article 4(5) expressly provides that participation of an international organization 'shall in no case confer any rights under this Convention on member States of the organization which are not States Parties to this Convention'.

The Convention on the Law of the Sea is, to some extent, a model for mixity as regards other multilateral instruments in the areas of transport, environmental protection, and fisheries. As a rule, Community participation in such instruments is *in tandem* with that of the Member States, and the requirement of submitting a declaration of competences is not unusual.

The 1970s and 1980s were also the period of development and expansion of the Community's relationships with the ACP countries, through the successive Lomé Conventions. Those conventions were all mixed agreements, as they were wide-ranging instruments for North–South co-operation, drawing extensively upon the Member States' resources. One important feature of the Lomé Conventions was that

---

[21] Ehlermann (n 5 above).

[22] See e.g. Council Decision 96/704 concerning the provisional application of the International Natural Rubber Agreement 1995 by the Community [1996] OJ L324/1.

[23] See Simmonds (n 20 above); M Ederer, *Die Europäische Wirtschaftsgemeinschaft und die Seerechtskonvention der Vereinten Nationen von 1982* (Verlag V. Florentz, 1988).   [24] Ibid, 115.

[25] Ibid, 108–9.

they generally took care to indicate whether the obligations they created were binding on the Community, on its Member States, or on both.[26]

Whereas mixity is clearly justified for these conventions, there can be more doubts as regards some of the association agreements concluded on the basis of Article 310 EC, where mixity is again the rule. The Court's ruling in *Demirel* clarified that the Community's powers under this provision are extensive, in the sense that it enables the Community to undertake commitments in all the areas covered by the Treaty.[27] It would therefore not require much creative effort or loss of subject matter to design association agreements in such a way that they may be concluded as pure Community agreements. Often the only justification for mixity is that such agreements also provide for a political dialogue, which is beyond the Community's competence.[28] Yet such a dialogue could easily be set up in parallel with the agreement. Similar considerations apply to partnership agreements and to certain types of bilateral agreement in the trade and investment domain.

In the 1980s and 1990s the most complex mixed negotiation was the GATT Uruguay Round, leading to the establishment of the WTO. In practice, however, the negotiations themselves did not give rise to particular problems of mixity, as the Community's preponderant role was recognized and accepted by the Member States.[29] It was only towards the end of the negotiations that the issue of mixity was raised, engendering the great legal battle of *Opinion 1/94*.[30] As regards the political sensitivity of the Member States' role in the creation of this new organization, one may again refer to the signing episode at the Marrakesh Ministerial Conference.[31] The Court's Opinion is extensively discussed in Chapters 2 and 3, and its statements on the duty of co-operation are examined below. There is however one aspect of the Opinion to which attention may be drawn here. The Commission's request for an Opinion was to some extent ambiguous on an issue which was crucial from the perspective of the law on mixity. The overall tenor of the Commission's submissions was to establish that the Community's competence over all matters covered by the WTO Agreement was exclusive,[32] yet there was some suggestion, particularly in the formulation of the actual questions, that the Commission was also inquiring into the scope of the Community's non-exclusive competences.[33] The Court, however, did not read the Commission's request in such a way and, prompted by submissions of the Council, ruled that the Opinion was concerned only with the question of

---

[26] See the case law discussed in Ch 4.

[27] Case 12/86 *Demirel v. Stadt Schwäbisch Gmünd* [1987] ECR 3719; see Ch 4.

[28] See e.g. Europe Agreements establishing an association between the European Communities and their Member States, of the one part, and the Republic of Hungary, of the other part [1993] OJ L347/2, Arts 2–5.

[29] P Van den Bossche, 'The European Community and the Uruguay Round Agreements', in JH Jackson and AO Sykes (eds), *Implementing the Uruguay Round* (OUP, 1997) 53–9.

[30] *Opinion 1/94 re WTO Agreement* [1994] ECR I–5267.   [31] See Ch 2.

[32] N Neuwahl, 'The WTO Opinion and Implied External Powers of the Community—A Hidden Agenda?', in Dashwood and Hillion (eds), (n 2 above), 141.

[33] See *Opinion 1/94* (n 30 above), at 5282–3. CWA Timmermans, 'Organising Joint Participation of EC and Member States', in Dashwood and Hillion (n 32 above), 240.

exclusive competence.[34] As a result, the Opinion does not systematically analyse whether the Community's concurrent competences in the areas of services and intellectual property cover the WTO Agreement. The Court did not pass the threshold of exclusivity, and declined to rule on whether mixity is permitted in the case of exercise of concurrent ('potential' or 'virtual') competences. That approach was markedly different from the intense scrutiny of mixity in *Opinion 1/76*. It is particularly in this regard, and arguably only in this regard, that *Opinion 1/94* can be said to be more conservative and deferential towards the Member States' international action than some earlier rulings.[35]

This survey may be concluded by referring to the latest practice as regards bilateral trade and co-operation agreements. Here it appears that the Court's judgment in *Portugal v. Council*, on the Co-operation Agreement with India,[36] has stimulated recourse to pure Community agreements. As Rosas reports, it is now the practice of the Community to conclude fairly comprehensive agreements, providing for co-operation in many different areas, on its own.[37]

Causes

It is useful to explore somewhat the causes and reasons for the persistent recourse to mixity. In this respect, the analysis by Ehlermann, even if it dates from the early 1980s, continues to stand out.[38] As he indicates, there appear to be few, if any, 'external' reasons for recourse to mixity: it is not the case in practice that non-member countries insist on mixity. Mixity is therefore almost exclusively the outcome of decision-making processes internal to the Community. Ehlermann points out that mixity could often be avoided if the Council wanted to avoid it, either by limiting the subject matter of an agreement to the Community's existing powers, or by adopting a broader interpretation of those powers. In particular, certain mixed agreements could be avoided if the Council were willing to make use of 'virtual', non-exclusive powers, but it is most reluctant to do so. One of the reasons for that attitude is purely political: 'Member States wish to continue to appear as contracting parties in order to remain visible and identifiable actors on the international scene'.[39] The European Commission often acquiesces in the use of mixity to avoid inter-institutional tension. In any event it could only challenge mixity before the Court of Justice,

---

[34] See *Opinion 1/94* (n 30 above), at 5282–3. CWA Timmermans, 'Organising Joint Participation of EC and Member States', in Dashwood and Hillion (n 32 above), 240.

[35] E.g. J de la Rochère, 'L'ère des compétences partagées' (1995) 390 RMCUE 446–8; JHJ Bourgeois, 'The EC in the WTO and Advisory Opinion 1/94: An Echternach Procession' (1995) 32 CML Rev 780–2; M. Hilf, 'The ECJ's Opinion 1/94 on the WTO—No Surprise, but Wise?' (1995) 6 EJIL 254 and 258.

[36] Case C–268/94 *Portugal v. Council* [1996] ECR I–6177; see Ch 4.

[37] Rosas (n 2 above), 218.

[38] Ehlermann (n 5 above), 4–9. The author was at the time Director-General of the Commission's Legal Service. See also JHJ Bourgeois, 'Mixed Agreements: A New Approach?', in JHJ Bourgeois, J-L Dewost, and M-A Gaiffe (eds), *La Communauté européenne et les accords mixtes—Quelles Perspectives?* (Interuniversity Press, 1997) 83–6; Helikoski (n 1 above), 9–21.   [39] Ibid, 6.

and recourse to the Court is considered as an instrument of coercion in a struggle for power. Acceptance of mixity may also be a means of achieving acceptance of Community participation, even in the case of agreements where the part covered by Community competence is small. Further, the mixed agreement formula avoids the necessity of agreeing on the exact delimitation of Community and Member States' powers, a subject of obvious complexity—unless of course non-member countries insist on such delimitation. Ehlermann sums his analysis up by concluding that 'the attempt to reach exclusive Community participation usually means tension and inter-institutional struggle while the mixed agreement formula is considered as implying mutual understanding, accommodation and peace-making'.[40] There is one further and obvious reason for mixity which Rosas notes:[41] mixed agreements to which all the Member States are parties inevitably require unanimity, since all the Member States need to conclude and ratify the agreement in accordance with domestic constitutional requirements, whereas pure Community agreements may be concluded by the Council with qualified majority voting, depending on the subject matter.[42] As an example of an area where such considerations no doubt play an important role one may refer to negotiations on trade in services in the WTO. *Opinion 1/94*,[43] by deciding that GATS comes within the joint competence of the Community and its Member States, enables each Member State government to insist upon agreeing with the detail of any GATS negotiation. The complex revision of Article 133 EC in the Treaty of Nice confirms the importance of the voting issue in these areas.[44]

Membership of international organizations

Membership and non-membership

There are no EC Treaty provisions generally regulating possible Community membership of an international organization.[45] Article 302 EC instructs the Commission 'to ensure the maintenance of all appropriate relations with the organs of the United Nations and of its specialized agencies', as well as 'to maintain such relations as are appropriate with all international organizations'. Article 303 EC provides that '[t]he Community shall establish all appropriate forms of cooperation with the Council of Europe', and Article 304 EC states that '[t]he Community shall establish close cooperation with the Organization for Economic Cooperation and Development,

---

[40] Ibid, 9.
[41] Rosas (n 2 above), 202; the author was at the time Director for External Relations in the Commission's Legal Service.   [42] Art 300(1) EC; see Ch 6.
[43] N 30 above.   [44] See Ch 2.
[45] General literature includes: Sack (n 20 above); R Frid, *The Relations between the EC and International Organizations—Legal Theory and Practice* (Kluwer, 1995); E Denza, 'The Community as a Member of International Organizations', in N Emiliou and D O'Keeffe, *The EU and World Trade Law after the GATT Uruguay Round* (John Wiley & Sons, 1996); Macleod, Hendry, and Hyett (n 1 above), Ch 7.

the details of which shall be determined by common accord'. Community membership of an international organization is clearly not envisaged in those Treaty provisions.[46] The EC Treaty is none the less not an obstacle to Community accession to an international organization. There is agreement that the Community may exercise its powers, in the external sphere, through accession to an organization which deals with matters coming within those powers.[47] External powers are not limited to concluding international agreements, but extend to joining international organizations and participating in their work.[48] Implicitly, that is confirmed by *Opinion 1/94*, where the Court acknowledged Community competence for the creation of the WTO.[49]

In practice, however, Community membership of international organizations stands in fairly sharp contrast to its treaty-making activity. Whereas the latter is fully fledged and largely corresponds to the Community's competences, even if agreements may be mixed, full Community membership of international organizations is much more limited. Following Sack's approach,[50] one can distinguish between accession to an international organization as such, i.e. an organization with an independent existence and a genuine membership structure, and participation in an international treaty on a specific subject which creates some sort of organizational structure. This section concentrates on the former category; as regards the latter, it is difficult to draw the dividing line with mixed agreements generally, as treaty-making, particularly at multilateral level, is increasingly accompanied by the creation of various institutions and bodies. At the level of international organizations as such, Community accession has been confined to the FAO, the EBRD, and the WTO.[51] The Community is not a member of the United Nations or of any of the major UN organizations, except for the FAO. It is not, for example, a member of the ILO, in spite of its significant competences and legislative activity in the field of social policy. It is not a member of the IMF or the World Bank. Nor is it a member of the Council of Europe. These are all international organizations dealing, at least from time to time, with matters within the province of the Community.

If the EC Treaty is not an obstacle, what then are the causes of the Community's apparent incapacity to join international organizations? Some of those causes are similar to those for recourse to mixed agreements. The Member States are reluctant to abandon their role in international organizations by promoting the EC's entry or even by ceding their place to the EC, essentially for reasons of sovereignty.[52] In contrast to mixed agreements, however, there are also significant difficulties at international level. The most basic of those is that, traditionally, and in particular within the UN system, international organizations permit accession only by States. Whenever

---

[46] A number of other Treaty provisions speak of co-operation with international organizations in specific areas, e.g. Art 174(4) EC.   [47] *Opinion 1/76* (n 10 above), para 5.

[48] See for a fuller analysis Frid (n 45 above), 119–32 and 345–59.   [49] N 30 above.

[50] Sack (n 20 above), 1238–9.

[51] In addition the EC is a member of a number of fisheries organizations, see Kapteyn and VerLoren van Themaat (n 1 above), 1264.   [52] Sack (n 20 above), 1233.

that is the case, Community accession requires modification of the organization's constitutional rules, and it may be difficult to persuade third countries, members of the organization, that such modification is in their interest or is appropriate. Such modification is not simply a threshold issue. When the Community does join, its Member States continue to be members, and this mixed membership gives rise to complex issues of participation in the organization's decision-making processes. A central issue concerns voting rights. How many votes will accrue to the Community? How does one allocate voting rights? Should this be on an alternative basis, or can the Community add its vote to those of the Member States? Other members of the organization would find the latter difficult to accept. Yet if the former approach is taken one needs to define in which cases the Community, and in which cases its Member States, have the right to vote. Third countries are also concerned about questions of responsibility and liability, and wonder whether the Community can require its Member States to keep to the commitments it has entered into. Also, there may be concern that Community participation would lead to the formation of 'blocks' within an organization.[53]

The apprehensive approach towards Community membership, particularly within the UN system, is well illustrated by an opinion of the UN legal office at the occasion of Community accession to the FAO. As regards the alternative exercise of membership rights, which was the solution adopted in the FAO for organizing participation by the Community and its Member States (see below), the opinion took the view that this should remain confined to the FAO and should not be used to justify attempts to encroach on the principle of 'one state one vote' contained in Article 18 of the UN Charter. A change in the Charter on this critical issue was considered to have no realistic probability of success, and the FAO solution was not to be invoked in the future as a precedent in the UN context.[54] It is doubtful, however, whether this approach carries conviction. Where an international organization takes decisions on matters coming within the Community's exclusive competences, the Member States are in any event required to adopt a common position and will form a block. Whether the expression of such a common position takes place by way of Member State voting, or by way of a Community vote, should not in any way alter the outcome of the process.

The types of difficulties to which the lack of Community membership of an international organization may give rise are exemplified by the relationship between the Community and the ILO.[55] The Community has only observer status in that organization, which has as its main task the negotiation and adoption of international labour conventions. The issue of Community participation in the negotiation of such conventions first arose as regards Convention No 153 on working hours and rest periods in transport (1977 to 1979). It proved impossible to find an arrangement

---

[53] Ibid, 1235–7.
[54] FAO Doc CL 100/9-Sup. 1, at 2–3, cited by FL Kirgis, *International Organizations in their Legal Setting* (2nd edn, West Publishing Company, 1993) 166.
[55] The following description is taken from *Opinion 2/91* (n 18 above), 1066–8.

then for such participation on account of fears held by employers and workers over their own position in the tripartite ILO approach towards rule-making. Documents drawn up by the Governing Body of the International Labour Office in 1981 and 1989 proposed that the Member States could authorize the Commission to propose amendments on their behalf, that the authority responsible for implementation might be the EC Council and that ratification could be done through an appropriate statement by the Community, provided that prior notification from all the Member States confirmed that this constituted ratification by them. The documents also referred to issues of liability. The problem of Community competence again arose in connection with Convention No 162 concerning safety in the use of asbestos (1983 to 1986), an area covered by four EC directives. As the Community could not take part in the Conference in 1986 the Council, after some skirmishes with the Commission, adopted a decision on Community participation in areas of exclusive Community competence. The decision imposed full compliance with the tripartite consultation procedure required by the ILO. It also stipulated that the Community replies to the ILO questionnaire (the instrument for consultation of both sides of industry) had to be adopted by the Council following a proposal from the Commission. In the Conference, the Commission would speak on behalf of the Community and act in close consultation with the Member States. The delegates of the Member States would retain their right to speak during the plenary session of the Conference. In 1988 then, several Member States contested the Community's exclusive competence as regards Convention No 170. There were again discussions between the Commission and the Council, the latter agreeing to re-examine its 1986 decision and to supplement it with provisions covering cases of joint competence. However, when, following the adoption of the Convention, the Commission wrote to the Council stating its view that the Member States should notify the ILO that the Community institutions were the competent authorities for the implementation of the Convention, several Member States indicated their refusal to accept that the Community had exclusive competence. The Commission then requested *Opinion 2/91*, asking for clarification of the competence question. The German Government contested the admissibility of the request, arguing that the Community was in any event incapable of concluding an ILO Convention, as it was not a member of the ILO. The Court rejected that argument, pointing out that the request did not concern the Community's capacity on the international plane, but only the question of Community competence, and that it was not for the Court to assess any obstacles which the Community might encounter in the exercise of its competence. In any event, Community competence could be exercised through the medium of the Member States acting jointly in the Community's interest.[56] Further in the Opinion, after having concluded that Convention No 170 came within the joint competence of the Community and its Member States, the Court referred to the duty of co-operation, which is analysed below. The Opinion did not however

---

[56] *Opinion 2/91* (n 18 above), paras 1–5.

resolve the differences between the Member States and the Commission, as Sack reported in 1995 that the Member States refused to make national ratifications of the conventions subject to a previous Council decision, and that the whole ratification process of ILO conventions was blocked.[57] The position has not changed since then.[58]

The duty of co-operation thus governs action by the Member States in international organizations of which the Community is not a member, in so far as that organization deals with matters coming within Community competence or governed by Community law. It may be noted that the EEC Treaty used to contain a more ambitious provision, Article 116, which provided that the Member States were required, in respect of all matters of particular interest to the common market, to proceed within the framework of international organizations of an economic character only by common action. The TEU deleted that provision, for reasons which are unclear.[59] It is true that Article 19(1) TEU, in the title on the CFSP, provides that the 'Member States shall coordinate their action in international organizations and at international conferences'. However, that provision cannot extend to Community action in light of Article 47 TEU.[60] In the sphere of monetary policy Article 111(4) EC provides that 'the Council, acting by a qualified majority on a proposal from the Commission and after consulting the ECB, shall decide on the position of the Community at international level as regards issues of particular relevance to economic and monetary union and on its representation, in compliance with the allocation of powers laid down in Articles 99 and 105'. This provision can be used for organizing the representation and defence of the Community's positions in international organizations which are of relevance to EMU.

If non-membership may create difficulties, so may membership. It is useful shortly to describe the organization of and experience with Community membership of the FAO and of the WTO.

The negotiations for Community accession to the FAO took four years,[61] and were successfully concluded in 1991.[62] As the FAO Constitution permitted accession only by States, its provisions had to be amended. Article II, as modified, permits admission of regional economic integration organizations, constituted by States

---

[57] Sack (n 20 above), 1239.

[58] See Denza (n 45 above), 10–11. In 1994 the Commission adopted a proposal for a Council Decision on the exercise of the Community's external competence at international labour conferences in cases falling within the joint competence of the Community and its Member States (COM(94)2 final). The Council did not act upon this proposal, which was withdrawn on 9 June 2000.

[59] The deletion is deplored by C Kaddous, *Le droit des relations extérieures dans la jurisprudence de la Cour de justice des Communautés européennes* (Helbing & Lichtenhahn, 1998) 187–8.   [60] See Ch 5.

[61] Sack (n 20 above), 1237.

[62] See also A Tavares de Pinho, 'L'admission de la Communauté économique européenne comme membre de l'Organisation des Nations Unies pour l'alimentation et l'agriculture' (1993) 370 RMCUE 656–73; R Frid, 'The European Economic Community A Member of a Specialized Agency of the United Nations' (1993) 4 EJIL 239–55; J Schwob, 'L'amendement à l'acte constitutif de la FAO visant à permettre l'admission en qualité de membre d'organisations d'intégration économique régionale de la Communauté économique européenne' (1993) 29 RTDE 1–16; Frid (n 45 above), Ch 5.

a majority of which are members of the FAO, and benefiting from a transfer of competence over a range of matters within the purview of the FAO. The regional economic integration organization has to submit a declaration of competence, and Member States of the organization are presumed to retain competence over all other matters. Subsequent changes in the distribution of competence need to be notified. Membership rights are exercised on an alternative basis, depending on where competence lies. The organization which joins the FAO shall have a number of votes equal to the number of its Member States which are entitled to vote, but voting rights can only be exercised by either the organization or its Member States. In accordance with those provisions, the Community submitted a declaration of competence. Moreover, the General Rules of the FAO were also modified so as to create more precision in the handling of joint membership. Rule XLI provides that any member of the FAO may request information regarding the division of competence in respect of any specific question. It also requires the member organization and its Member States to indicate, before any FAO meeting, where competence lies in respect of any specific question to be considered and which, as between the member organization and its Member States, shall have the right to vote in respect of each particular agenda item. Where an agenda item covers matters of mixed competence, both the member organization and its Member States may participate in the discussion, but the meeting, in arriving at its decisions, shall take into account only the intervention of the party which has the right to vote.[63]

Those provisions have been described as a straitjacket,[64] and it is easy to see that, when applied strictly, they risk becoming a source of constant tension, particularly within the Community where decisions on competence and voting rights need to be taken constantly in light of the multitude of FAO meetings. It is also obvious that such complex rules require some form of agreed decision-making process within the Community. The Commission and the Council therefore concluded an arrangement in 1991, providing for co-ordination meetings at various levels, for mechanisms ensuring an adequate flow of information, for rules on interventions and voting at FAO meetings, and for rules on participation in drafting committees. Some of the provisions of that arrangement are further examined below, in the section on the duty of co-operation. At this stage it is sufficient to indicate that, at least in the view of the Commission, Community participation in the work of the FAO has not worked well, due to the constant haggling over issues of competence and voting rights.[65] This has led the Commission to involve the Court of Justice, in a case brought against the Council for its alleged failure to apply the arrangement correctly (see below). Perceptions will of course differ, and the Commission may simply be unhappy with the limits on its proper role in FAO activities. Yet given the legal complexities of the division of competences between

---

[63] This provision appears to require that other FAO members have special powers so as to participate in a discussion with both a member organization and its Member States but to take into account only the intervention of the party with the right to vote.   [64] Sack (n 20 above), 1243.
[65] Ibid, 1245–6.

the Community and its Member States in their external relations and the constant tension between supranationalism and intergovernmentalism in the European integration process as a whole, a system whereby competences need to be defined and allocated for every item on the agenda of every meeting of an international organization is no doubt an ideal recipe for malfunctioning.

The case of the WTO can in some sense be contrasted with that of the FAO. The antecedents are very different, because the Community was already a *de facto* member of GATT (itself a *de facto* international organization), owing to its extensive and exclusive competences in matters of tariffs and trade. The Community was one of the main players in the Uruguay Round, which led to the establishment of the WTO. The Uruguay Round negotiations were conducted by the Commission, and the Council of Ministers was the central organ for deciding the EC common position. It was therefore only natural for the Community to become a founding member of the WTO, and the question was rather what type of role would be available for the individual Member States. Article XIV of the WTO Agreement simply provides that the agreement is open for acceptance by contracting parties to GATT 1947 and the European Communities. There is no requirement for a declaration of competence, and there are only a few basic provisions on voting: Article IX provides that each WTO member has one vote; that the EC has a number of votes equal to the number of its Member States which are members of the WTO; and, in a footnote, that the number of votes of the EC and its Member States shall in no case exceed the number of the Member States. The latter provision suggests alternating exercise of voting rights, but as the WTO is an organization where voting rarely takes place, the issue is largely theoretical. There appears to be nothing else in WTO law regulating membership by the EC and its Member States. Nor is there much more at internal Community level. After the conclusion of the Uruguay Round negotiations, but before the Court issued *Opinion 1/94*, the Council, the Commission, and the Member States did manage to agree on a 'code of conduct' for future negotiations on services. That code, which is quoted in the factual part of *Opinion 1/94*,[66] provides that the Commission should continue to negotiate on behalf of the Community and the Member States; that it should fully inform the Member States; that it should express positions reached on all issues according to the relevant decision-making procedures (with a footnote expressing disagreement between the Commission and the Council about what that means); that it should ensure that representatives of Member States are in a position to attend all substantive meetings and negotiations; and that it should promptly circulate all notes. The code also provides that the Council resolves to review regularly the progress of negotiations, and that it will consider the formulation of negotiating objectives and reserves the right to give the Commission appropriate directives. Then came the Court's Opinion, in which it emphasized the duty of co-operation, without, however, further spelling out the consequences of that duty (see below). The Commission, the

---

[66] *Opinion 1/94* (n 30 above), 5365.

Council, and the Member States subsequently entered into negotiations on a general code of conduct for the Community's and the Member States' participation in the operation of the WTO, but that negotiation was never concluded, as it became part of the 1996 IGC leading to the Amsterdam Treaty, which only managed to achieve a limited modification of Article 133 EC.[67] As a result, eight years into the operation of the WTO there is still no general document on Community and Member States' participation. None the less, there appear to be few serious problems, as the practice of acting in common and allowing the Community to be the central player in the system is continued. Even at the level of dispute settlement, when a third country brings a complaint against an EC Member State, it is the legal service of the Commission which takes up the defence.[68] There are no doubt a number of factors which explain the success of this joint membership, which in effect comes close to exclusive Community membership. Perhaps the most important one is that the legal, economic, and diplomatic expertise in trade issues is generally located in the Community institutions, particularly the Commission.

International organizations and the autonomy of the Community legal order

A separate point which deserves to be discussed with respect to the EU's relationship with international organizations is case law which emphasizes that Community participation in agreements setting up their own institutions must not affect the autonomy of the Community legal order.

Opinion 1/76 was the first case in which the Court identified that principle.[69] It concerned the European laying-up fund for inland waterway vessels, to be established by the Community, some of its Member States, and Switzerland. The legal system contained in the draft agreement provided for the grant of certain powers to the Fund Tribunal, composed of six judges from the ECJ and one judge from Switzerland. The Tribunal was to have the power to give preliminary rulings concerning not only the validity and interpretation of decisions adopted by the organs of the Fund but also the interpretation of the agreement itself. The Court pointed out that, once the agreement was concluded, it would itself have jurisdiction to interpret its provisions. It examined the hypothesis that the jurisdiction of the Tribunal and of the Court would be parallel so that it would be for the national court of a Member State to refer the matter to one or other of the two legal organs. The Court drew attention to the risk of conflicts of jurisdiction. It recognized that the need to establish judicial remedies and legal procedures which would guarantee the observance of the law could justify the principle underlying the system

---

[67] See Ch 2.

[68] See e.g. *EC—Measures Affecting Asbestos and Asbestos-Containing Products* (WT/DS/135), a case brought by Canada against French legislation. See further Helikoski (n 1 above), 178–93.

[69] N 10 above.

adopted. None the less, a difficulty would arise because the six members of the Court required to sit on the Fund Tribunal could be prejudicing their position as regards questions which could come before the Court after having been brought before the Tribunal, and vice versa. The arrangement could conflict with the obligation on the judges to give a completely impartial ruling on contentious questions when they came before the Court. In extreme cases the Court could find it impossible to assemble a quorum. For those reasons, the Fund Tribunal could be established only on condition that judges belonging to the Court of Justice were not called upon to serve on it.[70]

The Court had similar objections to the first version of the EEA Agreement. That agreement was an ambitious attempt to extend the policies, principles, and rules of the internal market to the EFTA countries without requiring them to become members of the Community.[71] In the original negotiation every effort had been made to ensure that the extension of the internal market was complete, and that the internal market would function in exactly the same way in the whole of the EEA. To achieve this the first version of the EEA Agreement copied EEC Treaty provisions as much as possible, and provided *inter alia* for extension of the case law of the Court of Justice, as well as for the creation of an EEA Court, composed of judges from the Court of Justice and from the EFTA countries, competent to interpret the agreement. The Court in *Opinion 1/91* emphasized the remaining differences between the objectives of the (then) EEC Treaty and those of the agreement, notwithstanding the negotiators' attempt to create as much homogeneity as possible.[72] It then examined the jurisdiction of the EEA Court, and objected to two of its dimensions.

First, the EEA Court would, when interpreting the term 'Contracting Party' in the agreement, have to rule on the respective competences of the Community and the Member States as regards the matters governed by the provisions of the agreement. It followed that the jurisdiction conferred on the EEA Court was likely adversely to affect the allocation of responsibilities defined in the Treaties and, hence, the autonomy of the Community legal order, respect for which had to be assured by the Court of Justice pursuant to (current) Article 220 EC. This exclusive jurisdiction was confirmed by Article 292 EC, under which the Member States undertook not to submit a dispute concerning the interpretation or application of the Treaty to any method of settlement other than those provided for in the Treaty.[73]

As a second point the Court examined the effect of the case law of the EEA Court on the interpretation of Community law. As in *Opinion 1/76* the Court recalled that it would have jurisdiction to interpret the EEA Agreement. It pointed out that where an international agreement provided for its own system of courts, including a court with jurisdiction to settle disputes between the Contracting

---

[70] Ibid, paras 17–22.   [71] Agreement on the European Economic Area [1994] OJ L1/3.

[72] *Opinion 1/91 re Agreement on the European Economic Area* [1991] ECR I–6079; see also Ch 8.

[73] Ibid, paras 31–35.

Parties, and, as a result, to interpret its provisions, the decisions of that court would be binding on the Community institutions, including the Court of Justice. An international agreement providing for such a system of courts was in principle compatible with Community law. The Community's competence in the field of international relations and its capacity to conclude international agreements necessarily entailed the power to submit to the decisions of a court which was created or designated by such an agreement as regards the interpretation and application of its provisions. The problem was however that the EEA Agreement took over an essential part of the rules which governed economic and trading relations within the Community and which constituted, for the most part, fundamental provisions of the Community legal order. The Court then referred to the agreement's provisions on homogeneity and uniformity, and came to the conclusion that in so far as it conditioned the future interpretation of the Community rules on free movement and competition the machinery of courts provided for in the agreement conflicted with (current) Article 220 EC and, more generally, with the very foundations of the Community.[74]

Moreover, the fact that judges from the Court of Justice were to sit on the EEA Court accentuated the general problems arising from the court system which the draft agreement purported to set up. Those judges would have to apply and interpret the same provisions (in the EC Treaty and in the EEA Agreement) but using different approaches, methods, and concepts in order to take account of the nature of each treaty and of its particular objectives. In those circumstances, it would be very difficult, if not impossible, for those judges, when sitting in the Court of Justice, to tackle questions with completely open minds where they had taken part in determining those questions as members of the EEA Court.[75]

After the Court's negative Opinion the agreement was renegotiated as regards the system of judicial supervision. The most significant modification was the replacement of the EEA Court with an EFTA Court, composed only of judges from the EFTA countries and with more limited jurisdiction. The Court then issued a positive Opinion.[76]

The principle of the autonomy of the Community legal order was also discussed in the context of *Opinion 2/94*, on the issue of accession to the ECHR.[77] The Council had requested the Court's Opinion on the question of Community competence to join the ECHR, and on the question whether accession would be compatible with the EC Treaty, in particular Articles 220 and 292 EC. However, the Court declined to reply to that question because it did not have sufficient information regarding the arrangements by which the Community envisaged submitting to the judicial control machinery established by the ECHR.[78]

In a recent Opinion, regarding the proposed agreement on the establishment of a European Common Aviation Area (ECAA), the Court again examined whether

---

[74] *Opinion 1/91 re Agreement on the European Economic Area* [1991] ECR I–6079, paras 37–46.
[75] Ibid, paras 47–52.
[76] *Opinion 1/92 re Agreement on the European Economic Area* [1992] ECR I–2821.
[77] *Opinion 2/94 re Accession to the ECHR* [1996] ECR I–1759; see also Ch 3.   [78] Ibid, para 20.

there were any threats to the autonomy of the Community legal order.[79] The agreement was modelled after the EEA Agreement. The Court recalled, and applied, the principles resulting from its previous case law. Where an agreement clearly separated the Community from the other Contracting Parties from an institutional point of view and did not affect either the exercise by the Community and its institutions of their powers by changing the nature of those powers, or the interpretation of Community law, the autonomy of the Community legal order could be considered to be secure.[80] After an extensive examination of the ECAA Agreement's provisions the Court concluded that those requirements were met.

This case law on the autonomy of the Community legal order is, notwithstanding its importance, of limited scope. Serious problems are likely to arise only with respect to agreements extending EU policies to neighbouring countries, where there risks being confusion as to the origin, nature, and methods of interpretation of duplicated legal provisions. The autonomy of the Community legal order is clearly not threatened by accession to an independent international organization with a dispute settlement system of its own, such as the WTO. The Court is particularly minded to safeguard its own autonomy in the interpretation of Community law, but at the same time recognizes that it may need to submit to the rulings of a dispute settlement organism of an agreement or organization which the Community has respectively signed or joined. Provided such an organism does not rule on pure questions of Community law, such as the division of powers between the Community and its Member States, the powers of the institutions, or provisions of the founding Treaties or of Community legislation, there can be no objections to such submission, which is an inherent feature of participation in international law making.

The duty of co-operation

The above survey of the practice as regards mixed agreements and mixed membership of international organizations reveals some of the problems and difficulties to which mixity gives rise. It may enable the reader better to appreciate the importance of the overarching legal principle governing mixity, namely the duty of co-operation. This section analyses the case law of the Court of Justice on the meaning of that principle, looks for its foundations, examines its legal consequences, and seeks to advance the debate on the forms and modalities of the principle's application.

The first judicial statements on the duty of co-operation were made in *Ruling 1/78*, an EAEC case.[81] In contrast with the EC Treaty, the EAEC Treaty expressly provides for parallelism between the EAEC's internal and external powers (Article 101). It also mentions mixed agreements in Article 102. Pursuant to Article 103 the Member States are required to communicate to the Commission all draft agreements

---

[79] *Opinion 1/00 re the ECAA Agreement* [2002] ECR I–3493.   [80] Ibid, para 6.
[81] N 17 above.

or contracts relating to matters within the purview of the Treaty. The Commission may then object, in which case the Member State may ask for a ruling by the Court of Justice. *Ruling 1/78* was made upon a request by the Belgian government, as regards competence to conclude the Convention on the Physical Protection of Nuclear Materials, Facilities and Transports. There is no need to examine the complex issues of competence, as analysed by the Court. Suffice it to say that the Court concluded that the Community could not be excluded from participation in the convention. In other words, the convention was to become a mixed agreement. The Court did not stop there, however. It drew attention to Article 192 EAEC, which is identical to Article 10 EC, formulating the principle of Member States' loyalty. The Court considered that there could be no doubt that unilateral action by the Member States, even if it were collective and concerted action, would have the effect of calling into question certain of the essential functions of the Community and of affecting detrimentally its independent action in external relations. It followed that the draft convention could be implemented as regards the Community only by means of a close association between the institutions of the Community and the Member States both in the process of negotiation and conclusion and in the fulfilment of the obligations entered into. The Court then reiterated the scope for concluding mixed agreements under the provisions of the EAEC Treaty. It added that it was not necessary to set out and determine, as regards other parties to the convention, the division of powers in this respect between the Community and the Member States, particularly as it could change in the course of time. It was sufficient, in the Court's opinion, to state to the other contracting parties that the matter gave rise to a division of powers within the Community, it being understood that the exact nature of that division was a domestic question in which third parties had no need to intervene. Lastly, as regards implementation of the convention, the same principles as governed the division of powers with regard to negotiation and conclusion applied: once the convention had entered into force, its application would entail close co-operation between the Community institutions and the Member States. The former would act within the scope of the Community competences, on the basis of the Treaty and the provisions of the convention. The Member States would have to adopt implementing provisions, each in its own territory, for matters not covered by Community competence. The Court concluded its analysis by stating that here 'there is to be found once more the necessity for harmony between international action by the Community and the distribution of jurisdiction and powers within the Community which the Court of Justice had occasion to emphasize in its case law originating with the [*AETR* judgment]'.[82]

There are a few points to be noted here. First, the fact that the case concerned the EAEC and not the EC Treaty appears to be of limited relevance. The Court itself makes the link between the two Communities by referring to the principle of loyalty and to the *AETR* judgment, and in later decisions under the EC Treaty it

---

[82] N 17 above, paras 33–36.

referred back to *Ruling 1/78*. Secondly, the principle of loyalty appears to be at the basis, to some extent at least, of the duty of co-operation as spelled out in the ruling. Thirdly, shared competence requires 'close association' in the process of negotiating, concluding, *and* implementing the mixed agreement. Implementing measures follow the division of competence; in other words, the conclusion of a mixed agreement does not permit the Community (or, for that matter, the Member States) to adopt implementing measures in areas which do not come within their competence. Fourthly, the comment on there being no need to clarify the division of powers is rather peculiar, as for third countries such clarification may well be a precondition for negotiating a mixed agreement. Fifthly, the Court was particularly concerned with achieving 'harmony' between internal and external action.

In *Opinion 2/91*, on ILO Convention No 170, the Court again had occasion to address the duty of co-operation. As discussed above,[83] the Court concluded in that case that the convention came within the joint competence of the Community and its Member States. The Court referred to its comments in *Ruling 1/78* on a close association between the Community institutions and the Member States both in the process of negotiation and conclusion and in the fulfilment of obligations entered into. This duty of co-operation also had to apply in the context of the EEC Treaty since it resulted from the requirement of unity in the international representation of the Community. The Court pointed out that in the case of the ILO co-operation was all the more necessary in view of the fact that the Community could not, as international law stood, itself conclude an ILO convention and had to do so through the medium of the Member States. It was therefore necessary for the Community institutions and the Member States to take all the measures necessary best to ensure such co-operation both in the procedure of submission to the competent authority and ratification of Convention No 170 and in the implementation of commitments resulting from that Convention.[84]

These statements constituted a useful recapitulation of the duty of co-operation. A new element is that this duty results from the requirement of unity in the international representation of the Community. By contrast, there is no mention of Article 10 EC. Nor did the Court expand much on how co-operation could be achieved; it merely demanded 'all the measures necessary', without attempting to define the content of such measures. Subsequent events demonstrated that the Opinion did not resolve the issues concerning Community involvement in the work of the ILO (see previous section).

Then came *Opinion 1/94* on the WTO Agreement, where the Court again, in the final part of the Opinion, turned to the duty of co-operation. At the hearing, the Commission had drawn the Court's attention to the problems which would arise, as regards the administration of the agreements, if there was shared competence. The Member States would undoubtedly seek to express their views individually on matters falling within their competence whenever no consensus was found.

---

[83] See Ch 3 and previous sect. [84] *Opinion 2/91* (n 18 above), paras 36–38.

Interminable discussions would ensue to determine whether a given matter fell within the competence of the Community, so that the Community mechanisms laid down by the relevant provisions of the Treaty would apply, or whether it was within the competence of the Member States, in which case the consensus rule would operate. The Community's unity of action *vis-à-vis* the rest of the world would thus be undermined and its negotiating power greatly weakened. The Court replied by stating that these concerns were legitimate, but that problems of co-operation could not modify the answer to the question of competence. It then recalled its statements on the duty of co-operation in *Ruling 1/78* and *Opinion 2/91*. It concluded by pointing out that the duty of co-operation was all the more imperative in the case of the substantive trade agreements annexed to the WTO Agreement, which were inextricably interlinked, and in view of the cross-retaliation measures established by the Dispute Settlement Understanding.[85] Here the Court appeared to assume that the Community and its Member States would each on their own participate in dispute settlement, but that is not what in effect happened. Again, however, the Court did not try to spell out in what way flesh could be put on the bones of the duty of co-operation.

The Court made its most significant statements on the duty of co-operation in *Commission v. Council* on participation in the FAO.[86] The general organization of joint membership by the Community and its Member States is described above. The Commission, however, became increasingly unhappy with Member States' reluctance to recognize and support the Community's role, particularly in cases of mixed competence. In practice, the provisions of the internal 'arrangement' which had been negotiated between the Commission and the Council proved crucial. It is therefore useful to elaborate a little on those provisions. Section 1.11 of the Arrangement provides that the Commission, in preparation for FAO meetings, communicates to the Member States its proposals concerning the exercise of responsibilities and interventions on a particular issue. Section 1.12 provides that, if no agreement is reached between the Commission and the Member States on those proposals, the question shall be settled in accordance with the rules and procedures of the Treaty and in accordance with agreed practice. If no agreement is reached on that basis the question is submitted to Coreper. Section 1.13 states that decisions referred to in Section 1.12 are without prejudice to the respective competences of the Community and its Member States. Section 2 lays down the rules on interventions and voting. Section 2.1 provides that where an item on the agenda concerns an area of exclusive Community competence the Commission is to take the floor and vote. Section 2.2 provides that where an item on the agenda concerns an area of national competence the Member States take the floor and vote. Section 2.3 deals with cases of shared competence, and provides that in such cases the aim will be to

[85] *Opinion 1/94* (n 30 above), paras 106–109.
[86] Case C–25/94 *Commission v. Council* [1996] ECR I–1469. See also J Helikoski, 'Internal Struggle for International Presence: The Exercise of Voting Rights Within the FAO', in Dashwood and Hillion (eds) (n 2 above), 79–99.

achieve a common position by consensus. If that is achieved, the Presidency of the Council shall express the common position when the thrust of the issue lies in an area outside the exclusive competence of the Community, the Member States and the Commission may speak to support or supplement, and the Member States will vote. When the thrust of the issue lies in an area within the exclusive competence of the Community the Commission shall express the common position, Member States may speak so as to support or supplement, and the Commission will vote. Lastly, Section 2.4 provides that, if a common position cannot be reached, the Member States are free to intervene and vote.[87]

The case brought by the Commission concerned the negotiation and adoption, in the framework of the FAO, of an agreement to promote compliance with international conservation and management measures by vessels fishing on the high seas. The details of the negotiation and contents of that agreement need not concern us here. Suffice it to say that there was disagreement within the Community on the division of competence, in particular as regards provisions on registration and flagging of fishing vessels. Throughout the negotiation, the Commission considered that the thrust of the agreement came within the Community's exclusive competence in the area of fisheries, so that it should have the right to vote under Section 2.3 of the Arrangement, whereas the Member States considered that they should have the right to vote. When, towards the end of the FAO negotiation, Coreper confirmed the latter position, the Commission brought the issue before the Council, which, two days before the agreement was finally adopted by the FAO, decided that indeed the Member States should vote. The Commission then challenged that Council decision before the Court.

It is worth noting that the dispute between the Commission and the Member States was confined to the issue of voting rights. Throughout the negotiation of the agreement, the Community and its Member States formulated and defended a common position, and there was no disagreement as to the substance of the negotiations. On that basis, Jacobs AG considered that the action was inadmissible, as in his Opinion there was no genuine dispute between the parties.[88] The Court took a different approach, however. It accepted the action, and, as it was generally acknowledged that there was shared competence, set out to examine whether the agreement concerned an issue whose main thrust lay in an area of exclusive Community competence (see Section 2.3 of the Arrangement). Its conclusion was that it did, and the Court then turned to the duty of co-operation, recalling its statements in *Ruling 1/78*, and *Opinions 2/91* and *1/94*. Then comes a vital paragraph, where the Court stated that Section 2.3 of the Arrangement between the Commission and the Council represented fulfilment of that duty of co-operation between the Community and its Member States within the FAO. It was clear, moreover, from the terms of the Arrangement that the two institutions intended to enter into a binding commitment towards each other, nor had the Council contested its effect at any moment

---

[87] See the description in the Opinion of Jacobs AG in *Commission v. Council* (n 86 above), paras 12–13.   [88] Ibid, para 59.

in the proceedings. Consequently, by giving the right to vote to the Member States the Council had acted in breach of Section 2.3 of the Arrangement which it was required to observe, and its decision had to be annulled.[89]

This judgment constitutes a major advance in the law on the duty of co-operation, but equally gives rise to many questions. The Court recognizes that it is possible, even informally, to conclude some form of interinstitutional agreement materializing and specifying the duty of co-operation in cases of mixed external action, and that such an agreement is binding on the institutions. Such recognition is not wholly without precedent, as in other areas too the Court has been giving effect to such agreements. The Community budget is an example.[90] The difference with other interinstitutional agreements, however, is that the FAO Arrangement concerns co-operation between the Community and its Member States, whereas other instances concern only interinstitutional co-operation. It is noteworthy that the Court recognizes the Arrangement, notwithstanding the fact that it was agreed between the Commission and the Council, and that the Member States did not formally agree to it in their individual capacity. The Court thus appears to accept that the Council may represent the Member States in this regard, possibly on the grounds that the duty of co-operation is a Community law principle.[91] What remains open, however, is the question whether such a pure interinstitutional agreement is binding on the Member States. The FAO case concerned a Council decision, but what if the Member States disregard the Arrangement?

The judgment does not indicate the legal basis for concluding such interinstitutional agreements. Are such agreements to be based on a provision of the Treaty, or is the duty of co-operation on its own a sufficient legal basis? What then is the appropriate decision-making procedure? Would it in all cases be sufficient to conclude the agreement between the Commission and the Council, or should there also be a role for the European Parliament?

A further question is whether, if it is possible to materialize the duty of co-operation by adopting a binding interinstitutional agreement, there is not also some form of obligation for the institutions to conclude such an agreement, at least as regards mixed membership in important international organizations, such as the WTO, or for Member States' participation in the work of organizations of which the Community cannot become a member, despite its competences in the matter, such as the ILO. Such an obligation could be enforced through an action for failure to act under Article 232 EC.

The above case law on the duty of co-operation and the Community's experience with work in international organizations suggest that the principle's effectiveness is limited if it is not fleshed out. There is an obvious case for creating some EC (or EU) Treaty language on this crucial principle for mixed external action. There

---

[89] *Commission v. Council* (n 86 above), paras 40–51 of the judgment.

[90] See for an overview J Monar, 'Interinstitutional Agreements: the Phenomenon and its New Dynamics after Maastricht' (1994) 31 CMLRev 693.   [91] Timmermans (n 16 above), 244.

is also an obvious case for basic legal texts on how to conduct co-operation in the framework of international organizations.

This section can be concluded by addressing the question as to the basis in Community law of the duty of co-operation itself, a question which has received some attention in the literature.[92] Judging from *Ruling 1/78*, the answer appeared simple enough: there the Court referred to the principle of loyalty, according to which the Member States shall take all appropriate measures to ensure fulfilment of the obligations arising out of the Treaty or resulting from action taken by the Community institutions; they shall facilitate the achievement of the Community's tasks; and they shall abstain from any measure which could jeopardize the attainment of the objectives of the Treaty (see, in the EC Treaty, Article 10). It is striking, however, that in the subsequent decisions the Court did not refer to Article 10. Timmermans takes the view that the duty of co-operation is more specific than the general principle of loyalty,[93] but that does not stand in the way of identifying the principle of loyalty as its foundation. He also draws attention to the Court's references to 'the requirement of unity in the international representation of the Community'. In a sense, that requirement of unity and the principle of loyalty can be seen as the twin foundations of the duty of co-operation. By insisting on unity, loyalty, and co-operation the Court expresses a particular conception of mixed external action, a conception which does not consist of simple recognition of split competences, possibly resulting in independent action by the Community and its Member States, but rather one where competences are truly shared or joint, necessitating a common approach maintaining unity.

Problems and questions

Having thus elaborated on the duty of co-operation, this chapter can now address some of the major problems and legal issues to which mixity gives rise, as the application of the duty of co-operation may contribute towards the resolution of at least some of them. The following analysis is structured according to the various stages of the life of a mixed agreement.

Negotiation

There are no established rules on how to negotiate a mixed agreement, in contrast with pure Community agreements, where Article 300(1) EC provides that the Commission conducts negotiations in consultation with special committees appointed by the Council and within the framework of directives issued by the Council.[94] In principle, a mixed negotiation could be divided into a Community

---

[92] Helikoski (n 1 above), 95–6 and Timmermans (n 16 above), 241.   [93] Ibid.
[94] See Ch 6.

and a Member States part, with different negotiators for each part. In practice, however, it does appear that most mixed agreements are negotiated under the Community method, albeit with a more preponderant role for Member States' representatives.[95] Much however will depend on the type of agreement and the type of negotiation. The duty of co-operation in any event requires 'close association' between the Community institutions and the Member States.

A reflection of those issues at the level of substance is whether a mixed negotiation always needs to be conducted on the basis of a common position, or whether it is sufficient that there is such a position for the Community part of the agreement.[96] Under a strict division-of-competences approach it would appear sufficient that there is a single negotiating stance for the Community part of the agreement. If however the above reading of the Court's case law on the duty of co-operation is correct, that duty would require that a common approach is maintained at all times. Experience teaches that it is difficult to distinguish and separate the Community and non-Community parts of an agreement any way, in light of the nature of Community competences and their linkages with national competences, and because a negotiation may float in different directions.[97]

In connection with mixed negotiations it is worth noting that the Community and its Member States are often a cumbersome partner to negotiate with, particularly, but not only, in a bilateral context. For third countries it often appears that the real negotiation takes place within the Community. Once a common position is reached, all flexibility is lost, and the other negotiating partner essentially needs to accept or reject the outcome. Mixed negotiations also offer temptations to Member States governments to extract particular concessions, as agreement by all Member States is necessary.[98]

Clarification of the division of powers

Third countries participating in a mixed negotiation may ask for clarification of the division of powers between the Community and its Member States, as happened as regards UNCLOS.[99] Such clarification may also be a precondition for joining an international organization, as in the case of the FAO (see above). The Community practice is for these clarifications to be fairly concise and basic, and that approach is no doubt appropriate in light of the complexities involved with defining the exact scope and nature of the Community's competences, and in light of the evolving

---

[95] Macleod, Hendry, and Hyett (n 1 above), 151–3; Helikoski (n 1 above), 78–80.

[96] Macleod, Hendry, and Hyett (n 1 above), 149–50.

[97] See for a good illustration the internal Community debate on competence in the context of the FAO case, as described by Jacobs AG (n 86 above), paras 15–22.

[98] That was the case in negotiations on trade with South Africa, where Italy and Greece sought concessions on ouzo and grappa: see BBC News at <http://news.bbc.co.uk/1/hi/business/604040.stm>.

[99] Rosas (n 2 above), 204.

character of Community competence, through both amendments of the Treaty and adoption of Community legislation creating an *AETR* effect.

In *Ruling 1/78* the Court stated that in a mixed negotiation there was no need to set out and determine, as regards other parties, the division of powers, which is an internal question.[100] That observation is somewhat curious, as surely third countries are not in any way bound by the Court's decisions, and may simply require clarification before allowing the negotiation to go ahead. The statement may in fact originate in a desire to stress the need for joint action in cases of mixity, and to move away from looking at a mixed negotiation through the prism of division of competence.[101]

The request for a clarification of the division of powers may in part be inspired by an understanding that the Community and its Member States, when concluding a mixed agreement, enter into the agreement and bind themselves only in so far as they are respectively competent to do so. Third countries may be concerned to have precise knowledge of the competences issue, so as to be clear about whether it is the Community or the Member States which may be held to account for possible violations.[102] It is doubtful however whether there is such a link between competence and responsibility. That issue is analysed below.

Clarification of competence may also be required in the day-to-day practice of an international organization, such as in the case of the FAO. Here the experience suggests that the Community should do its utmost to avoid such a requirement being imposed on it.[103] In a recent case concerning the EAEC's accession to the Nuclear Safety Convention the Court entertained an action for annulment which the Commission had brought against the Council's accession decision, in so far as that decision included a declaration of competences which the Commission considered incorrect.[104] Such a declaration was required pursuant to Article 30(4)(iii) of the Convention. The Court clarified that the Council, when it approved accession to an international convention without any reservation, had to respect the conditions for accession laid down by that convention, since an accession decision which did not comply with those conditions would be in breach of the Community's obligations from the moment it entered into force. In the case at hand, Article 30(4)(iii) of the Convention had, in the interest of the other contracting parties, to be interpreted to mean that the declaration of competences under that provision had to be

---

[100] N 17 above; see previous sect.

[101] In his Opinion in Case C–29/99 *Commission v. Council* [2002] ECR I–11221, at paras 112–113, Jacobs AG points out that in the context of *Ruling 1/78* 'the Commission had asked the Court to state that the usual practice for mixed agreements should be followed, namely that the internal division of powers between the Community and the Member States was not to be defined as far as third parties were concerned', and that '[t]he Court's statement . . . must therefore be read as a mere endorsement of the practice of the Communities of avoiding as far as possible at the negotiating stage the indication to third parties of the internal division of powers between the Community and its Member States. In view of the considerable legal and political difficulties of drafting declarations of competence that practice is indeed to be endorsed, since it allows the Communities and their Member States to focus on more important matters such as the substantive provisions of the agreement.'

[102] Kapteyn and VerLoren van Themaat (n 1 above), 1263.   [103] Sack (n 20 above), 1243–7.

[104] *Commission v. Council* (n 101 above).

complete. It followed that the Council was, under Community law, required to attach a complete declaration of competences to its decision approving accession to the Convention.[105] The Court subsequently made a careful examination of the scope of the EAEC's competences in relation to the Convention, and annulled the incomplete Council declaration. The judgment, whose principles can no doubt be transposed to EC law, emphasizes the importance of full respect for the Community's competences when making a declaration. It is also noteworthy that the Court did not make any distinction between exclusive and shared competences, implicitly confirming the conception that 'virtual' or 'potential' external competences are as real as exclusive competences, or competences in areas in which the Community has already legislated.[106]

Ratification and conclusion

Most international agreements of some significance do not merely require signing by the contracting parties for their entry into force, but also a further act of municipal endorsement in accordance with a State's constitutional provisions on participation in international law making. In the case of pure Community agreements, the procedure is rather straightforward, in particular where the European Parliament's assent is not required.[107] Mixed agreements, however, need to be concluded and ratified by each Member State. Depending on the subject matter of the agreement, procedures within a Member State may be complex and time-consuming, particularly in federal countries in which the component entities have a role to play in the endorsement of the agreement.[108] Some international agreements are of such political importance that these difficulties are easily overcome. The WTO Agreement, for example, was ratified and concluded by the Community institutions and by the Member States in the period between 15 November 1994, when the Court delivered *Opinion 1/94*, and 1 January 1995, when the agreement entered into force. Such swiftness is however most exceptional. It is a recurring problem of mixed agreements that their entry into force is delayed because some Member States do not manage to ratify. In a fast-evolving international constellation this may undermine the effectiveness of the Community's external action. Rosas reports the extreme case of the agreement on customs union and co-operation with San Marino, where after eight years the agreement had not yet entered into force for lack of ratification by some Member States.[109] It has to be noted that the Community's practice is that the Council will conclude a mixed agreement only

---

[105] *Commission v. Council* (n 101 above), paras 67–71.
[106] On the consequences under international law of a declaration of competences see Macleod, Hendry, and Hyett (n 1 above), 161–2.   [107] See Art 300 EC, further analysed in Ch 6.
[108] See e.g., with respect to ratification of the WTO Agreement, P Eeckhout, 'Belgium', in Jackson and Sykes (n 29 above), 108–10 and M Hilf, 'Negotiating and Implementing the Uruguay Round: The Role of EC Member States—The Case of Germany', in ibid, 125–32.   [109] Rosas (n 2 above), 208.

once all the Member States have ratified.[110] That is no doubt a safe practice, as otherwise problems of so-called partial mixity may be created (see below).

The Community developed two methods for handling these temporal problems. The first, for agreements containing a trade dimension, is to conclude an interim agreement on trade, which is a pure Community agreement and which can enter into force by way of a simple Council decision.[111] The second method is to provide for provisional application of the agreement at the time of signature, as permitted and regulated by Article 25 VCLT. Since the Amsterdam Treaty, Article 300(2) EC also expressly provides for that opportunity. It is obvious however that those methods cannot fully replace the definitive entry into force of the entire agreement.

The question thus arises whether a Member State which does not manage to ratify a particular mixed agreement is in breach of the duty of co-operation. There are arguments for and against such a view. On the one hand, one could argue that, once a Member State has signed the agreement, it has already expressed its willingness to enter into the agreement together with the Community and the other Member States, and therefore should not hold back on ratification. The reply to that argument from a domestic constitutional perspective would be that municipal procedures deserve to be taken seriously as they constitute the exercise of sovereign national powers, not transferred to the Community. In practice, therefore, much will depend on the reasons for delay. There have been cases where the need for ratification at Member State level became a tool for extracting last-minute commercial concessions from a third country.[112] Such cases may well constitute misuse of national powers, in violation of the duty of co-operation.

Representation and voting

Once a mixed agreement has been concluded, or the Community has joined an international organization, questions of representation and voting rights arise. As the duty of co-operation requires a 'close association' between the Community institutions and the Member States one would expect a common representation in the bodies set up under a mixed agreement or in an international organization. As to voting rights, the difficulties associated with the allocation of such rights have already been considered above, in connection with the Community's membership of the *FAO*. In that organization the alternative exercise of voting rights appears to be the greatest obstacle for an effective joint participation.

The *FAO* judgment points the way towards organizing the representation of the Community and its Member States. An interinstitutional agreement can regulate

---

[110] Art 102 EAEC Treaty expressly provides for such an approach as regards mixed agreements concluded under that Treaty. See however Helikoski (n 1 above), 93, pointing to derogations from this practice.

[111] E.g. Europe Agreements with Central and East European countries, see M Maresceau, 'On Association, Partnership, Pre-Accession and Accession', in M Maresceau (ed), *Enlarging the European Union* (Longman, 1997) 7.   [112] Agreement with South Africa (n 98 above).

this, and is binding on the institutions because it constitutes implementation of the duty of co-operation.

Implementation, interpretation, and effect

In *Ruling 1/78* the Court of Justice clearly stated that the implementation of a mixed agreement follows the division of powers between the Community and the Member States.[113] Thus, the Community can only implement the provisions of the agreement in the areas of its proper competence, and provisions not coming within the Community's competence can only be implemented by the Member States. Mixed agreements do not therefore entail an expansion of Community competence, even in relation to the particular agreement in question.

That approach is confirmed in a recent judgment in an enforcement action for failure to fulfil Treaty obligations between the Commission and Ireland.[114] Under Article 5 of Protocol 28 of the EEA Agreement, a mixed agreement, the Contracting Parties undertook to obtain their adherence before 1 January 1995 to the Berne Convention for the Protection of Literary and Artistic Works. The Commission brought an action for Ireland's failure to do so. The Court, referring to its judgment in *Demirel*,[115] held that mixed agreements had the same status in Community law as pure Community agreements, in so far as they contained provisions coming within Community competence. As a consequence, the Member States, in ensuring respect for commitments arising from an agreement concluded by the Community, fulfilled an obligation in relation to the Community, which had assumed responsibility for the due performance of the agreement. The Court then stated that, as the provisions of the Berne Convention covered an area which came in large measure within the scope of Community competence, the requirement of adherence to it came within the Community framework. Accordingly, the Commission was competent to assess compliance with that requirement, subject to review by the Court.[116] Ireland was thus found to have failed to fulfil its obligations under the Treaty.

The Commission can therefore monitor compliance by the Member States with a mixed agreement only in so far as that agreement comes within Community competence. The judgment also illustrates, however, that such competence may extend to provisions of a mixed agreement which require the Member States to act in a particular way. It is not the case that the Community part of a mixed agreement cannot impose any obligations on the Member States. On the contrary, that part may contain disciplines for, or require particular action by, the Member States. It is a general feature of Community law that the implementation of Community acts often needs to take place at national level. There is thus a distinction between competence and legal effects of an agreement.

---

[113] *Ruling 1/78* (n 17 above), para 36.
[114] Case C–13/00 *Commission v. Ireland* [2001] ECR I–2943.   [115] N 27 above.
[116] *Commission v. Ireland* (n 114 above), paras 14–20.

There is also apparently a distinction between Community competence and the jurisdiction of the Court of Justice to interpret the provisions of a mixed agreement. It is established case law that pure community agreements are acts of the Community institutions, and that, as such, the Court has jurisdiction to interpret their provisions in the preliminary rulings procedure (Article 234 EC).[117] It is logical that that approach is extended to mixed agreements, in so far as they come within Community competence. The Court, however, has gone further in a couple of judgments on the TRIPs Agreement in the context of the WTO. In *Hermès* and *Christian Dior* the Court interpreted Article 50 of TRIPs, a provision on judicial enforcement of intellectual property rights, in cases involving domestic law on trade marks and patents.[118] The Court appeared to base itself on the fact that the same provision also governed EC law intellectual property rights, such as the Community trade mark, and that a uniform interpretation was therefore required. It also based its decision on the fact that the WTO Agreement was concluded by the Community and ratified by the Member States without any allocation between them of their respective obligations towards the other contracting parties. In other words, the Community and Member States' parts of the agreement are not expressly identified. Arguably, therefore, if there were a mixed agreement which makes such distinctions, the Court's interpretative juridisction would in any event be limited to the Community part, as only that part would be an act of the Community institutions. This case law is further analysed in Chapter 8.

A final important question is to what extent Community law governs the type of legal effect a mixed agreement may have in the Community's and the Member States' legal orders. For pure Community agreements the Court may or may not recognize the direct effect of the agreement, a concept which is hugely significant for day-to-day legal practice. Again this is a subject which will be looked at in Chapter 8. Suffice it to say that, as regards mixed agreements, the Court confines its decisions on direct effect to the part of the agreement which comes within Community competence.[119] For other parts of the agreement, the question of internal legal effect of the agreement is governed by the law of the Member State in which the agreement is relied upon. That approach is not without dangers from a perspective of legal clarity and certainty. Those dangers are especially present in the case of the WTO Agreement, where the Court has denied direct effect to the provisions coming within Community competence. In principle national jurisdictions are free to take a different line as regards provisions coming within national competence. That, however, presupposes that the respective competences can be clearly delineated, which is obviously not a foregone conclusion. In many cases, the competence question will need to be clarified before a domestic court would be able to decide on the effect of the provision in question. There is also a possibility that a domestic court decides on direct effect, whereas the Court of Justice may have jurisdiction

---

[117] See Ch 8.
[118] Cases C–53/96 *Hermès v. FHT* [1998] ECR I–3603 and C–392/98 *Parfums Christian Dior v. Tuk Consultancy* [2000] ECR I–11307.   [119] Ibid.

to lay down a uniform interpretation of that provision, as its jurisdiction is broader than the provisions of WTO law covered by Community competence. So much follows from *Christian Dior*, where the Court adopted an interpretation but left the question of direct effect for the referring court to decide.[120]

International responsibility

Mixed agreements may raise delicate questions concerning the respective international responsibilities of the Community and of the Member States. Intuitively, one may be inclined to allocate responsibility according to the division of competences between the Community and its Member States.[121] Each could be held responsible only within the scope of its competences. There is however no support for that approach in either the literature or the case law, in particular in cases where the division of powers was not clarified at the time of the negotiation and conclusion of the agreement. The prevailing view is thus that, where no declaration of competences was made and the agreement contains no indication of which obligations were entered into by which party (Community or Member States), there is joint responsibility. In such cases the Community and its Member States are jointly liable for the performance of the agreement.[122] In *Parliament v. Council*, regarding Lomé IV, Jacobs AG stated that under a mixed agreement the Community and the Member States are jointly liable unless the provisions of the agreement point to the opposite conclusion.[123] In *Hermès*, which concerned the WTO Agreement, the Court referred to the fact that the agreement was concluded by the Community and ratified by its Member States without any allocation between them of their respective obligations towards the other contracting parties.[124]

The analysis can perhaps be taken a little further.[125] One can distinguish three kinds of mixed agreements. The first category is those agreements which expressly indicate which provisions are binding on which party, the Community or the Member States. Responsibility for the implementation of such an agreement will be limited to the commitments actually entered into, and the Community will not as a rule be liable for breaches by the Member States of provisions it has not committed itself to (and vice versa). The second category are agreements where a declaration of

---

[120]   See Ch 8 for further analysis.

[121]   This approach is advocated by C Kaddous, *Le droit des relations extérieures dans la jurisprudence de la Cour de justice des Communautés européennes* (Helbing & Lichtenhahn, 1998) 173–4.

[122]   E Stein, 'External Relations of the European Community: Structure and Process', in *Collected Courses of the Academy of European Law (1990)—Community Law*, Vol I, Book 1 (Martinus Nijhoff, 1991) 162; G Gaja, 'The European Community's Rights and Obligations under Mixed Agreements', in O'Keeffe and Schermers (n 5 above), 135; C Tomuschat, 'The International Responsibility of the European Union', in E Cannizzaro (ed), *The European Union as an Actor in International Relations* (Kluwer Law International, 2002) 185.

[123]   Case C–316/91 *Parliament v. Council* [1994] ECR I–625, para 69.

[124]   *Hermès* (n 118 above), para 24; see also the Opinion of Tesauro AG, paras 14 and 20, and *Dior* (n 118 above), para 33.   [125]   See also Macleod, Hendry, and Hyett (n 1 above), 158–60.

competences was made, but without a precise indication of how the division of competences affects the provisions of the agreements, and of which obligations are entered into by whom. In such cases it would seem that both the Community and the Member States could be held liable for any of their acts which violate a provision of the agreement, even if such acts do not correspond to the declaration of competences. The Community could not defend itself by arguing that it had acted outside the sphere of its competences, or of its declared competences. Where, however, the alleged violation of the agreement consists of a failure to act, the declaration of competences could be relied upon, e.g. by the Community, to argue that it cannot incur responsibility because it had no competence to perform the required acts. The third category are agreements with no allocation of commitments and no declaration of competences. Here the Community and its Member States would seem truly jointly liable, and other contracting parties could bring claims against either the Community, or the Member States, or both. The current practice in the WTO reflects this, as other WTO members have brought cases against the Community and against one or more Member States, whereas the defence has invariably been taken up by the Community.

Partial mixity

Many of the above problems and questions become even thornier in cases of partial mixity, where not all the Member States are parties alongside the Community. A clarification of the division of powers becomes more important, arrangements for representation may become more difficult, and there are likely to be more significant issues of implementation, interpretation, legal effect, and international responsibility. As Article 300(7) EC provides that agreements concluded by the Community are binding on the institutions *and* on the Member States, a Member State which does not participate in the conclusion of a mixed agreement risks none the less being bound by its provisions. A partially mixed agreement should therefore clarify the commitments entered into by the Community, and indicate the limits of the Community's participation, or the division of responsibility between the Community and the Member States.

Conclusions

Weiler has defended mixity on the ground that it offers an alternative to a centralist and unitarist model of external relations, avoiding a multiplicity of external relations and a weakening of the strength inherent in united action.[126] There are indeed no doubt certain advantages to mixed external action, but this chapter demonstrates that they can hardly be outweighed by the disadvantages. In many cases, mixity is

---

[126] JHH Weiler, *The Constitution of Europe* (CUP, 1999) 184–6.

an unnecessary burden, making the EU a more cumbersome and inflexible international actor, difficult to negotiate with and slow to ratify agreements. Third countries risk being confused as regards the division of competences between the Community and the Member States; indeed actors within the Community run the same risk. Third countries may also be uncertain as to which party, the Community or the Member States, can be held liable for failure to implement the agreement. As regards decision-making within the Council mixity implies unanimity, whereas many pure Community agreements can be concluded by qualified majority. Within the Community legal order, mixity gives rise to most intricate questions concerning jurisdiction to interpret and legal effects. By contrast, from a legal perspective there seem to be few, if any, advantages to a mixed agreement. Pure Community agreements are also fully binding on the Member States and, where directly effective, prevail over national law.

Mixity is therefore best avoided, even if it will never be eradicated as long as the EU is based on the principle of limited powers. Nevertheless, there may be increasing opportunities for avoiding mixity, in particular if the draft Constitution were to be enacted and enter into force. At present, many cases of mixity are justified on the basis of the inclusion in an agreement of provisions on a political dialogue. With the development of the CFSP, and with the abolition of the pillar structure, it will become possible to conclude agreements with both a 'Community' and CFSP dimension. The establishment of a political dialogue will no longer be able to justify the participation by Member States. The Treaty of Nice also broadened the EC Treaty provisions on co-operation with third countries, offering further opportunities for avoiding mixity.

The Court should also become more proactive in cases involving mixity. It should in particular enforce the principle that, when the Community decides to exercise its competences by concluding an international agreement, it cannot at will do so only partially. Where an agreement wholly comes within the Community's non-exclusive external competences, and the Community concludes the agreement, there is no legal justification for mixity. The requirement of unity in the international representation of the Community demands pure Community agreements in such cases.

As regards EU membership of international organizations there is still a long road to travel before such membership will reflect the EU's competences. The reasons therefor are as much located in resistance by international organizations themselves and by third countries, as in traditional concerns over sovereignty in the Member States. The Community's and the EU's international legal personality are fully recognized at the international plane in so far as the conclusion of international agreements is concerned, but much less so with respect to membership of international organizations.

It is true that EU law offers remedies for non-membership, but those are only second-best alternatives. There are strong legal rules centred on the duty of co-operation, but the practice shows that such remedies cannot replace full membership. Even where there is such membership, mixity may present problems. The duty of co-operation is an abstract principle which requires embodiment. The case law shows the way forward, through the rule that interinstitutional agreements on representation in an international organization are binding and can be enforced. However, the practice also shows that a lot may depend on other factors, in particular the location of relevant expertise: there is no general interinstitutional agreement on representation in the WTO, yet the organization of Community and Member States membership appears to raise few problems, and the Community is genuinely able to exercise its competences.

8

The courts and international agreements

Introduction

International agreements are an important instrument of lawmaking by the European Union. Where States or, as in this case, international organizations act under international law there are, of necessity, two legal dimensions to their action.

First, of course, their legal acts produce effects under international law itself. That is particularly the case where an international agreement is concluded. Such an agreement is binding, and questions of interpretation or effect may at some stage be submitted to an international judicial organ. As regards the EU's participation in treaty-making the most obvious example is the WTO Agreement, under which dispute panels and the Appellate Body decide whether a member violates provisions of the covered agreements. Other agreements may also include some form of dispute settlement system, involving some type of international judicial action.[1] The EU's position and role before international jurisdictions do not in principle differ from those of a State acting under international law, and do not require particular attention in this book.[2]

Secondly, however, international agreements may also produce effects in the internal legal order of the State or organization concluding such agreements. As law making through international action continues to increase, it will come as no surprise that international agreements are used in argument before domestic courts. Such use raises at least two kinds of questions. First, does the domestic court have jurisdiction to consider the agreement? Secondly, on the assumption that the reply to the first question is positive, what are the precise legal effects of the agreement in the domestic legal order? It is to those two questions that this chapter and the next respectively turn.

This chapter examines the position of international agreements under the main heads of jurisdiction of the EU's courts: in the first place the Court of Justice and the Court of First Instance, but also, in particular as regards questions of interpretation or validity of Community law, courts at the level of the Member States. The types of jurisdiction looked at are the following. First, before an agreement is concluded it may form the subject of a request for an Opinion by the ECJ as to its compatibility

---

[1] MA Gaudissart, J-V Louis, and L Van den Hende, 'Les clauses de règlement des différends dans les accords internationaux conclus par les communautés européennes', in *Arbitration and European Law* (Bruylant, 1997) 141–81.   [2] See Ch 7 for a few comments on dispute settlement in the WTO.

with the EC Treaty (Article 300(6) EC). Secondly, once an agreement is concluded and has entered into force, interpretation of its provisions may form the subject of a question for a preliminary ruling by the ECJ (Article 234 EC). Thirdly, an agreement may be relied upon to challenge the legality (or validity) of an act of an institution, in a direct action for annulment (Article 230 EC), or again in a question for a preliminary ruling (Article 234 EC). Fourthly, a party may invoke breach of the provisions of an international agreement in the context of a claim concerning the Community's non-contractual liability (Articles 235 and 288 EC). Fifthly, the Commission (or a Member State) may rely upon an agreement concluded by the Community in an enforcement action against a Member State (Article 226 EC). Those are the main types of jurisdiction, but the chapter does not end there. It goes on to consider some issues of interpretative approach as regards provisions of international agreements. It must also be noted that the Courts unfortunately have no jurisdiction over agreements concluded by the EU on the basis of Article 24 TEU.[3]

Chapter 9 will then analyse the legal effects of international law, including international agreements, in Community law. It is important however to bear in mind the interconnections between the two chapters. The separate treatment of jurisdiction and effects is merely an analytical tool, and in reality the two are indissociably linked. For example, the interpretation of the provisions of an international agreement by the Court of Justice in a preliminary ruling case cannot be separated from the legal effects which that agreement produces, for the act of interpreting does not take place in a legal vacuum but will rather serve a particular legal purpose. It is none the less appropriate first to discuss issues of jurisdiction, as prior understanding of the forms of action in which international agreements may become relevant is indispensable for a proper understanding of the effects of such agreements. Too often, as will be seen, the question of the 'direct effect' of international law is approached without full consideration of important jurisdictional issues, leading to confusion as to what direct effect does and does not entail.

Lastly, it may be noted that, underneath the terse and technical surface of the procedural issues which this chapter addresses, important aspects of the relationship between the international and the EC legal order are lurking.

Requests for an Opinion

Article 300(6) EC provides that the Council, the Commission, or a Member State may obtain the Opinion of the Court of Justice on whether an envisaged agreement is compatible with the provisions of the EC Treaty. Where the Opinion is adverse, the agreement may enter into force only in accordance with the procedure for amendment of the founding Treaties (i.e. Article 48 TEU). The ratio of the latter provision is of course that, where an agreement is incompatible with the EC Treaty,

---

[3] The draft Constitution purports to change that, as Art III–227, regarding agreements concluded by the Union, including CFSP agreements, is within the jurisdiction of the Court of Justice.

following the procedure for amendment cures any such incompatibility. Article 300(6) also clarifies that the Court's Opinions are binding on the institutions, which is not immediately apparent from the ordinary meaning of the term 'opinion'.[4]

The procedure was not available to the European Parliament, in spite of its important role in the conclusion of some types of international agreements, but the Treaty of Nice rectified this lacuna. Private parties are incapable of requesting an Opinion, which is understandable from the perspective that they are not directly involved in the negotiation of agreements. Also, private requests for an Opinion could interfere with the actual negotiation process.[5]

Already in its first Opinion the Court identified the general purpose of the procedure. *Opinion 1/75* concerned a draft 'Understanding on a Local Cost Standard', drawn up within the OECD.[6] The Commission asked whether the Community had competence to conclude this Understanding, and whether its competence was exclusive. In a section on the admissibility of the request, the Court stated that the compatibility of an agreement with the provisions of the Treaty had to be assessed in the light of all the rules of the Treaty, i.e. both those rules which determined the extent of the powers of the institutions and the substantive rules. This followed from the purpose of what is now Article 300(6) EC, which was to forestall complications which would result from legal disputes concerning the compatibility with the Treaty of international agreements binding upon the Community. In fact, the Court continued, a possible decision of the Court to the effect that such an agreement was, by reason either of its content or of the procedure adopted for its conclusion, incompatible with the provisions of the Treaty could not fail to provoke serious difficulties, not only in a Community context but also in that of international relations, and might give rise to adverse consequences for all interested parties, including third countries. For the purpose of avoiding such complications the Treaty had recourse to the exceptional procedure of a prior reference to the Court, which therefore had to be open for all questions capable of submission for judicial consideration, either by the Court or possibly by national courts, in so far as such questions gave rise to doubt as to either the substantive or formal validity of the agreement with regard to the Treaty. The Court then pointed out that the question whether the conclusion of a given agreement was within the power of the Community and whether such power had been exercised in conformity with the provisions of the Treaty was, in principle, a question which could be submitted

---

[4] See *inter alia* V Christianos, 'La compétence consultative de la Cour de justice à la lumière du Traité sur l'Union européenne' (1994) 374 RMCUE 37; C Kaddous, *Le droit des relations extérieures dans la jurisprudence de la Cour de justice des Communautés européennes* (Helbing & Lichtenhahn 1998) 112–25; R Plender, 'The European Court's Pre-Emptive Jurisdiction: Opinions under Article 300(6) EC', in D O'Keeffe and A Bavasso (eds), *Judicial Review in European Union Law—Liber Amicorum in Honour of Lord Slynn of Hadley* (Kluwer Law International, 2000), i, 203–20.

[5] Plender (n 4 above), 219 none the less pleads for allowing private parties who are directly and individually concerned to seise the Court. It is not however easy to see which type of international agreement would be of direct and individual concern.

[6] *Opinion 1/75 re Local Cost Standard* [1975] ECR 1355; see Ch 2.

to the Court, either directly, under what are now Articles 226 and 230 EC, or in accordance with the preliminary rulings procedure. It therefore had to be admitted that the matter could be referred to the Court in a request for an Opinion.[7]

This is a clear ruling on the rationale and scope of Opinions. The complications to which the Court alludes are not difficult to understand. Once an agreement is concluded under international law, a contracting party cannot invoke the unlawfulness of that agreement under its municipal law, except under the restrictive conditions of Article 46 VCLT.[8] Where the act of concluding an agreement is annulled for violation of municipal law, the contracting party is faced with the awkward position of continuing to be bound under international law. It is then, one presumes, obliged to terminate or renegotiate the agreement, a position clearly to be avoided. An Opinion may thus, in case of doubts, clarify (in)compatibility and thereby prevent such difficulties. By taking this approach in *Opinion 1/75* the Court also decided that it indeed has jurisdiction to rule on the legality, under Community law, of the conclusion of an international agreement (see also below on actions for annulment and questions of validity).

In *Opinion 1/75* the Court also clarified that the term 'agreement' in (current) Article 300 EC has to be broadly interpreted as including 'any undertaking entered into by entities subject to international law which has binding force, whatever its legal designation'.[9] Such a broad interpretation corresponds to the general purpose of the Opinion procedure: the above complications may arise in connection to any type of international law commitment.[10]

It follows from the general purpose of the procedure that an Opinion is appropriate only where an agreement is 'envisaged', and is not yet concluded. In subsequent cases, the Court looked at the two outer boundaries of the notion of an envisaged agreement. Which are the conditions for there to be an agreement which is genuinely envisaged, so that the Court does not look into a mere flight of fancy of an institution or a Member State? And at what point is the agreement no longer merely envisaged, but rather definitive, such that the procedure may no longer serve its purpose?

The first question came up in *Opinion 2/94*. That case concerned EC accession to the ECHR, which has been a contentious issue for decades. For a long time there was no consensus among Member States that such accession is required or appropriate for strengthening Community fundamental rights protection. None the less, in late

---

[7] Ibid, 1360–1. On competence and legal basis, see also *Opinion 2/00 re Cartagena Protocol on Biosafety* [2001] ECR I–9713, paras 1–19.

[8] Art 46 provides:

'1. A State may not invoke the fact that its consent to be bound by a treaty has been expressed in violation of a provision of its internal law regarding competence to conclude treaties as invalidating its consent unless that violation was manifest and concerned a rule of its internal law of fundamental importance.

2. A violation is manifest if it would be objectively evident to any State conducting itself in the matter in accordance with normal practice and in good faith'.

[9] *Opinion 1/75* (n 6 above), 1360.

[10] See further Plender (n 4 above), 207, where he argues that the word agreement is wide enough to embrace undertakings expressed by the casting of votes in international organizations.

1993 the Belgian Presidency again put the issue on the agenda of the Council, and managed to persuade the Council to request the Court's Opinion on (a) whether there was competence under the EC Treaty to join the ECHR, and (b) whether accession would be compatible with the Treaty. The Council could decide to make such a request by simple majority. Before the Court, the governments of Ireland, the UK, Denmark, and Sweden submitted that the request was inadmissible, or at any rate premature. In their view, an agreement could not be said to be envisaged where the Council had not even adopted a decision in principle to open negotiations. In its reply, the Court recalled the general purpose of the procedure. It then indicated that no negotiations had been commenced, nor had the precise terms of accession been determined. In order to assess the extent to which this affected the admissibility of the request, the Court felt it necessary to distinguish the purposes of the request. As regards the question of Community competence, the Court held that it was in the interests of the Community institutions and of the States concerned, including non-member countries, to have that question clarified from the outset of negotiations and even before the main points of the agreement were negotiated. The only condition was that the purpose of the envisaged agreement be known before negotiations were commenced. That was clearly the case as regards Community accession to the ECHR, as the general purpose and subject matter of the ECHR and the institutional significance of accession for the Community were perfectly well known. The fact that the negotiations had not been commenced did not stand in the way of admissibility. As regards compatibility of the accession agreement with the Treaty, however, matters were different. Here the Court needed sufficient information regarding the arrangements by which the Community would envisage submitting to the judicial control machinery established by the ECHR. As no such information was available the Court was not in a position to give its Opinion on this aspect.[11]

It is doubtful whether the Court's reasoning is entirely convincing. Much as the purpose of the envisaged agreement was clear, so were the general institutional consequences of accession: the Community would be bound by the provisions of the ECHR, as authoritatively interpreted by the ECtHR. But this leads us into questions of substance which cannot be further considered here.

Two other cases concern the point at which the agreement is no longer 'envisaged', but has become binding. In *Opinion 1/94*, concerning the WTO Agreement, the Spanish government argued that the request was inadmissible because the agreement had already been signed, entailing an obligation on the part of the signatories to submit it for the approval of their respective authorities. The Court brushed this objection aside, pointing out that it may be called upon to state its Opinion at any time before the Community's consent to be bound by an agreement is finally expressed (thereby referring to conclusion of the agreement by the Council). Unless and until that consent is given, the agreement remains an envisaged agreement.[12]

---

[11] *Opinion 2/94 re Accession to the ECHR* [1996] ECR I–1759, paras 1–22.
[12] *Opinion 1/94 re WTO Agreement* [1994] ECR I–5267, paras 10–12.

Whilst the Court delivered *Opinion 1/94* in time for the Council to be able to conclude, and for the Member States to be able to ratify, the WTO Agreement before 1 January 1995,[13] it did not manage to do the same with respect to *Opinion 3/94*. That case is part of the bananas saga.[14] At some point in the unfolding saga, only a couple of weeks before the signing of the WTO Agreement, the Commission negotiated a 'framework agreement' on imports of bananas with a number of Latin American countries, and then made the substance of that agreement part of the Community's GATT tariff schedules, which are in turn an integral part of the WTO Agreement. Disagreeing with that course of action, Germany requested the Court's Opinion on the compatibility of the framework agreement, as incorporated in the WTO Agreement, with the EC Treaty. It made the request in July 1994, three months after the signature of the WTO Agreement. The Court managed to produce its Opinion only in December 1995, one year after the Council concluded the WTO Agreement.

In light of that state of affairs, the Court addressed the question whether, for it to be able to deliver an Opinion, it is sufficient that the agreement be envisaged when the request is lodged, or whether it must still be so when the Court delivers the Opinion. The Court considered the text and purpose of (current) Article 300(6) EC. At the textual level, the Court drew attention to the fact that, where the Court's Opinion was adverse, the agreement could enter into force only in accordance with the procedure for amendment of the Treaties. It would therefore be contrary to the internal logic of the relevant Treaty provision to accept that it was appropriate for the Court to rule on the compatibility of an agreement which had already been concluded, since a negative Opinion would not have the prescribed legal effect. The purpose of the procedure confirmed this: the preventive intent of an Opinion could no longer be achieved if the Court ruled on an agreement which had already been concluded. Nor was the Court convinced that considerations of judicial protection altered that conclusion. Requests for an Opinion did not aim to protect the interests and rights of the Member State or the institution which had made the request. In any event, that State or institution could bring an action for annulment of the Council's decision to conclude the agreement and could in that context apply for interim relief. The Court's conclusion was that the request for an Opinion had become devoid of purpose, and that there was accordingly no need to respond.[15]

The Court's reasoning is surely correct, but it does not in any way address what should be the conduct of the various institutions and, where applicable, Member States, when a request for an Opinion is made and the Court may not be able to deal with it before the agreement is concluded.[16] Is the Council required to await

---

[13] Council Decision 94/800 concerning the conclusion on behalf of the European Community, as regards matters within its competence, of the agreements reached in the Uruguay Round multilateral negotiations (1986–1994) [1994] OJ L336/1.   [14] See Ch 10 for an account.

[15] *Opinion 3/94 re Framework Agreement on Bananas* [1995] ECR I–4577.

[16] See also Plender (n 4 above) 213–15; I Macleod, ID Hendry, and S Hyett, *The External Relations of the European Communities* (OUP, 1996) 113.

the Court's Opinion before concluding the agreement? If so, does it then not risk becoming the hostage of actors which are opposed to the agreement and which make a request for dilatory purposes? Should not the Court be more proactive in ensuring that Opinions are delivered before the agreement is concluded, particularly in those cases where there is urgency? Questions and problems of this kind can only be resolved through a concerted effort by all the actors involved, which, unfortunately, was lacking in the case of *Opinion 3/94*. However, there has been only one such episode so far, and one may hope that there will be no sequel.

A major part of the Court's Opinions concerns questions of external competence, rather than questions of substantive compatibility.[17] By assuming this type of jurisdiction, the Court significantly contributed to shaping the legal principles governing the Community's external action. There can be little doubt that there would have been fewer opportunities to do so had the procedure not existed. It is reasonable conjecture to assume that the Commission, for example, would have found it much harder to question, in law, the scope and the nature of the Community's various external powers if it had been obliged to proceed by way of actions for the annulment of Council decisions whereby agreements were concluded. Such actions challenge definitive agreements, and give rise to the political and legal complications referred to above. The Opinion procedure has in effect amounted to some type of coalition between the Commission and the Court for strengthening the legal dimension of the Community's external relations, as is also clear from previous chapters. The Court's eagerness to rule on questions of competence in Opinions is illustrated by *Opinion 2/91*, concerning ILO Convention No 170. There the objection was that no Community agreement was envisaged, since the EC is not a member of the ILO and since only members may ratify ILO conventions. The Court retorted that the request for an Opinion did not concern the Community's capacity on the international plane but related to the scope of the Community's competence under Community law.[18] It is doubtful, however, whether this approach is still in line with the general purpose of the procedure, which is to avoid complications arising from challenges to the lawfulness of a concluded agreement: the ILO Convention could never be a Community agreement.[19]

The Commission and the Court have certainly not always agreed on the precise outcome, but they have together injected a strong dose of legality into the Community's external policies. How strong the effects of that dose on the Community's practice have been is open to debate.

---

[17] See A Dashwood, Annotation Opinion 2/00 (2002) 39 CMLRev 366 for a list of competence issues.   [18] *Opinion 2/91 re ILO Convention No 170* [1993] ECR I–1061, paras 1–5.
[19] See also *Opinion 2/92 re Third Revised Decision of the OECD on national treatment* [1995] ECR I–521, paras 9–14 and *Opinion 2/00* (n 7 above), paras 1–9, both as regards the issue of legal basis, where again the Court adopted a broad approach towards its jurisdiction. Plender (n 4 above) 212 defends the approach.

Preliminary rulings on questions of interpretation

General

The procedure of Article 300(6) EC is confined to envisaged agreements. Once concluded, an agreement may form the object of a reference under Article 234 EC. Such a reference may concern the validity of the agreement, in which case the issues are similar to those arising in the context of actions for annulment. The next section examines such challenges to the lawfulness of an agreement. However, most references for a preliminary ruling involving an international agreement concluded by the Community are concerned with the interpretation of such an agreement. It is obvious that the reference to the Court of Justice, by a court or tribunal in a Member State, of questions of interpretation of an agreement is useful only if (a) the Court has jurisdiction to interpret and (b) the referring court may or must give effect to the provisions of the agreement in the case before it. The effects of an agreement are analysed in the following chapter. This section examines the Court's jurisdiction to interpret.[20] As will be shown, the Court readily accepted that it has such jurisdiction, and even extended it to acts adopted under an agreement. The most difficult issue concerns mixed agreements: what is the scope of the Court's jurisdiction over provisions in an agreement concluded by both the Community and its Member States?

The first reference which came to the Court as regards an agreement was *Haegeman*. The Haegeman company imported wines from Greece into Belgium. At the time Greece was not yet a Member State, but was linked to the Community through an association agreement (the Athens Agreement). Haegeman had to pay a countervailing charge on the wines it imported, and claimed that the charge was not in conformity with the association agreement. The Tribunal de Première Instance of Brussels referred a question of interpretation of the agreement's provisions (as well as a question of validity of a regulation, in light of the agreement) to the Court of Justice. The latter did not agree with Haegeman's submissions, but it did accept jurisdiction. It referred to the first paragraph of (current) Article 234 EC, according to which 'the Court shall have jurisdiction to give preliminary rulings concerning . . . the interpretation of acts of the institutions of the Community'. As the Athens Agreement was concluded by the Council it was, in so far as concerned the Community, an act of one of the institutions. The Court added that the provisions of the agreement, from the coming into force thereof, formed an integral part of Community law. Thus, within the framework of Community law, the Court had jurisdiction to give preliminary rulings concerning the interpretation of the agreement.[21]

---

[20] See also Kaddous (n 4 above), 70–86.
[21] Case 181/73 *Haegeman v. Belgium* [1974] ECR 449, paras 2–6.

Since *Haegeman* there have been many more cases in which provisions of agreements concluded by the Community came up for interpretation, and the Court has never hesitated to reply to them (with qualifications, however, in the case of mixed agreements: see below). None the less, the assumption of jurisdiction is criticized. Hartley argues that there is a distinction between an agreement and the decision of conclusion, and that the Court has jurisdiction to interpret the latter, which is properly an act of an institution, but not the former, which is an act of the Community as a whole, and not of an institution of the Community.[22] That argument is not persuasive. It is artificial not to regard an international agreement as an act of the institutions of the Community, simply on the grounds that it is not unilateral. Article 234 EC does not restrict the notion of an act of an institution to unilateral acts. It is true that the agreement as such is to be distinguished from the act of conclusion, but the former is as much an act of the institutions (together with the other contracting parties) as the latter. The Court has generally, and correctly, adopted a broad interpretation of its jurisdiction to interpret Community law in the setting of the preliminary rulings procedure.[23] Its jurisdiction effectively extends to interpreting all rules of Community law. By not assuming jurisdiction over the interpretation of agreements concluded by the Community the Court would have introduced an awkward dichotomy between 'internal' and 'external' Community law, and it would have engaged in an inappropriate judicial *non liquet* as regards the Community's international action.[24]

The broad approach to jurisdiction was confirmed in cases concerning decisions of bodies set up under an agreement. *Sevince* concerned decisions of the Association Council set up to implement the Ankara Agreement establishing an association between the EEC and Turkey (a mixed agreement).[25] The Association Council comprises, on the one hand, members of the governments of the Member States, of the Council, and of the Commission and, on the other hand, members of the Turkish government. It has the power, acting unanimously, to take decisions in order to obtain the objectives laid down by the agreement. As regards free movement of workers, the Association Council had adopted two decisions containing provisions on access to employment in the Member States. Sevince was a Turkish national residing in the Netherlands who relied on those decisions against the refusal of a residence permit. The Court recalled the principle that the provisions of an agreement concluded by the Community form an integral part of the Community legal system as from the entry into force of that agreement. It then referred to a previous decision in which it had held that, since they were directly connected with the agreement to which they gave effect, the decisions of an Association Council, in the same way as the agreement itself, formed an integral part, as from their entry into

---

[22] TC Hartley, *The Foundations of European Community Law* (4th edn, OUP, 1998) 263.

[23] D Anderson and M Demetriou, *References to the European Court* (2nd edn, Sweet & Maxwell, 2002) 58.

[24] Cf I Cheyne, 'International Instruments as a Source of Community Law', in A Dashwood and C Hillion (eds), *The General Law of EC External Relations* (Sweet & Maxwell, 2000) 257–8; Kaddous (n 4 above), 72.   [25] [1964] JO 217.

force, of the Community legal system.[26] Therefore, since the Court had jurisdiction to give preliminary rulings on the agreement, in so far as it was an act adopted by one of the institutions of the Community, it also had jurisdiction to give rulings on the interpretation of the decisions adopted by the authority established by the agreement and entrusted with responsibility for its implementation. That finding, the Court continued, was reinforced by the fact that the function of (current) Article 234 EC was to ensure the uniform application throughout the Community of all provisions forming part of the Community legal system and to ensure that the interpretation thereof did not vary according to the interpretation accorded to them by the various Member States.[27]

The Court's reasoning in this case followed the logic of *Haegeman* and of the Court's general approach towards its preliminary rulings jurisdiction. Perhaps the most remarkable aspect of the decision is that it concerned a mixed agreement, and that the Court made no effort to examine whether the decisions of the Association Council, on which the Member States are also represented as such and which concerned access to employment, came within the scope of the Community's powers or of those of the Member States. The Court had however previously decided, in *Demirel*, that the provisions of the Ankara Agreement on movement of workers came within the Community's powers,[28] and it may therefore have assumed that those powers extended to the decisions in issue.

Deutsche Shell extended interpretative jurisdiction to non-binding recommendations made under an agreement. The case concerned a 'resolution' adopted by the Joint Committee set up under the 1987 Convention on a Common Transit Procedure between the EEC and the EFTA countries. The Court examined whether a non-mandatory measure, adopted on the basis of an agreement concluded by the Community, forms part of the Community legal order. Recalling *Sevince*, the Court found that the recommendation was directly linked to the convention and concerned its implementation. The recommendation therefore formed part of Community law. In line with other case law, the fact that the measure had no binding effect did not preclude the Court from ruling on its interpretation. Although the recommendations of the Joint Committee could not confer upon individuals rights which they could enforce before national courts, the latter were nevertheless obliged to take them into consideration in order to resolve disputes submitted to them, especially when they were of relevance in interpreting the provisions of the convention.[29]

That decision is perfectly in line with previous judgments. It also illustrates that interpretation may not only be sought for identifying enforceable rights for a private party: provisions of an agreement or acts adopted under an agreement may produce other types of effect. In Chapter 9 we will further explore those effects.

---

[26] Case 30/88 *Greece v. Commission* [1989] ECR 3711, para 13.
[27] Case C–192/89 *Sevince* [1990] ECR I–3461, paras 8–11.
[28] Case 12/86 *Demirel v. Stadt Schwäbisch Gmünd* [1987] ECR 3719.
[29] Case C–188/91 *Deutsche Shell v. Hauptzollamt Hamburg-Harburg* [1993] ECR I–363, paras 14–18.
See also Case C–162/97 *Nilsson and Others* [1998] ECR I–7477, para 49.

Mixed agreements—first developments

The most complex questions concerning the Court's jurisdiction to interpret provisions of an agreement arise as regards mixed agreements.[30] In principle, a mixed agreement does not wholly come within the Community's competence. One of the difficulties, however, is that the division of competence between the Community and the Member States may not be clarified in either the agreement or the decision to conclude it. That is precisely one of the advantages of mixed agreements, as it avoids the often difficult, disputed, and therefore tortuous delineation of powers. None the less, intuitively at least it would seem logical to assume that the Court's interpretative jurisdiction is limited to the provisions of a mixed agreement which are covered by Community competence.[31] Is the Court to determine then, in each reference involving a mixed agreement, whether the provisions forming the object of questions of interpretation come within Community competence?

The foundational *Haegeman* judgment itself concerned a mixed agreement, but the Court did not consider the issue.[32] In *Demirel*, a case concerning the provisions on movement of workers in the Ankara Agreement, the German government argued that those provisions did not come within Community competence, and that the Court therefore did not have jurisdiction. The Court, however, disagreed with the German competence analysis, and stated that the question whether it had jurisdiction to rule on the interpretation of a provision in a mixed agreement containing a commitment which only the Member States could enter into in the sphere of their own powers did not arise.[33] It is indicative, though, that the Court mentioned the issue as a question rather than simply confirming that its interpretative jurisdiction is coextensive with Community competence.

For a long time the Court managed to steer clear of the jurisdiction question. As indicated, *Sevince* also concerned a mixed agreement, but the Court did not mention that aspect.[34] In the later *Kus* case, which was also on the decisions of the EC–Turkey Association Council on movement of workers, the German government attempted to persuade the Court to reverse *Sevince*, by arguing *inter alia* that the decisions of the Association Council dealt with matters coming within the competence of the Member States and thus were not acts of a Community institution.

---

[30] See Ch 7; P Koutrakos, 'The Interpretation of Mixed Agreements under the Preliminary Reference Procedure', (2002) 7 EFA 25–52; A Dashwood, 'Preliminary Rulings on the Interpretation of Mixed Agreements', in O'Keeffe and Bavasso (eds) (n 4 above), 167–75.

[31] E.g. HG Schermers, 'The Internal Effect of Community Treaty-making', in HG Schermers and D O'Keeffe (eds), *Essays in European Law and Integration* (Kluwer, 1982) 174–5; E Stein, 'External Relations of the European Community: Structure and Process', in *Collected Courses of the Academy of European Law (1990)—Community Law*, Vol I, Book 1 (Martinus Nijhoff, 1991) 165; L Hancher, 'Constitutionalism, the Community Court and International Law' [1994] NYIL 284–5; CWA Timmermans, 'The Implementation of the Uruguay Round by the EC', in JHJ Bourgeois, F Berrod, and E Gippini Fournier (eds), *The Uruguay Round Results—A European Lawyers' Perspective* (European Interuniversity Press, 1995) 507; Macleod, Hendry, and Hyett (n 16 above), 157.   [32] *Haegeman* (n 21 above).

[33] *Demirel* (n 28 above), paras 6–12.   [34] *Sevince* (n 27 above).

The Court, however, saw no reason to depart from *Sevince*, and did not give a material reply to the German arguments on competence.[35]

Mixed agreements—case law on TRIPs

The jurisdiction question came squarely before the Court in *Hermès*, which concerned provisions of the TRIPs Agreement.[36] TRIPs is a broad agreement on intellectual property protection which is part of the package of trade agreements managed by the WTO (and is legally part of the overall WTO Agreement). The question of the Court's jurisdiction over trade agreements coming under the WTO umbrella is of great significance, for essentially two reasons. First, those agreements cover a wide range of areas and contain many significant provisions for the conduct of international trade and for international economic relations. Depending on the effects which courts are willing to give to the agreements, those provisions could easily be regularly used in court proceedings. Secondly, as is well known and will be analysed in the next chapter, the Court denies the provisions of the WTO Agreement direct effect in Community law. The lack of direct effect seriously restrains the scope for application of the WTO Agreement at the instance, for example, of private parties to a dispute before a national court. It is here that the jurisdiction point becomes significant. In so far as the Court of Justice declines jurisdiction to interpret parts of the WTO Agreement, national courts might be inclined to plot their own course on the effects of the agreement, rather than follow the Court's ruling on the lack of direct effect. One need only think of the controversy in some Member States over the Community's banana import regime, and its incompatibility with WTO law, to realize that such developments are not inconceivable.

The case of the WTO Agreement is also significant because it illustrates the difficulties associated with taking the Community's competence as the criterion for the Court's jurisdiction. The WTO Agreement covers areas where Community and national competence appear particularly entangled, as is demonstrated by the complexity of *Opinion 1/94*.[37] If competence is the criterion for jurisdiction, the latter will be the hostage of the complexity of the former.

The facts of *Hermès* were as follows. Article 50 TRIPs concerns the ordering of provisional measures by judicial authorities to prevent certain infringements of intellectual property rights. The Hermès company is the proprietor of the name 'Hermès' and the name and device 'Hermès' as trade marks in the Benelux countries. Hermès applies those trade marks to *inter alia* neckties which it markets in the Netherlands. In the course of 1995 Hermès took the view that the company FHT

---

[35] Case C–237/91 *Kus v. Landeshaupstadt Wiesbaden* [1992] ECR I–6781, para 9; Darmon AG referred to *Demirel*: see paras 17–18 of his Opinion.
[36] Case C–53/96 *Hermès International v. FHT* [1998] ECR I–3603.
[37] *Opinion 1/94* (n 12 above); see Chs 2 and 3.

Marketing Choice BV was marketing copies of its ties. It applied to the President of the Amsterdam District Court for an interim order requiring FHT to cease infringement of its copyright and trade mark. The order was granted, but further issues arose regarding the right to seek revocation of that order and regarding the period within which Hermès should initiate proceedings on the merits of the case. Those issues turned on the interpretation of Article 50 TRIPs, and the President of the District Court referred a question concerning that interpretation to the Court of Justice. The Netherlands, French, and UK governments argued before the Court that it had no jurisdiction to reply to the question. In support, they referred to paragraph 104 of *Opinion 1/94*,[38] in which the Court held that the provisions of TRIPs on measures to secure effective protection of intellectual property rights fell essentially within the competence of the Member States, and not that of the Community. Thus, Article 50 TRIPs did not fall within the scope of application of Community law and the Court had no jurisdiction to interpret that provision.[39] The Commission, by contrast, argued that there was no necessarily absolute parallelism between the Community's competence to conclude agreements and the Court's interpretative jurisdiction. A mixed agreement was a single agreement whose interpretation and application had to be uniform, and the WTO agreements formed a whole that required interpretation based on the same criteria, avoiding the risk of diverging interpretations by the Court and the national courts on questions of major importance, such as direct effect.[40]

In a long and powerfully argued Opinion, Tesauro AG disagreed with that argument and proposed that the Court reply to the question of interpretation. In essence, the Advocate General considered that the principle that the Court had jurisdiction to interpret only the provisions that come within the Community's competence was only superficially clear and simple, but in fact proved to be fraught with problems. Provisions of one and the same agreement could be interconnected, and a given 'national' interpretation could affect the application of 'Community' provisions and/or the functioning of the system as a whole. The requirement of uniformity in interpretation and application could therefore quite properly be regarded as fundamental. The Advocate General also drew attention to the international responsibility of the Community, which extended to all of the WTO agreements. In his view, this meant that the Court of Justice had jurisdiction to ensure uniformity in interpretation and application throughout the Community and to protect the Community's interest in not being obliged to assume responsibility for infringements committed by one or more Member States. As a third point, the Advocate General referred to the duty of co-operation and the requirement of unity in the international representation of the Community, which extended to the negotiation, conclusion, and implementation of the commitments entered into. From that perspective it had to be recognized that the absence of centralized interpretation

---

[38] *Opinion 1/94* (n 12 above); see Chs 2 and 3.
[39] *Hermès International* (n 36 above), paras 22–33.
[40] Ibid, para 17 of the Opinion of Tesauro AG.

could completely undo the results achieved by the obligation to co-operate in the negotiation and conclusion of the provisions in question: the possibility could not be ruled out that, on the very points on which a consensus had been reached, the national courts might suddenly produce fifteen different interpretations, making an absolute nonsense of co-operation when it came to applying the provisions in question. Thus, interpretation by the Court could represent its contribution to the fulfilment of the duty of co-operation between institutions and Member States. Lastly, the Advocate General made a comment of a more general nature. Although the Community legal system was characterized by the simultaneous application of provisions of various origins, international, Community, and national, it nevertheless sought to function and to represent itself to the outside world as a unified system. That was, in the Advocate General's view, the inherent nature of the system which, while guaranteeing the maintenance of the realities of States and of individual interests of all kinds, also sought to achieve a unified *modus operandi*. Its steadfast adherence to that aim was lent considerable weight by the judicial review mechanism which was defined in the Treaty and relied on the simultaneous support of the Community court and the national courts.[41]

The Court largely followed the approach which Tesauro AG had advocated. It started its analysis by pointing out that the WTO Agreement was concluded by the Community and ratified by its Member States without any allocation between them of their respective obligations towards the other contracting parties. Equally, the Court continued, without there being any need to determine the extent of the obligations assumed by the Community in concluding the agreement, it had to be noted that at the time of signature of the WTO Agreement Council Regulation 40/94 on the Community trade mark had been in force.[42] The Court then identified the legal relationship between that regulation and Article 50 TRIPs. Article 99 of the regulation concerned 'provisional, including protective, measures'. The Court admitted that the measures there envisaged and the relevant procedural rules were those provided for by the domestic law of the Member State concerned for the purposes of the national trade mark. However, since the Community was a party to TRIPs and since that agreement applied to the Community trade mark, the courts referred to in Article 99 of the regulation, when called upon to apply national rules with a view to ordering provisional measures for the protection of rights arising under a Community trade mark, were required to do so, as far as possible, in the light of the wording and purpose of Article 50 TRIPs. It followed, the Court continued, that it had, in any event, jurisdiction to interpret that provision. It was immaterial that the dispute in the main proceedings concerned Benelux trade marks. First, it was solely for the national court to assess the need for a preliminary ruling and, where the question referred to it concerned a provision which it had jurisdiction to interpret, the Court of Justice was in principle bound to give a ruling. Secondly, where a provision could apply both to situations falling within the scope of national law and to

---

[41] Ibid, paras 20–21.   [42] [1994] OJ L11/1.

situations falling within the scope of Comunity law, it was clearly in the Community's interest that, in order to forestall future differences of interpretation, that provision should be interpreted uniformly, whatever the circumstances in which it was to apply. The Court therefore had jurisdiction.[43]

The Court's reasoning appears to consist of three parts. First, by referring to the absence of any allocation of obligations between the Community and its Member States, the Court suggests that, from an international law point of view, the Community is bound by all the provisions of the WTO Agreement. This is a significant point. If the international responsibility of the Community could be invoked in connection with any provision of the WTO Agreement, should this not be reflected in the scope of the Court's jurisdiction? Does it not mean that the entire WTO Agreement forms part of the body of Community law which the Court may be called upon to interpret on a reference from a national court? However, the Court does not develop the point, and it is therefore difficult to measure the precise implication of this observation.

The second part of the Court's reasoning concerns the effect of Regulation 40/94. The Court considers that, as Article 99 of that regulation deals with provisional measures in respect of Community trade marks, Article 50 TRIPs may affect the interpretation of that regulation. It is of no relevance here that Article 99 is to be applied by national courts, under national procedural rules. Therefore, the Court in any event has jurisdiction to interpret Article 50 TRIPs.

The third part of the Court's reasoning is a reply to the objection that the *Hermès* case did not concern a Community trade mark, but rather a Benelux trade mark, not covered by Regulation 40/94. Here the Court refers to some general principles concerning its jurisdiction under Article 234 EC. It is indeed solely for the national court to assess the need for a preliminary ruling, and, where it has jurisdiction, the Court is in principle bound to reply. Further, even though in the *Hermès* case Article 50 TRIPs applied to a situation falling within the scope of national rather than Community law, its interpretation by the Court could forestall future differences of interpretation. The idea seems to be that, if the Court were to decline jurisdiction, national courts might develop their own interpretation of Article 50 TRIPs, which at a later stage may prove conflicting with the interpretation given by the Court in, for example, a case concerning the Community trade mark.

The *Hermès* judgment appeared decisive as regards the Court's jurisdiction to interpret Article 50 TRIPs, no matter which intellectual property right, harmonized at Community level or not, was in issue. The Court none the less saw fit to add a layer of complexity in *Parfums Christian Dior*.[44] That case—in fact two joined references from Dutch courts—also concerned Article 50 TRIPs. One of the references was made by the Dutch Supreme Court (Hoge Raad) in a case involving wrongful copying of an industrial design, a type of intellectual property right for

[43] *Hermès International* (n 36 above), paras 24–33.
[44] Joined Cases C–300/98 and C–392/98 *Parfums Christian Dior v. Tuk Consultancy* [2000] ECR I–11307.

which there was no Community harmonization at the material time, in contrast with trade marks. The Supreme Court therefore asked whether the scope of the *Hermès* judgment, relating to the jurisdiction of the Court of Justice to interpret Article 50 TRIPs, was restricted solely to situations covered by trade-mark law.

Cosmas AG argued that there was no jurisdiction. In his view it was decisive that otherwise the Court would unduly interfere with the institutional balance between the Court and the Community's other institutions. As those institutions had competence to adopt legislation regarding intellectual property, central and uniform interpretation by the Court of applicable provisions of TRIPs, before such legislation was adopted, would establish a binding legal framework and would amount to substituting the Court's competence for that of the Community legislature.[45] With respect, it is difficult to share the Advocate General's concern. By adopting a uniform interpretation of the Community's obligations under TRIPs the Court would in no way assume the function of a legislature laying down new rules on intellectual property. In practice, the legislative institutions might indeed feel compelled to ensure that there is no conflict between newly adopted legislation and preceding case law on TRIPs. That does not however amount to the Court usurping the role of the legislature.

The Court did not follow the Advocate General's approach. It did however operate a distinction between (a) trade marks where, as regards provisional measures covered by Article 50 TRIPs, there was Community legislation in so far as the Community trade mark is concerned, but not as regards national trade marks; and (b) industrial designs, for which there was no Community legislation at all at the material time. The distinction is not immediately apparent in the section of the judgment dealing with the Court's jurisdiction, but it does appear more clearly in the section on the legal effect (direct or not) of Article 50. In the section on jurisdiction the Court first held that, as TRIPs was concluded by the Community and its Member States under joint competence, the Court had jurisdiction to define the obligations which the Community had assumed and, for that purpose, to interpret TRIPs. It then distinguished two situations, whilst referring to *Hermès*. First, the Court had jurisdiction to interpret Article 50 TRIPs in cases involving provisional measures for the protection of rights arising under Community legislation falling within the scope of TRIPs; in other words intellectual property rights harmonized by Community law. Secondly, where a provision such as Article 50 could apply both to situations falling within the scope of national law and to situations falling within that of Community law, as was the case in the field of trade marks, the Court had jurisdiction to interpret it in order to forestall future differences of interpretation. The Court then built on that rule, by referring to the obligation of close co-operation in fulfilling the commitments undertaken under joint competence, an obligation to which Tesauro AG referred in *Hermès*,[46] but which the Court itself did not mention in that judgment. Since Article 50 constituted a procedural provision which

---

[45] Ibid, paras 46–51 of the Opinion of Cosmas AG.   [46] See also Ch 7.

should be applied in the same way in every situation falling within its scope and was capable of applying both to situations covered by national law and to situations covered by Community law, the obligation of close co-operation required the judicial bodies of the Member States and the Community, for practical and legal reasons, to give it a uniform interpretation. The Court then stated that it alone, acting in co-operation with the courts and tribunals of the Member States, was in a position to ensure such uniform interpretation. The jurisdiction of the Court to interpret Article 50 TRIPs was thus not restricted solely to situations covered by trade-mark law.[47]

It is not easy to see why the Court introduced the duty of co-operation in this judgment, not having mentioned it in *Hermès*.[48] Furthermore, in the next section of the judgment, on direct effect of TRIPs, the Court distinguished between the field of trade marks, where the Community had already legislated, and industrial designs, where that was not yet the case. As regards the former, the case law regarding the effects in Community law of the WTO Agreement applied: the provisions of TRIPs did not have direct effect, but the judicial authorities of the Member States were required by virtue of Community law, when called upon to apply national rules with a view to ordering provisional measures for the protection of rights falling within such a field, to do so as far as possible in the light of the wording and purpose of Article 50 TRIPs. In other words, the duty of consistent interpretation applied,[49] even where, for example, national trade-mark law was concerned, and provisional measures were taken, on which there was no Community legislation. On the other hand, however, in a field in respect of which the Community had not yet legislated and which consequently fell within the competence of the Member States (such as *in casu* industrial designs), the protection of intellectual property rights, and measures adopted for that purpose by the judicial authorities, did not fall within the scope of Community law. Accordingly, Community law neither required nor forbade that the legal order of a Member State should accord to individuals the right to rely directly on Article 50 TRIPs or that it should oblige the courts to apply that rule of their own motion.[50] In other words, the question of legal effect of Article 50 is then left to national law, and the relevant Community law principles do not apply.

In the subsequent *Schieving-Nijstad* case Jacobs AG commented that it is not easy to understand why Community law governs the effects of Article 50 TRIPs not only where a Community trade mark is involved but also in situations concerning national trade marks.[51] One feels bound to agree, and as this book attempts to unfold the complexities of mixed agreements,[52] it must be noted that the above judgments do not contribute to simplification. The bottom line is that, in any event, the Court has jurisdiction to interpret Article 50 TRIPs. However, whether or not the referring

---

[47] *Dior* (n 44 above), paras 33–39.   [48] Koutrakos (n 30 above), 38.   [49] See Ch 7.
[50] *Dior* (n 44 above), paras 46–48.
[51] Case C–89/99 *Schieving-Nijstad v. Groeneveld* [2001] ECR I–5851, para 40 of the Opinion. In the judgment the Court simply confirmed its jurisdiction to interpret Art 50 TRIPs in the context of trade marks: see para 3.   [52] See also Ch 7.

court has to apply the Community law principles regarding the effects in Community law of the WTO Agreement depends on whether the intellectual property right in question has formed the subject of some degree of harmonization. This is liable to create differences in the effect of the Court's rulings on interpretation. In cases coming within the scope of Community law there is no direct effect, but the principle of consistent interpretation applies. In cases coming within the scope of national law, whether or not there is direct effect or consistent interpretation or any other type of effect, depends on national law. Given that the case law so far applies to only one TRIPs provision, one wonders whether the current maelstrom of jurisdiction and legal effect contributes much to an effective and workable implementation and application of WTO law at judicial level.

Review of legality

Under Article 230 EC the Court of First Instance and the Court of Justice have jurisdiction to review the legality of acts adopted by the EC institutions. Such so-called direct actions for annulment, which are available to natural and legal persons only under the restrictive conditions of Article 230, fourth paragraph, are complemented by the opportunity for national courts to refer questions of validity of acts of the institutions to the Court of Justice under Article 234 EC. This is a different procedure, but as regards the grounds for review questions of validity are treated in an identical way to review of legality in a direct action.[53] In Article 230 the Treaty lists those grounds as including lack of competence, infringement of an essential procedural requirement, infringement of the Treaty or of any rule of law relating to its application, or misuse of powers.

Agreements concluded by the Community may be relevant for cases involving review of legality in two contrasting ways. The conclusion of the agreement itself may be subject to review, and, conversely, an 'internal' act of an institution may be reviewed on grounds of violation of a Community agreement. This section looks at those types of review in turn.

Review of an agreement

As analysed above, in *Opinion 1/75* the Court identified the rationale of requests for an Opinion under (current) Article 300(6) EC as the prevention of complications which would result from legal disputes concerning the compatibility with the Treaty of international agreements binding upon the Community, thereby clarifying that, in principle, such agreements may be subject to review.[54] It took until 1994,

---

[53] M Brealey and M Hoskins, *Remedies in EC Law* (2nd edn, Sweet & Maxwell, 1998) 228.

[54] *Opinion 1/75* (n 6 above). The Court expressly mentioned Art 173 EEC (now Art 230 EC) in its judgment. For a general analysis see Kaddous (n 4 above), 40–61.

however, before there was a first challenge to a concluded agreement.[55] *France v. Commission* concerned the Agreement between the Commission and the United States regarding the application of their competition laws.[56] France objected to the Commission having concluded this agreement on its own, without involving the Council, and argued that this was contrary to the provisions of Article 300 EC.[57] As France had challenged the agreement as such, the Commission raised the question whether the action should have been directed at the Commission decision whereby it authorized its Vice-President to sign the agreement, rather than at the agreement itself.

Tesauro AG was unimpressed by the Commission's arguments. He referred to *Opinion 1/75* and to *Haegeman*[58] as authority for the view that an international agreement is as much an act of the institutions as is the decision to conclude it. He further considered that the question was merely one of form, and that, under the Community legal system which made provision for judicial review, without exception, of all the acts and practices of the institutions, of individuals and of the Member States, which affected the system itself, it was not reasonably possible to exclude review of the legality of the procedure for concluding an agreement with a non-member country. The possibility of doing so on the basis of a complaint expressly directed at the agreement as such, or at the act connected therewith, or else at an implied act, struck the Advocate General as a secondary and wholly irrelevant matter.[59]

The Court was equally unimpressed, but developed slightly different reasoning. It recalled that for an action under (current) Article 230 EC to be admissible the contested act had to be an act of an institution which produced legal effect. It then found that, as was apparent from its actual wording, the agreement in issue was intended to produce legal effects, and that, consequently, the act whereby the Commission sought to conclude the agreement had to be susceptible to an action for annulment. The Court stressed that the exercise of powers delegated to the Community institutions in international matters could not escape judicial review. It concluded that France's action had to be understood as being directed against the act whereby the Commission sought to conclude the agreement, and that the action was admissible.[60]

The Court is right in principle to exercise review of acts through which the Community concludes an agreement.[61] If agreements, on the grounds of their international law character, were outside the Court's jurisdiction, it would be impossible to uphold the rule of law in a significant segment of EC policy- and law-making. As to the specific reasoning, the Advocate General's approach is more convincing. If, in the context of questions for a preliminary ruling, the agreement itself

---

[55] Case 165/87 *Commission v. Council* [1988] ECR 5545 concerned a challenge to the Council decision concluding the International Convention on the Harmonized Commodity Description and Coding System, on the basis of incorrect legal basis. The Court dismissed the application.
[56] Case C–327/91 *France v. Commission* [1994] ECR I–3641.   [57] See Ch 6.
[58] N 21 above.   [59] *France v. Commission* (n 56 above), paras 9–11 of the Opinion of Tesauro AG.
[60] Ibid, paras 13–17 of the judgment.   [61] *Contra* Kaddous (n 4 above).

is an act of the institutions, as the Court decided in *Haegeman*, one cannot see why that should not also be the case as regards actions for annulment. The slight artificiality of having to (re)direct the action against the decision of conclusion of the agreement is then avoided. Moreover, there may be cases where the alleged illegality arises, not so much from the procedure followed for the conclusion of the agreement (as was the case in *Commission v. France*), but from substantive provisions of the agreement itself. That such provisions, too, are subject to review was borne out by the subsequent *Germany v. Council* case on the Framework Agreement on Bananas.[62] In that case the applicant and the Court maintained the *France v. Commission* approach of understanding the action as being directed against the decision to conclude the agreement. That decision concerned the conclusion of the entire WTO Agreement, as the Framework Agreement on Bananas formed part of the Community's tariff schedule for bananas. The Court found that the Framework Agreement, by creating an unjustified difference in treatment between various categories of importers of bananas, violated the general principle of non-discrimination. Accordingly, it annulled the Council decision to conclude the WTO Agreement 'to the extent that the Council thereby approved the conclusion of the Framework Agreement on Bananas . . . , in so far as that Framework Agreement exempts Category B operators from the export-licence system for which it provides'. The judgment shows that partial annulment of an agreement (formally the act concluding the agreement) is possible, much as such partial annulment is possible with respect to any other act subject to judicial review.[63] It thereby raises the question of the legal effects of annulment. Those effects are identical to the effects of annulment of 'internal' acts: the act is null and void *ab initio*, and the institutions concerned are required to take the necessary measures to comply with the judgment of the Court (Article 233 EC). Under international law, however, the agreement remains valid unless the Community is able to argue invalid consent under the law of treaties.[64] The Court of Justice has in any event no jurisdiction to annul the agreement itself as an act of international law.[65] In practice, therefore, an agreement affected by an annulment verdict by the Court will have to be renegotiated or terminated; if not, the Community will find itself in a position of conflicting Community law and international law obligations.[66]

Alternatively, the Court may limit the effects of annulment. That is what it did in *Parliament v. Council*, a case involving a challenge to Council decisions on the

---

[62] Case C–122/95 *Germany v. Council* [1998] ECR I–973; see also Ch 10.

[63] Brealey and Hoskins (n 53 above), 329.

[64] See Art 46 VCLT, cited in n 8, and Art 46(2) of the Vienna Convention on the Law of Treaties Between States and International Organizations or Between International Organizations (1986) (VCLTIO), which provides: 'An international organization may not invoke the fact that its consent to be bound by a treaty has been expressed in violation of the rules of the organization regarding competence to conclude treaties as invalidating its consent unless that violation was manifest and concerned a rule of fundamental importance'.

[65] Cf K Lenaerts and E de Smijter, 'The European Union as an Actor under International Law' (1999/2000) 19 YEL 102–4.

[66] For further discussion see Macleod, Hendry, and Hyett (n 16 above) 130–1.

conclusion of a government procurement agreement with the US and on the extension of the benefits of a Community directive to the US.[67] The Court annulled the decisions on the ground that they were adopted on the wrong legal basis, but decided to grant the Council's request to limit the effects of annulment. It observed that if the decisions were simply annulled, this would be liable adversely to affect the exercise of rights arising under them. Account also had to be taken of the fact that the agreement had already expired. In those circumstances there were important reasons of legal certainty, comparable to those which arose where certain regulations were annulled, which warranted the Court's exercising the power conferred upon it by (current) Article 231, second paragraph, EC where a regulation was annulled and indicating the effects of the decisions which had to be conserved. In the specific circumstances, all the effects had to be conserved.[68]

In *Germany v. Council* the Council also argued that the action was inadmissible because the Framework Agreement represented only one of the many agreements reached in the Uruguay Round and that its annulment would compromise the delicate balance of the reciprocal commitments and concessions negotiated in that context. The Court, however, brushed aside this objection on the ground that the Council had not given any specific indication of how annulment would render inoperative such other reciprocal commitments and concessions.[69] The Court thus showed that it is not easily impressed by arguments derived from the special nature of international relations and agreements so as to resist annulment of acts concluding agreements.

France v. Commission and *Germany v. Council* also exemplify on what grounds the act of concluding an international agreement may be challenged. Those grounds are in practice (if not in theory) limited to the Treaty itself, with the provisions on competence and procedure for the conclusion of agreements as the most likely basis for challenge, and to general principles of Community law, such as non-discrimination, proportionality, and fundamental rights. As Community legislation (regulations, directives, etc.) itself needs to conform to agreements binding on the Community, it cannot form the basis for challenging the legality of an agreement.

Review on grounds of violation of an agreement

'Internal' acts of the Community institutions may themselves be in conflict with provisions of an international agreement binding on the Community.[70] The question then arises whether the violation of an agreement can be invoked to challenge the legality or validity of such acts. That question is of far greater practical significance than the issues discussed in the previous subsection. In light of the scale of

---

[67] Case C–360/93 *Parliament v. Council* [1996] ECR I–1195.

[68] Ibid, paras 32–36. Art 231, second para, EC provides: 'In the case of a regulation, however, the Court of Justice shall, if it considers this necessary, state which of the effects of the regulation which it has declared void shall be considered as definitive'.   [69] *Germany v. Council* (n 62 above), paras 43–45.

[70] See also Kaddous (n 4 above), 62–9.

both the Community's internal legislative activity and its participation in international treaty-making, and in light of the increasing interconnectedness of those two dimensions of Community action, there is much scope for argument that provisions of Community legislation may not conform to the Community's international commitments.

It is thus no surprise that the issue came before the Court fairly early. In the 1972 *International Fruit Company* case an importer of apples questioned before a court in the Netherlands the validity of a number of Community regulations restricting such imports, arguing that the regulations violated Article XI GATT.[71] The court referred the case to the Court of Justice, its first question being 'whether the validity of measures adopted by the institutions of the Community also refers, within the meaning of (current) Article 234 EC, to their validity under international law'. The Court of Justice decided that, before the compatibility of a Community measure with a provision of international law can affect the validity of that measure, the Community must first of all be bound by that provision.[72] That condition is rather obvious, but in the case of GATT it posed some problems, because the Community had never formally signed or joined GATT. The Court none the less found, for reasons which need not be explored here,[73] that the Community was bound by the provisions of GATT. However, the Court also introduced a second condition. It stated that, before invalidity can be relied upon before a national court, the provision of international law must also be capable of conferring rights on citizens of the Community which they can invoke before the courts.[74] The Court did not indicate on what grounds it introduced this second condition, but it clearly followed the Opinion of Mayras AG. The Advocate General argued that, before regulations could be held invalid under the provisions of the law of an international agreement, which was outside the legal system of the Community, the applicants had to be able to rely on rights deriving from those provisions. In other words, he continued, those provisions had to have a *direct effect* within the Community.[75] The Advocate General referred to the principle of direct effect as it had been established by the Court's case law. He pointed out that it was applied in the relationship between Community law and national law, and considered that it also had to be applied in the relations between international law and Community law.[76] The Advocate General thus equated the conferral of rights on individuals with direct effect, but it may be noted that the Court itself did not refer to the concept of direct effect in its judgment. In all other respects the reasoning of the Advocate General and the Court were similar, as they respectively concluded, on the same grounds, that GATT was not directly applicable in the Community legal system and did not confer rights on individuals. Ever since, *International Fruit Company* has been commented upon, and has been much criticized, as the judgment which denied the provisions of GATT direct effect.

[71] Joined Cases 21 to 24/72 *International Fruit Company v. Produktschap voor Groenten en Fruit* [1972] ECR 1219.   [72] Ibid, para 7.
[73] See Ch 12.   [74] *International Fruit Company* (n 71 above), para 8.
[75] Ibid, 1234, emphasis in the original.   [76] Ibid, 1234–5.

There will be opportunity in the next chapter to analyse the concept of direct effect, its relationship with the notion of conferring rights on individuals, and the lack of direct effect of GATT and WTO law. What is of interest for the present discussion is that *International Fruit Company* concerned a reference for a preliminary ruling on the validity of Community acts, and not a direct action for annulment. Moreover, the Court appeared to have established a link between the condition that an agreement confer rights on private parties and the type of action: that condition must be fulfilled '[b]efore invalidity can be relied upon before a national court'.[77] Some commentators therefore took the view that the rights (or direct effect) condition did not apply to direct actions for annulment.[78] They reasoned that direct effect, as a principle, could only be relevant in cases before national courts where Community law is relied upon, and that the Court had never spoken of direct effect as a condition for relying on certain provisions of Community law in direct actions for annulment. Their opinion appeared vindicated by the *Nakajima* judgment.[79] That case involved a challenge to an anti-dumping regulation in which the applicant relied *inter alia* on the then GATT Anti-Dumping Code. The Council replied that the Code, like GATT, did not confer rights on individuals and that its provisions were not directly applicable within the Community. The Court considered this irrelevant. It pointed out that Nakajima was not relying on the direct effect of the Code. The applicant was in fact questioning, in an incidental manner under (current) Article 241 EC, the applicability of the basic anti-dumping regulation by invoking one of the grounds for review of legality referred to in (current) Article 230 EC, namely that of infringement of the Treaty or of any rule of law relating to its application.[80] At the time it was reasonable to read the judgment as authority for the view that direct effect or applicability, or the conferring of rights was not a precondition for relying on an agreement concluded by the Community in a direct action for annulment.[81] That suggested that there was a dichotomy between validity questions under the preliminary rulings procedure and legality review in an action for annulment.

---

[77] *International Fruit Company* (n 71 above), para 8.
[78] M Maresceau, 'The GATT in the Case Law of the European Court of Justice', in M Hilf, FG Jacobs, and E-U Petersmann, *The European Community and GATT* (Kluwer, 1986) 114–18; PJG Kapteyn, 'Quelques réflexions sur les effets des accords internationaux liant la Communauté dans l'ordre juridique communautaire', in Pérez González *et al* (eds), *Hacia un nuevo orden internacional y Europeo—Estudios en homenaje al Professor Don Manual Diez de Velasco* (Tecnos, 1993) 1014–15; Hancher (n 31 above), 280.
[79] Case C–69/89 *Nakajima v. Council* [1991] ECR I–2069. See also Case 70/87 *Fediol v. Commission* [1989] ECR 1781.
[80] *Nakajima* (n 79 above) paras 27–28. The reference to (current) Art 241 EC complicates matters a little, but is not difficult to understand. Nakajima was in fact arguing that a provision of the basic anti-dumping regulation, which had been crucial to the determination of dumping in the specific regulation it was challenging, was contrary to the Anti-Dumping Code. Under Art 241 any party may, in proceedings in which a regulation is at issue, plead the grounds specified in the second paragraph of Art 230 in order to invoke the inapplicability of that regulation. Arguably, this element had no bearing on the Court's ruling that Nakajima could effectively rely on the Anti-Dumping Code in a direct action for annulment.
[81] See e.g. the German Government's arguments in the *Bananas* case (n 82 below), see para 125 of the Opinion of Gulmann AG; J Vanhamme, *Volkenrechtelijke beginselen in het Europees recht* (Europa Law Publishing, 2001) 192.

The Court's judgment in Germany's challenge to the 1993 EC banana regime, however, showed this to be an erroneous reading of *Nakajima*.[82] Germany brought an action for the annulment of Council Regulation 404/93 on the common organization of the market in bananas,[83] arguing *inter alia* that the regulation violated a number of GATT provisions. Not only was this a direct action for annulment; it had been brought by a Member State, not by a private party, and it was therefore not unreasonable to assume that the condition of the agreement conferring rights on private parties would not apply. The assumption proved incorrect, however. The Court, following the Opinion of Gulmann AG, recalled the reasons for its earlier, settled case law that the GATT did not confer rights—reasons which will be further explored in the next chapter. It then held that the relevant features of GATT also precluded the Court from taking provisions of GATT into consideration to assess the lawfulness of a regulation in an action brought by a Member State under the first paragraph of (current) Article 230 EC. The Court made an exception, however, thereby at the same time explaining its ruling in *Nakajima*, for cases in which the Community was intending to implement a particular GATT obligation or in which the Community act expressly referred to GATT.[84] Again, that exception to the lack of direct effect of GATT is analysed in the next chapter. For the purposes of the present discussion, however, the ruling in the *Bananas* case clarified that there is no dichotomy between preliminary rulings cases on validity and direct actions for annulment, nor between the position of private parties and that of Member States. Whether or not an international agreement can be relied upon in order to challenge the legality or validity of an internal Community act depends on the direct effect (to use that concept here) of the agreement, and it does not matter (a) whether the agreement is relied upon in a direct action for annulment, (b) whether that action was brought by a private party, a Community institution, or a Member State, or (c) whether the agreement is relied upon before a national court to question the validity of a Community act.

From the perspective of a coherent approach towards the review of the legality of Community acts this seems eminently defensible.[85] When the Court determines on which grounds a Community act may be illegal, it should indeed not matter under which procedure the question of legality is posed, nor should the identity of the party posing that question matter. There are differences between, on the one hand, Community institutions and Member States, and, on the other, private parties, as regards standing before the Courts in actions for annulment (see Article 230, fourth paragraph, EC). However, once standing is granted it is hardly defensible to argue that, on the substance of what may be fully identical claims, the Court should rule differently according to the identity of the claimant.

The Court's approach is also coherent with the notion of direct effect. Without pre-empting the discussion in the next chapter, the issue of the direct effect of agreements

---

[82] Case C–280/93 *Germany v. Council* [1994] ECR I–4973; see also Ch 10.

[83] [1993] OJ L47/1.   [84] *Germany v. Council* (n 82 above), paras 105–111.

[85] Cf M Waelbroeck, 'Effect of GATT within the Legal Order of the EEC' (1974) 8 JWTL 622.

concluded by the Community concerns the relationship between the international legal order and the Community legal order. Applied to challenges to the legality/ validity of Community acts, it concerns the question whether that relationship is such that the provisions of international law may form a basis for judicially enforceable illegality. Forms of action or identities of plaintiffs are and should be irrelevant in that respect.

The judgment in *Germany v. Council* was none the less much criticized,[86] in particular as at the time, before the establishment of the WTO, the Community was not a formal GATT Contracting Party, in contrast to its Member States. The judgment effectively meant that Germany, as a GATT Contracting Party, was obliged to apply provisions of Community law on imports of bananas, provisions which GATT and later on WTO dispute settlement established to be in breach of the General Agreement, without being able to challenge the legality of those provisions, on that basis, before the Community Court.

Once the WTO Agreement had entered into force, the Court extended the above approach to that agreement, even if it advanced partially different reasons for not permitting review on the basis of violation of WTO law provisions, compared to the previous case law on GATT. In *Portugal v. Council*, again a case brought by a Member State, the Court decided that the WTO agreements are not in principle among the rules in the light of which the Court is to review the legality of measures adopted by the Community institutions.[87] It may be noted that here the Court did not speak of either direct effect or conferring rights, but simply denied WTO law the capacity to serve as a basis for the legality review of Community acts. The Court then completed the circle in *Parfums Christian Dior*, in which it was asked whether Article 50(6) TRIPs has direct effect, by stating that, for the same reasons as those which it mentioned in *Portugal v. Council*, the provisions of TRIPs, an annex to the WTO Agreement, are not such as to create rights upon which individuals may rely directly before the courts by virtue of Community law.[88] In *International Fruit Company* the Court had started its case law on GATT by denying that the provisions of GATT created rights for individuals; in *Parfums Christian Dior* it rounded off its case law on the effects of the WTO Agreement by denying that the provisions of WTO law create such rights.[89]

It is reasonable to conclude, on the basis of the above case law, that direct effect, or whichever other concept one prefers, is required if an agreement is to form the basis for review of the legality or validity of Community acts. Hitherto, this has formed a stumbling block only for GATT and WTO law, as the EU Courts have for no other agreements decided against direct effect. In light of the broad scope of WTO law, however, one should not underestimate the practical size of this obstacle.

---

[86]　MJ Hahn and G Schuster, 'Le droit des Etats membres de se prévaloir en justice d'un accord liant la Communauté' (1995) 99 RGDIP 367; U Everling, 'Will Europe Slip on Bananas? The Bananas Judgment of the Court of Justice and National Courts' (1996) 33 CMLRev 421–3; Kaddous (n 4 above), 68–9.

[87]　Case C–149/96 *Portugal v. Council* [1999] ECR I–8395, para 47.

[88]　*Dior* (n 44 above), para 44.　　　[89]　See also Ch 9.

As a last point, though, it is necessary to draw attention to the Netherlands' recent challenge to the directive on the protection of biotechnological inventions.[90] One of the arguments was that the directive violated both TRIPs and the Agreement on Technical Barriers to Trade (TBT, one of the WTO agreements), as well as the European Patent Convention and the Convention on Biological Diversity. A particular feature of the case is that Article 1(2) of the directive provides that it is without prejudice to the obligations of the Member States pursuant to international agreements, and in particular TRIPs and the Convention on Biological Diversity. As regards the European Patent Convention the Court pointed out that, as the Community was not a party to that agreement, the lawfulness of a Community instrument did not depend on conformity with it (thus applying the first condition of *International Fruit Company*). As regards TRIPs and TBT the Court first referred to *Portugal v. Council*, thus initially declining review. However, it then complicated matters in two different ways.

First, as regards the Convention on Biological Diversity the Court stated that the sort of exclusion from judicial review applicable to WTO law could not be extended to the Convention, which, unlike the WTO Agreement, was not strictly based on reciprocal and mutually advantageous arrangements. It then curiously held that, even if, as the Council had maintained, the Convention contained provisions which did not have direct effect, in the sense that they did not create rights which individuals could rely on directly before the courts, that fact did not preclude review by the courts of compliance with the obligations incumbent on the Community as a party to that agreement.[91] This paragraph is difficult to understand in the light of previous case law which, at least as regards GATT and the WTO Agreement, appeared to treat direct effect, the creation of rights, and inclusion in grounds of review as synonymous from the perspective of review of legality or validity. As the Court has it here, an agreement may, notwithstanding its incapacity to create rights, be included in the grounds for review of a Community act. Whether that approach is convincing remains to be seen.

The second complication is that the Court then stated that, in any event, the plea based on the violation of those four agreements had to be understood as being directed, not so much at a direct breach by the Community of its international obligations, as at an obligation imposed on the Member States by the directive to breach their own obligations under international law, while the directive itself claimed not to affect those obligations.[92] The Court accordingly proceeded to examine the alleged violations of those agreements, but found none.

The reasoning of the Court as to the basis for exercising this type of review, despite the lack of direct effect of WTO law and the fact that the Community is not bound by the European Patent Convention, is elliptical and leaves many questions

[90] Directive 98/44 of the European Parliament and the Council [1998] OJ L 213/13; Case C–377/98 *Netherlands v. European Parliament and Council* [2001] ECR 7079.

[91] Ibid, paras 52–54. On the last point the Court referred to Case C–162/96 *Racke* [1998] ECR I–3655; see Ch 9.   [92] Ibid, para 55.

unanswered. First, it is not clear whether the directive's providing that it is without prejudice to the obligations of Member States pursuant to international agreements is a decisive factor for the exercise of review. If it is, then it is difficult to understand: the directive could then, if it did indeed violate such agreements, be annulled for breach of its own provisions. If it is not, then it is unclear how much legal weight it carries. Secondly, particularly as regards the European Patent Convention the judgment appears to imply that Community legislation may not violate agreements to which only the Member States are party. That would be an important novel principle of Community law, which should hardly be introduced in the stealth-like fashion of this judgment.[93] Thirdly, the Court does not clarify whether this type of reasoning is specific to directives, which are, in contrast with regulations, addressed to the Member States, which need to transpose them in national law. Fourthly, neither does the Court clarify whether this type of review is available to all types of applicants, or whether only Member States which are themselves bound by the agreement allegedly violated may initiate it.

One possible reading of the judgment is indeed that the Court feels embarrassed by the incapacity of the Member States to seek judicial review on grounds of violation of agreements, particularly mixed agreements, to which they are themselves as much committed as is the Community, because the Court generally refuses such review. In other words, *Netherlands v. European Parliament and Council* may be an escape route for *Germany v. Council* and *Portugal v. Council*. Further case law is in any event needed for shedding more light on the current state of the law.

Non-contractual liability

By virtue of Articles 235 and 288, second paragraph, EC the Court of First Instance and, on appeal, the Court of Justice have jurisdiction in disputes relating to the non-contractual liability of the Community. The Treaty provision obliges the Community to make good, in accordance with the general principles common to the laws of the Member States, any damage caused by its institutions or by its servants in the performance of their duties. At first sight this type of action may seem an unlikely setting for any significant role for international agreements concluded by the Community. However, from the early stages the Court of Justice recognized that the Community may incur non-contractual liability for certain types of wrongful normative action.[94] More recently, the Court in *Bergaderm* re-examined the relevant principles. Community law confers a right to reparation where three conditions are met: the rule of law infringed must be intended to confer rights on individuals; the breach must be sufficiently serious; and there must be a direct causal link between the breach of the obligation resting on the State and the damage

---

[93]   On agreements concluded by the Member States, see also Ch 9.
[94]   See A Arnull, 'Liability for Legislative Acts under Article 215(2) EC', in T Heukels and A McDonnell, *The Action for Damages in Community Law* (Kluwer Law International, 1997) 129.

sustained by the injured parties. As to the second condition, the decisive test for finding that a breach of Community law is sufficiently serious is whether the Community institution concerned manifestly and gravely disregarded the limits on its discretion. The general or individual nature of a measure taken by an institution is not a decisive criterion for identifying the limits of the discretion enjoyed by the institution in question.[95]

International agreements may be relevant to the application of those principles.[96] In particular, breach of the provisions of an agreement binding on the Community may in principle form the basis for a claim in damages. However, in accordance with *Bergaderm* the provisions in question must be intended to confer rights. As all of the cases so far in which an action in damages was brought on the basis of violation of an agreement concerned WTO law, no claims have been successful.[97] In the *Biret* cases the Court of First Instance described the relevant principles as follows: it is clear from the case law which is now firmly established that in view of their nature and structure the WTO Agreement and its annexes do not in principle form part of the rules by which the Court of Justice and the Court of First Instance review the legality of acts adopted by Community institutions under (current) Article 230 EC, that individuals cannot rely on them before the courts, and that any infringement of them will not give rise to non-contractual liability on the part of the Community. The Court added that the purpose of the WTO agreements is to govern relations between States or regional organizations for economic integration and not to protect individuals.[98] The next chapter will further analyse the relevant concepts of direct effect and the creation of rights.

In theory, the conclusion of an international agreement may itself be an act causing damage to a private party. It is however difficult to envisage a realistic scenario in which the relevant conditions would be met, and there are no cases hitherto.

Enforcement actions

Under Article 226 EC the Commission may, after having issued a reasoned opinion, bring a Member State before the Court of Justice where it considers that that

---

[95] Case C–352/98 P *Laboratoires Pharmaceutiques Bergaderm v. Goupil* [2000] ECR I–5291.

[96] See also Kaddous (n 4 above), 108–12.

[97] Case T–18/99 *Cordis v. Commission* [2001] ECR II–913; Case T–30/99 *Bocchi Food Trade International v. Commission* [2001] ECR II–943; Case T–52/99 *T Port v. Commission* [2001] ECR II–981; Case T–2/99 *T Port v. Council* [2001] ECR II–2093; Case T–3/99 *Bananatrading v. Council* [2001] ECR II–2123; Case T–174/00 *Biret International v. Council* [2002] ECR II–17; Case T–210/00 *Etablissements Biret v. Council* [2002] ECR II–47.

[98] *Biret International* (n 97 above), paras 61–62. See however the Opinions of Alber AG in Case C–93/02 P *Biret International v. Council* and Case C–94/02 P *Etablissements Biret v. Council*, 15 May 2003, in which he argued in favour of the direct effect of decisions by the WTO Dispute Settlement Body (DSB). In its judgments the ECJ held that the CFI had made errors of law by not addressing the argument that the legal effects of the DSB decision regarding hormones called into question the lack of direct effect of WTO law and provided grounds for a review by the Community courts of the legality of the relevant EC legislation (judgments of 30 September 2003, not yet reported, paras 56–59). On the facts of the case, however, those errors turned out to be irrelevant, and the ECJ therefore upheld the CFI's judgments.

Member State has failed to fulfil an obligation under the Treaty. This power of the Commission enables it to exercise its important function of guardian of the Treaty, defined in Article 211 EC as the duty to ensure that the provisions of the Treaty and the measures taken by the institutions pursuant thereto are applied. In principle, it is also open to a Member State to bring another Member State before the Court of Justice on the same ground (Article 227 EC), but in practice the Member States, with very few exceptions, refrain from doing so.

As Article 300(7) EC provides that agreements concluded by the Community are binding on the institutions of the Community and on Member States, the Treaty contains a clear obligation for the Member States to respect such agreements in all their provisions.[99] Much as the Member States need to comply with the provisions of the founding Treaties and of Community legislation, they are required to act in conformity with Community agreements. There can therefore be no doubt that the Commission may bring an enforcement action under Article 226 EC against any Member State which fails to act in accordance with that principle, and in the first couple of cases involving pure Community agreements which it has dealt with the Court has not even bothered to express the principle, but has confined itself to examining whether the alleged non-compliance had taken place.[100] In *Commission v. Germany* on the International Dairy Arrangement, where there was some debate whether the Commission should have awaited the opinion of the (then) Article 113 Committee, the Court simply confirmed the Commission's autonomous power to bring enforcement actions. It stated that, under (current) Article 211 EC the Commission was responsible for ensuring the application of the Treaty and, accordingly, compliance with international agreements concluded by the Community which, pursuant to (current) Article 300 EC, were binding both on the Community institutions and the Member States. For the Commission to succeed in that task, it could not be hindered in the exercise of its power under (current) Article 226 EC to bring proceedings before the Court, and the initiation of such proceedings could not depend on the outcome of consultations within the Article 113 Committee. *A fortiori* it could not hinge on whether a consensus between the Member States had first been found to exist within the Committee with regard to the interpretation of the Community's commitments under international agreements.[101]

Those statements are no doubt correct in principle, and would not be remarkable were it not for the type of agreement which was in issue in *Commission v. Germany*: the International Dairy Arrangement was an agreement concluded at the end of the GATT Tokyo Round, and although a separate agreement, it was clearly part of the GATT family of agreements before the establishment of the WTO. It would therefore appear that there is no requirement of direct effect or creation of

---

[99] See in general Kaddous (n 4 above), 34–40.

[100] See e.g. Joined Cases 194 and 241/85 *Commission v. Greece* [1988] ECR 1037; Case C–228/91 *Commission v. Italy* [1993] ECR I–2701.

[101] Case C–61/94 *Commission v. Germany* [1996] ECR I–3989, para 15. See also *Opinion 1/91 re EEA Agreement* [1991] ECR I–6079, para 38.

rights, or any other form of requirement, for an agreement to qualify as the basis for an enforcement action. The position of the Member State in question is not enviable: in 1994 it found itself unable to challenge the legality of the Community banana regulation on grounds of violation of GATT,[102] and in 1996 it had to defend itself (unsuccessfully) for failing correctly to implement a GATT agreement.

The sole issue with respect to enforcement actions based on non-respect of an agreement binding on the Community appears to concern mixed agreements. Much as in the case of jurisdiction to interpret a mixed agreement (see above), various alternative approaches could be envisaged. The question has come up in a recent case, *Commission v. Ireland*, concerning Ireland's failure to adhere to the Berne Convention for the Protection of Literary and Artistic Works (Paris Act).[103] The obligation for Member States to join that convention is laid down in a protocol to the EEA Agreement, which is a mixed agreement. Before the Court Ireland accepted its failure to fulfil its obligations, but the United Kingdom, which had intervened, argued that the Court had no jurisdiction to hear the dispute as the Paris Act of the Berne Convention does not fall wholly within the Community's competence. The Court rejected that argument as inadmissible, because an intervener has no standing to raise a plea of inadmissibility not raised by the defendant, but none the less examined its jurisdiction of its own motion. The Court stated that it was necessary to examine whether the obligations devolving on Ireland came within the scope of Community law. It referred to previous case law according to which mixed agreements had the same status in Community law as pure Community agreements, in so far as they contained provisions coming within Community competence. As a consequence, the Member States, in ensuring respect for commitments arising from an agreement concluded by the Community institutions, fulfilled, within the Community system, an obligation in relation to the Community, which had assumed responsibility for the due performance of the agreement. The Court then applied those principles to the case at hand, and considered that there could be no doubt that the provisions of the Berne Convention covered an area which came in large measure within the scope of Community competence. First, the protection of literary and artistic works was to a very great extent governed by Community legislation. Secondly, the Court previously had occasion to rule, in the *Phil Collins* case,[104] that copyright and related rights fell within the scope of application of the Treaty. The Berne Convention thus created rights and obligations in areas covered by Community law, and there was therefore a Community interest in ensuring that all Contracting Parties to the EEA Agreement adhered to that convention.[105]

The Court's approach to determining Community competence over the Berne Convention is looser than its reasoning in *Opinion 1/94* on TRIPs.[106] The Court

---

[102] *Germany v. Council* (n 82 above).
[103] Case C–13/00 *Commission v. Ireland* [2002] ECR I–2943; see also Ch 7.
[104] Joined Cases C–92/92 and C–326/92 *Phil Collins and Others* [1993] ECR I–5145, para 28.
[105] *Commission v. Ireland* (n 103 above), paras 14–20.   [106] *Opinion 1/94* (n 12 above); see Ch 3.

does not establish that there is Community competence for the whole of the convention. Also, the reference to *Phil Collins* is not convincing, as that case was not concerned with the Community's lawmaking competence; it concerned the scope of application of the EC Treaty with a view to applying the principle of non-discrimination on grounds of nationality embodied in (current) Article 12 EC, which is a different question. The Court's analysis is none the less essentially correct, for it was sufficient that there was some degree of Community competence in relation to the Berne Convention for the duty to join that Convention to be considered a Community law obligation.[107]

It is lastly worth comparing *Commission v. Ireland* with the Court's jurisdiction to interpret provisions of a mixed agreement in a reference for a preliminary ruling (see above). In its case law on such jurisdiction the Court makes little or no reference to Community competence, and arguably adopts a broader approach. It is questionable whether that approach should be extended to enforcement actions. The Court may have jurisdiction to interpret Article 50 TRIPs in cases concerning national trade-mark law or national law on the protection of industrial designs, but that does not imply that the implementation and application of this provision in such cases is a Community law obligation for the Member States which could be sanctioned with an enforcement action.

Methods of interpretation

Introduction

It is clear from the preceding analysis that the EU courts may find occasion to interpret and apply provisions of international agreements binding on the Community in different contexts. Such agreements form part of Community law, and as such come within the courts' jurisdiction. They are none the less different from other segments of the EU legal order in that they are also part of international law. Thus, the courts when interpreting provisions in an agreement are interpreting what is essentially an act of international law. Indeed, it would be wrong to conclude from the fact that agreements form part of the EU legal order that they are automatically and fully assimilated to 'internal' Community law, in particular as regards methods of interpretation. The agreement, despite being integrated in the EU legal order, remains an act of international law. When concluding the agreement with the Community the other contracting parties do not of course intend to have Community law methods of interpretation extended to the agreement, unless expressly indicated. For them, the agreement is simply an act under international law, to be interpreted in accordance with recognized methods of interpretation of

---

[107] See the comments by Mischo AG on the indivisibility of the Berne Convention: as States cannot adhere to the Berne Convention in part, Community law could only require adherence to the Convention as a whole (*Commission v. Ireland* (n 103 above), paras 47–48 Opinion).

international treaties and agreements, and where the EU courts are to interpret those agreements they should follow those methods if they wish the Community law effects of the agreements to correspond with their substance, as governed by and interpreted under international law.

The above already suggests that there may be differences in the methods of interpreting, respectively, Community (EU) law and international law. It is clear that, at face value, i.e. at the level of general expressions of methods of interpretation, there are variations, at least in emphasis. The international law rules of treaty interpretation are embodied in Articles 31 and 32 VCLT, which is recognized as codifying customary law.[108] The basic principle of those provisions is that a 'treaty shall be interpreted in good faith in accordance with the ordinary meaning to be given to the terms of the treaty in their context and in the light of its object and purpose' (Article 31(1)), and both international practice[109] and commentaries[110] emphasize the central position of the ordinary meaning of terms in an agreement as the most reliable expression of the intentions of the contracting parties. In EU law, by contrast, there is a greater tendency to stress the objectives pursued by the act or provision in question, in particular (but not exclusively) as regards essential provisions of the founding treaties. This is the so-called teleological method of interpretation, and even if its importance is sometimes exaggerated, it is indisputable that it plays a significant role in the case law of the EU Courts. An example is Article 28 EC, which prohibits quantitative restrictions on imports 'and all measures having equivalent effect'. An interpretation of that provision which regards the ordinary meaning of its terms as crucial would take as a starting point whether a particular measure has effects equivalent to a quota. There is however virtually no trace of such an interpretation in the case law of the Court of Justice. Instead, the Court almost immediately adopted a broad definition of 'measures having equivalent effect', as encompassing all measures liable to hinder, directly or indirectly, actually or potentially, intra-Community trade,[111] on the ground that the fundamental objective of building a common (later internal) market required such a broad approach. It suffices to consult any overview of the case law to be quickly appraised of the plethora of state measures which, under Community law, are considered to have an effect equivalent to a quota.

The different methods of interpretation need not of themselves lead to difficulties. The EU courts are perfectly capable of applying the correct method, depending on

---

[108] See WTO Appellate Body, *United States—Standards for Reformulated and Conventional Gasoline*, WT/DS2/AB/R, adopted 20 May 1996, with further references. On the relationship between the EC and the second Vienna Convention see P Manin, 'The European Communities and the Vienna Convention on the Law of Treaties between States and International Organizations or between International Organizations' (1987) 24 CMLRev 457.

[109] Cf D McRae, 'The WTO in International Law: Tradition Continued or New Frontier?' (2000) 3 JIEL 35–6.

[110] E.g. R Jennings and A Watts (eds), *Oppenheim's International Law* (9th edn, Longman, 1992) 1271; I Brownlie, *Principles of Public International Law* (6th edn, OUP, 2003) 602; P-M Dupuy, *Droit international public* (6th edn, Dalloz, 2002) 309.

[111] Case 8/74 *Procureur du Roi v. Dassonville* [1974] ECR 837.

the act before them. The issue is none the less worth exploring further, because of the tendency to include provisions in international agreements concluded by the Community which are materially similar or even identical to provisions of EU law.[112] That tendency, which is not confined to technical issues but largely manifests itself in connection with basic principles of free movement of goods and persons, puts the respective methods of interpretation in the spotlight. To take the above example of measures having equivalent effect, how should one interpret a provision in an agreement between the Community and a third country prohibiting quantitative restrictions and measures having equivalent effect? Should one completely disregard the 'internal' Community law interpretation of that notion, or are there grounds for extending that interpretation to the agreement? Which, if any, may be those grounds? Those are taxing questions with which the EU courts have had to deal, and this section explores the courts' case law which has attempted to answer them.[113] Such an exploration may be useful, from the perspective of putting some flesh on the bones of both the Courts' jurisdiction over international agreements, and the legal effects of agreements (see the next chapter). It is also useful from the perspective of exemplifying and illustrating at least some of the contents of the Community's wide-ranging treaty-making practice, and its potential relevance for daily legal life. The analysis first focuses on the early case law of the Court of Justice. It then looks at some restatements of the relevant principles in decisions of the early 1990s. It separately analyses the approach towards the EEA Agreement, which is the strongest attempt to extend Community law principles to relations with third countries. And it concludes by looking at the most recent case law, concerned with free movement of persons rather than goods.

Early case law

In the 1979 *Bouhelier* case the Court was asked whether agreements with Greece, Spain, and Austria (all third countries at the time) prohibited certain types of export licence or certificate required under French legislation.[114] The case followed an earlier judgment by the Court in which it had held that the legislation, in so far as it applied in the context of intra-Community trade, contravened EEC Treaty provisions on the free movement of goods.[115] For various reasons the agreements in question did not apply, but the Court already emphasized that the agreements had to be considered on their own terms. Capotorti AG considered that the agreements, as instruments of commercial policy, had their own objectives, and that this obviously implied that even when they were similar in content to certain provisions of the Treaty they were not necessarily identical in meaning. The important consideration,

---

[112] In some cases the origin of the provision may lie further back, e.g. in GATT.
[113] See also Kaddous (n 4 above), 325–46.   [114] Case 225/78 *Bouhelier* [1979] ECR 3151.
[115] Case 53/76 *Procureur de la République v. Bouhelier* [1977] ECR 197.

he stated, was the context of each agreement, which had to be interpreted without regard to that of the Community Treaty.[116]

That is however easier said than done when the agreement and the Treaty are identical or very similar in wording, and the Treaty provision in question has been interpreted in a particular way. In three 1982 cases the Court was invited to extend interpretations of Treaty provisions on the free movement of goods to trade with third countries with which the Community had concluded agreements. The first case was *Polydor*, where the issue was whether the internal market doctrine of the exhaustion of intellectual property rights also applied to trade with Portugal, by virtue of the free trade agreement with that country, which contained provisions materially identical to (current) Articles 28 and 30 EC.[117] The Court started its analysis by referring to the general purpose of the agreement (which was part of a string of free-trade agreements between the Community and the then EFTA countries), i.e. to consolidate and extend the economic relations with Portugal and to ensure the harmonious development of commerce. To that end the contracting parties decided to eliminate progressively the obstacles to substantially all their trade, in accordance with Article XXIV(8) GATT on free-trade areas. The Court then described the provisions in the agreement on trade in goods, and found that they were expressed in terms which in several respects were similar to those of the (then) EEC Treaty. However, the Court went on, such similarity of terms was not a sufficient reason for transposing to the provisions of the agreement the case law on exhaustion of rights in intra-Community trade. The scope of that case law indeed had to be determined in the light of the Community's objectives and activities as defined by Articles 2 and 3 of the Treaty, which, by establishing a common market and progressively approximating the economic policies of the Member States, sought to unite national markets into a single market having the characteristics of a domestic market. Having regard to those objectives, the Court had developed its case law on exhaustion of rights. The considerations which led to that interpretation of (current) Articles 28 and 30 did not apply in the context of the relations between the Community and Portugal. It was apparent from an examination of the agreement, the Court continued, that it did not have the same purpose as the EEC Treaty, inasmuch as the latter sought to create a single market. It followed that in the context of the agreement restrictions on trade in goods could be considered to be justified on the ground of the protection of industrial and commercial property in a situation in which their justification would not be possible within the Community. Such a distinction was all the more necessary, the Court concluded, inasmuch as the instruments which the Community had at its disposal in order to achieve the uniform application of Community law and the progressive abolition of legislative disparities within the common market had no equivalent in the context

---

[116] *Bouhelier* (n 114 above), 3164.

[117] Case 270/80 *Polydor v. Harlequin Record Shops* [1982] ECR 329. Under the exhaustion of rights doctrine intellectual property rights may not be relied upon so as to restrict imports into a Member State where the product was placed on the market by the proprietor of the right or with its consent.

of the relations between the Community and Portugal. The principle of exhaustion of rights could therefore not be extended to trade with Portugal.[118]

While in *Polydor* the Court firmly established the principle that provisions in an agreement identical to provisions of 'internal' Community law should not by definition be interpreted the same way, a few months later it also made clear that there may be cases in which such identical interpretation may indeed be called for. *Pabst & Richarz* concerned the Association Agreement with Greece, Article 53(1) of which prohibited tax discrimination in terms similar to those of (current) Article 90 EC. In issue was a German system of tax relief for spirits which Pabst & Richarz claimed to be discriminatory towards imports. The Court first established that (current) Article 90 EC applied, in so far as imports from other Member States were concerned. It then pointed towards the similar wording of Article 53(1) of the agreement, and stated that that provision fulfilled, within the framework of the Association Agreement with Greece, the same function as that of (current) Article 90: it formed part of a group of provisions the purpose of which was to prepare for the entry of Greece into the Community by the establishment of a customs union, by the harmonization of agricultural policies, by the introduction of free movement for workers, and by other measures for the gradual adjustment to requirements of Community law. The Court concluded that it followed from the wording of Article 53(1) and from the objective and nature of the association agreement that it also precluded the tax relief in question, in so far as imports from Greece were discriminated against.[119]

Then came the Court's judgment in *Kupferberg*,[120] which again concerned the free-trade agreement with Portugal, not as regards the prohibition of quantitative restrictions and measures having equivalent effect, but as regards the prohibition of tax discrimination. Article 21, first paragraph, of the agreement stated, in terms which were comparable but clearly not identical to (current) Article 90 EC, that the contracting parties were to 'refrain from any measure or practice of an internal fiscal nature establishing, whether directly or indirectly, discrimination between the products of one Contracting Party and like products originating in the territory of the other Contracting Party'. Like *Pabst & Richarz* the case concerned a German system of tax on spirits and spirituous products. The first part of the first question which the *Bundesfinanzhof* (Federal Finance Court) referred to the Court of Justice was whether Article 21 had direct effect. The Court found that that was the case, on the basis of an analysis which will be looked at in the next chapter. The second part of that question was whether Article 21 contained a prohibition of discrimination in like terms to those of (current) Article 90, first paragraph, EC. Here the Court replied that, although Article 21 and (current) Article 90 EC had the same object inasmuch as they were aimed at the elimination of tax discrimination, both provisions, which were moreover worded differently, had to be considered and

---

[118] *Polydor* (n 117 above), paras 10–22.
[119] Case 17/81 *Pabst & Richarz v. Hauptzollamt Oldenburg* [1982] ECR 1331, paras 25–28.
[120] Case 104/81 *Hauptzollamt Mainz v. Kupferberg* [1982] ECR 3641.

interpreted in their own context. The Court then referred to its statements in *Polydor* on the different objectives of the Treaty and the agreement. It followed that the interpretations given to (current) Article 90 of the Treaty could not be applied by way of simple analogy to the free-trade agreement. Article 21 had to be interpreted according to its terms and in the light of the objective which it pursued in the system of free trade.[121] The Court subsequently proceeded to examine the tax in issue in the light of those findings, adopting a narrow interpretation of the 'like products' concept, and holding that there was no tax discrimination where there was no like product on the market in the Member State in question.

On the basis of those three judgments it looked as though the nature of the agreement—whether it established an association preparing for accession, or whether it merely established free trade—was decisive as regards the extension of interpretations of 'internal' Community law to the provisions of an agreement. With respect to trade in goods the Association Agreement with Greece and the free-trade agreement with Portugal appeared to be treated differently, notwithstanding similar wording, on the sole basis of the difference in objectives. The former was interpreted in accordance with case law on the common market, while the latter was not. However, a further string of cases from the beginning of the 1990s made clear that no such generalization is possible.

Case law of the early 1990s

In *Legros and Others* the Court analysed the system of '*octroi de mer*' (dock dues) applicable to imports into Réunion, a French overseas department to which the free movement of goods in the Community extends (see Article 227(2) EEC, since amended). The Court had little problem establishing that the dock dues were effectively a charge having equivalent effect to customs duties, contrary to (current) Articles 23 and 25 EC in so far as imports from other Member States were concerned. It then examined whether those dues were also in breach of Article 6 of the free-trade agreement with Sweden, which equally prohibited charges having equivalent effect. France argued that the *Polydor* principle applied, and that the Treaty interpretation should not be extended to the agreement with Sweden. This time, however, the Court did consider such an extension appropriate. It described the purpose of the free-trade agreement in the same terms as it had done in *Polydor*, referring to the objective of establishing a free-trade area in accordance with Article XXIV(8) GATT. It then stated that it followed that, in the context of the objective of eliminating obstacles to trade, elimination of customs duties was of prime importance, as was elimination of charges having equivalent effect, which, according to the Court's case law, were closely linked to customs charges *sensu stricto*. The Court concluded that the agreement would have been deprived of much of its effectiveness if the term 'charge having equivalent effect' contained in Article 6 were to be interpreted

---

[121] Ibid, paras 28–31.

as having a more limited scope than the same term appearing in the (current) EC Treaty.[122]

It thus became clear that it is not ruled out that provisions in a 'mere' free-trade agreement, identical or very similar in wording to provisions of the Treaty, are also identically interpreted. This was confirmed in two further cases. *Commission v. Italy* concerned Italian systematic health inspections on imports of fish as well as a prohibition of imports of certain kinds of fish. The Court found that the Italian measures were contrary to the provisions of (current) Articles 28 and 30 EC, and then examined whether they were also, in so far as they applied to imports of fish from Norway, in violation of the free-trade agreement with Norway. The Court established that Articles 15 and 20 of that agreement contained rules identical to those of (current) Articles 28 and 30 EC. It then simply stated that there were no grounds, in the case before it, for interpreting those rules differently from those articles of the Treaty. It accordingly extended the interpretation of the Treaty to the agreement, including the application of the principle of proportionality.[123]

Eurim-Pharm concerned parallel imports of pharmaceutical products from Austria into Germany. The German authorities required that Eurim-Pharm produce certain documents concerning the product (a medicine called Adalat R), notwithstanding the fact that the marketing of the product had previously been authorized in Germany, that the authorities were therefore in possession of those documents, and that there was no doubt that the Adalat R imported by Eurim-Pharm was genuine and identical to the Adalat R already on the market. The *De Peijper* case had clarified that, in intra-Community trade, the parallel importer of medicines is not required to produce such documents.[124] As regards imports from Austria, Eurim-Pharm relied on Articles 13 and 20 of the free-trade agreement with that country, which substantially reproduced (current) Articles 28 and 30 EC, arguing in favour of an extension of the *De Peijper* case law to trade with Austria. However, the United Kingdom and Italian governments and the Commission argued against such an extension, on the ground that the agreement made no provision either for harmonization of legislation or for administrative co-operation in the pharmaceutical sector. The Court did not accept that objection. It stated that, even on assumption that its case law on (current) Articles 28 and 30 EC could not be applied to the interpretation of Articles 13 and 20 of the agreement, it was sufficient to note that, since the German health authority already possessed all the necessary information about the medicine and there was no dispute that the imported medicine and the authorized medicine were identical, the authority had no need to secure co-operation of any kind from the Austrian authorities. In those circumstances, the Court concluded, to hold that Articles 13 and 20 of the agreement did not preclude rules of the kind at issue in the case would have deprived those articles of much of their effectiveness.[125]

---

[122] Case C–163/90 *Administration des douanes et droits indirects v. Legros and Others* [1992] ECR I–4625.
[123] Case C–228/91 *Commission v. Italy* [1993] ECR I–2701.
[124] Case 104/75 *De Peijper* [1976] ECR 613.
[125] Case C–207/91 *Eurim-Pharm v. Bundesgesundheitsamt* [1993] ECR I–3723.

In the *Eurim-Pharm* case Tesauro AG also made some interesting and convincing general statements concerning the issue of extension of interpretation. He referred to the *Polydor* and *Kupferberg* judgments, according to which the interpretation of provisions in the EEC Treaty cannot be applied by way of simple analogy to the corresponding provisions of a free-trade agreement. However, he continued, whilst that statement of principle was perfectly acceptable in itself, it had to be seen in its proper perspective and was certainly not intended to encourage or justify in general terms divergent interpretations of the Treaty and the corresponding rules in free-trade agreements to which the Community is a party. The ruling in question really constituted, in his view, no more than the application of a general principle of legal interpretation, which was also taken up in the VCLT, whereby a rule was to be interpreted having regard to the most general context in which it appeared. He concluded that, whilst it was true in principle that an interpretation given by the Court in the context of the EEC Treaty was not automatically applicable in the context of an agreement with a non-member country, it was equally true that, when faced with provisions drafted in substantially identical terms and laying down rules of fundamental importance in the context either of the EEC Treaty or of a free-trade agreement, it was still necessary to determine the specific reasons which could lead to a divergent interpretation. That, in the Advocate General's view, was the more correct reading of the *Polydor* judgment, confirmed by *Legros and Others*.[126]

A few months later, in *Metalsa*, the Court itself re-stated the relevant principles.[127] The case concerned the question whether the Court's ruling in *Drexl* could be extended to imports from Austria.[128] In that case the Court had held that national legislation which penalized offences concerning the payment of value added tax on importation more severely than those concerning the payment of value added tax on domestic sales of goods was incompatible with (current) Article 90 EC, in so far as that difference was disproportionate to the dissimilarity between the two categories of offences. As Article 18 of the free-trade agreement with Austria also prohibited tax discrimination, the question was whether the same interpretation should prevail. The Court started its analysis by pointing out that, although the wording of Article 18 differed from that of the first paragraph of (current) Article 90 EC, the object of both provisions was to prohibit all direct or indirect fiscal discrimination against products of the other Contracting Party, in the first case, and of Member States, in the other. It then referred to the case law analysed above, drawing attention to the fact that in some cases it had considered an extension of interpretation appropriate, while in others it had not. The Court continued that it was clear from the case law that the extension of the interpretation of a provision in the Treaty to a comparable, similarly or even identically worded provision of an agreement concluded by the Community with a non-member country depended, *inter alia*, on the aim pursued by each provision in its particular context and that a comparison between the objectives and context of the agreement and those of the Treaty was

---

[126] Ibid, paras 15–17 of the Opinion of Tesauro AG.
[127] Case C–312/91 *Metalsa* [1993] ECR I–3751.
[128] Case 299/86 *Drexl* [1988] ECR 1213.

of considerable importance in that regard. The Court subsequently referred to the VCLT: an international treaty must not be interpreted solely by reference to the terms in which it is worded but also in the light of its objectives; Article 31 VCLT stipulated in that respect that a treaty was to be interpreted in good faith in accordance with the ordinary meaning to be given to its terms in their context and in the light of its object and purpose.[129]

Applying those principles, the Court found that the *Drexl* interpretation had been based on the far-reaching objective of establishing a single market, an objective which the free-trade agreement with Austria did not pursue. Accordingly, the interpretation could not be extended. Article 18, first paragraph, of the agreement was limited to prohibiting discrimination resulting from any measure or practice which had a direct or indirect effect on the calculation, applicability, and methods of collection of taxes on products of the other Contracting Party, but did not require that there be any comparison between the penalties imposed by Member States for tax offences occurring on importation of goods from Austria and those imposed for tax offences arising on domestic transactions or on imports from other Member States.[130]

The EEA Agreement

Metalsa was not the first case in which the Court expressly referred to the VCLT in support of its reasoning as regards interpretation of agreements. A couple of years earlier the Community had concluded the Agreement on the European Economic Area (EEA), a most ambitious attempt to extend the policies, principles, and rules of the internal market to the EFTA countries without requiring them to become members of the Community.[131] In the original negotiation every effort had been made to ensure that the extension of the internal market was complete, and that the internal market would function in exactly the same way in the whole of the EEA. To achieve this the first version of the EEA Agreement copied EEC Treaty provisions as much as possible, and provided *inter alia* for extension of the case law of the Court of Justice, as well as for the creation of an EEA Court, composed of judges from the Court of Justice and from the EFTA countries, competent to interpret the agreement. However, in light of the ambition and novelty of the agreement the Commission first requested the Opinion of the Court of Justice under (current) Article 300(6) EC on the compatibility of the EEA Agreement with the Treaty, in particular as regards the system of judicial supervision.[132] The Court issued a negative Opinion, in which it emphasized the remaining differences between the objectives of the EEC Treaty and those of the EEA Agreement, notwithstanding the strenuous attempts to create as much homogeneity as possible between those two international agreements. The Opinion is a landmark in the case law on the autonomy and fundamental characteristics of the Community legal order.[133] It need not

---

[129] *Metalsa* (n 127 above), paras 9–12.   [130] Ibid, paras 15–20.   [131] [1994] OJ L1/3.
[132] *Opinion 1/91 re EEA Agreement* [1991] ECR I–6079.   [133] See Ch 7.

be fully analysed here, but in the context of the present survey it is necessary to describe what the Court said regarding extension of interpretation.

The Court started its analysis by comparing the aims and context of the agreement with those of Community law. It again recalled the principle that identical wording does not necessarily mean identical interpretation, because under Article 31 VCLT an international treaty was to be interpreted not only on the basis of its wording, but also in the light of its objectives. The Court then compared those objectives, observing that the agreement was concerned with the application of rules on free trade and competition in economic and commercial relations between the Contracting Parties while, as far as the Community was concerned, those rules on free trade and competition had developed and formed part of the Community legal order, the objectives of which went beyond that of the agreement. It followed *inter alia* from (then) Articles 2, 8a, and 102a of the EEC Treaty that the treaty aimed to achieve economic integration leading to the establishment of an internal market and economic and monetary union. Article 1 SEA made it clear moreover that the objective of all the Community treaties was to contribute together to making concrete progress towards European unity. It followed that the EEC Treaty provisions on free movement and competition, far from being an end in themselves, were only means for attaining those objectives. The Court also considered that the context in which those objectives were situated differed: the EEA Agreement merely created rights and obligations between the contracting parties, and involved no transfer of sovereign rights to the intergovernmental institutions which it set up, whereas the EEC Treaty constituted the constitutional charter of a Community based on the rule of law and established a new legal order, including transfer of sovereign rights, primacy, and direct effect. The Court concluded that homogeneity of the rules of law throughout the EEA was not secured by the fact that the provisions of Community law and those of the corresponding provisions of the agreement were identical in their content or wording.[134]

After the Court's negative Opinion the agreement was renegotiated as regards the system of judicial supervision. The most significant modification was the replacement of the EEA Court with an EFTA Court, composed only of judges from the EFTA countries and with more limited jurisdiction. The Court then issued a positive Opinion which need not be further discussed here.[135] The revised and definitive version of the EEA Agreement continues to aim at as much homogeneity as possible, notwithstanding the Court's scepticism. To that effect it *inter alia* contains a provision on interpretation:

Without prejudice to future developments of case-law, the provisions of this Agreement, in so far as they are identical in substance to corresponding rules of the [EEC Treaty and the ECSC Treaty] and to acts adopted in application of these two Treaties, shall, in their implementation and application, be interpreted in conformity with the relevant rulings of the Court of Justice of the [EC] given prior to the date of signature of the agreement.

---

[134] *Opinion 1/91* (n 132 above), paras 13–22.
[135] *Opinion 1/92 re EEA Agreement* [1992] ECR I–2821.

The reason for the limitation to prior case law is that the EFTA countries did not wish to commit themselves to future, unforeseeable developments in the case law of the EU courts on which they are not represented.

The EEA Agreement has lost much of its practical significance by reason of the accessions of Austria, Finland, and Sweden, and is now confined to trade and economic relations with Norway, Iceland, and Liechtenstein. There is none the less a significant amount of EU courts' case law which interprets the agreement. Despite the Court of Justice's emphasis on the differences in objectives, nearly all of the case law readily accepts that Community law interpretations of provisions in the Treaty or in legislation are to be extended to the whole of the EEA, thereby applying Article 6 of the agreement.[136]

An interesting application is *Opel Austria*.[137] In that case the Court of First Instance examined the issue of identical interpretation. The case concerned the legality of a Council regulation withdrawing tariff concessions for imports of certain types of car gearboxes from Austria. The regulation had been adopted just a few days before the EEA Agreement entered into force, but the Court of First Instance none the less decided, on grounds which will be discussed in the next chapter, to examine its compatibility with that agreement. Opel Austria argued that the regulation was in breach of Article 10 EEA, which prohibited customs duties and charges having equivalent effect. The Council contended, however, that this provision should not be interpreted in the same way as the corresponding provisions of the EC Treaty (current Articles 23 and 25), because there were major differences between the EC Treaty and the EEA Agreement. The Court of First Instance did not accept that argument. It engaged in an extensive examination of the objectives and content of the EEA Agreement, emphasizing the high degree of integration aimed at, with objectives exceeding those of a mere free-trade agreement, and with strong mechanisms to ensure homogeneity. The Court did not feel that *Opinion 1/91* was particularly relevant: in that case the Court of Justice was considering the judicial system contemplated by the EEA Agreement for the purpose of ascertaining whether that system might jeopardize the autonomy of the Community legal order in pursuing its own objectives; and not a specific case in which it was necessary to determine whether a provision of the EEA Agreement identical in substance to a provision of Community law had to be interpreted in conformity with the rulings of the Court of Justice and the Court of First Instance. The conclusion was that Article 6 EEA, on extension of interpretation, fully applied, and that Article 10 EEA had to be interpreted in the same way as (current) Articles 23 and 25 EC.[138]

The Court of First Instance's reasoning is convincing. The differences in objectives on which the Court based its analysis in *Opinion 1/91* were no doubt relevant to the general issue of the autonomy of the Community legal order and of its judicial system. They are however much less relevant to the interpretation of specific

---

[136] e.g. Case C–355/96 *Silhouette International Schmied v. Hartlauer Handelsgesellschaft* [1998] ECR I–4799.   [137] Case T–115/94 *Opel Austria v. Council* [1997] ECR II–39.
[138] Ibid, paras 103–111.

provisions, and in light of Article 6 EEA as well as other provisions emphasizing homogeneity there would have to be strong reasons for not extending Community law interpretations.

Recent case law

All of the case law so far discussed concerns trade in goods.[139] There are however also judgments relating to the movement or treatment of persons under provisions of an agreement which are similar or identical to EC Treaty provisions on free movement of persons. There is a long line of cases on the association agreement with Turkey, but most of those are less relevant because they turn on the interpretation of specific provisions of decisions adopted by the Association Council, provisions which do not copy 'internal' EC law provisions. One decision is worth mentioning, though. In *Bozkurt* the Court was asked whether a Turkish international lorry driver employed by a Netherlands company was a worker for the purpose of applying the association agreement and its implementing decisions. Mr Bozkurt relied on the Court's judgment in *Lopes da Veiga*, which concerned the free movement of workers within the Community.[140] The Court agreed to the extension on the basis that Article 12 of the agreement provided that the Contracting Parties agreed to be guided by (current) Articles 39 to 41 EC for the purpose of progressively securing freedom of movement for workers between them. As the relevant decision of the Association Council was aimed at going one stage further in that respect, the Court considered it essential to transpose, so far as was possible, the principles enshrined in those Treaty provisions to Turkish workers who enjoyed the rights conferred by the decision.[141]

Recently, the Court decided five cases on the interpretation and effect of provisions on free movement of persons in the Europe Agreements with Central and East European countries. The judgments again illustrate the nuanced approach by the Court, under which the reply to the question of extension of interpretation depends on the objectives of the agreements, the wording of the provisions in their context, and the facts of cases.

In three judgments of the same date the Court refused to extend the interpretation of (current) Article 43 EC to similarly worded provisions in the Europe Agreements with the Czech Republic, Bulgaria, and Poland. The three cases concerned nationals of those countries who had fraudulently obtained leave to enter the United Kingdom, and subsequently claimed the right to establish themselves there. The Court referred to the difference in objectives: the Europe Agreements were designed simply to create an appropriate framework for gradual integration into the Community, with a view to possible accession, whereas the purpose of the

---

[139] See also Joined Cases C–114/95 and C–115/95 *Texaco and Olieselskabet Danmark* [1997] ECR I–4263, paras 27–33.   [140] Case 9/88 *Lopes da Veiga v. Staatssecretaris van Justitie* [1989] ECR 2989.
[141] Case C–434/93 *Bozkurt* [1995] ECR I–1475, paras 15–20.

Treaty was to create an internal market. It also referred to the wording of the Europe Agreements, which each contained a further provision clarifying that the rights of entry and residence conferred as corollaries of the right of establishment were not absolute privileges, inasmuch as their exercise could, where appropriate, be limited by the rules of the host Member State concerning entry, stay, and establishment of nationals of the countries concerned.[142]

In two other cases, by contrast, the Court considered an extension of interpretation appropriate. *Jany and Others* concerned Polish and Czech prostitutes active in the Netherlands. One of the questions was whether their activity came within the scope of the concept of 'economic activities as self-employed persons' to which freedom of establishment under the relevant Europe Agreements extended. The Court referred to the similar concept of 'activities as self-employed persons' included in (current) Article 43 EC. It again described the objective of the Europe Agreements, but concluded that there was nothing in the context or purpose of the Europe Agreements to suggest that the parties intended to give the expression 'economic activities as self-employed persons' any meaning other than its ordinary meaning of economic activities carried on by a person outside any relationship of subordination with regard to the conditions of work or remuneration and under his own responsibility. Consequently, there was in this respect no difference in meaning between Article 43 EC and the relevant provisions of the Europe Agreements.[143]

The Court adopted a similar approach in *Pokrzeptowicz-Meyer*. That case concerned Article 37(1) of the Europe Agreement with Poland, which prohibited discrimination based on nationality as regards workers of Polish nationality legally employed in the territory of a Member State. Mrs Pokrzeptowicz-Meyer, a Polish-language assistant at the University of Bielefeld, objected to her fixed-term contract, and argued for the extension of the Court's ruling in *Spotti* to the above non-discrimination provision. In *Spotti* the Court had decided that the provisions on fixed-term contracts for foreign-language teachers violated (current) Article 39(2) EC and could therefore not be applied to nationals of other Member States.[144] The Court agreed. It followed from a comparison of the aims and context of the Europe Agreement with those of the EC Treaty that there was no ground for giving Article 37(1) a meaning different from that of (current) Article 39(2) EC as found in *Spotti*. In particular, it followed from the wording of Article 37(1) as well as from its aims that the prohibition of any kind of discrimination against Polish workers based on their nationality applied just as much to direct discrimination as to indirect discrimination which might affect their conditions of employment.[145]

---

[142] Case C–235/99 *The Queen v. Secretary of State for the Home Department, ex parte Kondova* [2001] ECR I–6427, paras 51–55; Case C–257/99 *The Queen v. Secretary of State for the Home Department, ex parte Barkoci and Malik* [2001] ECR I–6557, paras 51–55; and Case C–63/99 *The Queen v. Secretary of State for the Home Department, ex parte Gloszczuk and Gloszczuk* [2001] ECR I–6369, paras 47–52.

[143] Case C–268/99 *Aldona Malgorzata Jany and Others v. Staatssecretaris van Justitie* [2001] ECR I–8615, paras 32–38.   [144] Case C–272/92 *Spotti* [1993] ECR I–5185.

[145] Case C–162/00 *Land Nordrhein-Westfalen v. Beata Pokrzeptowicz-Meyer* [2002] ECR I–1049, paras 31–42.

The analysis in these judgments is convincing, except perhaps for the treatment of the objectives of the Europe Agreements in the *Kondova* group of cases. As the Europe Agreements prepared for accession to the EU it is difficult to envisage agreements whose objectives come closer to those of the founding Treaties. Surely this must be a strong argument for extension of interpretation as regards similarly or identically worded provisions. However, it was not so much the difference in objectives that was crucial, as the fact that the Europe Agreements expressly subjected the exercise of the right of establishment to compliance with the provisions in Member States on entry and residence. That is not the case with the EC Treaty. It was thus the difference in overall wording which justified the difference in interpretation.

Assessment

The case law on extension of interpretation of 'internal' Community law provisions to similarly or identically worded provisions in agreements binding on the Community is, on the whole, careful and convincing.[146] The Court has avoided easy generalizations, in the direction of either automatic transposition or automatic refusal. It has correctly based the interpretation of provisions in agreements on the relevant rules of customary international law. One can none the less make a few small observations, by way of footnotes to the case law.

The very starting point of similarly or identically worded provisions has some distortive effects, in particular where there are previous interpretations of 'internal' Community law which appear relevant. Notwithstanding the principle that each agreement should be interpreted on its own terms, the issue then really becomes one of extending or not extending such interpretations. That may not always be to the benefit of an independent interpretation of the agreement. One can for example argue that the Court's interpretation of the prohibition of tax discrimination in the *Kupferberg*[147] and *Metalsa*[148] cases is insufficiently considered and sophisticated; one can also argue that the application of the principle of proportionality to the free-trade agreement with Norway (*Commission v. Italy*)[149] finds little basis in the actual agreement. To some extent, therefore, the issue of extension of interpretation may be a red herring leading away from the real questions of interpretation.

As a second point, the Court's emphasis on differences in objectives between the EC Treaty and agreements concluded by the Community is arguably too strong. There is no denying such differences. However, on occasion the Court has exaggerated them; *Opinion 1/91* and the *Kondova* line of cases are instances of such exaggeration. It is also questionable whether under international law the objectives of an agreement are as vital for determining their meaning as is the case in the Court's judgments. There are in any event respected international courts and tribunals which put greater emphasis on the ordinary meaning of the terms of agreements as

---

[146] *Contra* Kaddous (n 4 above), 346.   [147] N 120 above.   [148] N 127 above.
[149] N 123 above.

opposed to aims and objectives.[150] The irony of the Court's case law is that the teleological method is often used for denying the extension of teleological interpretations of 'internal' Community law.

A last footnote is that the Court's characterization of free-trade agreements appears to play down the significance of such agreements, particularly in the setting of the GATT or the WTO. Agreements establishing a free-trade area are advanced and demanding agreements, going beyond standard GATT disciplines. It is questionable whether the Court's interpretation of those agreements has always corresponded to their importance. The case law on tax discrimination, in particular,[151] does not take into account the GATT origin of the prohibition in question (which is binding on all GATT Contracting Parties or, at present, WTO Members, and is not confined to free-trade areas). It would be worth examining whether that case law is in conformity with the interpretation of Article III(2) GATT, the source and foundation of all prohibitions of tax discrimination, including that in Article 90 EC, as developed in GATT and WTO dispute settlement. Such an examination, however, is beyond the scope of the present analysis.[152]

Conclusions

This chapter examined a variety of issues concerning the courts' jurisdiction over international agreements concluded by the Community. They cannot all be returned to in these conclusions. Instead, this concluding section offers some further reflections concerning two important problems: jurisdiction to interpret mixed agreements,[153] and the position of the Member States as regards compliance with Community agreements.

The Court, having steered clear of the question of its jurisdiction to interpret provisions in a mixed agreement, was forced in *Hermès* and *Parfums Christian Dior* to address that question as regards Article 50 TRIPs. It clearly adopted a broad approach towards its own jurisdiction, but the judgments are disappointing for failing to clarify the general rules or principles which apply. The Court has mentioned the fact that the WTO Agreement (like most other mixed agreements) was concluded without an express allocation and division of competence between the Community and its Member States, suggesting that the Community's international law obligations may cover the entire agreement. It has not however clarified the relevance of that factor for determining its jurisdiction. In *Hermès* it based its reasoning on the existence of Regulation 40/94 on the Community trade mark, whose provisions on provisional measures are subject to Article 50 TRIPs. That, together

---

[150]   Cf McRae (n 109 above).   [151]   *Kupferberg* (n 120 above) and *Metalsa* (n 127 above).

[152]   Cf M Slotboom, 'The Elimination of Discriminatory Internal Taxes in EC and WTO law' (2001) 4 JIEL 557.

[153]   See also JHJ Bourgeois, 'The European Court of Justice and the WTO: Problems and Challenges', in JHH Weiler, *The EU, the WTO and the NAFTA* (OUP, 2000) 85–8.

with the principle that it is for national courts to decide which questions to refer to the Court, was sufficient to establish jurisdiction, even if the case was concerned with a national trade mark not governed by the regulation. What the Court did not discuss, however, in either *Hermès* or *Parfums Christian Dior* is the issue of Community competence: under the principles of Community law governing implied powers one could have expected the Court to state that, as Article 50 TRIPs affects a piece of Community legislation, the *AETR* principle applies, and there is exclusive Community competence (even if Article 50 also governs national intellectual property law).[154] That would clearly have been sufficient to establish jurisdiction. In *Hermès*, however, the Court contrasts its reasoning with that of the Member States which had argued for competence as the criterion for jurisdiction. We are left in the dark as to the relevance of the competence aspect. In *Parfums Christian Dior*, then, the Court bases the extension of its jurisdiction to cases concerning intellectual property rights which are not subject to any harmonization whatsoever on the duty of co-operation between the Community institutions and the Member States, which extends to fulfilling the commitments entered into, and thus to judicial interpretation. It is not however clear why the Court did not refer to that duty in *Hermès*, declining the invitation by Tesauro AG. We thus appear to be left with four different reasons for broad jurisdiction: scope of the Community's obligations, relationship with harmonized Community law, approach towards references by national courts, and the duty of co-operation. As argued by Koutrakos, our understanding of the mechanisms of interpretation and application of mixity would be greatly enhanced by a clearer reasoning.[155]

It is submitted that the underlying principle which should govern the Court's jurisdiction over mixed agreements is whether the provisions in issue come within the scope of Community law. There are a number of different manifestations of that principle.

First, where the agreement itself, or the act of concluding it, clarifies which commitments are entered into by the Community and which are not, only the relevant provisions come within the scope of Community law. There is then clearly a part of the agreement which comes within the Court's jurisdiction, because it is a Community act, and another part which is an act of the Member States which the Court cannot interpret. Such agreements are rare, however.

Secondly, provisions of an agreement which affect other provisions of Community law, in particular Community legislation, also come within the scope of Community law and should be subject to the Court's jurisdiction. The case of Article 50 TRIPs, which affected the Community trade-mark regulation, is an example. This is not a question of Community competence, even if owing to the *AETR* principle there is exclusive Community competence where the provision of

[154] See Ch 3.
[155] Koutrakos (n 30 above), 52; see also J Helikoski, *Mixed Agreements as a Technique for Organizing the International Relations of the European Community and its Member States* (Kluwer Law International, 2001) 59–61.

an agreement affects a Community act. A special case of this second alternative is where the Court is asked to interpret a provision which affects a Community act, but the reference to the Court is made in a case where the provision affects national law, and not Community law. *Hermès* and *Parfums Christian Dior* were such instances. Here the Court has jurisdiction in principle, because the provision comes within the scope of Community law, but the case itself is *prima facie* not concerned with Community law. There may be doubts here whether it is appropriate for the Court to accept jurisdiction where the case itself does not appear to concern Community law.[156] However, the third alternative would govern such cases, and justify the Court's jurisdiction.

This third alternative takes Community competence as a criterion for the Court's jurisdiction. What if the Court is asked to interpret a provision in a mixed agreement, where the agreement does not distinguish between a Community and a non-Community part, and the provision does not affect any Community acts? Should the Court decline jurisdiction on the ground that the provision does not come within the scope of Community law? The answer must be negative, it is submitted, where the provision comes within Community competence. It is such competence which was exercised at the occasion of the conclusion of the agreement. The provisions of a mixed agreement therefore come within the scope of Community law in so far as they come within Community competence. One may connect this principle to the international law dimension. Where the Community concludes an agreement it commits itself under international law within the areas of its competence. It should therefore ensure that the relevant provisions are applied and enforced, also in relation to the Member States and national law. To take an example, let us assume that Article III:2 GATT, on national treatment of imports in matters of taxation, does not affect any Community acts. Article III:2 none the less comes within the Community's exclusive competence pursuant to Article 133 EC.[157] It follows that the Court has jurisdiction to interpret this provision in cases involving national taxation.

Is such jurisdiction limited to areas of exclusive Community competence? Arguably, it is not. As analysed in previous chapters, non-exclusive external competences are as genuine and real as those which are exclusive. By definition, such competences have been exercised where an agreement has been concluded. They are at that stage certainly no longer 'potential' or 'virtual'.[158] The Community has committed itself to ensuring good-faith performance of the agreement. It cannot, under Community law, act beyond the limits of its powers, but within those limits it is required to ensure correct implementation. The relevant provisions of the agreement therefore come within the scope of Community law.

Those should be the relevant criteria for determining the Court's jurisdiction. They should also be applied to the question whether Community law determines

---

[156] See further Case C–306/99 *BIAO v. Finanzamt für Grossunternehmen in Hamburg* [2003] ECR I–1, paras 40–70 of the Opinion of Jacobs AG.   [157] See Ch 2.
[158] See Ch 7.

the legal effects of the provisions of a mixed agreement. Again, the reply to that question should depend on whether the provisions come within the scope of Community law. The Court should therefore not have ruled in *Schieving-Nijstad* that national law governed the legal effect of Article 50 TRIPs in so far as industrial designs were concerned, on which there was no Community legislation at the time. The cleavage between jurisdiction to interpret and authority to determine legal effects is not convincing. The question of the legal effects of the provisions of an international agreement is closely connected to those provisions' interpretation, indeed one could say that it is itself a specific question of interpretation concerning the agreement.

A second issue deserving some further comments concerns the position of the Member States, in particular where they seek to ensure that the Community fulfils its international obligations. The current constellation is not satisfactory. Where an agreement does not have direct effect (to use that particular shorthand), neither a private party nor a Member State government is capable of relying on the agreement in cases involving judicial review of Community acts. It was argued above that, in principle, this equal treatment of all parties is correct. The judgment in *Netherlands v. Council* suggests that there may be certain ways in which a Member State can none the less base a claim on non-respect of an agreement which lacks direct effect. The reasoning in that judgment is not particularly clear, however.

Given the special position of the Member States in the EU construction and its legal system there are certainly arguments in favour of enabling the Member States to challenge non-respect of the Community's international obligations. However, actions for annulment are not necessarily an appropriate remedy. It must be borne in mind that annulment operates *ex tunc*, and is therefore a most drastic type of remedy. A different type of remedy may be more suitable. Unfortunately, the Treaty does not provide for an action for a declaration. Such a type of action would allow a Member State to seek a declaration by the Court of Justice that the Community has failed to fulfil an international obligation. It would be more akin to an enforcement action brought by the Commission against a Member State. In the absence of such an action for a declaration, it may be worth examining whether a Member State could make use of Article 232 EC, the action for failure to act. Could such an action be brought, not against the Community's failure to act as such, but against its failure to act in accordance with its international obligations? In any event, it would seem desirable to continue the search for ways to enable the Member States to engage in judicial action against the Community's non-respect of its international obligations, even where the agreement does not have direct effect.

9

The legal effects of international law

Introduction

Direct effect

This chapter explores the legal effects of various forms of international law, i.e. international agreements to which the Community is a party; rules of general international law; and agreements to which the Community is not a party, but one or more Member States is. This is a subject which is at the centre of the law of the EU's external relations. It is one thing for the EU to engage in international affairs and to give effect to such engagement by acting under international law. Such action creates important links and produces many types of legal effect in international law. What, however, are the legal effects of such action, not at the international plane, where the relevant actors remain by and large States and international organizations, but within the internal legal order? What are the effects in EU law (or Community law, to which the practice is so far limited) of an agreement concluded by the Community? What are the effects of a general rule of international law, or of provisions in an agreement binding on one or more Member States? Is international law, in doctrinal terms, separate from 'internal' EU law, or are there channels connecting one with the other? If so, which are those channels, and what is the effect of the international law rules flowing through them? May or must the EU's courts, including courts and tribunals at the level of Member States, apply such international law rules? What effect are they to give to such rules? Can private parties base their claims on rules of international law? In other words, may international law create rights for individuals?

The last set of questions creates an association with the concept of direct effect. The fact that provisions of Community law may have direct effect in the legal orders of the Member States is one of the very hallmarks and defining features of the EU's constitution. When the Court in *Van Gend en Loos* decided that the EEC Treaty had set up a new legal order, whose subjects included not just States but also their citizens, it started a legal revolution.[1] That revolution effectively involved setting Community law apart from all other forms of international law. Even though the

---

[1] Case 26/62 *Van Gend en Loos v. Nederlandse Administratie der Belastingen* [1963] ECR 1.

Court spoke of 'a new legal order of international law', it soon became clear that, particularly in the early stages, Community law was defining itself in opposition to, rather than in conformity with, the 'old' legal order of international law.[2] That may be less so at present, yet it remains indisputable that direct effect and supremacy continue to be the foundations of the Community legal order. Through those concepts Community law is the law of the land, taking precedence over any conflicting rules of national law. That is not merely the theory, but also very much the practice, as private parties have effective remedies for ensuring that Community law is correctly applied, so that they may benefit from any rights which Community law may confer on them. International law, by contrast, does not of itself have the characteristics of direct effect and supremacy. A State may, under its constitution, confer these features on international law, but it is not required by international law to do so. The latter only demands, in very general terms, that it is complied with. Precisely which effects international law may have in domestic or 'municipal' legal systems is a matter largely left to such a system's basic rules.

It is this ancestry of the concept of direct effect which renders the subject of this chapter so fascinating. Indeed, to some extent the Community legal order defined itself in opposition to international law, by the creation of direct effect. Ever since, Community law has been distinct from international law. Yet what, then, is the relationship between them? Like any other municipal legal order Community law itself largely determines the effects of international law rules in its legal system. What are those effects? Is the Community legal order prepared to give direct effect to international law under the same conditions as those which apply to 'internal' Community law? Or is there unwillingness to do so, perhaps inspired by the birth-giving act of opposition? Is the Community willing to extend its own approach to transnational legal relations to rules of law created outside its own legal premises? The question of the effects of international law in the Community legal order strikes at the heart of the EU's constitution.

The title of this chapter generally refers to the effects of international law. The choice is deliberate. In judicial and academic discussion it is customary to refer to the concept of direct effect as a shorthand for the issue of the relationship between international and Community law. However, shorthands have drawbacks.[3] A close reading of the case law leads one to conclude that international agreements and other forms of international law may produce many different types of legal effect, and an exaggerated use of the direct-effect notion may lead to some degree of myopia, resulting in failure to see the full picture. It is none the less the case that the question of direct effect occupies a central position in the case law, compelling us to examine it carefully, and to attempt to understand it.

---

[2] CWA Timmermans, 'The EU and Public International Law' (1999) 4 EFA Review 181–4; see also D McGoldrick, *International Relations Law of the European Union* (Longman, 1997) 23–5.

[3] Cf J Klabbers, 'International Law in Community Law: The Law and Politics of Direct Effect' (2002) 21 YEL 263.

Agreements are binding

Article 300(7) EC provides that agreements concluded under the conditions set out in the article shall be binding on the institutions of the Community and on Member States. This is first of all an expression of the vital international law principle of *pacta sunt servanda*. The provision's interest lies in the second part, where it indicates the actors which are bound: not just the Community institutions, but also the Member States. By doing so the provision clarifies that it addresses the effects of agreements in Community law, and not their effects in international law. The Member States are not *prima facie* bound under international law by agreements concluded by the Community, unless those agreements are mixed and have the Member States as contracting parties together with the Community.

The extension of the binding effect of Community agreements to the Member States need not surprise the observer.[4] One should avoid the fallacy that, because the Community may only conclude agreements which come within its treaty-making powers, such agreements cannot contain provisions which require action by the Member States. On the contrary, this is a classic function of Community law, a staple feature of the basic Treaties, of Community legislation (EC directives are by definition addressed to the Member States), and indeed of agreements. To give just one example, in *Opinion 1/94* the Court of Justice had little or no difficulty in deciding that the WTO agreements on trade in goods (Annex 1A of the WTO Agreement, which includes GATT 1994) come within the Community's exclusive competence to carry on the common commercial policy.[5] Yet many of the GATT provisions have limited relevance for the Community as such, and are mostly targeted, in the Community context, to the Member States. Article III:2 GATT, for example, prohibits discrimination against imported products in matters of taxation. As indirect taxation remains largely in the province of the Member States, the provision primarily affects national tax laws and regulations.

Article 300(7) refers only to agreements concluded by the Community. It does not refer to other forms of international law, such as general rules of international law. The Court has none the less recognized the binding effect of such general rules, and has without reservation accepted that the Community is bound by international law. The precise legal effects of those other forms of international law, however, remain to be examined. Also, as regards international agreements to which the Community itself is not a party, but which are binding on the Member States, there is the separate provision of Article 307 EC. That provision concerns the consequences of rights and obligations contracted by Member States before they became a Member of the Community.

---

[4] I Macleod, ID Hendry, and S Hyett, *The External Relations of the European Communities* (OUP, 1996) 125–8 rightly argue that this is a rule of Community law, and that the Member States are not bound by a Community agreement under international law.

[5] *Opinion 1/94 re WTO Agreement* [1994] ECR I–5267; see Ch 2.

In that connection, in the case of one agreement, namely the GATT in its original 1947 version, the Court of Justice has accepted that the Community was bound by its provisions, notwithstanding the absence of formal signature, conclusion, or accession.[6] This appears to have been a special case, resulting from the Community's exclusive competence in matters of tariffs and commercial policy. It is difficult to envisage similar cases.

One could view Article 300(7) EC as establishing full direct effect and supremacy, in Community law, of agreements concluded by the Community. In other words, that provision could be read as confirming a monist approach towards international law.[7] However, the Treaty nowhere expressly introduced the concepts of direct effect and supremacy, and when the Court in *Van Gend en Loos* confirmed the direct effect of Community law there was a fair amount of opposition from some founding Member States.[8] From that perspective it is not convincing to consider that the Treaty drafters intended international agreements to have such effect. Once the Court had established direct effect and supremacy, through its act of interpreting the Treaty, it of course became arguable that that approach should be extended to international agreements. However, the Court did not, as we will see, take that course (or at least not completely). The Court's case law may be criticized, but to base such criticism on Article 300(7) is not persuasive. The provision is limited to expressing the binding character of agreements concluded by the Community, and it does not describe the legal consequences or effects of this characteristic. Furthermore, full monism did not and does not reflect the legal traditions of the Member States as regards the relationship between international and domestic law.[9] If that had been otherwise, arguments based on Article 300(7) EC would have been more convincing, since the provision could then have been read as an expression of those traditions. It is thus clear that the wording of the Treaty does not exhaust the legal effects of agreements concluded by the Community.

Transposition and implementation

In its case law on the effects of agreements the Court has consistently held that as from the entry into force of the agreement, its provisions form an integral part of the Community legal system.[10] There is therefore no need for any particular act of transposition; it is sufficient that an agreement is concluded by the Council in

---

[6] Joined Cases 21 to 24/72 *International Fruit Company v. Produktschap voor Groenten en Fruit* [1972] ECR 1219.

[7] On monism and dualism, see e.g. FG Jacobs, 'Introduction', in FG Jacobs and S Roberts (eds), *The Effect of Treaties in Domestic Law* (Sweet & Maxwell, 1987) pp. xxiv–xxvi; JH Jackson, 'Status of Treaties in Domestic Legal Systems: A Policy Analysis' (1992) 86 AJIL 313–15; L Henkin, *International Law: Politics and Values* (Martinus Nijhoff, 1995) 64 ff.

[8] *Van Gend en Loos* (n 1 above), observations of the Netherlands and Belgian governments, at 6.

[9] Cf Jacobs and Roberts (n 7 above).

[10] Case 181/73 *Haegeman v. Belgium* [1974] ECR 449, paras 2–6.

accordance with the Article 300 EC procedure for it to produce full effect.[11] Of course, the type of effect which the agreement produces may differ, depending on the nature of the agreement and on its provisions, as analysed below.

The fact that no act of transposition is necessary is not to be confused with questions of implementation.[12] Whether the correct application of an agreement requires particular implementing measures again depends on the nature and provisions of the agreement. In *Kupferberg* the Court pointed out that the measures needed to implement the provisions of an agreement concluded by the Community were to be adopted, according to the state of Community law for the time being in the areas affected by the provisions of the agreement, either by the Community institutions or by the Member States.[13] In other words, the binding effect of agreements is automatic and extends to the requirement of implementation, both as regards the Community as such (the Community institutions) and as regards the Member States. To take the above example of Article III:2 GATT, a Member State may be required by that provision to amend its tax legislation without there being any need for a separate Community act requiring such amendment. As regards the Community institutions, too, the provisions of an agreement are a sufficient legal basis for adopting acts of implementation or application.[14]

It is difficult, if not impossible, to generalize about questions of implementation and application, as each agreement is different and may thus require different types of action or inaction. This may *inter alia* involve: no action at all, either because Community or national law already complies with the agreement, or because the agreement imposes a requirement of refraining from certain action; the adoption of general implementing legislation, which is needed so as to adjust either Community or national law to the Community's international commitments; taking certain forms of administrative or executive action; or the incurring of certain expenditure. In light of this variety it is not possible to point to any consistent implementation practice. There have been cases, however, where no implementing legislation was adopted even where at least for reasons of transparency such legislation was desirable.[15]

Judicial application—direct and indirect effects

As a rule the Community and its Member States faithfully implement and apply Community agreements, and they abide by the general rules of international law.

---

[11] Cf J Rideau, 'Les accords internationaux dans la jurisprudence de la Cour de justice des Communautés européennes' (1990) 94 RGDIP 308–12.

[12] Macleod, Hendry, and Hyett (n 4 above), 128.

[13] Case 104/81 *Hauptzollamt Mainz v. Kupferberg* [1982] ECR 3641, para 12. In para 13 the Court added that, in ensuring respect for commitments arising from an agreement concluded by the Community institutions, the Member States fulfilled an obligation not only in relation to the non-member country concerned but also and above all in relation to the Community which had assumed responsibility for the due performance of the agreement.

[14] See, for an example, Case 30/88 *Greece v. Commission* [1989] ECR 3711, paras 10–17.

[15] Cf P Eeckhout, 'The Domestic Legal Status of the WTO Agreement: Interconnecting Legal Systems' (1997) 34 CMLRev 25.

However, a rule will only exercise the strongest legal force when it is capable of being applied by the judiciary. If that is the case, and if there is a judicial system offering effective remedies, a rule may be regarded as legally perfect from the point of view of its application or enforcement. In the context of Community agreements, parties to litigation before the EU courts (which include national courts when dealing with questions of EU law) may seek to enforce agreements or general rules of international law where that is in their interest. It is at this point that the direct effect doctrine comes into play. Under what conditions may parties to litigation, in particular but not exclusively private parties, rely on such provisions or rules of international law? That question is vital, not because of any misguided overrating of judicial applications as opposed to other forms of implementing or applying international law. Indeed it is clear that most provisions of agreements will never come before the courts, and none the less need to be applied. However, the type of effect courts are willing to give to particular rules is bound to have a significant impact on the attitude towards those rules, and action taken by institutional actors such as the EU's political institutions and legislatures and public authorities at national level. Where, for example, it is clear that a provision has direct effect, so that it confers rights on individuals which they may enforce in court, a public authority will endeavour to avoid court action by applying those provisions in accordance with the courts' interpretation. If this sounds abstract, it becomes much less so when one looks, for example, at the case law of the Court of Justice on the rights of Turkish workers in the Community.[16] It is by no means certain that these people would have been in the same legal (and factual) position in matters of employment and social security in the absence of this case law.

There are forms of judicial application of Community agreements where, apparently, the binding effect as formulated in Article 300(7) EC is sufficient for the agreement to be fully applied; where, in other words, no further conditions, such as direct effect, are imposed. As discussed in the previous chapter, an agreement may form the basis for actions against Member States for failing to fulfil Treaty obligations (Article 226 EC): where a Member State violates a Community agreement the Commission need only prove such violation. This is a particular type of action. Another form of judicial application, unrelated to any specific judicial action, is the principle of consistent interpretation, discussed in a separate section below. According to that principle 'internal' Community law has to be interpreted in the light of the Community's international commitments. Again there are no further conditions.

For other forms of judicial application, however, there are such further conditions, commonly denominated with the concept of direct effect. The previous chapter already described the direct effect requirement as applying in the context of review of the legality or validity of Community acts (whether challenged before a domestic court—see Article 234 EC—or challenged directly before the EU Courts

---

[16] See the cases cited in n 53 below.

under Article 230 EC); in the context of the non-contractual liability of the Community (Articles 235 and 288 EC); and in the context of actions before national courts where a party relies on an agreement as against national law.

The concept of direct effect does not however exhaust all forms of judicial application where conditions are imposed for an agreement to be relied upon. In the context of its case law on the lack of direct effect of GATT and WTO law the Court has allowed certain forms of application of such law, where the Community intended to implement a particular obligation or where a Community act expressly refers to such law. This may be called indirect effect, or the principle of implementation. Furthermore, there are suggestions in recent case law that there may be still other forms of judicial application.

Before examining all of this, and before exploring in particular direct effect as a condition for certain forms of judicial application of rules of international law, it is necessary to make a comment on the concept of direct effect as such. One of the problems of that concept is that its use is not limited to the forms of international law which we are discussing here, but was first developed in the setting of 'internal' Community law, and then transposed to international law. This extension should not conceal that we are dealing with different issues; nor should we fail to define, in a correct manner, the sources of law involved. In 'internal' Community law the concept of direct effect is used in order to denote the relationship between Community law—provisions of the Treaty or of Community legislation—and national law. A provision of the Treaty which has direct effect needs to be applied and respected, even in the face of inconsistent national law. By contrast, as regards Community agreements and other forms of international law the concept of direct effect is used in order to denote the relationship between international law and Community law. A provision of a Community agreement which has direct effect needs to be applied and respected, even in the face of inconsistent 'internal' Community law. Moreover, as Community law overrides national law, and as the provisions of a Community agreement are an integral part of Community law, such provisions also have direct effect in national law. There is thus an important distinction between 'internal' and 'external' direct effect, which arguably justifies some differences in the way in which the concept is handled and applied.

Structure of the chapter

The structure of this chapter is as follows. The next section aims to provide a survey of the Court of Justice's approach towards the direct effect of agreements concluded by the Community.[17] That survey serves as a basis for the discussion, in the following

---

[17] See also C Kaddous, *Le droit des relations extérieures dans la jurisprudence de la Cour de justice des Communautés européennes* (Helbing & Lichtenhahn, 1998) 353–80; I Cheyne, 'Haegeman, Demirel and their Progeny', in A Dashwood and C Hillion (eds), *The General Law of EC External Relations* (Sweet & Maxwell, 2000) 20–41; Klabbers (n 3 above), 274–85.

section, of the grounds for recognizing or denying direct effect. As will be seen, those grounds can be classified in two different categories, the first relating to the nature of an agreement as such, the second concerning the characteristics of the specific provisions at issue. Subsequent sections examine the principle of consistent interpretation and the principle of implementation. Then follows a section on the effects of general international law. The chapter concludes with an investigation into the distinct question of the effects of agreements concluded by the Member States (Article 307 EC).

A survey of the case law on direct effect

GATT and Yaoundé

The Court's exploration of the realm of the direct effect of international agreements concluded by the Community started with the judgment in *International Fruit Company*.[18] In issue was, on a reference by a Netherlands court, the validity of an EEC regulation restricting imports of apples. International Fruit Company argued that the regulation violated Article XI GATT. The Court, following the Opinion of Mayras AG, which in turn largely followed the position of the Commission, found that, for the incompatibility of a Community measure with a provision of international law to affect the validity of that measure, the Community first had to be bound by that provision.[19] Secondly, before invalidity could be relied upon before a national court, that provision of international law also had to be capable of conferring rights on citizens of the Community which they could invoke before the courts.[20] International Fruit Company's claim stumbled over the second condition. With a view to establishing whether that condition was fulfilled the Court examined what it called 'the spirit, the general scheme and the terms of the General Agreement'.[21] It considered that GATT, which according to its preamble was based on the principle of negotiations undertaken on the basis of 'reciprocal and mutually advantageous arrangements', was characterized by great flexibility, particularly as regards derogations, safeguard measures, and settlement of disputes. The Court analysed the relevant provisions, drawing attention to the importance of consultations between the contracting parties; to the various alternatives offered by Article XXIII GATT in case of disputes; to Article XIX on safeguard measures. The conclusion was that Article XI GATT was not capable of conferring rights on citizens.[22] The Court itself did not expressly refer to the concept of direct effect, but

---

[18] N 6 above.   [19] See above on the binding effect of the GATT of 1947.
[20] *International Fruit Company* (n 6 above), paras 7–8.
[21] Ibid, para 20. In the French version of the judgment the Court speaks of '*l'esprit, l'économie et les termes de l'Accord général*'. In the 1973 *Schlüter* judgment the same terms are expressed in English as 'the meaning, the structure, and the wording of the General Agreement': Case 9/73 *Schlüter v. Hauptzollamt Lörrach* [1973] ECR 1135, para 28.   [22] Ibid, paras 21–27.

the Opinion of Mayras AG spoke of conferring rights and direct effect as one and the same issue.[23] The Advocate General also distinguished the direct effect of international law from that of 'internal' Community law, and he considered the issue of direct effect to be a problem of interpretation requiring various judicial and technical processes, including: analysis of the provisions; examination of the context and general scheme of the treaty; aim of the provision in question, having regard to the overall objective of the measure; and circumstances in which the contracting parties had decided to apply the treaty.[24]

Four years later, in *Bresciani*, the *Tribunale* of Genoa asked the Court whether Article 2(1) of the Yaoundé Convention of 1963 had 'immediate' effect so as to confer on Community citizens an individual right, which the courts had to protect, not to pay to a Member State a charge having an effect equivalent to customs duties (which that article prohibited). The Yaoundé Conventions were the predecessors of the Lomé Conventions and of the current Cotonou Convention. They followed the association with overseas countries and territories provided for by the Fourth Part of the original EEC Treaty. This case did not concern the validity of a Community act, but the direct effect of the Convention, so as to set aside inconsistent national law. The Court stated that, simultaneously, regard had to be paid to the spirit, general scheme, and the wording of the Convention and of the provision concerned. It recalled the roots of the Yaoundé Conventions, which were intended to maintain the association with former overseas countries and territories. It then analysed the Convention's provisions on charges having equivalent effect, pointing out that the Community had committed itself to abolishing those charges on a non-reciprocal basis. The Court considered that it was apparent from those provisions that the Convention was not concluded in order to ensure equality in obligations, but in order to promote the development of the associated States. This imbalance, which was inherent in the special nature of the Convention, did not prevent recognition by the Community that some of its provisions had direct effect. Under Article 2 the Community was automatically to proceed to the abolition of charges having equivalent effect, and as that provision referred to (then) Article 13 EEC the Community undertook precisely the same obligation to abolish such charges as, in the Treaty, the Member States assumed towards each other. Since the obligation was specific and not subject to any implied or express reservation, it was capable of conferring rights on citizens.[25]

The Court followed the Opinion of Trabucchi AG, who made some interesting general statements on the direct effect of international law. The Advocate General expressed scepticism as regards the extension of the 'internal' direct effect doctrine to international agreements, particularly with respect to agreements containing identical mutual obligations, based strictly on the criterion of reciprocity—not, he said, in making the direct applicability of its provisions dependent on the extent to which, in practice, they were observed by the third State concerned but

---

[23] *International Fruit Company* (n 6 above), 1234.   [24] Ibid, 1235.
[25] Case 87/75 *Bresciani v. Amministrazione Italiana delle Finanze* [1976] ECR 129, paras 16–26.

in establishing whether the agreement was, in principle, capable of creating directly applicable provisions. He felt that in *International Fruit Company* the Court had rightly refrained from automatically applying to the relationship between Community law and international law the concepts and criteria which it had accepted in comparing Community law with national law, in view of the differences between the Community and the international legal order. However, those considerations did not apply to the Yaoundé Conventions, which were 'the perfect continuation of the system which was originally laid down in the [EEC] Treaty'. The conventions were mainly concerned with privileges granted by the Community and its Member States to the associated countries in order to help their development. The alignment of individual rights with the obligations imposed on Member States by the conventions in question therefore appeared to be consistent with the nature and purpose of the conventions.[26]

The Court confirmed its ruling in *International Fruit Company* in *Schlüter*,[27] in *SIOT*,[28] and in *SPI and SAMI*.[29] *SIOT* was a case concerning Italian charges on transit of goods, and it therefore differed from *International Fruit Company* in that it did not concern the validity of a Community act. Here the Court used the concept of direct effect, by stating that the GATT provision in question could not have direct effect for the reasons stated in *International Fruit Company*, and that therefore individuals could not rely on it in order to challenge the (national) charges in question.[30] It is also worth noting that Reischl AG agreed with the Court's analysis in *International Fruit Company*, by noting that GATT was flexible and that direct effect was connected with rigidity. He also pointed out that nearly all Member States rejected direct effect of GATT in their internal legal order, that this was also the case for other GATT contracting parties, and that if the Community did recognize direct effect it would impair its negotiating power and its capacity to react to infringements by other parties.[31]

In *Razanatsimba* the Court turned to the first Lomé Convention, the successor of the Yaoundé Conventions, but as it considered the relevant provision inapplicable it did not expressly rule on direct effect. Reischl AG was of the opinion that the convention was capable of having direct effect. However, as the provision at issue contained an open-ended reservation, granting the participating States a wide discretionary power, it was impossible to consider its direct application.[32]

Early case law on free-trade and association agreements

In the 1980s the Court had the opportunity to clarify whether the free-trade agreement with Portugal (part of the group of free-trade agreements with the EFTA

---

[26] Ibid, para 5 of the Opinion of Trabucchi AG.   [27] N 21 above.
[28] Case 266/81 *SIOT v. Ministero delle Finanze* [1983] ECR 731.
[29] Joined Cases 267 to 269/81 *Amministrazione delle Finanze dello Stato v. SPI and SAMI* [1983] ECR 801.
[30] Ibid, para 28.   [31] Ibid, 790–1.
[32] Case 65/77 *Razanatsimba* [1977] ECR 2229, Opinion of Reischl AG at 2243–4.

countries) as well as association agreements with Greece and Turkey were directly effective.

In *Pabst & Richarz* the question was whether an importer of spirits could rely on the prohibition of tax discrimination in Article 53 of the association agreement with Greece. The Court considered that that provision had to be interpreted in the same way as (current) Article 90 EC. It then simply established that Article 53 contained a clear and precise obligation which was not, in its implementation or effects, subject to the adoption of any subsequent measure, and that, accordingly, it had to be considered as directly applicable.[33] These are the classic direct effect conditions, to which the Court constantly refers when examining the direct effect of 'internal' Community law. The swiftness with which the Court concluded that there was direct effect appeared to indicate that association agreements are in principle capable of producing direct effect.

Around the same time the Court was confronted with provisions in the free-trade agreement with Portugal. In *Polydor*, where the question was whether the prohibition of measures having equivalent effect involved exhaustion of intellectual property rights, the Court said nothing about direct effect, since it did not in any event agree with the proposed interpretation.[34] A few months later, in *Kupferberg*, the Court did however address the issue, in connection with claims based on the prohibition of tax discrimination in the agreement with Portugal.[35] Rozès AG had argued against direct effect, on the basis that the reasoning of *International Fruit Company* should be extended to free-trade agreements based on reciprocity.[36] The Court did not follow her Opinion, and took the opportunity to elaborate on the direct effect of agreements concluded by the Community. *Kupferberg* still contains the fullest general statement to date on the issue.

The Court first pointed to the binding effect of agreements, as expressed in (current) Article 300(7) EC. It then made a few statements on the implementation of agreements, as a responsibility of the Community institutions or of the Member States, depending on the circumstances (see previous section). The Court did however emphasize the Community nature of provisions in an agreement concluded by the Community, from which it followed that their effect could not be allowed to vary according to whether their application was in practice the responsibility of the Community institutions or of the Member States and, in the latter case, according to the effects in the internal legal order of each Member State which the law of that State assigned to international agreements. It was therefore for the Court, within the framework of its jurisdiction in interpreting the provisions of agreements, to ensure their uniform application throughout the Community.[37] This is an important starting point: even if implementation of a Community agreement may be the responsibility of the Member States, Community law exclusively governs

---

[33] Case 17/81 *Pabst & Richarz v. Hauptzollamt Oldenburg* [1982] ECR 1331, paras 25–27.
[34] Case 270/80 *Polydor v. Harlequin Record Shops* [1982] ECR 329.
[35] Case 104/81 *Hauptzollamt Mainz v. Kupferberg* [1982] ECR 3641.   [36] Ibid, 3674.
[37] Ibid, paras 11–14.

the legal effects which the agreement may produce, including its effects in national law.

The Court then described arguments by Member States which had submitted observations to the effect that the provisions of a free-trade agreement were not directly effective, in light of the principle of reciprocity, the institutional framework for settling disputes, and safeguard clauses.[38] It did not however agree with those arguments.

It was true, the Court said, that the effects within the Community of provisions of an agreement could not be determined without taking account of the international origin of the provisions in question. In conformity with the principles of public international law Community institutions which had power to negotiate and conclude an agreement with a non-member country were free to agree with that country what effect the provisions of the agreement were to have in the internal legal order of the contracting parties. Only if that question had not been settled by the agreement, the Court continued, did it fall for decision by the courts having jurisdiction in the matter, and in particular by the Court of Justice within the framework of its jurisdiction under the Treaty, in the same manner as any question of interpretation relating to the application of the agreement in the Community.[39] Those are two important principles. First, the agreement may itself determine its effects. That, however, is in practice the exception rather than the rule.[40] As States, under their constitutional rules, have different approaches towards the legal effects of agreements, and as they may have different attitudes towards international law, they tend rarely to agree on precise legal effects of agreements in the municipal legal order, and to keep matters at the general level of the international law principle of *pacta sunt servanda*.[41] Secondly, if the agreement does not determine its legal effects, it is for the Court of Justice to do so, as a matter of interpretation of the agreement.

The Court then turned towards the arguments which had been advanced against the direct effect of the agreement with Portugal. First, as regards reciprocity, the Court made the following statements. It referred to the international law principle of *bona fide* performance of every agreement, adding that, although each contracting party was responsible for executing fully the commitments which it had undertaken, it was nevertheless free to determine the legal means appropriate for attaining that end in its legal system, unless the agreement itself specified those means. Subject to that reservation the fact that the courts of one of the parties considered that certain of the stipulations in the agreement were of direct application, whereas the courts of the other party did not recognize such direct application, was not in itself such as to constitute a lack of reciprocity in the implementation of the agreement.[42] In other words, direct effect does not in principle depend on whether the courts in the other contracting parties also recognize it. As we will see, however, there may

---

[38] Ibid, paras 15–16.   [39] Ibid, para 17.

[40] D McGoldrick, *International Relations Law of the European Union* (Longman, 1997) 127. For such an exception see Case C–1/96 *R v. MAFF, ex parte Compassion in World Farming* [1998] ECR I–1251, para 35.

[41] Cf Henkin (n 7 above), 63.   [42] *Kupferberg* (n 35 above), para 18.

none the less be cases where this is an important factor: in its case law on the lack of direct effect of WTO law the Court does refer to it.

Secondly, the Court examined the institutional framework of free-trade agreements, consisting of joint committees responsible for the administration of the agreements and for their proper implementation. It considered that the mere fact that the contracting parties had established a special institutional framework for consultations and negotiations *inter se* in relation to the implementation of the agreement was not in itself sufficient to exclude all judicial application: the fact that a court of one of the parties applied to a specific case before it a provision of the agreement involving an unconditional and precise obligation and therefore not requiring any prior intervention on the part of the joint committee did not adversely affect the powers which the agreement conferred on that committee.[43] This is classic direct-effect reasoning. Also as regards 'internal' Community law the Court has always taken the approach of considering the absence of certain implementing measures irrelevant if the provision in question is sufficiently clear, precise, and unconditional.[44]

Thirdly, as regards safeguard clauses the Court observed that they applied only in specific circumstances, and as a general rule after consideration within the joint committee in the presence of both parties. Apart from specific situations which could involve their application, the existence of such clauses, which did not affect the provisions prohibiting tax discrimination, was not sufficient in itself to affect the direct applicability which could attach to certain stipulations in the agreement.[45]

From all this, the Court concluded that neither the nature nor the structure of the agreement with Portugal prevented a trader from relying on its provisions before a court in the Community. However, that was not the end of the matter. It was still left for the Court to examine whether the provision in issue was unconditional and sufficiently precise to have direct effect, a question which had to be considered in the context of the agreement of which it formed part. In other words, it was necessary to analyse Article 21 of the agreement in the light of both the object and purpose of the agreement and of its context.[46]

The Court then described the purpose of the agreement (essentially to create a system of free trade), and stated that the function of Article 21 in that context was to prevent the liberalization of trade in goods from being rendered nugatory by fiscal practices of the contracting parties. From that it appeared that the provision imposed on the contracting parties an unconditional rule against discrimination in matters of taxation, which was dependent only on a finding that the products affected by a particular tax system were of like nature, and the limits of which were the direct consequence of the purpose of the agreement. As such this provision could be applied by a court and thus produce direct effects throughout the Community. The overall conclusion was that the provision was directly applicable and capable of conferring upon individual traders rights which the courts had to protect.[47]

[43] *Kupferberg* (n 35 above), paras 19–20.
[44] e.g. Case 2/74 *Reyners v. Belgium* [1974] ECR 631, para 26.
[45] *Kupferberg* (n 35 above), para 21.   [46] Ibid, paras 22–23.   [47] Ibid, paras 24–27.

This second part of the judgment confirmed that the direct effect analysis does indeed consist of two parts. The first part involves an examination of whether the nature and structure of the agreement, as such, prevent direct effect. It was appropriate for the Court to put this in the negative for, as we will see, the Court rarely considers this to be a problem. The second part concerns an examination of the specific provisions relied upon: whether those provisions, interpreted in the light of the objective of the agreement and of their context, are clear, precise, unconditional; in other words the classic conditions for direct effect.

In *Kupferberg* the Court recognized the direct effect of free-trade agreements, thereby clarifying that such effect was not limited to association agreements. A few years later, in *Demirel*, the Court denied direct effect to certain provisions in the association agreement with Turkey.[48] The case concerned a Turkish national, Mrs Demirel, who, having joined her husband in Germany, claimed the right to remain there on the basis of the agreement. The Court made a careful examination of the objective and provisions of the agreement in the field of movement of workers. At the outset it stated, apparently summarizing *Kupferberg*, that a provision in an agreement concluded by the Community had to be regarded as directly applicable when, regard being had to its wording and the purpose and nature of the agreement itself, the provision contained a clear and precise obligation which was not subject, in its implementation or effects, to the adoption of any subsequent measure.[49] That was to become the standard statement concerning direct effect of international agreements, to be repeated in nearly all the relevant case law. As can be seen, however, it does not put in much relief the distinction between the structure and nature of the agreement as such, and the conditions for direct effect of specific provisions.

The Court then described the purpose and content of the association agreement. It noted that, in structure and content, the agreement was characterized by the fact that it set out the aims of the association and laid down guidelines for the attainment of those aims without itself establishing the detailed rules for doing so. In order to achieve the aims, the agreement conferred decision-making powers on the Association Council. As regards freedom of movement of workers, Article 12 provided that the contracting parties agreed to be guided by (current) Articles 39 to 41 EC for the purpose of progressively securing freedom of movement for workers. Article 36 of the Additional Protocol provided that freedom of movement was to be secured by progressive stages, and that the Association Council is to decide on the rules necessary to that end. The Court then pointed out that this provision gave the Association Council exclusive powers to lay down detailed rules for the progressive attainment of freedom of movement for workers in accordance with political and economic considerations; and that the only decision which the Association Council had adopted on the matter did not concern the sphere of family reunification. The Court therefore concluded that Article 12 of the agreement and Article 36 of the protocol essentially served to set out a programme and were

---

[48] Case 12/86 *Demirel v. Stadt Schwäbisch Gmünd* [1987] ECR 3719.   [49] Ibid, para 14.

not sufficiently precise and unconditional to be capable of governing directly the movement of workers. That conclusion was not affected by Article 7 of the agreement, which, in very general terms, provided that the contracting parties were to take all appropriate measures, whether general or particular, to ensure fulfilment of the obligations arising from the agreement and that they were to refrain from any measures liable to jeopardize the attainment of the objectives of the agreement: that provision imposed no more than a general obligation of co-operation and could not directly confer on individuals rights which were not already vested in them by other provisions of the agreement.[50] This was again a classic direct effect analysis. The Court could in fact have been considerably shorter: there simply was, at the time, no provision in the association agreement which specifically provided for the rights of family reunification to which Mrs Demirel laid claim. The problem did not therefore reside in the structure and nature of the agreement as such, but in its specific content.

Further case law on co-operation, free-trade, and association agreements

In the subsequent case law on direct effect of free-trade, co-operation, and association agreements the Court has never decided against direct effect on the basis of the structure and nature of the agreement as such. Nearly all questions of direct effect revolve around the clear, precise, and unconditional nature of the provisions in issue. What follows is a short overview of the most interesting cases and statements.

As regards the association agreement with Turkey the Court had pointed out in *Demirel* that most of the agreement itself was programmatic, and that its implementation required decisions by the association council. In *Sevince* the question arose whether such decisions could have direct effect. The Court decided that the same conditions applied as those governing the agreement itself. It referred to the standard statement in *Demirel* (see above), and proceeded first to examine the terms of the provisions in question, which dealt with (a) the right of a Turkish worker, after a number of years' legal employment in a Member State, to enjoy free access to any paid employment of his choice; and (b) a prohibition to introduce new restrictions on the conditions of access to employment applicable to workers legally resident and employed. The Court found that those provisions were clear, precise, and unconditional, and that the finding that they were capable of having direct effect was confirmed by the purpose and nature of the decisions of which they formed part and of the agreement to which they related. The fact that the decisions stated that the procedures for applying the rights conferred on Turkish workers were to be established under national rules was no obstacle for direct effect: those provisions merely clarified the obligation of the Member States to take such administrative

---

[50] Case 12/86 *Demirel v. Stadt Schwäbisch Gmünd* [1987] ECR 3719, paras 15–25.

measures as could be necessary for the implementation of the provisions in question, without empowering them to make conditional or restrict the application of
the precise and unconditional rights which the decisions granted. Nor was non-
publication of the decisions an obstacle, or the safeguard clauses, which applied only
to specific situations.[51]

Sevince confirmed that there is no objection in principle to recognizing the direct
effect of the association agreement with Turkey, including the decisions of the association council. In *Kziber* the Court extended this approach to the EEC–Morocco
co-operation agreement. Miss Kziber claimed rights under Article 41(1) of the
agreement, which provided for non-discriminatory treatment of workers of
Moroccan nationality as well as members of their families in the field of social security. The Court followed the *Sevince* scheme of analysis, first referring to the standard statement on direct effect in *Demirel*, then examining the terms of the
provision, and concluding its analysis by looking at the purpose and nature of the
agreement. As regards the terms of Article 41(1) the Court considered that they were
clear, precise, and unconditional. The fact that paragraphs (2) to (4) of the article laid
down certain limits to that prohibition as regards specific social security issues did
not bar direct effect, as it did not divest the prohibition of discrimination of its
unconditional character in respect of any other question which arose in the field of
social security. As regards the purpose and nature of the agreement the Court stated
that those factors did not contradict direct effect. The object of the agreement was to
promote overall co-operation between the contracting parties, in particular in the
field of labour. The fact that the agreement was intended essentially to promote
the economic development of Morocco and that it confined itself to instituting
co-operation without referring to Morocco's association with or future accession
to the Community did not prevent direct effect.[52]

Kziber was the first case in which the Court recognized the direct effect of provisions of a 'mere' co-operation agreement, in a sense the weakest type of bilateral
agreement between the Community and a third country. It confirmed that, for such
agreements, too, structure and nature of the agreement are unlikely to form an
obstacle to direct effect. In a number of subsequent cases the Court either proceeded
to interpret provisions in agreements without even mentioning direct effect or
established such effect with little or no problem.[53] A few judgments are worth a
short discussion.

---

[51] Case C–192/89 *Sevince* [1990] ECR I–3461, paras 14–26. See also the Opinion of Darmon AG for
an extensive analysis of the nature of the agreement, comparing it with the association agreement with
Greece. See further P Gilsdorf, 'Les organes institués par des accords communautaires: effets juridiques
de leur décisions', (1992) 357 RMCUE 328.

[52] Case C–18/90 *Kziber* [1991] ECR I–199, paras 15–23.

[53] Case C–163/90 *Administration des Douanes et Droits Indirects v. Legros and Others* [1992] ECR I–4625
(assumes direct effect free-trade agreement with Sweden); Case C–237/91 *Kus v. Landeshauptstadt
Wiesbaden* [1992] ECR I–6781, paras 27–31 (reiterates *Sevince*); Case C–207/91 *Eurim-Pharm v.
Bundesgesundheitsamt* [1992] ECR I–3723 (assumes direct effect free-trade agreement with Austria);
Case C–432/92 *Anastasiou and Others* [1994] ECR I–3087, paras 23–27 (direct effect association agree-
ment with Cyprus); Case C–58/93 *Yousfi* [1994] ECR I–1353, paras 16–19 (reiterates *Kziber*);

Taflan-Met was a reference for a preliminary ruling on the direct effect of Decision 3/80 of the EEC–Turkey association council. That decision set out to co-ordinate Member States' social security schemes with a view to enabling Turkish workers employed or formerly employed in the Community, members of their families, and their survivors to qualify for benefits in the traditional branches of social security. Its provisions referred for the most part to particular provisions of the well-known Regulation 1408/71 on social security,[54] and, less frequently, to Council Regulation 574/72 laying down the procedure for implementing Regulation 1408/71.[55] The Court compared Decision 3/80 with the two regulations, and came to the conclusion that the decision did not contain a large number of precise, detailed provisions, even though such were deemed indispensable for implementing Regulation 1408/71. The Court held that, by its nature, the decision was intended to be supplemented and implemented in the Community by a subsequent act of the Council. At the time, there was indeed a proposal for a Council regulation, but it had not yet been adopted. It followed that, even though some of its provisions were clear and precise, Decision 3/80 could not be applied as long as supplementary measures had not been adopted by the Council.[56]

A few years later, however, the Court in *Sürül* qualified that assessment by clarifying that some provisions of the decision could be directly effective. It pointed out that *Taflan-Met* was concerned with co-ordination rules regarding invalidity or survivors' pensions, and that the Court's reasoning there applied to all the provisions of the decision which required additional measures for their application in practice. However, that reasoning could not be transposed to the principle of equal treatment in the field of social security, embodied in Article 3(1) of the decision, which was the

---

Case C–355/93 *Eroglu v. Land Baden-Württemberg* [1994] ECR I–5113, para 11 (reiterates *Sevince*); Case C–103/94 *Krid v. CNAVTS* [1995] ECR I–719, paras 21–24 (direct effect co-operation agreement with Algeria); Case C–434/93 *Bozkurt v. Staatssecretaris van Justitie* [1995] ECR I–1475 (EEC–Turkey association); Case C–469/93 *Amministrazione delle Finanze dello Stato v. Chiquita Italia* [1995] ECR I–4533, paras 30–35 (direct effect of the Fourth Lomé Convention; reiterates *Bresciani*); Case C–126/95 *Hallouzi-Choho v. Bestuur van de Sociale Verzekeringsbank* [1996] ECR I–4807, paras 19–20 (reiterates *Kziber*); Case T–115/94 *Opel Austria v. Council* [1997] ECR II–39, paras 100–102 (Court of First Instance; direct effect of the EEA Agreement); Case C–171/95 *Tetik v. Land Berlin* [1997] ECR I–329 (EEC–Turkey association); Case C–386/95 *Eker v. Land Baden-Württemberg* [1997] ECR I–2697 (EEC–Turkey association); Case C–285/95 *Kol v. Land Berlin* [1997] ECR I–3069 (EEC–Turkey association); Joined Cases C–114/95 and C–115/95 *Texaco and Olieselskabet Danmark* [1997] ECR I–4263 (assumes direct effect free-trade agreement with Sweden); Case C–36/96 *Günaydin v. Freistaat Bayern* [1997] ECR I–5143 (EEC–Turkey association); Case C–98/96 *Ertanir v. Land Hessen* [1997] ECR I–5179 (EEC–Turkey association); Case C–113/97 *Babahenini v. Belgian State* [1998] ECR I–183, paras 17–18 (reiterates *Krid*); Case C–1/97 *Birden v. Bremen* [1998] ECR I–7747 (EEC–Turkey association); Case C–416/96 *Eddline El-Yassini v. Secretary of State for the Home Department* [1999] ECR I–1209, paras 25–31 (reiterates *Kziber*); Case C–179/98 *Belgian State v. Mesbah* [1999] ECR I–7955 (EEC–Morocco agreement); Case C–340/97 *Nazli v. Stadt Nurnberg* [2000] ECR I–957 (EEC–Turkey association); Joined Cases C–102/98 and C–211/98 *Kocak and Örs* [2000] ECR I–1287 (EEC–Turkey association).

[54] Council Regulation 1408/71 on the application of social security schemes to employed persons and their families moving within the Community [1971] OJ Spec Ed (II), 461.

[55] [1972] OJ Spec Ed (I), 159.

[56] Case C–277/94 *Taflan-Met and Others* [1996] ECR I–4085, paras 23–38.

provision at issue in *Sürül*. That provision did not require further implementation, and the circumstances of the case (alleged discrimination in the grant of family allowances) were not such as to give rise to problems of a technical nature relating in particular to the aggregation of periods completed in different Member States, to non-overlapping of benefits paid by different competent institutions or to determination of the applicable national legislation. The Court therefore proceeded to examine whether Article 3(1) was directly effective, examining its wording as well as the purpose and nature of the agreement. After a lengthy analysis, which merely reiterated previous case law, it found in favour of direct effect.[57]

The Court again looked at the association agreement with Turkey in *ex parte Savas*. The question in this case was whether Article 13 of the agreement and Article 41(1) of the additional protocol had direct effect. Article 13 provided that the contracting parties agreed to be guided by (current) Articles 43 to 46 and Article 48 EC for the purpose of abolishing restrictions on freedom of establishment between them. The Court considered that, like Article 12 on free movement of workers (which it had held not to be directly effective in *Demirel*),[58] Article 13 did no more than lay down in general terms the principle of eliminating restrictions on freedom of establishment, and did not itself establish precise rules for the purpose of attaining that objective. Further, the association council had adopted no measures to implement freedom of establishment. Article 13 was therefore incapable of directly governing the legal situation of individuals and could not have direct effect. Article 41(1) of the protocol, by contrast, provided that the contracting parties were to refrain from introducing between themselves any new restrictions on the freedom of establishment and the freedom to provide services. The Court stated that the very wording showed that this provision laid down, clearly, precisely, and unconditionally, an unequivocal 'standstill' clause. It was thus capable of directly governing the legal position of individuals, and this conclusion was not invalidated by an examination of the purpose and subject matter of the agreement. In this respect the Court referred to previous case law on association agreements.[59]

In *Racke* the Court recognized the direct effect of the co-operation agreement with Yugoslavia,[60] but as the importance of the judgment lies in the effect it gives to rules of customary international law it is more convenient to discuss it in the section on general international law, below.

Lastly, in a string of recent judgments the Court, logically, acknowledged that provisions on freedom of establishment and non-discrimination of legally employed workers in association agreements with Poland, Bulgaria, and the Czech Republic (so-called Europe Agreements) have direct effect. The Court followed the classic pattern of analysis, first examining whether the wording of the provisions in question, in their context, was clear, precise, and unconditional, and then finding that the

---

[57] Case C–262/96 *Sürül v. Bundesanstalt für Arbeit* [1999] ECR I–2685, paras 48–74.
[58] N 48 above.
[59] Case C–37/98 *The Queen v. Secretary of State for the Home Department, ex parte Savas* [2000] ECR I–2927, paras 41–55.   [60] Case C–162/96 *Racke v. Hauptzollamt Mainz* [1998] ECR I–3655.

conclusion of direct effect was not invalidated by an examination of purpose and nature of the agreement.[61]

GATT and WTO law

In the last part of this survey it is necessary to return to the lack of direct effect of GATT and WTO law; in fact the GATT and WTO agreements are the only ones which the Court of Justice has considered not to be capable of producing direct effect in light of the structure and nature of the agreements as a whole.[62]

As described above, the Court in *International Fruit Company* held that the GATT of 1947 did not confer rights on individuals.[63] In subsequent case law on the original GATT the Court maintained that approach, clarifying that the lack of direct effect prevented parties from relying on the provisions of GATT, both in cases of judicial review of Community acts and in cases involving national law.[64] In *Fediol*[65] and *Nakajima*,[66] however, the Court none the less proceeded to examine the legality of Community acts in the light of provisions of, respectively, GATT itself and the GATT Anti-Dumping Code. The Court considered that those cases did not

---

[61] Case C–235/99 *The Queen v. Secretary of State for the Home Department, ex parte Kondova* [2001] ECR I–6427, paras 30–39; Case C–257/99 *The Queen v. Secretary of State for the Home Department, ex parte Barkoci and Malik* [2001] ECR I–6557, paras 30–39; Case C–63/99 *The Queen v. Secretary of State for the Home Department, ex parte Gloszczuk and Gloszczuk* [2001] ECR I–6369, paras 29–38; Case C–268/99 *Aldona Malgorzata Jany and Others v. Staatssecretaris van Justitie* [2001] ECR I–8615, paras 26–28; Case C–162/00 *Land Nordrhein-Westfalen v. Beata Pokrzeptowicz-Meyer* [2002] ECR I–1049, paras 19–30.

[62] Literature on the subject includes Kaddous (n 17 above), 389–401; A Rosas, 'Annotation Case C–149/96, *Portugal v. Council*' (2000) 37 CMLRev 797; M Hilf and F Schorkopf, 'WTO und EG/ Rechtskonflikte vor den EuGH?' (2000) 35 Europarecht 74–91; GA Zonnekeyn, 'The Status of WTO Law in the Community Legal Order: Some Comments in the Light of the *Portuguese Textiles* Case' (2000) 25 ELRev 293; A Desmedt, 'ECJ Restricts Effect of WTO Agreements in the EC Legal Order' (2000) 3 JIEL 191; S Griller, 'Judicial Enforceability of WTO Law in the European Union: Annotation to Case C–149/96, *Portugal v. Council*' (2000) 3 JIEL 441; F Berrod, 'La Cour de justice refuse l'invocabilité des accords OMC: essai de régulation de la mondialisation' (2000) 36 Revue trimestrielle de droit européen 419; I Cheyne, 'International Instruments as a Source of Community Law', in Dashwood and Hillion (eds) (n 17 above) 266–72; JHJ Bourgeois, 'The European Court of Justice and the WTO: Problems and Challenges', in JHH Weiler, *The EU, the WTO and the NAFTA* (OUP, 2000) 104–21; S Peers, 'Fundamental Right or Political Whim? WTO Law and the European Court of Justice', in G de Búrca and J Scott (eds), *The EU and the WTO—Legal and Constitutional Issues* (Hart Publishing, 2001) 111–30; A von Bogdandy and T Makatsch, 'Collision, Co-existence or Co-operation? Prospects for the Relationship between WTO Law and European Union Law', in de Búrca and Scott, ibid, 143–50; N van den Broek, 'Legal Persuasion, Political Realism and Legitimacy: The European Court's Recent Treatment of the Effect of WTO Agreements in the EC Legal Order' (2001) 4 JIEL 411; J Vanhamme, *Volkenrechtelijke beginselen in het Europees recht* (Europa Law Publishing, 2001) 200–21; A von Bogdandy, 'Legal Equality, Legal Certainty and Subsidiarity in Transnational Economic Law—Decentralized Application of Art 81.3 EC and WTO Law: Why and Why Not', in A von Bogdandy, P Mavroidis, and Y Mény (eds), *European Integration and International Co-ordination—Studies in Transnational Economic Law in Honour of Claus-Dieter Ehlermann* (Kluwer Law International, 2002) 13; T Cottier, 'A Theory of Direct Effect in Global Law', in ibid, 99.   [63] N 6 above.

[64] See case law at nn 27–29 above and *Chiquita Italia* (n 53 above).

[65] Case 70/87 *Fediol v. Commission* [1989] ECR 1781.

[66] Case C–69/89 *Nakajima v. Council* [1991] ECR I–2069.

raise issues of direct effect in an analysis which is discussed and examined in the section on the principle of implementation.

In *Germany v. Council*, on the legality of the 1993 banana regime, the Court recalled the features of GATT which stood in the way of direct effect, as identified in *International Fruit Company*. It then stated that those features, from which it had concluded that an individual could not invoke GATT in a court to challenge the lawfulness of a Community act, also precluded the Court from taking provisions of GATT into consideration to assess the lawfulness of a regulation in an action brought by a Member State under (current) Article 230 EC. The special features of GATT showed that the GATT rules were not unconditional and that an obligation to recognize them as rules of international law which were directly applicable in the domestic legal systems of the contracting parties could not be based on the spirit, general scheme, or terms of GATT. In the absence of such an obligation following from GATT itself, it was only if the Community intended to implement a particular obligation entered into within the framework of GATT, or if the Community act expressly referred to specific provisions of GATT, that the Court could review the lawfulness of the Community act in question from the point of view of the GATT rules (*Fediol* and *Nakajima*).[67] The judgment was especially noteworthy for extending the direct effect requirement (even if the Court did not refer to the concept of direct effect) to an action brought by a Member State.[68]

Shortly after the judgment in the *Bananas* case the WTO Agreement entered into force.[69] The establishment of the WTO, as a successor to, but at the same time a significant expansion and upgrade of the GATT of 1947, clearly injected a much stronger legal dose into the multilateral trade agreements.[70] Not only was the territory of such agreements expanded so as to include trade in services and the protection of intellectual property, the latter, of course, an inherently rights-oriented subject. The GATT itself, some of whose provisions are indeed general and vague, employing complex and economically-oriented concepts, was given much more precision through a number of further agreements or 'understandings on interpretation'.[71] Two of those agreements subjected the important international trade sectors of agriculture and textiles and clothing to a process of liberalization which stands in stark contrast to the preceding lack of real disciplines (agriculture) or even organized protectionism (textiles and clothing).[72] The scope for exceptions, derogations, and safeguard measures under GATT was reduced by other agreements and understandings.[73] Most importantly, however, the WTO's institutional basis is much stronger than that of the GATT of 1947. That institutional basis includes an

[67] Case C–280/93 *Germany v. Council* [1994] ECR I–4973, paras 103–112.   [68] See Ch 8.
[69] 1 January 1995.
[70] See e.g. J Scott, 'GATT and Community Law: Rethinking the "Regulatory Gap" ', in J Shaw and G More (eds), *New Legal Dynamics of European Union* (Clarendon Press, 1995) 153.
[71] See the texts in Annex 1A of the WTO Agreement.
[72] Agreement on Agriculture, and Agreement on Textiles and Clothing.
[73] See e.g. the understandings concerning waivers, balance-of-payments provisions, and the interpretation of Art XXIV GATT (regional integration), as well as the Agreement on Safeguards.

advanced, sophisticated, and in many respects judicialized system of dispute settlement.[74] In contrast to the previous panel system, which was dependent on political consensus within the GATT both as regards the establishment of panels and as regards approval of panel reports, the present system is much more compulsory. WTO members can now ask for submission of a dispute to a panel as of right, and the consensus rule for adoption of panel reports has been reversed: it is only in the (very unlikely) event of a negative consensus among the WTO members that a report is not adopted. Furthermore, the diplomatic elements in the dispute-settlement system and the approach towards GATT law as a more or less self-contained system have much diminished as a result of the introduction of an appeal system, on points of law, before a standing Appellate Body. There is no denying that the case law of that organ—which could as well be called the World Trade Court[75]—has contributed much to the legalization of international trade relations. It is probably fair to say that, as a result, WTO law has a stronger bite than many other international agreements, including agreements which the Court of Justice recognized to be directly effective.

The establishment of the WTO triggered a great debate on the direct effect of WTO law, at political, judicial, and academic levels. The importance of the question could hardly be overestimated. In light of the broad scope of WTO law, covering trade in goods, trade in services, and intellectual property law, and in light of its many connections with EC law, the recognition of the direct effect of WTO law provisions would have opened up large avenues for claims based on WTO law, claims no doubt often directed at invalidating or setting aside either Community or national legislation. At political level, the Council and the Commission clarified from the outset that they were opposed to the recognition of direct effect. Their position is reflected in two legal documents. First, the Schedule of Commitments of the Community and its Member States under the GATS states in an introductory note that the rights and obligations arising from the GATS, including the schedule of commitments, shall have no self-executing effect and thus confer no rights directly on individual natural persons or juridical persons. Secondly, the Council Decision concluding the WTO Agreement on behalf of the EC states, in its preamble, that by its nature the agreement, including the annexes, is not susceptible to being directly invoked in Community or Member State courts.[76]

The academic debate on the question of direct effect of WTO law cannot be summarized in just a few sentences; there will be opportunity in the next section to discuss some of the main elements of that debate. At judicial level, Cosmas AG opened the discussion in *Affish* by arguing for a continuation of *International Fruit Company*. He considered that the WTO Agreement was still characterized by great

---

[74] See the Dispute Settlement Understanding (DSU).

[75] JHH Weiler, 'The Rule of Lawyers and the Ethos of Diplomats: Reflections on the Internal and External Legitimacy of WTO Dispute Settlement' (2001) 35 JWT 202.

[76] Council Decision 94/800 concerning the conclusion on behalf of the European Community, as regards matters within its competence, of the agreements reached in the Uruguay Round multilateral negotiations (1986–1994) [1994] OJ L336/1.

flexibility, and he was not impressed by the modifications to the dispute-settlement system and to the conditions for taking safeguard measures.[77] As the case concerned the SPS Agreement, he also analysed the provisions of that agreement, coming to the view that it required various implementing measures, an obstacle to recognition of direct effect. He finally pointed to the preamble to Decision 94/800,[78] which, in the absence of a corresponding provision in the text of the decision itself, could not by itself preclude direct effect, but none the less confirmed the fact that the weighty reasons against direct effect as expressed in the case law had not ceased to apply.[79] The Court, however, did not consider those issues, as it decided that they were not within the terms of the reference by the national court.

Almost a year later Tesauro AG delivered a powerful and thoroughly considered Opinion in *Hermès*,[80] both as regards the Court's jurisdiction to interpret the WTO Agreement[81] and as regards direct effect. The Advocate General first looked at the statement in the preamble to Decision 94/800, but was of the opinion, like Cosmas AG, that it did not bind the Court. He referred in that connection to the analysis in *Kupferberg*,[82] according to which, in the absence of the agreement itself laying down its effects, it was for the Court to determine them. In contrast to Cosmas AG, however, Tesauro did not accept that the *International Fruit Company* line of reasoning could as such be extended to the WTO Agreement. He first expressed some scepticism as regards that case law, taking the view that the characteristics of GATT were not very different from those of agreements which the Court recognized to be directly effective. He then looked at the modifications by the WTO Agreement, and considered that, as regards the flexibility which was at the basis of *International Fruit Company*, there were fundamental changes. The relationship between rules and exceptions as regards waivers and other exceptional measures had changed, and the dispute-settlement system had undergone a Copernican revolution through the reversal of the consensus requirement. The Advocate General was not impressed by the still available opportunity of compensation instead of compliance, pointing out that this was a purely provisional measure. His conclusion from all this was that the Court could not credibly maintain the *International Fruit Company* line of reasoning. He none the less left the door open for a continued denial of direct effect. He looked at the issue of reciprocity, pointing out that some other WTO members (notably the United States, Canada, and Japan) did not recognize direct effect, and that, in the absence of reciprocity in this respect, direct effect would place Community traders at a disadvantage compared with their foreign competitors.

---

[77] Tesauro AG referred *inter alia* to an influential analysis by CWA Timmermans, 'The Implementation of the Uruguay Round by the EC', in JHJ Bourgeois, F Berrod, and E Gippini Fournier (eds), *The Uruguay Round Results—A European Lawyers' Perspective* (European Interuniversity Press 1995) 501.

[78] N 76 above.

[79] Case C–183/95 *Affish v. Rijksdienst Keuring Vee en Vlees* [1997] ECR I–4315, paras 112–128 of the Opinion.

[80] Case C–53/96 *Hermès v. FHT* [1998] ECR I–3603. In the meantime Elmer AG had also argued against direct effect, but his Opinion contained little reasoning: see Joined Cases C–364/95 and C–365/95 *T Port v. Hauptzollamt Hamburg-Jonas* [1998] ECR I–1023, paras 27–31 of the Opinion.

[81] See Ch 8.   [82] N 35 above.

He then examined the Court's previous statements on reciprocity, particularly in *Kupferberg*.[83] The Advocate General effectively turned the Court's analysis there on its head: from the formulation that lack of reciprocity as regards direct effect did not in itself constitute lack of reciprocity as regards implementation of the agreement he concluded that there might be cases where one did lead to the other. As regards the WTO Agreement there could be no doubt that reciprocity was required, not only in the negotiation of the agreement but also in its performance, and the absence of recognition of direct effect by some other contracting parties could not but lead, at the very least, to an imbalance in the fulfilment of commitments. The Advocate General left it to the Court to undertake the, necessarily abstract, evaluation of whether the lack of reciprocity as regards direct effect would actually lead to lack of reciprocity in implementation. He concluded by reiterating his opinion that the *International Fruit Company* line of reasoning was no longer convincing, and that, if the Court intended to leave to the 'political' institutions the interpretation and, more generally, the 'management' of the provisions at issue, it should opt for reciprocity.[84]

In *Hermès*, too, the Court managed to avoid deciding the issue, by considering that the case was simply one of consistent interpretation and not of direct effect. Again a year later the Court had to rule in *Portugal v. Council*, a case concerning the legality of a Council decision concluding agreements on trade in textile products with Pakistan and India. Portugal claimed that the decision constituted a breach of certain rules and fundamental principles of the WTO, in particular those of GATT 1994, the Agreement on Textiles and Clothing, and the Agreement on Import Licensing Procedures.[85] Here the Court could no longer avoid the issue.

Saggio AG argued that Portugal should be entitled to rely on WTO law. He was perplexed as regards the *International Fruit Company* line of cases, in so far as the Court imposed the requirement of direct effect in actions concerning the legality or validity of Community acts. In his view all agreements binding on the Community could, on the basis of (current) Article 300(7) EC, form the basis for challenging Community acts, and such review could not be conditional upon direct effect.[86] He was not impressed by arguments based on reciprocity, drawing attention to the means available under general international law for taking action against the failure of another contracting party to implement an agreement. Nor did he feel that the statement in the preamble to Council Decision 94/800 was relevant: the Council did not have the authority to interfere with the operation of (current) Article 300(7) EC or with the jurisdiction of the Court of Justice or of national courts.[87]

The Court, however, did not follow the Advocate General's Opinion as regards direct effect. It effectively maintained its existing case law, but based it on a different reasoning. The analysis consists of two parts. In the first part[88] the Court started

---

[83] N 35 above.   [84] *Hermès* (n 80 above), paras 28–35 Opinion of Tesauro AG.
[85] Case C–149/96 *Portugal v. Council* [1999] ECR I–8395.   [86] See also Ch 8 and below.
[87] *Portugal v. Council* (n 85 above), paras 18–24 of the Opinion of Saggio AG.
[88] Ibid, paras 34–41 of the judgment.

by referring to *Kupferberg*: contracting parties were free to agree what effect the provisions of an agreement were to have, but if the question was not settled by the agreement it was for the Court to decide, as with any question of interpretation; also, according to the general rules of international law there had to be *bona fide* performance of every agreement, but although each contracting party was responsible for executing fully the commitments which it had undertaken it was nevertheless free to determine the legal means appropriate for attaining that end in its legal system, unless the agreement, interpreted in the light of its subject matter and purpose, itself specified those means. On that basis, the Court examined the WTO Agreement. It acknowledged the strengthening of the system of safeguards and the mechanism for resolving disputes, but nevertheless considered that the resulting system accorded considerable importance to negotiation between the parties. To demonstrate that, the Court turned to the dispute-settlement system, and in particular to the scope for compensation under the provisions of Article 22(1) and (2) DSU. It conceded that Article 22(1) showed a preference for full implementation of a recommendation to bring a measure into conformity with the WTO agreements in question, but pointed out that under Article 22(2), in the event of failure to implement, a member was required to enter into negotiations with a view to finding mutually acceptable compensation. Consequently, the Court continued, to require the judicial organs to refrain from applying the rules of domestic law which were inconsistent with the WTO agreements would have the consequence of depriving the legislative or executive organs of the contracting parties of the possibility afforded by this provision of entering into negotiated arrangements even on a temporary basis. It followed that the WTO agreements, interpreted in the light of their subject matter and purpose, did not determine the appropriate legal means of ensuring that they were applied in good faith in the legal order of the contracting parties.

At first glance this reasoning may seem conclusive (leaving aside whether it is convincing; see in that respect the discussion in the next section). Yet the Court added a second part,[89] which can only be understood against the background of its previous case law on direct effect. Indeed, the Court readily recognizes the direct effect of other international agreements, even though most of them do not 'determine the appropriate legal means of ensuring that they are applied in good faith etc.' either. So there needed to be further reasons for denying WTO law direct effect.

The Court opened this second part by indicating that it concerned, 'more particularly', the application of the WTO agreements in the Community legal order. It noted that the WTO was still founded, like GATT 1947, on the principle of negotiations with a view to 'entering into reciprocal and mutually advantageous arrangements' (see the preamble), and was thus distinguished, from the viewpoint of the Community, from agreements concluded between the Community and non-member countries which introduced a certain asymmetry of obligations or created

---

[89] Ibid, paras 42–49.

special relations of integration with the Community, such as the agreement which the Court was required to interpret in *Kupferberg*. The Court added that it was common ground that some of the contracting parties, which were among the most important commercial partners of the Community, had concluded from the subject matter and purpose of the WTO agreements that they were not among the rules applicable by their judicial organs when reviewing the legality of their rules of domestic law. The Court then acknowledged its statements on reciprocity in *Kupferberg*, but considered that in the case of the WTO agreements, based as they were on reciprocity, lack of reciprocity as regards judicial application could lead to disuniform application of the WTO rules. It added that to accept that the role of ensuring that Community law complied with those rules devolved directly on the Community judicature would deprive the legislative or executive organs of the Community of the scope for manœuvre enjoyed by their counterparts in the Community's trading partners. The Court concluded that it followed from all those considerations that, having regard to their nature and structure, the WTO agreements were not in principle among the rules in the light of which the Court was to review the legality of measures adopted by the Community institutions. That interpretation moreover corresponded with the statement in the preamble to Council Decision 94/800. Finally, the Court maintained the *Fediol* and *Nakajima* exception: it was only where the Community intended to implement a particular obligation assumed in the context of the WTO, or where the Community measure referred expressly to the precise provisions of the WTO agreements, that it was for the Court to review the legality of the Community measure in the light of the WTO rules.

In *Portugal v. Council* the Court did not mention the concept of direct effect, but that was not illogical: neither did the Court do so in *International Fruit Company* or in *Germany v. Council*, also cases concerning the validity/legality of Community acts. As analysed above, under the case law on the GATT of 1947 the same reasons led to (a) the conclusion that GATT does not confer rights on citizens, (b) the exclusion of GATT from grounds of review of the legality/validity of Community acts, and (c) the lack of direct effect of GATT in proceedings before national courts involving challenges to national law. As regards WTO law the Court takes the same approach. In *Dior* national courts expressly referred to the Court the question whether Article 50(6) TRIPs had direct effect, and the Court simply replied by stating that, for the reasons set out in *Portugal v. Council*, the provisions of TRIPs, an annex to the WTO Agreement, were not such as to create rights upon which individuals could rely directly before the courts by virtue of Community law. In the next paragraph the Court called this 'the finding that the provisions of TRIPs do not have direct effect'.[90]

---

[90] Joined Cases C–300/98 and C–392/98 *Parfums Christian Dior v. Tuk Consultancy* [2000] ECR I–11307, paras 41–45. See also Case C–89/99 *Schieving-Nijstad v. Groeneveld* [2001] ECR I–5851, paras 52–55.

It may be added that the Court, in light of the mixed character of the WTO Agreement, confined this lack of direct effect to fields in respect of which the Community has already legislated, as was the case with trade marks. On the other hand, stated the Court, in a field in respect of which the Community had not yet legislated and which consequently fell within the competence of the Member States, the protection of intellectual property rights, and measures adopted for that purpose by the judicial authorities (the subject matter of Article 50(6) TRIPs), did not fall within Community law. Accordingly, Community law neither required nor forbade that the legal order of a Member State should accord to individuals the right to rely directly on the provision in question or that it should oblige the courts to apply that provision of their own motion.[91] In other words, the lack of direct effect extended only to provisions coming within Community competence.

In the meantime the Court maintained the principle of implementation (*Fediol* and *Nakajima*), so that there are cases in which it is possible for a party to rely on WTO law (see below). It must also be noted that in the appeals against the CFI's *Biret* judgments, on non-contractual liability for failing to comply with WTO law as regards legislation on beef treated with hormones, Alber AG made a strong case for the direct effect of rulings by the WTO Dispute Settlement Body (DSB).[92] He distinguished such direct effect from the general direct effect of WTO law, reasoning that the objections of *Portugal v. Council* did not apply in cases where the DSB had made a ruling against the Community, with which the latter needed to comply pursuant to WTO law. The Court appeared receptive to the Advocate General's case. It held that the CFI had made errors of law by not addressing the argument that the legal effects of the DSB decision regarding hormones called into question the lack of direct effect of WTO law and provided grounds for a review by the Community courts of the legality of the relevant EC legislation. Those statements were in the nature of *obiter dicta*, because on the facts the CFI's errors turned out to be irrelevant. The Court therefore upheld the CFI's judgments. The question of the direct effect of DSB decisions adopting WTO panel or Appellate Body reports thus remains open.[93]

Other multilateral agreements

All of the above case law concerns either GATT and WTO law or bilateral and multilateral agreements with non-member countries aimed at developing a particular kind of general relationship with such countries (co-operation, free-trade, or association). There are however very few cases on the legal effects of other

[91] *Dior* (n 90, above), paras 46–48. See also Ch 8.
[92] Opinions of Alber AG in Case C–93/02 P *Biret International v. Council* and Case C–94/02 P *Etablissements Biret v. Council*, 15 May 2003, paras 70–119.
[93] Ibid., judgments of 30 September 2003, not yet reported. See further Eeckhout (n 15 above), 51–5.

multilateral agreements, for example in the field of environmental protection. Only two judgments are worth mentioning.

Ex parte Compassion in World Farming concerned a challenge to the validity of a directive on minimum standards of protection of calves,[94] in connection with the use of the so-called veal crate system. Compassion in World Farming argued that the directive was in breach of the European Convention for the Protection of Animals kept for Farming Purposes,[95] drawn up within the Council of Europe, and of the Recommendation concerning Cattle adopted within the framework of that convention. The Court did not agree. It considered that it was clear from the actual wording of the convention that the contracting parties had considerable discretion in the choice of appropriate methods for implementing it. The concern expressed in the convention to make the contracting parties aware of the need to maintain rearing conditions which respect the well-being of animals in vital areas was not followed up by the definition of standards whose non-observance could affect the validity of the directive. The recommendation, on the other hand, provided expressly that it was not directly applicable in the national law of the contracting parties and that it was to be implemented according to the method that each party considers adequate. The Court further considered that a document of that kind did not contain legally binding obligations.[96]

In *Netherlands v. European Parliament and Council* the applicant argued that the directive on the legal protection of biotechnological inventions[97] was in breach of *inter alia* the Convention on Biological Diversity.[98] The Court contrasted that convention with WTO law, and stated that the exclusion from grounds of review relating to WTO law could not be applied to the convention, which, unlike the WTO Agreement, was not strictly based on reciprocal and mutually advantageous arrangements. It then stated, without further explanation, that, even if the convention contained provisions which did not have direct effect, in the sense that they did not create rights which individuals could rely on directly before the courts, that fact did not preclude review by the courts of compliance with the obligations incumbent on the Community as a party to that agreement.[99] Thus, the Court appeared to disentangle direct effect from grounds of review of Community acts, but it did not further clarify that, as it subsequently turned its reasoning to a different type of argument: that the Netherlands' plea should be understood as being directed, not so much at a direct breach by the Community of its international obligations, as at an obligation imposed on the Member States by the directive to breach their own obligations under international law.[100]

---

[94] Council Directive 91/629 [1991] OJ L340/28.
[95] Approved by Council Decision 78/923 [1978] OJ L323/12.
[96] *Compassion in World Farming* (n 40 above), paras 30–37.
[97] Directive 98/44 of the European Parliament and the Council [1998] OJ L213/13.
[98] Approved by Council Decision 93/626 [1993] OJ L309/1.
[99] Here the Court referred to *Racke* (n 60 above); see below on general international law.
[100] Case C–377/98 *Netherlands v. European Parliament and Council* [2001] ECR I–7079, paras 52–55.

Grounds for recognizing or denying direct effect

The distinction between structure and nature of the agreement and direct effect of specific provisions

At this point it is appropriate to examine and discuss the grounds for the Court's recognition or denial of direct effect of an agreement concluded by the Community. The first issue to consider is the distinction which the Court makes between the direct effect of an agreement as such, or as a whole, and the direct effect of specific provisions of an agreement.[101] It is clear from the case law that the Court is favourably disposed towards recognizing that an agreement may as such have direct effect. There is in fact at the time of writing only one type of agreement, those in the context of the GATT and the WTO, which the Court denies direct effect in principle, and the Court regularly formulates the issue of direct effect in terms of a presumption in favour of direct effect: precise, clear, and unconditional provisions of an agreement have direct effect, unless the nature and structure of the agreement prevent that.

This favourable disposition towards direct effect, and the distinction between, on the one hand, the nature and structure of the agreement, and, on the other, the clear, precise, etc. character of the agreement's provisions is theoretically convincing. By taking such an approach the Court fosters general receptiveness to international agreements, a receptiveness which is justified in light of Article 300(7) EC, in light of the basic principle that agreements concluded by the Community form an integral part of the Community legal order, and in light of the EU's own origins. Indeed, one should not lose sight of the fact that the whole of the EU structure had, and continues to have, its basis in international treaties which, the Court recognized, had the capacity to create a new legal order. It would hardly be appropriate for EU law to develop an attitude of hostility towards other international treaties or agreements, which, of course, do not create a new legal order, but are none the less in essence identical legal instruments. On the other hand, precisely because of the distinction between the EU's own new legal order and classic international law it is appropriate that direct effect should not be automatic, and that there may be agreements which, in light of their nature and structure, cannot produce such effect. If that were not the case then agreements concluded by the Community would fully benefit from direct effect, and from its supremacy twin, in exactly the same way as 'internal' Community law. They would, effectively, be clothed with the imperial gowns of constitutionalism.

The distinction which the Court makes is therefore convincing in theory. It is however another question whether the way in which, in practice, the Court makes that distinction is also persuasive. We must therefore now turn to the Court's analyses of nature and structure of agreements from the perspective of direct effect.

---

[101] Cf Cheyne (n 17 above), 40; Kaddous (n 17 above), 382.

Structure and nature of GATT

It may be helpful to state at the outset of the analysis one of the main theses which this chapter advances. That thesis is that the denial of the direct effect of GATT and WTO law is appropriate and justified, but that the current distinction between the WTO agreements and other agreements (see *Portugal v. Council*), which are all recognized as having direct effect, is much less persuasive.

In *International Fruit Company*, the Court for the first time referred to the structure and nature of an agreement, which at the time it called 'spirit, general scheme and terms',[102] In essence, the Court considered the GATT of 1947 to be too flexible to be given direct effect. If the Court was right about the flexibility of GATT, then it was surely correct that it was not capable of conferring rights on citizens. Where an international agreement really only constitutes a flexible framework for relations between contracting parties and for further negotiations, and where the scope for derogations, exceptions, and reservations is such that an agreement effectively cannot impose strict legal discipline on the contracting parties, it would hardly be appropriate to give the agreement's provisions direct effect in the internal legal order, and to allow parties to claim rights under the agreement. It is in such a case not sufficient to apply the traditional direct-effect criteria of clarity, precision, etc. to individual provisions of the agreement: there may well be clear and precise provisions in such a flexible agreement, but the overall flexibility may be such that one should not focus too narrowly on individual provisions which, because they are part and parcel of the whole agreement, do not in the end lay down clear and precise obligations.

Was the Court right about the flexibility of the GATT of 1947? Many commentators criticized this case law,[103] yet the Court was on firm ground. It was generally recognized that the GATT was a mixture of law and diplomacy, most aptly described by Jackson's distinction between power-oriented and rule-oriented diplomacy.[104] The Court was essentially right to refer to the scope for exceptions and derogations, and to the political element of the dispute-settlement system. If a contracting party to GATT was able to oppose adoption of a panel report concluding that it violated GATT rules, and thus to oppose an official GATT finding of a violation, how could it be said that GATT provisions were sufficiently unconditional and inflexible as to have direct legal effect in the Community legal order?

Much of the criticism of the Court's case law was clearly inspired by a desire to reinforce the legal dimension of GATT. That was arguably a noble ambition, and it

---

[102] N 6 above.

[103] E.g. E-U Petersmann, 'The EEC as a GATT Member—Legal Conflicts between GATT Law and European Community Law', in M Hilf, FG Jacobs, and E-U Petersmann (eds), *The European Community and GATT* (Kluwer, 1989) 53–9; KJ Kuilwijk, *The European Court of Justice and the GATT Dilemma* (Nexed Editions, 1996).

[104] JH Jackson, *The World Trading System* (2nd edn, MIT Press, 1988) 109–12. It may be noted that even as of today, in the context of the WTO, there is authoritative discussion of the diplomatic component: see Weiler (n 75 above).

has led to the legally much stronger WTO. However, it was not for the European Court of Justice to take a 'progressive' stand in the debate about law and diplomacy, and to try to push the GATT towards a stronger legalization by recognizing the direct effect of its provisions. It is also true that, in the course of the 1970s and 1980s, the GATT itself travelled some way towards legalization, but not in such a way as to justify the quantum leap of giving direct effect.

In any event, the GATT of 1947 no longer exists, subsumed as it has been in the establishment of the WTO. At this stage it is therefore more important to examine and discuss the reasons for not giving direct effect to WTO law. Indeed, as Tesauro AG pointed out in *Hermès*,[105] the *International Fruit Company* line of reasoning was no longer justified once the WTO had been established. The Court recognized this by developing a new reasoning in its judgment in *Portugal v. Council*.[106] A careful analysis of that reasoning is crucial for understanding on what grounds the nature and structure of an agreement may preclude direct effect.[107]

Structure and nature of the WTO Agreement

As was mentioned, the reasoning of the Court in *Portugal v. Council* is divided into two parts. The Court starts by recalling the relevant principles: an agreement concluded by the EC may itself determine its effects in the laws of the contracting parties; where that is not the case, it is for the Court to decide those effects. Accordingly, the first part of the judgment examines whether the WTO Agreement itself provides, expressly or implicitly, that there is to be direct legal effect. As the conclusion is that it does not, the second part contains the Court's own assessment of the effect of WTO law. The relationship between the two parts is intricate, in particular because in the first part the Court does not merely look for a clear statement in the WTO Agreement *pro* direct effect, but goes on to examine whether a direct-effect requirement can be inferred from the WTO provisions on dispute settlement. In its other case law on the direct effect of agreements the Court devotes hardly any attention to the preliminary point of establishing whether the agreement itself provides for direct effect.[108] So this is the only judgment where the Court engages so deeply in this exercise. By doing that, however, the judgment raises the question of the relationship between this first part and the second part, where the Court examines, autonomously as it were, whether there is to be direct effect under EC law. If the reply to the question of the first part is negative, does that not pre-empt the discussion in the second part? What elements could be relevant to the Court's autonomous assessment, other than the agreement itself? As we will see, the Court does return to the WTO Agreement in the second part; but it also brings

---

[105] N 80 above.   [106] N 85 above.

[107] See also P Eeckhout, 'Judicial Enforcement of WTO Law in the European Union' (2002) 5 JIEL 83.

[108] In *International Fruit Company* (n 6 above), the Court did not make any distinction between examining the agreement itself and making an autonomous EC law assessment.

in considerations which are indeed autonomous, predicated on the EU's constitutional order.

How should we evaluate this first part? By going beyond a search for a clear-cut direct effect provision in the WTO Agreement the Court has not played safe, and some of the criticism is harsh. It is suggested that the Court has misinterpreted the DSU provisions. There is in fact no option for non-compliance under WTO law. Retaliation and compensation are mere temporary alternatives to full compliance, and the latter is absolutely mandated by the DSU.[109] But that critique, with respect, does not capture the essence of the Court's reasoning. The Court does not examine whether the WTO Agreement contains a commitment of full compliance. What the Court examines is whether the WTO Agreement mandates direct effect.[110] Those are two distinct and different questions of law. There is much to be said for the view that the DSU, properly interpreted, requires full compliance, yet that is not to be equated with direct effect. International agreements generally require full compliance, yet international law does not generally mandate direct effect. Where it comes to establishing direct effect, it is indeed meaningful that compensation and retaliation are temporary alternatives to compliance. Even if one may argue about the exact meaning of the relevant DSU provisions, it is clear that current WTO practice bears out that the above is essentially correct.[111] If direct effect were given, those alternatives would no longer be at the EU's disposal. Any private party could then claim the illegality of EC (or Member State) legislation, cutting off all attempts at buying time for amendment or for settlement.

The Court could have highlighted another feature of WTO dispute settlement which also shows that the DSU does not mandate direct effect as we know it in EC law. WTO dispute-settlement rulings are prospective. The WTO member found to have violated the agreement is requested to bring its laws and practices into compliance for the future, but there is no requirement of reparation for past misconduct—no compensation for either WTO Members or private parties.[112] However, direct effect as it was sought in *Portugal* and in other cases is not merely prospective. If WTO law were a basis for challenging the legality of an EC act, either under Article 230 EC or through a reference to the Court of Justice under Article 234 EC, successful challenges would lead to annulment *ex tunc*,[113] which is inherent to the EC judicial review process.[114] Depending on the circumstances, compensation

---

[109] Griller (n 62 above), 450–4, referring to JH Jackson, 'The WTO Dispute Settlement Understanding—Misunderstandings on the Nature of Legal Obligation', in J Cameron and K Campbell, *Dispute Resolution in the World Trade Organization* (Cameron May, 1998) 73.

[110] Cf Bourgeois (n 62 above), 109.

[111] See e.g. the protracted nature of the bananas and hormones disputes.

[112] But see WTO Panel Report, *Australia—Subsidies Provided to Producers and Exporters of Automotive Leather—Recourse to Article 21.5 of the DSU by the United States* ('Australia—Leather'), WT/DS126/RW, adopted 11 February 2000.

[113] JHJ Bourgeois, 'The European Court of Justice and the WTO', in JHH Weiler (ed), *The EU, the WTO and NAFTA* (OUP, 2000) 121.

[114] Joined Cases 97, 99, 193, and 215/86 *Asteris v. Commission* [1988] ECR 2181, para. 30. See M Brealey and M Hoskins, *Remedies in EC Law* (2nd edn, Sweet & Maxwell, 1998) 328–30.

might have to be awarded to private parties. Direct effect would therefore entail much more important legal, and in some cases financial, consequences of non-compliance than a prospective WTO ruling.

In the second part of *Portugal v. Council* the Court examines whether, notwithstanding the conclusion that the WTO Agreement itself does not mandate direct effect, such effect would flow from applying autonomous principles of EC law. Such an examination was necessary in light of the fact that previous case law readily accepted direct effect of other international agreements—most, if not all, of which are equally silent as regards direct effect. So, if in the case of other agreements the fact that they do not impose direct effect is no barrier for granting them such effect, why not give direct effect to WTO law? The obstacle in this case, according to the Court, is reciprocity. A popular reading of *Portugal v. Council* is that the Court has finally shown its hand. It has often been suggested that the 'real' reason for the lack of direct effect of the GATT of 1947 was the fact that other GATT contracting parties did not recognize such effect.[115] In *Portugal v. Council*, so it seems, the Court has been outed. It is the fact that the US and Japan (and others) are denying WTO law direct effect in their domestic laws which stops the Court from recognizing its direct effect in EC law.

We need however to take a closer look at the Court's analysis. The starting point is that the WTO Agreement, like the GATT of 1947, is still based on reciprocity. That distinguishes it, in the Court's view, from other agreements concluded by the EC, which introduce a certain asymmetry of obligations or create special relations of integration. The Court then points to the lack of direct effect in the legal systems of the most important commercial partners of the EU. It attempts to strengthen that point by stating that those partners 'have concluded from the subject matter and purpose of the WTO agreements' that they are not to serve as a basis for judicial review of domestic legislation. There is a suggestion here that those commercial partners have created some kind of precedent as regards legal assessment of the WTO Agreement's lack of direct effect. However, as regards the US at least, it is probably fair to say that the refusal of direct effect was more in the nature of a policy decision, inspired by concerns over sovereignty rather than being based on a legal reading of WTO law.[116]

The Court subsequently faces up to the main hurdle for invoking reciprocity. Had it not emphatically stated in *Kupferberg* that lack of reciprocity in the recognition of direct effect is not in itself such as to constitute a lack of reciprocity in the implementation of the agreement?[117] Nevertheless, in the case of WTO law the Court does see a clear link between the two. Lack of reciprocity in direct effect may lead to a disuniform application of the WTO rules. Then comes the final, and

---

[115] M Hilf, 'The Role of National Courts in International Trade Relations' (1997) 18 Michigan Journal of International Law 324.

[116] See DW Leebron, 'Implementation of the Uruguay Round Results in the United States', in JH Jackson and AO Sykes, *Implementing the Uruguay Round* (OUP, 1997) 209–18.

[117] *Kupferberg* (n 35 above), para 18.

arguably decisive point: to accept that the role of ensuring that EC law complies with WTO rules devolves directly on the Community judicature would deprive the legislative and executive organs of the Community of the scope for manœuvre enjoyed by their counterparts in the EU's trading partners. The conclusion is that WTO law is not among the rules in light of which the Court is to review the legality of measures adopted by the EC institutions. The Court also expressly refers to the fact that that conclusion corresponds to what is stated in the preamble to the Council's decision to conclude the WTO Agreement.[118]

This full account of the Court's reasoning is necessary for revealing the core meaning of *Portugal v. Council*. Reciprocity is indeed the cornerstone, but ultimately it is not reciprocity as such which leads the Court to deny WTO law direct effect. Rather, it is the impact of direct effect on the EU's political institutions. If direct effect were granted, those institutions would lose the scope for manœuvre which they currently have as regards implementation of WTO law, particularly in case of disputes with other WTO Members. The hands of those institutions would be much more tied than the hands of their US, Japanese, and other counterparts. Ultimately, the Court is unwilling to take that step of tying the hands of the EU's legislative and executive organs. This is the clear constitutional dimension of *Portugal v. Council*, and it goes beyond the issue of reciprocity in international trade relations. The Court defers to the EC legislature, in terms of respecting both the statement in the preamble and any specific policies, now or in the future, which may cause WTO friction.[119]

The Court's reference to reciprocity and its desire not to interfere with the EU's political institutions may be looked at as overt judicial policy-making. It is submitted, however, that such policy-making was in any event unavoidable. Whatever the Court decided in *Portugal v. Council*, and whichever way it chose to present the arguments in support of its ruling, there was in any event wide judicial discretion which could only be filled through judicial policy-making. The WTO Agreement itself is clearly not conclusive as to its domestic legal effect. It is not interpreted by the WTO organs as requiring any particular type of domestic legal effect, let alone full direct effect. The EC legislature, when concluding the agreement, made no more than a preambular statement about undesired effect. Whether *pro* or *contra* direct effect, the Court could not avoid reaching a decision on grounds other than judicial policy. Any formal legal reasoning could only serve to dress up (and disguise?) the judicial decision.

Griller argues that the Court is simply giving a licence to the EU institutions to violate WTO law, and that giving such a licence runs counter to Article 300(7) EC.[120] This critique is however grounded in an approach towards compliance with WTO law which is too formal and places too much faith in judicial enforcement. Judicial rulings are by no means the only or even most appropriate method for ensuring that

---

[118] Council Decision 94/800 (n 76 above).

[119] Cf Cheyne (n 17 above) 272, who presages and defends this approach on the basis of the 'need to avoid unnecessary conflict with the political institutions in an area where the policy choices are so significant and the implications so diverse that it is not an area which is appropriate for judicial involvement'.

[120] Griller (n 62 above), 454 and 460–1.

the EU (or any other WTO Member) complies with its WTO law commitments. In *Portugal v. Council* the Court is merely saying that, as a rule, it will not act as a judicial enforcer of WTO law. It is essentially leaving it to the political institutions to determine the scope and meaning of the EC's obligations. That may well be the most appropriate course of action for a legal system such as that set up by the WTO Agreement, a legal system which is still young and much contested, not only politically, but also as to the precise scope and meaning of its wide-ranging and multifarious provisions. It is vital to bear in mind that, as long as the WTO dispute-settlement organs have not reached a final ruling in a case, violations of WTO law are presumptive. As long as Geneva has not ruled against them, the EU's political institutions are entitled to argue that they do comply with WTO law. General direct effect would confer on the courts the task of reviewing claims and arguments concerning violations, giving them the authority to judge compliance. Dozens of cases could be brought in which private parties would invoke WTO law against EC acts or against acts of the EC Member States. There is little doubt that a majority of those would be cases which have no counterpart in WTO dispute settlement, such that it would not be possible for the courts to rely on panel or Appellate Body rulings as specific authority for resolution of the case. European courts, with the Court of Justice at the apex, might become day-to-day interpreters and enforcers of WTO law, with little or no guarantee that their rulings actually amounted to a correct interpretation of WTO law, or at least an interpretation with which the Appellate Body (the WTO's final judicial interpreter) and the WTO Members (the ultimate interpreters of WTO law: see Article IX(2) WTO Agreement) would agree.[121]

Nor does direct effect guarantee full compliance. A WTO dispute may be brought against the EU in a case which was never submitted to the domestic courts. Or a case may first be brought before the European courts, and they may conclude that there is no violation, whereas WTO dispute settlement may come to a different view later on. One would then have a clash between, for example, the Court of Justice and the Appellate Body. That would not make matters any better for the faithful EU implementation of commitments.

All of this is different, of course, in those cases in which a WTO dispute has run its full course, where a panel and, if called upon, the Appellate Body have spoken, and the DSB has sanctioned their rulings. In such cases the scope and meaning of WTO law are beyond legal dispute, as is the violation, where established. But one cannot base a general direct effect theory on those actual WTO cases. They raise a different issue, namely the issue of the domestic legal effect of actual WTO dispute-settlement rulings.[122]

The absence from the WTO's institutional constellation of a mechanism akin to the EC preliminary rulings procedure raises further issues.[123] Indeed, the question

---

[121] Cheyne (n 17 above), 267–8.   [122] See n 93 above.
[123] See also M Krajewski, *Verfassungsperspektiven und Legitimation des Rechts der Welthandelsorganisation (WTO)* (Duncker & Humblot, 2001) 63–7 and Rosas (n 62 above), 812.

is whether in the current procedural matrices direct effect of WTO law would actually contribute to the proper development of WTO law and of the WTO as such. As mentioned above, if direct effect of WTO law were recognized there would be much domestic litigation in which parties would aim to rely on WTO law. Think only of TRIPs, with its potential impact on daily practice in intellectual property law. How many of the questions of law raised in such domestic proceedings would ever reach WTO dispute settlement? Very few, one may suspect. In those circumstances, which would be the methods for ensuring a more or less uniform interpretation of WTO law? Which would be the methods for avoiding domestic courts adopting interpretations which are completely out of touch with prevailing Geneva views and may therefore cause more harm than good?

Direct effect could also interfere with the rationale and operating method of WTO dispute settlement. It is fairly obvious that the Appellate Body has so far been a cautious judicial operator, showing much awareness for the sensitivity of WTO law and taking care to gauge and calibrate the acceptability of its interpretations and rulings.[124] This has led to a marked case-by-case approach, focused more on leaving some scope for manœuvre for future cases than on creating much legal certainty. Prime examples are the Appellate Body's approach to the concept of like products, central to WTO non-discrimination rules, and the concept of necessity under Article XX GATT, the general exceptions clause. In the case of like products the Appellate Body even goes so far as to use the image of an accordion to indicate that the concept can be stretched and squeezed.[125] This approach may be well suited to WTO dispute settlement, and it may be appropriate for the gradual development of WTO law through dispute settlement in a manner acceptable to the broad WTO membership. However, if there were direct effect, the WTO dispute-settlement organs would also need to keep an eye on the interpretation and application of WTO law by domestic courts. It could be very difficult to combine all that, for domestic courts are not well served by the degree of elaboration and sophistication which WTO dispute settlement appears to require.[126] For direct effect to work well, there would need to be much more clarity, precision, and conciseness.

At present the WTO as an organization is called into question. This is not the place to engage in the globalization debate, or to discuss the merits of the various critiques which are made of the role and impact of the WTO. The European experience since the Maastricht Treaty none the less teaches that general contestation needs to be taken seriously, whether one regards it as well founded or not. One cannot divorce the law from this context. To the extent that there are doubts about the levels of democracy, transparency, and legitimacy (to mention just those) in and of the WTO,[127]

---

[124] Weiler (n 75 above); R Howse and E Tuerk, 'The WTO Impact on Internal Regulations—A Case Study of the Canada–EC Asbestos Dispute', in de Búrca and Scott (n 62 above), 304–6.

[125] WTO Appellate Body Report, *Japan—Taxes on Alcoholic Beverages*, WT/DS8/AB/R, WT/DS10/AB/R and WT/DS11/AB/R, adopted 1 November 1996.

[126] Cf von Bogdandy (n 62 above), 31.

[127] See e.g. M Krajewski, 'Democratic Legitimacy and Constitutional Perspectives of WTO Law' (2001) 35 JWT 167.

it is obvious that full-scale direct effect becomes difficult to defend; even more so where one advocates that it is for a court to decide this, contrary to the expressed view of the political institutions.

The conclusion must therefore be that the Court is right not to give WTO law direct effect. One should also not lose sight of the fact that, under certain conditions, the Court is prepared to interpret and apply WTO law: as we will see the principle of consistent interpretation extends to WTO law, and the principle of implementation (*Fediol* and *Nakajima*) permits judicial review on grounds of WTO law where Community legislation implements or refers to WTO law. Those forms of judicial application of WTO law are useful, even if they do not go as far as full direct effect, and they create channels of communication between EC and WTO law. The judgment in *Portugal v. Council* none the less raises a number of further issues regarding the general approach towards direct effect of international agreements. They include the role of the EU's political institutions; the contrast with other international agreements; and the relationship between direct effect and rights of private parties.

The role of the political institutions

In *Portugal v. Council* the Court was unwilling to tie the hands of the EU's political institutions, and left them scope for manœuvre in their dealings and negotiations with other WTO members. It added that the lack of direct effect was confirmed by the statement in the preamble to Council Decision 94/800, but it did not base its decision on that statement. The Court none the less followed the position of the Commission and the Council. All this raises the question of the role of the EU's political institutions, which constitute the EU's legislature and executive, in the process of determining the legal effects of agreements concluded by the Community.

It may be appropriate to look first at the legal value of the statement in the preamble to Decision 94/800. The Advocates General who examined this issue came to the view that it was not binding on the Court of Justice, applying the principle in *Kupferberg* that, if the agreement itself does not determine its legal effects this is for the Court to decide as a question of interpretation of the agreement.[128] Most of the literature on the subject follows the same approach.[129] Advocates General Cosmas and Tesauro did however note that the statement was only part of the preamble, and was not reflected in the operative part of the decision. They thus implicitly left open the question whether the operative part of a Council decision concluding an agreement could determine the legal effects of the agreement. There are forceful arguments in support of a positive reply to that question.

---

[128] *Affish* (n 79 above), para 127 of the Opinion of Cosmas AG; *Hermès* (n 80 above), para 24 of the Opinion of Tesauro AG; *Portugal v. Council* (n 85 above), para 20 of the Opinion of Saggio AG.

[129] E.g. G Gaja, *Introduzione al diritto comunitario* (Editori Laterza, 1996) 161.

In *Kupferberg* the Court took as a starting point that 'Community institutions which have power to negotiate and conclude an agreement with a non-member country are free to agree with that country what effect the provisions of the agreement are to have in the internal legal order of the contracting parties', and that 'only if that question has not been settled by the agreement does it fall for decision by the courts having jurisdiction in the matter, and in particular by the Court of Justice'.[130] The Court there effectively stressed the power of the (now) EU institutions which negotiate agreements to agree on internal effects with the other parties. It did not however expressly contemplate the situation where it proves impossible to find such agreement, but where the institutions none the less have strong views on the effects which the agreement should or should not have. It is actually difficult to see on what grounds the political institutions would not have the power unilaterally to determine the effects in Community law of an agreement. The institutions responsible for negotiating and concluding an agreement, i.e. the Commission, the Council, and to some degree the European Parliament, have the authority to determine, in agreement with the other contracting parties, the international obligations which the Community enters into. It is their task to define and accept the substance and content of such obligations, including, depending on the case, methods for enforcing such obligations, at the international or internal level. This task is political. Yet the internal legal effects of an agreement clearly affect the nature of the obligations which the Community undertakes, as the case of the WTO Agreement demonstrates. If the political institutions have the authority to determine, by agreement, substance, content, and methods of enforcement of international obligations, why should they not have the authority, where it proves impossible to agree with the other contracting parties on the internal legal effects of the agreement, to determine those effects in certain ways? This is essentially a political function, as the case law on the lack of direct effect of WTO law illustrates, and it is more legitimate for the political institutions to determine internal legal effects of an agreement than for the judiciary, particularly where the issue is much contested. Ideally, of course, those institutions would have greater democratic legitimacy; in other words, the role of the European Parliament in the negotiation and conclusion of agreements should be strengthened.[131] In the case of the WTO Agreement the European Parliament did not, unfortunately, adopt a position on the effects of that agreement in Community law.[132] If however there were ever a firm decision by the Commission, the Council, and the European Parliament on what should or should not be the internal legal effect of an agreement, the Court should consider itself bound by such

---

[130] *Kupferberg* (n 35 above), para 17.   [131] See Ch 6.

[132] See however the Parliament's Resolution on the relationships between international law, Community law, and the constitutional law of the Member States, in which the Parliament 'calls for a clear statement of the relationship between international law and European law to be written into the EC Treaty, in terms of the EC being equated with nation states, which means that international law is applicable not directly but only after it has been declared applicable by an internal legal act of the EC or after its substance has been transposed into EC legislation': [1997] OJ C325/26, para 14.

a decision, on the grounds of basic constitutional principles governing the division of powers between the institutions. This would correspond with the approach in many other legal systems.[133]

The position defended here does not amount to a revolution in the current doctrine of direct effect of international agreements. The first question would continue to be whether the agreement itself determines the effects it is to have in the legal order of the contracting parties, and the Community institutions would be bound by that. Also, where the political institutions do not adopt a position on the effects of the agreement, which under current practices is the rule, the Court would continue to decide whether there was direct effect or not. However, where the political institutions do lay down the effects the agreement is to have, the Court should defer to that decision.

The contrast with other international agreements

In *Portugal v. Council* the Court emphasized the fact that the WTO continues to be based on the principle of negotiation with a view to 'entering into reciprocal and mutually advantageous arrangements', and considered that it was thus distinguishable from agreements which introduce a certain asymmetry of obligations or create special relations of integration with the Community.[134] In this respect it referred to the free-trade agreement with Portugal, in issue in *Kupferberg*.[135] In other words, the WTO is based on reciprocity and thereby differs from the agreements which have direct effect.

As it is stated in the judgment, that distinction is not convincing, and several criticisms can be made.[136] To start with, the WTO Agreement also contains provisions establishing an asymmetry of obligations: those on more favourable and differential treatment of developing countries. Yet the Court does not mention or analyse them, and considers that the whole of the WTO Agreement lacks direct effect. The very agreement in issue in *Portugal v. Council*, on trade in textiles and clothing products, was designed to give better access to developed country markets for imports from developing countries. It may be difficult to differentiate between parts of the WTO Agreement for the purpose of granting or denying direct effect; the symmetry or asymmetry in obligations is really located in the bilateral relations between the EC as a WTO member and third country members, in so far as they are governed by WTO law.[137] It is none the less the case that WTO law and policies have a strong asymmetric dimension, which may be increasing, as exemplified by the current Doha 'development round'.

---

[133] E.g. the UK: see R Higgins, 'United Kingdom' in Jacobs and Roberts (n 7 above), 123–31; Italy, see G Gaja, 'Italy', in ibid, 87; Germany, see J Frowein, 'Germany', in ibid, 71–2; the US, see Leebron (n 116 above).

[134] *Portugal v. Council* (n 85 above).   [135] N 35 above.

[136] Cf van den Broek (n 62 above), 411.

[137] J Pauwelyn, 'The Nature of WTO Obligations', Jean Monnet Working Paper No 1/02, <www.jeanmonnetprogram.org/papers/02/020101.html>.

Moreover, when one looks at it more closely the idea of reciprocity versus asymmetry is difficult to capture. In formal terms all international agreements establish reciprocal obligations. One needs to look at substantive commitments to make an assessment of whether there is reciprocity or asymmetry, and making such an assessment may become increasingly difficult. The Yaoundé and Lomé Conventions, which the Court held to be directly effective, were clearly asymmetrical, but the current Cotonou Convention is much less so. Would that mean that it is not capable of producing direct effect?

It is also worth noting that there are misconceptions in the appreciation of reciprocity in the context of the GATT and the WTO. Commentators often refer to the argument that, if there were direct effect, European companies or traders would be at a disadvantage compared with, say, their American counterparts. The underlying assumption is that direct effect would give foreign exporters to Europe a weapon for obtaining market access which European exporters to other WTO members do not have at their disposal. However, the calculation of trade advantages cannot be reduced to such a simple equation. As international trade theory has taught for decades, a country's economy generally benefits from free imports, because of reduced prices for local importers and consumers. From a purely economic perspective, therefore, there is no cost to free trade. However, the Court in *Portugal v. Council* does not refer to the effect on private companies; instead it refers to the effect on the scope for manœuvre of the EU's political institutions, which is more convincing.

In the judgment the Court also distinguishes the reciprocity-based WTO from agreements which create special relations of integration with the Community. That distinction is convincing as regards association agreements, in particular those which prepare third countries for accession to the EU. As such agreements establish the closest type of relationship, in many respects modelled on EU law and policies, the extension of the EC law concept of direct effect is appropriate. However, the Court has clearly cast the direct-effect net more widely. The free-trade agreements with the EFTA countries, preceding the EEA, did not establish special relations of integration other than the creation of a free trade area in conformity with Article XXIV GATT. It therefore seems that the mere fact of creating preferential trade relations, going beyond and derogating from the GATT most-favoured-nation principle, is sufficient for direct effect. That, however, comes dangerously close to a political preference for regional integration over a multilateral framework based on non-discrimination. The Court also runs the risk of being seen to recognize the direct effect of agreements of which the EC is clearly the dominant contracting party, and not to recognize such effect for agreements where there is real, political reciprocity or multilateralism.

A rights-based approach towards direct effect

In *International Fruit Company* the Court stated that the GATT did not confer rights on citizens. The relationship between the concept of direct effect and the creation of 'rights' calls for some further exploration.

Petersmann has been the exponent of a current of thought which considers that GATT and WTO law include and confirm constitutional-type rights of free trade, logically flowing from Western constitutional traditions which emphasize concepts of non-discrimination and are free-market oriented.[138] Seen in such light, GATT and WTO law clearly ought to have direct effect so as to enable citizens to enforce the rights which such law, having a constitutional function, confers on them. The argument has a lot of merit, but it ultimately stumbles over the obstacle that neither the contracting parties to the original GATT nor the members of the current WTO have ever confirmed it. There is nothing in the agreements which suggests that the parties view those agreements as creating the kind of rights referred to above.[139] It is true that GATT and WTO law include a number of fundamental principles, such as non-discrimination,[140] but those principles are merely fundamental to the system of GATT and WTO law itself, a system which the membership generally continues to regard as purely international—as governing their trade relations at the international plane, and not as directly creating rights for citizens.

The rights argument does not therefore work well as regards GATT and WTO law. More in general, however, there would be scope in the case law on direct effect of international agreements for more analysis of whether an agreement confers rights. The above survey of the case law shows that the Court employs hardly any rights language. It has essentially transposed the 'internal' Community law approach towards direct effect of international agreements, with the proviso that the structure and nature of an agreement may preclude direct effect. That 'internal' Community law approach does not focus on whether a provision of EC law is intended to confer rights; the creation of rights is seen as a consequence of direct effect, which is very much the rule. The Court was obliged to adopt such an approach if it was to confirm the direct effect of EC law, and of the Treaty in particular, for the simple reason that in its original form the Treaty had virtually no rights language. Direct effect was really a tool for the effective enforcement of Community law, and such effective enforcement was greatly enhanced by permitting private parties to rely on provisions of Community law. This enlisting of the individual as an agent for the enforcement of Community law is well documented.[141]

One may have doubts whether the same approach should apply to international agreements. In view of the difference between the EC and the international legal order the approach towards direct effect should arguably not only focus on the mere operational character of the rules in question (whether they are clear, precise, etc.) as this is essentially an enforcement approach. It would be useful to combine that

---

[138] See e.g. 'Rights and Duties of States and Rights and Duties of their Citizens', in *Recht zwischen Umbruch und Bewahrung—Festschrift für Rudolf Bernhardt* (Springer, 1995) 1087–128; 'National Constitutions and International Economic Law', in M Hilf and E-U Petersmann (eds), *National Constitutions and International Economic Law* (Kluwer, 1993) 3–52.

[139] Cf von Bogdandy (n 62 above), 32.

[140] See WTO Apellate Body, *US—Section 211 Omnibus Appropriations Act 1988*, WT/DS176/AB/R, adopted 1 February 2002, para 233.

[141] See e.g. D Curtin and K Mortelmans, 'Application and Enforcement of Community Law by the Member States: Actors in Search of a Third Generation Script', in T Heukels (ed), *Institutional Dynamics of European Integration: Essays in honour of Henry G. Schermers—Volume II* (Martinus Nijhoff, 1994) 426–66.

with some measure of analysis of whether the provisions of an agreement confer rights. An example may illustrate this. From a perspective of direct effect and the creation of rights for private parties the case law on the direct effect of provisions in agreements on non-discrimination and movement of workers, or rights of establishment, appears more convincing than the case law on the direct effect of the prohibition of 'measures having equivalent effect' in the free-trade agreement with Portugal. The decisions of the EC–Turkey association council on the treatment of Turkish workers, for example, are eminently suitable for direct effect as they are clearly intended to give rights to individuals.

The suggestion here is not that the Court should become much more restrictive in its direct-effect analysis, by confining direct effect to provisions which expressly address the position of individuals. Rather, this is an extra dimension of the direct-effect issue, which should also be taken into account. It is for example remarkable that the case law on the lack of direct effect of WTO law in no way concentrates on the issue of rights, whereas it would have been relatively straightforward for the Court to establish that the WTO Agreement is not intended to confer rights.

Clear, precise, and unconditional

Once the hurdle of the structure and nature of an agreement is taken, the Court examines whether the provisions in issue, interpreted in their context and in the light of the objectives of the agreement, are sufficiently clear, precise, and unconditional. This is a classic direct-effect analysis, which is geared towards establishing whether a provision is sufficiently operational for judicial application.[142] The Court's approach here is very similar to its approach towards 'internal' Community law. Of prime importance, so it seems, is whether the provisions of an agreement require further implementation. If that is the case, as it was in *Demirel*[143] and in *Taflan-Met*,[144] there can be no direct effect. The analysis is however nuanced, and on a case-by-case basis, as demonstrated by *Sürül*,[145] where the Court, notwithstanding its conclusion in *Taflan-Met* that the relevant decision of the EC–Turkey association council on social security was in need of further implementation, recognized the direct effect of the non-discrimination principle, which stood on its own and was apt for judicial application.

The principle of consistent interpretation

Direct effect is not the only type of effect which an agreement may produce. The Court has also confirmed the principle of consistent interpretation. In *Commission v. Germany* the Court referred to that principle in general terms. It reasoned that,

---

[142] Case C–128/92 *Banks* [1994] ECR I–1209, para 27 of the Opinion of Van Gerven AG.
[143] N 48 above.   [144] N 56 above.   [145] N 57 above.

when the wording of secondary Community legislation is open to more than one interpretation, preference should be given as far as possible to the interpretation which renders the provision consistent with the Treaty, and that, likewise, an implementing regulation must, if possible, be given an interpretation consistent with the basic regulation. Similarly, the Court continued, the primacy of international agreements concluded by the Community over provisions of secondary Community legislation means that such provisions must, so far as is possible, be interpreted in a manner that is consistent with those agreements.[146] This principle is logical and obvious. The coherence of a legal system requires that its various provisions are as much as possible interpreted in light of each other, so as to avoid conflict between them, and consistent interpretation is a preferred judicial technique for such conflict prevention. As international agreements concluded by the Community form an integral part of the Community legal order it is logical that Community legislation, which should comply with such agreements because the latter are binding on the Community institutions, be interpreted in conformity with them.

The technique of consistent interpretation is not often applied for the simple reason that most agreements have direct effect, leading to their direct application and obviating the need for consistent interpretation. It is none the less a useful instrument, in particular as regards agreements which are not directly effective, i.e. GATT and the WTO agreements. The EU Courts have never hesitated to make use of consistent interpretation for the purpose of applying GATT and WTO law.[147] Again that is logical, because consistent interpretation does not lead to a direct application of the provisions involved. The legal instrument that is applied is the piece of Community legislation in issue, which is simply interpreted in a particular way. Interesting examples of the application of the consistent interpretation technique involving GATT are the Court's judgments in *Werner* and *Leifer*. In those cases the question arose whether Article 1 of Regulation 2603/69 establishing common rules for exports, which prohibits 'quantitative restrictions on exports', extends to national licensing requirements for exports of so-called dual-use goods. The Court gave an affirmative reply, and stated that its finding was supported by Article XI GATT, which could be considered to be relevant for the purposes of interpreting a Community instrument governing international trade. Article XI, headed 'General Elimination of Quantitative Restrictions', refers in its first paragraph to 'prohibitions or restrictions other than duties, taxes or other charges, whether made effective through quotas, import or export licences or other measures'.[148]

It is also clear from the case law that the principle of consistent interpretation has general application, and that a party invoking the principle need not show that

---

[146] Case C–61/94 *Commission v. Germany* [1996] ECR I–3989, para 10.

[147] See e.g. Case 92/71 *Interfood v. Hauptzollamt Hamburg* [1972] ECR 231, para 6; Case C–79/89 *Brown Boveri* [1991] ECR I–1853, paras 15–19; Joined Cases T–163/94 and T–165/94 *NTN Corporation and Koyo Seiko v. Council* [1995] ECR II–1381, para 65; *Commission v. Germany* (n 146 above); *Hermès* (n 80 above).

[148] Case C–70/94 *Werner v. Germany* [1995] ECR I–3189, para 23 and Case C–83/94 *Leifer and Others* [1995] ECR I–3231, para 24.

the Community legislation in issue was adopted with a view to implementing the international agreement influencing its interpretation.

Furthermore, a parallel may be drawn with the legal effects of directives. As is well known, directives lack so-called horizontal direct effect, in the sense that a directive cannot as such impose obligations on a private party.[149] As a result, there is pressure to apply the principle of consistent interpretation in cases between private parties involving an unimplemented directive. It is fair to say that, as a result, the Court has undertaken some creative interpretation so as to give effect to directives, stretching the language and meaning of the interpreted provisions.[150] One may wonder whether the Court would be willing to do the same as regards international agreements which are not directly effective, in particular the WTO agreements.

The principle of implementation

Both in *Germany v. Council*, as regards the lack of direct effect of the GATT of 1947,[151] and in *Portugal v. Council*, concerning the lack of direct effect of the WTO Agreement,[152] the Court made an exception: it is only where the Community intended to implement a particular obligation assumed in the context of the (now) WTO or where the Community measure refers expressly to the provisions of the WTO agreements that it is for the Court to review the legality of the Community measure in the light of the WTO rules. That exception is now established case law, and it is therefore necessary to examine its origins, rationale, and application.

Origins

The origins of this exception go back to the judgments in *Fediol*[153] and *Nakajima*.[154] In *Fediol* the EEC Seed Crushers' and Oil Processors' Federation challenged a Commission decision rejecting their complaint under what at the time was called the New Commercial Policy Instrument.[155] That instrument, which was the predecessor to the current Trade Barriers Regulation,[156] allowed Community producers to lodge a complaint with the Commission regarding illicit commercial practices by third countries, so as to initiate an examination procedure which could ultimately result in the adoption of commercial policy measures (i.e. sanctions) against the country concerned. Fediol's complaint concerned practices by Argentina

---

[149] Case 152/84 *Marshall v. Southampton and South-West Hampshire Area Health Authority (Teaching)* [1986] ECR 723, para 48.   [150] See e.g. Case C–106/89 *Marleasing* [1990] ECR I–4135.
[151] N 67 above.   [152] N 85 above.   [153] N 65 above.   [154] N 66 above.
[155] Council Regulation 2641/84 on the strengthening of the common commercial policy against illicit practices [1984] OJ L252/1.
[156] Council Regulation 3286/94 laying down Community procedures in the field of the common commercial policy in order to ensure the exercise of the Community's rights under international trade rules, in particular those established under the auspices of the WTO [1994] OJ L349/71; see Ch 10.

which, in its opinion, violated Articles III, IX and XXIII GATT. The Commission, however, disagreed with that analysis and rejected the complaint. Before the Court the Commission maintained that, in view of the lack of direct effect of GATT, Fediol could not challenge the decision on grounds of wrong interpretation of the relevant GATT provisions. Van Gerven AG did not concur with the Commission's defence. He distinguished the lack of direct effect of GATT from cases where a Community act referred to GATT, as did, implicitly, the New Commercial Policy Instrument. He likened such cases to the private international law instrument of *renvoi* to provisions of foreign law. In a footnote, he made interesting general statements about this type of effect. Van Gerven was of the opinion that a provision (like those of GATT) which did not have direct effect *per se* could none the less be transformed within a particular legal order, by a rule of that legal order, into a rule having direct effect, that is to say a rule which could be invoked by individuals; for instance, GATT provisions which were taken over in a Community regulation or to which a Community regulation referred and from which individuals could therefore to a greater or lesser extent derive rights pursuant to and within the limits of that regulation.[157]

The Court essentially followed that approach. It acknowledged the lack of direct effect of GATT, but considered that it could not be inferred from the case law that citizens could not rely on the provisions of GATT in order to obtain a ruling on whether conduct criticized in a complaint lodged under Regulation 2641/84 constituted an illicit commercial practice within the meaning of that regulation: the GATT provisions formed part of the rules of international law to which that regulation referred. As regards the flexibility of GATT, that did not prevent the Court from applying the rules of GATT with reference to a given case, in order to establish whether certain specific commercial practices should be considered incompatible with those rules, as the GATT provisions had an independent meaning which, for the purposes of their application in specific cases, was to be determined by way of interpretation. The fact that Article XXIII GATT provided a special procedure for the settlement of disputes did not preclude interpretation by the Court. Here the Court referred to its judgment in *Kupferberg*, where it had stated that the mere fact that the contracting parties had established a special institutional framework for consultations and negotiations *inter se* in relation to the implementation of the agreement was not in itself sufficient to exclude all judicial application of the agreement. It followed that, since the regulation entitled the economic agents concerned to rely on the GATT provisions in the complaint which they lodged with the Commission in order to establish the illicit nature of the commercial practices which they considered to have harmed them, those same economic agents were entitled to request the Court to exercise its powers of review over the legality of the Commission's decision applying those provisions.[158]

---

[157] *Fediol* (n 65 above), paras 11–13 of the Opinion of Van Gerven AG, in particular n 8.
[158] Ibid, paras 19–22 of the judgment.

The judgment in *Fediol* was logical. There was a Community regulation which required the Commission to examine whether third-country commercial practices were illegal under international law, and judicial review of that examination would have been meaningless if the Court could not look at the provisions of GATT. In *Fediol* the Court did not find that the Commission had erroneously interpreted GATT, but even if it had, the result would only have been that the Commission's rejection of Fediol's complaint would have been annulled on grounds of wrong implementation of the regulation. That does not amount to giving direct effect to GATT.

In *Nakajima* the applicant challenged a Council regulation imposing a definitive anti-dumping duty on imports of serial-impact dot-matrix printers originating in Japan. One of its claims was that the basic regulation on anti-dumping in force at the time was in breach of the GATT Anti-Dumping Code.[159] The Council objected that, like GATT, the Anti-Dumping Code lacked direct effect. Lenz AG did not agree with that objection, but it is not completely clear from the Opinion on which grounds he felt that review should be possible. In any event, he considered that there was no violation of the Code.[160] The Court took as its starting point that Nakajima was not relying on the direct effect of the provisions of the Code. Rather, it was questioning, in an incidental manner under (current) Article 241 EC, the applicability of the basic regulation by invoking one of the grounds for review of legality referred to in (current) Article 230 EC, namely that of infringement of the Treaty or of any rule of law relating to its application. The Court then noted that, like GATT, the Anti-Dumping Code was binding on the Community. It further noted that, according to the second and third recitals in the preamble to the basic anti-dumping regulation, it was adopted in accordance with existing international obligations, in particular those arising from Article VI GATT and from the Anti-Dumping Code. It followed that the basic regulation, which the applicant had called in question, was adopted in order to comply with the international obligations of the Community, which, as the Court had consistently held, was therefore under an obligation to ensure compliance with the GATT and its implementing measures.[161] The Court accordingly examined whether the basic regulation was in breach of the Code, but came to the conclusion that it was not.

The reasoning in *Nakajima* was more difficult to understand than that in *Fediol*. As stated in Chapter 8, it was reasonable at the time to read the judgment as establishing that the direct-effect requirement did not apply to direct actions for annulment under (current) Article 230 EC. However, the judgment in *Germany v. Council* on the banana regulation proved that that reading was incorrect.[162] There the Court declined to examine alleged violations of GATT provisions on the same grounds as those which precluded direct effect. It did however maintain the *Fediol* and

[159]   Council Regulation 2423/88 on protection against dumped or subsidized imports from countries not members of the EEC [1988] OJ L209/1.
[160]   *Nakajima* (n 66 above), paras 52–57 of the Opinion of Lenz AG.
[161]   Ibid, paras 28–32 of the judgment.   [162] N 67 above.

Nakajima case law, and for the first time stated the principle of implementation. It did not however clarify scope or rationale of the principle. The Court followed the Opinion of Gulmann AG on this point. The Advocate General had analysed the statements in *Fediol* and *Nakajima*, considering it decisive that in both judgments the Court based its reasoning on the fact that by reasons of references to the relevant GATT rules there were special reasons for undertaking review as regards compliance with GATT. There was no doubt, in his view, that in the banana regulation the Community legislature did not refer to GATT in such a way that the agreement should be incorporated into the legal basis for the Court's review of legality.[163]

Rationale and further application

As was mentioned, the *Fediol* type of application of GATT or WTO law is relatively straightforward; it is also of limited scope, and currently probably applies only to the Trade Barriers Regulation.[164] However, the Court consistently expresses the principle in more general terms: where the Community intended to implement a particular obligation assumed in the context of the WTO or where a Community act expressly refers to WTO law, judicial review on grounds of violation of WTO law will be undertaken. At first sight, this exception to the lack of direct effect may seem self-defeating and not very useful: where WTO rules are implemented there will be much less need for judicial review based on those rules than in other cases, where *ex hypothesi* those rules were not taken into account or observed. It may however be possible to define a basis for the exception. The theoretical justification could be that, even if WTO law does not as such have direct effect, in those cases where it has been transformed and incorporated into Community law by the Community legislature it becomes part of Community law in the sense and to such an extent that it can be relied upon in court proceedings concerning the legality or validity of Community acts. The act of implementing WTO law makes such law fit for full judicial application, and the exception may therefore be called the principle of implementation. Such an approach clearly has a dualist element. In a sense the Court is saying that the Community institutions need to be consistent in their legislative and administrative action. If an international agreement binding on the Community does not as such have direct effect, the institutions are none the less required to observe its provisions in those areas where the agreement has been implemented. In so far as there is implementation, the agreement ceases to be a mere instrument of international law. After implementation the obligation to implement correctly and in good faith, which is an obligation of international law and of Community law (see Article 300(7) EC) obviates the need for direct effect. The EU institutions have then used and forfeited the international scope for manœuvre which the agreement may have given them.

---

[163] Ibid, paras 147–150 of the Opinion of Gulmann AG. The banana regulation did not expressly refer to GATT, and clearly did not reflect any particular GATT provisions or obligations. It had none the less been adopted in full knowledge of the potential difficulties with GATT.   [164] N 156 above.

Why does the Court make such an exception?[165] A possible reading is that the Court attempts to strike some balance between lack of direct effect and respect for the EC's international commitments. To put it differently, the principle of implementation may well reflect some type of compromise reached within the Court. If that is the case, the future interpretation and application of the implementation principle risk not being guided by any particular underlying rationale, but rather being the outcome of internal struggle—between monists and dualists, one might say. This may be all the more so as the formulation of the implementation principle is fairly cryptic, particularly as to its first limb: when does the EC 'intend' to implement a 'particular obligation'?

There is some case law, but it appears to move in different directions. The principle of implementation is regularly, and almost as a matter of course, applied in the field of anti-dumping, where part of its ancestry lies.[166] That is natural, given how closely EC anti-dumping legislation tails the WTO Anti-Dumping Agreement, and given that the EC legislation was indisputably adopted so as to give effect to the particular obligations which WTO law imposes in this respect. It is none the less worth noting that, in this area, there appears to be no particular emphasis on the reference to 'particular' obligations, as opposed, possibly, to wholesale implementation of general WTO texts.

There are other examples of a receptive approach to the implementation principle. In *Italy v. Council* the Italian government sought the annulment of a Council regulation concerning tariff quotas for imports of rice, which had been adopted pursuant to agreements concluded between the EC and Australia and Thailand, subsequent to GATT Article XXIV(6) negotiations required by the accession of Austria, Finland, and Sweden. It was argued that the regulation was in breach of Article XXIV(6) and of paragraph 5 *et seq.* of the Understanding on the Interpretation of Article XXIV. The Council relied on the lack of direct effect of GATT, but the Court referred to the principle of implementation, and held that by adopting the regulation pursuant to agreements concluded with non-member countries following negotiations conducted on the basis of Article XXIV(6) of GATT, the Community sought to implement a particular obligation entered into within the framework of GATT.[167]

In one further case the Opinion of Ruiz-Jarabo Colomer AG again contained an interesting application of the implementation principle. *Kloosterboer Rotterdam* concerned a challenge by a Dutch customs agent to a Commission regulation concerning the establishment of the import price of frozen chicken fillets, for the purpose of applying additional customs duties. Kloosterboer Rotterdam argued that the regulation did not comply with the basic Council regulation on the common

---

[165] Cf Cheyne (n 67 above), 33.
[166] Case C–69/89 *Nakajima v. Council* [1991] ECR I–2069, para 31; Case C–188/88 *NMB v. Commission* [1992] ECR I–1689, para 23; Case T–162/94 *NMB and Others v. Commission* [1996] ECR II–427, para 99; Case T–256/97 *BEUC v. Commission* [2000] ECR II–101.
[167] Case C–352/96 [1998] ECR I–6937, para 20. See also the Opinion of Mischo AG at paras 21–22.

organization of the market in poultry. The latter regulation had been amended in 1995 so as to implement Article 5(1)(b) of the WTO Agreement on Agriculture which provides for establishment of the relevant import prices on the basis of cif prices. The Council regulation therefore also referred to cif prices, but the Commission implementing regulation contained exceptions to that rule. Advocate General Ruiz-Jarabo Colomer considered that this called for application of the implementation principle. He pointed out that the Council regulation had been amended with a view to implementing the Agreement on Agriculture, particularly as to its provisions on additional duties—that emerged from the preamble to the amending regulation. The amendments also charged the Commission with adopting implementing rules, particularly as regards the application of Article 5 of the Agreement on Agriculture. The Commission had thus been instructed by the Council to adopt implementing rules complying with the relevant WTO provisions, but had failed to do so, as the Agreement on Agriculture only permitted the use of cif prices. Most interestingly, the Advocate General sought and found confirmation of this interpretation of the relevant provisions of WTO law in the Appellate Body's report in *EC—Measures affecting the importation of certain poultry products*.[168] That case dealt with exactly the same issue, and the Advocate General relied on it without reservation, considering that this was a clear case for applying the implementation principle. The Court, however, did not mention the implementation principle, and looked only at the relationship between the basic and the implementing regulation.[169]

There is also recent case law which does not give much weight to the implementation principle. In three judgments on actions for damages based on the violation of WTO law in the context of the EC's banana import regime the Court of First Instance declined to apply the implementation principle. The actions challenged a 1998 Commission regulation, adopted in implementation of the amendments to the EC's banana import regime which the Council of Ministers introduced, also in 1998, subsequent to the EC's defeat in the WTO. The Court stated that neither the reports of the WTO Panel of 22 May 1997 nor the report of the WTO Standing Appellate Body of 9 September 1997 which was adopted by the Dispute Settlement Body on 25 September 1997 included any special obligations which the Commission 'intended to implement', within the meaning of the case law, in the challenged Commission regulation. That regulation did not make express reference either to any specific obligations arising out of the reports of WTO bodies or to specific provisions of the agreements contained in the annexes to the WTO Agreement.[170] With respect, that statement by the CFI is not convincing. It is true

---

[168] WT/DS69/AB/R, adopted 23 July 1998.
[169] Case C–317/99 *Kloosterboer Rotterdam* [2001] ECR I–9863, paras 28–38 of the Opinion of Ruiz-Jarabo Colomer AG and paras 23–36 of the judgment.
[170] Case T–18/99 *Cordis Obst und Gemüse Grosshandel v. Commission* [2001] ECR II–913, para 59; Case T–30/99 *Bocchi Food Trade International v. Commission* [2001] ECR II–943, para 64; Case T–52/99 *T Port v. Commission* [2001] ECR II–981, para 59. See also Case C–307/99 *OGT Fruchthandelsgesellschaft v. Hauptzollamt Hamburg-St. Annen* [2001] ECR I–3159.

that the Commission regulation did not in any way refer to WTO provisions or to the WTO dispute. However, it was adopted on the basis of the amended basic Council regulation on banana imports, the amendments to which expressly referred to the Council's desire that the EC comply with its international commitments (including WTO law) and instructed the Commission to adopt implementing rules which would achieve that aim.[171] The Commission, however, did not manage to achieve that in 1998, as the modified regime was found wanting, too.[172] As to the 'particular obligations' which the EC intended to implement, again it is not difficult to identify those: the panel and Appellate Body reports, as confirmed by the DSB, instructed the EC to bring its laws and regulations into conformity, and identified the relevant WTO provisions. In fact, it is hard to envisage a more precise identification of relevant obligations than that resulting from WTO dispute settlement.

In defence of the Court of First Instance, it must be said that the applicants in the banana cases did not build their case on the implementation principle, and appeared merely to refer to it in a rather confusing way at the oral hearing. They may not have made the argument that the Commission failed to adhere to the Council's instructions, and that the Council, as the EC legislator on banana imports, intended to comply.[173] The Court may have to reconsider this in a case brought by Chiquita.[174]

The last case to be mentioned in this short review is *Netherlands v. European Parliament and Council*,[175] in which the Netherlands government sought the annulment of the directive on the legal protection of biotechnological inventions.[176] One of its arguments was that the directive violated both the TRIPs Agreement and the TBT Agreement. Jacobs AG considered that the implementation principle applied as regards the former, since the preamble to the directive referred to the TRIPs provisions on patent protection, and since Article 1(2) of the Directive provided that it was without prejudice to the obligations of the Member States pursuant to *inter alia* the TRIPs Agreement. He did not however feel that review on the basis of the TBT Agreement was possible, as the directive did not refer to it and as it was not suggested that the directive intended to implement it.[177] The Advocate General thus examined compliance with TRIPs, but found no violation. However, it is worth adding that he also expressed the view that 'it might be thought that it is in any

---

[171] Council Regulation 1637/98 amending Regulation (EEC) No 404/93 on the common organization of the market in bananas [1998] OJ L–210/28, para (2) of the Preamble and Art 20 (e) of the amended basic Regulation.

[172] WTO Arbitrators, *European Communities—Regime for the Importation, Sale and Distribution of Bananas—Recourse to Arbitration by the European Communities under Article 22.6 of the DSU*, WT/DS27/ARB, 9 April 1999 and WTO Panel Report, *European Communities—Regime for the Importation, Sale and Distribution of Bananas—Recourse to Article 21.5 by Ecuador*, WT/DS27/RW/ECU, 12 April 1999.   [173] See the cases in n 170 above.

[174] Case T–19/01 *Chiquita v. Commission*, pending.

[175] N 100 above; see also however Case C–76/00 P *Petrotub and Republica v. Council* [2003] ECR I–79, paras 53–58 where the Court combines the implementation principle and the principle of consistent interpretation so as to give effect to the WTO Anti–Dumping Code.   [176] [1998] OJ L 213/13.

[177] *Netherlands v. European Parliament and Council* (n 100 above), paras 146–158 of the Opinion of Jacobs AG.

event desirable as a matter of policy for the Court to be able to review the legality of Community legislation in the light of treaties binding the Community. There is no other court which is in a position to review Community legislation; thus if this court is denied competence, Member States may be subject to conflicting obligations with no means of resolving them'.[178]

The Court of Justice, however, did not apply the implementation principle. It referred to the lack of direct effect of WTO law, but then considered that the plea of the Netherlands government was to be understood as being directed, not so much at a direct breach by the Community of its international obligations, as at an obligation imposed on the Member States by the directive to breach their own obligations under international law, while the directive itself claims not to affect those obligations.[179] It then proceeded to investigate the plea, but found no violations of either the TRIPs or TBT Agreement. This new method of approaching compliance with international commitments adds a further layer of complexity to the case law. Indeed, the Member States are all themselves founding WTO Members, and as such bound by all of the WTO agreements. The question thus becomes which types of EC acts could be considered to impose an obligation on the Member States to breach their obligations under WTO law. Also, is it necessary for this type of review for the EC act expressly to state that it does not affect the international obligations of the Member States? Or can it be argued that, in any event, the EC does not have the authority to require its Member States to violate their international obligations?[180]

The principle of implementation clearly offers nice opportunities for communication between the vessels of EU and WTO law, and between the judicial operators of both systems. It would be particularly useful if it were applied, not only in straightforward cases of EC acts expressing the implementation of parts or provisions of WTO law, but also in the more politically charged context of implementation of WTO dispute rulings. The *Bananas* case perfectly exemplifies the scope for EU judicial involvement. After the WTO banana litigation was lost in 1997, the Council of Ministers amended the basic regulation clearly in order to comply with WTO law. It accordingly instructed the Commission to adopt implementing rules on licence allocation—the crux of the WTO issue—and mandated compliance. The Commission, however, did not manage to achieve that, as at WTO level the revised regime was considered mostly to continue the original, unlawful regime. Such a case calls for application of the implementation principle. Where the competent EU institution, in this case the Council, clearly expresses intention to implement, the European Courts should review adopted acts on the basis of WTO law, and should look at the relevant WTO dispute rulings.

Some may feel that the European Courts should not in any event interfere in complex WTO disputes, and that it is best to let those cases run their full course in Geneva. But the *Bananas* case in fact shows that the issues and tensions may not be confined to the relationship between the EU and other WTO members.

---

[178] Ibid, para 147.   [179] Ibid, para 55 of the judgment.   [180] See also Ch 8.

The Member States themselves are often split on bananas, and the 1998 implementation attempt appears to reveal discord between the Council of Ministers, as the chief legislator, and the Commission, as the administrative legislator. The issues and tensions are therefore as much domestic as international, and it is certainly not inappropriate for the EU Courts to intervene in such a context. Court intervention may in effect and on aggreggate be beneficial to all involved, as it may settle issues through an authoritative ruling, which crystallizes the law and which may enable definitive resolution. Conversely, there is a danger that, if the EU Courts persistently refuse to intervene in cases which are litigated at WTO level, even where there is at some stage a clear intention to implement WTO law, in the meaning of the above case law, tension may build up between the EU judiciary and the WTO panels and Appellate Body. One may then end up with a situation in which the perception is one of non-communication and judicial blindness.

General international law

International law does not merely consist of international agreements. There are also general rules of international law, such as customary international law and general principles of law.[181] It is plain that the EU cannot take part in international treaty-making without respecting and applying general international law. The Court of Justice has therefore, without any difficulty, recognized that such general international law is binding on the Community. As with international agreements, however, that recognition does not of itself resolve all questions concerning the legal effects which such law may produce in the Community legal order. There is further case law in which the Courts have attempted to spell out those effects, even though there are fewer judgments than on the effects of agreements. This section analyses the various rulings and provides a general assessment.[182]

Early case law

In the well-known *Van Duyn* case, concerning exceptions to the free movement of workers in the Community, the Court referred to 'a principle of international law', namely that a State is precluded from refusing its own nationals the right of entry or residence, which the (then) EEC Treaty could not be assumed to disregard in the relations between Member States.[183] That was a very succinct statement, but it did at least express the Court's willingness to interpret the Treaty in accordance with

---

[181] See Art 38(1) Statute ICJ.
[182] For an in-depth study see Vanhamme (n 62 above); see also K Lenaerts and E de Smijter, 'The European Union as an Actor under International Law' (1999/2000) 19 YEL 122–6; J Klabbers, 'Re-Inventing the Law of Treaties: The Contribution of the EC Courts' (1999) 30 NYIL 45.
[183] Case 41/74 *Van Duyn v. Home Office* [1974] ECR 1337, para 22.

rules of general international law. Such willingness was confirmed in *Ahlström v. Commission*, a challenge to a decision establishing that a number of non-Community undertakings had engaged in concerted practices to agree on prices of wood pulp in the Community, contrary to (current) Article 81 EC.[184] The Commission had applied the so-called effects doctrine, according to which Article 81 applies to anti-competitive practices which produce effects in the Community, even if the conduct itself takes place outside the Community. The applicants challenged the decision *inter alia* on grounds of breach of international law principles concerning a State's jurisdiction. Neither the Advocate General nor the Court dwelled at length on the effects of international law principles. Darmon AG none the less considered, after having identified the correct interpretation of Article 81 in light of previous case law, that it was necessary to ascertain whether or not the interpretation was in conformity with the requirements and practice of international law.[185] The Court similarly examined arguments to the effect that the Commission decision was incompatible with public international law, but did not accept such arguments on their substance, thereby implicitly recognizing that Article 81 had to be interpreted in accordance with public international law.[186]

The Court was only a little more explicit on the precise effects of general international law in *Poulsen and Diva Corp.*[187] That case concerned the interpretation of a provision in a regulation on fisheries, effectively prohibiting the fishing of salmon and sea trout in certain regions of the high seas, as well as the retention on board, transshipment, landing, transportation, storage, selling, etc. of such fish. The provision was applied against a Panamanian vessel which had entered a Danish port. The case exemplified problems resulting from flags of convenience, as the captain and former owner of the vessel, as well as the crew, were all Danish, and as the vessel operated out of a Danish port. Several questions concerning the correct interpretation of the regulation were referred to the Court of Justice, most of them requiring an analysis of general international law. Indeed, as Tesauro AG pointed out, it was clear that a number of fundamental principles of general international law were at issue or, in any event, had to be closely scrutinized, namely: the freedom to fish on the high seas, navigation in the territorial waters of another State and the related right of innocent passage, the exercise by a coastal State of criminal jurisdiction over foreign vessels, the 'immunity' of a vessel that has taken refuge in a foreign port because it is in distress, and finally the respect to be paid to flags of convenience. The Advocate General was of the firm opinion that the regulation in question could not but be interpreted in conformity with the applicable rules of international law.[188] He engaged in an extensive and learned analysis of the relevant principles of the law of the sea so as to arrive at the correct interpretation of the regulation.

---

[184] Joined Cases 89, 104, 114, 116, 117, and 125 to 129/85 *Ahlström v. Commission* [1988] ECR 5193.
[185] Ibid, para 18 of the Opinion of Darmon AG.
[186] Ibid, paras 15–23 of the judgment.
[187] Case C–268/90 *Poulsen and Diva Corp.* [1992] ECR I–6019.
[188] Ibid, para 4 of the Opinion of Tesauro AG.

The Court took a similar approach, even if it did not in all respects follow the Advocate General's analysis. It did however also clarify the starting point of its interpretative act, which was that the Community must respect international law in the exercise of its powers and that, consequently, the relevant provision of the regulation had to 'be interpreted, and its scope limited, in the light of the relevant rules of the international law of the sea'.[189]

The Court's statement confirmed that Community legislation needs to be interpreted in accordance with principles or rules of general international law. It did not expressly address the question whether a Community act could also be held unlawful or invalid on grounds of breach of such law. The statement was somewhat ambiguous by also mentioning that the scope of the regulation could be limited on the basis of international law, which could be interpreted in different ways. Also, one could argue that the logical consequence of the principle that the Community must respect international law in the exercise of its powers is that any failure to do so results in unlawfulness of the act in question. However, as we have seen as regards international agreements, there may be further conditions: the Court recognizes that the Community must respect WTO law, but it does not generally accept that breach of WTO law leads to a finding of unlawfulness.

Opel Austria

In *Opel Austria v. Council* the applicant challenged before the Court of First Instance a regulation withdrawing tariff concessions for imports of gearboxes from Austria.[190] The regulation was a reaction to aid granted by the Austrian government to Opel Austria which the Commission saw as contrary to the provisions of the 1972 free-trade agreement with that country. However, the Council adopted the regulation on 20 December 1993,[191] whereas it had on 13 December adopted its decision to conclude the EEA Agreement,[192] leading to the entry into force of the EEA Agreement on 1 January 1994. Article 10 of the EEA Agreement prohibited all customs duties and charges having equivalent effect, and Opel Austria argued that the withdrawal of tariff concessions was a violation of that provision. It was fairly obvious that, in substance, that was indeed the case, but the Court of First Instance faced the problem that it could not directly apply the EEA Agreement because in the context of an application for annulment the legality of the contested measure had to be

---

[189] *Poulsen and Diva Corp.* (n 187 above), para 9 of the judgment.

[190] Case T–115/94 *Opel Austria v. Council* [1997] ECR II–39.

[191] Council Regulation 3697/93 withdrawing tariff concessions in accordance with Art 23(2) and Art 27(3)(a) of the Free Trade Agreement between the Community and Austria (General Motors Austria) [1993] OJ L343/1.

[192] Decision 94/1 on the conclusion of the Agreement on the European Economic Area between the European Communities, their Member States and the Republic of Austria, the Republic of Finland, the Republic of Iceland, the Principality of Liechtenstein, the Kingdom of Norway, the Kingdom of Sweden and the Swiss Confederation [1994] OJ L1/1.

assessed on the basis of the facts and the law as they stood at the time when the measure was adopted. Since the EEA Agreement had not yet entered into force on 20 December 1993, it appeared as if the Court would be unable to review the regulation on grounds of violation of the agreement. Opel Austria also argued, however, that by adopting the regulation the Council had infringed a principle of public international law, i.e. the principle of good faith, according to which, pending the entry into force of an international agreement, the signatories to that agreement could not adopt measures which would defeat its object and purpose. The Court essentially agreed with that argument. It stated that the principle was a rule of customary international law whose existence was recognized by the ICJ and which was therefore binding on the Community. It referred to Article 18 VCLT as codifying the principle. It then recalled the sequence of events, pointing out that at the time of adoption of the regulation the Communities were aware of the date of entry into force of the EEA Agreement. The Court, in a second point, stated that the principle of good faith was the corollary in public international law of the principle of protection of legitimate expectations which formed part of the Community legal order: any economic operator to whom an institution had given justified hopes could rely on the latter principle. The Court concluded that, in a situation where the Communities had deposited their instruments of approval of an international agreement and the date of entry into force of that agreement was known, traders could rely on the principle of protection of legitimate expectations in order to challenge the adoption by the institutions, during the period preceding the entry into force of that agreement, of any measure contrary to the provisions of that agreement which was to have direct effect on them after it had entered into force. Consequently, the applicant was entitled to require a review of the legality of the contested regulation in the light of the provisions of the EEA Agreement which had direct effect after its entry into force.[193] The Court then established that Article 10 EEA had direct effect, and that it precluded the withdrawal of tariff concessions in issue. Accordingly, it annulled the regulation.[194]

In this judgment the Court of First Instance effectively gave strong force to a rule of customary international law. It none the less did not apply that principle on its own, but channelled it into the Community law principle of legitimate expectations. The correct reading of the judgment appears to be that, in the particular context of conclusion and entry into force of agreements which have direct effect, the international law principle of good faith is a component of the Community law principle of legitimate expectations. Private parties have an enforceable expectation that the Community will not act contrary to the principle of good faith. However, not every rule of general international law will come within such a category, and *Opel Austria* left open the question whether Community acts could be annulled on grounds of breach of such general international law as such, in the absence of links with general principles (or other rules) of Community law.

---

[193] *Opel Austria* (n 190 above), paras 90–95.   [194] See also Ch 8.

Racke

Where *Opel Austria* concerned the conclusion and entry into force of an international agreement, the *Racke* case concerned its termination.[195] As the facts and legal context were rather complex it is appropriate to set them out in some detail. The case followed the suspension and termination of the 1983 co-operation agreement with Yugoslavia as a result of the break-up and war in that country in the early 1990s. The Community and its Member States attempted to play an active role in putting an end to the conflict, within the framework of what was then called European Political Co-operation, by *inter alia* contributing to a ceasefire agreement which was reached in The Hague in October 1991. When the ceasefire was not respected, the Community and its Member States issued a declaration appealing for compliance, and threatening to terminate the co-operation agreement if that did not happen. As the war continued, on 11 November 1991 the Community and its Member States adopted a decision suspending the agreement with immediate effect (the Suspension Decision).[196] The preamble to that decision stated that the pursuit of hostilities and their consequences on economic and trade relations constituted a radical change in the conditions under which the co-operation agreement was concluded. On the same day the Council also adopted a regulation suspending the trade concessions provided for by the co-operation agreement, again with immediate effect and on the same grounds (the Suspension Regulation).[197] Two weeks later, on 25 November 1991 the Council denounced and terminated the co-operation agreement, pursuant to Article 60 of the agreement, which permitted denunciation with six months' notice.[198]

Whereas the definitive termination of the agreement fully complied with its provisions, the decision of immediate suspension had no specific basis in the agreement. Racke had imported into Germany wines from Kosovo up to April 1992, several months after the suspension of the agreement, but none the less argued that those imports should benefit from the preferential rates of customs duty for which the co-operation agreement had provided. The case went to the *Bundesfinanzhof* (Federal Finance Court), which referred to the Court of Justice the question whether the Suspension Regulation was valid. The *Bundesfinanzhof* had doubts regarding the regulation's validity on grounds of international law, in particular the lawfulness of the unilateral suspension of the co-operation agreement. As the agreement did not provide for suspension, the Community decision had to be in conformity with customary international law rules on suspension and termination of treaties, codified as they were in the relevant provisions of the VCLT. Arguments focused on the

---

[195] N 60 above.

[196] Decision 91/586 of the Council and the Representatives of the Governments of the Member States, meeting within the Council, suspending the application of the Agreements between the European Community, its Member States and the Socialist Federal Republic of Yugoslavia [1991] OJ L315/47.

[197] Council Regulation 3300/91 suspending the trade concessions provided for by the Cooperation Agreement between the EEC and the Socialist Federal Republic of Yugoslavia [1991] OJ L315/1.

[198] Council Decision 91/602 [1991] OJ L325/23.

rule of *rebus sic stantibus*, reflected in Article 62 VCLT. According to that provision, a fundamental change of circumstances which has occurred with regard to those existing at the time of the conclusion of a treaty, which was not foreseen by the parties, may not be invoked as a ground for terminating or withdrawing from the treaty, or for suspending its operation, unless: (a) the existence of those circumstances constituted an essential basis of the consent of the parties to be bound by the treaty; and (b) the effect of the change is radically to transform the extent of obligations still to be performed under the treaty. The *Bundesfinanzhof* had doubts whether the suspension of the co-operation agreement complied with those provisions. It reasoned that, if the Suspension Regulation was invalid, the co-operation agreement had continued to apply, and that Racke was entitled to reduced customs duties on the basis of the direct effect of the relevant provision of the agreement (i.e. Article 22).

Jacobs AG distinguished the case from *Poulsen* and *Opel Austria*, in the sense that it was the first in which a Community regulation was sought to be declared invalid on the sole basis of an alleged violation of customary international law. He referred to *International Fruit Company*, where the Court had laid down the conditions for challenging the validity of a Community act on the basis of rules of international law.[199] He focused in particular on the second question, i.e. that the international law rule in question had to be capable of conferring rights on citizens, and proceeded to examine whether that was the case for rules of customary international law. The Advocate General saw two sources of inspiration for finding an appropriate answer to that question, i.e. the Court's own case law on direct effect of international agreements and the approach in the legal systems of the Member States towards the effect of customary international law. From a comparative examination of those legal systems he concluded that they did attempt to give some effect to rules of customary international law but that they were cautious as to the effect of such rules on the validity of domestic legislation, and that there was no case, so far as could be seen, in any national court where an effect similar to that claimed by Racke had been recognized. As regards the Court's approach to direct effect of agreements, the Advocate General inferred from the case law on the lack of direct effect of GATT that there were limits to the direct effect of agreements, and that an obstacle could lie in the overall purpose and nature of international law provisions. In the light of that, there also had to be limits to the effect of rules of customary international law relating to treaties, since the overall nature and purpose of the law of treaties was to lay down rules applying in the relations between States (and international organizations), and that it was not intended to create rights for individuals. The Advocate General did note that there could be other types of rules of customary international law which did intend to confer rights, for example rules of international humanitarian law. As regards the particular rules in issue, the Advocate General also pointed out that the notion of *rebus sic stantibus* was notoriously difficult and contested, and that it was therefore questionable whether the relevant provisions were sufficiently

---

[199] *International Fruit Company* (n 6 above).

clear and precise to confer rights. There were thus good reasons for not allowing individuals to challenge Community acts on the basis of the law of treaties. None the less, Jacobs AG considered that such challenges could not be wholly excluded, for the following reasons. First, where an agreement had direct effect and created rights for individuals, the beneficiaries of such rights could have legitimate expectations as to the correct and proper implementation of the agreement, as was recognized in *Opel Austria*. To some extent those expectations could extend to the life itself of the agreement: where the agreement, as in *Racke*, provided for denunciation with six months' notice, it could be legitimate for an individual to expect that the agreement would not suddenly be suspended without due cause. Secondly, such entitlement to some measure of protection of legitimate expectation was further supported by the strength of the basic principle of the law of treaties, i.e. *pacta sunt servanda*; the stability of treaty relations required that the plea of fundamental change of circumstances be applied only in exceptional cases.[200]

In conclusion the Advocate General was of the opinion that the Court should review only manifest violations of the law of treaties to the detriment of the individual concerned. Where there were such violations, there could be a breach of the Community law principle of the protection of legitimate expectations, and the breach of that principle, comporting at the same time a manifest violation of the law of treaties, could give rise to annulment of the Community act in issue, to a declaration of invalidity, or to a claim for damages. By allowing such review an appropriate balance was struck between the rights of the individual and the decision-making powers of the Community institutions. There had to be a relatively wide margin of discretion for those institutions to take decisions concerning the life of an agreement, in accordance with their powers under the Treaty, as it was only logical that this life should be primarily in the hands of the contracting parties, and as there was an important political dimension to the conclusion and termination of agreements which did not lend itself readily to judicial review.[201]

The Advocate General then proceeded to exercise such limited review, finding that there was indeed a fundamental change of circumstances, and that the Community institutions could reasonably consider that the effect of that change was such as radically to transform the extent of obligations still to be performed by the Community and its Member States. There was no point in continuing to grant preferences, with a view to stimulating trade, in circumstances where Yugoslavia was breaking up in a way which was strongly disapproved of by the international community.[202]

It is noteworthy that Jacobs AG, whilst first distinguishing *Racke* from *Opel Austria*, in the end applied a similar test to that of the Court of First Instance, combining the law of treaties with the principle of legitimate expectations. It is true that the Court of First Instance did not require a 'manifest' violation, but arguably the act in issue in *Opel Austria* constituted such a violation.

---

[200] Jacobs AG referred here to ICJ, *Gabcíkovo-Nagymaros Project (Hungary/Slovakia)* [1997] ICJ Rep 7, para 104.   [201] *Racke* (n 60 above), paras 76–90 of the Opinion of Jacobs AG.

[202] Ibid, paras 92–93.

The Court of Justice adopted the test proposed by the Advocate General, but the reasoning through which it arrived at that test was different and, it must be said, not easy to follow. It took Article 22 of the co-operation agreement, which laid down the tariff preferences for imports of wines, as a starting point, by stating that the question whether the disputed regulation was valid having regard to customary international law had arisen incidentally in a dispute in which Racke claimed that Article 22 should be applied. The Court therefore first examined whether that provision had direct effect, finding that that was indeed the case. It then investigated whether an individual could challenge the validity under customary international law rules of the Suspension Regulation. It rejected arguments of the Council relating to the Suspension Decision, pointing out that it was only the validity of the regulation which was in issue. The Court then stated that, if the Suspension Regulation had to be declared invalid, the trade concessions granted by the agreement would remain applicable until the Community brought the agreement to an end in accordance with the relevant rules of international law. Thus, a declaration of invalidity would allow individuals to rely directly on the rights to preferential treatment granted by the agreement.[203]

The Court then referred to the Commission's doubts whether the relevant international law rules formed part of the Community legal order. The Court replied to that by referring to *Poulsen*,[204] and confirmed that the Community had to respect international law in the exercise of its powers, and was required to comply with the rules of customary international law when adopting a regulation suspending the trade concessions granted by an agreement. It followed that the customary international law rules concerning the termination and the suspension of treaty relations by reason of a fundamental change of circumstances were binding upon the Community institutions and formed part of the Community legal order.[205]

The Court subsequently returned to the point that Racke was incidentally challenging the validity of the regulation in order to rely upon rights which it derived from the agreement, and stated that, therefore, the case did not concern the direct effect of customary international law. It further pointed out that Racke was invoking fundamental rules of customary international law against the disputed regulation, which was taken pursuant to those rules and deprived Racke of the rights under the agreement. In this respect the Court referred to the *Nakajima* judgment,[206] which it described as involving a comparable situation in relation to basic rules of a contractual nature. The Court then recalled the importance of *pacta sunt servanda*, as underlined by the ICJ. It concluded that, in those circumstances, an individual could rely on rules of customary international law. However, it added, because of the complexity of the rules in question and the imprecision of some of the concepts to which they referred, judicial review necessarily had to be limited to the question whether the Council made manifest errors of assessment concerning the conditions for applying those rules.[207]

---

[203] Ibid, paras 29–43 of the judgment.   [204] N 187 above.
[205] *Racke* (n 60 above), paras 44–46.   [206] N 66 above.   [207] *Racke* (n 60 above), paras 47–52.

On the substance, the Court's reasoning was similar to that of Jacobs AG, finding that there was no manifest violation of the law of treaties. The Suspension Regulation was therefore not considered invalid.

Assessment

The basis on which the Court in *Racke* accepted that it should review the validity of the Suspension Regulation can be criticized. The Court twice emphasized that Racke's challenge to the regulation was merely incidental, and that Racke in fact relied on Article 22 of the co-operation agreement. The Court added that the case did not concern the direct effect of rules of customary international law. Yet when one compares the facts of and claims in *Racke* with, for example, those in *International Fruit Company*, it is difficult to find any material differences. The question which the *Bundesfinanzhof* referred to the Court of Justice concerned the validity of a regulation on imports into the Community, as in *International Fruit Company*. Both cases concerned the validity of a regulation under rules of international law. It is true that in *Racke* a finding of invalidity would have led to the further application of the provisions of the co-operation agreement, up to the point in time when the agreement was terminated. Again, however, the position in *International Fruit Company* was not dissimilar: if the regulation restricting imports of apples had been declared invalid, International Fruit Company would have benefited from the right to free importation under the then applicable Community law rules. Yet in *International Fruit Company* the Court required that the provisions of international law confer rights on citizens. It is thus submitted that, effectively, the *Racke* case was concerned with the direct effect of rules of customary international law, contrary to the Court's own assessment.

Nor is it clear why the Court refused to examine the Council's arguments relating to the Suspension Decision (in contrast to the Suspension Regulation). A finding of invalidity of the latter was obviously not sufficient for the further application of the co-operation agreement: that agreement was suspended by the Suspension Decision, and unless that decision was also invalid, the agreement was no longer in operation. The case therefore concerned the validity of both the regulation and the decision.

A further criticism is that the reference to *Nakajima* is unclear and unconvincing. The case did not concern implementation of customary international law rules in the same way as *Nakajima* concerned implementation of the GATT Anti-Dumping Code. If the passing reference in the preamble to the Suspension Decision and the Suspension Regulation to a radical change of circumstances was sufficient to regard those instruments as triggering the principle of implementation, then the Court should have indicated and clarified that.

None the less, the outcome of the Court's reasoning and the test which it applied is satisfactory. Taken together, *Opel Austria* and *Racke* signify that the Courts are willing to exercise some measure of review of Community acts in the context of the entry into force, the suspension, and the termination of an international agreement concluded by the Community, if it is an agreement which has direct effect. As directly effective agreements confer rights on individuals, it is logical that there should be review of measures which affect the operation of those rights, even if such measures concern the life itself of an agreement. In its case law on the direct effect of international agreements the Court accepts that acts of the institutions, including legislative acts, need to comply with the provisions of a directly effective agreement. It would be awkward if decisions concerning the life itself of the agreement were not reviewable at all. Take an agreement which confers rights to free importation, such as the co-operation agreement with Yugoslavia. Those rights are fully enforceable, and private parties can challenge any Community (or national) acts which affect those rights. It would be akward if, none the less, the Council could, at will and in violation of the law of treaties, suspend such an agreement, without those same private parties being able to challenge such suspension in any way. Review on the basis of the law of treaties is therefore a complement to the direct effect of agreements.

The Court is also right to limit review to manifest violations. As it pointed out in *Racke*, the law of treaties is complex and the relevant provisions of the VCLT are not very precise, leaving scope for argument as to their correct interpretation and application. And as Jacobs AG pointed out in connection with the *rebus sic stantibus* rule, there is an important political dimension which does not lend itself easily to judicial review. It is indeed appropriate for the judiciary to refrain from making an essentially political assessment as to whether there is a fundamental change of circumstances justifying suspension or termination of an agreement. It is thought proper for the courts to limit their interference to cases of manifest violation of the relevant international law rules.

Opel Austria and *Racke* concerned only the law of treaties, and the other judgments on general international law do not teach us much about the effects of such law. There are therefore many questions which still need to be resolved. It is however submitted that the Jacobs AG's approach of investigating whether the purpose and nature of the rules at issue are such as to confer rights on citizens is correct. Rules of international humanitarian law, for example, should have direct effect, and it should be possible for private parties to challenge EU acts which violate such rules, if that were ever the case.

Agreements binding on the Member States

When the EEC Treaty was drafted the negotiators realized that the new Treaty could entail obligations and commitments for the Member States which would turn out to be in conflict with other international law commitments of the Member States, in particular as they resulted from international agreements which were in force. In so far as such prior agreements had only the Member States themselves as parties the new EEC Treaty would simply override them,[208] but the Treaty could not of course do likewise with agreements between a Member State and a third country. For the purpose of resolving problems of conflicting commitments the negotiators drafted (current) Article 307 EC:

The rights and obligations arising from agreements concluded before 1 January 1958 or, for acceding States, before the date of their accession, between one or more Member States on the one hand, and one or more third countries on the other, shall not be affected by the provisions of this Treaty.

To the extent that such agreements are not compatible with this Treaty, the Member State or States concerned shall take all appropriate steps to eliminate the incompatibilities established. Member States shall, where necessary, assist each other to this end and shall, where appropriate, adopt a common attitude.

In applying the agreements referred to in the first paragraph, Member States shall take into account the fact that the advantages accorded under this Treaty by each Member State form an integral part of the establishment of the Community and are thereby inseparably linked with the creation of common institutions, the conferring of powers upon them and the granting of the same advantages by all the other Member States.

The concept of this provision is straightforward, in particular as regards the first two paragraphs. The first paragraph recognizes what is in effect an established principle of international law, whereas the second paragraph instructs the Member States to resolve any problems of incompatibility to which the application of that principle may give rise. The meaning of the third paragraph is less straightforward, and there appears to be no case law clarifying that meaning in any substantial way. The case law has concentrated on interpreting and applying the first two paragraphs, and is analysed below.[209]

First paragraph

Article 307 EC refers to agreements concluded before 1 January 1958, when the EEC Treaty entered into force, or, for acceding States, agreements concluded before their accession. The latter element was inserted by the Treaty of Amsterdam, reflecting the principle contained in all accession treaties. The clarification is useful and highlights the actual relevance of Article 307, which is much greater for acceding and recently acceded Member States than for the original six. The term agreements refers to all types of international treaty obligations.[210]

Timing of agreements

Article 307 EC does not mention agreements concluded by the Member States after their accession. It is sometimes suggested that the rules and principles which

---

[208] See Art 30(4)(b) VCLT.
[209] See also Kaddous (n 17 above), 273–300; Lenaerts and de Smijter (n 182 above), 114–22.
[210] Case C–62/98 *Commission v. Portugal* [2000] ECR I–5171, para 43.

the provision introduces could, by analogy, be applied to such agreements. Particularly in cases where, at the time of the conclusion of the agreement, there is no incompatibility with Community law, but where that changes as a result of new Community acts being adopted, such an application by analogy would not seem inapposite. The case law none the less does not support such an extension of Article 307 EC. Capotorti AG considered the point in *Procureur Général v. Arbelaiz-Emazabel*, a case concerning fisheries. He addressed the argument that the institutions' obligations under Article 307 EC (see below) also applied to a later agreement, concluded before the Community exercised its powers in this area. He considered, though, that such a view conflicted with the wording of the first paragraph of (current) Article 307 EC and with the Court's case law. It seemed to him unacceptable, particularly since the provision was one of an exceptional nature, in so far as it ensured on a temporary basis the observance of obligations towards non-member States which were incompatible with Community law.[211]

The question of the date of birth of an agreement arose as regards the transition from the original GATT to the establishment of the WTO. That transition was regulated in the WTO Agreement, which refers to 'GATT 1947' and 'GATT 1994', and provides that they are legally distinct.[212] In *T. Port v. Council*[213] and *Banatrading v. Council*[214] the applicants sought damages from the Community, *inter alia* on the ground that the Council had violated (current) Article 307 EC by adopting legislation on imports of bananas which was in breach of certain GATT provisions.[215] The Court of First Instance pointed out that GATT 1994 had been concluded after the entry into force of the Treaty, and did not accept the argument that GATT 1994 replicated GATT 1947. It referred to the rule that both agreements were legally distinct, and cited with approval an earlier Opinion of Elmer AG.[216] The Advocate General considered that it followed from Article 59(1)(a) VCLT[217] that GATT 1994 had replaced GATT 1947 with effect from 1 January 1995. The WTO Agreement and GATT 1994 were concluded, as regards commercial policy, by the Community which, under (then) Article 113 EC, had exclusive competence for commercial policy. Accordingly, claims arising from GATT 1994 could be addressed only to the Community and not the various Member States. The Court added that

---

[211] Case 181/80 *Procureur Général v. Arbelaiz-Emazabel* [1981] ECR 2961, para 4 of the Opinion; for the same views, see, Opinion of Van Gerven AG, para 17, in Case C–23/92 *Grana-Novoa v. Landesversicherungsanstalt Hessen* [1993] ECR I–4505.

[212] See Art II(4) WTO Agreement, and the provisions of GATT 1994, as part of Annex 1A to the WTO Agreement.   [213] Case T–2/99 *T Port v. Council* [2001] ECR II–2093.

[214] Case T–3/99 *Banatrading v. Council* [2001] ECR II–2123.

[215] See Ch 10 for an overview of the banana saga.

[216] Joined Cases C–364/95 and C– 365/95 *T Port v. Hauptzollamt Hamburg-Jonas* [1998] ECR I–1023, para 16 of the Opinion.

[217] '1. A treaty shall be considered as terminated if all the parties to it conclude a later treaty relating to the same subject matter and: (a) it appears from the later treaty or is otherwise established that the parties intended that the matter should be governed by that treaty'.

obligations arising from GATT 1994 fell not on the Member States but on the Community.[218]

That reasoning is not wholly persuasive. From a formal point of view the Court is correct that GATT 1947 and GATT 1994 are legally distinct, but a large number of Member States' obligations were identical in both agreements, and were transferred as smoothly as possible from the old agreement to the new one. Nor is it correct that GATT 1994 obligations fall only on the Community. Both the Community and the Member States are founding members of the WTO, and as such bound by WTO law.[219] GATT 1994 provisions, such as Article III:2 on national treatment in matters of taxation, may affect national measures as much as Community measures. No allocation of obligations or commitments took place at the time of the conclusion of the WTO Agreement. The argument that the Member States have been bound, in a continuous way since 1947, by a number of GATT obligations is difficult to rebut. However, one also needs to determine the third country to which the Member States may be committed: in another *T Port* ruling the Court of Justice correctly pointed out that, in a case involving imports in 1995 of bananas from Ecuador, (current) Article 307 EC could not be relevant because Ecuador joined the WTO only in 1996.[220] There was also a lot of debate on the timing of agreements, from the point of view of Article 307 EC, in the air transport cases.[221] Those cases concerned bilateral air transport agreements between, on the one hand, a large number of Member States and, on the other, the United States. The Commission claimed that those agreements, the original versions of which pre-dated the Treaty or accession, but which had been renegotiated in 1995 and 1996, violated exclusive Community competence as well as (current) Article 43 EC on the right of establishment. The Court for the most part rejected the claim of exclusive competence, but held that provisions on national ownership and control of airlines were in breach of Article 43 EC. The Court did not examine the Commission's alternative claim that the Member States in question had violated their obligations under (current) Article 307 EC. It did not feel the need to rule conclusively on the question whether the renegotiations led to the existence of new agreements. It was satisfied that the renegotiations had led to new and significant international commitments and held in one of the judgments that, although (current) Article 307 EC applied to rights and obligations flowing from agreements concluded by Member States before the Treaty entered into force, it could not apply to amendments which Member States made to such agreements by entering into new commitments after the entry into force of the Treaty.[222]

---

[218] *T Port* (n 213 above) and *Banatrading* (n 214 above), respectively paras 78–82 and 73–76. In *OGT* (n 170 above), para 29, the ECJ also expressed doubts whether (current) Art 307 EC applied to GATT 1994.

[219] Cf *Hermès* (n 80 above), para 24.   [220] *T Port* (n 80 above), paras 62–63.

[221] Case C–466/98 *Commission v. UK* [2002] ECR I–9427; Case C–467/98 *Commission v. Denmark* [2002] ECR I–9519; Case C–468/98 *Commission v. Sweden* [2002] ECR I–9575; Case C–469/98 *Commission v. Finland* [2002] ECR I–9627; Case C–471/98 *Commission v. Belgium* [2002] ECR I–9681; Case C–472/98 *Commission v. Luxembourg* [2002] ECR I–9741; Case C–475/98 *Commission v. Austria* [2002] ECR I–9797; and Case C–476/98 *Commission v. Germany* [2002] ECR I–9855; see Ch 3.

[222] *Commission v. Germany*, (n 221 above), para 69.

Rights and obligations

The very first case on (current) Article 307 EC also concerned the relationship between the GATT and Community law. The Commission claimed that customs duties which Italy applied to imports from other Member States violated the Treaty, and Italy sought to defend itself by invoking the provisions of the 1956 Geneva Protocol to GATT. The Court agreed with the Commission that the term 'rights and obligations' in (current) Article 307 EC referred, as regards the 'rights', to the rights of third countries and, as regards the 'obligations', to the obligations of Member States and that, by virtue of the principles of international law, by assuming a new obligation which was incompatible with rights held under a prior treaty a State *ipso facto* gave up the exercise of these rights to the extent necessary for the performance of its new obligations. In matters governed by the EEC Treaty, that Treaty took precedence over agreements concluded between Member States before its entry into force, including agreements made within the framework of GATT.[223]

The Court thus confirmed from the outset that the first paragraph of Article 307 EC only concerns the rights of third countries and the corresponding obligations of the Member States. Indeed, as Mischo AG stated in *Commission v. Portugal*, the provision is merely declaratory, an expression of the fundamental principle of *pacta sunt servanda*.[224] In relations between the Member States the Treaty obligations automatically prevail over prior agreements, again in accordance with international treaty law,[225] as the Court often recalled.[226] Also, Article 307 EC is inapplicable where an agreement allows, but does not require, a measure which appears to be contrary to Community law.[227]

It is none the less not excluded that, also in relations between Member States, it may be necessary for a Member State to respect obligations towards third countries. As Warner AG pointed out in *Henn and Darby*, a multilateral agreement concluded by Member States and third countries may create multilateral obligations between all the parties to it, so that third countries have a right to the observation of its provisions even in relations between Member States (for example in intra-Community trade).[228] International environmental agreements are often considered to create such multilateral obligations.[229]

It is hardly worth adding that the rights and obligations in question need to be still in force; developments in international law, in the form of conclusion of further, incompatible international agreements by a Member State, may be such that

---

[223] Case 10/61 *Commission v. Italy* [1962] ECR 1, para 10.

[224] *Commission v. Portugal* (n 210 above), para 56 of the Opinion of Mischo AG.

[225] See Art 30 VCLT.

[226] e.g. Case 121/85 *Conegate v. HM Customs & Excise* [1986] ECR 1007, para 25; Case 286/86 *Ministère public v. Deserbais* [1988] ECR 4907, para 18; Case 235/87 *Matteuci v. Communauté française of Belgium* [1988] ECR 5589, para 21; Case T–69/89 *RTE v. Commission* [1991] ECR II–485, paras 102–103.

[227] Case C–324/95 *Evans Medical and Macfarlan Smith* [1995] ECR I–563 and Case C–124/95 *The Queen, ex parte Centro-Com v. HM Treasury and Bank of England* [1997] ECR I–81, para 60.

[228] Case 34/79 *Regina v. Henn and Darby* [1979] ECR 3795, 3833.

[229] Pauwelyn (n 137 above).

an agreement concluded before the entry into force of the Treaty no longer produces effect.[230]

Legal effects

The first paragraph of Article 307 EC provides that rights and obligations 'shall not be affected'. The effects of that provision were considered in cases concerning a French prohibition on nightwork for women. That prohibition implemented ILO Convention No 89, which France had concluded before the entry into force of the EEC Treaty. It was argued that the prohibition was contrary to Community law on sex equality. In *Stoeckel* the Court did not examine the effects of (current) Article 307 EC, and simply established a breach of Community law. However, Tesauro AG did look at the Convention, but considered that it could not be relied upon because Community law did not require nightwork for women. It was open to France to prohibit all nightwork, thereby removing the discrimination, or else to denounce the Convention.[231]

Two years later the issue was again before the Court in *Levy*, in which the referring court expressly inquired into the relationship between Convention No 89 and Community law. Again Mr Tesauro was Advocate General, but he took a slightly different line. He recalled that France should remove any incompatibility by either prohibiting all nightwork or denouncing the Convention. He then distinguished the second paragraph of Article 307 EC, which was the basis for that obligation, from the first. He regarded the two paragraphs as separate, and considered that, as the French legislation stood, there was a clear conflict between a Community rule and an earlier contractual provision. That conflict was governed by the first paragraph of (current) Article 307 EC, according to which priority was to be given to the Member State's international obligations. The national court could not give precedence to Community law on the ground that France had not taken all the necessary steps to ensure that Community law was observed, because of the letter and spirit of (current) Article 307 EC: such a decision would lead to the penalization not only and not so much of the Member State concerned, but precisely of those non-member countries whose rights Article 307 EC was intended to protect.[232] Unfortunately, the Court did not engage with those issues, and simply left it to the referring court to determine which obligations the Convention imposed and to ascertain to what extent its provisions constituted an obstacle to the application of Community law.[233]

The Opinion of Tesauro AG in *Levy* can be contrasted with the Opinion of Lenz AG in *Ministère public v. Asjes*, where he considered that a national court should

---

[230] Case C–158/91 *Levy* [1993] ECR I–4287, paras 19–20.
[231] Case C–345/89 *Stoeckel* [1991] ECR I–4047, para 11 of the Opinion of Tesauro AG.
[232] *Levy* (n 230 above), paras 6–8 of the Opinion of Tesauro AG.
[233] Ibid, para 21 of the judgment.

examine whether the Member State in question had complied with the second paragraph of (current) Article 307 EC. If the conclusion was that it had not, the national authorities could not rely upon their unlawful omission to take measures against transport operators on the basis of pre-Treaty international commitments.[234]

On balance the approach by Tesauro AG is preferable. Were a national court to give precedence, on the basis of Community law principles, to Community law over a Member State's international obligations, the Treaty instruction of respect for international law embodied in Article 307 EC would not in effect be respected, and Community law would impose a breach of international law.

In the earlier *Burgoa* case the Court clarified other aspects of the rule in the first paragraph of Article 307 EC. The Court reasoned that the provision could not have the effect of altering the nature of the rights which might flow from the international agreements in question. From that it followed that that provision did not have the effect of conferring upon individuals who relied upon such agreements rights which the national courts of the Member States had to uphold. Nor did it adversely affect the rights which individuals might derive from such an agreement.[235] In other words, Article 307 EC is completely neutral as to any rights which individuals may have under the provision of an international agreement concluded by a Member State before the entry into force of the Treaty.[236] For example, where a national legal order does not recognize the direct effect of such an agreement, individuals cannot invoke Article 307 EC to circumvent that non-recognition. As Capotorti AG pointed out in that case, Community law does not require performance by a Member State of the agreements in question.[237]

In the context of the legal effects of the first paragraph of Article 307 EC one should also mention the division of judicial functions between the Court of Justice and national courts under the preliminary ruling system. The Court's jurisdiction under Article 234 EC is limited to interpreting Community law or ruling on its validity; it is not within the Court's province to interpret national law, or indeed a Member State's international commitments. In *Henn and Darby* Warner AG considered that where an international agreement had a bearing on a question referred to the Court, and no one suggested that the agreement was open to different interpretations, the Court could answer the question on the assumption that the agreement meant what it apparently said. But if there was dispute over the meaning of the agreement, the Court had to give alternative answers and leave it to the national court or tribunal to decide.[238] In *Levy*,[239] *Minne*,[240] and *Centro-Com*[241] the Court

---

[234] Joined Cases 209 to 213/84 *Ministère public v. Lucas Asjes* [1986] ECR 1425, 1453.

[235] Case 812/79 *Attorney General v. Burgoa* [1980] ECR 2787, para 10.

[236] In *OGT* (n 170 above), para 30, the ECJ recalled that the first para of (current) Art 307 EC does not confer rights; the Court of First Instance similarly held in *T Port* (n 213 above), para 83 and *Banatrading* (n 214 above), para 81, that the provision is not intended to confer rights on individuals, as required by the principles of non-contractual liability.

[237] *Burgoa* (n 235 above), para 3 of the Opinion of Capotorti AG.

[238] *Henn and Darby* (n 228 above), 3853.   [239] N 230 above, para 21.

[240] Case C–13/93 *Minne* [1994] ECR I–371, para 18.   [241] N 227 above, para 58.

each time left it to the referring court to determine the extent of the Member State's international obligations. It is none the less possible to read into the Court's ruling in *Centro-Com* some degree of scepticism as to whether there was actually a conflict between the Community law provisions and the international obligation.[242]

Obligations of the institutions

In *Burgoa* the Court, following Capotorti AG, clarified that, although the first paragraph of (current) Article 307 EC mentioned only the obligations of the Member States, it would not achieve its purpose if it did not imply a duty on the part of the institutions of the Community not to impede the performance of the obligations of the Member States which stemmed from a prior agreement. However, that duty of the institutions was directed only to permitting the Member State concerned to perform its obligations under the prior agreement and did not bind the Community as regards the non-member countries.[243]

That principle was invoked in *T Port* and *Banatrading*,[244] where the applicants claimed that the violation of (current) Article 307 EC triggered the Community's non-contractual liability. As mentioned, the Court of First Instance first of all held that GATT 1994 constituted a new agreement. It further recalled that (current) Article 307 EC was not intended to confer rights, with the result that one of the conditions for non-contractual liability was not complied with.

Second paragraph

The second paragraph requires that the Member States take all appropriate steps to eliminate any incompatibilities. In most cases this will involve the renegotiation of the international agreement. Obviously, a Member State will need the co-operation of the third countries concerned. Such co-operation may be more or less forthcoming, depending on the interests of those countries or other factors. The ultimate question is therefore how a Member State needs to act where a third country is unwilling to renegotiate.

In *Lucas Asjes* Lenz AG remarked that, in such cases, the Member States were required to denounce the agreement,[245] and in *Stoeckel*[246] and *Levy*[247] Tesauro AG took the same view. The Court of Justice addressed the issue in two *Commission v. Portugal* cases.[248] Those cases concerned Portugal's obligations under a regulation concerning freedom to provide services in the maritime transport sector.[249] The regulation provided that the Member States had to phase out or adjust cargo-sharing

---

[242] See Ch 12 for further details.   [243] *Burgoa* (n 235 above), para 9.

[244] Nn 213 and 214 above.   [245] *Lucas Asjes* (n 234 above), 1453.

[246] N 234 above, para 11 of the Opinion.   [247] N 230 above, para 6 of the Opinion.

[248] *Commission v. Portugal* (n 210 above) and Case C–84/98 *Commission v. Portugal* [2000] ECR I–5215.

[249] Council Regulation 4055/86 [1986] OJ L378/1.

arrangements contained in existing bilateral agreements with third countries by a given date (Articles 3 and 4). The Commission claimed that Portugal had breached those obligations by neither adjusting nor denouncing agreements with Angola and with the Federal Republic of Yugoslavia. It did not therefore base its action on failure to comply with (current) Article 307 EC, but in its defence Portugal relied on that provision, arguing that the article required denunciation only exceptionally and in extreme circumstances. It further argued that, in the circumstances, denunciation would involve a disproportionate disregard of the interests linked to its foreign policy as compared with the Community interest.

Mischo AG considered that denunciation of a bilateral agreement could indeed be an act which governments found intrinsically repugnant, but the principle of uniform implementation of Community law carried with it requirements that should override the diplomatic interests of Member States. In his view it would be rather paradoxical if, having required Member States to ensure that Community law takes precedence even over their constitutional rules, case law should allow their diplomatic interests, the definition of which was very often somewhat vague, to prevail over that same law. It followed that denunciation was among the 'appropriate steps' required by the second paragraph of (current) Article 307 EC.[250]

The Court followed the Opinion. It recalled that the purpose of the first paragraph of (current) Article 307 EC was to make it clear, in accordance with the principles of international law, that application of the EC Treaty did not affect the duty of the Member State concerned to respect the rights of third countries under a prior agreement and to perform its obligations thereunder. It followed that Portugal had to respect in all cases the rights which Angola (and the FRY—see the other case) derived from the contested agreement. However, that agreement contained a denunciation clause, so that denunciation would not encroach upon the rights which the other party derived from that agreement. Although the Member States had a choice as to the appropriate steps to be taken, they were nevertheless under an obligation to eliminate any incompatibilities existing between a pre-Community convention and the Treaty. If a Member State encountered difficulties which made adjustment of an agreement impossible, an obligation to denounce that agreement could therefore not be excluded. As regards the argument that such denunciation would involve a disproportionate disregard of foreign-policy interests of the Portuguese Republic as compared with the Community interest, it had to be pointed out that the balance between the foreign-policy interests of a Member State and the Community interest was already incorporated in (current) Article 307 EC, in that it allowed a Member State not to apply a Community provision in order to respect the rights of third countries deriving from a prior agreement and to perform its obligations thereunder. The article allowed them to choose the appropriate means of rendering the agreement concerned compatible with Community law.[251]

---

[250] *Commission v. Portugal* (n 248 above), paras 60–61 of the Opinion of Mischo AG.
[251] Ibid, paras 44–50 of the judgment.

The Court thus shows itself willing to accept that a Member State may face difficulties in removing incompatibilities with Community law, but ultimately, where the other party is intransigent, an agreement must be denounced. Foreign-policy interests of the Member States cannot override that obligation, and a Member State cannot in principle argue that denunciation would be too harmful to those interests. That approach is also evident in the air transport cases,[252] where a number of Member States argued that the United States proved unwilling to renegotiate clauses on national ownership and control of airlines. The Court held that the Member States could simply not, when renegotiating the agreements, maintain in force a clause which infringed rights of Community airlines arising from (current) Article 43 EC.[253] Particularly indicative is the Court's statement in *Commission v. Belgium* that the efforts made by Belgium in 1995 to eliminate the incompatibility of the clause with (current) Article 43 EC, however commendable, were clearly insufficient to disturb the finding of a breach of that Treaty provision.[254]

Those are the principles resulting from the case law. There is no suggestion that there may ever be cases where the Community itself is required to act so as to remove incompatibilities, for example by amending Community law. In practice, however, there may well be such instances. In political terms it may in some cases be preferable to engage in such action rather than requiring the Member States to renegotiate or denounce their international treaty obligations. Particularly where important multilateral agreements are involved it may not always be possible to take the logic of Article 307 EC to its ultimate conclusion. One may think of the UN Charter or the ECHR, even if both those agreements have a particular link with Community law and may each, in one way or other, be regarded as binding the Community.[255]

Conclusions

This chapter has extensively examined the various legal effects which different forms of international law produce in the EU legal order. The task of discovering and determining those effects has fallen almost exclusively on the Court of Justice. The case law in this area is very much the counterpart of the case law on the direct effect and supremacy of the Treaties and of internal legislation, the defining features of European constitutionalism. Because the Court had decided to set Community law, as a new legal order, apart from international law, it was forced to construct a relationship between those two legal systems. The Court was compelled to engage in judicial policy-making,[256] as the Treaty only provided that agreements concluded by the Community were binding, and contained no further instructions. One may surmise that this gave rise to tension between two possible directions. On the one hand, the Court could give priority to the desire to affirm the new legal order by

---

[252] N 221 above.   [253] See e.g. *Commission v. Denmark* (n 221 above), para 134.
[254] *Commission v. Belgium* (n 221 above), para 143.   [255] See Chs 3, 12, and 13.
[256] McGoldrick (n 221 above), 134.

distinguishing it clearly from international law, which could be done by restricting the effects of international law in Community law. On the other hand, it seemed incongruous for a legal order which owed its very birth and existence to international law to become unreceptive to the latter.

After more than thirty years of case law one can certainly not conclude that the EU legal order is hostile towards international law. The lack of direct effect of GATT and WTO law has always occupied a central position in analyses and assessments of the Court's attitude towards international law, not unjustifiably in the light of the importance of those agreements, in particular for the Community and its policies. However, the general picture is positive.[257] The Court readily accepts that international agreements may have direct effect, and unless the structure and nature of the agreement preclude such effect, which hitherto is the case only for the GATT and the WTO Agreement, the same criteria and reasoning apply as in the case of 'internal' Community law. The Court also accepts that there may be cases where effect needs to be given to general international law in ways which have hitherto not been customary (at least not in practice) in the legal systems of the Member States.[258]

This receptive attitude towards international law has an important political dimension. It reflects the EU's active and ever-growing involvement in international relations. Indeed, the EU has not in any way proved to be an inward-looking organization of States, however much one may feel inclined to criticize certain external (and internal) policies. On the contrary, it is an exporter of international co-operation, witness the very dense network of bilateral agreements with third countries and the very active involvement in multilateral negotiations and law making. The current situation is such that European preference for international co-operation is even becoming an issue of international politics, as it is contrasted with the hegemonic approach of the United States.[259] This is reflected in the draft Constitution, which in Article I–3, on the Union's objectives, provides that the Union 'shall contribute . . . to strict observance and development of international law, including respect for the principles of the United Nations Charter'.

The case law on the lack of direct effect of WTO law may seem a rather ugly blot on this general picture. However, it is not only, as was argued, justified in the current constellation; it is also of more limited scope than is often thought. The principles of consistent interpretation and of implementation do permit that effect be given to WTO law in certain cases. One may, for example, contrast the recent decision in *Petrotub*,[260] where the Court effectively imposed compliance with a WTO dispute ruling in the field of anti-dumping, with a decision of the US Court of International Trade which, faced with very similar issues, shows much greater hostility.[261]

---

[257] Contrary to evaluations in some of the literature, e.g., ibid, 129; M Cremona, 'External Relations and External Competence: The Emergence of an Integrated Policy', in P Craig and G de Búrca, *The Evolution of EU Law* (OUP, 1999) 144.   [258] See the analysis by Jacobs AG in *Racke* (n 60 above).

[259] R Kagan, *Of Paradise and Power: America and Europe in the New World Order* (Alfred Knopf, 2003).

[260] N 175 above.

[261] US Court of International Trade, *The Timken Company v. United States*, Slip opinion 02–106, available at www.cit.uscourts.gov/slip.op/Slip.op02/Slip Op 02-106.pdf.

The lack of direct effect of WTO law is closely linked to the fact that the WTO has its own sophisticated system of dispute settlement—or better, its own judicial system. The evolution of the doctrine of direct effect of international law cannot be properly understood without involving the relations between the various judicial actors. The international legal order is increasingly judicialized, and giving direct effect to an international agreement may involve submitting to the case law of an international court or tribunal. That may in effect be the biggest obstacle for greater receptiveness to international law. In the case of the Court of Justice it is interesting to juxtapose the Court's relationship with two of the most significant international judiciaries from the perspective of EU law, i.e. the WTO's Appellate Body, and the European Court of Human Rights. There is no complete submission in either case, in the former on the ground of the lack of direct effect of WTO law, in the latter because the Community is not yet a party to the ECHR, partly owing to *Opinion 2/94*.[262]

This chapter also shows, if need be, that the concept of direct effect itself, and its relationship with the various forms of actions and remedies which the Treaties offer, continue to be enigmatic. Over the last decade the Court has not attempted to keep the concept of direct effect nice and simple, either in the internal or the external sphere.[263] Perhaps this is unavoidable, but the effectiveness and coherence of the EU legal order none the less require clarity at this foundational conceptual level. Perhaps, as was suggested, it is time to concentrate more on the question whether a provision confers rights, or is intended to confer rights, on private parties. The EU citizen and the rights conferred on the citizen are becoming more central to the EU legal order. We should thus move away from focusing too closely on the abstract enforcement dimension of direct effect. Looking at the subject more from the rights angle would also permit better connection with the system of remedies: where a directly effective right is recognized, there should be a remedy, following the treasured principle of English law, *ubi ius, ibi remedium*.

---

[262] *Opinion 2/94 re Accession to the ECHR* [1996] ECR I–1759.
[263] Cf S Prechal, 'Does Direct Effect Still Matter?' (2000) 37 CMLRev 1047.

Part III

Policies

10

Common commercial policy

Introduction

The common commercial policy is clearly the EU's most developed external policy. It is part of the essential arrangement of the European (Economic) Community, based as the Community is on a customs union (Article 23 EC), the GATT definition of which requires not only a common customs tariff on imports from third countries but also a common policy on other trade matters. As was analysed in Chapter 2, the Community's power in external trade matters is exclusive, which means that, in principle, it is completely in the hands of the Community institutions, and the Member States have no powers in this field. In practice, though, this lack of national powers needs to be qualified. First, if one considers that all policies covered by the WTO are trade policies, then it is clear that the Member States have hitherto retained certain powers, in particular as regards services and intellectual property.[1] Secondly, external trade policy interfaces with general foreign policy, and to the extent that the Member States continue to have powers in that area there is a frontier zone where the principle of exclusivity does not fully come into play. Also, the EU's common foreign and security policy affects the exercise of commercial policy powers in various ways.[2]

The common commercial policy none the less remains the centrepiece of the EU's external policies. Nearly all agreements which the Community concludes, at a bilateral level, with third countries open with a chapter on trade, which is often the core of the bilateral relationship. That is so in particular because many of those agreements establish preferential trade relations, notwithstanding the non-discrimination principles of WTO law. Trade is also at the heart of the EU's 'external' legislation: as there has so far been little harmonization of Member States' policies on immigration and movement of people across the EU's external borders, the regulation of imports and exports is where such external legislation is mainly located. Furthermore, the common commercial policy has a strong legal dimension, because of the extensive use of various types of legal instruments for over forty years now. This is a long history of lawmaking, with a large measure of judicial overview owing to the European Courts' full jurisdiction in trade matters.

---

[1] However, the draft Constitution purports further to broaden the scope of the common commercial policy: see Article III–217.   [2] See Ch 11.

This chapter aims to conduct a survey of the main legal components of that policy, so as to complement the chapter on the Community's powers in this field by giving some insights into the legal dimension of the practical operation of external trade policy.[3] The chapter consists of four general sections. The first briefly examines a few essential principles of the common commercial policy (there are not many). The second section provides an overview of the main legal instruments through which the policy is conducted, particularly at the internal, legislative level. The third section briefly discusses the actors of the common commercial policy, i.e. the institutions which are involved. The last section aims to discuss some aspects concerning judicial review of commercial policy measures. It also offers a case study of judicial review of the EC banana legislation, which enables us to bring together many different dimensions of the law of the EU's external relations.

Principles

As is mentioned in Chapter 2, the EC Treaty does not contain much on what the common commercial policy should look like or how it should be conducted. Article 131 EC provides that, by establishing a customs union, the Member States aim to contribute, in the common interest, to the harmonious development of world trade, the progressive abolition of restrictions on international trade, and the lowering of customs barriers. The common commercial policy should therefore generally be geared towards trade liberalization, and should not simply be an instrument of trade protection. The wording of the article is aspirational, however, and the Court of Justice has refused to use it as a benchmark for the review of particular trade measures.[4]

Article 132 EC concerns the specific issue of Member States' aid systems for exports to third countries.[5] Article 133 EC gives some description of the content of the common commercial policy. It states that the policy shall be based on uniform principles, particularly in regard to changes in tariff rates, the conclusion of tariff and trade agreements, the achievement of uniformity in measures of liberalization, export policy and measures to protect trade such as those to be taken in the event of dumping or subsidies. Again as analysed in Chapter 2, the Court has stated that this is a non-exhaustive enumeration. The Treaty of Nice added complex provisions regarding trade in services and intellectual property rights. Article 133 also describes the procedure for adopting trade policy measures and for concluding agreements in this field. Article 134 EC concerns the specific phenomena of trade deflection and economic difficulties connected to a non-uniform commercial policy; its meaning is analysed in the following subsection.

---

[3] See also I Macleod, ID Hendry, and S Hyett, *The External Relations of the European Communities* (OUP, 1996) Ch 12.

[4] Case 112/80 *Dürbeck v. Hauptzollamt Frankfurt am Main-Flughafen* [1981] ECR 1095 para 44.

[5] See below the subsection on export policy.

In Article 133 the Treaty proclaims that the common commercial policy must be based on uniform principles. Uniformity, which is the substantive counterpart of the rule of exclusive Community competence, is indeed a core feature of the policy. It is a notion which has given rise to some case law, which is analysed in the next subsection. From the case law on imports of goods one may further distill what may be called the principle of assimilation: once goods have been imported into the Community they fully benefit from the EC internal market. This is in fact as much a principle of the internal market as it is a principle of the common commercial policy, but it is none the less worth exploring a little further. The third subsection examines whether there is also a principle of non-discrimination in the EU's external trade relations.

The principle of uniformity

It is partly on the basis of the principle of uniformity that the Court in *Opinion 1/75* decided that the Community's competence in trade matters is exclusive.[6] Not only should all essential rules concerning external trade be adopted by the Community, but they should also lay down a uniform regime for imports and exports. As was mentioned, this is required, at least to a large degree, by the provisions of Article XXIV GATT, which provide that a customs union must constitute a single customs territory where 'substantially the same duties and other regulations of commerce are applied by each of the members of the union to the trade of territories not included in the union'.[7] It is also required by the operation of the internal market. Due to the principle of assimilation (see below), all goods imported from third countries fully benefit from the internal market once they have cleared customs. That principle can function effectively only in the presence of a uniform external trade regime. If the common commercial policy were to lay down that a particular non-Community product cannot be imported into a particular Member State, but can be imported into some or all other Member States, then free circulation in the internal market could be used for the purpose of circumventing the prohibition on importation, and the differential policy would be defeated.

Despite the Treaty's insistence on uniformity which, according to the pre-Amsterdam version, had to be achieved by the end of the transitional period (1 January 1970), it took much longer before a satisfactory level of uniformity was reached. The customs union in a strict sense, i.e. the abolition of customs duties in trade between Member States and the adoption of the common customs tariff, was completed in the course of 1968. However, at the time the Member States continued to apply quantitative restrictions on imports of certain products from certain non-member countries, and the Community proved unable either to abolish such quotas

---

[6] *Opinion 1/75 re Local Cost Standard* [1975] ECR 1355; see Ch 2.
[7] Art XXIV:8(a) GATT. On the interpretation of this phrase, see WTO Appellate Body, *Turkey—Restrictions on Imports of Textile and Clothing Products*, WT/DS34/AB/R, adopted 19 November 1999.

or to replace them with Community-wide quotas. The Community regulations on imports of goods simply recorded the existing quotas in their annexes, effectively providing for exceptions to the principle of uniformity as regards imports.[8] Quotas which Member States thus individually operated could not be circumvented by importing the goods in question into another Member State, so as to benefit from free circulation in the internal market, and to be marketed in the Member State with a quota: on the basis of current Article 134 EC (at the time Article 115 EEC) a Member State could be permitted by the Commission to control such so-called indirect imports.

The legality of that system under the provisions of the Treaty was tested in the *Donckerwolcke* case.[9] A couple of Belgian firms had imported textiles into France, declaring that the goods originated from Belgium. An inquiry by the French customs authorities showed that the declaration was false, and that the true origin was Syria and Lebanon. Prosecution followed, and the case was referred to the Court of Justice to establish whether France could lawfully monitor indirect imports. The Court established the principle of assimilation, analysed in the next section. It then accepted that, notwithstanding the requirement in the Treaty that the common commercial policy be uniform by the end of the transitional period, the Member States could continue to apply the quotas in question, and that (then) Article 115 EEC could be used to authorize Member States to monitor indirect imports. However, the Court imposed a number of conditions on the operation of this system. One of those was that the measures of commercial policy adopted by the importing Member State (in other words, the quotas) were in accordance with the Treaty. As full responsibility in the matter of commercial policy was transferred to the Community, the Court stated, measures of commercial policy of a national character were permissible after the end of the transitional period only by virtue of a specific authorization by the Community.[10] *Donckerwolcke* thus clarified that the Member States could not autonomously maintain exceptions to uniform import rules. At the same time the judgment created authority for the Community to permit the Member States to adopt certain commercial policy measures which derogate from the principle of uniformity.

The notion of a specific authorization is central to this effective exception to uniformity and to exclusive competence. The 1986 judgment in *Bulk Oil* showed that the Community authorization need not be too specific.[11] Since 1979 it had been United Kingdom policy to authorize the exportation of petroleum of United Kingdom origin only to Member States of the Community, member States of the International Energy Agency, and countries with which there was 'an existing pattern of trade'. The case concerned a dispute over exports to Israel, which the United Kingdom did not authorize, and the question arose whether such refusal was in accordance with the Community's commercial policy. At the time, Article 10

---

[8] E.g. Council Regulation 288/82 on common rules for imports [1982] OJ L31/1.
[9] Case 41/76 *Donckerwolcke v. Procureur de la République* [1976] ECR 1921.
[10] Ibid, paras 31–32.   [11] Case 174/84 *Bulk Oil v. Sun International* [1986] ECR 559.

of the Community regulation on exports, which was adopted in 1969, excepted crude oil and petroleum oils from the principle of free exportation in Article 1 of the regulation.[12] Bulk Oil argued that the United Kingdom's policy was not specifically authorized by the Community, and that Article 10 did not amount to such an authorization, especially since the UK's policy was adopted long after the entry into force of the regulation. The Court disagreed. It described Article 10 as limiting the scope of the principle of free exportation on a transitional basis with regard to certain products, until such time as the Council had established common rules applicable to them. It was therefore satisfied that Article 10 constituted a specific authorization permitting the Member States to impose quantitative restrictions on exports of oil to non-member countries, and there was no need to distinguish in that regard between previously existing quantitative restrictions and those which were subsequently introduced.[13] The judgment suggests that the notion of specificity does not relate to the precise national commercial policy measure in issue. It was sufficient for the Court that the regulation listed the products in question. The Court did however refer to the transitional character of the exception, thereby implying that there should be a common policy at some stage.

Bulk Oil provided authority for the view that the notion of specific authorization need not be interpreted too strictly. Around the same time the question arose whether that notion also covered the organization of the Community's policy on imports of textile products, as it then stood. In that sector, too, there were national quotas on imports, but in contrast with policies for other products those quotas were laid down in Community regulations, which provided for a Community-wide quota, divided into national subquotas. In other words, here it was the Community regulation itself which created a non-uniform commercial policy. In the *Tezi* cases the Court none the less accepted that regime, too.[14] It characterized the regime as a step towards the establishment of a common commercial policy for the products concerned.

It was essentially the effort to complete the internal market by the end of 1992 which led to a more uniform common commercial policy, and which enabled the Community to abolish the remaining national quotas for imports of products such as textiles and clothing, Japanese cars, and bananas.[15] As the internal market required the abolition of all controls on intra-Community trade it proved impossible to continue the application of (then) Article 115 EEC so as to control indirect imports. The remaining quotas were in any event of doubtful legality under GATT law, and the economic circumstances were such that the Member States were willing to agree to a common regime and to give up restrictions at national level. However, in the case of imports of bananas, the new Community regime led to a prolonged

---

[12] Council Regulation 2603/69 [1969] OJ Spec Ed (II) 590.

[13] *Bulk Oil* (n 11 above), paras 32–33.

[14] Case 59/84 *Tezi v. Commission* [1986] ECR 887 and Case 242/84 *Tezi v. Minister for Economic Affairs* [1986] ECR 933.

[15] See P Eeckhout, *The European Internal Market and International Trade—A Legal Analysis* (OUP, 1994) Chs 5 and 6.

trade war with the United States and other American countries[16] and created serious friction within the Community.[17]

As there is now a common and uniform regime of imports and exports for nearly all products, the question arises to what extent the Community can still lawfully authorize the Member States to adopt commercial policy measures which derogate from the principle of uniformity. It is arguable that the Court's liberal approach to the notion of a specific authorization in the above case law was inspired by patience rather than principle. In its judgments the Court consistently mentioned the transitional character of the exceptions to uniformity. It is therefore submitted that the Community could not now authorize the Member States to adopt national restrictions on imports and exports in the same way as it could in the 1970s and 1980s. That applies in particular to restrictions for purely economic reasons.

However, the completion of the internal market and the corresponding completion of the common commercial policy did not lead to absolute uniformity in the conditions for imports and exports. All the basic regulations on imports and exports contain a provision permitting the Member States to adopt measures on non-economic grounds such as public policy, public security, and public health.[18] There thus remains scope for national measures directly affecting imports and exports.[19] The principle of uniformity is none the less a cornerstone of the common commercial policy, and the instruments of that policy need to be interpreted and applied in the light of the principle.[20]

The principle of assimilation

In the *Donckerwolcke* case the Court also established the principle of assimilation. The Court referred to (current) Article 23 EC, which provides that the Community shall be based upon a customs union which shall cover all trade in goods between Member States. According to Article 23(2) the provisions adopted for the liberalization of intra-Community trade apply in identical fashion to products originating in Member States and to products coming from third countries which are in 'free circulation' in the Community. The Court further stated that products in free circulation were to be understood as meaning those products which, coming from third countries, were duly imported into any one of the Member States in accordance with the requirements laid down by (current) Article 24 EC. The Court then held that it appeared from Article 23 that, as regards free circulation of goods within the Community, products entitled to free circulation were definitively and wholly assimilated to products originating in Member States. The result of this assimilation

---

[16] For an in-depth analysis see F Breuss, S Griller, and E Vranes, *The Banana Dispute—An Economic and Legal Analysis* (Springer, 2003).

[17] U Everling, 'Will Europe Slip on Bananas? The Bananas Judgment of the Court of Justice and National Courts' (1996) 33 CMLRev 401.

[18] See the subsection on import and export regulations, below.   [19] See also Ch 12.

[20] See e.g. the common customs tariff below.

was that the provisions of (current) Article 28 concerning the elimination of quantitative restrictions and all measures having equivalent effect were applicable without distinction to products originating in the Community and to those which were put into free circulation in any one of the Member States, irrespective of the actual origin of these products.[21]

The judgment established the principle of assimilation in strong terms, and appeared to leave no room whatsoever for any qualifications. It may in fact be noted that, a few years earlier, the Court delivered its seminal judgment on (current) Article 28 EC in the *Dassonville* case, which concerned trade in Scotch whisky between France and Belgium, at a time when the United Kingdom was not yet a Member State.[22] That, too, was therefore a case concerning third-country products in free circulation, even if the Court did not mention that expressly.

The *Donckerwolcke* judgment permitted one exception to the principle of assimilation, i.e. the application of (then) Article 115 EEC. Under that provision the Commission could authorize the Member States to derogate from the principle of free circulation to protect national measures of commercial policy (in practice import quotas: see previous subsection). Article 115 was applied until 1993, when the Community managed to abolish the last remaining national import quotas, on bananas. The current version of Article 134 EC, as amended by the Maastricht Treaty, has never been used. It is arguable that the provision is in fact redundant, because the national commercial policy measures which it was designed to protect no longer exist, and could not lawfully be re-introduced after the completion of the common commercial policy (again see above).[23]

It is remarkable that so few problems have arisen with the application of the principle of assimilation. In one respect, its precise contours remain to be determined for lack of case law. In the famous *Cassis de Dijon* judgment the Court of Justice established the rule that, as a result of (current) Article 28 EC, any product lawfully produced and marketed in a particular Member State is in principle entitled to free circulation within the Community.[24] This is the rule of mutual recognition, a cornerstone of the internal market, not only in the context of case law on the free movement of goods, but also in that of harmonization of legislation. However, it is based on the idea that products are produced in one Member State, in accordance with the laws, regulations, or traditions of that Member State, and that other Member States should recognize that. How does that principle function in the case of third-country products, which were not produced in a Member State?

That question may be easier to resolve than it may seem. The principle of mutual recognition is in effect a convenient denominator for case law which in practice focuses not so much on the issue whether a product was lawfully produced and marketed in a Member State, but simply examines whether any trade restrictions by

---

[21] *Donckerwolcke* (n 9 above), paras 14–18.
[22] Case 8/74 *Procureur du Roi v. Dassonville* [1974] ECR 837.
[23] The draft Constitution no longer contains this provision.
[24] Case 120/78 *Rewe v. Bundesmonopolverwaltung für Branntwein* [1979] ECR 649.

the importing Member State are justified or not.[25] Under the case law on the free movement of goods there are two essential questions to be answered. The first is whether a particular measure constitutes a restriction on trade within the meaning of Article 28 EC. If that is the case, the second question is whether the restriction can be justified on grounds of the so-called mandatory requirements or of Article 30 EC. That method of examination can be fully transposed to third-country products. All that is required is that the products are in free circulation.

Through the principle of assimilation the common commercial policy displays openness towards trade with third countries. The internal market is not there merely for the benefit of EC products. Once goods have been imported, they can fully benefit from the internal market. There are of course various types of restrictions at the EU's external borders, but there are no further trade restrictions in the internal market other than those which also apply to EC products.

Towards a principle of non-discrimination?

The Community is a party to the WTO Agreement and is thus bound by the GATT non-discrimination principles, in particular most-favoured-nation treatment (prohibiting discrimination between third countries, members of the WTO) and national treatment (prohibiting discrimination against imported products). Those principles are clearly an important component of the common commercial policy, even if the EU makes extensive use of the scope under GATT Article XXIV to conclude preferential trade agreements establishing free-trade areas or customs unions, thereby derogating from the MFN principle. However, the GATT rules are not of themselves justiciable, as they do not have direct effect.[26] It is therefore, as a rule, not possible for private parties to enforce them.

That raises the question to what extent the principle of equal treatment or non-discrimination, as a general principle of Community law,[27] is relevant to, and can be enforced in the context of, the Community's external trade.[28] The Court of Justice has hitherto not been willing to accept that there is a requirement of equal treatment of third countries in the absence of specific provisions mandating such equal treatment. In *Faust v. Commission*, a case involving protective measures relating to imports of preserved mushrooms, the Court admitted that Taiwan appeared to have been treated less favourably than certain non-member countries. It stated, however, that there existed in the Treaty no general principle obliging the Community, in its external relations, to accord to non-member countries equal treatment in all respects. The Court also added that, if different treatment of non-member countries was compatible with Community

---

[25] P Eeckhout, 'The European Court of Justice and the Legislature' (1998) 18 YEL 19.
[26] See Ch 9.
[27] On general principles of Community law see T Tridimas, *The General Principles of EC Law* (OUP, 1999).
[28] See for further analysis M Cremona, 'Neutrality or Discrimination? The WTO, the EU and External Trade', in G de Búrca and J Scott (eds), *The EU and the WTO—Legal and Constitutional Issues* (Hart Publishing, 2001) 151.

law, different treatment accorded to traders within the Community also had to be regarded as compatible with Community law, where that different treatment was merely an automatic consequence of the different treatment accorded to non-member countries with which such traders had entered into commercial relations.[29]

On the other hand, the Court of Justice does apply the principle of equal treatment as regards EU-based importers, even if it does not appear to do that in a very strict way. In the 1994 *Germany v. Council* case, concerning the EC regime for imports of bananas, the Court did not uphold the claim of unequal treatment of various categories of importers (called operators under the relevant rules), notwithstanding the grave effects of the system of import licence allocation on importers of so-called third-country bananas. The Court considered that the difference in treatment was justified in light of the aims of the regulation, which were the integration of previously compartmentalized markets in the Community and the protection of Community and traditional ACP producers of bananas.[30] The judgment can be criticized on the ground that there was no strong link between treating operators differently, effectively giving one category of importers clear advantages, and the aims of the regulation. On proportionality grounds, the Court should have struck down the regulation for involving a greater measure of differential treatment than could be justified. Four years later, however, the Court did strike down further amendments to the banana regime, which aggravated the difference in treatment. The Community had concluded an agreement with a number of Latin American exporting countries so as to resolve the GATT dispute. That agreement provided for the allocation of export quotas to those countries, and introduced a system of export licences complementing the system of import licences. Again however a distinction was made between the different categories of operators, with those trading in Community and ACP bananas being exempted from the export licence system. The Court established that this difference in treatment had significant financial consequences for importers of third-country bananas, and that the further differential treatment could not be justified on the ground of maintaining an appropriate balance between the various categories of operators: the framework agreement had not disturbed the balance between them, and there was therefore no justification for the difference in treatment.[31]

Instruments

Conventional and autonomous instruments

There are basically two types of legal instruments which contain rules on external trade, adopted in the framework of the common commercial policy. Such rules may be included in bilateral or multilateral treaties or agreements between the

---

[29] Case 52/81 *Faust v. Commission* [1982] ECR 3745, para 25.
[30] Case C–280/93 *Germany v. Council* [1994] ECR I–4973.
[31] Case C–122/95 *Germany v. Council* [1998] ECR I–973, paras 59–72; Joined Cases C–364/95 and C–365/95 *T Port v. Hauptzollamt Hamburg-Jonas* [1998] ECR I–1023, paras 78–89.

Community and third countries (e.g. the WTO Agreement); and they may also flow from internal Community legislation. This chapter does not offer a survey of the first category. Previous chapters have examined the procedure for concluding such agreements, the role of the courts, and the legal effects of international law rules. As was mentioned, trade policy is almost invariably at the heart of bilateral agreements between the Community and third countries. In many cases such agreements set up preferential trade relations, through the establishment of a customs union or a free-trade area, or in the context of development co-operation policy (the Lomé and Cotonou conventions). The Community is moreover a key player in the WTO. The scale and scope of these conventional trade policies is such that their study would require an anaysis of its own, which cannot be undertaken here.

This section concentrates on the Community's trade legislation. It may therefore appear to show only half the picture. However, most of the regulations discussed below are closely connected with the rules of certain agreements, in particular those of the GATT, now part of the WTO Agreement: they are based on those rules, they aim to implement them, or they contain procedures for starting dispute settlement at international level in connection with trade matters.

This section analyses only the main pieces of legislation on imports and exports of goods.[32] It does not cover services or intellectual property, and deals mostly with general rules, applying to all imports or exports. In specific agreements with third countries one may find derogations from those general rules. Such derogations are contained in bilateral agreements, or in multilateral agreements with groups of countries, such as the EEA Agreement and the Cotonou Convention. The provisions of agreements establishing a free-trade area or a customs union with specific third countries derogate from the Common Customs Tariff, in that there are as a rule no customs duties on imports of goods from such countries.

The scope for such derogations must be kept in mind, since agreements concluded by the Community are binding on the Community institutions and in principle prevail over Community legislation.[33] In many cases, however, the trade provisions of an agreement are implemented by way of internal legislation.

This section discusses the Common Customs Tariff (CCT); derogations from the CCT through the generalized system of preferences; instruments for applying the CCT; the general import regulations; the Community's anti-dumping and anti-subsidy policies; the so-called trade barriers instrument; and the Community's export policy.

Common Customs Tariff

The Community is based upon a customs union, which implies common customs duties on imports. The CCT was established by 1968, more than a year before the end of the transitional period of the original EEC Treaty. The CCT is genuinely

---

[32] See also PJG Kapteyn and P VerLoren van Themaat, *Introduction to the Law of the European Communities* (3rd edn, by LW Gormley, Kluwer Law International, 1998) 1295–320.
[33] See Ch 9.

uniform in character. There are no differences in customs duties according to the Member State of importation, and the requirement of uniformity is confirmed in the case law of the Court of Justice. The position here can be contrasted with the Court's acceptance of national quotas on imports which benefited from a specific authorization (see above). In the *Generalized System of Preferences* case the Court examined whether it was permissible to divide tariff quotas (quotas involving reductions in customs duties) between the Member States. The Court emphasized that the CCT was intended to achieve an equalization of customs charges levied at the frontiers of the Community on imports from non-member countries, in order to avoid any deflection of trade and any distortion of free internal circulation or of competitive conditions. The Court accepted that a scheme of national shares could be justified by administrative, technical, or economic constraints which precluded the administration of the quota on a Community basis. However, such a scheme had to include machinery to ensure that, until the overall Community quota was exhausted, goods could be imported in any Member State, even if that Member State's share of the quota was exhausted. It was not acceptable that, in such a situation, goods would have to bear customs duties at the full rate or would have to be re-routed via another Member State.[34] In other words, the scheme of national shares had to be purely technical, and economically and fiscally neutral. Moreover, with the development of information technology the need for national shares has disappeared, and tariff quotas are now fully administered at central Community level.

The current version of the CCT is found in Regulation 2658/87 on the tariff and statistical nomenclature and on the Common Customs Tariff.[35] That regulation contains both the so-called 'combined nomenclature' (CN) and the prevailing rates of duty. The CN is based on the International Convention on the Harmonized Commodity Description and Coding System, to which the Community is a party.[36] The CCT consists of autonomous and conventional rates of duty. The autonomous rates are the original rates as of 1968; the conventional rates are those negotiated in the GATT, the so-called 'bound' duties. In practice, the latter are applied to all imports, including those from non-GATT (or non-WTO) members.[37] The current average tariff on industrial products is around 4.1 per cent.[38] There are however many derogations from the application of the conventional rates of duty set out in the CCT. The three most significant kinds of derogations are: (a) elimination of customs duties on imports from countries with which the Community concluded an agreement establishing a free-trade area or a customs union; (b) elimination of customs duties on imports from ACP countries, by virtue of the Cotonou Convention;[39]

---

[34] Case 51/87 *Commission v. Council* [1988] ECR 5459, paras 6–9.   [35] [1987] OJ L256/1.
[36] Council Decision 87/369 concerning the conclusion of the International Convention on the Harmonized Commodity Description and Coding System and of the Protocol of Amendment thereto [1987] OJ L198/1.
[37] ELM Völker, *Barriers to External and Internal Community Trade* (Kluwer, 1993) 51.
[38] WTO, EU Trade Policy Review, Report by the WTO Secretariat, WT/TPR/S/102, 26 June 2002, at p. x.   [39] [2000] OJ L317/3.

and (c) partial or full suspension of customs duties on imports from developing countries, covered by the GSP system (see below).

For imports of most agricultural products there are additional levies, besides the conventional rates of duty set out in the CCT. Various sets of rules apply to those levies, according to the type of common market organization concerned.

Lastly, other kinds of charges may be connected with the importation of goods into the Community. Such charges, imposed by the Community or by individual Member States, are generally indicated by the term 'charges having equivalent effect'. In intra-Community trade such charges are expressly prohibited (Article 25 EC). The Treaty does not contain such an express prohibition as regards imports from third countries. However, it is settled case law that no such charges may be applied by the Member States. In *Aprile v. Amministrazione delle Finanze dello Stato* the Court recalled the applicable principles.[40] The case involved a dispute between Aprile, a company in liquidation, and the Finance Department of Italy which refused to repay certain charges in respect of customs transactions. In previous judgments the Court had decided that those charges, in so far as intra-Community trade was involved, were collected in breach of Community law. The question now arose whether the same conclusion had to be reached where imports from the EFTA countries were involved.

The Court first examined whether the Member States were entitled unilaterally to impose charges having equivalent effect in trade with non-member countries. It pointed to the function of the customs union of avoiding trade diversion and distortion of competition. It also stated that the common commercial policy implied that national disparities of a fiscal and commercial nature affecting trade with non-member countries had to be abolished. The Court then held that both the unicity of the Community customs territory and the uniformity of the common commercial policy would be seriously undermined if the Member States were authorized unilaterally to impose charges having equivalent effect to customs duties on imports from non-member countries. It followed that it was for the Community alone to determine the level of duties and taxes payable on products from those countries.[41]

In the second part of the judgment the Court determined the scope of the prohibition of charges having equivalent effect contained in agreements concluded with non-member countries or in Community regulations governing trade with such countries. Here the Court considered that there was no reason to interpret such prohibitions differently from the prohibition of charges having equivalent effect in intra-Community trade. The agreements and regulations would be deprived of much of their effectiveness if the term 'charge having equivalent effect' contained in them were to be interpreted as having a more limited scope than the same term appearing in the Treaty.[42]

---

[40] Case C–125/94 *Aprile v. Amministrazione delle Finanze dello Stato* [1995] ECR I–2919.
[41] Ibid, paras 32–37.   [42] Ibid, paras 38–41.

The judgment did not answer the question of how to interpret the prohibition for Member States to introduce charges having equivalent effect in the absence of express provision in agreements or in Community regulations. It is however difficult to see any reasons for adopting a narrower interpretation of the concept in such a context.

Generalized tariff preferences

The system of generalized tariff preferences (GSP) was developed at the instigation of UNCTAD. It is however an autonomous measure of the Community; there are no international agreements on such preferences, except for a decision of the GATT contracting parties which established that preferences in favour of developing countries are permanently compatible with the GATT.[43] The Community system consists essentially of the full or partial reduction or suspension of the customs duties set out in the CCT with a view to facilitating the importation of certain products from developing countries. It was established for the first time in 1971. The current scheme is found in Regulation 2501/2001, and follows a reform of the system initiated in 1994.[44] In the preamble to the 1994 regulation it was stated that the scheme should become more development-oriented, focusing on the poorest countries; that it should be complementary to GATT instruments and should foster the integration of developing countries into the world economy and the multilateral trading system; and that consequently preferences should be seen as a transitional measure. The current regulation makes provision for the removal of a country from the list of beneficiaries where the country is classified by the World Bank as a high-income country and the country's development index reaches a certain level.[45] The current regulation on the other hand incorporates the 'everything but arms' initiative, under which all quotas and duties on all products except arms from the world's forty-eight least-developed countries are eliminated.[46]

The new system is also the first general commercial policy instrument which contains references to environmental protection and workers' rights. The link between trade policies and protection of the environment and fundamental social rights is increasingly emphasized, and the regulation manifests that. Its preamble refers to the promotion of sustainable development in developing countries as one of the objectives of the Community's development policy, and states that the common commercial policy must be consistent with and consolidate those objectives.

---

[43] Decision of 25 June 1971 L/3545, BISD 18 Supp. (1972) 24.

[44] Council Regulation 2501/2001 applying a scheme of generalized tariff preferences for the period from 1 January 2002 to 31 December 2003 [2001] OJ L346/1. The scheme is a continuation of the 1998–2002 scheme: see Council Regulation 2820/98 [1998] OJ L357/1, and of the 1994–1998 scheme: see Council Regulation 3281/94 [1994] OJ L348/1.

[45] Art 3 of Regulation 2501/2001 (n 44 above).

[46] Council Regulation 416/2001 [2001] OJ L60/43.

The regulation accordingly provides for special incentive arrangements for the protection of labour rights and of the environment. Those arrangements consist of a further reduction of customs duties. As regards labour rights such a reduction may be granted to countries which effectively apply the standards laid down in a number of ILO Conventions.[47] As regards environmental protection the additional preferences are limited to products of the tropical forests, and they may be granted to countries which effectively apply internationally acknowledged standards and guidelines concerning sustainable management of such forests.[48] The success of those incentive arrangements appears to be limited, as only Moldova benefits from the arrangement for the protection of labour rights, and no country benefits from the arrangement for environmental protection.[49] The regulation also provides for special arrangements to combat drug production and trafficking.[50]

The special incentive arrangements may be contrasted with the scope for withdrawing tariff preferences. Article 26 of Regulation 2501/2001 lists seven grounds for such withdrawal, which refer to labour standards, drugs policies, fraud, unfair trading practices, and fish conservation policies. The provision has been employed against Myanmar.[51]

Applying the CCT

The application of the CCT is left to national authorities, in conformity with the relevant provisions of Community law. Those provisions are the subject of an extensive body of technical legislation, mostly laid down in regulations. The basic instrument is Council Regulation 2913/92 establishing the Community Customs Code.[52] The Code contains, for example, rules on classification (where it refers to the CN contained in Regulation 2658/87), on valuation for customs purposes, and on the origin of products. Cases on the exact classification of products often end up in the Court of Justice, as a question of interpretation of the CN.[53] Again the principle of uniformity is essential, as can be illustrated by a few comments of Jacobs AG in *Neckermann Versand*, a case on the definition and classification of nightdresses. The referring court had mentioned the possibility of classifying goods on the basis of the generally accepted view in trade in the Member State of importation. That seemed to imply that the classification might vary depending on the point of entry into the customs territory of the Community. The Advocate General thought it conceivable that a garment might, as a result of climatic and cultural differences in the Member

---

[47] See Art 14 of Regulation 2501/2001 (n 44 above), which refers to ILO Conventions Nos 29 and 105 on forced labour, Nos 87 and 98 on the freedom of association and the right to collective bargaining, Nos 100 and 111 on non-discrimination in respect of employment and occupation, and Nos 138 and 182 on child labour. Those are the so-called fundamental ILO Conventions.

[48] Art 21 of Regulation 2501/2001 (n 44 above).   [49] See Annex 1 of 4 ibid.

[50] Art 25 of ibid.   [51] Para 23 of the preamble to ibid.   [52] [1992] OJ L302/11.

[53] See the Opinion of Jacobs AG in Case C–338/95 *Wiener v. Hauptzollamt Emmerich* [1997] ECR I–6495, for an overview of the relevant principles of interpretation.

States, be considered suitable for outdoor wear in one country but fit only for wearing in bed in another country. However, the very concept of a common customs tariff implied that goods imported into the Community should be subject to the same rate of duty regardless of the Member State of importation, and it was important to avoid using any criteria that might lead to a different classification depending on the country of importation. The Advocate General added that the suitability of a garment for wearing in bed had to be assessed in the light of the habits, not of one Member State, but of the Community as a whole. It could be difficult in practice for national authorities to make such an assessment, but the attempt had to be made.[54]

Rules of origin serve to identify the origin of products, with a view to determining the applicable customs regime. For imports subject to tariff preferences, for example in the context of a free-trade area, there are so-called preferential rules of origin, which are detailed and technical, and vary according to the country of exportation. For other purposes the general rules of origin apply. The most important provision is Article 24 of the Community Customs Code, according to which goods whose production involved more than one country shall be deemed to originate in the country where they underwent their last, substantial, economically justified processing or working in an undertaking equipped for that purpose and resulting in the manufacture of a new product or representing an important stage of manufacture.[55]

Although for some products there are more specific rules, for most products origin has to be determined, in cases of doubt, on the basis of the above general rule. It goes without saying that that is not always an easy matter, and that it gives rise to litigation. Generally, the Court of Justice takes the view that origin should be determined on the basis of technical, and not economic, criteria. In one case, involving the difficult issue of assembly operations, the Court also took the value added to the product in such operations into account.[56]

General import regulations

Regulation 3285/94 applies to most imports into the EC.[57] It contains the basic principle that imports are free, i.e. that they are not subject to any quantitative restrictions. The regulation also contains provisions on safeguard measures. They state under what conditions such measures may be taken, and effectively implement the WTO Agreement on Safeguards. The provisions are detailed and contain rules on the investigation procedure, where interested parties may have to be heard, and

---

[54] Case C–395/93 *Neckermann Versand v. Hauptzollamt Frankfurt am Main-Ost* [1994] ECR I–4027, para 14 of the Opinion of Jacobs AG.   [55] Regulation 2913/92 (n 52 above).

[56] Case C–26/88 *Brother International v. Hauptzollamt Giessen* [1989] ECR 4253.

[57] Council Regulation 3285/94 on the common rules for imports and repealing Regulation (EC) No 518/94 [1994] OJ L349/53.

on how injury is to be established. The Community, however, rarely takes safeguard action on the basis of those rules.[58]

There is a separate regulation governing imports from former Soviet Union republics and from China,[59] a left-over of those countries' state-trading and non-market economy status. The regulation also provides for free importation, but does lay down quotas for imports of certain products from China.[60]

Imports of most textile products are governed by Council Regulation 3030/93 on common rules for imports of certain textile products from third countries.[61] International trade in textiles has been subject to restrictions for decades, mostly in the framework of the Multi-Fibre Agreement. Those restrictions are phased out over a period of ten years, pursuant to the Agreement on Textiles and Clothing, which is part of the WTO Agreement.

Anti-dumping

Article VI of the GATT allows the GATT Contracting Parties to take action against dumping, defined as the practice 'by which products of one country are introduced into the commerce of another country at less than the normal value of the products'. Normal value is in principle the price for the like product when destined for consumption in the exporting country. Anti-dumping action may however be taken only where dumping causes or threatens to cause material injury to an established domestic industry, or materially retards the establishment of such an industry.

Such action consists of the levying of an anti-dumping duty (effectively a tax on imports). The current version of the basic EC legislation is contained in Council Regulation 384/96 on protection against dumped imports from countries not members of the European Community.[62] That regulation implements the new Anti-Dumping Code which resulted from the Uruguay Round negotiations, and which is part of the WTO Agreement. The regulation is very technical, and its application requires intimate knowledge of its provisions and of accounting and pricing policies of companies. However, in practice it is those technicalities which may determine the outcome of proceedings. What follows is a short description of the main elements of an investigation.

To determine whether dumping takes place one first needs to establish the *normal value* of the product.[63] For imports from market economy countries normal value is the price paid or payable, in the ordinary course of trade, by independent customers

---

[58] The only recent application concerns steel products: see Commission Regulation 560/2002 [2002] OJ L85/1.

[59] Council Regulation 519/94 on common rules for imports from certain third countries and repealing Regulations (EEC) Nos 1765/82, 1766/82, and 3420/83 [1994] OJ L67/89.

[60] Ibid, Annex II (footwear, tableware, and kitchenware).   [61] [1993] OJ L275/1.

[62] [1996] OJ L56/1. See *inter alia* I Van Bael and J-F Bellis, *Anti-Dumping and other Trade Protection Laws of the EC* (3rd edn, CCH Editions, 1996); E Vermulst and P Waer, *EC Anti-Dumping Law and Practice* (Sweet & Maxwell, 1996); S Farr, *EU Anti-Dumping Law* (Palladian Law Publishing, 1998).   [63] Art 2(A).

in the exporting country. For imports from non-market economy countries, however, different rules on normal value apply. The idea there is that the domestic prices in such a country are unreliable, and that therefore reference needs to be made to the prices in a market-economy country.

After establishing normal value one needs to establish the *export price*.[64] Once the normal value and the export price are established, they can be compared. That is no problem in those cases where domestic sales and exports take place under identical conditions, but in practice that is rarely the case. The regulation therefore provides that a fair *comparison* must be made.[65] After comparison, the *dumping margin* can be established.[66]

As mentioned, anti-dumping duties may be applied only if the dumping causes injury to the Community industry. There are also rules on the *determination of injury* and a definition of the term Community industry—normally the Community producers, as a whole, of the like products.[67]

Anti-dumping proceedings are as a rule initiated upon a written, substantiated complaint on behalf of the Community industry.[68] The Commission must examine such complaint, and take a decision on whether there is sufficient evidence to justify the initiation of an anti-dumping investigation. The Commission conducts this investigation,[69] which covers a period of not less than six months immediately prior to the start of the investigation. The Commission investigates whether over that period there was dumping and injury. Interested parties have a right to be heard, and there are specific provisions on verification visits;[70] sampling;[71] non-co-operation by interested parties;[72] confidentiality;[73] and disclosure of essential facts and considerations on the basis of which measures are imposed.[74]

In the course of the investigation the Commission may impose provisional anti-dumping duties, on the basis of a provisional establishment of dumping and injury.[75] Provisional duties are not immediately collected, but require to be secured by a guarantee; they are collected when the investigation is completed, resulting in definitive anti-dumping duties. The latter are the outcome of a definitive finding of dumping and injury.[76] There is however no obligation for the Community to adopt duties upon such a finding. First, there is a measure of discretion in so far as it needs to be established whether such duties would be in the Community interest.[77] That interest is defined as including interests of the domestic industry and users and consumers, with special consideration for the need to eliminate the trade-distorting effects of injurious dumping and to restore effective competition. Secondly, the Commission may accept undertakings from the exporters relating to prices and exports.[78] The Commission is however under no obligation to do so, nor are the exporters required to enter into them.

Definitive anti-dumping duties may not exceed either the dumping or injury margin (the so-called lesser duty rule).[79] The duties are normally individualized

---

[64] Art 2(B).   [65] Art 2(C).   [66] Art 2(D).   [67] Art 3.   [68] Art 5.
[69] Art 6.   [70] Art 16.   [71] Art 17.   [72] Art 18.   [73] Art 19.   [74] Art 20.
[75] Art 7.   [76] Art 9.   [77] Art 21.   [78] Art 8.   [79] Art 9(4), last sentence.

for each supplier of dumped products, reflecting the fact that an anti-dumping investigation is in principle targeted at the pricing policies of individual exporters. Definitive duties expire after five years, but may be continued if the dumping and injury persist.[80]

Anti-dumping policy also offers an illustration of the Community's desire to respect WTO law, and to ensure that WTO dispute settlement rulings are easily implemented. Council Regulation 1515/2001 concerns measures which may be taken following a WTO dispute settlement report concerning anti-dumping or anti-subsidy matters.[81] It enables the Council to adopt, on a proposal from the Commission and by simple majority, any appropriate measures which may be required by a WTO ruling, either in a case involving a Community measure or in other cases.

Anti-subsidy

Action may also be taken by the Community against subsidized imports. As with anti-dumping, new basic legislation was adopted following the conclusion of the Uruguay Round. The current version is Council Regulation 2026/97 on protection against subsidized imports from countries not members of the European Community,[82] which implements the Agreement on Subsidies and Countervailing Measures, part of Annex 1A to the WTO Agreement. The structure of anti-subsidy investigations and action is similar to anti-dumping. The Community does not however take anti-subsidy action very often.[83]

The trade barriers instrument

Part of the package of trade policy instruments adopted in December 1994 is Council Regulation 3286/94 laying down Community procedures in the field of the common commercial policy in order to ensure the exercise of the Community's rights under international trade rules, in particular those established under the auspices of the WTO.[84] That regulation is generally referred to as the trade barriers instrument. Under the regulation the Community industry has the right to lodge a complaint with the Commission as regards obstacles to trade that have an effect either on the Community market or on the market of a third country. In practice,

---

[80] Art 11.   [81] [2001] OJ L201/10.   [82] [1997] OJ L288/1.

[83] See further K Adamantopoulos and MJ Pereyra-Friedrichsen, *EU Anti-Subsidy Law and Practice* (Palladian Law Publishing, 2001); M Sanchez-Rydelski, *EG und WTO Antisubventionsrecht* (Nomos, 2001).

[84] [1994] OJ 1994 L349/71. For a recent analysis see M Bronckers and N McNelis, 'The EU Trade Barriers Regulation Comes of Age', in A von Bogdandy, P Mavroidis, and Y Mény (eds), *European Integration and International Co-ordination—Studies in Transnational Economic Law in Honour of Claus-Dieter Ehlermann* (Kluwer Law International, 2002) 55.

the instrument is mainly used for channelling complaints concerning unfair trade practices in third-country markets which hinder market access. One of the innovations, compared to the previous instrument,[85] is that, where obstacles on the market of a third country are complained of, such a complaint may be lodged by a single Community enterprise which is affected. The regulation contains detailed rules on the examination procedure which needs to be followed if the Commission decides that the complaint contains sufficient evidence and that an examination is in the Community interest. If as a result of the examination it is found that action by the Community is necessary, the regulation allows the Community institutions to adopt any type of measures aimed at combating the obstacles to trade. Examples are: the suspension or withdrawal of concessions, the raising of customs duties or the introduction of a charge on imports, and the introduction of quantitative restrictions. However, such measures must be compatible with existing international obligations and procedures. The regulation does not therefore permit any action which would not be in full compliance with the Community's international commitments, particularly in the WTO. The regulation is clearly aimed at encouraging Community enterprises to trigger Community action in the WTO against foreign trade barriers.

Export policy

The Community also has legislation on exports to third countries. The general rules are contained in Council Regulation 2603/69 establishing common rules for exports.[86] Article 1 of that regulation lays down the principle of freedom of exportation. There are basically two categories of exceptions. The first concerns petroleum products (see *Bulk Oil*, where the Court accepted that the Council could exclude petroleum products from the scope of the regulation).[87] Secondly, there is Article 11 of the regulation, which is a copy of Article 30 EC. It has been invoked in the context of so-called strategic export controls, a subject analysed in Chapter 12. That chapter also looks at Community legislation on export controls, and the EU's policy on economic sanctions, which often involve trade embargoes.

Actors

One can be short on the role of the various institutions in the conduct of the common commercial policy. As of the time of writing, Article 133 EC mentions only two institutions: the Commission and the Council. The long evolution towards greater involvement of the European Parliament in EC policy-making has not yet reached this important domain. Accordingly, the Treaty procedure is very simple: the

---

[85] Council Regulation 2641/84 on the strengthening of the common commercial policy with regard in particular to protection against illicit commercial practices [1984] OJ L252/1.
[86] N 12 above.   [87] Art 10(2) and n 11 above.

Council acts, by qualified majority, on a proposal from the Commission. That procedure not only applies to the adoption of internal commercial policy acts, but extends to the negotiation and conclusion of international agreements. The Treaty does not even provide for mere consultation of the Parliament, the weakest form of parliamentary involvement.

There may have been a time when the technicality of commercial policy could justify this absence of parliamentary scrutiny. In today's societies, however, this approach can clearly not be maintained if there is to be even a semblance of democratic decision-making. This was realized by the members of the Convention on the Future of Europe, and the draft Constitution provides that the legislative procedure, i.e. co-decision, will extend to the common commercial policy (see Article III–217). That is one of the important modifications to EU decision-making which the draft Constitution would introduce.

In practice, fortunately, the Parliament is to some extent involved in the formulation of the common commercial policy. It is regularly informed and consulted,[88] and may have to be consulted about or even give its assent to certain international agreements with a trade dimension, either because the agreement is not limited to trade, or because it comes within one of the categories requiring Parliamentary assent. The conclusion of the WTO Agreement, for instance, had to receive the Parliament's assent because it established a specific institutional framework (see Article 300(3) EC).[89]

The day-to-day conduct of the common commercial policy none the less remains a rather bureaucratic endeavour. Most of the technical expertise is located in the Commission, which has represented the Community and its Member States in the GATT and then the WTO for decades, and which is the negotiator of international agreements. The Commission is assisted and supervised by an important committee of Member State representatives, the so-called 133 Committee, which is expressly referred to in Article 133(3) EC in connection with the negotiation of trade agreements. Its role also extends to the formulation of commercial policy legislation and the adoption of commercial policy measures.[90]

The Council adopts commercial policy acts by qualified majority. There are however exceptions to that rule. Anti-dumping and anti-subsidy measures are taken by simple majority, on a proposal from the Commission.[91] This reflects the administrative dimension of such measures, which conclude a factual investigation by the Commission. The rule of simple majority amounts to a more preponderant role for the Commission, whose proposals are more easily adopted.

---

[88] E.g. through annual reports on anti-dumping and anti-subsidy policy: see e.g. Commission, Twentieth Annual Report on the Community's Anti-Dumping and Anti-Subsidy Activities, COM(2002)484 final.

[89] Council Decision 94/800 concerning the conclusion on behalf of the European Community, as regards matters within its competence, of the agreements reached in the Uruguay Round multilateral negotiations (1986–1994) [1994] OJ L336/1.

[90] See Kapteyn and VerLoren van Themaat (n 32 above) 1282.

[91] Art 9(4) of Regulation 384/96 (n 62 above) and Art 15(1) Regulation 2026/97 (n 82 above).

Lastly, the Court of Justice and Court of First Instance often need to deal with cases involving commercial policy measures. The subject of judicial review of such measures deserves separate treatment.

Judicial review of commercial policy measures

General observations

It will be clear from the above that the EC's external trade policy is sophisticated, and that it is implemented through myriads of commercial policy measures. Such measures obviously affect a range of economic interests and actors—producers, importers, exporters, consumers. In many cases, the measures which the EC adopts have a specific and significant impact, creating strong incentives for judicial challenge. There is, as a result, a large body of case law on judicial review of commercial policy measures. Within the scope of this chapter it is not possible to offer a complete survey and analysis of this area of judicial review.[92] Instead, this section aims to offer some insights into some of the most important issues arising in this context. It is followed by a small case study of one of the most fascinating sagas of legal contestation of EC legislation on external trade, namely the legislation on imports of bananas.

Commercial policy measures, whether in the form of general legislation, such as the basic regulations on imports, exports, anti-dumping, etc., or in the form of more specific measures or even decisions, are subject to the general system of judicial review set up by the EC Treaty and applied by the EU courts. There are essentially three forms of action.

The first is the action for the annulment of an act of an EC institution (Article 230 EC). As is well known, and much debated, private parties ('natural or legal persons') can bring such actions only against decisions addressed to them, or against a decision which, although in the form of a regulation or a decision addressed to another person, is of direct and individual concern to them. In practice, access to the courts (the Court of First Instance and, on an appeal on points of law only, the Court of Justice) turns on the notion of direct and individual concern, which is strictly interpreted.[93] As a result it is, generally speaking, not possible for private parties directly to challenge EC regulations, as they are not considered to be individually concerned by them. However, in the trade policy field there are significant exceptions to that rule. As analysed below, the courts have been willing to accept that anti-dumping regulations can be challenged by certain categories of affected

---

[92] For a case study concerning imports of Chinese toys see F Snyder, 'Judicial Review in the Age of Globalization: Chinese Toys in the European Court of Justice', in D O'Keeffe and A Bavasso (eds), *Judicial Review in European Union Law—Liber Amicorum in Honour of Lord Slynn of Hadley, Vol I* (Kluwer Law International, 2000) 651–64.

[93] See most recently Case C–50/00 P *UPA v. Council* [2002] ECR I–6677.

economic operators. The reasoning underlying such acceptance is however based on the specific nature of anti-dumping measures, and cannot readily be transposed to other commercial policy measures in the form of regulations, let alone general external trade legislation.

The restrictions on direct access or standing do not put general commercial policy measures beyond judicial review, which brings us to the second form of action. As such measures are typically implemented at the level of the Member States, where import and export transactions are administered, it is open to any affected economic operator to challenge such implementation before the competent national court or tribunal, on the basis that the EC measures are invalid. If such an operator manages to persuade that court or tribunal that there are indeed serious doubts as regards the validity of the EC measure, a reference will be made to the Court of Justice under Article 234 EC. The object of that reference is the question whether the commercial policy measure, which may be of a general, legislative character, is valid.

The grounds for challenging the validity of EC acts by way of a preliminary reference are identical to those which may be advanced in an action for annulment,[94] so from that perspective there are no drawbacks to this alternative route for judicial review. There are however other disadvantages, which arguably result in the preliminary rulings procedure offering a less effective remedy than the action for annulment.[95] First, an economic operator may for various reasons find it difficult to locate and challenge a national implementing measure before a court in a Member State. It may even have to infringe the law so as to trigger some form of prosecution, in the context of which a challenge to the EC measure can be made, which is not a particularly attractive proposition. There may be difficulties of obtaining standing before the competent court or tribunal. Secondly, the economic operator needs to be able to persuade the national court that the validity of the EC act is genuinely in doubt. It is indeed that court which has sole authority to decide that a reference needs to be made, and parties have no right to a reference. There may be cases where the operator is obliged to appeal against rulings declining the making of a reference, up to the highest court, which is obliged to refer in any case which turns on a point of EC law.[96] Thirdly, it may be more difficult to obtain interim measures, such as measures suspending the operation of the challenged EC act or legislation, and the national court is not particularly well placed to operate the balancing of interests which the decision on interim measures may require. Fourthly, and most significantly, because of its indirect character the preliminary rulings procedure is not well adapted to the challenge of commercial policy measures, particularly where such measures are fact-intensive and of an administrative character. The whole case before

---

[94] M Brealey and M Hoskins, *Remedies in EC Law* (2nd edn, Sweet & Maxwell, 1998) 228.

[95] Cf Opinion of Jacobs AG in *UPA v. Council* (n 93 above).

[96] See Art 234 EC, third para. For an example of a successful challenge to the validity of a commercial policy measure on a reference by a highest court (the German *Bundesfinanzhof* or Federal Finance Court), see Case C–24/90 *Hauptzollamt Hamburg-Jonas v. Werner Faust* [1991] ECR I–4905.

the Court of Justice will be defined by the order for reference, which may not always provide sufficient information, the proceedings are not adversarial (there is no exchange of written pleadings), and as a result the Court of Justice may not be in a good position to engage in full investigation and review of all the facts and issues that may arise. For example, as further analysed below, EC importers of products which are subject to anti-dumping duties do not as a rule have standing in direct actions for annulment, and are therefore compelled to use the indirect preliminary reference route. It is however clear that judicial review of anti-dumping regulations may require intense scrutiny of the administrative investigation which led to the adoption of the duties, and it is plainly more difficult for the Court of Justice to engage in such scrutiny on a reference than it is for the Court of First Instance in a direct action for annulment. Moreover, the latter Court was set up with the specific instruction to deal with fact-intensive cases of an administrative character,[97] and it would seem logical that it could hear all challenges to commercial policy measures which come within that category.

Those problems can however be resolved only through a general reconsideration of the system of remedies under EU law, particularly as regards direct access to the EU courts for the purpose of challenges to EU acts. The Court of Justice is unwilling to do so by way of re-interpretation of the notion of direct and individual concern.[98] It is therefore up to the Member States to modify the system, a task which they should urgently undertake.[99]

There is a third form of action which is available to an economic operator seeking judicial review: it may invoke the non-contractual liability of the Community (Articles 235 and 288, second paragraph, EC). The EC is obliged to compensate any damage resulting from wrongful behaviour, but in the case of rule-making it is only where there is a sufficiently serious violation of a rule intended to confer rights on private parties that compensation may be granted.[100] This means that a mere illegality will not always be sufficient, and there are very few examples of successful cases in this area.

The above is the general picture of judicial review of commercial policy measures. The following subsections analyse three further topics. The first concerns access to court, or standing, in the context of anti-dumping. The second relates to the standards of review which the Court of Justice and Court of First Instance operate in the area of commercial policy. The third is a short survey of the banana saga, which introduces further elements of judicial review: the fact that EC commercial policy measures may be challenged not only before the courts in Luxembourg, but also before the dispute-settlement organs of the WTO and before national constitutional courts.

[97] Council Decision 88/591 establishing a Court of First Instance of the European Communities [1988] OJ L319/1, the preamble to which states that 'in respect of actions requiring close examination of complex facts, the establishment of a second court will improve the judicial protection of individual interests'.   [98] *UPA* (n 93 above).

[99] The draft Constitution introduces a broadening of standing to all regulatory measures of direct concern; it does not permit standing in cases involving legislative measures (see Art III–270(4)).

[100] Case C–352/98 P *Laboratoires Pharmaceutiques Bergaderm v. Goupil* [2000] ECR I–5291.

Standing in anti-dumping cases

In the very first action for the annulment of an anti-dumping measure before the
Court of Justice the question of standing immediately surfaced. The cases concerned
imports of ball-bearings from Japan and were brought by a series of Japanese
exporters and their European subsidiaries. As anti-dumping measures are adopted
by way of regulations the issue was whether the companies were directly and individually concerned. The Court admitted the actions on rather narrow grounds.[101]

A few years later, in 1984, the Court in *Allied Corporation and Others* made a
broader ruling on standing of exporters affected by anti-dumping measures.[102]
The cases concerned provisional duties imposed by the Commission on exports of
fertilizers by the applicants, who were expressly named in the regulation. VerLoren
van Themaat AG referred to the Commission's plea in support of admissibility of
actions brought by exporters. The Commission based its reasoning on the principle
of reciprocity, pointing out that in the United States there was effective legal protection for exporters. It also indicated that exporters could not bring a direct action
in the national courts of the Member States against anti-dumping duties imposed
in specific cases, and that therefore a declaration of inadmissibility by the Court of
Justice would deprive them of any legal protection whatsoever. The Advocate
General accepted those arguments, and invited the Court to make a ruling of principle. He added another argument, namely that dumping is a phenomenon by
nature related to forms of distortion of competition which, under the system of the
(then) EEC Treaty, were normally countered by means of decisions.[103]

The Court agreed. It pointed out that, in the light of the criteria of (current)
Article 230, fourth paragraph, EC, anti-dumping measures were, as regards their
nature and scope, of a legislative character, inasmuch as they applied to all the traders
concerned, taken as a whole. None the less, the provisions of anti-dumping regulations could be of direct and individual concern to those producers and exporters
who were charged with practising dumping. It was in particular clear from the provisions of the then applicable basic anti-dumping regulation (which have, as to their
essence, not hitherto been modified) that anti-dumping duties could be imposed
only on the basis of findings resulting from investigations concerning the production and export prices of undertakings which had been individually identified. It
was thus clear that measures imposing anti-dumping duties were liable to be of
direct and individual concern to those producers and exporters who were able to
establish that they were identified in the measures adopted by the Commission or
the Council, or were concerned by the preliminary investigations. The Court added

---

[101] Case 113/77 *NTN Toyo Bearing Company v. Council* [1979] ECR 1185; Case 118/77 *ISO v. Council*
[1979] ECR 1277; Case 119/77 *Nippon Seiko v. Council and Commission* [1979] ECR 1303; Case 120/77
Koyo Seiko v. Council and Commission [1979] ECR 1337; Case 121/77 *Nachi Fujikoshi v. Council* [1979]
ECR 1363.
[102] Joined Cases 239 and 275/83 *Allied Corporation and Others v. Commission* [1984] ECR 1005.
[103] Ibid, 1037–45.

that there was no risk of duplication of means of redress since it was possible to bring an action in the national courts only following the collection of an anti-dumping duty which was normally paid by an importer residing within the Community, and since in the context of a reference it was for the Court of Justice alone to give a final decision on the validity of the contested regulations.[104]

The ruling of the Court in *Allied Corporation* signified that exporters would as a rule have standing to challenge anti-dumping duties affecting their exports. Indeed, anti-dumping investigations are normally conducted on the basis of the individual pricing practices of companies which take part in the investigation and are named in the regulations.[105] Since the judgment there has been a long procession of exporters affected by anti-dumping duties before the Court of Justice and, later on, before the Court of First Instance. In the great majority of cases, however, they were unsuccessful (see below).

The Court also admits actions for annulment brought by complainants, as became clear in the *Timex* case.[106] In issue were definitive anti-dumping duties on imports of mechanical wrist-watches originating in what was then the Soviet Union. The Council had adopted those duties following an investigation initiated by a complaint on behalf of Timex Corporation, among others. Timex considered the duties to be insufficient and brought an action for annulment. The Court repeated that anti-dumping measures were, in fact, legislative in nature and scope, inasmuch as they applied to traders in general, but that their provisions could nevertheless be of direct and individual concern to some of those traders. It was in this regard necessary to consider the part played by the applicant in the anti-dumping proceedings and its position on the market to which the contested legislation applied. The Court pointed out that the complaint had originated with Timex, and that Timex was heard during the procedure. It also referred to the fact that Timex was the leading manufacturer of mechanical watches and watch movements in the Community and the only remaining manufacturer of those products in the Community. Furthermore, the conduct of the investigation procedure had been largely determined by Timex's observations and the anti-dumping duty had been fixed in the light of the effect of the dumping on Timex. The contested regulation was therefore based on the applicant's own situation. It followed that the contested regulation constituted a decision which was of direct and individual concern to Timex within the meaning of (current) Article 230 EC.[107]

For importers of dumped products, who actually pay the anti-dumping duties, matters are altogether different. The Court looked at the position of importers in general in the *Alusuisse* case.[108] The applicant imported orthoxylene as an

---

[104] Ibid, paras 11–13.
[105] Among the exceptions are cases involving non-market economy countries, where no account is taken of individual companies' pricing practices: see e.g. P Eeckhout, 'European Anti-Dumping Law and China' (1997) 1 EIoP No 7 (⟨http://eiop.or.at/eiop/texte/1997-007a.htm⟩).
[106] Case 264/82 *Timex v. Council and Commission* [1985] ECR 849.   [107] Ibid, paras 12–16.
[108] Case 307/81 *Alusuisse v. Council and Commission* [1982] ECR 3463.

independent importer, that is an importer who is not linked to a manufacturing or exporting company, from *inter alia* the United States and Puerto Rico. In the course of 1981 provisional and definitive anti-dumping duties were imposed on those imports. Alusuisse challenged the relevant regulations in an action for annulment. The Court referred to the language of (current) Article 230, fourth paragraph, EC, and stated that an action for annulment was not admissible in so far as it was directed against a regulation having general application, the test for distinguishing between a regulation and a decision being whether or not the measure in question had general application. It was therefore necessary to appraise the nature of the contested measures and in particular the legal effects which they were intended to produce or did in fact produce. The Court found that the measures in issue constituted, as regards independent importers who, in contrast to exporters, were not expressly named in the regulations, measures having general application within the meaning of (current) Article 249 EC, because they applied to objectively determined situations and entailed legal effects for categories of persons regarded generally and in the abstract. The Court rejected the argument that Alusuisse formed part of a closed category of traders, because a measure did not cease to be a regulation where it was possible to determine the number or even the identity of the persons to whom it applied at any given time, as long as it was established that such application took effect by virtue of an objective legal or factual situation defined by the measure in relation to its purpose. The Court also rejected the argument based on Alusuisse's participation in the procedure leading to the adoption of the duties: the distinction between a regulation and a decision could only be based on the nature of the measure itself and the legal effect which it produced, and not on the procedures for its adoption. The Court lastly pointed out that this was in conformity with the system of remedies provided for by Community law, since importers could contest before the national court individual measures taken by the national authorities in application of the Community regulations. Alusuisse was therefore refused standing.[109]

Not all importers are refused standing. Those which are not independent but are associated with the exporters concerned may be able to bring an action for annulment under certain circumstances, e.g. where their resale prices formed the basis for a constructed export price.[110] As regards independent importers the Court again considered the issue of lack of standing in *Extramet*.[111] The applicant was an undertaking producing granules of calcium metal by a redistillation process which it had developed and patented. The calcium metal market was characterized by a very small number of producers, only one of which, Péchiney, was based in the EC. The latter was therefore the only producer of calcium metal in the EC, and Extramet was the largest importer of calcium metal, essentially from China and what was then the Soviet Union. On a complaint on behalf of Péchiney the Council, after an investigation,

[109] Case 307/81 *Alusuisse v. Council and Commission* [1982] ECR 3463, paras 8–14.
[110] See e.g. *ISO v. Council* (n 101 above); Joined Cases C–305/86 and C–160/87 *Neotype Techmashexport v. Commission and Council* [1990] ECR I–2945, paras 17–22.
[111] Case C–358/89 *Extramet Industrie v. Council* [1991] ECR I–2501.

imposed definitive anti-dumping duties. Extramet however alleged that the increase in imports was due to the fact that Péchiney refused to supply it with calcium metal, because Péchiney was itself developing its own process for producing calcium granules. Extramet had even lodged a complaint against Péchiney with the *Conseil Français de la Concurrence* (French Competition Council).

Jacobs AG argued in favour of a generally more liberal approach towards standing of importers. He pointed out that, in so far as the earlier case law on inadmissibility was based on the fact that an importer could not prove that the measure was in substance a decision, it was inconsistent with more recent case law, which did not treat the requirement of a decision as independent of the requirement of individual concern. In so far as the case law suggested that the procedure leading to the adoption of an anti-dumping regulation could not affect the question of standing, it could not be reconciled with the case law on the standing of complainants. The Advocate General also referred to the fact that, in other contexts too, such as state aid, the Court had accepted that participation in a procedure culminating in a quasi-judicial determination of a party's rights could be enough to establish a person's standing to challenge that determination. He further looked at the acceptance of standing of associated importers, and considered that the fact that the Commission had taken account of an importer's resale prices did not in itself establish that that importer was affected more immediately than, or in a qualitatively different way from, other importers whose resale prices had not been taken into account. Those considerations suggested that there was no logical basis for distinguishing rigidly in this respect between producers, exporters, complainants, and importers. The Court should in the Advocate General's view accept that similar criteria should be applied in determining the admissibility of actions brought by undertakings in each of these categories, and there was a particularly strong case for acknowledging the admissibility of an action brought by an undertaking whose participation in the proceedings before the Commission could be regarded as having affected their outcome.[112]

In *Extramet* Jacobs AG also compared the preliminary rulings procedure with the action for annulment, and referred to the disadvantages of the former, some of which were discussed above. He mentioned the fact that national courts were not the most appropriate forum for challenges to anti-dumping regulations; the fact that such cases were likely to involve substantial extra delay and costs; the problem of interim measures, which in any event were confined to the Member State in question when ordered by a national court; and the fact that the Court of Justice might not have as full an opportunity to investigate the matter as in a direct action, for example because of the generality of the reference.[113]

The Court did not follow the Opinion, despite the strength of the argument. It admitted Extramet's action, but did so on narrow grounds. The Court referred to its earlier case law in the field of anti-dumping, recalling that independent importers do not have standing, in contrast to exporters and associated importers.

---

[112] Ibid, paras 55–66 of the Opinion of Jacobs AG.   [113] Ibid, paras 69–74.

It then indicated, however, that it was in any event open to any category of trader to show that it was individually concerned, in application of the famous *Plaumann* formula:[114] where such traders could point to certain attributes which were peculiar to them and which differentiated them from all other persons. The Court considered that the applicant had in fact established that. It was the largest importer of the product forming the subject of the anti-dumping measure and, at the same time, the end-user of the product. In addition, its business activities depended to a very large extent on those imports and were seriously affected by the contested regulation in view of the limited number of manufacturers of the product concerned and of the difficulties which it encountered in obtaining supplies from the sole EC producer, which, moreover, was its main competitor for the processed product.[115]

The admissibility of Extramet's action was clearly based on the specific, and exceptional, facts of the case, and there are no other examples of successful actions for annulment, in terms of standing, by independent importers.

It is unfortunate that the Court did not follow the approach advocated by Jacobs AG. Anti-dumping regulations are clearly of an administrative rather than legislative character. It is true that they lay down general rules on the duties to be levied on all imports of the dumped products, yet such general rules are only the end result of what is essentially an administrative process, focusing on the pricing policies of exporters and on the effects of dumped imports on EC producers, importers, and consumers. Indeed, the basic anti-dumping regulation recognizes that those are the various interests which need to be looked at and balanced, under the heading of Community interest.[116] It also recognizes that interested parties, including importers, have a right to be heard and to participate in the investigation.[117] It would be but a small step to accept that such recognition at legislative level of the various interests and interested parties needs to be transferred to the interpretation and application of the notion of individual concern in Article 230, fourth paragraph, EC.

Since the most recent developments in the case law on standing[118] it does however appear that only a general constitutional reform of the system of remedies, by way of Treaty amendment, will lead to modification. As the Court of Justice has decided to stick to the *Plaumann* test, there seems little scope for any significant change in the above case law on importers based on arguments limited to the field of anti-dumping. There is in any event no complete absence of judicial remedy, as affected importers can challenge the anti-dumping duties at national level and seek a preliminary reference.

Standards of review

Difficult as it may be to generalize as regards the standards or intensity of review which the Court of Justice and Court of First Instance operate in the trade policy area, it is none the less necessary to make the attempt in order to shed more light on the subject

---

[114] Case 25/62 *Plaumann v. Commission* [1963] ECR 95.
[115] *Extramet Industrie* (n 111 above), paras 15–17.
[116] Art 21 of Regulation 384/1996 (n 62 above).   [117] Ibid, Art 6.   [118] *UPA* (n 93 above).

of judicial review of commercial policy measures. The starting point is that the Courts have traditionally recognized a significant margin of discretion, where both legislative acts and economic policy-making are concerned.[119] That starting point applies to review of legality in actions for annulment and review of validity in prelim-inary rulings cases, where the same grounds and standards of review apply. It applied even more to actions in damages, where the traditional case law required a suffi-ciently characterized breach of a higher rule of law designed to protect the indi-vidual.[120] As will be seen below, however, that case law was recently modified, and we will have to examine the (potential) effects of that modification on review of trade policy measures.

The approach of recognizing discretion is no doubt correct, in particular where general normative action of a legislative kind is involved. The Courts would be transgressing their judicial function if they scrutinized too closely the merits of EC legislation on external trade.[121] Discretion none the less needs to be put in the perspective of the nature of the measure in issue. There is in fact in EU law a broad spectrum of legal acts, ranging from the most generally normative to very specific decisions. There is, moreover, no firm legal framework or established constitutional doctrine or theory for the classification of different acts, and for determining the legal consequences of such classification. This can most clearly be seen in the use of regulations as legal instruments. Some regulations, based directly on the Treaty, are legislative in character. They may themselves form the basis for implementing regu-lations, which are obviously of a different nature from the basic regulation. And in the context of implementation, there may be a further layer of regulations, even more specific than the general implementing ones.[122]

As the common commercial policy is a wide-ranging and sophisticated policy it makes use of much of the spectrum of EU law making. This may be illustrated by anti-dumping policy. There is obviously a difference in legal character between: (a) the basic anti-dumping regulation, reflecting the policy choices of the EC legis-lature in that field; (b) anti-dumping regulations imposing provisional or definitive anti-dumping duties, in application of the basic regulation; and (c) decisions which the Commission takes in the context of an anti-dumping investigation, e.g. on interested parties' right to be heard. Even within those categories there may, from the perspective of discretion, be significant differences. For example, with every amendment the basic regulation becomes more detailed and precise on how to calculate normal value or how to assess injury to domestic producers, in this respect arguably removing some of the scope for discretion in a particular investigation. In other areas, by contrast, the basic regulation continues to call for what is largely a discretionary assessment: that is the case for the Community interest clause,[123] which is open-ended as to how to balance the various interests involved, and leaves

---

[119] See e.g. K Lenaerts and D Arts, *Procedural Law of the European Union* (R Bray (ed and trans) Sweet & Maxwell, 1999) 198.

[120] Case 5/71 *Zuckerfabrik Schöppenstedt v. Council* [1971] ECR 975, para 11.

[121] Cf Eeckhout (n 25 above), 25–7.   [122] See e.g. the daily Commission regulations.

[123] N 77 above.

the Commission and Council much leeway in striking that balance. It follows that
judicial scrutiny of the determination of normal value or injury will need to be
closer than that of the Community interest determination.

The following paragraphs start by looking at some of the hallmarks and instances
of judicial review in this field of anti-dumping, which has given rise to a large body
of case law. They then discuss some cases in other areas. The objective is not to
provide a rounded assessment of standards of review of commercial policy measures,
as that would require a separate study. The objective is rather to illustrate the level
of review, and in particular to point to some of the defects of the current system.

With respect to anti-dumping there is the benefit of an authoritative survey and
assessment by Jacobs AG, extra-judicially, covering the period up to the transfer of anti-
dumping cases to the Court of First Instance (1994).[124] The conclusions of his analysis
were that, at the time, the Court took an active, and perhaps it could be said more
balanced, role than earlier in reviewing anti-dumping measures. The case law suggested
that the Court exercised control in relation to the following issues: (a) whether the
procedural rules were correctly observed, including procedural requirements that went
beyond those set out in the legislation; (b) whether the facts were accurately stated;
(c) whether there had been a manifest error of appraisal or misuse of powers; (d) whether
the reasoning was adequate; and (e) whether there was a violation of any provisions of
the Treaty, of the enabling legislation or of fundamental principles of Community law,
or of the GATT Anti-dumping Code.[125] On the other hand, Jacobs considered that
challenges to the Commission's methodology had generally not succeeded, nor had
challenges based on such matters as comparisons with sales on the domestic market,
attribution of costs to domestic sales and exports, etc. It seemed questionable to him,
from such comparative surveys as had been undertaken, whether the courts of other
jurisdictions carried out more extensive review of anti-dumping measures.

The 1991 *Nölle* judgment offers a good illustration of the Court of Justice's
willingness to exercise significant review of anti-dumping measures.[126] The case
concerned imports of paint brushes from China. As China was a non-market
economy country the normal value of the paint brushes had to be determined on
the basis of prices in a reference country, which according to the basic regulation
the Commission was required to choose 'in an appropriate and not unreasonable
manner'. The Commission had opted for Sri Lanka, but Nölle, the importer,
considered that that choice was inappropriate and unreasonable. The Court started
its analysis by acknowledging that the choice of reference country was a matter
falling within the discretion enjoyed by the institutions in analysing complex
economic situations. However, it went on to state, the exercise of that discretion was
not excluded from review by the Court, which had consistently held that it would
verify whether the relevant procedural rules had been complied with, whether the

---

[124] FG Jacobs, 'Court of Justice Review of Community Trade Measures', in BE Hawk (ed),
International Antitrust Law & Policy 1994 (Fordham Corporate Law Institute, 1995) 434.
[125] See Ch 9 on the principle of implementation.
[126] Case C–16/90 *Nölle* [1991] ECR I–5163.

facts had been accurately stated, and whether there had been a manifest error of appraisal or a misuse of powers. The Court then examined Nölle's arguments, agreeing with several of them. It established that production volumes of paint brushes in Sri Lanka represented only 1.2 per cent of the volume of Chinese exports to the EC, and considered that to be an indication that the market in Sri Lanka was not very representative. It also found that Sri Lankan industry had to import the raw materials for paint brushes, including pig bristle, whereas China had almost 85 per cent of the market in pig bristle. The Commission should have taken the comparability of access to raw materials into account, which it had not. The Court also went along with Nölle's argument that, as there were only two producers in Sri Lanka, one of whom was a subsidiary of an EC producer involved in the complaint, there was no natural competition, making prices in Sri Lanka inappropriate. The Court in fact found that prices in Sri Lanka were higher than those of two representative EC producers. In conclusion, the Court considered that Nölle had produced sufficient factors to raise doubts whether the choice of Sri Lanka as a reference country had been appropriate and not unreasonable. Moreover, during the investigation the Commission had not pursued a suggestion by Nölle that Taiwan was a more appropriate reference country, notwithstanding clear indications that this was indeed the case. The Commission's attempts to obtain further information on prices in Taiwan had been minimal and insufficient. The Court concluded that the reference country had not been determined in an appropriate and not unreasonable manner, and declared the anti-dumping regulation invalid.[127]

In 1994 anti-dumping cases were transferred to the Court of First Instance, and in 1995 that Court delivered its first judgment in this area, striking down an anti-dumping regulation imposing duties on imports of ball-bearings from Japan.[128] That seemed promising from the perspective of strict review of anti-dumping policy, particularly as the Court of First Instance's founding brief instructed it to look closely at the facts of cases (see above). Subsequent case law did not however confirm any such tendency. Few challenges to anti-dumping regulations are successful, and even though that may in principle simply be due to the correct and diligent attitude of the Commission and the Council, there are examples of excessive deference to the views of those institutions. One such instance is *Sinochem*, in which the question arose as to how to interpret a provision in the basic regulation concerning injury. At the time the regulation required that injury to the 'Community industry' be shown, the latter being defined as 'Community producers as a whole of the like product or . . . those of them whose collective output of the product constitutes a major proportion of the total Community production'. The challenged anti-dumping regulation had been based on injury to one single producer, who was the complainant, and represented 35 per cent of the Community industry. The

---

[127] Ibid, paras 11–37.
[128] Joined Cases T–163/94 and T–165/94 *NTN Corporation and Koyo Seiko v. Council* [1995] ECR II–1381.

question thus arose whether that constituted a major proportion. The Court of First Instance simply accepted, in a single sentence devoid of all reasoning, that the expression 'major proportion' should be interpreted not as a proportion of 50 per cent or more, but rather as 25 per cent or more.[129]

Another example which may show that there is scope for closer scrutiny of anti-dumping measures is the sequel to the *Nölle* case.[130] The importer in question brought an action in damages against the Community, following the Court of Justice's decision to declare invalid the anti-dumping regulation on imports of paint brushes. That case came before the Court of First Instance. The Court considered that anti-dumping measures constituted legislative action involving choices of economic policy and that, as a result, Community liability could be incurred by virtue of such measures only if there had been a sufficiently serious breach of a superior rule of law for the protection of individuals. Applying that test, the Court found that the Community institutions had breached the duties of care and proper administration, but that the violation was not manifest and serious. It referred to the judgment of the Court of Justice, and considered that the Court had not held the choice of Sri Lanka to be inherently wrong, but had simply considered that the Commission ought to have carried out a more detailed investigation in order to determine whether Taiwan might be a more appropriate choice. Damages were therefore denied.[131]

The Court of First Instance's judgment is not convincing. There can be doubts whether anti-dumping measures constitute legislative action involving choices of economic policy, leading to a high threshold for non-contractual liability claims. Even if that were so, the judgment of the Court of Justice was itself based on recognition of the discretion of the Community institutions, and the Court had examined whether there had been a manifest error of appraisal, arriving at an affirmative conclusion. Of course the Court of Justice had not examined whether there was a 'sufficiently serious breach', as that question was not before it. The Court of First Instance made no attempt, however, to engage in a further, autonomous examination of what had taken place.

More recently the Court of Justice aligned the test for non-contractual liability for wrongful normative action with the principle of Member State liability, thereby modifying the *Schöppenstedt* test. In *Bergaderm* the Court emphasized that the decisive test for finding that a breach of Community law was sufficiently serious was whether the Member State or the Community institution concerned manifestly and gravely disregarded the limits on its discretion. It also established that where the Member State or the institution in question had only considerably reduced, or even no discretion, the mere infringement of Community law could be sufficient to establish the existence of a sufficiently serious breach.[132] The Court of Justice has

---

[129] Case T–161/94 *Sinochem Heilongjiang v. Council* [1996] ECR II–695, para 89; the Court's interpretation conformed to the later version of the basic regulation, but it is not clear whether it complies with the Anti-Dumping Code.   [130] N 126 above.

[131] Case T–167/94 *Detlef Nölle v. Council* [1995] ECR II–2589.

[132] *Bergaderm* (n 100 above), paras 43–44.

therefore abandoned the notion of legislative measures, focusing instead on the degree of discretion.[133] In the context of anti-dumping, and commercial policy measures more generally, this should lead to a less generalized approach towards damages claims. Indeed, in many respects the Community institutions have considerably reduced discretion in this field.

Outside the field of anti-dumping, most other cases concerning review of commercial policy measures relate to imports of agricultural products. Although the Court in that area too generally acknowledges that the Community institutions have a wide margin of discretion, it has intervened on occasion, for example where general principles of Community law such as legitimate expectations or proportionality were not observed. Two judgments offer nice illustrations.

Sofrimport concerned imports of dessert apples. In 1988 the Commission took a number of protective measures. After having introduced special surveillance of imports the Commission decided to suspend the issue of import licences because of the threat of a serious disturbance to the Community market. Sofrimport had shipped a cargo of apples, originating in Chile, before the Commission took its decision. It asked for import licences while the apples were being transported, but the licences were refused, notwithstanding a provision in the basic regulation that the Commission should take account of the special position of products in transit to the Community.[134] The Court decided that the effect of that provision was to enable an importer whose goods were in transit to rely on a legitimate expectation that, in the absence of an overriding public interest, no suspensory measures would be applied to him. It did not accept the Commission's arguments to the effect that it had extended the period of validity of import licences or that a reasonably careful trader could have expected that it might at any time take protective measures. The Court stated that simply to inform traders of the possibility of protective measures could not be regarded as sufficient, and that the measure should also have indicated the situations in which the public interest could justify the application of suspensory measures with regard to goods in transit. The Commission had not demonstrated the existence of any such overriding public interest, and the Court annulled the measure in this respect.[135]

In *Werner Faust* a reference was made concerning the validity of a regulation imposing an additional amount (effectively an additional import duty) on imports of preserved mushrooms from third countries.[136] The regulation was part of a series of measures taken since 1978 with a view to addressing disturbances of the Community

---

[133] There are doubts whether the Court of First Instance immediately grasped the ramifications of *Bergaderm*, see its reasoning in Case T–178/98 *Fresh Marine Company v. Commission* [2000] ECR II–3331; see also T Tridimas, 'Liability for Breach of Community Law: Growing Up and Mellowing Down?' (2001) 38 CMLRev 330–1.

[134] Art 3(3) of Council Regulation 2707/72 laying down the conditions for applying protective measures for fruit and vegetables [1972] OJ L291/3.

[135] Case C–152/88 *Sofrimport v. Commission* [1990] ECR I–2477, paras 14–20. It is also noteworthy that the action was declared admissibile in so far as it related to products in transit.

[136] Case C–24/90 *Werner Faust* [1991] ECR I–4905.

market caused by lower prices of imported mushrooms, which were put on the market in large quantities. The regulation imposed an additional levy of ECU 175 per 100 kg for imports exceeding a certain quota. The referring court asked whether the additional amount, and in particular the level at which it was fixed, were appropriate.

The Court of Justice took as a starting point that it followed from the principle of proportionality that measures imposing financial charges on economic agents were lawful provided that the measures were appropriate and necessary for the attainment of the objectives legitimately pursued by the legislation in question. Where there was a choice between several appropriate measures, the least onerous measures had to be used and the charges imposed could not be disproportionate to the aims pursued. The Court then examined the relevant Community legislation and the objective of the measure in issue. The Council regulation permitting the Commission to take protective measures provided that those measures could be taken only to such extent and for such time as was strictly necessary, and that they could be restricted to products imported from or originating in certain countries, to exports to particular countries, or to particular qualities or types of presentation. The Court accepted that the levy of an additional amount was an appropriate and necessary measure for the purpose of protecting the Community market in mushrooms which was threatened with serious disturbances. The Commission had considered it appropriate, in view of traditional trade flows with non-member supplier countries, not to apply measures to suspend imports but to make imports exceeding the traditional volume subject to the less restrictive measure of imposing an additional levy. The Court did not however stop there, and went on to examine whether the additional amount had been set at an appropriate level, particularly as there was no provision for it to be set at different levels according to the quality of the goods and the circumstances in which they were imported. The Court rejected the defence that the amount had to be high in order to constitute a deterrent on the ground that the objective of the measure was not to penalize imports but to protect the Community market.[137] The Commission then explained that the level of the additional amount corresponded to the cost price of grade 1 preserved mushrooms from France, sold on the German market—France being the leading producer and Germany the main purchaser in the Community. The Court however pointed out that the effect of the level of the additional amount was that the cost of preserved mushrooms produced, like those in the main proceedings, in China, was significantly increased in relation to the cost of preserved mushrooms produced in the common market. Moreover, as the additional amount was based only on the cost of grade 1 mushrooms it had much more serious effects on imports of lower-grade mushrooms. The Court concluded that the additional amount functioned as an economic penalty for traders who had imported goods without a licence, and that this was disproportionate.[138]

---

[137] Cf the dictum by Jacobs AG (ibid, para 46 of the Opinion) that 'the use of a canonball to kill a fly cannot be defended on the ground that a nuclear missile might have been used instead'.

[138] Ibid, paras 15–30 of the judgment.

If those two judgments are examples of rather strict review of import legislation in the agricultural field in the light of general principles of Community law, the banana saga offers a contrasting story of greater judicial deference to the policy choices of the Community institutions. It also exemplifies the complexities of some commercial policy measures and the different avenues for challenge.[139]

Bananas: a case-study in judicial review of commercial policy measures

The banana imports regime

It took until 1993 before the EC managed to adopt uniform legislation on imports of bananas. Before that, the Member States had varying policies on such imports. The United Kingdom and Italy preferred imports from former colonies, and so did France, which also produced bananas in its overseas territories. Spain and Portugal had production of their own, which they sought to protect. All those Member States therefore operated restrictions on imports of bananas from Latin America.[140] By contrast, a number of other Member States, led as it were by Germany, were mainly supplied from Latin America. Germany was even entitled to import bananas free of customs duties, pursuant to a protocol attached to the EEC Treaty.

Matters were complicated by the fact that exports of bananas from former colonies were protected under the provisions of the successive Lomé Conventions, which included clauses to the effect that no banana-exporting ACP country would be put in a less favourable position.

The absence of a uniform import regime was contrary to the Treaty requirement of a uniform commercial policy. Moreover, the different import systems could be maintained only through the application of (then) Article 115 EEC, pursuant to which the Commission authorized Member States to operate restrictions on intra-Community trade in bananas from third countries. When the EC sought to complete the internal market it became clear that those restrictions could not be maintained, and that a uniform import regime was required. The institutions chose the establishment of a common market organization, based on the Treaty's agricultural policy provisions, but in the light of the limited production of bananas in the EU it was obvious that the most significant provisions of the regulation concerned imports from third countries.[141] The essential aim of those provisions was to continue the protection of both EC and ACP bananas, by introducing restrictions on imports of Latin American ('third-country') bananas. Without such restrictions it was feared that EC and ACP bananas would not be able to face up to the competition, and the EC felt obliged to honour its commitments under the Lomé Convention. On the other

---

[139] See also A Davies, 'Bananas, Private Challenges, the Courts and the Legislature' (2002) 21 YEL 299.
[140] So-called dollar bananas or, in the language of the regulation, third-country bananas.
[141] Council Regulation 404/93 [1993] OJ L47/1.

hand, however, there were the rules of GATT which generally provide for non-discriminatory policies and do not in principle permit import quotas.[142]

The attempt to square the circle consisted of the introduction of an annual tariff quota for imports of bananas from third countries. Imports in excess of the quota were subject to a prohibitively high tariff.[143] By contrast, 'traditional' imports of ACP bananas were free from customs duties, the term traditional referring to the level of imports from each ACP country prior to the adoption of the regulation. Such a system of tariff quotas is not uncommon for agricultural products, the difference in the case of bananas however being that traditional ACP imports were exempted, which as will be seen would lead to difficulties in the GATT, and later on in the WTO.

The institutions also considered that a mere tariff quota would not be sufficient for the purposes of integrating strongly compartmentalized markets and of protecting EC and ACP bananas. They therefore introduced a system of access to the tariff quota for third-country bananas, by way of licences, which would prove particularly controversial. Instead of distributing all those licences to companies which had traditionally imported third-country bananas, the regulation limited those traditional importers' access to the tariff quota to 66.5 per cent, whilst giving 30 per cent to companies which had traditionally marketed/imported EC or ACP bananas. As a result, traditional importers of third-country bananas saw their capability to import drastically reduced, and in order to overcome that, they needed either to purchase EC or ACP bananas, or to acquire licences from traders in EC and ACP bananas (licences were tradeable). The negative effects of that licence allocation system were strongly felt in Germany, where many traditional importers of third-country bananas were established. The German government had voted against the adoption of the regulation, and it challenged its lawfulness in an action for annulment before the Court of Justice.

The challenge to the banana regulation before the ECJ

In *Germany v. Council* the applicant sought the annulment of Title IV of the banana regulation, which concerned trade with third countries, and of Article 21(2), which abolished the tariff quota laid down in the Banana Protocol attached to the EEC Treaty.[144] The pleas in law which it advanced alleged breaches of essential procedural requirements, of substantive rules and fundamental principles of Community law, of the Lomé Convention, of the GATT, and of the Banana Protocol. Under the pleas concerning substantive rules and fundamental principles of Community law came: infringement of (then) Article 39 EEC; exceeding the

---

[142] See Arts I, III, and XI GATT.
[143] The original tariff quota was 2 million tonnes; the customs duty for excess imports was ECU 850 per tonne.   [144] *Germany v. Council* (n 30 above).

limits of (then) Articles 39, 42, and 43 EEC; breach of the principle of undistorted competition; and breach of fundamental rights and general principles of law. The list illustrates the breadth of the case, and the many possible dimensions of judicial review of commercial policy measures.

Among the strongest arguments were those based on GATT (see below). The Court did not however examine those arguments, because it considered that Germany could not invoke the provisions of GATT in order to challenge the lawfulness of an EC regulation. It referred to its established case law on the lack of direct effect of GATT, and stated that the features of GATT which precluded direct effect were equally relevant in an action for annulment brought by a Member State.[145] The issues of lack of direct effect of GATT and WTO law and of the exclusion of such law from grounds of review in actions for annulment were examined and discussed in Chapters 8 and 9. *Germany v. Council* illustrated the significance of those issues for judicial review of commercial policy measures. It also highlighted the contrast between GATT and WTO law and other international agreements binding on the Community. Even if the Court found no breach of the Lomé Convention, it had no problems whatsoever in accepting that Germany could rely on the provisions of that agreement.[146] There is other case law on bananas which displays the dichotomy between GATT and the Lomé Convention as regards direct effect.[147] The irony of that dichotomy is that a GATT panel regarded the whole trade preferences system of the Lomé Convention as in breach of the provisions of GATT (again see below), thereby compelling the EC to obtain a waiver in the GATT, and later on the WTO, so as to be able to continue to grant those preferences.[148]

Under the heading of breach of fundamental rights and general principles of law Germany mainly challenged the subdivision of the tariff quota and the licence allocation system. Here, too, its arguments were strong, but not strong enough to persuade the Court of Justice to annul the relevant part of the regulation. The judgment shows the type of reasoning which the Court develops in such cases and highlights the potential links between commercial policy measures and fundamental rights. It may therefore be useful to summarize that part of the judgment.

First, Germany argued that the subdivision of the tariff quota constituted unjustified discrimination against traders in third-country bananas. The Court referred to (current) Article 34(2) EC on common market organizations, prohibiting discrimination between producers or consumers within the Community. That prohibition was only a specific expression of the general principle of equality, one of the fundamental principles of Community law, which required that comparable situations were not treated in a different manner unless the difference in treatment was objectively justified. The Court had no problems in recognizing that banana traders were also entitled to equal treatment. It therefore proceeded to

---

[145] Ibid, paras 103–112.   [146] Ibid, paras 100–102.
[147] Case C–469/93 *Amministrazione delle Finanze dello Stato v. Chiquita Italia* [1995] ECR I–4533
[148] *GATT Activities 1994–1995*, 106–7.

examine whether the regulation treated comparable situations differently. The
Court referred to the pre-regulation situation, consisting of open and protected
national markets, governed by different regimes. It also indicated that the selling
price of EC and ACP bananas had been appreciably higher than that of third-
country bananas. It was therefore clear that before the regulation was adopted
the situations of the categories of economic operators among whom the tariff
quota was subdivided were not comparable. The Court recognized that, since
the regulation had come into force, those categories of economic operators had
been affected differently. It none the less accepted that such difference in treatment was inherent in the objective of integrating previously compartmentalized
markets, bearing in mind the different situations of the various categories
before the establishment of the common market organization. The regulation was
intended to ensure the disposal of Community production and traditional ACP
production, which entailed the striking of a balance between the two categories of
economic operators in question. There was thus no violation of the principle of
non-discrimination.[149]

Secondly, Germany argued that the regulation, by depriving of market shares
operators who traditionally marketed third-country bananas, was in breach of the
right to property and of the freedom to pursue their trade or business. The Court
recognized that the right to property and the freedom to pursue a trade or business
formed part of the general principles of Community law, but emphasized that
those principles had to be viewed in relation to their social function. The exercise
of such right and freedom could be restricted, particularly in the context of a common market organization, provided that those restrictions corresponded to objectives of general interest pursued by the Community and did not constitute a
disproportionate and intolerable interference, impairing the very substance of the
rights guaranteed. The Court then pointed out that the right to property did not
actually apply, as no economic operator could claim a right to property in a market
share, which constituted only a momentary economic position exposed to the risks
of changing circumstances. Nor could an economic operator claim an acquired
right or even a legitimate expectation that an existing situation which was capable
of being altered by decisions taken by the Community institutions within the limits of their discretionary power would be maintained. As regards, on the other hand,
the freedom to pursue a trade or business, the Court recognized that the regulation
altered the competitive position of German traders, but considered that the restrictions corresponded to objectives of general Community interest and did not impair
the very substance of that right. The Court referred to the various objectives of the
regulation, and accepted the necessity of the machinery for dividing the tariff quota.
As regards the transferability of licences, the Court considered that the financial
advantage which such a transfer could in some cases give traders in EC and ACP
bananas was a necessary consequence, and was a means intended to contribute to

---

[149] *Germany v. Council* (n 30 above), paras 64–75.

the competitiveness of operators marketing EC and ACP bananas and to facilitate the integration of the Member States' markets.[150]

Thirdly, Germany argued breach of the principle of proportionality. In its view the objectives of supporting ACP producers and guaranteeing the income of EC producers could have been achieved by measures having less effect on competition and on the interests of certain categories of economic operators. In its reply the Court referred to the broad discretion of the Community legislature in matters concerning the common agricultural policy (and it could have added the common commercial policy). The lawfulness of a measure could be affected only if the measure was manifestly inappropriate having regard to the objective which the competent institution was seeking to pursue. More specifically, where the legislature was obliged to assess the future effects of certain rules, which could not be accurately foreseen, its assessment was open to criticism only if it appeared manifestly incorrect in the light of the information available to it at the time of the adoption of the rules in question. That was particularly the case where the Council had to reconcile divergent interests and thus select options within the context of the policy choices which were its own responsibility. The Court then described those divergent interests. In reply to the argument that less onerous measures, such as more extensive aid for EC and ACP producers, could have been chosen, the Court considered that it could not substitute its assessment for that of the Council, if the measures in question were not manifestly inappropriate. Germany had not shown that.[151]

The judgment in *Germany v. Council* can be criticized.[152] The structure of the Court's reasoning is not convincing, in that proportionality is examined separately, and not in connection with the alleged breaches of the principle of equal treatment and of the freedom to carry out a trade or business. The critical point was indeed whether the licence allocation system did not go too far in terms of unequal treatment and freedom of business. The Court was clearly right to point out that banana traders in the various Member States were not in the same position when the regulation was adopted, but it is questionable whether the dissimilarity was such as to justify the significant redistribution of market shares and the financial transfers resulting from trade in licences. Nor is it clear that this furthered the aims of the regulation. The Court spoke of integration of compartmentalized markets, but such integration was achieved through the adoption of a common import regime and the abolition of controls on indirect imports, and did not require this type of licence allocation system. The Court also mentioned the aim of furthering sales of EC and ACP bananas. In this respect it is correct that the licence allocation system appeared to stimulate such sales, by encouraging traders in third-country bananas to market EC and ACP bananas to obtain more licences for importing third-country bananas in following years. In practice, however, that has not appeared to be the effect of the regulation; traders in third-country bananas rather purchased licences from traders in

---

[150] Ibid, paras 77–87.   [151] Ibid, paras 88–89.
[152] See also Everling (n 17 above); MJ Hahn and G Schuster, 'Le droit des Etats membres de se prévaloir en justice d'un accord liant la Communauté' [1995] RGDIP 367.

EC and ACP bananas. Of course it may have been difficult for the Court to acknowledge that at the time of the judgment. None the less, it was clear on its face that the licence allocation system, including the transferability of licences, was a rather indirect system for supporting production and trade in EC and ACP bananas. Aiding companies involved with marketing those bananas did not automatically assist the producers of such bananas, as those companies could well use the additional income for other purposes. The licence allocation system thus amounted to a form of protection of these companies, rather than stimulating the production and disposal of EC and ACP bananas, and it is questionable whether such protection was justified.

It needs to be acknowledged on the other hand that the Court was right to emphasize the discretion of the EC legislature in such general regulatory matters. In these cases judicial review should indeed be limited to manifest violations. The threshold should none the less not be so high as to make review meaningless. The principle of proportionality is crucial in this respect. There is clearly some tension between the statement that review of the proportionality of general legislation is possible and the limitation of such review to manifest violations.[153] If the violation needs to be truly manifest then the test is really one of reasonableness rather than proportionality. Given that proportionality does not stand on its own, but is the very touchstone of what constitutes acceptable and unacceptable interferences with fundamental rights and principles (such as equal treatment, right to property, freedom of business, and others), it should not be emasculated.

One may add that, if the Court had struck down the banana regulation, it could have saved the EU a lot of trouble in the WTO, by forcing the legislature to go back to the drawing board.

Challenges in the context of GATT and in the WTO

When the 1993 banana regulation was adopted it was immediately challenged by a number of (then) GATT Contracting Parties, and the pre-WTO GATT produced a panel report establishing that the new import regime violated several GATT provisions.[154] The panel report was never adopted by the Contracting Parties, the Community objecting to its content.[155] The EC started negotiations with Colombia, Costa Rica, Guatemala, Nicaragua, and Venezuela under Article XXIII:1 GATT with a view to resolving the dispute. Those negotiations resulted in a so-called framework agreement, which was integrated in the EC's schedule of tariff concessions.[156] The implementation of that framework agreement involved an increase of the tariff quota for third-country bananas, as well as the introduction of

---

[153] Eeckhout (n 25 above).
[154] GATT, *EEC—Import Regime for Bananas*, DS38/R, XXXIV [1994] ILM 177.
[155] Under the GATT of 1947 the adoption of panel reports required consensus.
[156] *Legal Instruments Embodying the Results of the Uruguay Round of Multilateral Trade Negotiations*, Vol 19, Schedules LXXX European Communities, 16373–7.

quotas per exporting country.[157] Germany challenged that framework agreement, too, and was partly successful (see below).

The GATT panel report was based on the assessment that the preferential terms of trade established by the Lomé Convention violated the provisions of GATT. Even if the report was not adopted the EC considered it appropriate to seek a GATT waiver for those trade preferences.[158] The framework agreement and the waiver did not however signify the end of the GATT dispute. Following the entry into force of the WTO Agreement a number of WTO members started new proceedings, this time in the knowledge that the EC would not be able to block the adoption of the dispute-settlement reports. Latin American banana-exporting countries were joined in their complaints by the United States which, although not itself exporting bananas to the EC, is home to some of the largest banana-trading companies, and considered that its rights under the new GATS were violated. It argued that distributors in the EC of bananas of US origin did not receive national treatment at the level of wholesale distribution of bananas, because of the licence allocation system, which was more beneficial to banana distributors of EC origin.

The panel and, on appeal, the Appellate Body agreed with most of the arguments of the complainants. They considered the allocation of tariff quotas to exporting countries to be in breach of Article XIII GATT. They also established that the licence allocation system violated both Articles III:4 (national treatment) and I:1 (most-favoured nation treatment). Perhaps the most far-reaching finding was that the licence allocation system did, as the US had argued, amount to a violation of GATS Article XVII on national treatment. Panel and Appellate Body established that wholesale trade services were covered by the EC's Schedule of Commitments, and that the EC was thus obliged to provide national treatment of foreign service suppliers. They accepted that one should specifically look at the market of wholesale trade services in bananas, where it was fairly obvious that there was a difference in treatment, and saw no objection to a simultaneous application of GATT and GATS.[159]

It took the EC some time to amend its banana import regime so as to achieve compliance with WTO law. In 1998 the Council adopted a number of changes,[160] which the Commission implemented.[161] The complainants did not however feel that those amendments led to full compliance, and the WTO dispute-settlement organs agreed with that.[162] Ecuador and the United States were then authorized to

---

[157] See Council Regulation 3290/94 [1994] OJ L349/105 and Commission Regulation 478/95 [1995] OJ L49/13.   [158] N 148 above.

[159] WTO Panel and Appellate Body, *EC—Regime for the Importation, Sale and Distribution of Bananas*, WT/DS27, adopted 10 October 1997.   [160] Council Regulation 1637/98 [1998] OJ L210/28.

[161] Commission Regulation 2362/98 [1998] OJ L293/32.

[162] WTO Arbitrators, *EC—Regime for the Importation, Sale and Distribution of Bananas—Recourse to Arbitration by the EC under Article 22.6 of the DSU*, WT/DS27/ARB, 9 April 1999, and WTO Panel Report, *EC—Regime for the Importation, Sale and Distribution of Bananas—Recourse to Article 21.5 by Ecuador*, WT/DS27/RW/ECU, 12 April 1999.

retaliate, which Ecuador did in the area of intellectual property rights rather than trade in goods.

It took until 2001 before the EC finally managed to devise an import regime for bananas which satisfied the WTO complainants and is, in all likelihood, compatible with its WTO obligations.[163]

Four observations are worth making as regards this particular case of WTO review of an EC commercial policy measure. The first is that the fight was acrimonious and long-drawn-out. The 1993 banana regime was immediately challenged in the GATT, and it took eight years before it was satisfactorily amended. Even if the WTO dispute-settlement mechanism is relatively speedy, the banana case shows that its ultimate effectiveness may be less so. The second observation is that the banana case triggered the demise of the long-established trade preference regime under the Lomé Convention. Until then there had been no GATT challenges to that regime, and one may wonder whether it was worth risking such challenge for the purpose of protecting EC and ACP bananas. Thirdly, the WTO banana case illustrates that, whereas WTO dispute settlement is a matter for WTO members as such, private interests may play an important role. It is no secret that US enthusiasm for following the WTO path was largely due to pressure by large US producers and distributors of bananas, in particular Chiquita. Fourthly, in the following subsection we will look at a number of further challenges to the banana regime and its various amendments before the EU courts, most of which in some way tried to rely on the established violations of WTO law. In Chapter 9 we looked at the lack of direct effect of WTO law, and the exceptions thereto, which were obviously relevant to those challenges. Bananas have been and are a test case for the relationship between WTO law and EC law.

Further case law by the EU courts—effects of GATT and WTO law

Germany also objected to the conduct and outcome of the GATT negotiations which had led to the framework agreement. Those negotiations were conducted by the Commission, which had not sought specific approval by the Council, but had in what was the final phase of the Uruguay Round inserted the agreement into the EC's schedule of tariff concessions. At Marrakesh, where the Uruguay Round Final Act was signed, the Council was therefore left with the choice of either accepting the banana framework agreement or creating a major political crisis by refusing to sign the Final Act. It of course opted for the former. Germany then brought a request for an Opinion under Article 300(6) EC, in which it challenged the Commission's actions. The Court did not however manage to deliver *Opinion 3/94*

---

[163] Council Regulation 2587/2001 of 19 December 2001 amending Regulation (EEC) No 404/93 on the common organization of the market in bananas [2001] OJ L345/13.

before December 1995, and by that time the WTO Agreement had entered into force and was no longer 'envisaged'. The Court therefore established that the request had become without object.[164]

Germany did not leave matters there, and also challenged the decision whereby the Council concluded the WTO Agreement, in so far as it contained the framework agreement on bananas.[165] The challenge was directed at the country quotas which the framework agreement had established: each of the banana-exporting countries which had signed the agreement had been allocated an export quota. It was also directed at the system of export licences which the agreement had introduced: under that system only category A and C operators (i.e. traders in third-country bananas) were required to obtain such licences, and not category B operators (traders in EC and ACP bananas). As obtaining licences involved the payment of charges to the issuing countries the system made imports from those countries more expensive, and Germany argued that it contravened the principle of non-discrimination.

On the first issue the Court recalled that there was no general principle of Community law obliging the Community, in its external relations, to accord third countries equal treatment in all respects. If different treatment of third countries was compatible with Community law, then different treatment accorded to traders within the Community also had to be regarded as compatible where it was merely an automatic consequence of the different treatment accorded to third countries with which such traders had entered into commercial relations.[166]

However, as regards the difference in treatment between various categories of operators, the Court emphasized that this was not the automatic consequence of any difference in treatment between third countries. It then established that different operators were clearly treated differently since, as Germany had claimed and the Council admitted, the export licence system led to a 33 per cent higher purchase price for category A and C operators, compared to category B operators. The question was thus whether such a difference was justified. The Court reiterated the original justification for treating the various categories of operators differently, which it had accepted in the first *Germany v. Council* judgment.[167] It also accepted that, where the balance between the various categories of operators was disturbed, the Council could act to restore that balance. However, the Court could not see in what way the balance had indeed been disturbed by the increase in the tariff quota and the introduction of country quotas for which the framework agreement provided. Nor did it accept the Council's argument that the system of export licences was also intended to provide financial aid for the third countries party to the framework agreement: the Council had been unable to show why the objective of compensating those countries for the restrictions on their exports had to be achieved by the imposition of a financial burden on only some of the economic operators importing bananas from those countries. The Court accordingly established a violation of the principle

---

[164] *Opinion 3/94 re Framework Agreement on Bananas* [1995] ECR I–4577. See also Ch 8.
[165] Decision 94/800 (n 89 above).   [166] *Germany v. Council* (n 31 above), paras 54–57.
[167] N 30 above.

of non-discrimination, and annulled the Council decision in issue in so far as it exempted category B operators from the export-licence system.[168]

On the same day as the second *Germany v. Council* judgment the Court gave a preliminary ruling in one of the *T Port* cases.[169] T Port was a German banana trader which was particularly affected by the banana regime, and which made various legal challenges (see below). The Court repeated its analysis of the framework agreement, but it also replied to a question concerning the legal effect of GATT. The referring court had asked whether certain provisions of the banana regulation could be disapplied on the ground that they were in conflict with GATT, which could take precedence by virtue of Article 307 EC.[170] The Court of Justice rejected that reasoning on the technical ground that the case concerned imports from Ecuador at a time when that country was not yet a member of the WTO, and there were therefore no GATT obligations towards it.[171]

There are quite a few banana cases in which parties attempted to rely on GATT or WTO provisions as against the banana import regime. In most of them the failure of such arguments could be predicted on the basis of the first *Germany v. Council* judgment,[172] which confirmed the impossibility of invoking GATT against the lawfulness of a Community act, and on the basis of the subsequent *Portugal v. Council* judgment in which the Court extended that approach to WTO law.[173] However, in both those judgments the Court accepted that there are circumstances in which GATT/WTO law-based judicial review is possible: where the Community intended to implement a specific GATT/WTO obligation or where a Community act expressly refers to GATT/WTO law.[174] No challenge to the original banana regulation was permitted on those grounds, as the Court confirmed in the first *Germany v. Council* decision,[175] but in 1998 the Council and the Commission modified the import regime, expressly with a view to complying with international commitments, including WTO law.[176] The question thus arose whether that did not enable parties to rely on WTO law in order to challenge the 1998 amendments, which the WTO dispute settlement organs established also to be in breach of WTO law.

That argument was made, in a rather confused way, in a number of actions in damages before the CFI. The Court decided however that the banana panel and Appellate Body reports did not include any special obligations which the Commission 'intended to implement' in its 1998 implementing regulation; nor did that regulation make express reference to any specific obligations arising out of the reports of the WTO bodies, or to specific provisions of the agreements contained in the annexes to the WTO Agreement.[177] The CFI's decision was clearly

---

[168] *Germany v. Council* (n 31 above), paras 59–72.

[169] Joined Cases C–364/95 and C–365/95 *T Port v. Hauptzollamt Hamburg-Jonas* [1998] ECR I–1023.

[170] See Ch 9.   [171] *T Port* (n 169 above), paras 58–65.   [172] N 30 above.

[173] Case C–149/96 *Portugal v. Council* [1999] ECR I–8395.   [174] See Ch 9.

[175] N 30 above.

[176] Regulation 1637/98 (n 160 above), para 2 of the preamble and Art 20(e) of the amended basic regulation.

[177] Case T–18/99 *Cordis Obst und Gemüse Grosshandel v. Commission* [2001] ECR II–913, para 59; Case T–30/99 *Bocchi Food Trade International v. Commission* [2001] ECR II–943, para 64 and

erroneous.[178] The Commission implementing regulation was adopted on the basis of the amended Article 20 of the basic banana regulation, which expressly instructed the Commission to ensure compliance with the Community's international obligations. It was therefore crystal clear that there was an express intention to implement WTO obligations. As to the question whether those obligations were 'special' (or 'particular', to use the language of the ECJ's judgments), it is difficult to envisage better specification of particular obligations than through WTO dispute settlement: the panel and Appellate Body reports identified the various violations of WTO obligations and recommended that the Community bring its laws and regulations into compliance with WTO law, a recommendation adopted by the Dispute Settlement Body.[179] The CFI may have to re-examine its approach in an action for damages by *Chiquita*.[180]

Cases in national courts—interim protection and fundamental rights

The EC banana import regime was also challenged before national courts, particularly in Germany. It is beyond the scope of this survey to offer a complete analysis of this litigation episode. As some of the cases went up to the German *Bundesverfassungsgericht* (Constitutional Court) it may be useful to concentrate on a couple of judgments, in particular as they threw up issues of interim judicial protection and protection against economic hardship, both connected with fundamental rights.

As national courts are unable to declare EC legislation invalid, they are required to refer questions of validity to the Court of Justice where they are persuaded that validity is in doubt. However, such references may put the case on hold for a couple of years, and in the mean time much harm may be caused by what may later turn out to be an invalid piece of legislation. It is therefore open to national courts to suspend the operation of an EC act or to take interim measures. That competence is however strictly circumscribed.[181]

Atlanta Fruchthandelsgesellschaft, a German banana trader, brought proceedings before the *Verwaltungsgericht* (Administrative Court) Frankfurt am Main, challenging the EC banana import regime and seeking interim protection. That court referred to the Court of Justice questions of validity,[182] as well as the question whether it was empowered to make an interim order so as provisionally to settle or regulate the disputed legal positions or relationships (by allocating additional import

---

Case T–52/99 *T Port v. Commission* [2001] ECR II–981, para 59. See also Case C–307/99 *OGT Fruchthandelsgesellschaft v. Hauptzollamt Hamburg—St. Annen* [2001] ECR I–3159; that Order by the ECJ did not however concern the 1998 amendments, but rather the original 1993 regulation.

[178] *Contra* Davies (n 139 above), 320.   [179] WTO Dispute Settlement Body, WT/DS27/12.
[180] Case T–19/01, *Chiquita v. Commission*, pending.
[181] Case C–143/88 *Zuckerfabrik Süderdithmarschen* [1991] ECR I–415.
[182] Case C–466/93 *Atlanta Fruchthandelsgesellschaft (II) v. Bundesamt für Ernährung und Forstwirtschaft* [1995] ECR I–3799.

licences to Atlanta).[183] The Court of Justice took the opportunity to refine its case law on interim protection by national courts. It restated the principle that national courts were required to ensure that individuals were given interim legal protection, both where the validity of national law under Community law was in issue and where the validity of an EC act under Community law was contested. Such interim protection not only needed to consist of the suspension of such an act but could also require positive interim measures. However, strict conditions applied. The national court had to refer the question of validity to the Court of Justice, and had to set out the reasons for which the Court should find the regulation in issue invalid. In this respect it had to take into account the margin of discretion for the EC institutions. The grant of relief had to retain the character of an interim measure. Relief was conditional upon urgency, i.e. to avoid serious and irreparable damage to the party seeking relief likely to occur before the judgment of the Court. Purely financial damage could not be regarded irreparable. The court granting relief had to take account of the Community interest, by examining whether the act would be deprived of all effectiveness if not immediately implemented. Here it should examine the damage which the interim measure could cause the legal regime established by the regulation for the Community as a whole. If there was a financial risk for the EC the national court should seek guarantees. It should also respect other case law by the Court of Justice and the Court of First Instance on the same issue.[184]

The message sent by *Atlanta Fruchthandelsgesellschaft (I)* was clear, particularly since the same day the Court rejected the challenge to the validity of the banana import regime in *Atlanta Fruchthandelsgesellschaft (II)*. When reading the judgment on interim measures one can sense the Court's concern that national courts should not unduly interfere with the uniform application of EC acts by granting interim measures where that is not justified.

Another group of cases on the protection of individual rights was initiated by the German banana trader T Port. In the first *Germany v. Council* case on bananas the Court of Justice had decided, in the context of an application for interim measures, that under Article 16(3) of the banana regulation the Community institutions were required to adjust the tariff quota, if that proved necessary to take account of exceptional circumstances affecting, in particular, import conditions (such as if the quota was insufficient to satisfy demand appropriately). Also, Article 30 required the Commission to take transitional measures, in particular in order to overcome difficulties of a sensitive nature.[185] T Port was particularly affected by the entry into force of the banana regulation, because it had been able to import only unusually small quantities of third-country bananas during the reference period for calculating licence entitlement, due to problems with a Colombian supplier. It argued that, as a result, it was suffering exceptional hardship, exacerbated by contractual commitments with Ecuadorian suppliers. It applied for additional import licences, but its

---

[183] Case C–465/93 *Atlanta Fruchthandelsgesellschaft (I) v. Bundesamt für Ernährung und Forstwirtschaft* [1995] ECR I–3761.   [184] Ibid, paras 19–51.
[185] Case C–280/93 R *Germany v. Council* [1993] ECR I–3667, paras 44–48.

applications were dismissed by the *Verwaltungsgericht* (Administrative Court) Frankfurt am Main and, on appeal, by the *Hessischer Verwaltungsgerichtshof* (Higher Administrative Court, Hesse). The *Bundesverfassungsgericht* then quashed the latter decision, on the ground that the lower courts had not duly applied the ECJ's case law on the possibilities for adjustment of the tariff quota in case of exceptional hardship. The *Verwaltungsgericht* should have dealt with the question whether the German authorities' failure to act in spite of the provision for hardship cases conflicted with the guaranteed protection of fundamental rights which applied also in Community law.[186]

The judgment of the *Bundesverfassungsgericht* could obviously be interpreted as expressing some concern as regards the effects of the banana regulation on individual traders. In the light of the past history of fundamental rights protection in the EC, and of the *Solange* case law of the *Bundesverfassungsgericht*, insisting on adequate protection of rights, there seemed to be the potential for a very damaging conflict between that court and the Court of Justice.[187] Some have indeed argued that this potential caused the Court of Justice to interfere in the second *Germany v. Council* case.[188] In any event, the *Hessischer Verwaltungsgerichtshof* duly complied with the judgment of the *Bundesverfassungsgericht* by referring questions to the Court of Justice on the precise meaning of Articles 16(3) and 30 of the banana regulation. The Court decided that, under Article 30, the Commission could, and was required to, depending on the circumstances, lay down rules catering for cases of hardship from the fact that importers met difficulties threatening their existence. The condition was that those difficulties should be inherent in the transition from the previous national arrangements to the common market organization, and that they were not caused by a lack of care on the part of the traders concerned. The Court did not however accept that the national courts could order provisional measures until such time as the Commission had adopted an act with legal effect to deal, in accordance with Article 30 of the regulation, with cases of hardship affecting traders. The Court's judgment therefore did not leave much scope for intervention by either national authorities or courts to respond to cases of economic hardship. The Commission did set up a reserve of 20,000 tonnes for hardship cases.[189]

Litigation in Germany none the less continued. In the *Atlanta Fruchthandelsgesellschaft* cases the *Verwaltungsgericht* Frankfurt am Main had asked the *Bundesverfassungsgericht* whether the EC banana regulation violated the German Constitution. The *Bundesverfassungsgericht* waited almost four years before deciding the case, but on 6 June 2000 it rejected the constitutional objections. It decided that, henceforth, constitutional challenges to EC acts were not admissible except where it was argued that fundamental rights protection in the EC, including the case law of the Court of Justice, had sunk beneath the required level.[190] In other words, the

[186] *T Port* (n 169 above), paras 5–8 of the Opinion of Elmer AG.
[187] Everling (n 17 above), 443–5.   [188] N 31 above.
[189] Commission Regulation 2601/97 establishing, pursuant to Art 30 of Council Regulation (EEC) No 404/93, a reserve for 1998 to resolve cases of hardship [1997] OJ L351/19.
[190] *Bundesverfassungsgericht*, 2 BvL 1/97 of 7 June 2000 (</www.bverg.de/>).

Bundesverfassungsgericht will only examine a general challenge to the level of fundamental rights protection in the EU, and will not hear claims of fundamental rights violations in individual cases. What was potentially a challenge to the uniformity of Community law and the case law of the Court of Justice became definitive confirmation of the *Bundesverfassungsgericht*'s acceptance of the EU level of fundamental rights protection.

Conclusions

The common commercial policy is clearly the most established and sophisticated external EU policy. This chapter has looked at a number of aspects, but is not complete. A comprehensive assessment would require all the bilateral and multilateral trade agreements which the EC has concluded to be examined. It would also require an in-depth study of WTO law, for such law is part and parcel of the EC law on external trade, and the WTO is the *locus* of further development of trade policy (and more than that) through its dispute settlement system and through its rounds of multilateral negotiations. It would further require more intense analysis of various trade policy instruments, in particular but not just anti-dumping. One would need to look intensely at the fiercely complex subject of trade policy for agricultural products.

The survey and discussion in this chapter none the less lead to a couple of conclusions. At the level of institutional actors, it is remarkable that commercial policy has remained for so long within the almost exclusive remit of the executive and of the Community's bureaucracy. Article 133 EC continues to refer to the Council and the Commission only, and not to the Parliament. The technicality of many decisions further enhances the powers of technocrats (including the 133 Committee) compared with those of elected politicians. There may be certain advantages in terms of stability and rationality of decision-making, but they arguably do not outweigh the lack of democratic input. The draft Constitution rightly rectifies this state of affairs, by fully involving the European Parliament through the extension of the legislative procedure to commercial policy.

The Courts are also important actors in the sphere of commercial policy, in contrast to other areas of EU external action, such as the CFSP (see next chapter). They hear many cases involving commercial policy measures, and interfere occasionally to ensure that adequate standards of legality are maintained. However, there may be scope for more intense scrutiny. When reading judgments involving some type of challenge to an EC commercial policy measure, and comparing them with rulings in cases involving 'internal' administrative acts (such as in competition law), one cannot escape the impression that the Courts are less inclined to assist private parties in the external trade field, some of which are of course companies which are identified as foreign rather than European. The banana saga exemplifies the difficulty of obtaining successful judicial review. It also exemplifies the interconnections between the internal and the external: in the end the regime affected domestic

European companies, importers of bananas, as much if not more than foreign exporters. The Court of Justice should have been more careful in its analysis of whether the banana regime was non-discriminatory and proportionate. The case law on judicial review of commercial policy measures further demonstrates the outdated approach to standing of private parties, and the difficulties for certain aggrieved parties to have access to an effective remedy. In addition, one should bear in mind the lack of direct effect of WTO law (Chapter 9), which also reduces the scope for judicial review.

At the level of autonomous commercial policy instruments there is limited scope for amendment or innovation owing to the obligations under WTO law. For example, it makes no sense to discuss the merits of anti-dumping policy solely within the EU. Such discussions need to take place at the global level. The only instrument which is less WTO-dependent is the GSP system, which only benefits from a general WTO imprimatur. The current system exemplifies the linkages between trade and non-economic policies which the EU is to some extent promoting, but again most of that debate needs to take place within the WTO.

11

Common Foreign and Security Policy

Introduction

In Chapter 5 we analysed the objectives of the CFSP and the powers conferred upon the EU to conduct a foreign and security policy. That analysis revealed that the CFSP is to a large extent supplementary to the Community's external policies, and that the actual terrain which it occupies consists mostly of forms of external action which cannot be undertaken by the Community, because it lacks the necessary powers. In this chapter we return to the CFSP in order to take a closer look at the actual policies which the EU pursues under the Second Pillar. However, as this book concentrates on the legal and constitutional foundations of external relations, there is no attempt to review the CFSP from a pure policy perspective. We leave that to international relations and political science experts, many of whom have indeed scrutinized the CFSP.[1] Academic lawyers, by contrast, have devoted remarkably less attention to the EU's foreign policy, even if they appear to be catching up.[2] That discrepancy is no coincidence. For a long time lawyers were at a loss when attempting to capture the CFSP in legal discourse. Law seemed to be kept out of the CFSP with a view to safeguarding its intergovernmental character and protecting it from supranational infection. The original TEU defined the objectives of the CFSP, and enabled the Council of Ministers to use legal instruments, in particular joint actions and common positions, but signally failed to clarify the nature and effect of those instruments. Even if the objective of their creation may have been to develop policy in a more systematic and formal way than under the preceding European Political Co-operation, as well as to reinforce the binding character of agreed policies,[3] the adoption of strong legal instruments was clearly not the primary objective.[4] The very terms 'joint action' and 'common position' do not evoke established legal instruments of either domestic, Community, or international law. The TEU provides that CFSP decisions are binding on the Member States, but it did not create any specific mechanisms of enforcement, other than supervision by the Council itself: the jurisdiction of the Court of Justice was not extended to CFSP

---

[1] See Ch 5, introduction.

[2] E.g. RA Wessel, *The European Union's Foreign and Security Policy—A Legal Institutional Perspective* (Kluwer, 1999); P Koutrakos, *Trade, Foreign Policy and Defence in EU Constitutional Law* (Hart Publishing, 2001); E Denza, *The Intergovernmental Pillars of the European Union* (OUP, 2002).

[3] S Keukeleire, *Het buitenlands beleid van de Europese Unie* (Kluwer, 1998), 181.

[4] Denza (n 2 above), 90.

matters, and the Commission was not made the guardian of the CFSP. The lack of Court jurisdiction also meant that no case law could develop on either the interpretation of certain TEU provisions or the effect of CFSP decisions. Could certain CFSP acts have direct effect? Does the principle of supremacy extend to the CFSP? The examination of such questions, interesting though they may be,[5] remained a matter of pure speculation in the absence of an ultimate judicial voice. Even on the very juridical nature of the EU, as distinct from the EC, it was almost impossible to determine the correct parameters of legal debate, let alone find some degree of consensus.[6] The debate on whether the EU has legal personality, sketched in Chapter 5, epitomized the academic quicksand lawyers were sucked into when attempting to analyse the legal dimension of the CFSP.

However, the actual conduct of policy does not have to be obstructed by lawyers' failure to apply their legal categories. A lot of practice developed under the CFSP, even if it rarely managed to capture the international political limelight. The first decade of CFSP practice, together with the Amsterdam and Nice Treaty modifications and the current constitutionalization process, allow for more significant legal analysis than was possible when the TEU entered into force.

This chapter focuses on the instruments and actors of the CFSP. In the first part it discusses the various instruments which are at the EU institutions' disposal for conducting the CFSP, including the budgetary means. It inquires into the nature and legal effect of those instruments, on the basis not only of the TEU's language but also the actual content of CFSP acts. International agreements concluded on the basis of Article 24 TEU are not covered, however, as the EU's treaty-making practice is discussed in previous chapters. Nor is there a specific analysis of the special case of economic and financial sanctions which may be adopted, pursuant to Articles 301 and 60 EC, in conjunction with a common position or joint action: such sanctions will be given closer scrutiny in the following chapter on the connection between trade and foreign policy.

In the second part this chapter concentrates on the role of the various institutions and agents involved in CFSP decision-making. The Council and its various organs and agents are the main players, but the analysis cannot be confined to them, in particular if one adopts the perspective of constitutionalism. Indeed, important questions of parliamentary and judicial scrutiny arise in connection with the CFSP, and require further examination. Those questions are not unconnected with the issue of the legal nature and effect of CFSP acts. Depending upon the strength and depth of commitments entered into, and on the legal force and effects of decisions, those questions may become more burning in a constitutional polity. It is from those angles that the role of the institutions is studied, and there is no attempt to offer a definitive institutional analysis, which would require a stronger interdisciplinary approach and would move us beyond external relations.

---

[5] On supremacy see CWA Timmermans, 'The Constitutionalization of the European Union' (2002) 21 YEL 9–11.   [6] Ch 5, introduction.

The final part of the chapter looks at the proposed modifications in the draft Constitution. At the level of instruments and actors of the CFSP those modifications are sufficiently significant to merit separate analysis.

Instruments

Introduction and overview

Article 12 TEU provides that the EU shall pursue the objectives of the CFSP, set out in Article 11, by:

—defining the principles of and guidelines for the common foreign and security policy;
—deciding on common strategies;
—adopting joint actions;
—adopting common positions;
—strengthening systematic co-operation between Member States in the conduct of policy.

That provision, enumerating the various tools and instruments of the CFSP, was inserted by the Treaty of Amsterdam. The original version of the TEU did not contain such enumeration, nor did it provide for common strategies as a specific instrument. It spoke of systematic co-operation between the Member States and of the gradual implementation of joint actions in areas where the Member States have important interests in common (Article J.1(3)). Member States were to inform and consult one another, and the Council could define common positions to which national policies had to conform. Member States were also to co-ordinate their action in international organizations and at international conferences (Article J.2). The Treaty provided for a procedure for the adoption of joint actions, but did not define the concept itself (Article J.3). The TEU appeared to have created some kind of halfway house between informal co-ordination of policies and the adoption of formal legal instruments with specific legal effects. CFSP acts were regarded as binding under international law,[7] but, as mentioned, no particular methods of enforcement were provided for. The lack of legal precision led to uncertainty and confusion, particularly as regards the distinction between joint actions and common positions, which became the core CFSP instruments.[8]

---

[7] Denza (n 2 above), 55; M Eaton, 'Common Foreign and Security Policy', in D O'Keeffe and P Twomey (eds), *Legal Issues of the Maastricht Treaty* (Chancery Law, 1994) 222.

[8] S Nuttall, *European Foreign Policy* (OUP, 2000), 186; E Decaux, 'Le processus de décision de la PESC: vers une politique étrangère européenne?', in E Cannizzaro (ed), *The European Union as an Actor in International Relations* (Kluwer, 2002) 42; Wessel (n 2 above), 129; G Edwards, 'Common Foreign and Security Policy' (1994) 14 YEL 545.

The Treaty of Amsterdam attempted to create more precision through the above enumeration, and by offering some type of definition of joint actions (they 'address specific situations where operational action by the Union is deemed to be required': Article 14(1) TEU) and of common positions (which 'define the approach of the Union to a particular matter of a geographical or thematic nature': Article 15 TEU). It introduced common strategies, decided by the European Council, and 'to be implemented by the Union in areas where the Member States have important interests in common' (Article 13(2) TEU).

Those are the three most formal instruments of the CFSP, together with international agreements, discussed in previous chapters. Beyond those instruments, there are other types of CFSP acts, such as statements and declarations and *sui generis* CFSP decisions.

Joint actions

Article 14(1) TEU defines joint actions as follows:

The Council shall adopt joint actions. Joint actions shall address specific situations where operational action by the Union is deemed to be required. They shall lay down their objectives, scope, the means to be made available to the Union, if necessary their duration, and the conditions for their implementation.

Further provisions in Article 14 address the duties of the Member States with respect to joint actions. Article 14(3) provides that 'they shall commit the Member States in the positions they adopt and in the conduct of their activity'. That obligation is fleshed out in Article 14(5), which provides *inter alia*:

Whenever there is any plan to adopt a national position or take national action pursuant to a joint action, information shall be provided in time to allow, if necessary, for prior consultations within the Council.

Article 14(6) addresses 'cases of imperative need arising from changes in the situation and failing a Council decision'; the Member States may then 'take the necessary measures as a matter of urgency having regard to the general objectives of the joint action'. Further, Article 14(7) provides that, '[s]hould there be any major difficulties in implementing a joint action, a Member State shall refer them to the Council which shall discuss them and seek appropriate solutions', which 'shall not run counter to the objectives of the joint action or impair its effectiveness'. Further duties of the Member States (and indeed of the Commission) are defined in Article 20 TEU, which provides *inter alia*:

The diplomatic and consular missions of the Member States and the Commission Delegations in third countries and international conferences, and their representations to international organizations, shall cooperate in ensuring that the common positions and joint actions adopted by the Council are complied with and implemented.

Other paragraphs of Article 14 concern the modification of joint actions and their implementation. As regards modification, Article 14(2) provides:

If there is a change in circumstances having a substantial effect on a question subject to joint action, the Council shall review the principles and objectives of that action and take the necessary decisions. As long as the Council has not acted, the joint action shall stand.

As regards implementation, Article 14(4) provides:

The Council may request the Commission to submit to it any proposals relating to the common foreign and security policy to ensure the implementation of a joint action.

It is also worth mentioning that joint actions may be used for implementing common strategies defined by the European Council, and that the Council generally acts by taking decisions 'necessary for defining and implementing the common foreign and security policy on the basis of the general guidelines defined by the European Council' (Article 13(3) TEU).[9]

What can be learned from those Treaty provisions as regards the nature and legal effects of joint actions? The definition of joint actions as instruments addressing specific situations where operational action is deemed necessary does not shed much light on their legal nature. Operational action is not a legal term of art, and appears to allow for various types of decisions and provisions. The qualification that joint actions shall lay down their objectives, scope, means, duration, and conditions is not of much further assistance. It is not clear, for example, whether joint actions can have some type of legislative scope, or whether they can have a normative function.

With respect to legal effects the Treaty language does emphasize that joint actions are binding on the Member States, as regards 'the positions they adopt and in the conduct of their activity'. The Treaty refers to national positions and national actions, not to national law. That appears to confirm that joint actions are not intended to be used as a legislative instrument, that we should not look at joint actions from the perspective of the relationship between EU and domestic *law*, but rather from the perspective of political statements and action. As mentioned before, it is not clear whether doctrines such as direct effect and supremacy can extend to Union law, as distinct from EC law.

The Treaty does not provide that joint actions also commit the EU institutions, in particular the European Commission, which is responsible for much external 'action' under the EC Treaty. The absence of such a provision (with the exception of Article 20 TEU on Commission Delegations) is no doubt linked to the relationship between the pillars, and the tension between supranationalism and intergovernmentalism. As discussed in Chapter 5, the Commission is concerned that CFSP decisions may interfere with its powers and prerogatives under the EC Treaty.

---

[9] Wessel reports that in an initial phase joint actions used to be based on European Council guidelines, but that this is no longer the practice (n 2 above, 119).

The Commission is none the less under an obligation, together with the Council, to ensure the consistency of the EU's external activities as a whole (Article 3 TEU).

In light of the lack of Treaty precision as regards the nature and effects of joint actions, it may be useful to take a closer look at the actual practice. It is clear from that practice that joint actions are in many respects the key vehicle of the CFSP.[10] It is in particular interesting to investigate what types of 'operational action' the Council undertakes. Joint actions have broadly concerned the following activities:

—support for democratic transition and democratic processes in third countries, through assistance in the preparation of elections and the monitoring of elections;[11]
—support for peace and stabilization processes, through the convening of an inaugural conference,[12] general support for a peace process,[13] financial assistance to help meet social welfare payments,[14] financial and logistical support for a meeting of Heads of State or Government,[15] the establishment of an EU Monitoring Mission,[16] a contribution to a conflict settlement process,[17] and to the capacity to support and protect an OSCE observer mission;[18]
—action in the sphere of production, trade, proliferation, and use of arms, weapons, and other military material;[19]
—protection against the effects of extra-territorial legislation;[20]

[10] Cf E Paasivirta, 'The European Union: From an Aggregate of States to a Legal Person?' (1997) 2 The Hofstra Law & Policy Symposium 51.

[11] E.g. Joint Action 93/678 concerning support for the transition towards a democratic and multi-racial South Africa [1993] OJ L316/45; Joint Action 96/406 concerning action by the Union to support the electoral process in Bosnia and Herzegovina [1996] OJ L168/1; Joint Action 98/302 concerning support for the electoral process in Bosnia and Herzegovina [1998] OJ L138/3; Joint Action 98/735 in support of the democratic process in Nigeria [1998] OJ L354/1.

[12] Joint Action 93/728 on the inaugural conference on the stability pact [1993] OJ L339/1.

[13] Joint Action 94/276 in support of the Middle East peace process [1994] OJ L119/1.

[14] Joint Action 98/301 in support of the Government of Montenegro [1998] OJ L138/1.

[15] Joint Action 2000/717 on the holding of a meeting of Heads of State or of Government in Zagreb (Zagreb Summit) [2000] OJ L290/54.

[16] Joint Action 2000/811 on the European Union Monitoring Mission [2000] OJ L328/53.

[17] Joint Action 2001/759 regarding a contribution from the European Union to the conflict settlement process in South Ossetia [2001] OJ L286/4.

[18] Joint Action 2002/373 regarding a contribution of the European Union towards reinforcing the capacity of the Georgian authorities to support and protect the OSCE observer mission on the border of Georgia with the Ingush and Chechen Republics of the Russian Federation [2002] OJ L134/1.

[19] Joint Action 96/588 on anti-personnel landmines [1996] OJ L260/1; Joint Action 97/288 on the European Union's contribution to the promotion of transparency in nuclear-related export controls [1997] OJ L120/1; Joint Action 1999/878 establishing a European Union Co-operation Programme for Non-proliferation and Disarmament in the Russian Federation [1999] OJ L331/11; Joint Action 2000/401 concerning the control of technical assistance related to certain military end-uses [2000] OJ L159/216; Joint Action 2002/589 on the European Union's contribution to combating the destabilizing accumulation and spread of small arms and light weapons and repealing Joint Action 1999/34 [2002] OJ L191/1.

[20] Joint Action 96/668 concerning measures protecting against the effects of the extraterritorial application of legislation adopted by a third country, and actions based thereon or resulting therefrom [1996] OJ L309/7.

—action in the sphere of policing, including sending a forensic experts mission,[21] contributing to the re-establishment of a viable police force,[22] and sending an EU Police Mission;[23]
—support for counter-terrorist activities;[24]
—establishment of institutes and centres;[25]
—appointment of a Special Representative;[26]
—and last but not least military operations.[27]

As can be seen this represents a wide range of acts and activities. Joint actions provide for financial expenditure and transfers. They involve sending missions, from election observers to military personnel, consisting mostly of persons seconded by the Member States. They provide for diplomacy, consultations, démarches, representation, and conferences. Joint actions instruct the Member States to take various forms of action, up to the adoption of legislation (including sanctions)[28] and the ratification of international conventions.[29] They may set up institutions and centres with legal personality.

The ill-defined nature of joint actions therefore appears to permit virtually any type of government activity, with the exception of general normative action creating rights and obligations for citizens. It is only in the latter sense that joint actions can be said to be non-legislative, and in material terms a number of joint actions do have legislative effect, albeit through legislative action which the Member States are instructed to take. This broad juridical scope of joint actions needs to be borne in mind when considering the involvement of the various institutions. In particular, from a perspective of constitutionalism the question arises whether the current standards of parliamentary and judicial supervision of joint actions are satisfactory.

Common positions

Article 15 TEU provides:

The Council shall adopt common positions. Common positions shall define the approach of the Union to a particular matter of a geographical or thematic nature. Member States shall ensure that their national policies conform to the common positions.

[21] Joint Action 98/736 concerning a forensic experts mission in the Federal Republic of Yugoslavia [1998] OJ L354/3.
[22] Joint Action 1999/189 concerning a contribution by the European Union to the re-establishment of a viable police force in Albania [1999] OJ L63/1.
[23] Joint Action 2002/210 on the European Police Mission [2002] OJ L70/1.
[24] Joint Action 2000/298 on a European Union assistance programme to support the Palestinian Authority in its efforts to counter terrorist activities emanating from the territories under its control [2000] OJ L97/4.
[25] Joint Action 2001/554 on the establishment of a European Union Institute for Security Studies [2001] OJ L200/1; Joint Action 2001/555 on the establishment of a European Union Satellite Centre [2001] OJ L200/5.
[26] Joint Action 2002/211 on the appointment of the EU Special Representative in Bosnia and Herzegovina [2002] OJ L70/7.
[27] Joint Action 2003/92 on the European Union military operation in the Former Yugoslav Republic of Macedonia [2003] OJ L34/26 and Joint Action 2003/423 on the European Union military operation in the Democratic Republic of Congo [2003] OJ L143/50.
[28] E.g. Joint Action 2000/401 (n 19 above).   [29] E.g. Joint Action 96/588 (n 19 above).

In contrast to joint actions there is no further Treaty language on the effects of common positions on the Member States,[30] or on amendment and implementation. The Treaty is thus even more silent on the nature and legal effects of common positions, and academic literature in fact agrees that the distinction with joint actions is unclear in either theory or practice.[31] Other than that the emphasis appears to be on political positions rather than operational action there is little that one can derive from the Treaty language. As can be seen from the above discussion of joint actions, the latter in practice also involve the adoption of political positions.

What does the practice as regards common positions show? Common positions have broadly concerned the following activities and positions:

—economic and financial sanctions, mostly in implementation of UN Security Council resolutions, and in combination with EC regulations based on Articles 301 and 60 EC;[32]
—other sanctions, in particular travel bans and visa restrictions,[33] and arms trade restrictions;[34]
—objectives, priorities, and activities towards specific third countries;[35]
—broad policy documents on general international problems, e.g. human rights and good governance in Africa;[36] conflict prevention, management, and resolution in Africa;[37] terrorism;[38]

[30] With the exception of Art 20 TEU: see above.
[31] E.g. Nuttall (n 8 above), 186; Decaux (n 8 above), 42–3.   [32] See further Ch 12.
[33] E.g. Common Position 98/240 on restrictive measures against the Federal Republic of Yugoslavia [1998] L95/1; Common Position 97/193 on restrictive measures aimed at persons having perpetrated violent acts during the incidents in Mostar on 10 February 1997 [1997] OJ L81/1; Common Position 99/318 concerning additional restrictive measures against the Federal Republic of Yugoslavia [1999] OJ L123/1; Common Position 98/409 concerning Sierra Leone [1998] OJ L187/1; Common Position 2001/357 concerning restrictive measures against Liberia [2001] OJ L126/1; Common Position 2001/542 concerning a visa ban against extremists in FYROM [2001] OJ L194/55; Common Position 2003/139 concerning restrictive measures against the leadership of the Transnistrian region of the Moldovan Republic [2003] OJ L53/60; Common Position 2003/297 on Burma/Myanmar [2003] OJ L106/36.
[34] Common Position 96/184 concerning arms exports to the former Yugoslavia [1996] OJ L58/1; Common Position 98/409 (n 33 above); Common Position 2001/357 (n 33 above); Common Position 2002/829 on the supply of certain equipment into the Democratic Republic of Congo [2002] OJ L285/1; Common Position 2003/297 (n 33 above).
[35] Common Position 94/779 on the objectives and priorities of the European Union towards Ukraine [1994] OJ L313/1; Common Position 95/91 with regard to Burundi [1995] OJ L72/1; Common Position 95/413 on Angola [1995] OJ L245/1; Common Position 96/407 concerning East Timor [1996] OJ L168/2; Common Position 96/697 on Cuba [1996] OJ L322/1; Common Position 97/357 on Albania [1997] OJ L153/4; Common Position 2002/401 on Nigeria and repealing Common Position 2001/373 [2002] OJ L139/1; Common Position 2002/495 on Angola and repealing Common Position 2000/391 [2002] OJ L167/9; Common Position 2002/830 on Rwanda and repealing Common Position 2001/799 [2002] OJ L285/3.
[36] Common Position 98/350 concerning human rights, democratic principles, the rule of law and good governance in Africa [1998] OJ L158/1.
[37] Common Position 2001/374 concerning conflict prevention, management and resolution in Africa [2001] OJ L132/3.
[38] Common Position 2001/930 on combating terrorism [2001] OJ L344/90.

    —support for democratic and peace processes;[39]
    —conflict prevention and non-proliferation;[40]
    —policy towards the international criminal courts and tribunals;[41]
    —temporary reception in Member States of particular persons.[42]

As can be seen the range of subjects addressed through common positions is as wide
as that covered by joint actions, and many subjects are similar, if not identical. There
are however a number of differences in the content of the respective measures.
Common positions do not appear to involve financial expenditure and transfers, the
sending of missions, or the establishment of institutes or centres. Those are therefore clearly forms of 'operational action' for which a common position is not the
appropriate instrument. Common positions do contain wide-ranging policy statements and instructions for action by the Member States. Again one can say that the
instrument is non-legislative because it does not directly regulate rights and obligations of citizens. Indirectly, however, and in a material sense, common positions do
have legislative character, even more so than joint actions. Many common positions
concern various forms of sanctions and restrictions, which acquire binding force
through implementation either by the Community, where the measures come
within Article 301 or 60 EC, or by the Member States (mostly visa and travel bans,
and restrictions on trade in military material and technologies).

    A good example of a common position with strong legislative purpose is the
common position on combating terrorism.[43] Under Article 1 the wilful provision

---

[39] Common Position 98/606 on the European Union's contribution to the promotion of non-
proliferation and confidence-building in the South Asian region [1998] OJ L290/1; Common Position
99/345 concerning a Stability Pact for South East Europe [1999] OJ L133/1; Common Position 99/691
on support to democratic forces in the Federal Republic of Yugoslavia (FRY) [1999] OJ L273/1 and
Common Position 2000/599 on support to a democratic FRY and the immediate lifting of certain
restrictive measures [2000] OJ L261/1; Common Position 2000/420 concerning EU support for the
OAU peace process between Ethiopia and Eritrea [2000] OJ L161/1; Common Position 2003/319 concerning European Union support for the implementation of the Lusaka Ceasefire Agreement and the
peace process in the Democratic Republic of Congo (DRC) and repealing Common Position 2002/203
[2003] OJ L115/87.
[40] Common Position 95/379 concerning blinding lasers [1995] OJ L227/3; Common Position
96/408 relating to preparation for the Fourth Review Conference of the Convention on the prohibition of the development, production and stockpiling of bacteriological (biological) and toxin weapons
and on their destruction (BTWC) [1996] OJ L168/3; Common Position 99/533 relating to the
European Union's contribution to the promotion of the early entry into force of the Comprehensive
Nuclear Test-Ban Treaty (CTBT) [1999] OJ L204/1; Common Position 2000/297 relating to the 2000
Review Conference of the Parties to the Treaty on the Non-proliferation of Nuclear Weapons [2000]
OJ L97/1; Common Position 2001/567 on the fight against ballistic missile proliferation [2001] OJ
L202/1; Common Position 2001/758 on combating the illicit traffic in conflict diamonds, as a contri-
bution to prevention and settlement of conflicts [2001] OJ L286/2; Common Position 2001/869 on participation by the EU in the Korean Peninsular Energy Development Organization (KEDO) [2001] OJ
L325/1.
[41] Common Position 2002/474 amending Common Position 2001/443/CFSP on the International
Criminal Court [2002] OJ L164/1; Common Position 2003/280 in support of the effective implementation of the mandate of the ICTY [2003] OJ L101/22.
[42] Common Position 2002/400 concerning the temporary reception by Member States of the EU
of certain Palestinians [2002] OJ L138/33.   [43] Common Position 2001/930 (n 38 above).

or collection of funds for terrorist purposes shall be criminalized. Article 2 concerns the freezing of funds held by terrorists. Article 8 provides that terrorists shall be brought to justice and that terrorist acts shall be established as serious criminal offences. Pursuant to Article 9 Member States must afford one another and third States assistance in connection with criminal investigations or proceedings. Article 10 requires that the movement of terrorists or terrorist groups be prevented by effective border controls. Article 14 provides that the Member States shall become parties as soon as possible to the relevant international conventions and protocols. These are just a number of examples of the kind of provisions a common position may contain. As with joint actions the question of parliamentary and judicial supervision arises.

Common strategies

Article 13(1) and (2) TEU defines the role of the European Council in the conduct of the CFSP. Article 13(1) provides that the European Council shall define the principles of and general guidelines for the CFSP. Every European Council meeting devotes considerable time to international affairs and external relations, and the Presidency Conclusions invariably contain policy statements and guidelines for further EU action. That has been the practice since the inception of the CFSP, but the Amsterdam Treaty introduced a further instrument for European Council involvement. Article 13(2) provides:

The European Council shall decide on common strategies to be implemented by the Union in areas where the Member States have important interests in common.

Common strategies shall set out their objectives, duration and the means to be made available by the Union and the Member States.

Article 13(3) clarifies that the Council 'shall recommend common strategies to the European Council and shall implement them, in particular by adopting joint actions and common positions'.

The ostensible purpose of common strategies is to create a general policy framework, in certain broader areas, leading to more coherent and unified CFSP actions. Indeed, Article 13(3) also instructs the Council, in connection with the adoption and implementation of common strategies, to ensure the unity, consistency, and effectiveness of Union action, thereby highlighting common strategies' rationale. There is however also a significant institutional and decision-making dimension to common strategies. Pursuant to Article 23(2) TEU the Council acts by qualified majority 'when adopting joint actions, common positions or taking any other decision on the basis of a common strategy', by way of derogation from the standard unanimity requirement. Throughout the inception and life of the CFSP there has been strong debate about the voting rules in the Council. Unanimity is regarded as safeguarding national sovereignty, whereas qualified majority is advanced as indispensable for effective decision-making. This debate took place at Amsterdam and in the Convention on the Future of Europe (see below). Common strategies are thus also some type of ceasefire in the constitutional politics of the EU as regards voting rules in CFSP matters.[44]

The broad, inclusive nature of common strategies raises questions concerning their relationship with EC policies. It would seem unavoidable that the policies set out in a common strategy extend to trade, economic, development, migration, and environmental policies conducted by the EC.[45] As with joint actions and common positions the Treaty does not clarify whether the Community is bound by a common strategy. Again this is left to the consistency requirement for which the Council and the Commission are responsible.

The common strategies hitherto adopted concern Russia, Ukraine, and the Mediterranean region.[46] They are thus geographical in character. They are also broad in terms of subject matter, addressing overall policy towards the countries concerned, and making reference to the entire gamut of external policies, conducted by the EU, by the Member States, *and* by the EC. Those common strategies do not, however, contain strict instructions for the Community; the European Council rather 'calls on the Council, the Commission and Member States', to 'review, according to their competencies and capacities, existing actions, programmes, instruments, and policies to ensure their consistency with this Strategy'.[47] Nor do they contain operational legal provisions, in contrast to joint actions and common positions. It is further notable that the three common strategies followed rather than preceded significant Community policies and instruments. In the cases of Russia and Ukraine the strategies make ample reference to the partnership and co-operation agreements with those countries,[48] whereas the strategy on the Mediterranean region expressly 'builds on the Euro-Mediterranean partnership established by the Barcelona Declaration and its subsequent *acquis*'.[49]

The common strategies instrument is not highly praised. The High Representative for the CFSP, Mr Solana, has produced a critical report arguing that the common strategies are rhetorical and descriptive of existing instruments.[50] In academic literature, too, one finds criticism: common strategies are said to equal joint actions, but adopted by the European Council, and it is argued that the EU none the less remains

---

[44] S Peers, 'Common Foreign and Security Policy' (1997) 17 YEL 546 suggests that this is the real purpose of common strategies; A Dashwood, 'External Relations Provisions of the Amsterdam Treaty', in O'Keeffe and Twomey (eds) (n 7 above), 212 speaks of the primary purpose.

[45] S Peers, 'Common Foreign and Security Policy' (2001) 20 YEL 540 argues that they should remain within the second pillar.

[46] Common Strategy 1999/414 on Russia [1999] OJ L157/1; Common Strategy 1999/877 on Ukraine [1999] OJ L331/1; and Common Strategy 2000/458 on the Mediterranean region [2000] OJ L183/5.

[47] E.g. Common Strategy 1999/414 (n 46 above), Instrument and Means, Section 2.

[48] Agreement on partnership and co-operation establishing a partnership between the European Communities and their Member States, of one part, and the Russian Federation, of the other part [1997] OJ L327/3 and Partnership and co-operation agreement between the European Communities and their Member States, and Ukraine [1998] OJ L49/3.

[49] Common Strategy 2000/458 (n 46 above), part I, para 4.

[50] Europe Documents, No 2228; see Denza (n 2 above), 292.

the prisoner of divided competences.[51] According to Denza, however, an overview of existing and projected programmes is presentationally helpful for the country or region concerned as well as for those working in a narrow area of the Council or the Commission. By formulating policy and objectives agreed unanimously by the Member States they open the way to co-ordinated implementing decisions (by qualified majority within the Second Pillar). The practice has been for each incoming Presidency to draw up a Work Programme for each common strategy, and in these documents the allocation between pillars and legal bases is made clear.[52]

Other instruments

The instruments of the CFSP are not confined to common strategies, joint actions, and common positions. The Council also frequently issues political statements and declarations on international developments of concern to the EU.[53] Those statements and declarations are the outcome of constant Council deliberations, one assumes in implementation of Article 16 TEU, according to which 'Member States shall inform and consult one another within the Council on any matter of foreign and security policy of general interest in order to ensure that the Union's influence is exerted as effectively as possible by means of concerted and convergent action'. Their precise legal effects are unclear, but it is worth recalling that unilateral declarations may have consequences under international law.[54]

The Treaty also presupposes that Council 'decisions' may be required for the purpose of implementing joint actions or common positions (see Article 23(2) TEU). In other places, too, the TEU refers to 'decisions', for example in Article 13(3), according to which the Council shall take the decisions necessary for defining and implementing the CFSP. However, the use of the term here may simply be generic, entailing a general reference to joint actions and common positions. Formal Council decisions under the CFSP, which are published in the Official Journal, are generally subordinate instruments, whose purpose is to implement details of common positions or joint actions, or to amend, extend, or repeal other CFSP instruments.[55] Dashwood argues that the Council is entitled to adopt *sui generis* decisions, just as it may do under the EC Treaty.[56] Provided a Council CFSP decision is in some way based on the Treaty or on another CFSP instrument there would indeed seem to be no reason for excluding the use of this instrument. As a matter of fact, common positions and joint actions are a form of Council decisions as well. However, as the Treaty does not define 'decisions', their legal effects are not clear cut.

---

[51] Decaux (n 8 above), 34–5 and 37–40.   [52] Denza (n 2 above), 292–3.
[53] For further details see Wessel (n 2 above), 185–8.
[54] M Koskenniemi, 'International Law Aspects of the Common Foreign and Security Policy', in M Koskenniemi (ed), *International Law Aspects of the European Union* (Kluwer Law International, 1998) 31.
[55] Denza (n 2 above), 149–50.   [56] Dashwood (n 44 above), 212–13.

In so far as Council decisions relate to joint actions and common positions (amending, extending, repealing, or implementing them) one should think the legal effects are identical to those of 'true' joint actions and common positions.

Budget

Many CFSP joint actions involve considerable expenditure, and the question therefore arises how financing is organized. When the TEU was negotiated it was not envisaged that the EU, as distinct from the EC, would require its own budget and financial resources. Article J.11 of the original TEU provided that administrative expenditure was to be charged to the EC budget. As regards operational expenditure, the Treaty left two options: either the Council decided unanimously that such expenditure was to be charged to the EC budget, in which case the relevant EC Treaty provisions applied, or it could determine that such expenditure be charged to the Member States, where appropriate in accordance with a scale to be decided. It may be noted that the first option effectively implied a measure of communitarization, as the Commission and the Parliament have significant powers and functions in relation to the budget.

These financial arrangements were criticized from the outset as showing that the EU lacked any financial autonomy, and in practice they soon proved to be divisive and time wasting.[57] The lack of automatic financial cover for CFSP decisions either led to prolonged wrangling or even prevented action.[58] The financing option created tension between the objective of keeping the CFSP intergovernmental and the concern to spare national budgets.[59] Gradually the practice moved towards the systematic use of the EC budget, but this in itself did not solve the issue of which institution would control the decision to finance a joint action, or who would control and oversee implementation.[60] In 1997 the Parliament, the Council, and the Commission concluded an interinstitutional agreement on provisions regarding the financing of the CFSP.[61] This agreement provided that CFSP expenditure was to be regarded as non-compulsory. It arranged for an overall structure of CFSP financing in the EC budget, with a particular CFSP chapter to be subdivided into certain categories. Transfers within the chapter were to be allowed, but any additional overall CFSP expenditure that proved necessary during the year was to be agreed under an urgent procedure. In the event of disagreement between the Council and Parliament an *ad hoc* concertation procedure was to be set up to expedite agreement, and the Parliament extracted significant commitments on information and consultation.[62]

---

[57] Denza (n 2 above), 57.
[58] J Monar, 'The Financial Dimension of the CFSP', in M Holland (ed), *Common Foreign and Security Policy—The Record and Reforms* (Pinter, 1997) 34.
[59] Wessel (n 1 above), 98; Nuttall (n 8 above), 265.   [60] Peers (n 44 above), 542.
[61] [1997] OJ C286/80.   [62] See also Peers (n 44 above), 544.

The Treaty of Amsterdam amended the TEU provisions on CFSP financing, effectively confirming actual practice. Article 28(3) TEU modified the provisions on operational expenditure, by providing that:

Operational expenditure to which the implementation of those provisions gives rise shall also be charged to the budget of the European Communities, except for such expenditure arising from operations having military or defence implications and cases where the Council acting unanimously decides otherwise.

In cases where expenditure is not charged to the budget of the European Communities it shall be charged to the Member States in accordance with the gross national product scale, unless the Council acting unanimously decides otherwise. . . .

In the meantime the above interinstitutional agreement has been replaced with the (general) interinstitutional agreement on budgetary discipline and improvement of the budgetary procedure,[63] but without material modification of the arrangements on CFSP expenditure. The most notable dimension of the CFSP financing saga is that it has led to greater Commission and Parliament involvement in CFSP matters than the TEU expressly provides for (see below).

Actors

European Council

The role and function of the European Council in EU policy-making are ever increasing. That is also the case with the CFSP. The original TEU referred to the European Council in the last part of the CFSP title. Article J.8(1) confined the role of the European Council to defining the principles of and general guidelines for the common foreign and security policy. The Treaty of Amsterdam enhanced the European Council's position and input.[64] The provision of Article J.8(1) was maintained, but it was moved further up in the CFSP title. Article 11 TEU describes the objectives of the CFSP, and the role of the Member States. Article 12 lists the policy instruments, and Article 13 starts by describing the function of the European Council. Paragraph 1 concerns the definition of principles and general guidelines, 'including for matters with defence implications'. Paragraph 2 adds that the European Council shall decide on common strategies, which are an additional instrument for European Council involvement. The Amsterdam Treaty also amended the provisions on a common defence policy, 'which might lead to a common defence, should the European Council so decide' (Article 17(1) TEU).[65] The draft Constitution further enhances the role of the European Council.

As mentioned, at every European Council meeting a substantial amount of time is devoted to international affairs and external relations, and Presidency conclusions

---

[63] [1999] OJ C172/1.   [64] Dashwood (n 8 above), 212.

[65] In that case the European Council is to recommend to the Member States the adoption of such a decision in accordance with their respective constitutional requirements.

invariably contain long passages on the EU's external policies, which indeed serve as guidelines for the daily work of the other institutions, in particular the Council. Council joint actions and common positions regularly refer to the European Council's deliberations, although there does not appear to be a fixed pattern. The common strategies instrument is less frequently used (see above), and it is not yet altogether clear whether it forms a significant contribution to policy-making, and whether it effectively increases the European Council's involvement.

However, the European Council's most important role is probably at constitutional and institutional level. For example, one of the most significant CFSP developments over recent years has been the construction of a European Security and Defence Policy (ESDP), which forms part of the CFSP, but with a clear separate identity, as confirmed in the draft Constitution.[66] This process has been driven by the European Council, in an attempt to strengthen the EU's crisis-management and conflict-prevention capabilities. The construction of the ESDP required significant institutional action, and it is at the level of the European Council that decisions were taken to convert the Political Committee (PC) into a Political and Security Committee (PSC); to create a European Union Military Committee (EUMC); and to set up a European Union Military Staff Organization (EUMS).[67]

Council

The Council is by far the most important institution for the conduct of the CFSP. Whereas EC policy-making is characterized by a strong division of powers between the Council, the Commission, and the Parliament, requiring constant co-operation between those institutions, as in most cases none of them can act on its own, the Council clearly dominates the CFSP. However, more than in any other area the Council is not merely the meeting of members of national governments. As the Council's functions in CFSP matters are, in traditional constitutional terms, both legislative and executive, many of its acts require a lot of further activity of different types, i.e., institutional, diplomatic, and even military. Also, the preparation of Council decisions requires a strong administrative framework. In performing its functions the Council is therefore served by other actors, bodies, and organs. Accordingly, this subsection first addresses the Council's powers under the relevant Treaty rules, it then looks at decision-making within the Council, and lastly discusses those other actors within the Council framework.

Powers

Article 13(3) TEU describes the Council's powers in general terms. It takes the decisions necessary for defining and implementing the CFSP on the basis of the

[66] See Arts III–210 to III–214.
[67] Nice Presidency Conclusion, Annex IV (<http://ue.eu.int/en/Info/eurocouncil/index.htm>).

general guidelines defined by the European Council. It shall recommend common strategies to the European Council, and shall implement them, in particular by adopting joint actions and common positions. It shall ensure the unity, consistency, and effectiveness of EU action. The Treaty provisions on joint actions and common positions are discussed above. The Council adopts both those instruments, and in the case of joint actions the Treaty specifies how the Council may modify such actions, and how it interacts with national positions or actions. Under Article 13(5), whenever there is any plan to adopt a national position or take national action pursuant to a joint action, information shall be provided in time to allow, if necessary, for prior consultations within the Council. Under Article 13(7), should there be any major difficulties in implementing a joint action, a Member State shall refer them to the Council which shall discuss them and seek appropriate solutions, which shall not run counter to the objectives of the joint action or impair its effectiveness. The Treaty also provides for Council decisions which aim at implementing joint actions or common positions (Article 23(2)).

The Council may conclude international agreements under Article 24 TEU.[68] It is generally the forum in which Member States shall inform and consult with one another on any matter of foreign and security policy of general interest in order to ensure that the EU's influence is exerted as effectively as possible by means of concerted and convergent action (Article 16 TEU).

Decision-making

Article 23 TEU contains the provisions on Council decision-making in CFSP matters. The rule is unanimity. There is one qualification to that rule, so-called constructive abstention, and three exceptions, where the Council decides by qualified majority.

Article 23(1) provides that the Council decides unanimously, whilst clarifying that abstentions shall not prevent the adoption of decisions. However, when abstaining any member of the Council may qualify its abstention by making a formal declaration. The Treaty provides that in that case the member in question shall not be obliged to apply the decision, but shall accept that the decision commits the Union. In a spirit of mutual solidarity, that Member State shall refrain from any action likely to conflict with or impede Union action based on that decision, and the other Member States shall respect its position. However, no decision can be adopted where the Member States qualifying their abstention represent more than one third of the votes weighted in accordance with Article 205(2) EC (on qualified majority voting).

This mechanism of constructive abstention is unique in Council decision-making under the EC and EU Treaties. It is clearly intended to lower, in some cases,

---

[68] See Ch 7.

the high hurdle of unanimous decision-making. Whether, however, it has much practical relevance is unclear. In 2001 Peers reported that the mechanism had never been used,[69] and this appears not to have changed in the meantime, in so far as joint actions and common positions are concerned.

Since the Treaty of Nice there have been three types of decisions which the Council adopts by qualified majority, pursuant to Article 23(2) TEU:

—when adopting joint actions, common positions, or taking any other decision on the basis of a common strategy;
—when adopting any decision implementing a joint action or a common position;
—when appointing a special representative in accordance with Article 18(5).[70]

The qualified majority operates in accordance with Article 205(2) EC, with a requirement of at least sixty-two votes in favour, cast by at least ten members. There are however two exceptions to the use of qualified majority. First, it does not extend to decisions having military or defence implications. Secondly, every member of the Council has a kind of veto right:

If a member of the Council declares that, for important and stated reasons of national policy, it intends to oppose the adoption of a decision to be taken by qualified majority, a vote shall not be taken. The Council may, acting by a qualified majority, request that the matter shall be referred to the European Council for decision by unanimity.

Hitherto, qualified-majority voting primarily takes place as regards implementation of joint actions and common positions.[71] There is also an example of a joint action adopted by qualified majority on the basis of a common strategy.[72]

It is obvious that the rule of unanimity may make it difficult for the EU to develop common policies on matters of general interest. For example, if one examines the joint actions and common positions of 2002 and of the first half of 2003 one finds no trace of the conflict in Iraq, which will come as no surprise to all those who have followed the events in question. Whether however the EU is ripe for more extended use of qualified-majority voting in the most sensitive areas of international politics is another matter.

Other actors

The Council is chaired by its Presidency, which rotates between Member States on a six-monthly basis. Article 18(1) and (2) TEU provides that the Presidency shall represent the EU in CFSP matters, and that it shall be responsible for the implementation

---

[69] Peers (n 45 above), 537.
[70] Art 18(5) provides that the Council may, whenever it deems it necessary, appoint a special representative with a mandate in relation to particular policy issues.
[71] Peers (n 45 above), 538–9.   [72] Joint Action 1999/878 (n 19 above).

of decisions; in that capacity it shall in principle express the position of the EU in international organizations and conferences.[73] It is the Presidency which, pursuant to Article 21 TEU, shall consult the Parliament on the main aspects and the basic choices of the CFSP and shall ensure that the views of the Parliament are duly taken into consideration. The Presidency is also responsible for the negotiation of international agreements, assisted by the Commission as appropriate (Article 24(1) TEU). It is thus clear that the Presidency performs important CFSP functions.

The Council and the EU institutions in general are greatly assisted by committees consisting of national representatives, often from national administrations (so-called comitology).[74] The most important of those committees is Coreper, the committee of Permanent Representatives of the Member States. Its role is described in Article 207 EC as preparing the work of the Council and carrying out the tasks assigned to it by the Council. Coreper is active throughout the work of the Council, but in CFSP matters there is a second committee, originally called the Political Committee and since the Treaty of Nice the Political and Security Committee (PSC), in order to reflect the increasing activity in the field of security and defence. Article 25 TEU describes the role of the PSC:

Without prejudice to Article 207 of the [EC] Treaty . . ., a Political and Security Committee shall monitor the international situation in the areas covered by the common foreign and security policy and contribute to the definition of policies by delivering opinions to the Council at the request of the Council or on its own initiative. It shall also monitor the implementation of agreed policies, without prejudice to the responsibility of the Presidency and the Commission.

Within the scope of this Title, this Committee shall exercise, under the responsibility of the Council, political control and strategic direction of crisis management operations.

The Council may authorize the Committee, for the purpose and for the duration of a crisis management operation, as determined by the Council, to take the relevant decisions concerning the political control and strategic direction of the operation, without prejudice to Article 47.

In literature the Political Committee has been described as the backbone of foreign policy co-ordination since the inception of European Political Co-operation.[75] It has also been noted that there have been power struggles between Coreper and the Political Committee, and that co-ordination between them is not straightforward.[76]

The second and third paragraphs of Article 25 TEU were inserted by the Treaty of Nice, and were immediately applied in the EU's military operations in FYROM and Congo. Both joint actions contain provisions reflecting the language of those paragraphs, and they confer on the PSC the powers to amend the operation plan, the chain of command, and the rules of engagement.[77]

---

[73] See further Art 19 TEU (see also Ch 7).

[74] See in general M Andenas and A Türk (eds), *Delegated Legislation and the Role of Committees in the EU* (Kluwer Law International, 2000); C Joerges and E Vos (eds), *EU Committees: Social Regulation, Law and Politics* (Hart Publishing, 1999).   [75] Peers (n 44 above), 551.

[76] Nuttall (n 8 above), 245 ff; Edwards, 'Common Foreign and Security Policy' (1993) 13 YEL 499; Wessel (n 2 above), 79.

[77] Art 4(1) Joint Action 2003/92 (n 27 above) and Art 7(1) Joint Action 2003/423 (n 27 above).

Coreper and the PSC have the function of representing the Member States and bridging the gap between national administrations and the Council. They do not however perform an administrative function for the Council. The CFSP is now so developed as a policy that it requires substantial administrative back-up. That function is performed by the Council's General Secretariat. Its name betrays its original function, but effectively the Council's administration has become the EU's second executive, after the Commission.[78] In addition, there has been a growing desire to put a face to the CFSP through the appointment of a distinguished politician responsible for moving the CFSP forward and for representing the EU in CFSP matters. The Treaty of Amsterdam thus created the position of High Representative for the CFSP, who is at the same time Secretary-General of the Council. As will be seen below, the draft Constitution develops this position into a Minister for Foreign Affairs.

The function and role of the High Representative are succinctly described in the Treaties. Article 207(2) EC provides that the Council shall be assisted by a General Secretariat, under the responsibility of a Secretary-General, High Representative for the CFSP. Article 26 TEU provides:

The . . . High Representative . . . shall assist the Council in matters coming within the common foreign and security policy, in particular through contributing to the formulation, preparation and implementation of policy decisions, and, when appropriate and acting on behalf of the Council at the request of the Presidency, through conducting political dialogue with third parties.

Further, Article 18(3) instructs the High Representative to assist the Presidency, which according to that provision has powers of representation and implementation (see above).

The creation of the position of High Representative was no doubt an important development.[79] Whereas the TEU describes his or her role as that of assisting the Presidency, recent joint actions go further. They do not, as a rule, provide for an important role for the Presidency, but instead confer powers on the High Representative and on the PSC. In the EU's military operations the role of the PSC is, as mentioned, preponderant. In other matters there is a more important role for the High Representative. For example, the High Representative gives operational direction to the EU Satellite Centre[80] and chairs the board of the EU Institute for Security Studies.[81] The joint action on the EU Monitoring Mission (EUMM) to the Western Balkans confers on the High Representative the power to give directions to that mission,[82] and to define the tasks of the mission 'acting in close coordination with the Presidency'.[83] The EUMM reports to the Council through the High Representative, who shall ensure that the mission functions flexibly and in a streamlined manner.[84]

---

[78] G Edwards, 'Common Foreign and Security Policy: Incrementalism in Action?', in Koskenniemi (ed) (n 54 above), 12.   [79] Decaux (n 8 above), 20.
[80] Art 4(1) Joint Action 2001/555 (n 25 above).
[81] Art 5(2) Joint Action 2001/554 (n 25 above).
[82] Art 1(1) Joint Action 2000/811 (n 16 above).   [83] Art 2(1), ibid
[84] Art 2(2) and (3), ibid

Indeed, Peers has criticized that joint action for delegating so much power to the High Representative as to raise serious questions about accountability.[85] However, one may take the view that those questions arise generally as regards the Council's role in CFSP matters, particularly in recent years, with stronger operational action, including action of a military kind. As regards military operations one must also mention the creation by the European Council of the EU Military Committee (EUMC) and the EU Military Staff Organization (EUMS). The TEU itself does not mention those organs.

For the sake of completeness one must also mention the so-called Troika, which since Amsterdam has consisted of the current Presidency and the next one,[86] and the policy planning and early warning unit, created by Declaration No 6 to the Amsterdam Treaty.[87]

As can thus be seen there is no dearth of actors within the Council framework as regards CFSP matters, and it may be doubtful whether such institutional proliferation contributes to more effective policies. The institutional evolution in the Council appears to move in the direction of a more important role for the permanent administration, headed by the High Representative, and politically controlled by the Council and the PSC. The draft Constitution builds on that evolution by having the foreign affairs Council chaired by the Minister for Foreign Affairs, who would take over the functions of the High Representative (see below).

Commission

Upon a mere reading of the TEU the Commission's role in CFSP matters appears strictly limited. Article 27 TEU provides that the Commission shall be fully associated with the work carried out in the common foreign and security policy field. The Treaty does not define what such association involves, and there are few other provisions which speak of Commission involvement. Article 18(4) TEU provides that the Commission shall (again) be fully associated with the Presidency's tasks of representing the EU, implementing decisions, and expressing the EU's position in international organizations and at international conferences. Article 20 TEU refers to the Commission Delegations in third countries and international conferences, and its representations to international organizations; they must co-operate in ensuring that common positions and joint actions are complied with and implemented. The most meaningful provision on Commission input is Article 22(1) TEU, which provides that the Commission (as well as any Member State) may refer to the Council any question relating to the CFSP and may submit proposals to the Council. In the negotiation of agreements the Presidency may be assisted by the Commission 'as appropriate' (Article 24(1) TEU).

That is all the Treaty provides for. The actual role of the Commission is however much more extensive. There are a number of factors contributing to such greater

---

[85] Peers (n 45 above), 536.   [86] Dashwood (n 8 above), 216.   [87] Ibid, 217.

involvement. The Commission has one of the largest foreign services in Europe (compared to those of the Member States), and it is through those delegations increasingly becoming a privileged interlocutor between third countries and the EU.[88] Related thereto there is the fact that the CFSP is but one segment of the EU's overall external action. As discussed in other chapters, the CFSP cannot be dissociated from the EC's external policies, in which the Commission generally plays a much more important role. It negotiates nearly all international agreements which the EC concludes, and it represents the EC in a number of international organizations, the most important of which is the WTO. For example, the EC is currently negotiating a trade and co-operation agreement with Iran, and at the time of writing those negotiations were becoming the linchpin of EU efforts to persuade Iran to be more co-operative with the international community as regards weapons of mass destruction. The Commission is involved automatically. The Commission is also very active in the area of development co-operation, other forms of co-operation with third countries, humanitarian aid, and external environmental policies. It is therefore not without reason that the TEU provides that the Commission must be fully associated with the CFSP. Consistent external action by the EU is not possible without Commission co-operation.

Even in strict CFSP matters the role of the Commission is more extensive than may appear at first. Under Article 274 EC it is the Commission which implements the Community budget, and, as analysed above, that budget is increasingly used to finance the CFSP. Joint actions requiring expenditure therefore invariably refer to the Commission as the institution responsible for implementing the policy in question. Indeed, some joint actions, which are limited to financial support for a particular cause or country refer almost exclusively to the Commission.[89]

In practice, therefore, the Commission is represented at all levels in the CFSP structure.[90] The Commission has also made use of its right to make proposals to the Council, and some of those have been accepted (even if in much modified form).[91]

Parliament

Under the terms of the TEU the Parliament's role in the conduct of the CFSP is even more limited than that of the Commission. Article 21 TEU alone addresses that institution:

The Presidency shall consult the European Parliament on the main aspects and the basic choices of the common foreign and security policy and shall ensure that the views of the European Parliament are duly taken into consideration. The European Parliament shall be kept regularly informed by the Presidency and the Commission of the development of the Union's foreign and security policy.

---

[88] Edwards (n 8 above), 12.   [89] E.g. Joint Action 1999/878 (n 19 above).
[90] Wessel (n 2 above), 91.   [91] Peers (n 44 above), 540.

The European Parliament may ask questions of the Council or make recommendations to it. It shall hold an annual debate on progress in implementing the common foreign and security policy.

The above provisions limit the Presidency's consultation duty to 'the basic choices', and do not provide for a right of consultation on all Council CFSP acts. The Parliament has the right to ask questions and make recommendations, but there could hardly be any doubt that a democratically elected legislature has those rights anyway, whether confirmed in the Treaty or not.

The Parliament is none the less very active in CFSP matters, exercises considerable influence, and the Council follows many of its views and recommendations.[92] It also manages to have a say in CFSP decisions through its budgetary powers (see above). As most CFSP operational expenditure is charged to the EC budget the Parliament is automatically involved. As described above, an interinstitutional agreement contains further provisions on budgetary matters. As CFSP expenditure is classified as non-compulsory the Parliament has the right to amend the draft CFSP budget.[93] Commentators agree that the budget has been a vital means for the Parliament to gain a wider role in the CFSP.[94] It is none the less the case that the Parliament has no formal legislative or decision-making powers in CFSP matters, and that the Council is not truly accountable before the Parliament. CFSP power is clearly concentrated in the executive.

Court of Justice

The Court of Justice and Court of First Instance have no jurisdiction in CFSP matters. Article 46 TEU provides that the EC Treaty provisions concerning the powers of the Court of Justice and the exercise of those powers apply only to a number of TEU provisions, which do not include those of Title V on the CFSP. According to Denza there were essentially two reasons for the exclusion of jurisdiction. The first related to the nature of CFSP instruments, which are short-term in character, potentially both wide-ranging and sensitive, and which are not designed to establish a permanent framework of mutual legal obligations. Measures to enforce compliance were not envisaged. The insistence on the continuation of ultimately sovereign policies, together with the need for speed in the resolution of differences, meant that the conditions for judicial resolution of disputes did not exist. The second reason concerned the nature and record of the Court, whose rulings in the sphere of external relations lay much more emphasis on the integrationist purpose of the Treaties and less on presuming a minimum derogation from individual sovereign powers. There was concern that doctrines such as that of exclusive external powers might find their way into the CFSP.[95]

---

[92] Denza (n 2 above), 337.
[93] PJG Kapteyn and P VerLoren van Themaat, *Introduction to the Law of the European Communities* (3rd edn, by LW Gormley, Kluwer Law International, 1998) 227.
[94] Edwards (n 2 above), 13; Wessel (n 2 above), 99.   [95] Denza (n 2 above), 312.

   The Court does have jurisdiction to interpret and apply Article 47 TEU, which provides that the TEU does not affect the EC Treaty. As analysed in Chapter 5, the Court showed its readiness to arbitrate the delimitation of the pillars in the *Airport Transit Visa* case.[96] The reader is referred to those pages for an extensive analysis of the ruling and its consequences.

   There is a further way in which CFSP acts are subject to Court jurisdiction. The EC law rules and principles on transparency and access to documents extend to all Council documents, including those which come within the scope of the CFSP. In *Svenska Journalistförbundet* the Court of First Instance decided that, and the ruling has since been confirmed.[97] This does not however mean that access must be granted to all CFSP documents. The current Regulation on access to documents provides for exceptions where disclosure would undermine the protection of the public interest as regards *inter alia* public security, defence and military matters, and international relations (Article 4(1)).[98] The Courts none the less show willingness to construe the principle of access to documents broadly, by applying the principle of proportionality and obliging the institutions to grant partial access where only parts of a document are protected.

   The case for exclusion of Court jurisdiction in CFSP matters is not persuasive in all respects. One can understand the apprehension that the Court might draw stronger legal consequences from the text of the Treaty than the Member States ever envisaged. Judicial decisions on the Member States' failure to comply with the CFSP are regarded as undesirable, and perhaps unworkable. There are however dimensions to the CFSP other than the relationship between CFSP acts and the Member States. Certain acts affect private persons, and there may even be doubts whether certain CFSP decisions, e.g. on sanctions, are in conformity with fundamental rights. The allegation that this may be the case only becomes stronger through the exclusion of Court jurisdiction. Further, certain CFSP acts are in substance of a legislative character, and their correct application would be greatly enhanced by a system of uniform interpretation, which is currently unavailable. There may even come a time when a Member State does not agree with a Council decision adopted by qualified majority, and again there is no mechanism for challenging such a decision.

The draft Constitution

The draft Constitution introduces significant changes to the CFSP, which can be summed up under two interconnected themes. First, the draft Constitution removes the pillar structure, in the sense that the CFSP will no longer be governed by

---

   [96] Case C–170/96 *Commission v. Council* [1998] ECR I–2763.

   [97] Case T–174/95 *Svensja Journalisförbundet v. Council* [1998] ECR II–2289, para 81 and Case T–14/98 *Hautala v. Council* [1999] ECR II–2489, para 42; see further A Tomkins, 'Transparency and the Emergence of a European Administrative Law' (1999/2000) 19 YEL 231–2.

   [98] Regulation 1049/2001 of the European Parliament and of the Council regarding public access to European Parliament, Council, and Commission documents [2001] OJ L145/43.

provisions in a separate Treaty, outside the sphere of Community law. Secondly, it introduces modifications to the institutional arrangements.

The disappearance of the pillar structure does not mean that all differences between the CFSP and other EU external policies are eliminated. The CFSP is governed by a separate chapter of the Constitution, and policy-making continues to be more intergovernmental in character. The unanimity rule is maintained, and the European Parliament, the Commission, and the Court of Justice continue to be far less involved than they are in other EU policies.

The draft Constitution none the less attempts to strengthen the institutional framework of the CFSP, by the creation of the position of Union Minister for Foreign Affairs. The Minister will be appointed by the European Council, with the agreement of the President of the Commission. The Minister will conduct the CFSP and will at the same time be one of the Vice-Presidents of the Commission, responsible there for handling external relations and for co-ordinating other aspects of the Union's external action (see Article I–27). It is thus clear that the creation of this position seeks, through so-called double-hatting, to bridge the gap which the Constitution maintains between the CFSP and other EU external policies.

Within the framework of the CFSP the Minister will have significant powers. According to Article III–197 the Minister 'shall chair the Council of Minister for Foreign Affairs, shall contribute through his proposals towards the preparation of the common foreign and security policy and shall ensure implementation' of CFSP decisions. The Minister shall also represent the Union for matters relating to the CFSP, conduct political dialogue on the Union's behalf, and express the Union's position in international organizations and at international conferences. The Minister shall be assisted by a European External Action Service.

The Minister will thus replace both the current High Representative and the Commission member responsible for external relations. As chair of the Council the Minister will also replace the Presidency. The current proliferation of actors involved in the conduct and implementation of the CFSP will thus be considerably reduced. There are no substantial changes to the limited roles of the Commission and of the European Parliament, even if one of the effects of the 'double-hatted' Minister may be that the Commission is more closely associated with the CFSP.

The Court of Justice continues to lack jurisdiction in CFSP matters (see Article III–282). There are however two exceptions, compared to the current position. First, Article III–282 provides for 'jurisdiction to rule on proceedings reviewing the legality of restrictive measures against natural or legal persons, adopted by the Council on the basis of Article III–224'.[99] CFSP sanctions against individuals will therefore be within the Court's jurisdiction. Secondly, there is a unified procedure for the negotiation and conclusion of international agreements (Article III–227), which also governs CFSP agreements and which is not located in the CFSP parts of the Constitution which are outside the Court's jurisdiction.

---

[99] Art III–198 is the legal basis for operational action by the Union (current joint actions).

As regards CFSP instruments there is little change other than in terminology. The Constitution speaks of European decisions on actions of the Union, positions of the Union, and implementation of actions and positions. The idea of common strategies is maintained, but is broadened to include both CFSP and other forms of external action. Under Article III–194 the European Council will identify the strategic interests and objectives of the Union, which 'shall relate to the [CFSP] and to other areas of the external action of the Union'.

Conclusions

The analysis of the actors and instruments of the CFSP shows that this policy continues to be in a precarious state, from a legal and institutional perspective. There is a range of legal instruments, but they are ill-defined and the practice does not bring much clarity. The precise legal effects are uncertain, be it in relation to the Member States, to the EU institutions, or to individuals. The institutional lacuna of lack of Court jurisdiction prevents authoritative clarification. The overall institutional arrangements are confused, with a variety of actors with uncertain remits within the Council framework (Coreper, PSC, High Representative, Presidency, Secretariat), and with subcutaneous involvement by the Commission and the Parliament through the linkages with, respectively, EC policies and the EC budget. In the eyes of the general public the CFSP is not credited with much success. This is partly due to lack of knowledge about its achievements, but one can indeed doubt whether the current constitutional framework is conducive to effective policy-making, even if one disregards the flagship unanimity/majority issue.

The draft Constitution aims to bring relief by homogenizing the institutional framework. The creation of the double-hat Union Minister for Foreign Affairs, heading a unified external action department, makes eminent sense. The current existence of parallel central administrations in the Council and the Commission is bound to be unproductive and to lead to turf battles rather than effective policy-making. It is in the end a fallacy that the Council Secretariat is more representative of national interests, because a developed central administration in any event needs to look for common denominators and for the general interest. There is no need for two such administrations.

However, it is at the level of parliamentary and judicial scrutiny that much remains to be done. Here, unfortunately, the draft Constitution makes little progress. The current state of affairs, it is submitted, is unacceptable in a polity governed by the rule of law. CFSP policies show signs of significant expansion, in particular in their natural terrain of security and defence policies. We now have joint actions involving military operations. The analysis above reveals, moreover, the many different objects of joint actions in particular, some of which appear to have indirect legislative scope. All these policies are over-dominated by the executive. The focus of debate should not continue to be the well-worn battle between supranationalism and intergovernmentalism, but should turn to issues of accountability. The latter is clearly no luxury in times when the EU is involved in military operations and the war against terrorism.

Parliamentary and judicial scrutiny is fortunately not as non-existent as the Treaty language suggests, owing to interactions between the pillars. In legal terms the scope of the CFSP is restricted to areas not covered by the EC Treaty (see Chapter 5). The Parliament has impact through its budgetary role, and the Court has jurisdiction in the area of sanctions (see also Chapter 12). That is not however sufficient. There is no reason in principle for excluding CFSP policies from full parliamentary and judicial scrutiny, even if there are difficult questions of finding a space for executive discretion. The exercise of arranging for such scrutiny would force the EU polity to come to terms with the reality of the attempt to construct a meaningful and work-able CFSP. The often lofty ideals and objectives of CFSP policies need to be matched with strong constitutionalism.

12

Trade and foreign policy

Introduction

It is one of the hallmarks of the European Union's external relations that trade policy and foreign policy are constitutionally separated, the first always having been at the very core of supranational integration and the second forming the subject of evolving, but still on the whole intergovernmental, co-operation. In Chapters 2 and 5 we examined the interface between trade policy and foreign policy from the angle of the respective competences of the EC, of the EU under the Second Pillar, and of the Member States. In Chapter 10 we briefly looked at the EC's import and export regulations, which are the legal cornerstones of external trade. Particularly as regards exports the analysis in that chapter is limited to the general export regulation, which provides for the freedom to export. Yet it is obvious that exports may be sensitive from a foreign and security policy perspective. As certain parts of the world are rather unstable and as certain countries' regimes are considered a threat to international peace and security, exports need to be monitored and controlled. Such controls do not of course cover just armaments, which are to some extent outside EC competence,[1] but also so-called dual-use goods which can be used for both civil and military purposes. Such goods are normally traded, and as such fully covered by the common commercial policy, but because they are sensitive their exportation is controlled under specific legal instruments which are based on foreign and security policy considerations. Next to such export controls, there is another obvious instance of a foreign policy instrument which directly affects trade, both imports and exports: embargo measures, or, to use the common EU law term, economic sanctions, which are adopted to force a State or regime to modify its behaviour.[2] It is in those areas of export controls and economic sanctions that the artificiality of the dichotomy between trade policy and foreign and security policy is most apparent. Other instruments of trade policy are of course also influenced by foreign policy considerations, but then at a general and aggregate level. Export controls and economic sanctions, however, are specific trade policy *instruments* which are exclusively employed for foreign policy *objectives*. In legal terms, this tension between instrument and objective connects those areas with exclusive EC competence

---

[1] See Art 296(1)(b) EC.   [2] See Ch 11.

under the commercial policy, with the CFSP, and with the Member States' autonomous powers over foreign policy. Export controls and economic sanctions are in a frontier between trade policy and foreign policy where it is difficult, if not impossible, to draw clear boundaries. To take the image a little further, one could say that they are in a no man's land between the front lines of the supranational and the intergovernmental.

The EU's policies on export controls and economic sanctions therefore offer an excellent case study of the evolving interaction between the EC's external trade policies, which are at the core of EC external relations, and the CFSP, as well as national foreign policy. In light of the abovementioned constitutional dichotomy it will come as no surprise that practice in this area has given rise to a series of legal developments, and has thrown up a number of issues and questions. This chapter aims to address the most significant ones. It shows that there is considerable evolution in these areas, generally towards more developed common policies. Indeed in the area of economic sanctions we have moved from Member State action, through the use of (current) Article 133 EC, in conjunction with decisions in the framework of European Political Co-operation, to a specific legal basis in the EC Treaty for the adoption of sanctions, based on decisions taken within the CFSP. In the field of export controls we have also moved from Member State action, through two combined instruments, one EC and one CFSP, to a single EC Treaty-based regulation.

Export controls and economic sanctions do not just offer case studies of the evolution of the interaction between trade policy and foreign policy. They also exemplify the difficulties associated with achieving consistency in the EU's external relations. They concern interaction between the supranational and the intergovernmental, and their study may reveal to what extent fears of encroachment upon the *acquis communautaire* and supranational integration mechanisms are warranted.[3]

This chapter first looks at the subject of economic sanctions. It starts with a short review of the history of EC/EU involvement, and then addresses four further topics which are of central importance, partly as a result of case law of the Court of Justice. The first concerns the methods of interpreting and applying sanctions instruments adopted by the EU. A discussion of that topic will include issues pertaining to the balance between the supranational and the intergovernmental. The second concerns the status of UN Security Council resolutions in EC law. The third relates to the relationship between EU economic sanctions and fundamental rights. The fourth topic is the question whether, or to what extent, the Member States continue to have autonomous legal capacity to adopt sanctions.

The chapter then looks at export controls. Here it first examines the disciplines which EC law imposes on such controls at Member State level, and then the evolving EU policy on export controls.

---

[3] See Ch 5 on consistency of external action.

Economic sanctions

A short history

It took until the 1980s before a pattern of EC involvement in the adoption of eco-nomic sanctions developed. Before that the Member States defended their powers to proclaim sanctions under the so-called Rhodesia doctrine, which was based on (cur-rent) Article 297 EC. The doctrine provided that Member States were deemed free to implement economic sanctions serving political aims against a third country under national rules justified on the basis of Article 297 EC.[4] The prevailing view was that economic sanctions were beyond the scope of the common commercial policy.[5] In the early 1980s European Political Co-operation, the predecessor to the CFSP, developed. This provided the basic institutional preconditions for a culture of consul-tation,[6] within which it became possible to adopt sanctions regulations on the basis of (current) Article 133 EC. The first such sanctions were directed against the Soviet Union, following the declaration of martial law in Poland.[7] In the same year the Council adopted sanctions against Argentina, for the first time expressly mentioning discussions in the context of EPC in the preamble.[8] That became the established practice: sanctions were based on Article 133 EC, and referred to preceding discussions in the framework of ECP as the political source for their adoption.[9] Commentators agree that this movement towards Community involvement was mainly the result of a concern to ensure the effective and uniform imposition of sanctions, rather than constituting a principled recognition of Community competence.[10] Regulations can be adopted relatively smoothly on the basis of Article 133 EC, as a Commission proposal and a qualified majority in the Council are sufficient. They are directly applic-able in all the Member States and automatically override all inconsistent national law.

This practice was codified in (current) Article 301 EC, introduced by the TEU:

Where it is provided, in a common position or in a joint action adopted according to the provisions of the Treaty on European Union relating to the common foreign and security pol-icy, for an action by the Community to interrupt or to reduce, in part or completely, economic relations with one or more third countries, the Council shall take the necessary urgent measures. The Council shall act by a qualified majority on a proposal from the Commission.

---

[4] Art 297 EC provides: 'Member States shall consult each other with a view to taking together the steps needed to prevent the functioning of the common market being affected by measures which a Member State may be called upon to take in the event of serious internal disturbances affecting the main-tenance of law and order, in the event of war, serious international tension constituting a threat of war, or in order to carry out obligations it has accepted for the purpose of maintaining peace and international security'.

[5] P Koutrakos, *Trade, Foreign Policy & Defence in EU Constitutional Law* (Hart Publishing, 2001) 58.

[6] Ibid, 63–4.   [7] Council Regulation 596/82 [1982] OJ L72/15.

[8] Council Regulation 877/82 [1982] OJ L102/1.

[9] PJ Kuijper, 'Trade Sanctions, Security and Human Rights and Commercial Policy', in M Maresceau (ed), *The European Community's Commercial Policy after 1992: The Legal Dimension* (Kluwer, 1993) 390.

[10] Koutrakos (n 5 above), 64.

A corresponding provision extends this approach to movement of capital and payments. Article 60 EC provides:

1. If, in the case envisaged in Article 301, action by the Community is deemed necessary, the Council may, in accordance with the procedure provided for in Article 301, take the necessary urgent measures on the movement of capital and on payments as regards the third countries concerned.

2. Without prejudice to Article 297 and as long as the Council has not taken measures pursuant to paragraph 1, a Member State may, for serious political reasons and on grounds of urgency, take unilateral measures against a third country with regard to capital movements and payments. The Commission and the other Member States shall be informed of such measures by the date of their entry into force at the latest.

The Council may, acting by a qualified majority on a proposal from the Commission, decide that the Member State concerned shall amend or abolish such measures. The President of the Council shall inform the European Parliament of any such decision taken by the Council.

As can be seen those provisions speak in general terms of interrupting or reducing economic relations. In practice the sanctions based on them include trade embargoes, prohibiting imports and exports; financial sanctions, banning transfers of funds, lending, or investment; and sanctions regarding means of transport or transport services.[11] Most EU sanctions implement UN Security Council resolutions. They are, in accordance with the above provisions, preceded by 'political' decisions under the CFSP.[12]

Koutrakos has usefully identified some of the common features of sanctions regimes adopted under Article 301 EC.[13] The CFSP common position refers to the political background and the main thrust of the sanctions regime. There is usually provision for certain exceptions, such as for humanitarian reasons. Scope for independent action is left to the Member States, in terms of allowing them to authorize deviations from the regime (either in accordance with the views of UN Sanctions Committees or autonomously). Sanctions regulations establish a co-operation procedure amongst the Member States, and between them and the Commission. Member States have the right to determine penalties for breach of the regulations. And special reference is made to the UN Sanctions Committee where a regulation implements a UN Security Council resolution.

Interpretation and application

Sanctions regulations, whether pre-TEU and based on (current) Article 133 EC, or post-TEU and based on Article 301 (and 60) EC, are EC acts open to interpretation by the Court of Justice. National authorities are required to implement and apply the regulations, and as the latter affect private companies engaged in trade, or

---

[11] Ibid, 69.   [12] Common positions: see Ch 11.   [13] N 5 above, 72–6.

providing transport or financial services, it is hardly surprising that their precise scope or application may be disputed, giving rise to litigation. National courts may be confronted with issues of interpretation or even validity, and may refer questions to the Court of Justice under Article 234 EC. A number of such cases have come before the Court, and they show the kind of issues to which sanctions regulations may give rise. This subsection looks at case law on how to interpret and apply sanctions regulations. The Court has had to grapple with the required method of interpretation of the terms of sanctions regulations, in particular where they find their origin in UN Security Council resolutions; with the territorial scope of such regulations; with sanctions and penalties applied by the Member States; with the application of the exceptions for which the regulations provide; and with their relationship with other instruments of Community law, in particular the general export regulation.[14]

Bosphorus

Bosphorus was the first case in which the Court had to interpret an EC sanctions regulation.[15] In implementation of UN Security Council resolutions the Council had adopted Regulation 990/93 concerning trade between the EEC and the Federal Republic of Yugoslavia (Serbia and Montenegro).[16] The sanctions were a reaction to the conflict in the former Yugoslavia, particularly in Bosnia-Herzegovina. They extended to means of transport: Article 8 of the regulation provided that all vessels, freight vehicles, rolling stock, and aircraft in which a majority or controlling interest was held by a person or undertaking in or operating from the FRY had to be impounded by the competent authorities of the Member States. That wording was in substance identical to the relevant passage in the Security Council resolution.[17] Bosphorus Airways was a Turkish air charter company, which in 1992 had leased two Boeing aircraft from Yugoslav Airlines (JAT). They were so-called dry leases, meaning that Bosphorus Airways provided the cabin and flight crew and had full day-to-day operational control and direction of the aircraft. The leases were themselves not in breach of the sanctions, the agreement between Bosphorus Airways and JAT was entirely *bona fide*, and Bosphorus Airways operated the aircraft for its charter operations, flying between Turkey and various EU Member States as well as Switzerland. JAT had no further involvement whatsoever with the use of the aircraft or the management and direction of Bosphorus Airways. In April 1993 one of the aircraft was flown to Dublin Airport for the purpose of maintenance. At that point the Irish authorities impounded the aircraft, in implementation of Article 8 of the sanctions regulation. They acted after having

---

[14] Council Regulation 2603/69 establishing common rules for exports [1969] OJ Spec Ed (II) 590.
[15] Case C–84/95 *Bosphorus v. Minister for Transport, Energy and Communications, Ireland and the Attorney General* [1996] ECR I–3953. For a full description of facts and law see the Opinion of Jacobs AG.
[16] [1993] OJ L102/14.   [17] Resolution 820 (1993), para 24.

consulted the UN Yugoslavia Sanctions Committee, which took the view that the aircraft came within the scope of the resolution and therefore had to be impounded. Bosphorus Airways then applied to the High Court in Dublin for judicial review. The High Court quashed the decision on the ground that the aircraft was not one in which a majority or controlling interest was held by a person or undertaking in or operating from the FRY. It considered that the aim of the sanctions regulation was to operate as a punishment, deterrent, or sanction against the people or government of the FRY, and that the type of interest referred to in Article 8 had to have been intended to identify a situation in which the person in or operating from the FRY could exercise a decision-making function in relation to the use on a day-to-day basis of the asset in question. Any other construction was both unreal and unjust, and the aim of the regulation was not to punish or penalize peoples or countries who had not in any way caused or contributed to the tragic events in Yugoslavia. The Irish Minister then appealed to the Supreme Court, which referred to the Court of Justice the question whether an aircraft such as that in issue was covered by Article 8 of the regulation.

Jacobs AG took the text of Article 8 as a starting point, and considered that it left little room for doubt. The term 'interest' was very broad, encompassing all types of property interest, and most other language versions of the regulation referred to the notion of property, instead of interest. As JAT continued to be the exclusive owner of the aircraft in question, Article 8 on its wording clearly applied. This conclusion was further strengthened by the requirement of uniform interpretation, to which the preamble to the regulation expressly referred. The issue was therefore whether there were any compelling reasons to interpret the regulation in a way which appeared to depart from its wording. The Advocate General examined that question in the light of the context and the objects of the regulation, which were the Security Council resolutions which it aimed to implement. He pointed out that the term 'majority or controlling interest' was reproduced verbatim from Resolution 820 (1993). He did not agree with the reasoning of the Irish High Court that the purpose of the relevant provision of the resolution was to deprive the FRY of recourse to the aircraft which could be used to transport goods in breach of the applicable trade embargo. It was not excluded that the Security Council had intended to go further, requiring the freezing of assets abroad. Jacobs AG was of the opinion that it was much more difficult to divine the precise purpose of a Community measure implementing a Security Council resolution than it would normally be to ascertain the purpose of an ordinary Community measure, because of the involvement of the intentions of the Security Council, an organ composed of many diverse States acting in highly charged political circumstances. He agreed with the Commission that the aim of the measure could also be to prevent persons or undertakings in the FRY to recover means of transport temporarily outside their control. He also found support for his view in other provisions of the resolution. The Advocate General lastly examined the weight of the opinion of the Yugoslavia Sanctions Committee, which had led to the impounding of the aircraft. He considered that due regard should be given to that opinion, but that it could not be regarded as binding, if only because such an effect was not provided for in the resolution, at least as regards the issue in question.[18]

The Court largely adopted the reasoning of Jacobs AG. Nothing in the wording of the regulation suggested a distinction between ownership and control. The regulation had to be interpreted in light of its context and aims, which included the UN resolutions. The wording of the resolution confirmed its application to any aircraft which was the property of a person or undertaking in the FRY, and confirmed that actual control was not required. The word 'interest' could not, on any view, exclude ownership as a determining criterion; the conjunction with the word 'majority' moreover clearly implied the concept of ownership. Other language versions of the regulation confirmed this. The Court also stated that the impounding contributed to restricting the exercise by the FRY and its nationals of their property rights, and was thus consistent with the aim of the sanctions, namely to put pressure on the FRY. By contrast, the use of day-to-day operation and control as the decisive criterion could jeopardize the effectiveness of the strengthening of the sanctions, as it would allow the FRY or its nationals to evade application of those sanctions through the mere transfer of day-to-day operation and control of means of transport.[19]

Both the Advocate General and the Court also examined whether the regulation, thus interpreted, was in breach of fundamental rights and the principle of proportionality. That question is however discussed below.

Bosphorus established a number of important principles. Sanctions regulations, in particular those adopted in implementation of UN Security Council resolutions, must be interpreted literally, in light not only of their own wording but also of that of the corresponding resolution. Whilst the Court appeared more willing to establish the aims of the sanctions than the Advocate General, one may none the less assume that the classic teleological method of interpretation of a Community act is not easily extended to sanctions regulations. Uniform interpretation is clearly paramount, as it is one of the main rationales for EC involvement in the adoption of sanctions. There is therefore little deference to the views of national authorities, including national courts. The case also put the legal status of Security Council resolutions and of opinions of Sanctions Committees established by such resolutions in the spotlight, but neither the Court nor the Advocate General felt compelled fully to clarify that legal status.

Ebony Maritime

In the subsequent case of *Ebony Maritime* the same Regulation, 990/93, was in issue.[20] The facts were a little more spectacular than those of *Bosphorus*. In April 1994 the

---

[18] *Bosphorus* (n 15 above), paras 31–47 of the Opinion of Jacobs AG.
[19] Ibid, paras 8–18 of the judgment.
[20] N 16 above; Case C–177/95 *Ebony Maritime and Loten Navigation v. Prefetto della Provincia di Brindisi and Others* [1997] ECR I–1111.

Lido II, a tanker flying the Maltese flag and owned by Loten Navigation Company Ltd, a Maltese company, left the Tunisian port of La Skhira bound for Rijeka, Croatia, with a cargo of petroleum products and motor spirit. The cargo was owned by Ebony Maritime, a Liberian company. At some point, when the vessel was in the Adriatic, the master sent out distress signals, because the *Lido II* began to take on water in the engine room. Stating that he was unable to contain the leak, he set course towards the Montenegran coast, which was nearest. Before the *Lido II* entered Yugoslav territorial waters, thus still being in international waters, a NATO/WEU helicopter landed on its deck and a Dutch military squad took control of the vessel, which was towed to Brindisi and placed at the disposal of the Italian authorities. The *Prefetto* (Prefect) of Brindisi decided to arrest the vessel and confiscate its cargo, in implementation of the sanctions laid down in Italian law for breach of the trade embargo. The companies involved brought proceedings before the competent Italian courts, and the *Consiglio di Stato* (Council of State) referred several questions to the Court of Justice.

The first issue in the case was whether Regulation 990/93 actually applied to the facts. The United Kingdom and France argued that it did not. They referred to Article 11, according to which the regulation applied within the territory of the Community and in any aircraft or vessel under the jurisdiction of a Member State, and to any person elsewhere who was a national of a Member State and any body elsewhere which was incorporated and constituted under the law of a Member State. The argument was that, as both Ebony Maritime and Loten Navigation Company were non-Community companies, as the *Lido II* flew the Maltese flag, and as it was taken control of when in international waters, none of the connecting criteria were present. The Court did not agree. It referred to Article 9, read in conjunction with Article 1(1)(c), and Article 10 of the regulation, according to which the competent authorities of the Member States were required to detain, pending investigations, all vessels and cargoes suspected of having breached the prohibition of entry into the territorial sea of the FRY for purposes of trade, and were permitted to confiscate vessels and cargoes once an infringement had been established. It followed from the wording of those provisions that the detention and confiscation measures applied to all vessels, irrespective of flag or ownership. Nor was the application of those measures subject to the condition that the breach of the sanctions should take place within Community territory—in any case the prohibition on entry into the territorial sea of the FRY could be breached only outside Community territory. Since under Article 11 the Regulation applied within the whole territory of the Community, Articles 9 and 10 were applicable once vessels were within the territory of a Member State and thus under the territorial jurisdiction of that State. That interpretation was borne out by the wording and purpose of Resolution 820 (1993), paragraph 25 of which expressly provided that all vessels suspected of violations that were found in the territory of a State had to be detained and, where appropriate, forfeited to that State.[21] Again the Court largely adopted

---

[21] Ibid, paras 15–21.

the reasoning of Jacobs AG, who in addition pointed out that the regulation needed to be interpreted so as to make the sanctions provided for by the resolution fully effective. He also considered that the Regulation was not thereby given an interpretation conflicting with rules or principles of international law, such as the principle of the freedom of the high seas, expressed in Articles 87 and 92 of the Convention on the Law of the Sea.[22] Measures adopted by the Security Council under Chapter VII of the UN Charter were binding on all UN member States (Article 25), and in the event of conflict between obligations under the Charter and under any other international agreement the former prevailed (Article 103).[23]

The second issue in *Ebony Maritime* arose because the *Lido II* had been taken over by NATO/WEU forces before its actual entry into the territorial waters of the FRY. The legal question was whether Articles 1(1)(c) and (d) of the regulation prohibited only actual entry of commercial traffic into the territorial sea of the FRY or whether it also prohibited conduct occurring in international waters which gave good reason to believe that the vessel concerned was on course for that territorial sea for the purposes of commercial traffic.[24] The Court noted that the prohibition on entry was introduced pursuant to Resolution 820 (1993), which was designed to reinforce the sanctions imposed against the FRY. In order to guarantee that those sanctions would be effective, it was deemed vital to prevent all commercial traffic in Yugoslav waters. The Court considered that effective prevention of all such traffic implied that the prohibition should apply not only to actual entries, but also to attempted entries by vessels in international waters. Any other interpretation would risk rendering the prohibition ineffective. The prohibition in Article 1(1)(d) on any activity the object or effect of which was to promote the entry of any commercial traffic into the FRY's territorial sea confirmed that a breach of the sanctions could result from conduct occurring in international waters.[25] In line with the broad territorial scope of the regulation, the Court thus opted for a broad interpretation of the prohibitions which it laid down, so as to ensure the effectiveness of the sanctions.

The third issue in *Ebony Maritime* was whether the Italian authorities were entitled to confiscate the cargo of the *Lido II*. There was some confusion about the actual wording of the regulation, because of differences in the various language versions. But the Court also addressed further issues. The companies involved argued that the confiscation ran counter to the principle of *nulla poena sine culpa*, in that no proof of fault on the part of the owner of the cargo was required, thereby implying a system

---

[22] Done at Montego Bay on 10 December 1982, 21 ILM 1261 [1998] OJ L179/3.

[23] *Ebony Maritime* (n 20 above), paras 21 and 27.

[24] Art 1(1)(c) and (d) provided:
'1. As from 26 April 1993, the following shall be prohibited:
. . .
(c) the entry into the territorial sea of the Federal Republic of Yugoslavia (Serbia and Montenegro) by all commercial traffic;
(d) any activity the object or effect of which is, directly or indirectly, to promote the transactions mentioned under (a), (b) or (c);
. . .'.

[25] *Ebony Maritime* (n 20 above), paras 22–27.

of strict criminal liability. They further contended that it was contrary to the principle of proportionality for the owner of the cargo to be penalized in the same way
as the owner of the vessel, regardless of their respective degrees of involvement. The
Court replied to those arguments by first referring to the basic principle that the
Member States were required to take all measures necessary to guarantee the application and effectiveness of Community law. While the choice of penalties remained
within their discretion, they had to ensure in particular that infringements of
Community law were penalized under conditions, both procedural and substantive,
which were analogous to those applicable to infringements of national law of a similar nature and importance and which, in any event, made the penalty effective, proportionate, and dissuasive. The Court then pointed out that it had already accepted
that a system of strict criminal liability penalizing breach of a regulation was not in
itself incompatible with Community law.[26] It was for the national court to determine whether the penalty of confiscation complied with the above principles and,
in particular, whether it was dissuasive, effective, and proportionate. In making that
determination, the national court had to take account, in particular, of the fact that
the objective pursued by the regulation, which was to bring to an end the state of
war in the region concerned and the massive violations of human rights and
humanitarian law in the Republic of Bosnia-Herzegovina, was one of fundamental
general interest for the international community.[27] The Court thus again hinted at
the overriding concern for making the sanctions effective.

Centro-Com

The third case involving sanctions against the FRY, *Centro-Com*,[28] concerned payment for authorized exports of medical products. The applicable sanctions regulation at the time of the facts was Regulation 1432/92,[29] which gave effect to UN
Security Council Resolution 757 (1992). Article 1(b) of the Regulation prohibited
all exports to Serbia and Montenegro, but Article 2(a) exempted exports of commodities and products intended for strictly medical purposes and foodstuffs notified to the UN Yugoslavia Sanctions Committee. Article 3 subjected such exports
to a prior export authorization, to be issued by the competent authorities of the
Member States. Centro-Com was an Italian trading company, specializing in the
supply of pharmaceutical goods. After having obtained the approval of the Sanctions
Committee and the prior authorization of the Italian authorities required by Article 3
of the Regulation, Centro-Com exported from Italy, between 15 October 1992 and
6 January 1993, fifteen consignments of pharmaceutical goods and blood-testing

---

[26] See Case C–326/88 *Anklagemyndigheden v. Hansen* [1990] ECR I–2911, para 19.
[27] *Ebony Maritime* (n 20 above), paras 28–39.
[28] Case C–124/95 *The Queen, ex parte Centro-Com v. HM Treasury and Bank of England* [1997] ECR
I–81; see also Ch 2.
[29] Council Regulation 1432/92 prohibiting trade between the European Economic Community and
the Republics of Serbia and Montenegro [1992] OJ L151/4.

equipment to two wholesalers in Montenegro. Payments for those exports were to
be debited from a bank account held by the National Bank of Yugoslavia with
Barclays Bank, London. Under the applicable United Kingdom law implementing
the financial sanctions against Serbia and Montenegro (which were not covered by
the sanctions regulation),[30] the Bank of England could authorize such payments,
and did indeed authorize them for eleven of the fifteen consignments. However,
following reports of abuse of the authorization procedure established by the
Sanctions Committee, such as misdescription of goods and unreliability of the documents issued, or apparently issued, by that Committee, the UK Treasury decided
to change its policy. Henceforth, payment from Serbian and Montenegrin funds
held in the UK for exports of goods exempt from the sanctions, such as medical
products, was to be permitted only where those exports were made from the United
Kingdom. One of the main reasons for the new policy was to enable the UK authorities to exercise effective control over goods exported to Serbia and Montenegro so
as to ensure that the goods exported actually matched their description and that no
debiting of accounts held with British banks was authorized for payments for
non-medical or non-humanitarian purposes. In implementation of this new policy,
the Bank of England did not permit Barclays Bank to transfer funds to Centro-Com
in payment of the four remaining consignments. Centro-Com challenged that
decision before the High Court, which refused its application, and in the appeal
proceedings the Court of Appeal referred a couple of questions to the Court of
Justice. The question which is of interest here was, in substance, whether the above
UK policy on release of funds was compatible with the Community's common
commercial policy, as implemented by the sanctions regulation.

The Court considered that that question raised two problems. The first concerned
the relationship between measures of foreign and security policy, such as those intended
to ensure effective application of Resolution 757 (1992), on the one hand, and the
common commercial policy, on the other. When analysing this problem the Court
discussed the scope of the common commercial policy, as examined in Chapter 2. The
United Kingdom argued that the measures in issue had been taken by virtue of its
national competence in the field of foreign and security policy and that performance
of its obligations under the Charter and under the resolutions of the United Nations
fell within that competence. The Court accepted that the Member States retained
competence in the field of foreign and security policy, but also emphasized that
national competences had to be exercised in a manner consistent with Community
law. The Member States could not treat national measures whose effect was to prevent
or restrict the export of certain products as falling outside the scope of the common
commercial policy on the ground that they had foreign and security objectives.[31]

The second problem concerned the scope of the common commercial policy
and of the relevant measures adopted pursuant to (then) Article 113 EEC. Here the

---

[30] The regulation was adopted on the basis of (then) Art 113 EEC. Current Art 301 and 60 EC were
not yet in force.   [31] *Centro-Com* (n 28 above), paras 23–30.

Court analysed the precise meaning and effect of the combined provisions of the sanctions regulation and of Regulation 2603/69 establishing common rules for exports (the export regulation).[32] The latter provides for a principle of free exportation, but allows for exceptions on grounds of public policy or public security. The Court construed the general prohibition of exports in the sanctions regulation as a derogation from the principle of free exportation in the export regulation. However, in so far as the sanctions regulation permitted exports of medical products, such exports remained subject to the common system provided for by the export regulation. As Article 1 of that regulation prohibited quantitative restrictions on exports the question arose whether restrictions on the release of funds held at a bank could constitute such a quantitative restriction.[33]

The Court replied to that question with the following reasoning. It noted that Article 1 of the export regulation implemented the principle of freedom to export at Community level and therefore had to be interpreted as covering measures adopted by the Member States whose effect was equivalent to a quantitative restriction where their application could lead to an export prohibition. National measures by a Member State preventing the release of Serbian and Montenegrin funds as payment for goods that could be legally exported to Serbia and Montenegro unless those goods were exported from its own territory constituted a restriction on the payment of the price of the goods which, like the supply of goods, was an essential element of an export transaction. Such measures were equivalent to a quantitative restriction since their application precluded the making of payment in consideration of the supply of goods dispatched from other Member States, and thus prevented such exports.[34]

The further question which then arose was whether the requirement that the authorized exports take place from United Kingdom territory was justified on grounds of public security, and could benefit from the exception in Article 11 of the export regulation. The United Kingdom argued that, having regard to the difficulties involved in applying the system of authorizations issued by the Sanctions Committee, that requirement was necessary in order to ensure that the sanctions imposed by Resolution 757 (1992) were applied effectively, since it allowed the United Kingdom authorities themselves to check the nature of goods exported to Serbia and Montenegro. Jacobs AG was of the opinion that the general question whether the United Kingdom policy was justified did not need to be resolved, since the specific decision in issue did not in any event comply with the principle of proportionality. When the Treasury changed the policy Centro-Com had already exported to Montenegro, having obtained the approval of the Sanctions Committee as well as an Italian export authorization. In those circumstances the refusal to release payment could not serve the objective of an effective implementation of the export ban, since the exports had already taken place.[35] The Court, however, went further,

---

[32] N 14 above.   [33] *Centro-Com* (n 28 above), paras 31–39.   [34] Ibid, paras 40–42.
[35] Ibid, para 71 of the Opinion of Jacobs AG.

and addressed the general question of justification. It first noted that the concept of public security within the meaning of Article 11 of the export regulation covered both a Member State's internal security and its external security and that the risk of a serious disturbance to foreign relations or to the peaceful coexistence of nations could affect the external security of a Member State. Therefore, a measure intended to apply sanctions imposed by a resolution of the UN Security Council in order to achieve a peaceful solution to the situation in Bosnia-Herzegovina, which formed a threat to international peace and security, fell within the exception provided for by Article 11 of the export regulation. However, a Member State's recourse to Article 11 ceased to be justified if Community rules provided for the necessary measures to ensure protection of the interests enumerated in that article. The sanctions regulation, which was designed to implement, uniformly throughout the Community, certain aspects of the sanctions imposed by the UN Security Council, laid down the conditions on which exports of medical products to Serbia and Montenegro were to be authorized (i.e. notification to the Sanctions Committee and export authorization by a Member State). In those circumstances, measures regarding the release of funds such as those adopted by the United Kingdom could not be justified, since effective application of the sanctions could be ensured by other Member States' authorization procedures, as provided for in the sanctions regulation, in particular the procedure of the Member State of exportation. The Member States had to place trust in each other as far as concerned the check made by the competent authorities of the Member State from which the products in question were dispatched. There was nothing in the case to suggest that the system of export authorizations had not functioned properly. Finally, it had to be borne in mind that, since Article 11 of the export regulation formed an exception to the principle of freedom to export, it had, on any view, to be interpreted in a way which did not extend its effects beyond what was necessary for the protection of the interests which it was intended to guarantee. Less restrictive measures were possible here, such as resorting to administrative collaboration with the authorities of other Member States. The Court therefore concluded that the United Kingdom policy was contrary to the combined provisions of the sanctions regulation and of the export regulation.[36]

The judgment in *Centro-Com* strongly enhanced the status and effect of EC sanctions regulations and external trade rules. On the issue of competence, even if the Court recognized that the Member States retained powers in the field of foreign and security policy and that the sanctions regulations constituted implementation of political decisions in the framework of EPC, it none the less emphasized that the Member States need to comply with the various commercial policy instruments, including sanctions regulations. The political subordination to foreign policy decisions was not matched by any form of legal subordination.[37] As regards the interpretation of the various provisions in the sanctions regulation and in the export

---

[36] *Centro-Com* (n 28 above), paras 44–53 of the judgment.   [37] See also Ch 2.

regulation, it is first of all noteworthy that the Court had no qualms about fully applying the principle of freedom of exportation resulting from Article 1 of the export regulation to exports authorized under the sanctions regulation. Secondly, the Court interpreted the principle of free exports broadly, as encompassing measures regarding payment for export. Thirdly, and most significantly, it did not accept recourse to the public security exception in Article 11 of the export regulation, on the ground that the sanctions regulation occupied the field. In this respect the judgment followed the general approach towards the relationship between free trade and free movement principles in the internal market, exceptions thereto, and Community harmonization. It is indeed established case law that exceptions to free movement can no longer be relied upon where the Community has harmonized the relevant laws and regulations of the Member States.[38] In *Centro-Com* the Court not only extended that approach to external trade; it did so in what was, from the perspective of national sovereignty, a most sensitive area. Notwithstanding the fact that the Member States are required, under international law, to abide by the UN Charter and by Security Council resolutions, and that they retain competence in the area of foreign and security policy, they can no longer act outside the EC law framework once a comprehensive sanctions regulation has been adopted. Jacobs AG summed up the position in stark terms. He considered that the United Kingdom's argument on national competence in the field of foreign and security policy appeared to suggest that the Member States had more leeway in interpreting, applying, or supplementing Community acts which had a foreign or security policy dimension than they had in respect of other Community acts. He rejected that view. The interpretation of a Community act depended on its objectives, its terms, and its context. The fact that it had a foreign or security policy dimension could therefore have an impact on its interpretation, but it did not in principle mean that the Member States had more leeway.[39]

In terms of the balance between the intergovernmental and the supranational the above case law on the interpretation and application of sanctions regulations thus strongly confirms the full scope and effect of supranational legal instruments. Their adoption may be conditioned on prior political decisions, but once adopted the regulations in question need to be uniformly interpreted and applied (*Bosphorus*); they need to be effective (*Bosphorus* and *Ebony Maritime*); they have broad territorial scope (*Ebony Maritime*); sanctions and penalties by Member States need to be effective, proportionate, and dissuasive (*Ebony Maritime*); and the Member States cannot freely decide how to enhance their effectiveness by imposing further requirements which do not conform to the regulations themselves (*Centro-Com*).

The significant legal effect of EC sanctions is further confirmed in a recent interim order by the President of the Court of First Instance. *Abdirisak Aden and Others v. Council and Commission* concerned a challenge to Council and Commission

---

[38] Case 5/77 *Tedeschi v. Denkavit* [1977] ECR 1555, para 35.
[39] *Centro-Com* (n 28 above), para 43 of the Opinion of Jacobs AG.

regulations imposing sanctions on the Taliban, including the freezing of assets of persons resident in the EU. The regulations were again adopted in implementation of UN Security Council resolutions. The applicants requested the provisional suspension of those regulations, but the President of the Court rejected that request on grounds of lack of urgency. In the order the President also examined whether the applicants lacked legal interest. The Council and the Commission had argued that, even if the regulations were suspended, Sweden was required to give effect to the UN resolutions, and would thus have to freeze the applicants' assets. The President did not agree. He first of all pointed out that there was no Swedish legislation which would apply if the regulations were suspended. He then went on to refer to the defendants' own argument (presumably in the main proceedings) that the regulations constituted exercise of an exclusive Community competence in the field of sanctions. Such exclusive competence of necessity had as its counterpart the lack of any Member States' competence.[40]

The legal status of UN Security Council resolutions

The case law on sanctions regulations draws attention to the relationship between EU law and UN Security Council resolutions, adopted under the UN Charter.[41] All of the regulations in issue had the implementation of such resolutions within the EU as their object. The EC is not however a member of the UN (nor, of course, is the EU), and that gives rise to various legal questions about the exact relationship between the UN Charter and Security Council resolutions, on the one hand, and EC law on the other. Those questions can be grouped into two categories. The first concerns the effect of the Charter and of the resolutions in EC law itself. Are the Charter and the resolutions binding on the Community? If so, what effect may they produce? The second group includes questions about the scope for the Member States of the EU to derogate from EC law so as to give effect to the Charter and the resolutions. Where, in particular, there is a sanctions regulation occupying the field, are the Member States still entitled to adopt divergent provisions on the ground that those provisions are required by a resolution?

Let us first examine whether the Charter and the resolutions are binding on the EC. This question has two dimensions. The first is whether, under international law, that is the case. *Prima facie* the answer appears to be negative. The Charter is an international treaty to which the EC is not a contracting party, as membership of the UN is limited to States. The language of the Charter does not suggest that it is binding on non-signatory States,[42] let alone other international or regional organizations.

---

[40] Case T–306/01 R *Abdirisak Aden and Others v. Council and Commission* [2002] ECR II–2387, paras 56–60; see also Case T–47/03 R *José Maria Sison v. Council*, Order of 15 May 2003, not yet reported.

[41] See also C Kaddous, *Le droit des relations extérieures dans la jurisprudence de la Cour de justice des Communautés européennes* (Helbing & Lichtenhahn 1998) 417–24.

[42] See however Art 2(6) on the attitude of the Organization towards non-signatory States.

Article 25 of the Charter provides that the members of the UN agree to accept and carry out the decisions of the Security Council in accordance with the Charter; it does not mention non-members. There is none the less some debate on whether Security Council resolutions have broader scope, and Bohr reports that some resolutions call on all States, including non-UN members, to act in accordance with their provisions, and that other resolutions refer to 'all States and international organizations'.[43]

As the UN Charter does not appear to bind the EU or the EC on the basis of international law, it is important to investigate whether there are none the less any grounds in EU law itself for characterizing the Charter or the resolutions as binding. The Court of Justice has so far not ruled on the issue.[44] Article 11(1) TEU defines the objectives of the CFSP as the safeguarding of the common values, etc, of the Union, 'in conformity with the principles of the United Nations Charter', and as the preservation of peace and the strengthening of international security, again 'in accordance with the principles of the United Nations Charter'. Even if those statements might have some effect on the relationship between the CFSP and the Charter, it would be difficult to distil from them a hard legal rule of binding effect for the EC. In the EC Treaty the United Nations are mentioned only in Article 302, which merely provides that the Commission is to ensure the maintenance of all appropriate relations with the organs of the United Nations. There are thus no express provisions confirming that the Charter or Security Council resolutions are binding on the Community. There is however scope for some further argument, on the basis of a couple of indirect precedents.

First, there is the Court's decision in *International Fruit Company*.[45] There the Court was asked to rule on the question whether a trade regulation was invalid for violation of the provisions of GATT. The Court therefore had to examine whether GATT was binding on the Community, notwithstanding the fact that the Community had never formally become a Contracting Party. The Court's conclusion was positive, on the basis of a number of considerations.[46] When the EEC was established the Member States were GATT Contracting Parties. By concluding a treaty between them they could not withdraw from their obligations to third countries. On the contrary, their desire to observe the GATT undertakings followed from the very provisions of the EEC Treaty and from their declarations in GATT. That intention was made clear in (old) Article 110 EEC, which sought the adherence of

---

[43] S Bohr, 'Sanctions by the United Nations Security Council and the European Community' 4 (1993) EJIL 262–3.

[44] In Case 204/86 *Greece v. Council* [1988] ECR 5323, paras 27–28, the Court declined to examine an alleged breach of a resolution on Cyprus in a challenge to a decision on financial co-operation with Turkey, by stating that the resolution was completely extraneous to relations between the EC and Turkey in the context of the association agreement. In *Bosphorus* (n 15 above), Jacobs AG at para 35 considered that the question whether resolutions bind the EC, though very interesting, did not fall to be decided.

[45] Joined Cases 21 to 24/72 *International Fruit Company v. Produktschap voor Groenten en Fruit* [1972] ECR 1219; see Chs 8 and 9. See also Bohr (n 43 above), 263–5; S Peers, 'Common Foreign and Security Policy' (1998) 18 YEL 671. [46] Ibid, paras 10–18.

the Community to the same aims as those sought by GATT, as well as by the first paragraph of (old) Article 234 EC on pre-EEC international commitments. The Community had assumed the functions inherent in the tariff and trade policy by virtue of (old) Articles 111 and 113 EEC. By conferring those powers on the Community, the Member States showed their wish to bind it by the obligations entered into under GATT. Since the entry into force of the EEC Treaty and the setting up of the common external tariff the transfer of powers had been put into concrete form in different ways within the framework of the GATT and had been recognized by the other contracting parties. The Community had appeared as a partner in tariff negotiations and as a party to all types of agreement in the framework of GATT. It therefore appeared that, in so far as under the EEC Treaty the Community had assumed the powers previously exercised by Member States in the area governed by GATT, the provisions of that agreement had the effect of binding the Community.

Much of that reasoning can be transposed to the relationship between the UN Charter and the EC, in so far as Security Council resolutions are concerned.[47] All the Member States are members of the United Nations. That in itself cannot be sufficient for concluding that the Charter is binding, for it would mean that all international agreements which are binding on all the Member States are *ipso facto* binding on the Community, and there is no basis for such a broad claim in either the Treaty or the case law of the Court of Justice. It is none the less a condition which is fulfilled. The further condition in *International Fruit Company* of a transfer of powers to the Community is also fulfilled, at least in so far as economic sanctions are concerned. Under Articles 301 and 60 EC there is now express competence for the adoption of such sanctions. It may be doubtful whether that competence is exclusive in character, in contrast to the common commercial policy, but in *International Fruit Company* the Court did not refer to exclusive competence— indeed it had not yet decided the issue.[48] Nor, in so far as one may detect an underlying rationale, would exclusive competence be required. The reasoning of the Court appears to be that the commitments under international agreements binding on all Member States need to be transferred to the Community where the Community may exercise powers in areas covered by such agreements. Such a transfer may prevent the Community from acting in breach of such commitments, which is highly desirable to avoid putting both the Community and its Member States in an awkward position: in the case of conflict the Member States would have to choose between their international and Community law obligations, and would be entitled under Article 307 EC to opt for the former, thereby rendering Community law ineffective. As the Community adopts economic sanctions under Articles 301 and 60 EC, mostly in implementation of Security Council resolutions, the transfer-of-powers reasoning would extend to the obligation to respect those resolutions.

---

[47] Cf Kaddous (n 41 above), 423–4.
[48] See *Opinion 1/75 re Local Cost Standard* [1975] ECR 1355.

However, in *International Fruit Company* the Court referred to a further element, namely the fact that the Community had in effect replaced the Member States in the framework of GATT. No such substitution has so far taken place in the UN or in the Security Council, even though the latter no doubt recognizes the role played by the Community. It would therefore remain to be seen to what extent the condition of substitution is essential, and, if so, whether it is fulfilled in the case of economic sanctions.[49]

Secondly, in addition to *International Fruit Company* there is the case law on international law generally. There are a number of rather vague and all-encompassing statements by the Court of Justice, such as that the Community must respect international law in the exercise of its powers.[50] The precise purport of such statements is not clear, and it is true that the relevant cases concerned rules of customary international law. The UN Charter is not among such rules, nor are resolutions of the Security Council. The statements could none the less be cited in a decision by the Court to characterize the Charter and the Security Council's efforts to maintain international peace and security as so vital for the international legal order that resolutions should be considered binding on the Community.

Thirdly, there may be some analogy with the legal treatment of international human rights instruments to which all the Member States are parties. In the absence, before the adoption of the Charter of Fundamental Rights, of a written catalogue of such rights, the Court developed the concept of general principles of EC law, which include fundamental rights as protected under such international instruments. The prime instance is the ECHR. The UN Charter is not of course a human rights instrument, and its provisions could hardly be characterized as general principles of EC law. It is none the less indicative that the Court seeks to give effect to human rights treaties to which all Member States are parties. From that perspective it may also be inclined to give effect to the UN Charter, again in light of its vital character for the international legal order.

In conclusion, the Court might well, if the question were ever to come before it, be inclined to recognize the binding character of the UN Charter and of Security Council resolutions, and could find support for such recognition in its own case law. However, a further question would then arise as to the precise legal effects of e.g. a resolution. In the case of GATT the Court accepted that the agreement was binding, but it did not recognize its direct effect. Could a Security Council resolution have direct effect? Could it confer rights on private parties? In practice, this would not be straightforward. The object of nearly all sanctions resolutions is to restrict the rights of certain private parties, rather than to expand and confirm them. Could a resolution which was not or was wrongly implemented be invoked, on the basis of Community law, against a private party? The analogy of directives comes to mind: as directives are addressed to the Member States they cannot, as such, impose

---

[49] Cf K Lenaerts and E De Smijter, 'The United Nations and the European Union: Living Apart Together', in K Wellens (ed), *International Law: Theory and Practice—Essays in Honour of Eric Suy* (Martinus Nijhoff, 1998) 447–8. [50] See Ch 9.

obligations on private parties.[51] Resolutions are similarly addressed to States, and there is clearly no basis for accepting that they are of themselves binding on individuals. The Community or a Member State could thus not rely on a resolution as against an individual. Could a resolution be relied upon to invalidate or annul a Community act? One feels inclined to argue that the Member States, at least, should be capable of making such a challenge, as they are members of the UN and therefore have a clear interest in ensuring that the Community does not violate Security Council resolutions. On the basis of *International Fruit Company*[52] and *Germany v. Council (bananas)*,[53] however, it seems that direct effect of the international rule is a precondition, even in the context of actions by Member States.[54]

If the UN Charter and Security Council resolutions were binding, a further question would concern the effect of decisions of the various sanctions committees, instructed by the Security Council to supervise the implementation of sanctions. As is clear from the practice of adopting such resolutions, including the above case law, the opinions of those committees are most influential, and are probably considered politically if not legally, binding, by most public authorities, both at a national and at a Community level. In *Bosphorus* Jacobs AG emphasized the importance of such committees, and stated that their views must carry considerable weight. He declined to regard the opinion of the Yugoslavia Sanctions Committee in that case as binding, 'if only because such an effect [was] not provided for by the relevant provisions of the resolutions'. He thus did not rule out that the approach might be different in cases where a resolution required prior approval, for example of a particular export transaction, by the competent committee.[55] If, where a committee has the power to make decisions in the context of sanctions, such decisions have the effect of binding the Community, awkward questions may arise. That is so particularly in light of the Security Council's recent anti-terrorism practice of freezing the assets of individuals.[56] What if, in a challenge to the legality of a Community implementing decision, it is shown that the inclusion of a person was wholly erroneous and violates that person's fundamental rights? If the source of the inclusion is a sanctions committee's decision, which rule would then take precedence: the protection of fundamental rights as general principles of EC law or the decision of the UN sanctions committee?

The second issue to be addressed in this section is whether there is scope for the Member States to give precedence to their obligations under the Charter, and thus not to apply Community law. It is indeed not inconceivable that there is a conflict

---

[51] Case 152/84 *Marshall v. Southampton and South-West Hampshire Area Health Authority (Teaching)* [1986] ECR 723, para 48.   [52] N 45 above.
[53] Case C–280/93 *Germany v. Council* [1994] ECR I–4973.   [54] Ch 8.
[55] *Bosphorus* (n 15 above), para 46.
[56] See e.g. Council Regulation 881/2002 imposing certain specific restrictive measures directed against certain persons and entities associated with Usama bin Laden, the Al-Qaida network, and the Taliban, and repealing Council Regulation (EC) No 467/2001 prohibiting the export of certain goods and services to Afghanistan, strengthening the flight ban and extending the freeze of funds and other financial resources in respect of the Taliban of Afghanistan [2002] OJ L139/9, which refers to several Resolutions.

between the provisions of a resolution and provisions of Community law. According to Article 103 of the UN Charter, in the event of a conflict between the obligations of the UN members under the Charter and their obligations under any other international agreement, their obligations under the Charter shall prevail. The position is therefore clear cut under international law: EU Member States are required to give precedence to obligations under the Charter. In any event, if the Charter were binding on the Community, Article 103 of the Charter would itself be a norm of Community law, and EC law provisions in breach of the Charter could be considered unlawful. However, the Member States would not even need to argue that the Charter is binding on the Community for the purpose of being permitted not to apply Community law. Article 307, first paragraph, according to which pre-E(E)C rights and obligations arising from agreements with one or more third countries are not affected by the provisions of the EC Treaty, regulates the matter.[57] The UN Charter is such an agreement for all the Member States, and they are therefore entitled not to fulfil their obligations under the EC Treaty if doing so would put them in breach of their obligations under the Charter.

Indeed this was argued in the *Centro-Com* case,[58] where the second question which the Court of Appeal referred to the Court of Justice concerned the scope of (current) Article 307. The argument of the United Kingdom was that its new policy on the release of funds was required to ensure the effectiveness of the sanctions imposed by Resolution 757 (1992). The Court recalled its settled case law, according to which the purpose of the first paragraph of (current) Article 307 EC is to make clear, in accordance with the principles of international law, that application of the Treaty does not affect the commitment of the Member State concerned to respect the rights of non-member States under an earlier agreement and to comply with its corresponding obligations. Consequently, in order to determine whether a Community rule could be deprived of effect by an earlier international agreement, it was necessary to examine whether that agreement imposed on the Member State concerned obligations whose performance could still be required by non-member States which were parties to it. The Court then pointed out that, in proceedings for a preliminary ruling, it was not for the Court but for the national court to determine which obligations were imposed by an earlier agreement on the Member State concerned and to ascertain their ambit so as to be able to determine the extent to which they thwarted application of the provisions of Community law in question. It therefore instructed the national court to examine whether, in the circumstances of the case before it, in which exports were approved by the United Nations Sanctions Committee and authorized by the competent authorities in the country of export, both the change of policy and the four decisions refusing to allow funds to be released were necessary in order to ensure that the Member State concerned performed its obligations under the UN Charter and under Resolution 757 (1992). The Court concluded its reasoning by recalling that, in any event, when

---

[57] See Ch 9.   [58] N 28 above.

an international agreement allowed, but did not require, a Member State to adopt
a measure which appeared to be contrary to Community law, the Member State
had to refrain from adopting such a measure.[59]

When reading the judgment one senses that the Court was not itself convinced
by the United Kingdom argument that its change of policy on the release of funds
was required to meet its obligations under the UN Charter. The Court felt the need
to refer to the circumstances of the case, in particular the approval of the exports by
the Sanctions Committee and the export authorization by Italy, and then added that
Article 307 covers only action which is required by the agreement in question. The
Court was however constrained by its previous case law, according to which it is for
the national court to determine the extent of a Member State's obligations.

The *Centro-Com* case shows what may in effect be the real issue concerning the
application of Article 307 EC with respect to Security Council resolutions. The legal
principle is not in any doubt: the Member States are entitled to give precedence to
their obligations under the UN Charter. The real issue is the locus of interpretation
and decision. Can a Member State freely determine the extent and effect of its UN
obligations, and can it freely decide that derogation from Community law is required?
Surely there must be some degree of supervision, for otherwise Article 307 EC may
amount to a blank cheque. Nearly all of the cases on Article 307 EC have been
requests for a preliminary ruling, and in that context it is no doubt appropriate for
the Court to leave the ultimate decision on the international obligations of the
Member State concerned to the national court. Indeed, the Court appears to have
no jurisdiction to make that decision, as its jurisdiction is limited to the interpretation (and validity) of Community law. In other types of proceedings, however,
the Court's jurisdiction may be more extensive. Enforcement proceedings under
Article 226 EC require the Court to determine whether a Member State fulfils its obligations under the Treaty. Where the Commission brings such a case on the basis that
a Member State was not in specific circumstances entitled to invoke Article 307 EC
the Court would surely need to look into the obligations imposed on that Member
State under the international agreement in question, for it is otherwise not in a position to exercise its jurisdiction. Even then, the Court may have to be more circumspect than in a case turning only on Community law. Some basic principles could
none the less be introduced. For example, where there is no clear-cut conflict
between the Member State's international obligations and the provisions of
Community law (such as in the *Centro-Com* case), the Court could hold that the
burden of proving such conflict rests on the Member State in question. In the context of preliminary rulings, the Court could emphasize that the national court must
itself be satisfied that the Member State's action is required under its international
obligations, and that it should not simply defer to the views of that Member State's
executive. The Court could also decide to rule on the issue itself, where it is manifest
that arguments based on Article 307 EC are unfounded.

---

[59] N 28 above, paras 56–60.

There appears to be another basis in the EC Treaty for recognizing an autonomous national power for the implementation of Security Council resolutions, enabling the Member States to derogate from their Community law obligations. Article 297 EC provides that the Member States shall consult each other with a view to together taking the steps needed to prevent the functioning of the common market being affected by measures which a Member State may be called upon to take *inter alia* in order to carry out obligations it has accepted for the purpose of maintaining peace and international security. In the literature it has been argued that this provision establishes a 'reserve of sovereignty' which could not be overridden by a commercial policy measure[60] (or, by analogy, a sanctions regulation). The case law of the Court of Justice, however, appears to treat Article 297 as an exception along with other exceptions. In *Johnston* the Court listed all 'public safety' exceptions in the Treaty (current Articles 30, 39, 46, 296, and 297), and held that they dealt with exceptional and clearly defined cases, and that because of their limited character those articles did not lend themselves to a wide interpretation.[61] The Court also stated that Article 297 concerned a wholly exceptional situation,[62] but there can be no doubt that the implementation of Security Council resolutions comes within the provision's scope. If Article 297 EC is an exception rather than a reserve of sovereignty, the legal position is that a Member State could rely on this provision to justify derogating from its obligations under the Treaty.[63] As such it would not in the context of obligations under the UN Charter seem to add much to the effect of Article 307 EC, discussed above. In fact it is arguable that Article 297 is *lex specialis* to Article 307 in the area of implementation of Security Council resolutions.

Would there be reasons for contending that, in light of the specific language of Article 297 EC, review by the Court of Justice of a Member State's use of that provision, as a basis for derogating from Community law, would need to be more limited than in the context of other exceptions or derogations, or in the context of Article 307 EC? In the FYROM case, discussed below,[64] Jacobs AG argued that judicial review of whether a Member State was justified in acting in a context of 'serious international tension constituting a threat of war', also referred to in Article 297 EC, had to be severely limited (see below). It is however submitted that the reasons which led the Advocate General to that conclusion, which were connected with the nature of the issues which war and a threat of war raise, cannot be transposed to the implementation of Security Council resolutions. There is no

---

[60] Cf I Canor, ' "Can Two Walk Together, Except They be Agreed?"—The Relationship Between International Law and European Law: The Incorporation of United Nations Sanctions Against Yugoslavia Into European Community Law Through the Perspective of the European Court of Justice' (1998) 35 CMLRev 172–3.

[61] Case 222/84 *Johnston v. Chief Constable of the Royal Ulster Constabulary* [1986] ECR 1651, para 26, confirmed in Case C–273/97 *Sirdar* [1999] ECR I–7403, para 16.

[62] *Johnston* (n 61 above), para 27.

[63] In *Sirdar* (n 61 above) La Pergola AG speaks of derogations from the system of the common market (para 21); he does not accept that the matter is outside the EC Treaty (para 25).

[64] Case C–120/94 *Commission v. Greece* [1996] ECR I–1513.

paucity of judicially applicable criteria here: it is standard business of courts to compare and interpret legal texts, and to determine the scope of legal obligations.

A further question is whether Article 297 EC can still be relied upon where there is an EC sanctions regulation constituting implementation of a Security Council resolution. In *Centro-Com* the Court took the view that, in so far as the relevant trade rules were laid down in Community law (and thus, in a sense, harmonized), the United Kingdom could no longer rely on the public security exception in Article 11 of the export regulation.[65] As the relevant sanctions regulation provided for a complete regime of prohibited and authorized exports, the Community had occupied the field and there was no further scope for autonomous Member State action. One does not see why the same reasoning would not apply to Article 297 EC.[66] The kind of situation referred to there may be 'wholly exceptional', but where the Community, under the powers conferred by the Treaty, has regulated the matter, the uniformity and effectiveness of Community law is unjustifiably undermined if the Member States none the less continue to benefit from an open-ended derogation such as that in Article 297 EC. Again the matter becomes one of locus of interpretation and decision. Unless a clear conflict between a resolution and the provisions of Community law could be shown, the latter should be respected by all Member States. That must be the proper reading of the current EC Treaty, which on the one hand gives power to the Community to adopt sanctions regulations, and on the other enables a Member State to derogate from its obligations where such derogation is required to carry out obligations for maintaining peace and international security. No such derogation is required where Community law itself constitutes implementation of the Member States' obligations.

Protection of fundamental rights

Economic sanctions are measures which do not simply affect countries or regimes. They have immediate effects, often of a stark nature, on people's or companies' economic activities. Those effects may be such that people's very lives are disrupted or even jeopardized. It is therefore not surprising that economic sanctions are often challenged from a human rights perspective. Such challenges are not confined to the level of policy-making. They may also take the form of legal action. EC economic sanctions, too, are not immune to attack on grounds of human rights violations, as the *Bosphorus* case showed.[67] Such human rights challenges to economic sanctions raise complex issues. Fundamental rights are protected as general principles of EC law, and before the EU Charter of Fundamental Rights was adopted there used to be no written catalogue of such rights. At the time of writing the Charter is still a legal instrument with uncertain legal effects, and the Court of Justice has not yet

---

[65] Regulation 2603/69 (n 14 above).
[66] See Bohr (n 43 above), 267–8. *Contra* R Pavoni, 'UN Sanctions in EU and National Law: The *Centro-Com* Case' (1999) 48 ICLQ 590–1.   [67] N 15 above.

referred to it.[68] Fundamental rights are none the less binding on the EU institutions, and the Court strikes down legal acts which violate such rights. In the case of economic sanctions, however, there is usually a strong political dimension, particularly where the sanctions implement Security Council resolutions. Challenges to EC economic sanctions may in effect be challenges to Security Council decisions, as private parties are not in a position to bring legal actions against Security Council decisions as such. At the level of international law it is not clear whether there is a hierarchical relationship between human rights law and action by the Security Council to maintain peace and international security, in the sense that the former would trump the latter. The discussion is in any event fairly theoretical, as there are no effective means for challenging Security Council decisions.[69] The issue therefore becomes, as it were, decentralized. Within a municipal legal order giving effect to Security Council resolutions, decisions need to be taken as to the relationship between fundamental rights protection and economic sanctions.

In *Bosphorus* the Turkish charter company argued that the impounding of its aircraft was contrary to legal certainty, proportionality, and respect for fundamental rights. Jacobs AG considered that this part of Bosphorus Airways' claim raised an important issue, which led him to examine the issue in some detail. The company specifically referred to the right to peaceful enjoyment of property, which is protected under the ECHR; the latter is for practical purposes part of Community law and can be invoked in the Court of Justice and in national courts where Community law is in issue, particularly where Member States implement Community law. Bosphorus Airways also referred to the right to pursue a commercial activity, which has also been recognized as a fundamental right by the case law of the Court of Justice. Jacobs AG then analysed the right to property as protected under Article 1 of the First Protocol to the ECHR. He carefully examined the relevant case law of the ECtHR, and established that the type of interest which Bosphorus Airways had in the impounded aircraft was covered by the ECHR. Article 1 recognized that States were entitled to control the use of property in accordance with the general interest, but a fair balance had to be struck between the demands of the general interest of the community and the requirements of the protection of the individual's fundamental rights. There were no decisions of the ECtHR dealing specifically with the impounding of assets in implementation of international sanctions, but there were judgments in which the ECtHR recognized that confiscation could be justified as a measure of enforcement against an innocent owner. The Advocate General then analysed the case law of the Court of Justice on the right to property, and referred to the statement in *Hauer* that it was necessary to identify the aim pursued by the disputed regulation and to determine whether there was a reasonable relationship between the measures provided for by the regulation and the aim pursued by the Community.[70] Jacobs AG concluded that the essential question was

[68] The draft Constitution incorporates the Charter.
[69] N Angelet, 'Protest against Security Council Decisions', in Wellens (ed) (n 49 above), 277.
[70] Case 44/79 *Hauer v. Land Rheinland-Pfalz* [1979] ECR 3727, para 23.

whether the obvious interference with Bosphorus Airways' possession of the aircraft was a proportionate measure in the light of the aims of general interest which the sanctions regulation sought to achieve. The Advocate General recognized that the impounding of the aircraft was a severe restriction on the exercise by Bosphorus Airways of its property rights, a restriction difficult to distinguish, in its effects, from a temporary deprivation. On the other hand it was also obvious that there was a particularly strong interest in enforcing embargo measures decided by the UN Security Council. Indeed it was difficult to think of any stronger type of public interest than that of stopping a civil war as devastating as the one which engulfed the former Yugoslavia, and in particular Bosnia-Herzegovina. Unavoidably, the sanctions decided by the international community to put pressure on the FRY affected property rights, including those of innocent economic operators. In that respect Bosphorus Airways was in no way in a unique position, as many others were likely to have suffered severe losses from the embargo measures. That did not mean that any type of interference with the right to property should be tolerated. In the case in issue, however, the Advocate General considered that the decision to impound the aircraft on the ground that it was owned by an undertaking in the FRY could not be regarded as unreasonable, in the light of the aims of the sanctions regulation (see above). He lastly examined the alleged drastic financial and commercial effects of the decision to impound. He pointed out that the financial consequences might vary (a lessee might simply be able to cancel the agreement and lease another aircraft), and did not in any case think that it was possible to set aside a general measure such as the sanctions regulation because of the financial consequences which it could have in a particular case. But even if it were relevant to take account of the losses allegedly incurred, the Advocate General did not think that the principle of proportionality would be infringed, in view of the importance of the public interest involved.[71]

The Court of Justice was shorter in its analysis, but in essence concurred with the reasoning of its Advocate General. It referred to settled case law that the fundamental rights invoked by Bosphorus Airways were not absolute and their exercise could be subject to restrictions justified by objectives of general interest pursued by the Community. It then pointed out that any measure imposing sanctions had, by definition, consequences which affected the right to property and the freedom to pursue a trade or business, thereby causing harm to persons who were in no way responsible for the situation which led to the adoption of sanctions. Moreover, the importance of the aims pursued by the regulation at issue was such as to justify negative consequences, even of a substantial nature, for some operators. The Court then sketched the aims and justifications of the sanctions. It concluded that, as compared with an objective of general interest so fundamental for the international community, which consisted of putting an end to the state of war in the region and to massive violations of human rights and humanitarian international law in the Republic of Bosnia-Herzegovina, the impounding of the aircraft in question, which

---

[71] *Bosphorus* (n 15 above), paras 49–66 of the Opinion of Jacobs AG.

was owned by an undertaking based in or operating from the FRY, could not be regarded as inappropriate or disproportionate.[72]

The judgment in *Bosphorus* has been severely criticized for failing to protect fundamental rights. Canor argues that the Court should have interpreted the sanctions regulation in a manner which afforded protection to Bosphorus Airways' right to property. She deplores that the Court dissociated the question of how to interpret the notion of 'interest' in the sanctions regulation from the issue of fundamental rights protection. In her view the text of the regulation was not as clear as the Court portrayed it, the notion of interest being sufficiently vague to be open to interpretation. Accordingly, it should have been interpreted in such a way that it did not apply to the kind of interest which JAT had in the leased aircraft, over which it did not have day-to-day control, and which could not therefore be used to evade or circumvent the sanctions. The Court should have given precedence to the rights of the innocent lessee.[73]

This critique may appear attractive if one focuses on the particular facts of the case. However, were the approach which Canor advocates to be generalized, the protection afforded to the right to property would be liable to undermine the entire sanctions regime. It is obvious that, in itself, the impounding of the aircraft in question is unlikely to have contributed much to the sanctions. But the same reasoning would be valid for many instances of application of the various sanctions. A specific small import or export transaction, though clearly prohibited under the trade embargo, would also not in itself undermine that embargo. Yet it needs to be prohibited because the sanctions can only be effective through their aggregate effect. Similarly, the Community agent of such a specific transaction could be as innocent as Bosphorus Airways. If, then, Bosphorus Airways' challenge had been successful, it could have opened up an avenue for a flood of litigation undermining the entire sanctions regime. It is, in the context of sanctions, difficult to conceive of a workable approach to human rights protection which focuses on the relationship between the specific facts of the case and the overall purpose of the sanctions. The reasoning of Jacobs AG is persuasive. It is only where the measure is wholly unreasonable that the Court should intervene. In *Bosphorus* that was not the case, because it was possible to see justification for a broad scope of the provision on impounding all means of transport; by contrast, the use of day-to-day operation and control as the decisive criterion could have jeopardized the effectiveness of the strengthening of the sanctions, as it would have allowed the FRY or its nationals to evade application of those sanctions through the mere transfer of day-to-day operation and control of means of transport.

Sanctions by the Member States

It is clear from the above analysis that the EC has extensive powers to adopt economic sanctions, previously on the basis of Article 113 EEC, currently on the

---

[72] Ibid, paras 21–26 of the judgment.   [73] Canor (n 60 above), 137–87.

grounds of Articles 301 and 60 EC. The practice is that virtually all Security Council resolutions imposing sanctions are followed by a CFSP common position, triggering EC sanctions regulations. That is now possible due to the extended legal basis in the Treaty, covering both trade and financial movements.[74] In effect, therefore, the Community occupies the field. The question none the less arises whether there remains scope for action by the Member States in this area. There are several angles to that question.

First, it is obvious that the Member States are under an obligation to implement and apply sanctions regulations adopted by the Community. As *Ebony Maritime* shows,[75] the Member States need to provide for effective, proportionate, and dissuasive penalties, and they are generally required to take all measures necessary to make the sanctions effective. Even if regulations are directly applicable in all the Member States, this requirement of effectiveness will lead to various forms of legislative and executive activity at national level. However, the *Centro-Com* judgment shows the limits of what action a Member State is entitled to take to ensure effectiveness of the sanctions.[76] Derogation from the terms of the applicable regulations is not permitted.

Secondly, what is the position where there are no EC sanctions regulations, or where a particular aspect of sanctions is not regulated at Community level? Is the Community's competence under the EC Treaty to adopt sanctions exclusive? There are no indications in Article 301 that this will be the case; on the contrary, the reference to a prior decision under the CFSP suggests that Community competence is conditional. That is clearly a strong argument against exclusivity: if there is no CFSP sanctions decision, for example because there is no unanimity, the Community cannot adopt sanctions. Surely this signifies that the Member States, which as the Court recognized remain competent in the area of foreign and security policy,[77] have the power to adopt sanctions. However, the position changes if one starts looking at the EC common commercial policy, which comes within the Community's exclusive competence.[78] Economic sanctions at national level cannot in principle be decreed in breach of EC competence in trade matters. Therefore, where a Member State seeks to adopt trade restrictions, let alone a trade embargo, it needs to comply with Community trade legislation.[79] So much follows from *Centro-Com*, where the Court verified whether the United Kingdom policy on the release of funds in payment of authorized export transactions complied with the relevant sanctions regulations *and* with the EC export regulation. The Court was unequivocal, both in that case and in the *Werner* and *Leifer* judgments:[80] measures whose effect is to prevent or restrict the export (or, by analogy, the import) of certain products cannot be treated as falling outside the scope of the common commercial

---

[74] But those provisions do not cover sanctions against individuals; accordingly, Art 308 EC was also referred to as legal basis for e.g. Regulation 881/2002 (n 56 above).   [75] N 20 above.

[76] N 28 above.   [77] Ibid.   [78] Ch 2.

[79] Cf Lenaerts and De Smijter (n 49 above), 449.

[80] Case C–70/94 *Werner v. Germany* [1995] ECR I–3189; Case C–83/94 *Leifer and Others* [1995] ECR I–3231; see Ch 2.

policy on the ground that they have foreign policy and security objectives, and national foreign and security policy measures have to respect the provisions adopted by the Community in the field of the common commercial policy. That does not however mean that there is no scope whatsoever for national economic sanctions affecting trade. The basic commercial policy instruments all contain an exception for public security, and in *Werner* and *Leifer* the Court accepted that a Member State could control exports on the basis of that exception (see below). It did not interpret the public security exception too strictly, as it was satisfied that the German legislation in issue, which not only referred to external security but also to the peaceful co-existence of nations and to Germany's external relations, came within it. On that basis it would be open to a Member State to adopt trade restrictions or an embargo on the ground that this is required from the perspective of public security.

As regards Article 60 EC the position appears different. There the Treaty provision suggests exclusive competence, because Article 60(2) spells out that, without prejudice to Article 297 EC, a Member State may, as long as the Council has not acted, take unilateral measures 'for serious political reasons and on grounds of urgency'. The Member State in question must inform the Commission and the other Member States, and the Council may by qualified majority decide that the Member State concerned shall amend or abolish such measures. Those provisions presuppose that EC competence is exclusive, for if it were concurrent with that of the Member States there would be no need for determining under which, rather exceptional, circumstances the latter may adopt financial sanctions. However, the exclusive character of Community competence is clear even in the absence of Article 60(2). One of the general principles of the Treaty chapter on capital and payments is that all restrictions on payments between Member States and third countries shall be prohibited (Article 56(2)). It is true that Article 57 recognizes and confirms certain restrictions in national law, but only those which existed on 31 December 1993, and from that date onwards only the Council may amend the basic rule of free movement. Any financial sanctions adopted by individual Member States would thus directly interfere with that basic rule and, in the absence of some kind of Treaty basis, be in violation of that rule. That may be the reason for the provisions of Article 60(2). Kuijper reports that the scope for Member States' action was included because financial assets can be removed from Community and Member States' jurisdiction at very short notice and that it may therefore be necessary to act at the very first hint of the flight of assets.[81] That is indeed a difference with a trade embargo, which in any event takes time to implement and produce effect.

In addition to Article 60(2), Article 58(1)(b) allows the Member States to take measures which are justified on grounds of public policy or public security. The observations above on the public security exceptions in the framework of the common commercial policy can therefore be extended to financial sanctions.

---

[81] Kuijper (n 9 above), 391; I Macleod, ID Hendry, and S Hyett, *The External Relations of the European Communities* (OUP, 1996) 355.

The Member States are in principle entitled to restrict financial movements to or from third countries if that is necessary on grounds of public security.

Thirdly, as discussed above in the section on the status of UN Security Council resolutions, the Member States can rely on Article 307 EC to fulfil their obligations under the UN Charter, including their duty to implement Security Council resolutions. Where there is a conflict with provisions of Community law, those international law obligations take precedence.

Finally, there is the provision of Article 297 EC, which refers to measures which a Member State may be called upon to take in the event of serious internal disturbances affecting the maintenance of law and order, in the event of war, serious international tension constituting a threat of war, or in order to carry out obligations it has accepted for the purpose of maintaining peace and international security. The latter ground is discussed above in the section on Security Council resolutions, where this chapter examined to what extent a Member State could derogate from its Community law obligations on the basis of Article 297, so as to implement a resolution. Article 297 can however also be relied upon in the event of serious internal disturbances, war, or serious international tension constituting a threat of war. There has been one case in which a Member State has invoked those exceptions in order to justify a trade embargo. The break-up of Yugoslavia in the early 1990s led to the formation of a number of new States, including the former Yugoslav Republic of Macedonia (FYROM). Greece strongly objected to the use of the name Macedonia, which it regards as part of its own cultural patrimony, and complained that FYROM promoted the idea of a unified Macedonia. After a series of further developments, interventions, and negotiations, culminating in the official recognition of FYROM by a number of EU Member States and by the United States, Greece adopted a trade embargo against its neighbour. In February 1994 it unilaterally prohibited trade, in particular via the port of Thessaloniki, in products originating in, coming from, or destined for FYROM, and imports into Greece of products originating in or coming from that Republic. It was clear that the embargo was in breach of the applicable EC law rules and instruments on trade with FYROM. Greece relied on (current) Article 297 EC, and the Commission immediately brought an action under Article 298 EC, which, by derogation from Articles 226 and 227, allows the Commission or any Member State to bring the matter directly before the Court of Justice if it considers that a Member State is making improper use of the powers provided for in Articles 296 and 297.

The Court never ruled on the Commission's action because the case was withdrawn after Jacobs AG delivered his Opinion, which therefore represents the only judicial authority.[82] The Advocate General first examined whether there were 'serious internal disturbances affecting the maintenance of law and order'. He took as a starting point that the situations covered by Article 297 were 'wholly exceptional',[83] as evidenced by the fact that they permitted suspension of all the ordinary rules

---

[82] *Commission v. Greece* (n 64 above).   [83] See *Johnston* (n 61 above).

governing the common market. He therefore considered that the provision envisaged a situation verging on a total collapse of internal security. In his opinion Greece had clearly failed to establish that in the absence of the trade embargo against FYROM civil disturbances would have taken place on such a scale that the means at its disposal for maintaining law and order would have been insufficient. Greece had made only vague and unsubstantiated assertions about massive demonstrations. The Advocate General therefore rejected the idea that Greece could rely on that particular ground in Article 297 EC.

Jacobs AG next considered whether Greece could invoke the notions of war or serious international tension constituting a threat of war. He considered that this question was far more complex and raised the fundamental issue of the Court's power to exercise judicial review in such cases. Whilst it was plain that the Court had power to review the legality of action taken by a Member State under this heading, the scope and intensity of such review were severely limited on account of the nature of the issues raised. There was a paucity of judicially applicable criteria, he argued, that would permit the Court, or any other court, to determine whether serious international tension existed and whether such tension constituted a threat of war.[84] That is a theme which runs through the whole Opinion. The Advocate General reiterated it when he looked at the Commission's argument that the action taken by Greece was likely to increase tension and thus adversely affect the internal and external security of Greece: that was very much a policitical assessment of an eminently political question, and there simply were no juridical tools of analysis for approaching such problems.[85] He also returned to the point when he examined whether Greece had made 'improper use' (see Article 298) of the powers provided for in Article 297. Again, if a Member State considered, rightly or wrongly, that the attitude of a third State threatened its vital interest, its territorial integrity, or its very existence, it was for the Member State and not for the Court of Justice to determine how to respond to that perceived threat, and there were no judicial criteria by which such matters could be measured. It was difficult to identify a precise legal test for determining whether a trade embargo was a suitable means of pursuing a political dispute between a Member State and a third country.[86]

Another theme which runs through the Opinion is that the question whether there was international tension constituting a threat of war had to be looked at, not from some outside objective perspective, but from the subjective point of view of the Member State concerned. War was by nature an unpredictable occurrence and the transition from sabre rattling to armed conflict could be swift and dramatic.[87] If the matter was looked at from Greece's subjective point of view and if due weight was attached to the geopolitical environment and the history of ethnic strife, border disputes, and general instability that had characterized the Balkans for centuries, then it could not be said that Greece was acting wholly unreasonably by taking the

---

[84] *Commission v. Greece* (n 64 above), paras 50–51 of the Opinion of Jacobs AG.
[85] Ibid, para 59.   [86] Ibid, para 65.   [87] Ibid, paras 54 and 52.

view that the tension between itself and FYROM bore within it the threat—even if it was long-term and remote—of war.[88] The Advocate General also referred to case law of the ECtHR according to which issues of national security were primarily a matter for the appraisal of the authorities of the State concerned.[89]

The Advocate General also stressed, perhaps to some degree in contrast to his other Opinions on trade and foreign policy,[90] that Article 297 EC recognized that foreign policy remained essentially a matter for the individual Member States, and that the Member States retained ultimate responsibility for their relations with third States. Notwithstanding the co-operation pursued within the framework of the provisions introduced by the SEA and the TEU, it was still for each Member State to decide in the light of its own interests whether to recognize a third State and on what footing to place its relations with such a State.[91] Articles 297 and 298 EC recognized that the autonomy left to Member States in the field of foreign policy was in stark contrast to the integration achieved in the field of economic and commercial policy, and they attempted to define the outer limits of the autonomy left to the Member States in the field of foreign policy.[92]

Jacobs AG also considered that there were no indications that Greece had made improper use of its powers in the sense of affording protection, instituting discrimination, or taking disproportionate action. As regards proportionality, he pointed out that the effect on the common market was the appropriate benchmark. As the embargo affected a tiny percentage of the total volume of Community trade and was unlikely to have any perceptible impact on the competitive situation in the Community, there was clearly no breach of the principle of proportionality.[93] Accordingly the Advocate General proposed that the Commission's action be dismissed.

The Opinion of Jacobs AG in the *FYROM* case is the EU judicial text which comes closest to establishing some kind of political question doctrine in the framework of EU constitutional law.[94] The emphasis on severely limited judicial review, on the paucity of judicially applicable criteria, and on the eminently political character of the issues involved may create an impression of judicial abdication in the face of a Member State's claims under Article 297 EC. The Advocate General also referred to similar approaches under German, United Kingdom, and ECHR law in support of judicial deference. However, the general language used does not perhaps completely match the type of review actually undertaken. Jacobs AG was surely right to point out that wars may flare up rather unexpectedly, and that a lot, if not everything, depends on the perception in the countries involved. The serious tension between Greece and *FYROM* was undeniable, as was the history of ethnic violence and conflict in the Balkans. On the facts, therefore, judicial deference and

---

[88] *Commission v. Greece* (n 64 above), para 56 of the Opinion of Jacobs AG.   [89] Ibid, para 55.
[90] Canor (n 60 above), 166.
[91] *Commission v. Greece* (n 64 above), para 64 of the Opinion of Jacobs AG.
[92] Ibid, para 66.   [93] Ibid, paras 69–72.
[94] It is perhaps no coincidence that Jacobs AG cites TM Franck, *Political Questions/Judicial Answers* (Princeton University Press, 1992).

acceptance were clearly warranted, and the Advocate General took great care in examining and reflecting on those facts. It is moreover doubtful whether such highly charged political issues can in any way be resolved by a judicial ruling.

The approach by Jacobs AG is warranted in the case of war, a situation which in any event will rarely be in doubt, or serious international tension constituting a threat of war. It should not be extended to the other grounds for Member State action, i.e. serious internal disturbances and obligations to maintain peace and international security. Indeed the Advocate General clearly distinguished the case of serious internal disturbances, swiftly discarding Greece's claim based on that limb of Article 297 EC as being unsubstantiated, and emphasizing that those disturbances should verge on a complete internal collapse. As regards obligations to maintain peace and international security, which were not in issue in the *FYROM* case, the observation that there are few judicially applicable criteria would clearly be incorrect. Determining the extent of a Member State's international obligations surely requires some degree of legal analysis which a court is perfectly capable of carrying out, even if there may be a margin of political appreciation.

The Advocate General also emphasized national competence as regards foreign and security policy. Here one wonders whether the emphasis has not shifted in the meantime. It is undeniable that there has been more movement towards common action in this area, not just in practice but also at constitutional level.[95] From that angle one should ask the question whether today, if a Member State were to find itself in a situation such as that of Greece, and the case were to come before the Court, that Member State should not have to prove that it has sufficiently attempted to follow the CFSP route, by involving the EU as a whole in negotiations aimed at reducing international tension. If a Member State can derogate from any of its common market obligations (effectively any of its Treaty obligations), then it is not excessive to require that Member State first to exhaust the EU political and diplomatic mechanisms and channels. The Court could exercise at least some review of that process.

Export controls

Within the same general context of interfaces between trade and foreign policy come policies concerning controls on exports of products and technologies which are sensitive from the perspective of external and international security. Ever since World War II and the subsequent Cold War, Western countries have operated sophisticated and secretive export control systems. Those systems not only concern arms and military material, i.e. products which are covered by the derogation clause in Article 296 EC, a provision which is not further analysed here. The now defunct COCOM framework of controlling exports to Communist countries during the Cold War focused on exports of dual-use goods, i.e. products which can be used for

---

[95] See the strengthening of CFSP by the Treaty of Amsterdam and the further strengthening in the draft Constitution.

both civil and military purposes. In the post-Cold War era and the current post-September 11 era that focus is maintained, even if there have been fundamental shifts in the predominant issues of international security. It is not difficult to grasp the broad scope of the notion of dual-use goods in highly technological societies. In the context of the European Union, this means that export control policies may affect a significant percentage of exports. In EU constitutional terms, therefore, this is another policy area where exclusive EC competence for trade policy meets foreign and security policy, both at the level of Member States and in the context of the CFSP.

This section first analyses case law on autonomous export controls by the Member States. It then turns to the developing EU policies in this area.

Member State action

The COCOM export control system was one in which nearly all Member States participated, without any involvement of the EC institutions. It took until 1991 before questions about the relationship between that system and EC law were referred to the Court of Justice. The case of *Richardt and 'Les Accessoires Scientifiques'*[96] had its origin in a contract which Mr Richardt concluded in 1984 with the Soviet central purchasing agency, Technopromimport, for the supply of a unit for the production of bubble memory circuits. The unit was said to be for use by the Soviet post office. Part of the unit was a so-called ten-inch microetch, manufactured in the US. Mr Richardt's company, LAS, applied to the competent French authority for a licence permitting the export of the entire unit to the Soviet Union, and was informed that no licence was required for *inter alia* the microetch. A contract was concluded with Air France for the transport of the microetch from Roissy to Moscow on board an Aeroflot flight which was due to leave Roissy on 14 May 1985. The flight from Roissy was cancelled, however, and Air France decided to transport the cargo to Luxembourg, from where there was an alternative Aeroflot flight. However, the Luxembourg authorities seized the microetch as it was being loaded on the plane. They took the view that under the relevant Grand Ducal regulation an export licence was required. Criminal proceedings were instituted against Mr Richardt and four other defendants, and after protracted proceedings the Luxembourg *Cour de Cassation* (Court of Cassation) referred to the Court of Justice a question concerning the impact of Community law. The question focused on the effect of a document (T1), issued pursuant to an EC regulation on transit, under cover of which the export had been due to take place. The *Cour de Cassation* inquired whether that document constituted unreserved valid authorization for the transit operation, irrespective of the nature of the goods transported and even if they endangered the external security of the State concerned, or whether, conversely, the regulation allowed a Member State to refuse to recognize the document when

---

[96] Case C–367/89 *Richardt and 'Les Accessoires Scientifiques'* [1991] ECR I–4621.

the national legislation considered the goods to be transported to be strategic equipment and, on external security grounds, made transit through its territory subject to the grant of special permission.

Jacobs AG considered that the transit regulation was in fact irrelevant as, at the time of the facts, the transit from France to Luxembourg had been completed. Rather, the dispute was concerned with the transport of the microetch from Luxembourg to the Soviet Union. Accordingly, the Advocate General examined the seizure by the Luxembourg authorities from the perspective of the common commercial policy, and in particular Regulation 2603/69 on exports.[97] He took the view that the seizure was in breach of the principle of free exportation for which the regulation provides, but could be justified under Article 11.[98] He had no doubt that the concept of public security was in principle broad enough to embrace restrictions on the transfer of goods or technology of strategic importance to countries which were thought to pose a military threat. He also referred to the principle of proportionality, which had to be complied with.[99]

The Opinion of Jacobs AG contained, in a nutshell, the approach which the Court was to follow in all other cases on trade and foreign policy. In the *Richardt* judgment, however, the Court did not refer to the common commercial policy. It did not concur with the Advocate General's analysis of the relevance of that policy, and considered that the problem was indeed one of intra-Community transit. Accordingly, it examined the seizure and confiscation of the microetch from the angle of (current) Article 30 EC. It recalled that Article 30 did not constitute a reserve of exclusive jurisdiction of the Member States, but rather an exception to the fundamental rule of free movement of goods, to be strictly interpreted. It also recalled the principle of proportionality, which required that a Member State take the least restrictive measure. However, the Court also accepted that the concept of public security covered both a Member State's internal security and its external security. It was common ground, the Court stated, that the importation, exportation, and transit of goods capable of being used for strategic purposes could affect the public security of a Member State. Accordingly, the Member States were entitled to make transit subject to the grant of a special authorization. As regards penalties, the Court added that a measure involving seizure or confiscation could be considered disproportionate in a case where the return of the goods to the Member State of origin could suffice. However, it was for the national court to determine whether the system complied with the principle of proportionality, taking account of all the elements of each case, such as the nature of the goods, the circumstances in which the breach was committed, and whether or not the trader was acting in good faith.[100]

Even if the Court did not in this case examine the restrictions from the angle of the common commercial policy, its approach contained many of the ingredients

---

[97] N 14 above.   [98] See above.
[99] *Richardt* (n 96 above), paras 13–29 of the Opinion of Jacobs AG.
[100] Ibid, paras 11–25 of the judgment.

of the subsequent case law: no reserved competences for the Member States, a broad
interpretation of the notion of public security, and application of the principle of
proportionality. It is also worth comparing the ruling in *Richardt* with that in
Centro-Com.[101] The difference is that, in *Richardt*, the fact that the French authorities
had authorized the exportation did not in any way bind the Luxembourg authorities, whereas in *Centro-Com* the United Kingdom was in essence required to respect
the export authorization granted by the Italian authorities. The justification for these
contrasting approaches lies in the fact that in the latter case there was Community
legislation in the matter, regulating the authorization of exports, whereas there was
no harmonization of export controls at Community level at the time of *Richardt*.

The *Richardt* case came at a time when the Community was in the process
of completing the internal market, and it highlighted the fact that the absence of
a Community policy on export controls was liable to affect, not just external
trade and the common commercial policy, but also the internal market. This led
to attempts to realize some degree of harmonization, as discussed in the next
subsection.

A couple of years later the Court was confronted with two references by German
courts where it was indisputable that the cases concerned external trade rather than
the internal market. *Werner v. Germany* related to the export to Libya of a vacuum
induction smelting and cast oven, for which Firma Fritz Werner Industrie-
Ausrüstungen GmbH had requested an export authorization, which had been
refused.[102] In *Leifer and Others* a number of people were criminally prosecuted for illegal export to Iraq, in the years 1984 to 1988, of plant, parts of plant, and chemicals.[103]
The German legislation in issue in both cases was the *Aussenwirtschaftsgesetz* (Law on
Foreign Trade, 'AWG'). Under paragraph 7(1) of the AWG contracts and activities
in the sphere of foreign trade could be curtailed in order to:

—guarantee the security of the Federal Republic of Germany;
—prevent a disturbance of peaceful coexistence;
—prevent the external relations of the Federal Republic of Germany from
   being seriously disrupted.

In issue in the *Werner* case were German regulations implementing the AWG and
subjecting the export to Libya of the type of oven in question to the issue of an
export licence. The justification was that it could be used by Libya for the production of missiles, and that Libya was suspected of attempting to produce medium-
range missiles, capable of reaching countries such as Israel and Italy. The Werner
company did not obtain an export authorization, and challenged that decision. The
Verwaltungsgericht (Administrative Court) Frankfurt am Main referred to the Court
the question whether (current) Article 133 EC precluded national provisions on
foreign trade requiring a licence for the export of a vacuum induction oven to
Libya which was refused on the ground that refusal was necessary in order to

---

[101] N 28 above.   [102] *Werner* (n 80 above).   [103] *Leifer and Others* (n 80 above).

protect the public security of the Member State owing to a feared disruption of foreign relations.

In *Leifer* the German authorities had, in 1984, amended the export control regulations implementing the AWG as a reaction to indications that Iraq was developing chemical weapons and had procured certain installations from a German firm. In the criminal proceedings against Leifer and others the *Landgericht* (Regional Court) Darmstadt had doubts regarding German competence to regulate export controls in the light of the common commercial policy. It referred to the Court of Justice questions regarding the effect of (current) Articles 133, 296, and 297 EC, and of the EC export regulation.[104] The national court was in particular uncertain whether national rules were capable of being justified, even if they were not aimed at safeguarding the security of the Member State in question, but were merely aimed at preventing considerable disturbance of the peaceful co-existence of nations or at preventing the external relations of the Member State concerned from being seriously disrupted. The *Landgericht* also referred questions on the burden of proof and on penalties.

The Court decided the two cases on the same day, and the judgments run in parallel, largely following the Opinion of (again) Jacobs AG. The Court started by pointing out that (current) Article 133 EC provided for a common commercial policy based on uniform principles, and that implementation of such a policy required a non-restrictive interpretation. It followed that measures such as those in issue in the two cases, whose effect was to prevent or restrict the export of certain products, could not be treated as falling outside the scope of the common commercial policy on the ground that they had foreign policy and security objectives. The specific subject matter of commercial policy required that a Member State should not be able to restrict its scope by freely deciding, in the light of its own foreign policy or security requirements, whether a measure was covered by Article 133. Since full responsibility for commercial policy was transferred to the Community, national measures of commercial policy were permissible only if they were specifically authorized by the Community.[105]

The Court subsequently examined the effect of the export regulation. Article 1 of that regulation prohibited quantitative restrictions (and not, expressly, measures having equivalent effect), and the first question was whether a national requirement for an export licence constituted a quantitative restriction in the meaning of that provision. The Court pointed out that in interpreting a provision of Community law it was necessary to consider not only its wording but also the context in which it occurred and the objectives of the rules of which it was part. A regulation based on Article 133 EC, whose objective was to implement the principle of free export at Community level, could not exclude from its scope measures adopted by the Member States whose effect was equivalent to a quantitative restriction where their application could lead, as was the case, to an export prohibition. That finding was

---

[104] N 14 above.   [105] *Werner* (n 80 above), paras 8–12; *Leifer* (n 80 above), paras 8–12.

moreover supported by Article XI GATT, which was relevant for the purpose of interpreting a Community instrument governing international trade.[106]

Having established that the German legislation was contrary to Article 1 of the export regulation, the Court examined whether it could be justified under Article 11, which referred to public security. The specific issue here was whether the German legislation could refer, in addition to the security of the Federal Republic, to the risk of disturbance of Germany's foreign relations and to peaceful coexistence of nations. The Court recalled its ruling in *Richardt and 'Les Accessoires Scientifiques'*,[107] according to which the concept of public security within the meaning of (current) Article 30 EC covered both a Member State's internal and external security. To interpret the concept more restrictively when it was used in Article 11 of the export regulation would be tantamount to authorizing the Member States to restrict the movement of goods within the internal market more than movement between them and non-member countries. The Court then referred to the Opinion of Jacobs AG, where the Advocate General had concentrated on the fact that it was difficult to draw a hard-and-fast distinction between foreign-policy and security-policy considerations, as well as to the fact that it was becoming increasingly less possible to look at the security of a State in isolation, since it was linked to the security of the international community at large, and of its various components. The Court therefore concluded that the risk of a serious disturbance to foreign relations or to peaceful coexistence of nations could affect the security of a Member State.[108] In *Leifer* it added that it was therefore unnecessary to examine whether the legislation could also be justified under Article 296 or 297 EC.[109]

Also in *Leifer* the Court then considered proportionality. Since Article 11 formed an exception to the principle of the freedom to export laid down in Article 1 it had to be interpreted in a way which did not extend its effects beyond what was necessary for the protection of the interests which it was intended to guarantee. The Court then recalled the various components of the proportionality test. However, it added that, depending on the circumstances, the competent national authorities had a certain degree of discretion when adopting measures which they considered to be necessary in order to guarantee public security. When the export of dual-use goods involved a threat to the public security of a Member State, those measures could include a requirement that an applicant for an export licence show that the goods were for civil use and also, having regard to specific circumstances such as *inter alia* the political situation in the country of destination, that a licence be refused if those goods were objectively suitable for military use. On the issue of criminal penalties for breaches of the licensing procedures, the Court again referred to proportionality. It recalled the criteria identified in *Richardt and 'Les Accessoires Scientifiques'*:[110] the national court had to take account of all the elements of each case, such as the nature

---

[106] Art XI speaks of 'prohibitions or restrictions other than duties, taxes or other charges, whether made effective through quotas, import or export licences or other measures'.   [107] N 96 above.
[108] *Werner* (n 80 above), paras 14–27; *Leifer* (n 80 above), paras 15–28.   [109] Ibid, para 31.
[110] N 96 above.

of the goods capable of endangering the security of the State, the circumstances in which the breach was committed, and whether or not the trader who had illegally exported the goods was acting in good or bad faith.[111] The Court finally confirmed the direct effect of the export regulation, in particular Article 1; that was not affected by the exceptions in Article 11 since they were open to judicial review.[112]

No further cases have come before the Court on national export controls, in part doubtless because of the establishment in 1994 of an EU regime for such controls (see the next section). The judgments in *Richardt and 'Les Accessoires Scientifiques'*, *Werner v. Germany*, and *Leifer and Others* may at first reading appear to subject national export controls to strict supervision as to their compliance with the rules and principles of the common commercial policy. The Court is unwilling to accept that their foreign policy and security objectives are capable of taking such controls outside the scope of Community law. However, a closer reading reveals that the Court essentially struck a balance between the demands of the common commercial policy and national export control policies, a balance which is not too intrusive for the latter. Indeed, the Court was willing to adopt a broad interpretation of the notion of public security, effectively expanding it so that it generally covers national foreign and security policies. That follows from the Court's acceptance of the three criteria in the German AWG. It based such acceptance on its assessment, taken from the Opinion of Jacobs AG, that in today's world foreign policy and security policy are difficult to distinguish (indeed the TEU lumps them together in the CFSP), and that a State's security is closely linked to the security of the international community at large. Moreover, when discussing proportionality, which is a customary tool in EC law for imposing discipline on the Member States where they seek to rely on exceptions to fundamental rules or principles, the Court acknowledged that national authorities have a significant degree of discretion. It did not spell out further criteria, other than as regards the application of criminal penalties, where it identified what are probably commonly applied criteria of criminal law in such circumstances: to take account of the facts of each case, i.e. the nature of the goods and the good or bad faith of the exporter. In all other respects it left the application of proportionality to the national court, thereby empowering the judiciary at national level to use that principle for the purpose of judicial review of export controls. However, one may doubt whether national courts are keen to wield the proportionality weapon in such politically sensitive contexts.

On the whole, therefore, the approach is one of judicial deference, perhaps more inspired by the inherent difficulties which courts face when interfering with this kind of foreign policy—a concern to which Jacobs AG again referred, recalling his Opinion in the *FYROM* case[113]—than by the desire not to upset the delicate balance between the common commercial policy, the emerging CFSP, and national foreign and security policies. Indeed, there are significant obstacles to judicial intervention

---

[111] *Leifer* (n 80 above), paras 32–40.   [112] Ibid, paras 44–45.
[113] *Commission v. Greece* (n 64 above).

in the assessment of public authorities as regards the threat posed by certain exports. There is the technical difficulty of establishing the potential use to which certain products may be put. There is the eminently political assessment of the international security situation. Such an assessment can often only be made on the basis, in part, of sensitive and secret information, which the authorities may not like to subject to open judicial analysis and discourse. It is therefore not unnatural for courts to engage in a tactical retreat in the face of such obstacles, and the above judgments can be read as constituting such a retreat. In the case of the Court of Justice there is an additional obstacle, at least to the extent that cases on national export controls come via the preliminary rulings procedure. In such cases the Court is ill placed to examine the facts, which are a matter for the national court, and judicial intervention in this context requires intimate factual knowledge.

The above judgments also stand in some degree of contrast to the case law on EC economic sanctions. The general principles and statements are the same, but it is obvious that there is much less leeway for national authorities when they implement an EC sanctions regulation (see *Bosphorus Airways*, *Centro-Com*, and *Ebony Maritime*) than when they apply national export controls. The bottom line is that real EU law impact depends on legislative action, which indeed the EU also developed in this area.

European Union action

By the time the Court delivered its judgments in *Werner v. Germany* and *Leifer and Others* Community legislation on export controls had been adopted. Already in 1989, after various scandals concerning the delivery of technical know-how on chemical weapons production to Libya,[114] the Council adopted a regulation based on (current) Article 133 EC concerning the export of certain chemical products.[115] The preamble referred to discussions in the context of European Political Co-operation which had led to a consensus that it was necessary to take urgent measures to control the export of certain chemical products which could be used for the production of chemical weapons. It also made clear that the choice of a Community regulation was made because it permitted the adoption of urgent and effective measures. The regulation contained a list of the products concerned, and subjected exports of those products to an export authorization by national authorities (Article 1). The regulation did not determine any dangerous destinations, but simply provided that no authorization could be issued if there was reason to believe that products under consideration would be used for the development or production of chemical weapons or that there was a risk of their being delivered directly or indirectly to belligerent countries or to areas of serious international tension (Article 2). It is obvious that the Community institutions' approach was inspired by the economic

---

[114] Kuijper (n 9 above), 401.
[115] Council Regulation 428/89 concerning the export of certain chemical products [1989] OJ L50/1.

sanctions practice: Article 133 EC was used because it permits swift and effective legislative action, uniformly applied throughout the EC, and the regulation was preceded by an EPC decision.

Export controls are not however confined to chemical products. In 1992 the Commission proposed more comprehensive legislation on export controls for dual-use goods.[116] It made the proposal in the context of the programme to complete the internal market, because diverse systems of export controls at national level also created obstacles to trade in the internal market, as the *Richardt and 'Les Accessoires Scientifiques'* case had clearly demonstrated.[117] EU involvement in this area was no doubt facilitated by the end of the Cold War, which led to the demise of COCOM and a re-focusing of policies. The legislative process was none the less a difficult one, not least because of discussions on competence.[118] A majority of Member States felt that the political elements of such legislation, i.e. the list of sensitive destinations and of dual-use goods, did not come within Community competence under (current) Article 133 EC. The Council accordingly decided to set up a dual legal instrument: EC Regulation 3381/94 setting up a Community regime for the control of exports of dual-use goods,[119] and CFSP Decision 94/942 on the joint action adopted by the Council on the basis of (then) Article J.3 of the Treaty on European Union concerning the control of exports of dual-use goods.[120] The regulation merely laid down the procedural requirements for the exportation of such goods, whereas the CFSP decision contained the lists of dual-use goods and sensitive destinations.

This approach was markedly different from that which had prevailed in the case of economic sanctions, even before the TEU came into effect.[121] As we have seen, in the latter context EPC and, later, CFSP involvement was limited to making the decision of principle as to the appropriateness of sanctions, and all material rules were put in EC regulations. In the case of exports of dual-use goods some of the most vital elements of the regime were in a CFSP decision, which did not come within the jurisdiction of the Court of Justice. The regime therefore did not offer the same guarantees of effectiveness and uniformity. One presumes that the CFSP decision had to be implemented at national level by way of legislation, because there is no indication that such a decision has direct effect. It was not possible to refer questions of interpretation of the decision to the Court of Justice. Those were all disadvantages of the new regime, at least in terms of effectiveness and uniformity, but the concerns over the issues of competence obviously weighed more heavily on the decision-making process. One needs to realize that, at the time, the Court of Justice had not yet interpreted the scope of Article 133 EC in the context of foreign and security policy, and that the regime was established shortly after the entry into force of the TEU, with all the attendant concerns to keep the CFSP intergovernmental. At EU constitutional level those were tense times, and there were fears that the supranational EC approach in the field of external relations would be emasculated

---

[116] COM(92)317 final.   [117] N 96 above.   [118] Koutrakos (n 5 above), 94–5.
[119] [1994] OJ L367/1.   [120] [1994] OJ L367/8.   [121] Koutrakos (n 5 above), 94.

by the predominance of the intergovernmental CFSP, and that the *acquis commu-nautaire* was under attack.[122] The new EU export control regime was one of the clearest examples of how such emasculation could take place, EC law being relegated to the rank of administrative implementation of a regime whose essential features were in a CFSP decision.

The case law of the Court of Justice on the relationship between commercial policy and foreign and security policy however led to a fundamental modification of the dual-use goods regime with dual (EC and EU) legal basis. In 1998 the Commission proposed a number of changes, the most significant being that the whole regime should be consolidated in an EC regulation, on the ground that the case law had effectively established that there was no need for a CFSP decision containing the lists of dual-use goods and sensitive destinations. The proposal was based on (current) Article 133 EC.[123] It took about two years to convince the Council, but in the end Regulation 1334/00 setting up a Community regime for the control of exports of dual-use items and technology was adopted,[124] and the 1994 CFSP decision repealed.[125] The preamble to this act referred to *Werner v. Germany*, *Leifer and Others*, and *Centro-Com*.[126] In the press release on the occasion of the adoption of the new regulation the Presidency of the Council indicated, as regards legal basis, that the Court had clearly established exclusive Community competence for export controls concerning dual-use goods. The Court had explicitly stated that neither the particular nature of the goods nor the fact that the control measures were taken in light of foreign policy or security considerations prevented Article 133 from being applicable. However, the Court had also ruled that Article 133 did not preclude national measures regarding export controls, provided this was done on the basis of a delegation of powers by the EC and within the limitations posed by the general export regulation. The press release further stated that the new regulation therefore struck a balance between the principle of Community competence and the legitimate concerns of Member States to remain in control of matters relating to their national security.[127]

Regulation 1334/00 applies to dual-use items, which include not only goods, but also software and technology. Reflecting the Court of Justice's approach to trade in services,[128] it does not apply to the supply of services or transmission of technology if it involves the movement of natural persons (Article 3(3)). It makes several references to the international commitments and responsibilities of the Member States as regards proliferation and export controls. The preamble states that further harmonization is required in order to guarantee effective application of the controls. It is however plain that the Member States retain a considerable margin of discretion. The regulation lays down common lists of dual-use items, destinations,

---

[122] See further Ch 5.   [123] COM(1998)257 final, [1998] OJ C399/1.
[124] [2000] OJ L159/1.
[125] Council Decision 2000/402 repealing Decision 94/942/CFSP on the joint action concerning the control of exports of dual-use goods [2000] OJ L159/218.   [126] Nn 80, and 28 above.
[127] 2278th Council Meeting, PRES/00/219 of 30 November 2000.   [128] Ch 2.

and guidelines, requiring the Member States to operate the export authorization system for exports covered by those lists. However, under Article 5(1) the Member States may prohibit or impose an authorization requirement for the export of items not listed, for reasons of public security or human rights considerations. Article 8 provides that the Member States, when granting an authorization, shall take into account all relevant considerations, including *inter alia* their non-proliferation and export control commitments; sanctions imposed by a common position or joint action, by an OSCE decision or by a binding UN Security Council resolution; and considerations of national foreign and security policy, including those covered by the EU Code of Conduct on arms exports.[129]

It is thus clear that the regulation involves only partial harmonization, and does not fully replace national export control policies. That approach surely complies with the case law, because the Court recognizes that the Member States may, on grounds of public security, restrict exports; Article 11 of the export regulation constitutes a specific authorization of export controls on such grounds. The new export control regulation is in effect a junction of various legal systems: EC law on exports, national law on export controls, and international commitments of the Member States and of the European Union as regards such controls. In various places the regulation appears to confirm national competence in relation to foreign and security policy, including Member States' competence to enter into international non-proliferation and export control commitments.[130] One must however take into account the case law on implied powers, according to which there is exclusive EC competence for the conclusion of international agreements which affect or alter the scope of an EC act.[131] On that basis there appears to be Community competence for future international negotiations in this area which affect the export control regulation. That competence may not extend to all such negotiations, or to every aspect of any particular negotiation. But at least some degree of mixity appears to be called for.

Conclusions

The analysis in this chapter shows that there are many connections between trade and foreign policy, throwing up a host of legal issues owing to the constitutional separation which characterizes the EU's external action. In these conclusions it is not possible to return to all those issues. Instead one may offer some further reflections on some likely evolutions and developments. Partly because of September 11 economic and financial sanctions are no longer exclusively geared towards countries, but increasingly focus on individuals. As the previous chapter shows, sanctions

---

[129] On the Code of Conduct see Koutrakos (n 5 above), ch 9.
[130] Regulation 1334/00 (n 124 above); para 7 of the preamble provides that decisions to update the common lists of dual-use items must be in full conformity with the obligations and commitments that each Member State has accepted as a member of the relevant international non-proliferation regimes and export control arrangements, or by ratification of relevant international treaties.   [131] Ch 3.

adopted under the CFSP also move in the direction of putting pressure on regimes through action against individuals (so-called smart sanctions). The draft Constitution reflects these developments: Article III–224(2) allows for the adoption of restrictive measures 'against natural or legal persons and non-State groups or bodies'. Cases have already been brought before the Court of First Instance concerning such sanctions against individuals.[132]

Such cases are likely to lead to confrontation between human rights law and foreign and security policy. The courts will have to face up to the delicate and sensitive task of striking the right balance between the various competing interests. They will have to struggle with the question whether there is anything like a political-question doctrine in EU law. It is not possible within the scope of these conclusions to propose a fully considered reply to that question. It is none the less submitted that there should be caution not to exaggerate judicial deference, and that the courts should not abdicate judicial review on the mere basis of the political sensitivity of the issues. In particular where sanctions against individuals are concerned, there are bound to be cases which raise significant human-rights issues and which call for judicial intervention. Such intervention cannot be denied on the ground that measures have their origin in a UN Resolution. Domestic courts, in our case both the EU Courts and national courts, effectively offer the only opportunity for judicial review of such measures. In the absence of such review, sanctions are pure executive acts, and no matter what type of foreign and security policy interests are at stake, it cannot be accepted in an organization based on the rule of law that executive acts which strongly affect people's lives are not subject to any effective judicial scrutiny.

There may be inherent difficulties in exercising judicial review, such as the inherently political nature of certain assessments, the complexity of facts, the secret character of sources of information, etc. Those difficulties cannot be denied, yet courts should face up to them in light of the importance of their task and position in these matters.

---

[132] *Abdirisak Aden* and *José Maria Sison* (n 40 above).

13

Human rights policy

Introduction

Over the course of the last fifteen years human rights, or fundamental rights as is the more generally used concept, have come to occupy an ever more central position in the EU's polity and legal system. The original treaties did not expressly refer to human or fundamental rights, which in the post-war construction of European integration were located in the European Convention on Human Rights and the Council of Europe. It was initially for the Court of Justice, in the course of the 1970s, to formulate and define the system of respect for fundamental rights, a system which it based on the unwritten, judicially discovered source of general principles of EC law.[1] The Court finds fundamental rights in the constitutional traditions common to the Member States and in international human rights instruments to which the Member States are parties (in particular the ECHR). On that basis it examines, in so far as it has jurisdiction, whether acts of the institutions do not trespass on fundamental rights. This general principle of respect was confirmed at Maastricht, in what is currently Article 6(2) TEU. Article 6(1) goes even further, by spelling out that the Union is actually founded on the principles of liberty, democracy, respect for human rights and fundamental freedoms, and the rule of law. This is not merely treaty rhetoric. The episode of an Austrian government being contested, including the far-right Freedom Party,[2] and the effective conditioning of accession to the EU on reaching certain standards of rights protection[3] confirm the centrality of human rights in EU integration.

Further prominent displays include the Charter of Fundamental Rights, proclaimed in 2000 at Nice, which the Convention on the Future of Europe proposes should be incorporated in the new Constitution;[4] and the projected EU accession to the ECHR.[5] In its policy-making and legislative activity, too, the EU has become more oriented towards fundamental rights. Here the outstanding examples are new

---

[1] See, for an overview, P Craig and G de Búrca, *EU Law—Text, Cases and Materials* (3rd edn, OUP, 2002) 319–27.

[2] Cf M Hofstätter, 'Suspension of Rights by International Organizations: The European Union, the European Communities and Other International Organizations', in V Kronenberger (ed), *The European Union and the International Legal Order: Discord or Harmony?* (TMC Asser Press 2001) 23; see also Art 7 TEU.

[3] M Nowak, 'Human Rights "Conditionality" in Relation to Entry to, and Full Participation in, the EU', in P Alston (ed), *The EU and Human Rights* (OUP, 1999) 687.

[4] As Part II of the Constitution.   [5] Art I–7(2) of the draft Constitution.

directives on non-discrimination law,[6] complementing long-established rules on sex equality.

Orientation towards human rights is not confined to the internal workings of the EU. On the contrary, most commentators agree that the external human rights policy is more meaningful than the internal one.[7] The constitutional roots of this external policy lie also in Maastricht, where EC development co-operation policy was defined, with the emphasis in (current) Article 177(2) EC on the 'general objective of developing and consolidating democracy and the rule of law, and . . . of respecting human rights and fundamental freedoms'.[8] The 1991 Maastricht negotiations coincided with the formulation of important policy reflections by the Commission and the Council in this field,[9] which continue to form the basis for the EU's external human rights policy.

This general centrality of human rights justifies this chapter's focus on external policies in this area. This book aims to identify the constitutional foundations of the EU's external relations, and it is a truism that human rights are at the core of modern, and perhaps even more of postmodern, constitutionalism. That in itself justifies exploring external human rights policy, but the subject offers other attractions as well. This policy is, more than any other external policy, horizontal and transversal, integrated—or so it should be—in substantive external policies, and yet with a distinctiveness of its own. Many CFSP decisions are motivated or inspired by human rights concerns.[10] Development co-operation must contribute to respect for human rights, and policies in this area have an important human rights component. Indeed, respect for human rights appears to be the central 'legal' element of EU development co-operation, both as objective and condition. Bilateral agreements with non-member countries, be they development-oriented, or directed at general co-operation, partnership, or association, are now all predicated on respect for human rights.[11] The common commercial policy has a human rights dimension in the context of GSP. Further study of external human rights policy therefore emphasizes the linkages and interconnections between discrete domains of external action, and in that sense complements the preceding chapter on trade and foreign policy.

This chapter focuses on four dimensions of external human rights policy. First comes a section following the trajectory of the definition and construction of such

---

[6] Council Directive 2000/78 establishing a general framework for equal treatment in employment and occupation [2000] OJ L303/16 and Council Directive 2000/43 implementing the principle of equal treatment between persons irrespective of racial or ethnic origin [2000] OJ L180/22.

[7] Cf P Alston and JHH Weiler, 'An "Ever Closer Union" in Need of a Human Rights Policy: The European Union and Human Rights', in Alston (n 3 above), 7.

[8] See Ch 4; see further DJ Marantis, 'Human Rights, Democracy and Development: The European Community Model' (1994) 7 Harvard Human Rights Journal 1.   [9] See below.

[10] A Clapham, 'Where is the EU's Human Rights Common Foreign Policy, and How is it Manifested in Multilateral Fora?', in Alston (n 3 above), 627.

[11] That this is not merely lip service is illustrated by the foundering of negotiations with Australia. See E Fierro, *The EU's Approach to Human Rights Conditionality in Practice* (Martinus Nijhoff, 2003), 287–302.

policy. Secondly, we need to return to the Treaty basis for action in the field of human rights,[12] for the constitutional foundations are much disputed. The following section looks at the instruments of human rights policy. The chapter then concentrates on the practice of including human rights clauses in agreements with non-member countries. It concludes by looking at autonomous trade measures designed to promote respect for human rights, in particular GSP.

Defining and developing the policy

The EEC's first significant exposure to the human rights question in its external policies was in the context of the Lomé Conventions with ACP countries.[13] In the course of the 1970s and 1980s there were significant human rights issues in a few of those countries, and the EEC found itself in the uncomfortable position of being legally committed under those conventions to continue aid, even in the face of grave violations.[14] Then came the fall of the Berlin Wall and the end of the Cold War, triggering the policy of reuniting the European continent and of expanding the EC, but also leading to the terrible conflict in ex-Yugoslavia, where again the EEC was struggling to act as a force for pacification and for putting an end to large-scale human rights violations.[15]

These factors, and others, led to political focus on the human rights question in 1991. The Commission adopted a communication,[16] which was followed by a Council resolution on human rights, democracy, and development.[17] That resolution sketched the links between human rights and development, and outlined the future policy. The Council reaffirmed that respecting, promoting, and safeguarding human rights is an essential part of international relations and one of the cornerstones of European co-operation, as well as of relations between the Community and its Member States and other countries. It stressed its attachment to the principles of representative democracy, of the rule of law, of social justice, and of respect for human rights. The Council considered it important that the Community and its Member States should have a common approach aimed at promoting human rights and democracy in developing countries. It recognized the necessity of a consistent approach; development co-operation was based on the central place of the individual and had, therefore, in essence to be designed with a view to promoting—in parallel with economic and social rights—civil and political liberties by means of

---

[12] See Ch 3 on *Opinion 2/94 re Accession to the ECHR* [1996] ECR I–1759 and Ch 4 on Arts 177(2) and 181a(1) EC.

[13] For a more detailed account of gradual involvement see Fierro (n 11 above), ch II.

[14] See also below.   [15] See below.

[16] Commission Communication on human rights, democracy and development co-operation, SEC(61)91 of 25 March 1991.

[17] Resolution of the Council and of the Member States meeting in the Council on human rights, democracy and development, 28 November 1991, Bull. EC 11/1991, 122–3.

representative democratic rule that is based on respect for human rights. On the basis of those principles the Council identified a number of approaches, instruments, and activities, which included both positive, or supportive, and negative, or coercive measures (carrot and stick).[18] The Community and its Member States would give high priority to a positive approach that stimulated respect for human rights and encouraged democracy. An open and constructive dialogue between them and the governments of developing countries could make a very important contribution to the promotion of human rights and democracy. The Council further stressed the importance of good governance. However, while, in general, a positive and constructive approach had to receive priority, in the event of grave and persistent human rights violations or the serious interruption of democratic processes, the Community and its Member States would consider appropriate responses in the light of the circumstances, guided by objective and equitable criteria. The Community's response to violations would avoid penalizing the population, and the Council recognized that building democracy was a gradual process which would sometimes take a relatively long period. The Council also attached great importance to the question of military spending, stressing the negative effects of excessive military spending on the development process. It lastly identified a vital legal component of the external human rights policy, namely that the Community and its Member States would explicitly introduce the consideration of human rights as an element of their relations with developing countries, and that human rights clauses would be inserted into future co-operation agreements.

Also in 1991, the Maastricht negotiations led to the formulation of (current) Article 177(2) EC in the context of development co-operation, and they set up the CFSP, the objectives of which included (and include): 'to develop and consolidate democracy and the rule of law, and respect for human rights and fundamental freedoms' (current Article 11(1) TEU). That indicated that external human rights policy had a vocation to transcend development co-operation.

On the basis of the Council resolution and the EC and EU Treaty provisions the EU started building a comprehensive human rights policy. However, 1996 became a year of constitutional question marks, as the Court in *Opinion 2/94 re Accession to the ECHR* stated that no Treaty provision conferred on the Community institutions any general power to enact rules on human rights or to conclude international conventions in this field.[19] In *Portugal v. Council*, on the co-operation agreement with India, the Court accepted the human rights clause in the agreement, but one passage of the judgment could be read as ruling out that human rights could be a specific field of co-operation.[20] Partly in response to the questions raised by those cases, in 1997 the Commission proposed a Council regulation on the development and consolidation of democracy and the rule of law and respect for human rights and

---

[18] B Brandtner and A Rosas, 'Trade Preferences and Human Rights', in Alston (ed) (n 3 above), 701.
[19] *Opinion 2/94* (n 12 above), para 27.
[20] Case C–268/94 *Portugal v. Council* [1996] ECR I–6177, para 28; see Ch 4.

fundamental freedoms,[21] which was to provide a legal basis for support for human rights projects. However, the Council Legal Service contested the EU's powers as regards human rights, and the legal picture was further complicated by a 1998 Court judgment, effectively meaning that many projects on human rights lacked a satisfactory legal basis. Indeed, in *United Kingdom v. Commission* the Court held that the implementation of Community expenditure relating to any significant Community action presupposed not only the entry of the relevant appropriation in the budget of the Community, which was a matter for the budgetary authority, but in addition the prior adoption of a basic act authorizing that expenditure, which was a matter for the legislative authority.[22] In other words, significant funding for human rights projects required legislation authorizing it, legislation itself requiring a basis in the Treaty.[23]

In 1999 the Council managed to adopt two regulations laying down the relevant rules for Community funding of human rights projects in third countries, one relating to 'development co-operation operations',[24] and the other to 'operations other than those of development co-operation policy'.[25] The first regulation was adopted on the basis of (current) Article 179 EC, which no doubt provided an adequate legal basis, but the second had to be adopted on the basis of (current) Article 308 EC, as there were at the time no specific Treaty provisions on co-operation with developed third countries, let alone an indication that such co-operation should also contribute to respect for human rights. In light of the limitations on the use of Article 308 EC imposed by the Court in *Opinion 2/94*, that legal basis appeared precarious. In the meantime the Treaty of Nice inserted Article 181a EC enabling co-operation with developed countries, which is also to contribute to respect for human rights. The combined provisions of Articles 177(2) and 181a EC now offer a broader basis for an external human rights policy, yet there remain significant questions. Could, for example, a pure trade agreement be predicated on respect for human rights?[26] Could the EC or the EU conclude international agreements on human rights standards and protection? Could it join international organizations focusing on protection of human rights? Even if *Opinion 2/94* and *Portugal v. Council* were analysed and commented upon in previous chapters, it is worth revisiting questions concerning the scope of EU powers in the field of human rights.

---

[21] COM(97)357 final, [1997] OJ C282/14.

[22] Case C–106/96 *United Kingdom v. Commission* [1998] ECR I–2729, para 26.

[23] See on this episode Fierro (n 13 above), 85–6; JHH Weiler and S Fries, 'A Human Rights Policy for the European Community and Union: The Question of Competences', in Alston (n 3 above), 147–52.

[24] Council Regulation 975/1999 laying down the requirements for the implementation of development co-operation operations which contribute to the general objective of developing and consolidating democracy and the rule of law and to that of respecting human rights and fundamental freedoms [1999] OJ L120/1.

[25] Council Regulation 976/1999 laying down the requirements for the implementation of Community operations, other than those of development co-operation, which, within the framework of Community co-operation policy, contribute to the general objective of developing and consolidating democracy and the rule of law and to that of respecting human rights and fundamental freedoms in third countries [1999] OJ L120/8.						[26] Fierro (n 13 above), 256.

The question of powers

It appears important to distinguish two different kinds of external action in the sphere of human rights. If one concentrates on the conclusion of international agreements, there are vital differences between (a) agreements which aim to legislate as regards human rights, in the sense of laying down rules and standards of human rights protection for all the contracting parties, and (b) agreements which do not have human rights as their main object, but which are predicated on respect for human rights, or contain provisions on co-operation in this field. Examples of the first category are the ECHR and its subsequent Protocols, the UN covenants, and arguably a number of ILO Conventions, or at least some of their provisions.[27] Within the second category come virtually all bilateral co-operation, partnership, and association agreements between the EC and third countries.

That distinction is required because EC competence for the first category is clearly more precarious and disputed—and indeed has not yet been exercised. There is no Treaty provision which confers on the Community institutions any general power to enact rules on human rights or to conclude international conventions in this field, as the Court pointed out in *Opinion 2/94*.[28] In the second category, by contrast, there is considerable practice. Such practice is based on express provisions in the EC Treaty, in particular Articles 177(2) and 181a EC, and the Court recognized it in *Portugal v. Council*.[29]

The distinction is not just an accident of Treaty drafting or jurisprudence. The first type of external competence reaches much further in constitutional terms than the second. Particularly in the context of the EU it is intimately linked with the federal question, i.e. the question of constitutional balance between the EU and its Member States.[30] Human rights protection is a core element of constitutionalism, and the power to define rules and standards of such protection, in legislative form, has indeed not been transferred to the EU in any general way. It is clear that the EU does not have general power to conceptualize, formulate, and define human rights, so as to make them binding throughout the EU, on all public authorities and, in so far as relevant, private actors. If it had such power, the EU constitution would, in this core area, transcend and dominate national constitutions. Following the general approach in this book, it is in this respect irrelevant whether such human rights power is exercised through internal lawmaking or by concluding international agreements. As such agreements are binding on the EU institutions and on the Member States, their effect is in many respects identical to that of Community legislation.

The above does not however mean that there is no Community power whatsoever to conclude human rights treaties coming within this first category. As analysed

---

[27] Cf A Rosas, 'The European Union and International Human Rights Instruments', in Kronenberger (n 2 above), 57–9.

[28] N 12 above.   [29] N 20 above.

[30] cf P Eeckhout, 'The EU Charter of Fundamental Rights and the Federal Question' (2002) 39 CMLRev 945–94.

in Chapter 3, the Court's decision in *Opinion 2/94* did not rule out EC participation in the negotiation and conclusion of such treaties, even if the Court established that there is no general EC power in this field. The decision focused on the constitutional and institutional consequences of EC participation in the ECHR system. The fact that the Court concentrated on those specific consequences would indicate that it did not wish to erect a general barrier for EC involvement with human rights treaties.[31] Indeed it is difficult to see what the constitutional basis for such a general barrier would be. As has been analysed elsewhere,[32] there is surely a functional EC competence to enact provisions on human rights protection, within the scope of EC policies and of the 'substantive' powers conferred by the Treaty. As the EU institutions are committed to respecting fundamental rights, there must be power to legislate so as to ensure such respect. The anti-dumping regulation, for example,[33] even if *prima facie* unconnected with human rights, must contain provisions on rights of defence. It is obvious that the requirement of 'respect' for fundamental rights cannot be a mere negative requirement, a mere condition of abstention, judicially enforced; it must also include positive obligations, as indeed the ECtHR emphasizes in its case law.[34] One may give another example, taken from actual case law. In *Matthews* the ECtHR decided that under Article 1 of Protocol 1 to the ECHR the citizens of Gibraltar must have the right to vote in elections for the European Parliament.[35] The implementation of that decision—indeed the realization of the right to vote generally—requires positive action setting up an election process. Such examples can be multiplied.

If, within its spheres of competence, the Community is under an obligation to respect fundamental rights and needs to have the legal tools to ensure such respect, it may also be necessary for the Community to commit itself at international level. Here too there appears to be an implied power to act. But the matter does not end there. Increasingly, the EU is active in areas which are either closely linked with the protection of fundamental rights, or which concern human rights as such. Instances of the former are asylum policy and co-operation in criminal matters. Instances of the latter are Community non-discrimination policies, originally confined to sex equality, but now greatly expanded by two directives based on Article 13 EC.[36] That provision confers powers on the Community in the field of human rights. As these powers have been exercised, the *AETR* principle applies to the conclusion of international agreements in this field. This is not mere theory. There is for example currently exclusive Community competence for the conclusion of Protocol 12 to the ECHR, which also deals with non-discrimination, in so far as the provisions of that Protocol affect Community legislation. There may be difficulties in exercising

---

[31] Cf A Arnull, 'Left To Its Own Devices? Opinion 2/94 and the Protection of Fundamental Rights in the European Union', in A Dashwood and C Hillion (eds), *The General Law of EC External Relations* (Sweet & Maxwell, 2000) 71–2.   [32] Eeckhout (n 30 above), 981–5.

[33] Council Regulation 384/96 on protection against dumped imports from countries not members of the European Community [1996] OJ L56/1.   [34] Cf Fierro (n 13 above), 278–9.

[35] ECtHR, App. No. 24833/94 *Matthews v. United Kingdom*, (1999) 28 EHRR 361.

[36] Directives 2000/43 and 2000/78 (n 6 above).

that competence, because under its current provisions the Convention and the Protocol can only be signed by States, but the EU Member States are none the less under an obligation to consult within the Council on this matter and to define a common approach enabling the defence of the Community interest.[37]

In conclusion, there is clearly some measure of Community competence to conclude international agreements which lay down specific rules or standards of human rights protection binding on all contracting parties; human rights treaties, in other words.

Competence to conclude the second type of agreements is less precarious,[38] because the Treaty expressly confirms that development co-operation and other co-operation policies must contribute to the general objective of developing and consolidating democracy and the rule of law, and to that of respecting human rights and fundamental freedoms. With the introduction of Article 181a EC by the Treaty of Nice all co-operation agreements with third countries, be they developing countries or not, should contribute to that objective, including association agreements, which are also mentioned in Article 181a. The Treaty bases therefore cover most of the bilateral contractual relations with third countries. But what about a pure trade agreement, concluded under Article 133 EC? Could there be a human rights clause in such an agreement, even if Article 133 does not mention respect for human rights?[39] The answer should be positive, on the basis of the language of various provisions of the EC and EU Treaties. Both Articles 177(2) and 181a(1) EC speak of a 'general objective' of respect for human rights, to which the respective policies must contribute. Those terms can only indicate that the objective transcends those specific policies. No other provision in the EC Treaty mentions this general objective, and the Treaty is therefore rather imprecise as to its scope. However, one should also look at the provisions of the TEU, and there one does find more guidance. Article 11(1) TEU provides that the Union 'shall define and implement a common foreign and security policy covering all areas of foreign and security policy, the objectives of which shall be . . . to develop and consolidate democracy and the rule of law, and respect for human rights and fundamental freedoms'. In the second part this is exactly the same language as in the discussed provisions of the EC Treaty. If one adds Article 3 TEU, requiring the EU to 'ensure the consistency of its external activities as a whole in the context of its external relations, security, economic and development policies', the picture becomes even clearer. The 'general objective' in Articles 177(2) and 181a(1) EC is a general objective of external EU action.

On that basis, all EU external policies, be they First or Second Pillar (or Third), are to contribute to the general objective of developing and consolidating democracy and the rule of law, and of respecting human rights and fundamental freedoms. What remains to be examined is the scope of that objective, and the corresponding limits to the relevant EC powers. In *Portugal v. Council* the Court accepted the 'essential

---

[37] Cf *Opinion 2/91 re ILO Convention No 170* [1991] ECR I–1061, para 6; see Chs 3 and 7.
[38] Cf S Peers, 'EC Frameworks of International Relations: Co-operation, Partnership and Association', in Dashwood and Hillion (eds), (n 31 above), 166–8.   [39] Fierro (n 13 above), 256.

element' clause, which could, if the above reasoning is correct, be part of any substantial agreement with a third country. In the EC–India agreement the clause was generally phrased, and did not refer to any specific sources for human rights protection, or standards of democracy or of the rule of law. As will be seen, the practice as regards the formulation of such clauses varies. Brandtner and Rosas have suggested that the clause is increasingly orientated towards the Universal Declaration on Human Rights, because this may be regarded as *ius cogens*, thereby avoiding debate about EC competence to lay down rules on human rights.[40] However, in light of the above analysis there must be some margin of discretion for the institutions for further defining what democracy, rule of law, and respect for human rights may mean in a particular bilateral relationship. As long as the institutions do not cross the line of exercising a legislative function as regards human rights, thereby also binding the Community to respect for newly defined or formulated human rights, it appears sufficient that the specific formulation be adequately reasoned. Exercise of a legislative function brings an agreement within the first category, and it would then need to be shown that such exercise is necessary to reach a specific, substantive objective of the Community.

An agreement providing for specific, concrete co-operation in the domain of human rights would need to be based on either Article 177(2) EC, in the case of developing countries, or on Article 181a(1) EC, for other third countries. As argued in Chapter 4, co-operation measures and agreements may be specifically orientated towards protection and promotion of human rights. That is particularly important for internal measures. The two 1999 regulations on co-operation as regards human rights[41] are clearly within the boundaries of Community competence.

All that is complemented by the CFSP, under which many instruments are directed towards respect for human rights or have a human rights dimension.

Instruments and scope

Whatever the precise boundaries of the EU's human rights powers, policies in this field are steadfastly expanding. Human rights concerns are increasingly integrated into the many different dimensions of EU external action (mainstreaming), and a growing number of instruments are used to consolidate democracy and the rule of law and to further human rights protection. Without claiming exhaustiveness, the following short inventory may illustrate the breadth and depth of the policy.[42]

> —High standards of democracy, rule of law, and protection of human rights
>   are a condition for accession to the European Union. They are a core

[40] B Brandtner and A Rosas, 'Human Rights and the External Relations of the European Community: An Analysis of Doctrine and Practice' (1998) 9 EJIL 475.

[41] Regulation 975/1999 (n 24 above) and Regulation 976/1999 (n 25 above).

[42] See further Alston (n 3 above), *passim*; Fierro (n 13 above); Brandtner and Rosas (n 40 above).

element of the Copenhagen criteria,[43] they played an important role in the accession process of a number of Central and East European countries, and are central to the dynamics of Turkey's accession claim.

—As mentioned before, all bilateral co-operation, partnership, and association agreements between the EU and third countries are consistently predicated on respect for human rights. The *sérieux* of this policy of human rights conditionality is illustrated by the collapse of negotiations with Australia and New Zealand on trade and co-operation agreements, caused by this very point.[44]

—Linked to such conditionality in bilateral agreements, the EU attaches great importance to human rights in its political dialogue with third countries.

—The EU has been prepared to implement human rights conditionality by suspending agreements and co-operation, even if such action is so far confined to ACP countries.

—The EU aims to speak with one voice during human rights debates at the United Nations, in particular in the General Assembly and in the UN Commission on Human Rights. Co-ordination takes place through the CFSP. In other international fora, too, there is an EU policy, an example being the issue of core labour standards, debated at the ILO and at the WTO.[45]

—Human rights problems and violations are a constant topic of CFSP common positions and joint actions. The CFSP is used to adopt sanctions such as visa bans and freezing of funds or assets.

—Autonomous EC trade measures may be linked to human rights protection. In the case of ex-Yugoslavia, trade preferences were granted only to Republics complying with UN Resolutions and protecting human rights. More generally, GSP has elements of conditionality and offers incentives predicated on respect for basic rights.

—Human rights are an important component of the EU's co-operation with third countries, in particular developing countries, and there is substantial financial support for human rights projects through the European Initiative for Democracy and Human Rights (EIDHR).[46]

A 2001 Commission communication took stock of the EU's external human rights policy, and projected its further development.[47] The Commission indicated that at least its own action in this field would be guided by compliance with the rights and principles contained in the Charter of Fundamental Rights. It identified three areas where the Commission could act effectively: (a) through promoting coherent and consistent policies in support of human rights and democratization; (b) through placing a higher priority on human rights and democratization in relations with third countries and taking a more pro-active approach; and (c) by adopting a more

---

[43] Nowak (n 3 above), 691–2.   [44] Fierro (n 13 above), 287–302.
[45] Clapham (n 10 above).   [46] See in particular the regulations, nn 24 and 25 above.
[47] The European Union's role in promoting human rights and democratization in third countries, COM(2001)252 final.

strategic approach to the EIDHR, matching programmes and projects in the field with EU commitments on human rights and democracy. The Commission insisted on the full involvement of the European Parliament. It drew attention to the fact that trade and investment were areas which in recent years had seen a proliferation of initiatives intended to promote human rights. As regards the EIDHR, the Commission proposed four thematic priorities: (a) support to strengthen democratization, good governance, and the rule of law; (b) activities in support of the abolition of the death penalty; (c) support for the fight against torture and impunity and for international tribunals and criminal courts; and (d) combating racism and xenophobia and discrimination against minorities and indigenous people. As regards the creation of a European Human Rights Agency, first suggested in the conclusions of the Cologne European Council of June 1999, the Commission was more reserved. Against this general background, the following sections concentrate on two major instruments of human rights policy.

Human rights clauses

Origins

The need for express references to respect for human rights in agreements with third countries first arose in the context of Lomé I.[48] Particularly in a number of African countries, such as Uganda and the Central African Empire, there were major human rights problems in the 1970s, but the Lomé I Convention did not permit suspension of the co-operation which it set up on such grounds. The EEC's approach therefore had to be based on the principle of *pacta sunt servanda*.[49] Negotiations on Lomé II did not yet lead to the insertion of a human rights clause, because of resistance by the ACP countries.[50] Nor did Lomé III include such a clause, *inter alia* because the EEC's negotiating position was weakened in light of its attitude towards South Africa.[51] The emphasis on human rights protection, and its link with development, none the less gradually strengthened, in large measure due to pressure exercised by the European Parliament.[52] In 1979 the EP was for the first time directly elected, and it quickly seized on human rights as a domain where it could play a significant role. In an important 1983 resolution on human rights in the world the EP expressed its opinion that human rights are universal and that the Community had a duty to encourage respect for those rights, in particular in countries with which it had close ties. Accordingly, the EP invited the Commission to draw up a proposal to incorporate human rights considerations into external relations with

---

[48] See also F Hoffmeister, *Menschenrechts- und Demokratieklauseln in den vertraglichen Aussenbeziehungen der Europäischen Gemeinschaft* (Springer, 1998); K Arts, *Integrating Human Rights into Development Cooperation: The Case of the Lomé Convention* (Kluwer Law International, 2000).
[49] Fierro (n 13 above), 42–7.   [50] Ibid, 47–55.   [51] Ibid, 55–9.   [52] Ibid, 59–63.

a view to the gradual establishment of a comprehensive human rights policy.[53] Ever since, the EP has been the strongest advocate of such a policy.

When Lomé IV was negotiated (1989) the Single European Act had given the EP a right of assent to association agreements, and it soon became clear that such assent would only be given to an agreement containing human rights provisions.[54] The negotiations did indeed lead to an extensively worded human rights clause.[55] Article 5 of Lomé IV highlighted that co-operation was directed towards development centred on man, thus entailing respect for and promotion of all human rights. A positive approach was called for, and emphasis was laid on the indivisibility of human rights, including economic, social, and cultural rights. As regards non-discrimination there was a reference to apartheid, and to the situation of migrant workers, students, and other foreign nationals legally within a contracting party's territory. At the request of ACP States financial resources could be allocated to the promotion of human rights in the ACP States. Article 5 was clearly carefully negotiated, emphasizing issues of concern to the ACP States, and containing no reference to respect for human rights as an essential element of the co-operation. Nor were there any express provisions on suspension of co-operation.

The provision none the less created a precedent. In the following years the Soviet bloc collapsed and the Community was thrust to the forefront of efforts to assist the transition process in Central and Eastern Europe, a process in which again great importance was attached to democracy and human rights. This led to the political and legislative developments discussed above in the EC, in the year 1991. In the course of the same year the Community suspended the co-operation agreement with Yugoslavia, in reaction to the break-up of that country and the unwillingness of Serbia and Montenegro to co-operate with Community efforts to reach a cease-fire. The suspension of the agreement was disputed under international law, as it had no express basis in the agreement, and was later challenged before the Court of Justice in *Racke*.[56] That episode made the institutions even more aware of the need for human rights clauses in bilateral agreements, coupled with mechanisms for suspension and termination. From 1991 onwards the Community consistently inserted human rights clauses into external agreements, following the approach outlined in the 1991 Council resolution.[57]

Typology of human rights clauses[58]

After the negotiation of Lomé IV the Community managed to include a so-called 'basis clause' in the Framework Agreement for trade and economic co-operation

---

[53] [1983] OJ C161/58.   [54] Fierro (n 13 above), 67.
[55] For Lomé IV see [1991] OJ L229/3.
[56] Case C–162/96 *Racke v. Hauptzollamt Mainz* [1998] ECR I–3655; see Ch 9.   [57] N 17 above.
[58] See also E Riedel and M Will, 'Human Rights Clauses in External Agreements of the EC', in Alston (n 3 above), 726–32; Fierro (n 13 above), Ch VI.

with Argentina,[59] later replicated in agreements with Chile, Uruguay, and Paraguay. According to this provision co-operation was 'based on respect for the democratic principles and human rights, which inspire the domestic and external policies of the Community and Argentina'. Such a basis clause left much room for interpretation, however. It was also doubtful whether, in case of human rights violations, it could justify recourse to Article 60(3)(b) VCLT, on termination or suspension of a treaty on grounds of material breach.[60]

The episode with the suspension of the Yugoslavia agreement convinced the Council that references to human rights needed to be strengthened so as to express true conditionality. In a declaration of May 1992 concerning relations with CSCE States the Council emphasized that respect for human rights and democratic principles formed an essential and integral part of agreements with those countries,[61] and from the agreements with the Baltic States onward the 'basis clause' was transformed into the 'essential element clause'.[62] Under such a clause respect for democratic principles and human rights constitutes an essential element of the agreement, thus expressly referring to the concept in Article 60(3)(b) VCLT.

The essential element clause was further enhanced by specific non-compliance clauses. The first type of such clauses emerged in the agreements with the Baltic States and with Albania (the so-called 'Baltic clause').[63] The clause provided that the parties reserved the right to suspend the agreement in whole or in part with immediate effect if a serious breach of its essential provisions occurred. However, the Baltic clause had certain disadvantages, such as its limitation to serious violations and the absence of provisions on dialogue and notification.[64] It was soon replaced by the so-called Bulgaria clause, which continues to be the relevant model.[65] The clause provides:

If either Party considers that the other Party has failed to fulfil an obligation under the Agreement, it may take appropriate measures. Before so doing, except in cases of special urgency, it shall supply the Association Council with all relevant information required for a thorough examination of the situation with a view to seeking a solution acceptable to the Parties.

In the selection of measures, priority must be given to those which least disturb the functioning of the Agreement. These measures shall be notified immediately to the Association Council and shall be the subject of consultations within the Association Council if the other Party so requests.

That clause introduces consultations, and requires a proportionate reaction to violations, but it is no panacea either, as consultations may serve to make the essential

---

[59] [1990] OJ L295/67.

[60] Art 60(3)(b) requires 'the violation of a provision essential to the accomplishment of the object or purpose of the treaty'. On those drawbacks of the basis clause see Riedel and Will (n 58 above), 728.

[61] Bull. EC 5-1992, pt. 1.2.13.

[62] E.g. Art 1, of the Agreement on trade and commercial and economic cooperation with Estonia [1992] OJ L403/2.   [63] Ibid, Art 21, third paragraph.

[64] Riedel and Will (n 58 above), 729 and Fierro (n 13 above), 222.

[65] Art 118(2) of the Europe Agreement with Bulgaria [1994] OJ L358/3.

element clause ineffective.[66] In the Partnership and Co-operation Agreement with Russia that potential problem was sought to be countered through a joint declaration clarifying that cases of special urgency meant cases of material breach defined in VCLT terms, thereby referring to the essential element clause.[67]

Insertion into a bilateral agreement of the essential element clause in combination with a suspension provision akin to the Bulgarian clause is currently standard EU practice. There are none the less variations, both as regards the formulation of what constitute essential elements, including references to international instruments, and as regards suspension provisions. As regards the former, the recent analysis by Fierro shows that there is a range of approaches. Some agreements refer to human rights and democratic principles *tout court*, without making reference to any specific instruments; other agreements also refer to OSCE documents and to the principles of market economy; and increasingly there is reference to the UDHR.[68] Rosas also notes the latter tendency, which in his view is based on the understanding that the principles contained in the Universal Declaration reflect existing general international law, whether seen as customary law or as general principles of law recognized by civilized nations. The EU's treaty practice is thus said to contribute to the reaffirmation of the status of the Declaration as an expression of general international law binding on all States.[69]

The most elaborate human rights provisions are found in the contractual relationship with the ACP countries, both as regards the essential element clause and suspension provisions.[70] Already the 1995 version of Lomé IV included a non-execution clause which was more developed than ordinary clauses,[71] and the current Cotonou Convention builds on that.[72] It is worth taking a further look at those provisions, in particular because they are the only ones which have been put to active use hitherto (see below).

Article 9(2) of the Cotonou Convention provides that 'respect for human rights, democratic principles and the rule of law, which underpin the ACP–EU Partnership, shall underpin the domestic and international policies of the Parties and constitute the essential elements of this Agreement'. A comparable clause in Article 9(3) concerns good governance, but here the term 'fundamental element' is used instead. Article 9(4) indicates that the Partnership shall actively support the promotion of human rights, processes of democratization, consolidation of the rule of law, and good governance, and that those areas will be an important subject for the political dialogue. Article 96 of the Convention concerns '[e]ssential elements: consolidation procedure and appropriate measures as regards human rights, democratic principles and the

---

[66] Riedel and Will (n 58 above), 730.

[67] Joint Declaration in relation to Article 107 [1997] OJ L327/3; this declaration was copied for other treaties with CIS countries.   [68] Fierro (n 13 above), 229–38.

[69] Rosas (n 27 above), 61.   [70] Fierro (n 13 above), 313–21.   [71] [1998] OJ L156/3.

[72] [2000] OJ L317/3; see also the Internal agreement between the representatives of the governments of the Member States, meeting within the Council, on measures to be taken and procedures to be followed for the implementation of the ACP–EC Partnership Agreement [2000] OJ L317/376.

rule of law'. Article 96(2) describes the procedure to be followed where, despite the political dialogue, a Party considers that the other Party has failed to fulfil an obligation referred to in Article 9(2). Such a Party shall, except in cases of special urgency, supply the other Party and the EU–ACP Council of Ministers with the relevant information required for a thorough examination of the situation with a view to seeking a solution acceptable to the Parties. Consultations shall be conducted at the level and in the form considered most appropriate for finding a solution, and there are provisions regarding the timing of such consultations. If the consultations do not lead to a solution acceptable to both Parties, if consultation is refused, or in cases of special urgency, appropriate measures may be taken. Such measures must be in accordance with international law, and proportional to the violation. In the selection of these measures, priority must be given to those which least disrupt the application of the agreement, and it is understood that suspension would be a measure of last resort. Different rules apply in cases of special urgency, defined as exceptional cases of particularly serious and flagrant violation of one of the essential elements referred to in Article 9(2), that require immediate action. The Party resorting to that procedure shall inform the other Party and the Council of Ministers separately of the fact, unless it does not have time to do so. If measures are taken in cases of special urgency, they shall be immediately notified to the other Party and the Council of Ministers; at the request of the Party concerned, consultations may then be called in order to examine the situation thoroughly and, if possible, find solutions.

At EU level, the internal agreement[73] gives the Council, on the initiative of the Commission or a Member State, the power to start consultations. The Council acts by qualified majority, and in consultations the Community is represented by the Presidency of the Council and the Commission. It is also the Council which decides on appropriate measures, again acting by a qualified majority, except in the case of a full suspension of application of the Convention in relation to the ACP State concerned, where it must act unanimously. The European Parliament is only 'immediately and fully informed' of any decision taken.

Application

It is obvious that the success and effectiveness of the human rights clauses should not be measured by the rate of application of formal consultation and suspension provisions. Such clauses are intended to be fully respected, and to form part of a constant political dialogue, and in that sense it would rather be the absence of any suspension practice which would point towards success. However, the assessment of human rights issues requires great realism and, subject to variation depending on the general economic and political significance of the relationship between a third country and the EU, the effectiveness of the external pressure exercised through

---

[73] Ibid, Annex.

an essential element clause no doubt has its limits. There are many human rights problems in third countries (as well as in the EU), and some may be of such gravity that they warrant application of the human rights mechanism in an agreement. Identifying and listing human rights violations which could have been so regarded is beyond the scope of the present analysis. It is none the less striking that, at the time of writing, suspension measures have been adopted only as against ACP countries. As Fierro points out, breaches of democratic principles or human rights have been recognized for the purpose of the clause in countries such as Comoro Islands, Ivory Coast, Togo, and Guinea Bissau, but not in Israel or Russia.[74] The author advances a number of explanations, such as the nature of human rights violations involved, consisting of a military coup or a flagrant interruption of the democratic process, as well as the long-standing focus on human rights in the EC–ACP context and the sophisticated procedural framework.[75] There may be further, and perhaps more significant reasons, though. Extensive development co-operation takes place within the Lomé/Cotonou framework, including large-scale financial aid. That puts more pressure on the EU to act under the human rights clause in order to avoid such aid, to which it is committed, continuing to flow to countries where there are grave violations. In relationships with countries with which co-operation is less developed, recourse to the human rights clause is likely to be less effective, and there may be less pressure by public opinion. Further, the balance of global political power is more conducive to strong action against ACP countries, compared to some other non-member States.

It is beyond the scope of this chapter to analyse all cases of suspension under the Lomé and Cotonou conventions. Some level of case study is none the less interesting, particularly as it reveals the interconnections between the EU pillars and policies, and the struggle to come up with a coherent set of measures in the face of constitutional fracture. The current sanctions against Zimbabwe offer such a case study. In the course of 2000 the political situation in that country deteriorated, particularly as regards election processes and illegal occupation of farm land. The European Parliament started churning out resolutions at a regular pace, in increasingly alarmist terms.[76] The problems expanded to government action to silence dissent and to undermine the independence of the judiciary, and the country gradually slid into a chaos of political violence, breakdown of law and order, and a worsening human rights situation. In 2001 those problems became the subject of political dialogue, culminating in a Council decision to open consultations with Zimbabwe pursuant to Article 96 of Cotonou.[77] Those consultations did not lead to satisfactory results, and in February 2002 the Council suspended the Cotonou Agreement and adopted a set of targeted (or 'smart') sanctions, for which the Parliament had

[74] Fierro (n 13 above), 309.   [75] Ibid, 309–13.
[76] Resolution of 13 April 2000 [2001] OJ C40/425; Resolution of 18 May 2000 [2001] OJ C59/241; Resolution of 6 July 2000 [2001] OJ C121/394; Resolution of 15 March 2001 [2001] OJ C343/304.
[77] Council ACP Working Party, Opening of consultations with Zimbabwe pursuant to Art 96 of the Cotonou Agreement, 18 December 2001, 15435/01 (< http://register.consilium.eu.int>).

called.[78] There were three Council acts. In an EC Decision the Council concluded the consultations with Zimbabwe. It noted that the essential elements cited in Article 9 of the ACP–EC Partnership Agreement had been violated by the government of Zimbabwe, and that specific commitments made by that government were insufficient. The decision listed seven measures, adopted as appropriate measures within the meaning of Article 96(2)(c) of the agreement, and to apply for a period of twelve months. Those measures included suspending certain types of financial support, and reorienting financing in direct support of the population.[79] In order to put further pressure on the regime, a Common Position was adopted concerning restrictive measures against Zimbabwe, on the basis of Article 15 TEU. Those measures involved a prohibition of supply or sale of arms and related material; a prohibition of arms-related training or technical assistance; a prohibition of supply of equipment which might be used for internal repression; a prohibition of entry into the EU (visa ban) and the freezing of funds and assets of listed regime members (defined as 'persons . . . who are engaged in activities that seriously undermine democracy, respect for human rights and the rule of law in Zimbabwe').[80] The common position was complemented with a Council Regulation concerning certain restrictive measures in respect of Zimbabwe, based on Articles 60 and 301 EC. The regulation contained further detail as regards the freezing of funds and assets, arms-related training or technical assistance, and supply of equipment which might be used for internal repression.[81] The regulation did not however cover the supply of arms and the visa ban, which were governed only by the common position.

Autonomous trade measures

Autonomous EC measures regarding imports or exports may also be used as a tool for improving human rights protection in third countries. The EU's internal market is of such dimensions that access to it is of great economic significance for many countries. Refusing such access (stick) or granting preferential terms of trade (carrot) is therefore likely to exercise considerable pressure for change. Further, import and export restrictions are a constant feature of economic sanctions, which are often connected to human rights violations. That subject is discussed in Chapter 12.

The scope for promoting respect for human rights through the introduction of autonomous import restrictions or preferences is in many cases strictly limited by international commitments, in particular within the WTO. The MFN principle resists different treatment of trading partners which are WTO members, and the

---

[78] Resolution of 15 March 2001 (n 76 above).
[79] Council Decision 2002/148 concluding consultations with Zimbabwe under Art 96 of the ACP–EC Partnership Agreement [2002] OJ L50/64.
[80] Council Common Position 2002/145 concerning restrictive measures against Zimbabwe [2002] OJ L50/1.
[81] Council Regulation 310/2002 concerning certain restrictive measures in respect of Zimbabwe [2002] OJ L50/4.

exceptions to that principle are basically confined to regional integration (customs unions or free-trade areas)[82] and preferences for developing countries.[83] As regional integration is itself regulated in international agreements, autonomous trade measures with human rights conditionality are effectively confined (a) to trade relations with countries which are not WTO members and with which there is no trade agreement, and (b) to trade relations with developing countries benefiting from the EC's GSP system.

An example of the first category was the conditionality policy towards certain countries of South-East Europe (former Yugoslavia).[84] When in 1991 the co-operation agreement with Yugoslavia was suspended, and later terminated, the trade preferences which the agreement conferred were recast as autonomous preferences for those republics which actively contributed to the peace process. Those preferences were annually renewed, until in 1996–7 the Council embedded them in an express conditionality policy, introducing a clear link between these countries' performance as regards *inter alia* democracy, the rule of law, and higher standards of human and minority rights.[85] That conditionality policy is currently subsumed in the Stabilization and Association process for South East Europe, a broadly based programme involving trade preferences, extensive co-operation, and the conclusion of stabilization and association agreements.[86] That whole process is predicated on and indeed aimed at the consolidation of democracy and the rule of law, and protection of human rights.

The Community's GSP system has since 1994 included both incentive and withdrawal mechanisms.[87] The current version of the basic regulation, applying a scheme of generalized tariff preferences for 2002–4,[88] contains special incentive arrangements for the protection of labour rights and for the protection of the environment. As regards the former, the focus is on so-called core labour rights, which can be regarded as fundamental rights. Article 14(2) of the regulation provides:

The special incentive arrangements for the protection of labour rights may be granted to a country the national legislation of which incorporates the substance of the standards laid down in ILO Conventions No 29 and No 105 on forced labour, No 87 and No 98 on the freedom of association and the right to collective bargaining, No 100 and No 111 on non-discrimination in respect of employment and occupation, and No 138 and No 182 on child labour and which effectively applies that legislation.

The incentive consists of a further reduction in customs duties, which are impressive in size, and which may be granted to certain sectors, and not only to entire

---

[82] Art XXIV GATT, Understanding on Article XXIV, and Art V GATS.   [83] Part IV GATT.
[84] Brandtner and Rosas (n 40 above), 709–13.
[85] Council Conclusions on the principle of Conditionality governing the development of the EU's relations with certain countries of south-east Europe, Bull. EU 4–1997, points 1.4.67 and 2.2.1.
[86] See The Stabilization and Association Process for South East Europe—First Annual Report, COM(2002)163 final.   [87] Ch 10.
[88] Council Regulation 2501/2001 applying a scheme of generalized tariff preferences for the period from 1 January 2002 to 31 December 2003 [2001] OJ L346/1.

countries. They do not however seem to be very successful as the basic regulation lists only Moldova as a beneficiary.[89]

There is, on the other hand, also scope for withdrawal of preferences for a number of reasons, including:[90]

(a) practice of any form of slavery or forced labour as defined in the Geneva Conventions of 25 September 1926 and 7 September 1956 and ILO Conventions No 29 and No 105;

(b) serious and systematic violation of the freedom of association, the right to collective bargaining or the principle of non-discrimination in respect of employment and occupation, or use of child labour, as defined in the relevant ILO Conventions;

(c) export of goods made by prison labour.

Brandtner and Rosas note that the prohibitions of slavery and forced labour are examples of fundamental human rights, perhaps of *ius cogens* character, which transcend the distinction between civil and political, and economic, social, and cultural rights. This procedure of withdrawal has so far been used against the Union of Myanmar (Burma), on grounds of use of forced labour.[91] A complaint was lodged against Pakistan on grounds of use of child labour, but in that case the Commission preferred a policy of encouraging compliance through incentives rather than coercive measures.[92]

The legality of special incentive arrangements under WTO law is currently contested in a complaint by India against the EC.[93] It thus remains to be seen whether even this type of human rights conditionality in the trade field is disciplined, or even prohibited, by WTO law.

Conclusions

The analysis of this chapter demonstrates that human rights policy, in its broad conception which includes democracy and the rule of law, is increasingly present throughout the EU's external relations and policies. Developing and expanding such a human rights policy, and making it the central component of external action, is arguably the most ambitious and noble target the EU can set itself for its relations with the rest of the world.

Unfortunately, however, there are significant constitutional hurdles on the road towards a more meaningful external human rights policy. The EU's powers in this field are much disputed, in light of the importance of human rights for the federal balance between the EU and its Member States. *Opinion 2/94* has not been very

---

[89] Ibid, Annex I.   [90] Ibid, Art 26(1).

[91] Council Regulation 552/97 temporarily withdrawing access to generalized tariff preferences from the Union of Myanmar [1997] OJ L85/8.   [92] Brandtner and Rosas (n 40 above), 717.

[93] See WT/DS246/5 of 6 March 2003 (constitution of a panel).

helpful, for reasons which have less to do with competence in the sphere of human rights as such than with institutional issues, including the relationship between the Court of Justice and the European Court of Human Rights. The current EC and EU Treaties none the less offer a firm basis for putting human rights at the heart of EU external action, through their emphasis on this 'general objective' as regards CFSP, development co-operation, and other co-operation policies. The draft Constitution would further strengthen this dimension, through its general emphasis on human rights and its unification of external action.

This chapter did not attempt to analyse all instruments and dimensions of external human rights policy, but concentrated on human rights clauses and autonomous trade measures. One should therefore refrain from evaluating the effectiveness of the EU's policy. The survey none the less exemplifies the inherent difficulties of constructing such an effective and even-handed policy. The real world of international politics is of course not a natural habitat for the enlightened ideals of human rights, democracy, and the rule of law. As a result, it is all the more necessary to strengthen the constitutional foundations of human rights policy, for without such strong foundations the policy risks becoming completely subordinate to international interests and politics. The survey also shows the limited scope for using economic means, in particular trade measures, to exercise pressure on foreign governments, due to the disciplines imposed by the WTO. The autonomous trade measures are largely confined to GSP, i.e. to preferences over and above GATT tariff bindings, and are none the less contested in the WTO. The human rights clauses in agreements have so far only been used in relations with ACP countries, no doubt in part because of the scope for restricting development aid. In relations with other countries trade may be the only effective means of applying pressure, but the potential difficulties under WTO law are immediately apparent. Accordingly, there needs to be further reflection on the relationship between trade policy and the protection of human rights, and the EU should stimulate such reflection.

Index